PRAISE FOR
Cleveland Ethnic Eats ...

"Dipping into Laura Taxel's book is like putting on a pair of magic glasses. Before, Northeast Ohio is meatloaf and peas. After, it's a colorful melting pot of Jamaican jerk wings and Hungarian stuffed cabbage, of reggae in the back room and curried goat in the kitchen...." – *Akron Beacon Journal*

"A jewel.... Good research, fine writing and touches of genuine love make this truly special.... Anything you might want to know about this area's ethnic restaurants and markets."
– Linda Griffith, *Currents*

"Good reading—and good eating, too." – *Northern Ohio Live*

"This lively and wide-ranging book is a welcome guide.... With tips on how to find anything from Asian basil to zucchini kugel, it could be as useful to serious cooks as serious eaters."
– *The Plain Dealer*

"An adventure in dining on every page"
– *The Morning Journal*

"If you are tired of going to the same places for dinner every Friday and Saturday night, you won't want to miss out on this fun and informative book" – *Call & Post*

"Taxel methodically covers nearly every corner of the Cleveland food world, helping readers find what they are look
– *Sun Ne..*

"Whatever type of exotic food y
a particular day, chances are th
you to a place to get it." – *West ...*

"A well-planned guide for diners s ...ntic culinary cuisine from around the world and for diners who simply want to try something different from their usual fare." – *The Gazette*

Cleveland
Ethnic
Eats

Jim — Wishing you many delicious meals!
3/04
♡ Sarah

LAURA TAXEL

GRAY & COMPANY, PUBLISHERS
CLEVELAND

To Barney, my partner in eating and driving as in all else.

This book is my way of expressing appreciation to all the members of the ethnic communities who so graciously opened their doors to me. It is dedicated to those people who generously shared their ideas, insights, suggestions, and stories, and to the restaurant owners, managers, merchants, chefs, and shopkeepers who were so hospitable and helpful. My thanks to each of you.

© 2003 by Laura Taxel

Illustrations © 1995 by Richard J. Konisiewicz

Designed by Laurence J. Nozik

Gray & Company, Publishers
1588 E. 40th St., Cleveland, OH 44103
(216) 431-2665
www.grayco.com

This guide was prepared on the basis of the author's best knowledge at the time of publication. However, because of constantly changing conditions beyond the author's control, the author disclaims any responsibility for the accuracy and completeness of the information in this guide. Users of this guide are cautioned not to place undue reliance upon the validity of the information contained herein and to use this guide at their own risk.

ISBN 1-886228-76-0

Printed in the United States of America

First Printing

CONTENTS

Introduction 7

1. Pacific Rim
Cambodian, Chinese, Philippine, Japanese, Korean, Thai, Vietnamese, mixed 17
Restaurants 21
Markets 56

2. Middle East, Africa, India
Ethiopian, Indian, Middle Eastern, Moroccan 67
Restaurants 70
Markets 86

3. Mediterranean
Greek, Italian, mixed 97
Restaurants 100
Markets 136

4. Europe East of the Danube
Croatian, Czech, Hungarian, Lithuanian, Polish, Russian, Slovenian, Ukrainian 149
Restaurants 152
Markets 165

5. Europe West of the Danube
British, French, German, Irish, mixed 177
Restaurants 180
Markets 191

6. Latin America
Jamaican, Mexican, Puerto Rican, mixed 201
Restaurants 203
Markets 224

7. American Regional
African-American/Southern, Jewish, Louisiana Cajun 231
Restaurants 235
Markets 244

8. International
Restaurants 249
Restaurants 250
Markets 253

9. All Ohio 261

Ethnic Festivals 268

Indexes
by Name 283
by Location in Cleveland . . . . 2__
by Country or Region . . . . 2__
Idea Indexes . . . . 2__
Eat Streets . . . . 2__

ACKNOWLEDGMENTS

If you've never done it, it's hard to imagine just what it takes to pull all the pieces of a book like this together. Trust me when I say that it is hard work, requiring long hours. My husband, Barney, my three sons, Ezra, Nathan, and Simon, and my parents, Elliott and Mitzi Faye gave me an immeasurable quantity of enthusiastic support for my efforts and patient tolerance of my absences, both physical and mental. Their encouragement and good humor kept me going. Their willingness to try almost anything made everything else possible.

Special thanks to Jane Snow, Food Editor for the *Akron Beacon Journal* and a woman who knows a good meal when she finds it, for her willingness to share her knowledge and expertise with me.

To my loyal, fearless, and always hungry band of eating adventurers, I can only tell you what you surely have already realized: I couldn't have done it without you. Many people ate out with me and for me, and though I am not listing them by name, they know who they are. They traveled far and wide, sampled dishes that lesser folk might shrink from, and stuffed themselves beyond the call of duty.

INTRODUCTION

I n this detailed guide to the authentic ethnic restaurants, bakeries, butcher shops, and grocery stores of Greater Cleveland, you'll find out who still makes strudel dough and sausages by hand—the old-world way; who sells imported basmati rice, loquats, or dates; and what's the only place in town that serves Moroccan sheriya bahara (noodles sweetened with sugar and cinnamon). Researching the book, I spoke with a true United Nations of Clevelanders, individuals who have a strong sense of their own ethnic background. I asked them to tell me where they and other people from their "home" country eat and shop for authentic meals. Housewives and community leaders were my expert advisors. With their help I was able to uncover the vast multicultural food world of Greater Cleveland. Even a quick flip though the pages of this book testifies to how interesting and varied a world it is.

More than a directory, *Cleveland Ethnic Eats* is a guide to eating as an adventurous experience. It's about where to go when you're looking for an alternative to typical American fare or have a yen for the taste of faraway places. It lets you know what to expect when you get there. It offers no guarantees that you'll like what you find, but every place I visited was in its own way worth the trip. Some offer the kinds of dishes your mother or your grandmother made. Others present foods you may never have seen or even imagined people eating. Almost everything—from pierogies to pakoras, linguine to lo mein—is available in Cleveland. It may surprise you to find out just how easy it is to get a bowl of real pad Thai noodles or Jamaican goat curry.

There are spots, hidden behind nondescript storefronts and tucked away in innocuous strip malls, where shopkeepers wear saris; menus, posted on the walls, are written in beautiful Oriental calligraphy; and friendly smiles rather than English may be the only common language. Without flying across an ocean, you can sample Ethiopian yebug alicha (lamb stew) under a thatched roof or sit at a Japanese sushi bar and watch a master slice and wrap raw fish. You can cross a threshold, and leave the sights and sounds of this city behind you as you enter stores filled with exotic smells and unfamiliar foods, close to home and yet as foreign to most of us as a Middle Eastern shouk (bazaar).

I know a couple who have made shopping in Cleveland's ethnic markets a lifelong hobby. They say it's exciting, like a visit to another country, and the foods they encounter always give them new ideas to use in their own kitchen. Eating in ethnic restaurants, they told me, is also a low-cost way to "travel," a chance to soak up the flavor of the people and the culture along with the sauce. After spending many years investigating more than 30 of the area's ethnic food communities, I have to agree with them.

Shopping was an outing, not a chore. Many of the markets, family-owned and -operated, offered the hospitality and personal service of an old-fashioned corner store. Eating out became more than just a meal in a restaurant; it was an opportunity to take a little trip into parts unknown, break away from the usual, and enlarge my view of what Cleveland is all about. I discovered that this is truly a "cosmopolis," a city inhabited by people from all parts of the world, and it's this variety that can make living here so much fun.

Discovering Cleveland's Ethnic Communities

In addition to being a dining guide, this is also a chronicle of the unique mix of peoples and cultures that come together in Northeast Ohio. Immigrants, representing more than 50 different nations, have contributed to the growth of Cleveland from its earliest days, changing it from a pioneer backwater to a thriving, culturally rich urban center. They have come with strong backs, skilled hands, and great minds that have helped to build this city and its institutions. And even as they forged new American identities, they kept alive the spirit of their homelands. The shops and restaurants they opened represent the need that each immigrant group has always had for a taste of home. The fact that as a country we've developed an appreciation for many of their distinctive dishes shows what a profound influence their presence has had on our national consciousness.

Some, like the Puerto Ricans and the Vietnamese, are relative newcomers, arriving in this region in significant numbers only within the past 25 years. Others, like the Germans and the Irish, were among the earliest settlers. The census of 1890 showed that more than half of the city's population was foreign born. The Haymarket area southwest of Public Square was called "Baghdad on the Cuyahoga" because so many different languages were spoken there. When Cleveland celebrated its 150th anniversary in 1946, the theme was "One World." The Chinese, Czechs, English, Finns, French, Germans, Greeks, Hungarians, Irish, Jews, Italians, Lithuanians, Poles, Scots, Slovaks, Slovenians, Spanish, Swiss, and Ukrainians living here all made floats for the parade.

But we don't have it all. Guides to eating ethnic in other cities include restaurants that feature the foods of Afghanistan and Russia, Malaysia and Tunis. Although Greater Cleveland boasts residents from Turkey, Armenia, and Cape Verde, those countries are not represented among our restaurants. An active community interest in ethnic foods demonstrates that we're not just a meatloaf and mashed potatoes town, as some have said, and will encourage other nationality groups to open restaurants and share their foods with us.

Nowadays, most ethnic communities in Cleveland are defined not so much by geographic boundaries as by a shared heritage. But in years past, nationality groups clustered in specific neighborhoods. There was Big and Little Italy, Greek Town, the Cabbage Patch and Chicken Village (Czech), Warszawa (Polish), and Chinatown. Remnants of some of those neighborhoods can still be found, and often that's also where there are still many stores and little hole-in-the-wall restaurants that offer foods unlike anything to be found on the shelves of an ordinary supermarket or under a heat lamp at a drive-thru. But special shops and restaurants are located in newer suburbs and shopping malls, too.

That means this book is also a kind of road map, showing you how to escape from the confines of your usual stomping grounds and explore parts of the city and the surrounding communities you may know little about or rarely have occasion to visit.

How the Restaurants and Markets were Chosen

My criteria for choosing what to include were ethnicity, authenticity, and personal recommendations from those who know the food best. This is a book with a theme, not a yellow pages, and that means there are many restaurants that I didn't include. That's not to say they aren't very good, but they didn't fit my definition. If I've missed a place you feel should be included, use the form at the back to tell me about it so I can check it out and possibly add it to the next edition.

There are no national chains in this guide, no places that offer only one or two ethnically inspired dishes, or places that feature what's lately been described as "fusion cuisine" (or, as I call it, blue corn pasta in peanut salsa with a side of herbed collard greens). I was looking for traditional food made with integrity and respect for the eating style of the culture from which it springs. I stretched my definition of ethnic as far as I could comfortably go, in an effort to include places that honor the foods, flavors, and preparation techniques of a particular geographic region or cultural group.

I didn't pass judgment on the restaurants I've included, or rate them with stars. That's for you to do, though I have to admit that many times I decided that there really was no reason for me to ever cook again. I wanted to offer information, not evaluations, and encourage readers to investigate and experiment. That's what I did, and I had a wonderful time; so did the all the folks who helped me. We met many fine people who are proud of where they come from, determined to link the best from their past with the present, and eager to share their customs and traditions. Hearing their stories and tasting their distinctive cuisines has been a process of building bridges, making connections, and opening doors.

Many of these cuisines almost qualify as endangered species. The "Americanization" of eating, with its emphasis on fast foods, continues to make inroads into traditional practices and lifestyles in Cleveland and around the world. Recognizing the value of Cleveland's ethnic restaurants and markets and patronizing these establishments is a way to preserve them and insure that the unique contribution each makes to the community will continue to nourish us.

"Through its food," Salvador Gonzalez, who came to Cleveland from Mexico, told me, "you can come to know the culture of any country." *Cleveland Ethnic Eats* is an invitation to participate in that fascinating cultural exploration, a journey around the world that can begin and end in Northeast Ohio.

Using This Book

How This Book is Organized

This book is divided into eight broad geographic regions. I've established areas that reflect physical proximity and kitchen commonalities rather than political affiliations or national borders. Within each of those chapters, ethnic groups are listed alphabetically. For each group, there is a section of restaurants and another of stores, introduced with information about the specific ingredients that define the cuisine of that country or culture. In her cookbook, *All Around the World*, author Sheila Lukins likens these staples and seasonings to a painter's palette, with each cuisine having its own collection of foods and flavorings that set it apart from all others. Of course, these tend to be general descriptions, and there are always distinctive regional differences within every country.

Greater Cleveland isn't the only place in Ohio where world foods can be found. At the end of the book is a special section that includes some of the most outstanding ethnic restaurants and markets from around the state. To make it easy to use, I've divided Ohio into five regions: Northwest, Northeast, Southwest, Southeast, and Central. Within each region, information is organized first by city, and within each city, by ethnicity. So you can locate interesting places to eat in little towns like Sharonville, Reynoldsburg, Celina, or Somerset, or find out if you can get Chinese dim sum anywhere in Columbus; handmade Italian gnocchi in Cincinnati; Indian pakoras in Dayton, and Middle Eastern tabouleh in Toledo.

The listings themselves go beyond just names, addresses, and telephone numbers. They'll tell you about parking, identify landmarks that make places easier to locate, and let you know when to call ahead for reservations and special orders. The market information makes rare and hard-to-find ingredients accessible, and points the way to one-of-a-kind treats like homemade meat pies and handmade dumplings. The restaurant information lets you know what sort of dress is appropriate, whether or not it's a good spot to bring the kids, and explains what goes into some of the foods featured on the menu. Using the descriptions, you can pick out a fancy, sophisticated place that serves bouillabaisse (a Mediterranean fish soup), an inexpensive little neighborhood hangout that has huevos rancheros (Mexican eggs), or a bar *cum* restaurant that offers moussaka (a Greek meat-and-eggplant dish) along with late-night jazz.

Some of the stores are big, brightly lit, and modern. Some are quaint, with a charming old-world ambience. Others are irritatingly small, or inconveniently hidden away on back streets, but they're open seven days a week and you're sure to find that jar of kimchee (pickled cabbage) essential for the Korean meal you want to prepare.

The same is true of the restaurants. A few may be well known to the general public and even qualify as trendy, but many serve mostly their own countrymen and a group of loyal fans who think of them as their own special secret "find." There are places that seat 120 and others that squeeze seven tables and a kitchen into a space not much bigger than the average living room. At one end of the spectrum are down-and-dirty joints where the linoleum is cracked and pinball machines provide the only background music; at the other, elegant, stylish dining rooms with well-dressed servers who bring artfully arranged food to your linen-covered table. And there is every variation in between. Some restaurants are located in neighborhoods that diners who come from beyond its borders might not consider the best. Many are unpretentious places, where a dollar goes a long way and the food makes you feel well fed and satisfied. Whether you're looking for upscale or downscale, this book is meant to help you find what you want.

Use it to figure out just how far you'd have to go in order to sample Vietnamese bun ga sao (stir fried chicken) or see what's available, ethnically speaking, in South Euclid (how about koussa mehshi—stuffed squash—at Amir's Marketplace Restaurant?). Whether you've a hankering for a cannoli and a loaf of crusty fresh-from-the-oven Italian bread or need green bananas and hot Scotch Bonnet peppers for a Caribbean dish you want to prepare, this book can help you find them.

If you've not been much of an eating adventurer, preferring steak and an iceberg lettuce salad, the predictability of a food franchise, or the familiarity of your own part of town, then this book can help you feel comfortable getting started as you venture out into the frontiers of new taste sensations. It's full of the kind of information that makes everybody an insider. And who knows, new places may soon become your old favorites.

What to Wear? Atmosphere and Attire

By "atmosphere" I refer both to the style of dress that seems to be the general rule at a restaurant and to the decor and tone of the place. These are connected: how the patrons dress is part of every dining room's particular ambience. Tank tops and shorts set one kind of mood; suits and ties, another. And if you know how people dress when they go to a particular restaurant, you'll have some idea of what to expect from the surroundings.

There is no denying that we're becoming a dress-down society in general, but around Cleveland tradition still holds on. Here, "dressing up" usually means more than just a jacket with jeans.

My four-step scale reflects local attitudes and standards for attire: Relaxed, Casual, Dressy, and Formal. (You may notice below that I have tended to define attire in terms of men's clothing. Please don't read into this any statements about politics or power. It's just a simpler way to make things clear. Men have fewer options, so it's simpler to base guidelines on their clothes.

Relaxed, for the purposes of this book, means almost anything goes, short of being barefoot and shirtless. Neither the management nor the other diners have any expectations you must meet. On the night I visited one such eatery, the couple ahead of me were dressed in warm-up suits; the woman behind me was wrapped in an ankle-length fur coat. The criterion to go by is what makes you comfortable—knowing, in advance, that it's next to impossible to be under-dressed.

Casual is one step up. Comfort is still the aim and informality the norm, but the unspoken code definitely calls for better than just a no-holes, clean-clothes style. Picture the look in terms of upscale play attire—what folks in the trendy mail-order catalogs and magazine ads wear when they're having fun. You can get away with wearing a T-shirt, but it shouldn't sport stains, brand names, or lewd remarks. Turtlenecks, sweaters, and jeans are all acceptable, but you'd still fit in if you chose to spruce up just a bit.

Dressy is what was once commonly called business attire and implies a moderate level of formality. It's an office look: shirts with collars, pressed slacks, and sport jackets. Ties are optional. In times past I think this look was described as "nice," as in your mother saying "Why don't you change into something nice?" or "Don't you have anything nicer than that?" before you went out on a date.

Formal indicates that coat and tie are required or strongly suggested. This means that male and female patrons dress up and dress well when they dine at such establishments, moving beyond looking merely nice to looking very nice. "The 'Tie required or suggested' criteria," says McCue, "is a good take-off point for women; they know how to choose a corresponding outfit, whether it's a dress or trousers and a silk blouse, from among the many different kinds of clothes available to them."

Spelling

Throughout the listings, you may notice many different spellings for the same word. That's the nature of transliteration. There's often more than one way to create the English equivalent of a foreign word. In general, I took my cues from the people I spoke with. So one store owner suggested I write "filo" dough while another spelled it out for me as "phyllo," and when I checked, I found both are used in other books. I also adopted a policy of matching my spellings to those that appear on the menu of each establishment I was writing about, except where there were obvious English misspellings.

Prices

I've used a scale of one to five dollar signs to indicate the relative cost of an average meal at each of the restaurants:

$$$$$	much lower than average
$$$$$	slightly lower than average
$$$$$	about average
$$$$$	slightly higher than average
$$$$$	much higher than average

Obviously, one person's "average meal" varies from another's—even at the same restaurant—depending on what and how much you order. To give a reasonable standard, though, I based my rating on the average dinner entree price from each restaurant's standard menu. I also considered other factors, such as whether entrees come with appetizer, or whether it's the kind of place that's intended for for a lavish multicourse meal rather than a simple sit-down dinner.

Don't Forget to Call Ahead!

Keep in mind that although the information is as accurate and up to date as possible, things can and will change. Hours don't always stay the same, policies and practices are altered, businesses come and go, and new owners often have new ideas. Moreover, if it's a long drive to an unfamiliar location, it's *highly recommended* that you call ahead for directions to save you time and to avoid confusion.

It is *always* best to call first.

Location

I've divided Greater Cleveland roughly into ten geographic areas: Downtown, Near West Side, West Side, Far West Side, Near East Side, East Side, Far East Side, Southeast, Southwest, and Far South. This is to help you tell from a glance at the listings approximately where a restaurant or market is located relative to where you live or plan to visit. The map above shows how these areas are divided. An area is indicated directly below each restaurant's and market's name, followed by specific city and street address information. Phone numbers appear next to each listing's name so you can call for directions.

Areas Covered in this Book

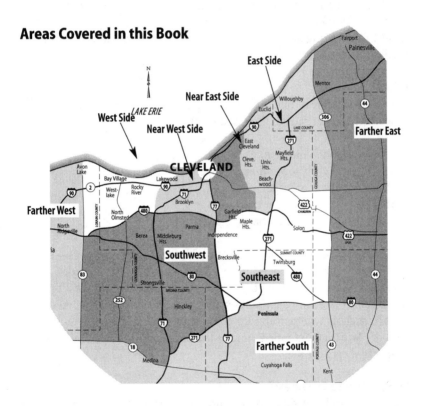

Cleveland
Ethnic
Eats

{ *Chapter 1* }

PACIFIC RIM

The region known as the Pacific Rim includes the vast and varied terrain of more than 10 different Far Eastern countries. The Cleveland area is home to markets and restaurants from the Rim nations of Cambodia, China, Japan, Korea, the Philippines, Thailand, and Vietnam.

The Chinese were the first Asian group to come to Cleveland, and their numbers began to grow significantly in the late 1800s. In its early days, Cleveland's Chinese community was made up primarily of immigrants from the southern Cantonese province of Guangdong who came by way of the West Coast. Later it came to include people from northern and central China, Hong Kong, and Taiwan. Cleveland's Chinatown, along Rockwell Avenue between 24th and 21st streets, was once densely populated with immigrants. Though small by the standards of New York or San Francisco, it is nonetheless the historical heart of the community. Now Chinese live in all parts of Greater Cleveland, but the recent $2.3 million renovation of an old warehouse into Asia Plaza on Payne created a modern, bustling Asian shopping and dining center that is a new hub for the old neighborhood.

The Organization of Chinese Americans of Greater Cleveland, which networks with other local groups like the Asian Pacific Federation, is a tightly knit association active in cultural education. "We feel that our traditions are very rich," said Frances Namkoong, founding president, "and they are important to us. Most Chinese Americans live with a foot in both worlds. We continue to be close to our immigrant ancestors and a world view that comes very much from their past. But at the same time, we are Americans."

Ms. Namkoong's sentiments are echoed by others in the Asian community. "We teach our children that their roots are in Korea but their home is in Cleveland," says Dr. Sakoo Lee, head of the Korean-American Association of Greater Cleveland. The organization now boasts more than 5,000 members.

Koreans did not become a visible presence here until the 1970s, when U.S. immigration quotas changed. According to Dr. Lee (and much to my surprise), one reason Koreans like Cleveland is our four-season climate, which is similar to, though slightly colder than, that of their homeland. But there's more to their attraction than weather.

"This city and the surrounding suburbs," said Dr. Lee, a physician with a family practice in Westlake, "are truly a multicultural melting pot. Every nationality group is unique with something to contribute. I've traveled in many other parts of the country, and Cleveland is one of those rare places where there's an understanding of that. Here, we can all live together, keeping what's best from our own heritage while becoming part of the community."

That receptivity and understanding were part of what helped the Japanese feel welcome in Cleveland after World War II. Forcibly removed from West Coast communities, they were encouraged to resettle here by the War Relocation Authority, and their numbers peaked in 1946. Filipinos, who settled here after 1950, make up another small subset of the Asian community. Like their Chinese and Japanese counterparts, many are professionals in the fields of medicine and technology. A large number of students from all three countries have come in recent years to take advantage of the area's colleges, medical schools and teaching hospitals, and industrial research facilities. According to Sunthorn Phetcharat, a Thai immigrant and former owner of the Thai Kitchen in Lakewood, there are not many people from Thailand living in Cleveland, and their stories would have to be told one by one, for they have come as individuals and not as a group.

Most Cambodians and Vietnamese began to arrive in Cleveland after 1970, driven to emigrate by war and its devastating aftermath. "My family is lucky," explained Liem Nguyen, a former South Vietnamese army captain (and prisoner of the North Vietnamese) now living on the city's West Side. "Once again we have a bright future. This is a chance to start a new life. We are willing to work very hard, night and day. We want to show our thanks and prove to Cleveland that we have much to give."

One of the things each of these ethnic groups has to give is its singular cuisine. Though influenced by geographic neighbors, each country possesses its own distinctive approach to food.

Chinese cooking represents one of the oldest continuing culinary traditions in the world. It is also the Asian cuisine most familiar to Americans. Won Kee opened Cleveland's first Chinese restaurant, on Ontario, before 1900; a second was added soon after on the west side of Public Square. Our taste for Chinese food has expanded in recent years beyond the now-familiar Cantonese and Mandarin to include the spicy styles of Szechuan and Hunan cooking. The Chinese New Year, celebrated in February, is a great opportunity to sample a wide variety of special traditional foods.

Korean food tends to be spicy, though not necessarily fiery hot. Kimchee appears on the table at every meal. It is a peppery, piquant condiment made primarily from pickled cabbage. Chili powder, vinegar, fermented bean pastes, and sesame seeds are important ingredients in the Korean kitchen. Bounded on three sides by water, Koreans have incorporated a wide variety of fish and seafood into their diet, though they also have a national enthusiasm for beef, an appreciation said to have been left behind by the invading Mongol hordes.

Japanese cooking, too, is dominated by seafood, much of it eaten raw and accompanied by varieties of pickles and pungent condiments like momiji oroshi, made from grated white radish with red chiles, or wasabi, a horseradish paste so strong that an overly large bite can bring on tears and provide instant cleansing of the sinuses. Classical Japanese cuisine shows virtually no signs of outside influences, perhaps because the country imposed a ban on foreigners from 1640 to 1868.

The same cannot be said for the cooking styles of Vietnam, Cambodia, and the Philippines. All bear the stamp of European colonial incursions into both their territory and their traditional ways of life. So Philippine food has a decidedly Spanish twist, and one of the most characteristic dishes, a chicken-and-pork stew called adobo, is reminiscent of Mexican cookery, which shares this Spanish influence.

From the French, who first arrived in the 16th century, the Vietnamese got a taste for sweetened milky coffee and also sausages, which they make from both meat and fish. Indian traders brought curry, used primarily by the southern Vietnamese, and the Buddhist influence means there are many vegetarian dishes. Traditional cooking uses raw greens, and food is often served on crisp lettuce leaves.

Thailand, though inspired by its culinary neighbors, China, India, Burma, and Laos, was never colonized, so its food has no Western leanings. Thai cooks make good use of all the tropical fruits and vegetables that grow in abundance throughout the country, and season them with fresh herbs like lemon grass, green coriander, lime leaves, mint, and Oriental basils. They make liberal use of coconut milk, chili peppers, peanuts, and sesame seeds. These same flavorings are used both by the Vietnamese and the Cambodians.

Soy is the salty condiment favored by the Chinese and Japanese; a similar effect is achieved by other Southeast Asian cooks through the use of a fermented fish sauce. Use of garlic, ginger, scallions, and hot capsicums (peppers) is universal, but cooks in each country, as well as in different regions, use them in quite different ways, and the results vary widely. Koreans, for example, often add the garlic at the end of cooking or eat it raw so that it keeps its bite.

Rice, of course, is an omnipresent staple. The Thai invitation to a meal translates as "Come and eat rice," while an age-old Chinese greeting is "Have you eaten rice yet?" All Asian cuisines rely on very fresh, seasonal foods and strive to retain rather than mask the natural flavors of each ingredient.

Eating styles throughout the Pacific Rim are very light and healthy. People eat few dairy products, meat in small quantities, and use only vegetable and bean oils. Rich desserts are the exception rather than the rule.

Technique and presentation are defining principles for all these Asian cuisines. Actual cooking methods tend to be quick and simple, reflecting the fact that food is eaten with chopsticks or spoons and so must be sliced and chopped into small pieces.

Delicate flavors come from painstaking preparation, with great attention to detail, and subtly seasoned sauces. The Chinese and the Japanese say that every dish must be made with four elements in mind: color, fragrance, flavor, and shape. Korean and Chinese cooks strive for balance and harmony among what they call the five basic flavors: sweet, sour, hot, tart, and salty. The equation for Thai cuisine is only slightly different: sweetness, sourness, saltiness, hotness, nuttiness, and bitterness.

We now have one Filipino restaurant and a few markets that carry ingredients for home cooking. There are a couple of Cambodian restaurants and a handful of Thai and Vietnamese ones. There are now a few Korean restaurants where Clevelanders can sample the food from "The Land of Morning Calm," and a few serving authentic Japanese cuisine. And although the list of Chinese restaurants is long, only a select few serve what the Chinese consider to be authentic, rather than American, Chinese food.

Frances Namkoong has some advice for those who want a true Asian eating experience. "Much of the best food is not on the English-language menus. But diners can ask for dishes they've heard about, enjoyed elsewhere, or things they notice other non-American people eating. A restaurant would feel honored if guests request recommendations from the kitchen."

DON'T FORGET: CALL AHEAD!

RESTAURANTS

Asian Mix

Little Orchid Cafe
☎ (440) 893-9495

CITY: **Chagrin Falls**   AREA: **Farther East**
ATMOSPHERE: **Casual**   COST: $$$$$

ADDRESS: 95 N. Main St.
HOURS: Mon–Thu 11 a.m.–9:30 p.m., Fri & Sat 11 a.m.–10:30 p.m., Sun 3–9 p.m.
RESERVATIONS: Taken, Suggested on weekends
PAYMENT: MC, VS **BAR:** None **TAKEOUT:** Yes
SMOKING: Smoke-Free **ACCESS:** ♿ Full access
OTHER ETHNIC SPECIALTIES: Thai, Chinese, and Vietnamese

This little corner of Main Street America was once a service station. My memory tells me it did time as a dry cleaner. Then it became a bakery. Now it's retooled, redecorated, and reincarnated as a charming restaurant that serves a mix of Thai, Chinese, and Vietnamese dishes. Chagrin Falls, a place that prides itself on its quaint, late-19th-century Midwestern look, seems more than a few steps away once you've walked in, sat down, and taken up the menu. Your mind may keep saying "Ohio," but it's hard to remember that when you wrap your mouth around a bite of tropical-tasting green papaya salad, suck up a spoonful of hot and sour shrimp soup, or feel the taste-bud tremors from an order of stir-fried beef in chili sauce (neu prig sod). This is travel by plate. Ask for moo prig khing (P1 on the menu, for the linguisti-

cally timid): the platter of pork, green beans, and carrots stir-fried with sweet basil and lemon in curry paste takes you to Thailand. Banh uot cha lua banh tom chien (say A12, or just point) gets you an appetizer of rice noodles with bits of pork roll and fried shrimp cake, and an epicure's ticket to Vietnam. Take a tour of China with Mongolian lamb, moo shu vegetables with Mandarin pancakes, or Szechuan green beans. The three small bright rooms, with seating for about 24 patrons, are decorated with orchids, both live and artificial. Tables and chairs are blond wood, floors are white tile, and strings of tiny white Christmas lights twinkle in the windows. The overall impression is crisp, clean, and attractive. There are only a few parking spaces in a small lot that wraps around the restaurant on two sides, but plenty of on-street spaces and a municipal lot near by.

Tea House Noodles
☎ (216) 623-9131

CITY: **Cleveland**   AREA: **Downtown**
ATMOSPHERE: **Relaxed**   COST: $$$$$

ADDRESS: 1900 E. 6th St.
HOURS: Mon–Fri 10:30 a.m.– 4 p.m.
RESERVATIONS: Not taken **PAYMENT:** Cash only
BAR: None **TAKEOUT:** Yes **SMOKING:** Smoke-free
ACCESS: ♿ Limited **OTHER ETHNIC SPECIALTIES:** Thai, Philippine, Indonesian, Chinese, Japanese

The ads for this place are intriguing: "The Sponge Mirrors Are Returning. Have You Checked Your Bags? (Stay Toned)"; or, "A Simple Alignment . . . Spin 33 Clockwise." You know there's got to be a story here. And there is. Restaurant owner Richard Baribalt, who traveled around Asia 30-something years ago when so many young folks sought adventure and answers in the East, is as interested in people's psyches as he is in their stomachs. Still in touch with that '70s mind-set, Baribalt views Tea House Noodles as a venue for business, philosophizing, and fun. (He talks about wanting good "vibes" in his kitchen, and speaks of spiritual growth in the same casual tones he uses for discussing the daily special.) Think of him and his operation as the Asian-food equivalent of Ben and Jerry's. His quirky koan-like ads are meant to be good for the mind, just as his rice-and-noodle dishes are good for the body. "I create the ads to make people curious, get their attention, and provide some brain exercise. I think that's healthy, just like my food. I figure if a person likes my ads, he or she will probably like my restaurant, too." The inspiration for the restaurant, which was originally located in the Old Arcade, came from the noodle shops he saw on almost every corner in the Asian countries he toured, the Asian answer to fast food, but—unlike its American counterparts—wholesome and flavorful.

Adding what he calls a "twist" to make everything "user friendly" and appealing to Cleveland diners, Baribalt begins with the same basic ingredients—rice noodles, steamed brown rice, and fresh Oriental vegetables. He creates a variety of sauces for them—a mild sesame ginger, a distinctive and very popular Thai peanut, a creamy Indonesian curry, and a zesty Filipino sweet-hot—or a miso broth or a chicken soup seasoned with lemon grass and ginger to float them in. He also offers the option of adding chicken and/or shrimp to the vegetarian combinations. Vegetable-filled, steamed rice-flour-dough buns topped with the same selection of sauces are another option. Steam table specials change daily and include soups such as a cold Asian gazpacho, Oriental vegetable, a spicy coconut chicken, and a hot and sour shrimp. Also offered are steamed wontons and heartier entrees such as a Balinese-style chicken prepared in a sweet and tangy sauce; Thai curry chicken with sweet potatoes; chicken and stir-fried vegetables made with coconut milk and mango; and steamed fish of the day. There are also salads, which you can choose to dress in either a lemon grass vinaigrette, mango cream, or gado-gado. Everything is made in-house. Friend and classically

trained chef Frank Ziff helped Baribalt create the menu. All the food is relatively low fat, low salt, and very nutritious, but a feather icon on the menu marks those that are especially light and healthy. The longest you can expect to wait for an order, which you place at the counter and pick up yourself, is three minutes. Takeout orders, placed in advance, are ready and waiting. There are no servers in this simple storefront space, and tables accommodate only 15. For menus, reviews, and words of wisdom, go to their website: www.teahouse-noodles.com.

Cambodian

Phnom Penh Restaurant
☎ (216) 251-0210

CITY: **Cleveland**   AREA: **Near West Side**
ATMOSPHERE: **Casual**   COST: $$$$$

ADDRESS: 13124 Lorain Ave.
HOURS: Mon–Thu 11 a.m.–9:30 p.m., Fri 11 a.m.–10 p.m., Sat 11 a.m.–11 p.m., Sun 3–9 p.m.
RESERVATIONS: Taken, recommended on weekends for groups of 4 or more
PAYMENT: Cash only **BAR:** Byob **TAKEOUT:** Yes
SMOKING: Smoke-free **ACCESS:** ⬥ Full access

Owner Mono Bun is a native of Cambodia, and his cuisine is traditionally a strongly flavored one characterized by the use of coconut milk, fermented fish sauce, and peanuts, and a variety of spices unfamiliar to Americans, such as galanga root (like ginger but milder), tangy Asian basil, lemon grass, aromatic mint, and kaffir lime leaves. The preparation and presentation are similar to the Chinese cooking Ohioans are more familiar with, but the sauces and seasonings render the taste quite different. The promise of "special sauce" here, unlike its burger-topping American counterpart, really delivers something special because sauces are made with spice-blend pastes similar to those of India, using turmeric, star anise, cloves, cinnamon, and nutmeg. Many dishes are made with noodles (wheat, rice, and potato based) that come soft and flat, round, crispy, stir-fried, sauteed, or pan-stirred. Plenty of options for the health conscious: vegetarian appetizers, soups, and entrees, a section of the menu devoted to "healthy traditional Cambodian dishes," and a flavorful low-fat dish called mikroolaa. The pronunciation of most items is a mystery to the untrained tongue, but never fear—each item on the menu has a number so you won't have to struggle with trying to ask for loath chha (noodles with vegetables and egg) or banh sough (rice noodles with vegetables, whipped co-conut milk, and crumbled spring rolls). For daily specials like the very unusual amok siemreap (spicy shrimp, scallops, crab, and catfish steamed in a bannana leaf), just point. Servers, who are almost exclusively Cambodian, speak English and will help diners find their way around the nine-page menu, which also provides short English-language explanations of each of the 136 dishes. The menu offers even more options by allowing some food play: add their homemade tofu to any order; add seafood or noodles to soup; substitute vegetable fried rice for steamed rice; and personalize the heat in any spicy dish by ordering mild, medium, or hot. Loyal customers come back regularly from as far away as Toledo. One enthusiast insists their Khmer shrimp and seafood rice soup is better than "Jew-ish penicillin" (chicken soup).

The L-shaped space is small, plain, and simple. A mirror on one wall creates the il-lusion of space, as do the big storefront windows. There's seating for about 50 pa-trons. There are a couple of round tables that can accommodate groups of six or eight, but most are four- and two-tops. Phnom Penh is usually busy at lunchtime and caters to a dinner crowd of relaxed food adventurers who are willing to bring their own beer and wine. For those who want to quench their thirst without alco-hol, there are some treats—a large variety of tropical fruit drinks, egg soda, soybean or coconut milk, and hot or cold French coffee. There is no waiting area to speak of, so you may find yourself standing in the entryway or outside until your table is ready, but I think it's worth it and appar-ently so do many other people who are willing to put up with the inconvenience. The restaurant's facade blends in so well with the other stores on the street that it's easy to miss when driving by. If you park in one of the few head-in spaces directly in front of it you're almost inside the dining room. Plenty of additional on-street park-ing in the neighborhood. Gift certificates are available.

Chinese

Bo Loong
☎ (216) 391-3113

CITY: **Cleveland**   AREA: **Near East Side**
ATMOSPHERE: **Casual**   COST: **$$**$$

ADDRESS: 3922 St. Clair Ave.
HOURS: Daily 10 a.m.–2 a.m.
RESERVATIONS: Taken, recommended for 6 or more **PAYMENT:** MC, VS, AX, checks **BAR:** Beer, wine, liquor **TAKEOUT:** Yes **SMOKING:** Yes
ACCESS: & Full access

This place is big, seating 400, and the first impression is of something be-tween a cafeteria and a university dining hall with a funky red-and-gold Oriental motif. But the fact that the decor lacks a slick look (part of its unique charm) does not keep this restaurant from being a hands-down favorite among Cleveland's Chinese families, and their regular, visible presence is a measure of the authentic quality of the food. Management is espe-cially proud of the dim sum, a large selec-tion of sweet and savory pastries, buns, and dumplings that can be ordered indi-vidually as an appetizer or in combination to create an entire meal. The number of choices is unequaled anywhere else in town, especially on the weekends. Some of the notable options include steamed or baked buns filled with barbecued pork; rice noodles stuffed with beef; sticky rice with pork; Chinese sausage, duck, and egg wrapped and steamed in a lotus leaf; fried dumplings stuffed with shrimp and vegetables; sesame seed pastry with a red bean paste filling; and an egg custard tart. They are also pleased to now offer patrons seafood so fresh that it's still swimming when you order it: lobster, eel, catfish, and tilapia are fished from the tank and immediately prepared. While many of the other dishes on the menu will be familiar, reflecting a variety of regional cuisines and including shark's fin soup, chicken in black bean sauce, salt-baked shrimp, and beef with ginger and scallions, others cater to a more Asian palate and feature such unusual ingredients as chicken feet, beef tripe, and quail eggs. If you're feeling experimental, this is a great place to put the menu aside, point to what's being eaten at another table, and have a tasting adventure by saying, "I'll have some of that." Also a great place for a late-night visit. Your evening may include performance art— the restaurant offers karaoke, 10 p.m. to closing, seven nights a week. To make it even more interesting, the thousands of songs would-be lounge crooners and rock stars can choose from are available in English, Cantonese, Mandarin, Korean, Vietnamese, and Japanese. Banquet facilities available.

Brand new digs in 2003 for this dual Asian eatery. Both Chinese and Japanese food is served, and the many Chinese and Japanese people who choose to eat here attest to its quality and authenticity. You can choose from traditional floor seating or Western-height tabletops. The menu features the Japanese dishes favored in this country, such as tempura, teriyaki, yakitori (skewered pieces of broiled chicken or beef), and sukiyaki. But the real standout is the extensive selection of sushi and sashimi, and the other fresh and raw fish creations served at the sushi bar. The chef, who enjoys entertaining his audience at the bar with his technique, works with flounder, salmon, red snapper, tuna, eel, octopus, sea urchin, and fish roe. Chunks, slices (30 different types), and rolls made with rice and seaweed are served on rectangular plates and small wooden cutting boards, garnished with paper-thin pieces of ginger and hillocks of sharp green wasabi. Japanese beer is available.

The opposite side of the restaurant is the Chinese half, with 110 items on the menu. Some of the notable house specialties are five-spiced pork chop, crystal shrimp (prepared in a garlic sauce), Szechuan hot braised lobster, ta-chien chicken (made with green and red peppers in a spicy sauce), fire pots, abalone with black mushrooms, and happy family bird's nest (shrimp, pork, chicken, and beef with vegetables served in a noodle basket). Dishes can be prepared without salt and/or MSG upon request, and with advance notice the chef will create a gourmet dinner of unique banquet dishes. Take special note of the fact that *only* Chinese food is available during the lunch hours. Japanese food service begins at 5 p.m. Also be aware that restaurants in Cuyahoga Falls are not licensed to serve liquor on Sundays.

Golden Dragon
☎ **(330) 929-1109**

CITY: **Cuyahoga Falls**   AREA: **Farther South**
ATMOSPHERE: **Casual**   COST: $$$$$

ADDRESS: 1634 State Rd.
HOURS: Mon–Thu 11 a.m.–10 p.m., Fri & Sat 11 a.m.–11:30 p.m., Sun noon-10 p.m.
RESERVATIONS: Not taken **PAYMENT:** MC, VS, AX, DIS **BAR:** Beer, wine, liquor **TAKEOUT:** Yes
SMOKING: Smoking section **ACCESS:** ⅊ None
OTHER ETHNIC SPECIALTIES: Japanese

Golden Swan
☎ (440) 684-9108

CITY: **Mayfield Heights**   AREA: **East Side**
ATMOSPHERE: **Casual**   COST: $$$$$

ADDRESS: 1463 SOM Center Rd.
HOURS: Mon–Thu 11:30 a.m.–9 p.m., Fri & Sat 11:30 a.m.–10 p.m., Sun noon–9 p.m.
RESERVATIONS: Taken, suggested for more than 6
PAYMENT: MC, VS, AX, DIS   BAR: Beer, wine, liquor
TAKEOUT: Yes   SMOKING: Smoking section
ACCESS: ♿ Full access

It's in a shopping center, and it's a Chinese restaurant. So you've got plenty of reasons not to expect much in terms of visual appeal. But the Golden Swan contradicts the predictable in a lovely way. It's got a modern and elegant decor. The floors are marble in some areas, thickly carpeted in others; booths and chairs are upholstered; the walls display mirrors, traditional artwork, and contemporary murals created by a Taiwanese artist specifically for this room; some tabletops are marble, others are covered in cloth with lace on top, and still others have a mirrored surface. Focused lighting serves to make each booth a space unto itself. A second dining area is slightly elevated, and sectioned off by a dark wood divider. The look of things is clearly important to owners Rita and Spencer Sien, and he extends this aesthetic sensibility beyond decorating to the presentation of food. Water is served in stemmed goblets. Cloth napkins are intricately folded, the serving dishes are attractively decorated, and the Chinese background music is relaxing. Every dish is beautifully garnished with vegetables artistically cut into flower shapes, lemons, limes, and parsley. It's all part of pleasing the customer, a job Sien takes seriously, and he has many loyal customers who appreciate his efforts. The menu is a mix of the Chinese standards you'd find in most restaurants and some house specialties: Oriental-style lobster; scallops in a Hong Kong–style sauce (XO scallops); whole roast Peking duck or crispy duck marinated and then fried; Firecracker Fish, a fillet in hot pepper sauce; and Chicken Curl, a dish for two made with minced chicken, water chestnuts, mushrooms, and eggs, wrapped in lettuce with plum sauce. There are also some American selections for those who want to go West rather than East. The barkeep, who tends a little six-seater counter, pours a respectable assortment of local, domestic, and imported beers, including the Chinese brew Tsingtao (say "ching-dow" if you want to sound like you know what you're talking about); Asian wines; a selection of California whites and reds, as well as two Australian vintages and one Italian; and sparkling wines, port, and sherry. The restaurant even has its own website (www.goldenswan.cjb.net) that includes a map with driving directions, the menu with prices, and pictures of many of the dishes.

House of Hunan
☎ (330) 864-8215

CITY: **Akron**   AREA: **Farther South**
ATMOSPHERE: **Casual**   COST: $$$$$

ADDRESS: 2717 W. Market St.
HOURS: Mon–Thu 11:30 am.–10 p.m., Fri 11:30 a.m.–11 p.m., Sat noon–11 p.m., Sun noon–10 p.m.   RESERVATIONS: Taken, suggested Fri & Sat nights   PAYMENT: MC, VS, AX, DIS
BAR: Beer, wine, liquor   TAKEOUT: Yes
SMOKING: Smoking section   ACCESS: ♿ Full access

An Akron favorite since 1983, this Chinese restaurant offers the familiar, dependable mix of Hunan, Mandarin, and Szechuan specialties. Yet, among the dishes most of us know and love are some surprises. Among the appetizers: steamed vegetable-and-shrimp dumplings, steamed meat buns, and the House Special Fire Pot soup. In the entree department: prawns with walnuts and hot chile sauce, a whole steamed flounder, Tokoyo Moon Land (a dish containing shrimp, pork, chicken, and

PACIFIC RIM

vegetables in brown sauce), spicy hot pork, Hunan lobster with black mushrooms, boneless tung ting duck, rose beef (I guessed a flowery roast, but it turns out to be filet mignon in a tangy sauce that's a combination of sweet and hot), and a braised tofu. If you prefer the tried and true, you'll be choosing from the likes of egg rolls, wonton soup, the general's chicken, kung bao-ed beef (on other menus it's usually spelled King Pao), sizzling this and that, sweet and sour stuff, the moo shu mix (this is non-dairy despite the name), shrimp and chicken the way the empress liked it, and those poems of the plate known as Dragon and Phoenix (lobster, vegetables, and chicken), Happy Family (shellfish, chicken, pork, and beef), and Lover's Dinner (a medley of meats, seafood, and vegetables for two—but you can just be friends). The menu even includes what the owners delightfully refer to as Old Fashion dishes, which are actually those Americanized Chinese concoctions that were once, back in those benighted and less sophisticated days, all most of us knew when it came to Pacific Rim cookery— fried rice, chow mein, chop suey, lo mein, and egg foo young. Their presence on the menu makes it clear they still are the food of choice for plenty of folks. A Japanese-style sushi bar and some cooked Japanese dishes are a fairly recent addition.

The combination of old and new attracts a diverse crowd—gray hairs and green hairs, the baby carriers and the cell phone set, the dressed for success and the dressed in sweats. It's a large, attractive place to eat. It doesn't seem sprawling because tables are on two levels. (If someone in your party has trouble with steps, make reservations and ask for a table on the lower level). There's some lovely traditional art on the walls, screens, a huge aquarium in the center, dragon statues, a burbling fountain, and lots of greenery. An eye-catching ceramic tile mural fills the back wall. The restaurant is located in Fairlawn Town Center, and it's easy to spot with its distinctive gold doors and bright red molding in classic Chinese style.

House of Hunan
☎ (330) 253-1888

CITY: **Akron**   AREA: **Farther South**
ATMOSPHERE: **Casual**   COST: $$$$$

ADDRESS: 12 E. Exchange St.
HOURS: Mon–Thu 11:30 am.–10 p.m., Fri 11:30 a.m.–11 p.m., Sat noon–11 p.m., Sun noon–10 p.m. RESERVATIONS: Taken, suggested Fri & Sat nights PAYMENT: MC, VS, AX, DIS BAR: Beer, wine, liquor TAKEOUT: Yes SMOKING: Smoking section ACCESS: ♿ Full access

The menu here is similar to the one at House of Hunan on W. Market St. (see above listing), but with more of a contemporary focus—no old-fashioned chop suey here.

Hunan by the Falls
☎ (440) 247-0808

CITY: **Chagrin Falls**   AREA: **Southeast**
ATMOSPHERE: **Casual**   COST: $$$$$

ADDRESS: 508 E. Washington St.
HOURS: Mon–Thu 11:30 a.m.–10 p.m., Fri & Sat 11:30 a.m.–11:00 p.m., Sun noon–9 p.m.; lunch menu available daily until 3:30 p.m.; kitchen does not close between lunch & dinner. RESERVATIONS: Taken, recommended, accepted for parties of 6 or more only Fri and Sat evenings PAYMENT: MC, VS, AX, DIS BAR: Beer, wine, liquor TAKEOUT: Yes SMOKING: Smoke-free ACCESS: ♿ Full access

This is innovative gourmet Chinese cuisine served in an equally modern and exceptional setting. Winner of numerous awards, including "Best"s from readers of *Northern Ohio Live*, *Cleveland Magazine*, and the *Chagrin Valley Times*, this 80-seat restaurant has grown steadily in popularity since it opened in 1993. Part of the draw is surely the attractive, contemporary-looking dining area, decorated with paintings by local artist Kasumi, and an indoor waterfall. But the real attraction is the food that chef Kwan Kuen Chau prepares. It's a mix of traditional Chinese regional cuisine, featuring such well-known dishes as General Tso's chicken, Mongolian beef, Mandarin orange duck, shrimp in black bean sauce, and lo mein. Some less familiar dishes also emerge from his kitchen: fire pots (casserole-type combinations of vegetables with seafood, meat, or tofu); fu yong don (a lighter, more typically Asian version of egg foo yong, with oyster flavor sauce); mala string beans, which are made with Chinese cabbage chile peppers, and garlic; Singapore-style noodles (chow me fun); and Asian taro basket, a weave of crisp fried strips of this tuber, made to hold vegetables and your choice of chicken, shrimp, or seafood. Chef Chau also produces some unique creations of his own: yau-tsoi (green leafy vegetables and portobello mushrooms sauteed in an oyster-flavored sauce); walnut prawns (prawns lightly floured, sauteed quickly in oil, and tossed in a walnut sauce); and red chili curry noodles (spicy rice noodles seasoned with cilantro, lemon grass, and basil). Some popular seasonal specials include tangerine roughy; a sauteed vegetable dish called dou mieu, made with peapod plants and garlic sauce; and ginger lamb. Many menu items for vegetarians, a nice wine list, and rich desserts. Service is attentive and personal, and kitchen staff will try to accommodate special requests and needs. Parking in back after 5 p.m.

liquor **TAKEOUT:** Yes **SMOKING:** Smoking section **ACCESS:** & Full access

A wall of large windows lets in plenty of light and opens out onto Coventry Road. The decor is fashionably elegant, though patrons—an eclectic crowd of every age—are as likely to dress in sweaters as suits. There are lovely details featured in the decor: framed Asian flower prints, a glass wall sandblasted in a flower motif to separate entrance from dining area, and indirect light from modern wall-mounted sconces. Rich-looking warm-colored wood, grey carpeting, and polished brass accent white walls and table linens. The food looks elegant too, often garnished with flowers or butterflies beautifully sculpted from a simple radish or wedges of tomato. The menu features a large selection of classic dishes, both Hunan spicy and not, and there are also some unexpected offerings tucked among the lo meins, kung paos, and moo shus: mussels in spicy garlic sauce, Shanghai chicken with honey walnuts, Mandarin noodles with sesame sauce, and Beijing-style lamb with scallions. Plentiful options for vegetarian diners. Portions are generous, service is attentive, and at the end of the meal you get not only a fortune cookie but a warm, individually wrapped, disposable cloth for freshening hands and face. A good place to eat, visit, and celebrate. A multistory parking garage is located across the street.

Hunan Coventry
☎ (216) 371-0777
CITY: **Cleveland Heights**   AREA: **East Side**
ATMOSPHERE: **Casual**   COST: $$$$$

ADDRESS: 1800 Coventry Rd.
HOURS: Tue–Thu 11:30 a.m.–9:45 p.m., Fri 11:30 a.m.–10:45 p.m., Sat noon–10:45 p.m., Sun 4–8:45 p.m.; closed Mon
RESERVATIONS: Taken, for parties of 6 or more only **PAYMENT:** MC, VS, AX, DIS **BAR:** Beer, wine,

Hunan East
☎ (216) 381-2266
CITY: **Richmond Heights**   AREA: **East Side**
ATMOSPHERE: **Relaxed**   COST: $$$$$

ADDRESS: 724 Richmond Rd.
HOURS: Mon–Thu 11 a.m.–9:30 p.m., Fri & Sat 11 a.m.–10:30 p.m., Sun noon–9 p.m.
RESERVATIONS: Not Taken **PAYMENT:** MC, VS, AX, DIS **BAR:** None **TAKEOUT:** Yes **SMOKING:** Smoke-Free **ACCESS:** & Full access

This restaurant has been here for years, but even I knew nothing about it until May of 2001. It's as ordinary as can be, outside and in, until you discover "the secret." I was clued in by Bob P., a man who is a true good-food enthusiast. And now you, too, can be in the know. The place looks like a million other little storefront Chinese restaurants, the kind that do more carryout than sit-down business. Its appearance has nothing to recommend it. And the typical American-style Chinese food they serve is nothing to write home about. But you can't go by appearances, and what you see is definitely not all you can get. Because there's another menu. That's the secret. It's in Chinese, so it's generally not presented to those who don't immediately appear likely to read the language. This menu features many of the same dishes that appear on the English version, but they are prepared in a completely different way aimed to please a Chinese rather than an American palate. Fresh ginger, garlic, and scallions are used more liberally. Uncommon Asian vegetables like Chinese broccoli, pea pod leaves, black ear and cloud mushrooms, baby choy, and miniature eggplants predominate. Those who have eaten here without knowing about this other menu may have harbored some suspicions about what was going on in the kitchen. The food on their plates looked and smelled quite different from what was being served to Chinese people at nearby tables—and every other table is nearby in this small room with only 60 seats. In fact, by pointing and asking if they can have "what those other people are eating," many diners discover "the secret." Once servers and management know you're interested in the Real Chinese Food, they'll do all they can to help, short of sitting down and translating every line on the multipage menu. You can tell them you want seafood, pork, or a noodle dish, something full of vegetables, or a dish that is highly spiced and laced with heat, and they'll make suggestions. Or you can choose something like kung poa chicken, crispy fish, or orange beef from the regular menu and ask them to prepare it Chinese style. But you have to make it clear you don't suffer from "fear of flavor." So "ask and ye shall receive." Once they understand that you are ready to go beyond pu-pu platters and chow mein, they'll take you there, into a world of taste that highlights regional specialties and intricately seasoned, complex dishes like Dragon Phoenix, Double Rainbow Delight, crispy Hunan fish, and Happy Family. Some authentic preparations require ingredients that are more costly, and the price will reflect this. If you don't want to be surprised by the bill, inquire about the cost of what you select from the Chinese menu up front. Don't expect anything exotic in the locale or setting. What could be more mundane than an aging shopping strip across from Richmond Mall? Industrial-strength carpeting covers the floor, and those predictable Chinese horoscope placemats grace the tables. The room is decorated with fake plants and fish tanks. Booths line each wall, and there are three tables in the center, one for six and two with eight chairs each. There's parking in the small front lot, and in another lot along the side.

Li Wah
☎ **(216) 696-6556**

CITY: **Cleveland**   AREA: **Near East Side**
ATMOSPHERE: **Dressy**   COST: $$$$$

ADDRESS: 2999 Payne/Asia Plaza
HOURS: Daily 10 a.m.–2 a.m.
RESERVATIONS: Taken, recommended for large groups of 10 or more **PAYMENT:** MC, VS, AX
BAR: Beer, wine, liquor **TAKEOUT:** Yes
SMOKING: Smoking section **ACCESS:** ♿ Full access

Chinese people eat here because they can get dishes they aren't likely to find on any other local restaurant menu: duck eggs with ginger; shredded chicken with jellyfish; pan-fried noodles with abalone; and dim sum that includes beef tripe, chicken feet, sticky rice with lotus leaf, and turnip cakes. But the spacious restaurant, which can seat up to 400, attracts people of every ethnicity because, in addition to an extensive selection of flavorful Chinese dishes, the setting is attractive, comfortable, and contemporary, and service is attentive and efficient. It's a place for dining out—not just chowing down—with an atmosphere that's conducive to good conversation, celebration, and gracious eating. Round tables for 10 or 12 with lazy Susans in the center are perfect for big groups. There's usually a sizable business lunch crowd. The location, in Asia Plaza, is convenient for folks who work downtown, and perfect if you want to do some shopping at the Tink Hall Food Market next door. (For more information about the market, see Tink Hall's listing further on in this chapter.) Dim sum, which translates roughly as "a little bit of whatever your heart desires," is available daily until 3 p.m., and the selection, made from carts wheeled up to your table, is sizable. On Saturday and Sunday, when the clientele is mostly Chinese, there are even more choices. One small detail is noteworthy because it's so rare and so important if you happen to have a baby with you, and representative of an unusual level of consideration for patrons: there's a diaper-changing station in the ladies' room. (Of course, in a perfect world, there'd be one in the men's room, too.) In February, when the Chinese New Year is celebrated, there is a most unusual banquet menu; tickets for this event should be purchased in advance.

Long Phung
☎ (216) 651-1119

CITY: **Cleveland**   AREA: **Near West Side**
ATMOSPHERE: **Relaxed**   COST: $$$$$

ADDRESS: 5107 Detroit Ave.
HOURS: Mon–Thu 11 a.m.–11 p.m., Fri–Sun 11 a.m.–midnight RESERVATIONS: Taken
PAYMENT: MC, VS, DIS BAR: None TAKEOUT: Yes
SMOKING: Smoking section ACCESS: ♿ Limited

A phoenix has risen out of what was once home to the now defunct Big Egg, a 24-hour greasy spoon. The Dragon and Phoenix to be exact. That's the meaning of the words "Long Phung," the name of the restaurant that opened in January 2003 at this location. This place is much, much easier on the eye and the digestion. It's been freshly painted, light wood accents and snow-white curtains have been added, chandeliers sparkle, and Asian bric-a-brac adds a cheery feel. The space, which is larger than it appears from the outside, is divided into two rooms, with one for smokers. Each table is stocked with a vase of cloth flowers, chopsticks, deep-bowled soup spoons, tiny dipping dishes, and squeeze bottles of soy, fish, sweet-and-sour, and hoisin sauces. The Chinese menu is large and is sure to please those with a taste for such things as sesame chicken, moo shu pork, and shrimp lo mein, but holds no surprises. The Vietnamese one, however, is an embarrassment of culinary riches. Each category offers something intriguing and unusual as well as the more popular and well-known dishes. In addition to rice-paper rolls, the appetizers include fried quail, ground shrimp on a sugarcane, and rare smoked young beef salad. Among the Vietnamese-style specials are shrimp sauteed in fish sauce; lemon grass chicken; and stir-fried squid. There are 24 hot pots—made with things like roast duck, marinated beef, steamed fish, squid, clams, or lobster; a selection of soups (pho); crepes; and 13 varieties of bún (vermicelli noodles). One of my measures of authenticity is a menu that includes things I'm pretty sure I've never eaten and hesitate to try. This place meets that criterion with pork stomach porridge; rice noodles with pork kidneys and liver; soup loaded with soft beef tendon and tripe; and spiny goby fish. The restaurant is a dream come true for owner Hanna To and her husband, Tung Nguyen, who are both are from Saigon. On weekends, between 9 p.m. and midnight, they plug in the karaoke machine, and there is much fun in many lan-

PACIFIC RIM

guages. There's a lot in back plus on-street parking in front.

New Wong's Chinese Restaurant
☎ **(216) 696-3811**

CITY: **Cleveland**   AREA: **Near East Side**
ATMOSPHERE: **Relaxed**   COST: $$$$$

ADDRESS: 3211 Payne Ave
HOURS: Daily 9 a.m.–2 a.m. **RESERVATIONS:** Not taken **PAYMENT:** MC, VS, DIS **BAR:** None
TAKEOUT: Yes **SMOKING:** Smoking section
ACCESS: ♿ Limited

Herein lies a potentially confusing story of ownership and change. New Wong's replaces Wong's Hunan Cuisine, which was formerly at this location (and listed in the first edition of *Cleveland Ethnic Eats*). The sign above the door of the old Wong's used to read "Che's" (yet another restaurant that was once on this spot), making the restaurant a bit hard to find. Now there's new management, a new, correct sign out front, and new decor. But the hours are the same, seven days a week and just seven hours shy of round the clock, and the kitchen continues to prepare many of the dishes that made the old place special. Barbecued ducks hang in the front window, just as they used to, and this is still the only place to find breakfast dim sum. As in the past, the clientele is primarily Chinese, especially in the morning and the evenings, so tables are set with chopsticks, not silverware. Menus are printed in both Chinese and English, and Chinese videos play on the wall-mounted television. A good selection of Chinese dishes favored by Westerners is listed, as well as others that are more suited to Asian tastes, such as the 15 varieties of noodle soup, nine versions of congee (a thick rice soup), and what they call barbecued steamed rice plates. The dining room has been spruced up: it's light and bright with blond wood accents, beige wallpaper that sports a contemporary-looking geometric-patterned border, and tables with white cloths. The setting is no

longer hole-in-the-wall spare, but this is still a small, simple Chinese restaurant off the beaten path that has much to offer those who are both gastronomically bold and hungry. How about a noodle bowl with pigs' feet, or a congee of pork and preserved eggs? For those with less daring palates, there's always Szechuan pork, shrimp with cashews, stir-fried string beans, beef lo mein, and sesame chicken. On-street parking available, as well as a very small lot beside the building.

Pearl of the Orient
☎ **(216) 751-8181**

CITY: **Shaker Heights**   AREA: **East Side**
ATMOSPHERE: **Casual**   COST: $$$$$

ADDRESS: 20121 Van Aken Blvd.
HOURS: Lunch Mond–Fri 11:30 a.m.–3 p.m.; Dinner Sun–Thu 5-10 p.m., Fri & Sat 5–11 p.m.; no lunch Sat & Sun **RESERVATIONS:** Taken, recommended **PAYMENT:** MC, VS, AX, DIS
BAR: Beer, wine, liquor **TAKEOUT:** Yes
SMOKING: Smoking section **ACCESS:** ♿ Full access **OTHER ETHNIC SPECIALTIES:** Thai

Cleveland Magazine readers have voted Pearl of the Orient the best Chinese restaurant 12 times, and owner Rose Wong is well known in the community both for her culinary creativity and her volunteer work. Her original East Side location has been in operation since 1979, and the second, West Side one has an 11-year track record. (For information about Pearl of the Orient in Rocky River, see next listing). The two restaurants are fundamentally the same, serving a combination of traditional dishes and inventive variations in handsome, modern, upscale settings. Wong believes she was the first area restaurateur to offer diners Szechuan-style dishes and a menu that did not include egg foo yong and chop suey. Though many offerings change seasonally, some of her customers' favorites that have a permanent place on the menu include the Pearl Wor Bar, a combination of shrimp, scallops, chicken, and vegetables on a bed of sizzling rice; Peking duck (24 hours' notice required); shrimp and chicken with cashews; and filet mignon in ginger mushroom sauce. Hot and spicy dishes, which can be ordered at three levels of burn, include Szechuan scallops; string beans in garlic sauce; black pepper chicken; beef with tangerine peel; shredded spice pork; and Singapore rice noodles. Among the more unusual entrees the kitchen turns out are wok-seared salmon in chili sauce; chicken with mangoes and honey walnuts; vegetables with roasted garlic cloves and toasted cashews; smoked duck breast with three types of mushrooms; a stir-fry of shrimp, melon, and strawberries; and calamari with black bean sauce. Brown rice can be substituted for white. A few classic Thai dishes are also featured: pad Thai; red curry chicken; vegetables in peanut sauce; and prawns with basil. The wine list is extensive, with many available by the glass, and there's also a sizable selection of beers, including a number of microbrews. Each location seats about 110 and provides ample, convenient parking.

Pearl of the Orient
☎ (440) 333-9902

CITY: **Rocky River**   AREA: **West Side**
ATMOSPHERE: **Casual**   COST: $$$$$

ADDRESS: 19300 Detroit Rd.
HOURS: Lunch Mon–Sat 11:30 a.m.–3:30 p.m.; Dinner Mon–Thu 3:30–9:45 p.m., Fri & Sat 3:30–10:45 p.m., Sun 4–8:45 p.m.; no lunch Sun
RESERVATIONS: Taken, recommended
PAYMENT: MC, VS, AX, DIS   BAR: Beer, wine, liquor
TAKEOUT: Yes   SMOKING: Smoking section
ACCESS: ☐ None   OTHER ETHNIC SPECIALTIES: Thai

See preceding listing for Pearl of the Orient in Shaker Heights.

Peking Gourmet
☎ (216) 397-9939

CITY: **South Euclid**   AREA: **East Side**
ATMOSPHERE: **Casual**   COST: $$$$$

ADDRESS: 13955 Cedar Rd.
HOURS: Mon–Thu 11:30 a.m.–10 p.m., Fri & Sat 11:30 a.m.–11 p.m., Sun 4–10 p.m.
RESERVATIONS: Taken, suggested at all times, but especially on weekends   PAYMENT: MC, VS
BAR: Beer, wine, liquor   TAKEOUT: Yes
SMOKING: Smoking section   ACCESS: ☐ None

The varieties and subtleties of Chinese cuisine available here are both a revelation and an education. To ascend to extraordinary heights of gastronomic delight, you descend below ground level, entering a "basement" restaurant, which is nonetheless elegantly appointed, attractive, and pleasant. Cecilia Huang and her daughter Angela, who own and operate the restaurant, are vegetarians, reflecting the influence of Angela's grandmother, who was a practicing Buddhist. They have brought this influence to bear on the menu, and the result is a vegetarian's dream come true—eight pages of dishes that contain neither meat nor fish, including many classical Zen specialties not available anywhere else in town. One of the more amazing aspects of some of these "fleshless" selections is that tofu, wheat paste, and other ingredients are used to create chicken, beef, pork, and seafood look-alikes and taste-alikes. So in addition to ordering vegetable bean curd soup, crystal spinach rolls, stuffed squash, Szechuan asparagus, and "vegetarian bundles" made with golden and shiitake mushrooms, carrots, and celery, those who choose not to eat anything that once walked or swam (as well as anyone else who likes good food) can enjoy Zen "chicken" in orange peel sauce; Zen sweet and sour "fish"; and Mu Shu Fantasia made with soy pate, bean noodles, cabbage, scallions, and wood ear mushrooms. These same dishes are ideal for those who are concerned with eating less fat, as are the delectable tofu desserts, which contain no fat or dairy products.

The menu has a section devoted to "Heart Smart Specials," and the restaurant has won accolades from local health and nutrition-conscious organizations and experts. But if indulgence rather than abstinence is what you're after, you'll also find it here, in an extensive array of the most popular, as well as some rare, Chinese dishes. There are three different types of pot stickers (a 20-minute wait, as they are always assembled and cooked to order); five different kinds of egg rolls, including one made with seaweed and another made with taro; unusual "starters" like pickled garlic, seaweed salad, and ginkgo nut soup; and regional specialties such as Hunan lamb; Peking-style duck or shrimp and scallops; Cantonese lobster; Taipei rice noodles or spicy Singapore mai fun noodles made with pork and shrimp; Mongolian beef; Szechuan whole fish; and an ever-changing list of chef's specials. Lavish desserts are also one of their trademarks—chocolate treats as well as Chinese specialties. The modest wine list has been designed to offer those vintages which complement the menu. Service is extremely gracious and efficient. I am embarrassed to admit that for more than 15 years I lived near this restaurant, which earned an unprecedented six chopsticks from a fellow food writer (five was his standard best), but I never ate here until I began to work on the second edition of *Cleveland Ethnic Eats*. But I've seen the error of my ways and fully expect I'll join the ranks of the regulars, whose photos and letters of thanks and appreciation line one entire wall. Limited metered parking in front. Plenty of free parking in the rear, but this entails either using one of the two alleys that lead to the front of the Cedar Center shopping plaza to reach the front entrance or coming in the rear door and making your way down a long, grim, winding corridor.

Ricky Ly's Chinese Gourmet
☎ (330) 492-5905

CITY: **Canton**   AREA: **Farther South**
ATMOSPHERE: **Relaxed**   COST: $$$$$

ADDRESS: 4695 Dressler Rd.
HOURS: Mon–Thu 11:30 a.m.–10:30 p.m., Fri 11:30 a.m.–11:30 p.m., Sat noon–11:30 p.m., Sun 11 a.m.–9 p.m. **RESERVATIONS:** Taken, suggested for 5 or more **PAYMENT:** MC, VS, AX, DIS **BAR:** Beer, wine, liquor **TAKEOUT:** Yes **SMOKING:** Smoking section **ACCESS:** ⑤ Full access **OTHER ETHNIC SPECIALTIES:** Thai and Japanese

Situated as it is in mall country, where every street features a shopping center that looks like it went up overnight and chain stores are the norm, this place could easily be mistaken for just another American-style Chinese restaurant, perhaps a franchise model where everything is planned by businessmen at some distant corporate headquarters. But it's not. It's a one-of-a-kind place run by Ricky Ly, who escaped from Vietnam on a fishing boat when he was 18 with help from members of his family, and it's been around since the 1980s. Servers wear Chinese dress. It's a spacious, upscale place with seating for about 150 and a modern look, inside and out. The lounge is also the dining area for smokers and and those patronizing the sushi bar (which represents the totality of Japanese cuisine available here). The menu has more Chinese than Thai dishes, but there's enough variety so that you can come back often and still not have to eat the same few things. There are many hot and spicy dishes in both Chinese and Thai style. Some of the more uncommon efforts from the kitchen include Szechuan lobster, Bangkok fish, Siam tofu, hot pepper chicken, Hong Kong steak, and macadamia nut squid. For mussel lovers like myself, the choice seems almost decadent: they do them Szechuan-style, with black bean sauce, in a clay pot, Siam style, and with Thai basil. Four special combination dinners for two offer intriguing possibilities with lyrical names: Emperor's Treasure combines Mongolian beef, almond chicken, and sauteed sea scallops; Three Moon's combo is a platter of Hunan shrimp, chicken with peapods, and sesame beef; Lover's Shrimp offers prawns two ways—half are done with wine sauce and the rest with red ginger sauce; and Swinging in the Stars is a sort of elaborate surf and turf made with scallops, chicken, beef, shrimp, pork, and Chinese vegetables. They make their own coconut ice cream, and other dessert options are banana fritters, mandarin oranges, and lychees. With 24 hours notice the chef will prepare an Imperial Gourmet Dinner for groups of six or more, and it's supposed to be a feast that is as beautiful as it is delicious. I have one complaint about the menu and pass it along as a warning—dishes are listed by name without any descriptive information. So while it's easy to decide if you want orange beef or curry duck, it's a good deal harder to know whether you'd prefer pataya pork, siracha shrimp, chicken shijing, gang shio prawns, Triple Delicacy, or Double Pleasure unless you've eaten them before or were raised or educated to know the difference between san shian and lard na. But don't be afraid to ask. Servers are friendly, and the management is quick to admit they like to spoil their customers. If you let them know about special dietary needs by phone or fax prior to your arrival, they'll go out of their way to be accommodating. They have banquet facilities, gift certificates, and outdoor seating (which unfortunately gives you a view of either the parking lot or busy Dressler Road).

Sun Luck Garden
☎ (216) 397-7676
CITY: **Cleveland Heights** AREA: **East Side**
ATMOSPHERE: **Casual** COST: $$$$$

ADDRESS: 1901 S. Taylor Rd.
HOURS: Lunch: Tue–Fri 11:30 a.m.–2 p.m.; Dinner Tue–Fri 4–9:30 p.m., Sat 4–10 p.m., Sun 4–8:30 p.m.; closed Mon **RESERVATIONS:** Taken, recommended on weekends and at all times for groups of 5 or more **PAYMENT:** MC, VS, AX, DIS **BAR:** Beer, wine **TAKEOUT:** Yes **SMOKING:** Smoke-free **ACCESS:** ♿ Full access

Let go of all preconceptions about what a Chinese restaurant is supposed to be before you walk in the door. Owner Annie Chiu has created a brilliant fusion of East and West, old and new. Daily specials highlight traditional ingredients and techniques in unlikely contemporary combinations, such as mussels in a spicy red garlic-laced broth; grouper baked Continental style and served sizzling with stir-fried Oriental vegetables; puff pastry filled with sa cha beef (meat in a kind of barbecue sauce); shrimp and scallions layered with phyllo dough; and steamed chicken dumplings with spinach, a dish Chiu created to satisfy her customers' needs for something very low fat and low calorie but just as delicious as everything else that comes from her kitchen. The decor reflects the blend of old and new. Original paintings by a local artist incorporate ancient Chinese mythological themes in a contemporary motif. Chiu serves special dishes rarely prepared in this country, never scrimping on rare or costly ingredients like baby ginger, dried Chinese scallops, Chinese chives, and saffron. Even familiar items like hot and sour soup and governor's chicken take on a new and intriguing identity here. For those in search of the Chinese food they know and love, her spicy kung pao shrimp, and yu shan scallops are popular choices. She does amazing things with tofu: her dark tofu is so meaty and flavorful that if you don't tell the kids or those who've dedicated themselves to avoiding anything that smacks of health, they'll never know what they're eating. Her ma pau tofu, considered to be a kind of Chinese comfort food, is a favorite with her Asian guests.

Much of what she knows, Chiu learned by studying with master chefs in China, apprenticeships arranged by her mother's brother, who is a renowned chef and teacher there. And hers is among the few Chinese restaurants around that offer extraordinary desserts. There's plum cheesecake daily, and if you're lucky, you'll visit on a day she's had the urge to whip up something even more unusual like pistachio mousse, French pear tart with homemade pear ice cream, strawberry chocolate soufflé roll, or chocolate pecan tarts. For those with a taste—or doctor's orders—for something lighter, she creates her own sorbets from the likes of grapefruits, passion fruit, mangoes, and rose petals. "People come here, before they know us," she said, "expecting the Chinese food they've eaten elsewhere. They quickly realize this is a place where they can taste something quite different than the usual." Be sure to get on Chiu's mailing list. She's also instituted a "What's Cooking at Annie's" hot line (216-556-1992) with a new message every Monday evening. Dial up to find out about the specials she's preparing for the week that take advantage of the best the markets have to offer and seasonal produce. Throughout the year she hosts special events, such as a unique Chinese English high tea. She's always on the lookout for unusual and outstanding wines from around the world that will complement her cooking; the selection is eclectic and ever changing. The restaurant is located at the end of Taylor Commons, a strip mall one-half mile north of Cedar Road; ample parking in front.

Szechwan Garden

☎ (216) 226-1987

CITY: **Lakewood**　　AREA: **West Side**
ATMOSPHERE: **Casual**　　COST: $$$$

ADDRESS: 13800 Detroit Ave.
HOURS: Lunch Mon–Sat 11:30 a.m.–2:30 p.m.; Dinner Mon–Thu 4:30–9:30 p.m., Fri & Sat 4:30–10:30 p.m., Sun 4–9 p.m.; closed between lunch & dinner RESERVATIONS: Taken, recommended on weekends PAYMENT: MC, VS, AX, DIS BAR: Beer, wine, liquor TAKEOUT: Yes

SMOKING: Smoking section ACCESS: ♿ Full access

Newcomers may be surprised to find that behind the unimpressive exterior of this little place located in an older neighborhood of small apartment buildings, single-family homes, and storefronts, is an exceptional restaurant. Once inside, patrons encounter booths and tables (seating about 60) set with peaked cloth napkins, expert service, and authentic regional Chinese dishes. A husband-and-wife team owns the restaurant and runs the kitchen, where they turn out house specialties including Hunan lobster, orange chicken, and Szechwan duck. Other interesting items on the menu are egg flower soup; a spicy pork dish with vegetables in a dark, pungent sauce; and Lake Tung Ting shrimp (made with beaten egg whites). The kitchen is willing to adjust the spiciness according to your preference for mild, medium, or hot. The atmosphere is warm and hospitable, and there's a steady flow of patrons at all hours, both for eat-in and takeout. Plenty of parking available.

Wu's Cuisine

☎ (216) 221-9030

CITY: **Lakewood**　　AREA: **West Side**
ATMOSPHERE: **Relaxed**　　COST: $$$$

ADDRESS: 14821 Madison Ave.
HOURS: Lunch Mon–Fri only, 11:30 a.m.–2 p.m., Dinner Mon–Thu 5–8:30 p.m., Fri & Sat 5–9:30 p.m.; kitchen closed between lunch & dinner; closed Sun RESERVATIONS: Not taken
PAYMENT: Cash only BAR: None TAKEOUT: No
SMOKING: Smoking section ACCESS: ♿ Limited

I was introduced to this restaurant by one of Cleveland's all-time great food enthusiasts, Saul Isler, a writer whose articles appeared in *The Plain Dealer* and the *Downtown Tab* until he emigrated to the West Coast in the spring of 1997. His specialty was tracking down cheap but excellent eateries. His primary purpose in bringing me here was to interview me about the first edition of *Cleveland Ethnic Eats*. But he also liked the idea of introducing me to a wonderful restaurant I didn't already know about. I met Lee Wu, a native of Taiwan, who greets and seats visitors to this very small, unadorned storefront restaurant (only 10 tables) that she operates with her husband, known to all as Chef Wu. Lee speaks enthusiastic English punctuated by her stunning smile; Chef Wu, who worked for 18 years in one of Taiwan's finest restaurants, not a word of it, but he communicates through his food. His menu features Szechuan, Mandarin, Hunan, and Taiwanese cuisine, including some dishes rarely found anywhere else in town, such as leung mein (diced chicken, cashews, and greens in a "pancake wrapper"), Mongolian butter beef, tomato chicken, four season string beans, spicy cabbage, and a braised duck stewed with onions, scallions, and carrots. He uses only fresh ingredients and makes all his own sauces from scratch. His hot and sour soup is a masterful blend of the two flavors, and the pieces of tenderloin in his yu hsiang pork manage to be both crisp and moist at the same time. There are some interesting choices for vegetarians, too. The sense of intimacy that's a function of the small size of the place is reinforced by Lee's friendliness. She keeps a big photo album of her family on the window ledge, and if you show any interest, she'll be more than glad to bring it out and proudly show you pictures of her children. According to Saul—and seconded by Lee—everyone he has brought here has come back and become a regular. What better recommendation could there be? Plenty of on-street parking on Madison, at Warren across from the famous Malley's Candy.

Filipino

Nipa Hut
☎ (440) 842-7333

CITY: **Parma Heights**   AREA: **Southwest**
ATMOSPHERE: **Relaxed**   COST: $$$$$

ADDRESS: 6775 W. 130th St.

HOURS: Mon–Sat 8:30 a.m.–7:30 p.m., Sun closed RESERVATIONS: Taken, suggested for 5 or more PAYMENT: MC, VS, DIS BAR: None
TAKEOUT: Yes SMOKING: Smoke-Free
ACCESS: ♿ Full access

This is the only place in the region where you can get freshly prepared Filipino food. Although Filipino chefs use many of the same ingredients found in Chinese, Japanese, Korean, and Thai cooking, the spicing is quite different, the Spanish influence is apparent, and the end result is food unlike any other in the Pacific Rim. This means that even though Nipa Hut is more market than restaurant—with only a few tables and some folding chairs, disposable plates and utensils, and a self-serve counter—it offers a not-to-be-missed dining experience. Poli Ignacio and his wife Mercy have been making delicacies from their homeland, many of which require time-consuming preparation and slow cooking, for 27 years, 17 of them at this location near Pearl Road. Not every dish on their menu is available every day, but you can call ahead to place a special order. The best selection is found on Saturdays, when they do their weekly buffet. It will likely include lumpia (egg rolls), marinated fried bangus (milkfish, the most popular fish in the Philippines), menudo (pork in a sauce made with garlic, tomatoes, and onions), pancit (rice stick noodles), barbecued chicken or pork, and sweets such as cassava cake, leche plan (flan), and purple rice cake. The daily menu requires some knowledge of the language and the cuisine because most items are listed only by their Filipino name. Here's an abbreviated glossary—but don't hesitate to ask the folks behind the counter for help. Chicken afritada and beef mechado are both meat-and-vegetable stews. Dinuguan is also a stew, but few Americans like it, according to Poli, as it is made with beef or pork blood. Empanadas are a cross between a pierogi and an egg roll—a fried pastry with a meat-and-vegetable filling. Pakbet is a mix of vegetables including long beans, Oriental eggplant, and okra. Kare-kare is oxtail soup. Ukoy is made with squash, onion, and fried shrimp. Pata is a dish of pork hocks that are boiled in a seasoned broth, dried, and then fried until crispy. Anything with palabok comes in a sauce of ground pork and oysters, clams, or mussels. In the dessert department, turon are fried bananas, puto is a sweet rice cake, bibingka is a confection of sticky rice and coconut milk, and hopia is a kind of cake. Kids under 12 get a bargain rate on the buffet, and those three and under eat free. Tables are actually opposite shelves filled with products from all the Asian nations. (For more information about the grocery store, see listing under same name in the market section of this chapter). Most of the restaurant business is actually carryout, which is a good thing because there's only seating for 24. A large green-and-white sign near the road makes the place easy to find.

Akira Sushi & Hibachi

☎ **(440) 349-6850**

CITY: **Solon**   AREA: **Farther East**
ATMOSPHERE: **Casual**   COST: **$$$$**$

ADDRESS: 6025 Kruse Dr.
HOURS: lunch: Mon–Fri 11:30 a.m.–2:30 p.m.; Dinner Mon–Thu 5 p.m.–10 p.m., Fri–Sat 5 p.m.–11 p.m., Sun 5 p.m.–9 p.m.
RESERVATIONS: Taken, Suggested weekends
PAYMENT: MC, VS, AX, DIS   BAR: Beer, wine, liquor
TAKEOUT: Yes   SMOKING: Smoke-Free
ACCESS: ⚬ Full access

A jewel of a place set in the ever-expanding mall district of this southeastern suburb, and one where diners are sure to find something wonderfully unique amidst the overabundance of national chains and name-brand merchandise. Owners Anna and Hank Saito, who came here from New York City, are determined to set themselves apart from other Japanese restaurants. They've crafted a menu that blends classic dishes with some of their own inspired creations, designed a space that is thoroughly contemporary but that subtly references traditional elements, and created an atmosphere that both welcomes children and appeals to adults.

Look for a mix of eating possibilities with presentation always treated as art. Some will challenge your palate to explore unusual textures and tastes like edamame (steamed soybeans); nabe yaki udon (noodles, tempura, and fish cakes in broth); and the raw fish selections. Sushi and sashimi are impeccably fresh, varied, and expertly prepared. Fish connoisseurs take note—this is the only restaurant in the Midwest, according to Anna Saito, to serve that infamous delicacy blowfish (fugu), when it is in season and available. They're also the only ones offering a cold summer version of a dish called shabu shabu, which they bring in a bowl made of ice. Generally served hot, and named for the sound the ingredients make when they hit the steaming broth, it features slices of tender, shaved beef, noodles, and sculpted vegetables. Other entrees are comfortingly familiar—teriyaki steak, shrimp tempura, and grilled swordfish. Dishes prepared tableside on the built-in hibachi grills offer eating-as-entertainment. Diners get a show that's sure to be a kid pleaser when the chef goes into action. He wheels a three-tiered cart over, laden with ingredients, and then masterfully plays with your food, flipping, swirling, and tossing everything including his utensils. A few surprising cross-cultural combinations, which too often produce a muddle of flavors, are culinary achievements here. Look for Latin American ceviche-style New Millennium sashimi; tuna carpaccio; and a deep-fried, Italian-influenced crispy roll, made with smoked salmon, asparagus, and mozzarella cheese. This last offering and their popular Volcano Roll, made with shrimp tempura and conch, feature fully cooked fish, perfect for those who cringe at the thought of eating seafood that hasn't seen a stove. For those who enjoy a drink with dinner, I recommend trying the chilled semi-dry sake. If you like the food, take note: not only do they do off-site catering, but they have a portable sushi bar that they can bring to you.

The decor is attractive and sleek, all earthy tones and natural wood. There's a 12-seat sushi bar. The spacious dining room is divided into discrete sections by half walls and sculptural semi-solid partitions. Anna, who serves as hostess and one-woman welcoming committee, organizes the seating so that the front portion of the space is reserved for adults dining without children, creating a sort of intimate bistro within the larger room. She also chooses the background music, and we have the same taste in tunes—Nora Jones, Ella Fitzgerald, the Temptations. Although the surroundings are stylish, many diners dress very casually.

Aoeshi
☎ (440) 716-0988

CITY: **North Olmsted**   AREA: **West Side**
ATMOSPHERE: **Casual**   COST: $$$$$

ADDRESS: 24539 Lorain Ave.
HOURS: Tue–Thu 11 a.m.–10 p.m., Fri–Sat 11 a.m.–10:30 p.m., Sun 11:30 a.m.–10 p.m., Mon closed RESERVATIONS: Taken, Suggested weekends PAYMENT: MC, VS, AX, DIS BAR: Byob
TAKEOUT: Yes SMOKING: Smoke-Free
ACCESS: ♿ Full access

Cleveland's own Joe Crea, food and restaurant editor at The Plain Dealer and a man with the experience and expertise to know fine food when he tastes it, described this restaurant as "a surprising little gem" and wrote that he had three of best maki rolls here that he ever had anywhere. Local celebrity chef Michael Symon, another guy who knows his way around the table, tipped him off, suggesting that the sushi was as good as that at Nobu's, a famous and pricey NYC eatery. That's high praise for a small mom-and-pop restaurant located in an out-of-the-way strip mall in North Olmstead, an area not exactly known as a hotbed of culinary innovation. Young Kim welcomes diners, and her husband, Chong, is the sushi master and chef. The selection is large and creative: there are 10 different seaweed-wrapped vegetarian maki; 22 nigri-sushi featuring such delicacies as smelt fish roe, quail egg, sweet shrimp, and river eel atop little mounds of rice; and cleverly named and conceived rolls— Three Amigo, Pink Lady, Dragon, and Rainbow. Sit at the sushi bar in one of the six seats and you'll have a great view of an artist at work as Chong Kim expertly slices whole fish and assembles his beautiful little packages and arranges his platters. The regular menu is just as enticing and eclectic. Look for steamed dumplings, salmon skin salad (don't be put off by the name), tempura, noodle dishes, and breaded and fried cutlets. The setting is modern and minimalist with a clean bright look. Seating for just 50, but there's enough parking in the strip mall's lot out front for an entire regiment.

Daishin
☎ (440) 899-9969

CITY: **Westlake**   AREA: **West Side**
ATMOSPHERE: **Casual**   COST: $$$$$

ADDRESS: 24545 Center Ridge Rd.
HOURS: Lunch Mon–Fri 11:30 a.m.–2 p.m.; Dinner Mon–Fri 5–10 p.m., Sat 4:30–10:30 p.m.; closed between lunch & dinner; closed Sun
RESERVATIONS: Taken, recommended
PAYMENT: MC, VS, AX, DIS BAR: Beer, wine, liquor
TAKEOUT: Yes SMOKING: Smoking section
ACCESS: ♿ Full access

Entering the vestibule, you leave behind the surrounding small strip mall and nearby office park. The sound of water in a fountain, trickling over stones, welcomes you. On the other side of the second door is a huge aquarium filled with tropical fish. Beyond that is an airy, spacious, white-walled room with natural blond wood accents. The room manages to convey both the quiet beauty of Japanese design and a sense of cosmopolitan style. To your left is a seven-seat sushi bar, where small pieces of raw fish are prepared with spoonfuls of rice. Chunks of octopus, tuna, shrimp, and salmon, colorful as jewels, are artfully displayed in a glass case. A large photo poster shows all the different kinds of sushi. Waitresses wear kimono jackets. Some tables that offer what appears to be traditional on-the-floor seating actually make a concession to Western habits: the tables are close to the floor, but the area under them is open so diners' legs actually hang down as in a chair, and cushions are equipped with rigid backs. The menu features 19 different appetizers, and the entrees, which come with miso soup and salad, represent a nice variety of seafood, chicken, and beef, with several options for vegetarians.

Daishin Hibachi Steak House
☎ (440) 979-1337
CITY: **North Olmsted**   AREA: **West Side**
ATMOSPHERE: **Casual**   COST: $$$$$

ADDRESS: 26092 Brookpark Rd.
HOURS: Lunch Mon–Fri 11:30 a.m.–2 p.m.; Dinner Mon–Fri 5–10 p.m., Sat 4:30–10:30 p.m.; closed between lunch & dinner; closed Sun
RESERVATIONS: Taken, recommended
PAYMENT: MC, VS, AX, DIS **BAR:** Beer, wine, liquor
TAKEOUT: Yes **SMOKING:** Smoking section
ACCESS: & Full access

A second location for Don Park, owner of the original Daishin Restaurant in Westlake. This one, equally as inviting, features the same large selection of sushi and sashimi, plus Hibachi dinners cooked tableside at built in grills. There are 12 grill tables, each seating 8. Diners can choose entrees prepared with chicken, salmon, steak, scallops, shrimp, lobster, or vegetables only. Child-sized hibachi portions are offered for kids under 10. The restaurant is located in Great Northern Mall.

Ginza Sushi House
☎ (216) 589-8503
CITY: **Cleveland**   AREA: **Downtown**
ATMOSPHERE: **Casual**   COST: $$$$$

ADDRESS: 1105 Carnegie Ave.
HOURS: Lunch Mon–Fri 11:30 a.m.–2:30 p.m.; Dinner Mon–Thu 5:30–9:30 p.m., Fri & Sat 5–10:30 p.m.; closed Sun; kitchen closed between lunch & dinner **RESERVATIONS:** Taken, evenings only **PAYMENT:** MC, VS, DIS **BAR:** Beer, wine **TAKEOUT:** Yes **SMOKING:** Smoking section
ACCESS: & Limited

Sonny Garcia, who is half Japanese and hails from the Philippines, is owner and chef here, and his mother, Virginia, is hostess and general PR person. To say that this family-run business is friendly is an understatement—it's not unusual to see "regulars" chat with "Mom" when they arrive and hug her when they leave. In between, regulars and newcomers alike have an opportunity to experience Sonny's artistry. He had 17 years of experience, much of it as a chef in local Japanese restaurants and the rest in Japan and Los Angeles, and now brings it all to bear in his own place in his preparation of nigiri sushi (small "fingers" of pressed rice and either raw or cooked seafood, mushroom, daikon, or egg); maki sushi (raw or cooked seafood or vegetables and rice hand-rolled in paper-thin sheets of seaweed); futomaki (extra-large maki); and sashimi (raw fish with sides of rice and vegetable). Sonny's signature creation is the Ginza roll, a futomaki made with three different fishes, avocado, and egg (tamago) arranged in eye-catching red, yellow, and green stripes. The fish, flown in daily, is always very fresh. Ordering is simple: a list you fill in yourself is provided: the numbered Japanese name is accompanied by a brief description of the contents. All you have to do is check off your choices. Sonny often prepares sushi creations that are not on the a la carte list, so be sure to ask about the chef's specials. Everyone in the family is glad to discourse on the healthful benefits of sushi, and will happily provide advice about how to eat it properly. One of their tips is to use the decorative ginger pickles on the serving bowl as a palette cleanser between each selection. For those who suffer from fear of fish, especially the raw variety, a visit to Ginza could be the beginning of a new era: writer Chris Shimp recounted in the *Free Times* that he brought his sushi-phobic parents here, and, much to their surprise as well as his, they loved everything. There are, however, ample alternatives for the hard-core carnivores and those who want to sample other Japanese dishes. A separate menu offers hot entrees such as hibachi-prepared chicken or steak, tempura, noodle-filled hot pots, and teriyaki. A bowl of miso soup and a side of seaweed salad are a light and flavorful accompaniment to any entree. Though it may not sound appetizing to most Americans, my eating troopers found green-tea or red-bean ice cream, imported from Japan, surprisingly refreshing as a finish to their meal. Japanese beers and both hot and cold sake are also available. Acknowledging the fact of their location just one block from Jacobs Field and the Gund Arena, Ginza offers boxed sushi-sashimi meals to go, and they have named one creation Gateway Maki. The restaurant is actually a few doors down from the original place, and it's larger and fancier. Clever use of wooden latticework dividers, and an area raised a few steps above the rest, maintain a sense of intimacy even though the seating capacity has doubled to about 90. The old place had a very casual East-meets-West decor; here the two cultures still combine forces, but the effect is much more elegant. A traditional motif that employs rice-paper screens and muted colors,

and some floor seating with cushions (there are also conventional tables and chairs) create that impression of quiet calm associated with Japanese interiors. The restaurant website, www.ginzasushi.com, provides directions, a menu, and an option for making large-group reservations (six or more) online, 24 hours in advance.

Matsu Japanese Restaurant
☎ (216) 767-1111

CITY: **Shaker Heights**   AREA: **East Side**
ATMOSPHERE: **Casual**   COST: **$$$**$$

ADDRESS: 20126 Chagrin Blvd.
HOURS: Mon–Thu 11:30 a.m.–2 p.m. & 5–10 p.m., Fri & Sat 11:30 a.m.–2 p.m. & 5–11 p.m., Sun 4–9 p.m., Mon closed
RESERVATIONS: Taken, suggested on weekends
PAYMENT: MC, VS, AX, DIS   BAR: Beer, wine, liquor
TAKEOUT: Yes SMOKING: Smoke-Free
ACCESS: ♿ Limited

Scott Kim is Korean by birth, so it would have been reasonable to expect that when he finally opened his own restaurant, after 15 years in the business working for other people, it would be a Korean restaurant. But it isn't. Kim serves Japanese food at Matsu, and his reasoning makes perfect sense. "I knew I could never be as good a Korean cook as my mother," says Kim, "so I decided to study Japanese cooking instead." It's evident he's mastered the art. The menu is varied and interesting, featuring a lengthy assortment of sushi and sashimi, tempura, and teriyaki combinations as well as hot and cold noodle dishes, and traditional "pot cooking" done tableside. His kitchen also turns out some offerings less commonly found here. Among the appetizers and salads are edamame (green soybeans), hiyayakko (chilled bean curd), unagi kabayaki (charbroiled eel), and sunomono (cucumbers, scallions, and seaweed). Entrees for those who want to go beyond sukiyaki include ton katsu (a breaded pork tenderloin), yakiniku (beef and vegetables in garlic sauce), and fish yakimono (a poached fillet in a spicy wine sauce). Desserts offer an opportunity to find out what the Japanese think is a treat: red-bean or green-tea ice cream with an optional sweet bean topping; steamed cheesecake; and mochi (ice cream in a sticky rice bun). More conventional mango sherbet, key lime pie, and a Kahlua brownie sundae are also available for a less challenging finish.

Presentation gets as much attention as preparation. In fact, every detail, from how food is arranged on the plate to how the room is lit, is part of a careful, conscientious effort to create something beautiful and appealing. Kim's wife Brenda, who works with him, insists that all of it reflects the vision in his mind's eye. "He knew just how he wanted it to look, and what you see is a reflection of his ideas." That being true, it must be said that he's got good ideas. And a flair for design. The decor includes modern elements—like metal chairs, blond wood, smoked-glass mirrors, a pale mauve color scheme, and updated track lighting that evokes associations with tightropes and suspension bridges—and combines then with a traditional Asian sensibility, expressed in the simplicity and openness of the floor plan, rice-paper shades and screens, and colorful Japanese paper parasols hung from the ceiling over the 10-seat sushi bar. The result is sleek, understated elegance. Despite the sophisticated atmosphere and menu, children are welcome, with high chairs and booster seats available, but in my opinion it would be unfair to other diners to bring those likely to disturb the calm and decidedly adult mood of the place. Although smoking is not allowed in the dining area, the Kims have created a hospitable alternative to huddling outside in the doorway—smokers may sit in a lounge area in the basement, and they are free to bring coffee, tea, or a drink with them. And there are some interesting drink options, including ten varieties of sake by the bottle (to be quaffed cold as the connoisseurs suggest), hot sake by the glass or bottle, and four Japanese beers that come

regular size (12-ounce Kirin), big (16-ounce Yebisu), bigger (21-ounce Sapporo), and almost embarrassingly huge (22-ounce Kirin Ichiban). There's also a full bar and a small selection of red and white wines by the glass and the bottle, and weekly wine specials. There is a buffet at lunchtime and an abbreviated version of the dinner menu. Free parking in a lot behind the restaurant and a rear entrance.

Otani
☎ (440) 442-7098

CITY: **Mayfield Heights**   AREA: **East Side**
ATMOSPHERE: **Dressy**   COST: **$$$**$$

ADDRESS: 6420 Mayfield Rd. (Golden Gate Plaza)
HOURS: Lunch Mon–Fri 11:30 a.m.–2 p.m., Sat noon–2 p.m.; Dinner Mon–Thu 5–10 p.m., Fri & Sat 5–10:30 p.m., Sun 4:30–8:30 p.m.; closed between lunch & dinner **RESERVATIONS:** Taken, recommended on weekends **PAYMENT:** MC, VS, AX, DIS **BAR:** Beer, wine, liquor **TAKEOUT:** Yes **SMOKING:** Smoking section **ACCESS:** ৬ Full access

Two dining areas are handsomely decorated with a mixture of traditional and contemporary Japanese artwork, plants, and lantern lights. The large rooms are divided into intimate spaces by partitions and subdued lighting, and guests can choose to be seated at regular tables or on low tables surrounded by cushions. There's also counter service at the sushi bar. Other "raw" choices include sashimi (fish without rice) and maki (rice and fish or vegetables wrapped in seaweed); the restaurant has a large selection of all three. The presentation is a feast for the eyes. If you're not in the mood for raw fish (or never will be), you can still eat here; choose teriyaki steak, tempura vegetables (batter dipped and deep fried), or ginger chicken. For special occasions, tableside cooking is popular; Shabu Shabu is a beef and vegetable dish diners cook themselves, one bite at a time. In addition to Japanese beer, hot sake, plum wine, and sakura (a noncarbonated

Japanese soft drink) are available. A nice setting for a celebration.

Pacific East
☎ (216) 320-2302

CITY: **Cleveland Hts.**   AREA: **Near East Side**
ATMOSPHERE: **Casual**   COST: $$$$$

ADDRESS: 1763 Coventry Rd.
HOURS: Lunch Mon–Fri 11 a.m.–3 p.m., Sat noon–3 p.m.; Dinner Mon–Thu 5 p.m.–10 p.m., Fri–Sat 5 p.m.–11 p.m., Sun 3 p.m.–10 p.m.
RESERVATIONS: Taken, Suggested weekends
PAYMENT: MC, VS, AX, DIS **BAR:** Beer, wine
TAKEOUT: Yes **SMOKING:** Smoke-Free
ACCESS: ♿ Full access

Pacific East opened for business in November 2002, and Coventry Village is a better place because of it. It's the only source of Japanese food in the neighborhood. The selection is extensive and interesting, and shows that chef Freeman Ngo wants to stake out new culinary territory. In addition to the standard miso soup, diners can choose from seven others including one made with shiitake mushrooms and another that features crabmeat. The list of appetizers and salads is even longer and equally innovative, and two or three of the 50 possibilities make a fine meal on their own. There's ankimo, a paste made from monkfish liver; poached bean curd in seaweed broth; broiled eggplant with sweet miso sauce; oshitashi, a spinach dish; grilled squid with daikon radish and ginger; and shrimp with asparagus in spicy dressing. The menu also includes a tempting array of noodle dishes (udon), rice bowls (don buri), tempura, teriyaki, yakitori (skewered, grilled meat, poultry, or fish), and bento box meals. And then there are the sushi bar entrees: generously cut slices of fish, artfully rolled and assembled into a multitude of combinations, and beautifully presented. The palate of special ingredients the chefs work with includes plum paste, pickled radish, fermented soybeans, fish roe, eel sauce, egg custard, and

fish powder. Not to be missed is chirashi, made with vividly colored slices of fresh fish atop a bed of seasoned rice. Groups can take advantage of the house's sushi and sashimi combos for a special treat—The Bridge serves two, The Boat is for three and is indeed served in a ship, and the glorious King and Queen feeds four royally. The space at the corner of Coventry and Mayfield, once an Indian restaurant, has been completely refurbished. The most striking feature is the color blue, so intense and pervasive that it's easy to imagine oneself underwater, hanging with the octopus, tuna, giant clams, and sea urchins that show up on the menu. Meters on the street and down the block in a garage.

Shinano Japanese Restaurant
☎ (440) 473-2345

CITY: **Richmond Heights**   AREA: **East Side**
ATMOSPHERE: **Casual**   COST: $$$$$

ADDRESS: 5222 Wilson Mills Rd.
HOURS: Lunch Mon–Fri 11:30 a.m.–2 p.m.; Dinner Mon–Thu 5:30–10 p.m., Fri & Sat 5:30–10:30 p.m.; Sun 5:30–10 p.m. (May–Sep), 4:30–9 p.m. (Oct–Apr); closed between lunch & dinner **RESERVATIONS:** Taken, recommended on weekends **PAYMENT:** MC, VS, AX, DIS **BAR:** Beer, wine **TAKEOUT:** Yes **SMOKING:** Smoking section
ACCESS: ♿ Full access

Natural wood, wallpaper with a bamboo motif, and paper lanterns and screens work together to create a Japanese ambience. A 15-seat sushi bar runs the length of one wall, and behind the chefs, who work with speed and grace, is a mural of white cranes and blue water on a field of gold. The restaurant is frequented by Japanese students and businesspeople, which may account for the fact that tables are set not with forks but with chopsticks. Silverware is available on request. Warm wet cloths for wiping hands and face come to the table in little wooden cradles before the food. There's a lunchtime buffet that includes a wide variety of traditional dishes such as tempura, sushi, and fried tofu. The bento box, a compartmentalized tray, offers an artful, visually appealing presentation plus a chance to sample a variety of meat, seafood, and vegetable dishes. There are also traditional hot pots—one-pot meals. Sushi can be ordered à la carte in 44 variations, or as special combination plates. Japanese beers and a number of different brands of sake, served hot and cold, are available. The restaurant is located in the Hilltop Plaza strip, across from Richmond Mall. Packaged Japanese sweets, cookies, and crackers are for sale at the register.

Shuhei Restaurant of Japan
☎ (216) 464-1720

CITY: **Beachwood**   AREA: **East Side**
ATMOSPHERE: **Casual**   COST: $$$$$

ADDRESS: 23360 Chagrin Blvd.
HOURS: Lunch Mon–Fri 11:30 a.m.–2:30 p.m., Sat 11:30 a.m.–2 p.m.; Dinner Mon–Thu 5:30–10 p.m., Fri & Sat 5:30–11 p.m., Sun 5–9 p.m.
RESERVATIONS: Taken, recommended
PAYMENT: MC, VS, AX, DIS **BAR:** Beer, wine, liquor
TAKEOUT: Yes **SMOKING:** Smoke-Free
ACCESS: ♿ Limited

Both atmosphere and food here are classically Japanese. The setting is serene, a calm and relaxing environment in which to sample raw fish from the sushi bar or a traditional nabe mono (a hot pot of noodles and vegetables, with optional meat or fish, in a seasoned broth). The menu is not intimidating for the less experienced, with detailed descriptions of every dish, and it is extensive: 30 appetizers, 37 entrees, plus daily specials. Portions are ample, and each dinner entree comes with a bowl of miso (a richly flavored soup made from fermented soybeans) and a choice of either a Western or a Japanese salad. All the female servers are dressed in beautiful traditional costumes. They watch over diners with great care and attention, quickly removing empty plates and supplying the chopstick-challenged with silverware. Guests of all ages will be appropriately dressed in anything from jeans to a business suit. A large sign close to the road pinpoints the office building location. The restaurant itself is in the back; turn into the parking lot and follow the driveway around to the rear.

Sushi 86
☎ (216) 621-8686

CITY: **Cleveland**   AREA: **Downtown**
ATMOSPHERE: **Relaxed**   COST: $$$$$

ADDRESS: 140 Euclid Ave.
HOURS: Mon–Fri 11 a.m.–6:30 p.m., Sat & Sun closed **RESERVATIONS:** Not Taken **PAYMENT:** MC, VS, AX, DIS **BAR:** None **TAKEOUT:** Yes
SMOKING: Smoke-Free **ACCESS:** ♿

At last, fast futo maki. Who knew the world was waiting? Apparently Rachel and Mike Hsu did. That's why they opened their little sushi takeout place on Public Square. If you need food on the go and you prefer flying fish roe, smoked salmon, or red clam to McFat, McSalty, and McGreasy, think Sushi 86. Designed with convenience and speed in mind, the operation is meant to have you in, out, and eating in double-quick time. Call in your order ahead of time and you can probably get away with parking where you shouldn't and running in to pick it up. There is room for seven bodies at the sushi bar if you don't want to take your eel-and-cucumber roll, seaweed salad, and miso soup with you. They also offer delivery service to a limited area downtown. It's free if your order totals $20 or more. Although they are closed on Saturday and Sunday, they will prepare party trays seven days a week, one day's notice required.

DON'T FORGET: CALL AHEAD!

Sushi on the Square Asian Grill

☎ (216) 921-7744

CITY: **Cleveland** AREA: **East Side**
ATMOSPHERE: **Casual** COST: $$$$$

ADDRESS: 13120 Shaker Square
HOURS: Lunch: Mon–Fri 11:30 a.m.–2:30 p.m.,
Sat noon–3 p.m.; Dinner: Mon–Thu 5–10 p.m.,
Fri & Sat 5–11 p.m.; Sun 5–9 p.m.
RESERVATIONS: Taken **PAYMENT:** MC, VS, AX, DIS
BAR: Beer, wine, liquor **TAKEOUT:** Yes
SMOKING: Smoke-Free **ACCESS:** ♿ Full access

No kimonos, floor cushions, or shoji screens at this Japanese restaurant. You can get traditional foods—sushi, futo maki, sashimi, udon, and tempura—but the setting is cosmopolitan, contemporary, and casually chic. "Glam" martinis are on the menu along with "sippin" sake (served stylishly chilled) and Kirin beer. This pairing of ethnic and urbane seems to have wide appeal. The place is typically bustling during mealtimes, and the crowd is a good mix—assorted ages, races, social sets, and fashion groups; families, couples, and a noticeable number of men and women who find this a comfortable spot for dining alone. Fish, especially in its raw form, dominates the menu. Tuna, bonito, salmon, shrimp, scallops, flounder, stripped bass, snapper, eel, octopus, clams, cockles, and more come rolled and wrapped. There are also some vegetarian varieties of nigiri sushi made with shiitake mushrooms, daikon sprouts, spinach, asparagus, or fried bean curd, as well as a short selection of vegetarian entrees. Notable starters include frog legs made with hot pepper and sake; soft-shell crab in a vinegary sunomono sauce; wasabi dumplings; and green mussels. A soup of the day, salads, three noodle dishes, and a selection of grilled meats, fish, and poultry round out the offerings. The dining room is divided into two distinct areas by a half wall. The lower level where you enter is backed by a long, curving sushi bar. There's seating here, and on the upper level, accessible by a ramp, are a combination of booths and tables. In warm weather, there's outdoor seating on the Square too. Park in front at meters or in back in a free lot and enter through a rear door.

Sushi Rock

☎ (216) 623-1212

CITY: **Cleveland** AREA: **Downtown**
ATMOSPHERE: **Dressy** COST: $$$$$

ADDRESS: 1276 W. 6th St.
HOURS: Mon–Thu 11:30 a.m.–2:30 p.m. &
5–10:30 p.m., Fri 11:30 a.m.–2:30 p.m. &
5 p.m.–midnight, Sat 5 p.m.–midnight, Sun
4 p.m.–9 p.m. **RESERVATIONS:** Taken, Suggested
Thu–Sat **PAYMENT:** MC, VS, AX, DIS **BAR:** Beer,
wine, liquor **TAKEOUT:** Yes **SMOKING:** Smoking
section **ACCESS:** ♿ Full access

Sushi is hot, it's in, and it has suddenly become cutting-edge cuisine rather than mere ethnic fare. The hottest, "in"-est, "cutting"-est place to eat these bite-sized morsels of raw seafood, the place to see and be seen, is Sushi Rock in the Warehouse District, open since February 2000. The place aims to be cool—cooler than Cleveland is generally judged to be—and just to be sure you get the message, the walls feature large, backlit photos of New York City, the penultimate metaphor for urban chic. I thought I had the name figured out after I walked in, saw the DJ perched in a pulpit above the teeming, feasting throngs, and heard (or perhaps it would be more accurate to say felt) the throbbing, high-intensity music. Okay, I thought, I get it: rock, roll, and fish. But a chat with the manager revealed that I had sort of missed the boat. While the allusion to a certain chain of cafes that want you to associate music with food is undeniable, the name is actually meant to reflect the unique two-sided menu concept that lets diners choose from food of the sea or more earthbound offerings like free-range chicken, flank steak, or pork tenderloin. It's a water and land, sea and earth, marriage of opposites thing: hence Sushi Rock. The watery side is Japanese style, which is where my interests lie. There's a long list of traditional sushi, sashimi (that's sushi without the rice), maki rolls, temaki (more of a cone), and the king-sized Big Rolls—each available by the piece so you can mix and match at will, and ordered by ticking off your choices on the printed form. The selection is vast and eclectic—tuna, salmon, eel, mackerel, octopus, snapper, sea urchin, clam, yellowtail, flying fish roe, and more. Combinations mix it up with cucumber, avocado, tofu, pickled radish, dried gourd, mountain carrot, and asparagus. Seaweed, baby octopus salad, and chirashi (a combination of vinegared rice, vegetables, and fish) round out the selection. Sushi arrives at your table on a black marble slab brought by a server, male or female, who is dressed in black and sure to be young and well-proportioned, with great hair, and probably sporting a piercing or two. This description fits the clientele equally well, the main difference being that most of them have cell phones glued to their ears or at the ready, and leather jackets on their backs or the backs of their chairs. In contrast, the sushi chefs on a raised platform at the back of the restaurant who prepare your order look like . . . well . . . sushi chefs. The lighting is carefully designed and dramatic, and the result is that the people and food all look appealing. Tables are packed tight on the first floor, and on weekends the crowd is also packed tight in the adjacent bar area, but there's a more expansive feel as well as room for larger groups upstairs. The bar serves martinis in "glam" glasses, some Japanese beers, and cold sake straight and flavored (the new "in" drink, in case you hadn't heard), nice wines by the glass, classy ports, and $3 bottles of water. The entire place resonates with action and potential action, a spot where you can eat ethnic and rev your social engines. Be forewarned: parking in this neighborhood, especially on Friday and Saturday nights, is a complex and potentially expensive undertaking. There are lots, but the price tag is significant, and the search for an on-street spot can be long or leave you with a long walk.

Korean

Korea House

☎ (216) 431-0462

CITY: **Cleveland**   AREA: **Near East Side**
ATMOSPHERE: **Casual**   COST: $$$$$

ADDRESS: 3700 Superior Ave.
HOURS: Mon–Sat 11 a.m.–9 p.m., Sun noon–8 p.m.; closed Tue   **RESERVATIONS:** Taken, recommended for groups of more than 4
PAYMENT: MC, VS, AX, DIS, checks   **BAR:** Beer, wine
TAKEOUT: Yes   **SMOKING:** Smoking section
ACCESS: ⟨♿⟩ Full access

From the outside, this place used to look more like a factory than a restaurant. And in fact, it is a commercial building, surrounded by aging manufacturing and commercial spaces. When owner Housden Chong first opened this restaurant, she concentrated on remodeling the interior space. Enter from a side door that opens into the parking lot, and you'll find pristine white walls and table linens, standing rice-paper and latticework screens, stylized lanterns, silk flowers, and a quiet, spare atmosphere of Asian charm. Now the exterior of the building has been renovated, too, so that it is more inviting and attractive, with the addition of large front windows that will, as Ms. Chong explains, let you see from the outside how great it is on the inside. And beyond the decor, what's great about the inside is the food. Korean food is not at all similar to Chinese food, so diners here should expect a very different eating experience. You'll encounter pot stews, ingredients like octopus, buckwheat noodles, and kimchee (a salty, fermented side dish made of cabbage). Many dishes are spicy, but the chef is happy to adjust the heat to your taste, so feel free to order mild, medium, or hot. Two of the most popular menu items for Americans are the Korean-style barbecued chicken and bul gogi jung sik (marinated sliced beef cooked, for two or more, right at the table). The family-style dinners are a good way to sample a variety of dishes if you're unfamiliar with Korean cuisine. Kim's, a Korean grocery store formerly on Payne, is now located behind the restaurant. (For more information about the store, see listing further on in this chapter).

Seoul Garden
☎ (330) 929-9971

CITY: **Cuyahoga Falls**   AREA: **Farther South**
ATMOSPHERE: **Relaxed**   COST: $$$$$

ADDRESS: 2559 State Rd.
HOURS: Tue–Sun 11:30 a.m.–2:30 p.m. & 5–10 p.m., Mon closed **RESERVATIONS:** Not Taken **PAYMENT:** MC, VS **BAR:** None
TAKEOUT: Yes **SMOKING:** All sections
ACCESS: ✗ None

We all know you shouldn't judge a book by its cover, but most of us do anyway, and we go for the attractive ones with real eye appeal. You shouldn't judge a restaurant by its decor either, but most of us do that, too. So when you walk into this tiny Korean joint you may feel a tremor of disappointment. It's true there's fake wood paneling on the walls (and not much else except for a single decorative black-and-white cloth hanging), but there's real food on the plates. What's lacking in atmosphere, service, and even English-language skills (I don't recommend attempting telephone conversations more complex than "Are you open?" or "A Number 7 and a Number 12 to go, please") is made up for in the authenticity of the food. Eat here and you eat as Koreans do. Entrees range from whole-meal soups like the beefy yook ge jang and nang myon (buckwheat noodles in cold broth) to broiled beef ribs (kalbi), a spicy rice-and-vegetable dish called dolsotbibimbab (better known as Number

16), and a meat dumpling and rice cake combo (ttok mandukuk). Most dishes come with a variety of side-dish condiments as well as steamed rice. If you like beef or you want a vegetarian dish, you'll have several choices. But there's only one pork dish, one chicken dish, and no fish dishes on the 21-item menu. Dessert comes in liquid form, and there are just two of them: sikye, which is a sweet rice drink, and sujong gwa, the intriguing persimmon punch. You'll find the restaurant in a tiny little shopping strip with parking in front.

Seoul Hot Pot
☎ (216) 881-1221

CITY: **Cleveland**   AREA: **Near East Side**
ATMOSPHERE: **Casual**   COST: $$$$$

ADDRESS: 3709 Payne Ave.
HOURS: Mon–Sat 10 a.m.–10 p.m.; closed Sun **RESERVATIONS:** Taken, recommended for large groups **PAYMENT:** MC, VS **BAR:** Beer
TAKEOUT: Yes **SMOKING:** Smoking section
ACCESS: ✗ None

This small restaurant (it seats about 40) was once the only place around where one person could order a meatball sub and the other jaeyook bokum (marinated pork) and twikim mandu (fried dumpling). When the owners, who came here from Korea, went into business they thought success was to be found in pizzas and subs, so they bought a downtown pizzeria, kept the name, and learned to cook Italian-style. But their Korean friends, including homesick exchange students, kept asking them to use the restaurant kitchen to make traditional Korean dishes. Fearing that Clevelanders would never take to Korean food, they decided the best business would be both businesses and for years served pizzas and naeng myun (noodles). But I'm pleased to report that since the publication of *Cleveland Ethnic Eats* there's been so much interest in the Korean half of the menu (which does a good job of explaining what goes into all the dishes so unfamiliar to most Americans), that the family has chosen to focus strictly on their native cuisine. So now those with bold palates can sample gejan bekban (raw crab in hot sauce) or kimbob (a sort of egg roll made with seaweed). Some tables have built-in grills for cooking your own meat, Korean-style. The beef is top quality, marinated, and cooks up so tender you can cut it with a fork. But you're not supposed to. The protocol, if you want to do as the Koreans do, is to wrap a bite-size piece in a lettuce leaf, pick it up with your hands, and pop the whole thing in your mouth. Like all the entrees, it is accompanied by a variety of side dishes and condiments, including pickled vegetables, rice, and hot sauce. Don't be put off by the uninviting exterior; the inside is simple but pleasant.

Thai

Bangkok Gourmet
☎ (330) 630-9789

CITY: **Akron**　AREA: **Farther South**
ATMOSPHERE: **Casual**　COST: **$$$**$$

ADDRESS: 1283 E. Tallmadge Rd.
HOURS: Mon–Thu 5–9:30 p.m., Fri & Sat 5–10 p.m., Sun 5 p.m.–9 p.m.
RESERVATIONS: Not taken　**PAYMENT:** MC, VS, AX, DIS　**BAR:** Beer, wine, liquor　**TAKEOUT:** Yes
SMOKING: Smoking section　**ACCESS:** ♿ Full access

In 1987 Sunanta Fogle opened her Thai restaurant on Merriman Road in Akron, and in 1998 it was relocated and reincarnated under the same name on East Tallmadge. Loyal customers followed, new ones were acquired, and the restaurant continues to be a showcase for Fogle's culinary artistry, a craft she learned working with her mother and grandmother at the restaurant they operated in Thailand. It's still a family undertaking that includes her

son, Ott, and daughter, Oui, doing everything from cooking to serving. Family recipes form the backbone of the menu, which features flavorful soups, a variety of curries, seafood, beef, pork, and poultry dishes, and rice and noodle dishes. In 1997 Ms. Fogle went back to Thailand to study classical cooking technique, and she's been putting what she learned to good use ever since. Her addition of a hot and spicy "drunken stir fry" (pad khee mao, made with whiskey, palm sugar, galanga, and fish sauce) has been especially popular, she says. She prides herself on offering some dishes rarely found in other Thai restaurants, and this is perhaps part of the reason her place has been designated "Best Thai Restaurant in Ohio" four times by the Zagat survey. A short list of these uncommon entrees includes pla sahm roet (a fish fillet sauced with three layers of flavor— sweet, salty, and sour); ok geai yad sai (a chicken breast stuffed with ground pork and beef, dried mushrooms, and water chestnuts); neva kreung thet, which translates as beef in the herb garden; hed hom pad med bua (black mushrooms with lotus seed); and gai savan or mu savan (honey, spiced chicken or pork that features an intriguing marinade of honey, coffee, and rice wine). Duck dishes are available Thursday through Sunday only and sometimes in limited quantities: choose from ped ob (young duck roasted Thai-style); ped sahm ro yod (duck with cashews); and gaeng phet ped yang (duck with red curry). Her ingredients, as you'll learn from reading the descriptions on the menu (available online at www.bangkok-gourmet.com, along with prices and other useful information), are not merely mixed, they're "married" or "melded." Sauces are not just spicy, they're "bold," "pungent," or, as in gung (shrimp) or gai (chicken) nan daeng, a "fragrant fire." Every meat, fish, rice, and noodle entree is available in a vegetarian version, with or without tofu.

Fogle brought back artwork from Thailand as well as recipes, and the walls here are tastefully decorated with paintings and

PACIFIC RIM

pieces of traditional embroidery. There are about 85 seats in one large room. The restaurant attracts a multi-aged, multi-nationality crowd, including families, and students from Akron University and Kent State—especially those from Thailand who are hungry for the home-cooked taste of red curry, dumplings, or pad Thai noodles. Even children who generally favor pizza and hot dogs will find something to like here; especially popular with that set is the chicken satay, the Thai version of barbecue that's made and served on a stick. Ingredients are always fresh, everything is cooked to order, no MSG is ever used, and all cooking oils are cholesterol-free. The atmosphere is relaxed, friendly, and casual—a good place for socializing. Bangkok Gourmet is located close to Chapel Hill Mall, at the intersection of Britain and East Tallmadge Roads.

Lemon Grass Thai Cuisine
☎ (216) 321-0210

CITY: **Cleveland Heights**   AREA: **East Side**
ATMOSPHERE: **Casual**   COST: $$$$$

ADDRESS: 2179 Lee Rd.
HOURS: Lunch Mon–Fri, 11:30 a.m.–2:30 p.m.; Dinner Mon–Thu 5–10 p.m., Fri & Sat 5–11 p.m.; Sun 4–9 p.m. RESERVATIONS: Taken, For parties of 6 or more PAYMENT: MC, VS, AX BAR: Beer, wine, liquor TAKEOUT: Yes SMOKING: Smoke-free ACCESS: ⚹ Full access

Eat here if you're a vegetarian or a die-hard carnivore; an enthusiast of the hot and spicy, in need of mild and light, or a devotee of fresh and healthy; a seeker of classic Thai cuisine or unusual Thai-inspired creations, some of which you can combine to your own taste. Lemon Grass has it all and offers diners a range of choices in environment and food. The 94-seat sunroom, so called because of all the windows that face onto a pocket park, has a laid-back feel with stone tile floors, a view of the bar, and big-screen televisions tuned to whatever game is the current hot

topic of conversation. The other room has a softer, more refined look and a quieter atmosphere. The warm-toned beige walls are decorated with works by Thai artists, the floor is covered in richly colored carpeting with a design inspired by Oriental rugs.

Both sides offer the same authentic dishes prepared by chef and owner Thosaporn "Paul" Wongngamdee and his staff. They offer the traditional pad Thai noodles; lemon grass soup; coconut shrimp; crispy duck in a brown lemon sauce; chicken prepared with pine nuts or cashews; a spicy cold beef salad; pork with jade noodles; and a variety of seafood dishes made with shrimp, mussels, squid, and fish fillets; and homemade coconut ice cream. The regular menu also has a varied selection of meatless dishes including spring rolls made with bean curd, cucumber, lettuce, and carrots; rice noodle and fried rice dishes; and "Green Garden," steamed vegetables in peanut sauce. There's always a choice of yellow, red, masaman, and green curries prepared with your choice of shrimp, tofu, duck, chicken, or beef: yellow is the mildest, red the hottest. All dishes are well described on the menu so you know just what you're getting into when you order, and the spicing can be adjusted at your request. Readers of Cleveland Magazine and Northern Ohio Live regularly vote this the best Thai in town. In good weather, there's an outdoor patio where this same food is also served. Plenty of parking in a city lot at the rear of the restaurant, and because it's just a few doors away from the Cedar Lee Theatre, a great choice for pre- or post-movie dining.

Mekong River
☎ (216) 371-9575

CITY: **Cleveland Heights**   AREA: **East Side**
ATMOSPHERE: **Casual**   COST: $$$$$

ADDRESS: 1918 Lee Rd.
HOURS: Mon–Thu 4–10 p.m., Fri & Sat 4–11 p.m., Sun 4–9 p.m. RESERVATIONS: Taken, suggested on weekends PAYMENT: MC, VS, DIS BAR: Beer,

wine, liquor **TAKEOUT:** Yes **SMOKING:** Smoke-Free **ACCESS:** & Full access *Not recommended for children

A board listing specials greets diners at the door. You might see crispy tangerine duck and wild rice, simmered lamb shanks; or a variation on one of the many Thai-style curries that are a part of the regular menu. And if that's not enough to get your juices flowing and your taste buds tingling, wait until you get beyond anticipation and start eating the highly spiced dishes that characterize Thai and Cambodian cooking. Expect an out-of-the-ordinary mix of tastes, textures, and colors, with crisp vegetables, chopped peanuts, overtones and undertones of coconut, lime, and cilantro, and, more often than not, the smack of hot chiles. If you're not sure what to order, owners Sophy and Sarin Chham, who is from Cambodia, will be glad to make a recommendation. Depending on your preferences, he can steer you toward some serious heat or help you identify the mild-to-your-mouth dishes that are also part of the culinary repertoire of Chef Kajohnsakoi Satayathum, fondly known to friends and co-workers as John-John. There's a good selection of the standard Thai foods found in restaurants here, plus a number of more unusual Thai and Cambodian specialties: lop (a Thai dish made with ground chicken or pork and roasted ground rice); Cambodian gumbo with papaya and pumpkin; plajian (fish with ginger gravy); and for dessert, sweet sticky rice with mango. The menu is also coded for heat: "no stars" means you're safe; one star has a bite; three stars are only for the very bold or the experienced. Appetizers like fish cakes, Mekong chicken wings, and Thai curry puffs plus a papaya salad make a meal. Vegetarian options get a page of their own on the menu. Chham started this restaurant in the space formerly occupied by Siam Cuisine. His former career involved neon, which accounts for the distinctive purple neon signage in the restaurant's front window. It's diagonally across the street from Cain Park, making it an excellent pit stop in the warm-weather months on your way to or from a play or a concert at the outdoor theaters there. But any time of year is a good time to take this taste trip to Southeast Asia. Expect a comfortable, casual atmosphere where jeans or jackets are acceptable, and you'll find people of all ages, from the high-chair set to card-carrying members of the Golden Buckeye club. Equally good for a date, a girls' night out, or a cross-generational gathering. A small five-seat bar area with chilled Thai beer at the ready. Parking on the street and at the rear of the building.

Pad Thai Restaurant
☎ **(330) 650-9998**

CITY: **Hudson**   AREA: **Farther South**
ATMOSPHERE: **Casual**   COST: $$$$$

ADDRESS: 5657 Darrow Rd.
HOURS: Lunch Daily 11 a.m.–3 p.m.; Dinner Sun–Thu 11 a.m.–10 p.m., Fri–Sat 11 a.m.–10:30 p.m. **RESERVATIONS:** Taken, Suggested weekends **PAYMENT:** Cash only **BAR:** None **TAKEOUT:** Yes **SMOKING:** Smoking section **ACCESS:** & Full access

Y ou can't miss this new addition to Hudson's dining scene. I mean that both in terms of it being easy to spot—a large, arresting stand-alone building with a beautiful Asian-inspired wooden entrance facade, with the restaurant's name lettered in both English and distinctive Thai script, a copper roof, and red awnings—and the fact that it's a must-visit place for fans of Thai food. It's owned and operated by Joanne and Timothy Ly, the same couple who do such a great job at Thai Gourmet, in Stow. Their menu features an abundant and distinctive array of appetizers; soups; salads; and chicken, beef, pork, seafood, and vegetarian entrees. Their green curry duck is an acknowledged standout. Two eggplant dishes, along with two others that feature hot curry paste and tomato chili

PACIFIC RIM

paste sauce, respectively, fresh basil rolls, marinated Cornish hen, and avocado ice cream are not often found in these parts. The spice "spigot" on everything can be adjusted to taste with merely a word to your server. The restaurant has banquet facilities and does catering for events on and off the premises. There are four dining areas, all tastefully appointed with colonial-style rattan-look chairs and traditional arts, crafts, and sculptures. The lounge area is inviting for drinking and eating. Plenty of parking in a lot that separates the restaurant from the traffic whizzing by.

Thai Gourmet
☎ (330) 688-0880

CITY: **Stow**　AREA: **Farther South**
ATMOSPHERE: **Casual**　COST: $$$$$

ADDRESS: 3732 Darrow Rd.
HOURS: Sun–Thu 11 a.m.–9:30 p.m., Fri & Sat 11 a.m.–10:30 p.m. **RESERVATIONS:** Taken, suggested for large parties **PAYMENT:** MC, VS, AX **BAR:** Beer, wine **TAKEOUT:** Yes **SMOKING:** Smoke-Free **ACCESS:** ♿ Full access **OTHER ETHNIC SPECIALTIES:** Chinese

According to a report on National Public Radio, there were 500 Thai restaurants in this country in 1990. Now there are more than 2,000. One of them is tucked between megamarts and chain stores at a busy intersection between Cleveland and Akron. It is an unlikely location for this top-quality one-of-a-kind place, a bright spot of uniqueness in a zone of mediocre commercial sameness. The strip-mall exterior is generic, but there are surprises and rewards inside for those who crave an extraordinary meal in pleasant and comfortable surroundings. It was risky, admits Joanne Ly, who runs the restaurant with her chef-husband, to open a Thai restaurant here. "We weren't sure if people in this area would be interested, and in the beginning many of our customers did choose familiar dishes from the Chinese section of our menu. They were afraid of the spici-

ness that is part of Thai cooking and very hesitant to try new things." So Joanne, who is beautiful, articulate, and personable, with a smile that makes you feel special, took it upon herself to coax, charm, and convince people to get acquainted with the food of her homeland—and she's succeeded. "In five years' time, we've developed a large group of enthusiastic regulars, many of whom had never tasted Thai food before coming here, and now they've graduated from wanting only mild spicing to asking for it very hot!" Fans come from as far away as Twinsburg and Hudson, some willing to drive 45 minutes to get a bowl of the savory coconut soup that is surely as much tonic as food, a platter of fish in chile pepper sauce, or an order of basil mussels. Once you've tried their Thai coconut spaghetti, your ideas of what's possible with pasta will be forever changed.

For ease of ordering, the menu is divided into separate Chinese and Thai sections, each with entries in every category from appetizers to entrees that combine frequently seen, popular items like pad Thai, red, green, and yellow curries, lo mein, governor's chicken, and orange beef with other, less common options including hot pepper duck, Bangkok fish, Siam eggplant, lobster with ginger sauce, crystal shrimp, and Szechuan bean curd. Dishes that pack heat are clearly marked. A large list of meatless dishes makes this a destination for vegetarians. To allay diners' concerns about fat and cholesterol, most vegetables are steamed, and coconut milk is used with a light hand. The seven dessert choices range from ordinary, non-Asian chocolate or vanilla ice cream, tiramisu, or walnut cake to homemade Thai coconut ice cream, banana dumplings, fried bananas with peanut or sesame topping, and shankaya (sweet brown coconut rice). This is a good place for celebrations; there are tables down the center that can easily be pushed together for large groups, and there's a birthday cake on the menu that serves four to 10 (to be sure one is prepared for you, let them know in advance that you'll be coming and tell them the number of people in your party). Beers from Thailand, Vietnam, India, Japan, and China are available along with brews from England, Ireland, Holland, Germany, and the U.S. of A. California reds and whites are available by the glass, as well as a small but interesting mix of domestic and imported wines by the bottle, plus plum wine and hot or cold sake. Though far from formal, the small restaurant aims for a certain polish. Cloth napkins are folded like fans and stand upright on each plate. The decorations and furnishings are tasteful, with seats that make it inviting to take your time. High chairs are available, and there's a small waiting area at the front. Off-site catering services. You'll never have to search for a parking spot in the massive lot out front, where Graham Road meets Route 91 (Darrow Road).

Thai Kitchen
☎ **(216) 226-4450**

CITY: **Lakewood**   AREA: **West Side**
ATMOSPHERE: **Casual**   COST: **$$**$$

ADDRESS: 12210 Madison Ave.
HOURS: Mon & Thu 11:30 a.m.–9 p.m., Wed 5–9 p.m., Fri & Sat 11:30 a.m.–10 p.m., Sun 1–9 p.m., closed Tue   RESERVATIONS: Not taken
PAYMENT: Cash only   BAR: None   TAKEOUT: Yes
SMOKING: Smoke-free   ACCESS: ♿ None

If there's such a thing as Thai kitsch, this is it. Every available surface, including the ceiling, is festooned with the Asian version of bric-a-brac, travel posters, and paper mobiles. But the result is a charmingly tacky backdrop for very interesting and extremely healthy food. There's a good selection of rice and rice noodle dishes, soups, curries, salads, and meat, vegetable, and seafood entrees flavored with the traditional aromatic Thai seasonings of lime, curry, basil, lemon grass, ginger, and coriander. Many dishes have a spicy bite that's balanced by the use of coconut milk, honey, or crisp vegetables. Peanut and fish sauces are common. The Thai Kitchen is frequented by many of Cleveland's Thai residents when they want "a taste of home." The chef prepares each dish using authentic Thai methods with traditional seasonings. She makes each item to order with only the freshest ingredients, honoring individual preferences for vegetarian, spicy, or mild dishes and never uses MSG. Although the names are often long and unfamiliar—khao bai-gra-pao khai-down (stir-fried chicken with sweet basil and hot chiles) and kaeny choed phug-gard-dong (pickled mustard vegetable soup with pork and sauteed garlic)—each dish is well described on the menu, and staff will happily answer all your questions. The restaurant is small, only six tables and 14 chairs grouped around the L-shaped kitchen. Recorded popular Thai music plays in the background. In terms of the setting, eating out doesn't get much homier than this. But the food will transport you to another world. Owners Suriya and Numtip Chuaypradit always welcome visitors warmly and treat every diner as if they were family.

Thai Orchid
☎ **(440) 461-8266**

CITY: **Lyndhurst**   AREA: **East Side**
ATMOSPHERE: **Casual**   COST: **$$$**$

ADDRESS: 5136 Mayfield Rd.
HOURS: Lunch: Tue–Fri 11:30 a.m.–2:30 p.m.; Dinner: Tue–Fri 5–10 p.m., Sat 4–10 p.m., Sun 5–9:30 p.m.   RESERVATIONS: Taken, recommended on weekends   PAYMENT: MC, VS, AX, DIS, checks   BAR: Beer, wine, liquor
TAKEOUT: Yes   SMOKING: Smoking section
ACCESS: ♿ Full access

This is a nice place to enjoy real Thai food. There are curries, many seafood dishes, and full-flavored noodles. House specials have musical names: River and Land (a stir-fry of shrimp, chicken, and beef with mustard, cabbage, and mushrooms), Fisherman's Party (a mix of sauteed scallops, shrimp, squid, and crab claw with vegetables, red pepper, and basil leaves), and Chicken Mango Lovers (chicken and mango with fresh garlic, onions, ginger, roasted chili, hot peppers, water chestnuts, red peppers, and scallions). A surprise is that some dishes are made with brown rice, which is also available as a side order. Owners Payao and Lek Sriweawnetr ran a restaurant in Boston before relocating here, but the couple are originally from Bangkok, where Lek was sous chef for a large hotel restaurant. Their Thai roots are reflected in the traditional design Lek has hand-stenciled on the walls, as well as in the artwork on display. One dining area is designated nonsmoking, and a completely separate dining room is for smokers. Although the sign over the front door facing Mayfield Road is what catches your eye, you can't enter through that door. Park in the large lot and use the side door.

V-Li's Thai Cuisine
☎ (330) 854-5344
CITY: **Canal Fulton**   AREA: **Farther South**
ATMOSPHERE: **Casual**   COST: $$$$$

ADDRESS: 129 N. Canal St.
HOURS: Tue–Fri 11:30 a.m.–2:30 p.m. & 5–9:30 p.m., Sat 4–9:30 p.m., Sun–Mon closed; closed first week in July RESERVATIONS: Not taken PAYMENT: MC, VS, AX BAR: Beer, wine, liquor TAKEOUT: Yes SMOKING: Smoke-Free ACCESS: ♿ Limited

This is an unlikely location for a restaurant so good that it received a Readers' Choice Award for "Best Thai" from *Northern Ohio Live* magazine. Canal Fulton, after all, would never be considered a hub of fine dining or an ethnic enclave. But V-Li Van Sickel lives nearby with her husband and family, and when she decided to open her own place, she chose a place close to home. She was also attracted to the building itself, a 100-year-old Federal-style brick structure on the town's picturesque Main

Street (also the main street), which once served as the Odd Fellows lodge. (Note to self—look up Odd Fellows on the Internet and find out, once and for all, who and what they are.) The restaurant has proved to be an important addition to local commerce as it draws a steady stream of customers, many willing to travel the distance from Akron, Cleveland, Wooster, and even a couple from Parkersburg, West Virginia (who usually leave with a big box of carryout to eat later). Highways make the trip easy and relatively fast, and V-Li's cooking makes it worth the effort. She has a sizable number of weekly "regulars," and even her employees come to the restaurant in their off-hours to eat her food. She learned to cook growing up in Thailand. After her marriage to Ohio native Roger Van Sickel in 1973, she came to America and perfected her skills working in restaurant kitchens. She loves to cook and passed that enthusiasm on to her son Phillip, who trained to be a chef and now works with her. Together they prepare a variety of Thai dishes, some familiar like satay, pad Thai, and red, yellow, or emerald curry, others less well known in these parts—cinnamon soup, honey pork, triple-flavored fish, and grilled giant prawns (a weekend special). All the food is light and healthy. Hot dishes get a one- or two-chile rating on the menu. Some of her customers are not the type to try new things, and members of this group tend to order the same one or two dishes they know and love. She brings them what they want, of course, but encourages them in her gentle, charming way to try new things, and willingly provides little "tastes" or sampler portions. Desserts offer a lovely choice: there's sweet rice with custard, fried bananas, coconut ice cream, her own Siam Sundae, and tapioca with young coconut meat. The wine list is good: there's a Reserve list of expensive bottles, a choice of quality reds and whites, both with good descriptions of each vintage, and four more ordinary house wines by the glass. The setting is pleasant and easy on the eyes: natural wood, a palette of natural colors, and lovely Thai artwork.

#1 Pho
☎ (216) 781-1176

CITY: **Cleveland**   AREA: **Near East Side**
ATMOSPHERE: **Casual**   COST: $$$$$

ADDRESS: 3120 Superior Ave.
HOURS: Sun–Thu 11 a.m.–1- p.m., Fri–Sat
11 a.m.–11 p.m. RESERVATIONS: Taken
PAYMENT: MC, VS, AX, DIS BAR: Beer, wine, liquor
TAKEOUT: Yes SMOKING: Smoke-Free
ACCESS: ♿ Limited

Soon after this place opened in September 2002, I began receiving e-mail messages from friends and readers who wanted to clue me in to what they variously described as their exciting, great, amazing new "find." And I'm so glad they did. It's a wonderful addition to the downtown dining scene, a lovely plus for the street, and a terrific, and popular, place to eat. The refurbished and remodeled double storefront building is attractive inside and out. The two dining rooms are spacious and nicely appointed with oak floors stripped, buffed, and varnished to a high shine, modern lighting, polished wooden tables, and a fashionable red and buttery cream color scheme. The menu qualifies as a tome, and you'll have to eat here many times in order to thoroughly sample all it has to offer. Soups, the mainstay of Vietnamese cuisine, dominate, of course, but they go way beyond the pho you know, or have yet to discover: soups include spicy lemon grass, tomato crab, and sweet and sour fish. There are 17 different appetizers that run the gamut from crispy spring rolls and shrimp on a sugarcane to the more esoteric lotus root salad and salt baked squid; a variety of bún (rice noodle) and còm tâm (broken rice) dishes; half a page of options for vegetarians; and 14 entrees made with shrimp, squid, or other fish. The beverages, which comprise a full page, are in a class by themselves and a liquid experience that will surely take most people's taste buds to new places. Consider some of the possibilities: drinks made with durian (not for the timid), soursop, mung beans, logan, and jackfruit. Service in this 80-seat eatery is consistently attentive, and there is a small but comfortable waiting area. Parking is free on the street, and spaces are generally plentiful.

Asia Tea House
☎ (216) 621-1681

CITY: **Cleveland**   AREA: **Downtown**
ATMOSPHERE: **Relaxed**   COST: $$$$$

ADDRESS: 3126 St. Clair Ave.
HOURS: Tue–Thu 11 a.m.–7 p.m., Fri –Sun
11 a.m.–8 p.m., Mon closed RESERVATIONS: Not
taken PAYMENT: MC, VS, AX, DIS BAR: None
TAKEOUT: Yes SMOKING: Smoke-Free
ACCESS: ♿ None

This small, plain, and thoroughly authentic Vietnamese eatery is hidden inside and at the back of the Asia Food Market. (For more information about the market, see listing later in this chapter.) There are seats for 30, but the restaurant's brisk takeout business accommodates many more who are hungry for goi cuon (chewy rice-paper rolls stuffed with crisp fresh vegetables and herbs, shrimp, and pork) or banh cuon cha lua (steamed rice roll with pork). I like to place my order, do some grocery shopping while it's being prepared and packed up, and then bring dinner home for the family along with supplies for the rest of the week. They don't cater much to Western tastes here. The menu is only 17 items long, featuring the most popular combination in homestyle Vietnamese cookery—noodles in soup. Pho Dac Biet, the house special soup, is made with a combination of rare and well-done beef. The kitchen also prepares broken-rice dishes, a specialty of central and southern Vietnam. Grains of jasmine rice that chipped and splintered during harvest and processing, called com tam, are the central

PACIFIC RIM

ingredient. In Vietnam this rice is less expensive than regular jasmine rice, but in America it's a sort of delicacy and costs more. In an article in the *L.A. Times*, Jonathan Gold writes that com tam is "one of the great Vietnamese working-class foods, the basis of a million lunch plates." At this inconspicuous little spot, broken rice can be ordered with grilled chicken, grilled pork chops, shredded pork, pork skin (big with Vietnamese, decidedly less so among most Americans), and egg. There are also a few Hong Kong–style dishes—roast pork and roast pig (I'm not sure of the difference—maybe a question of body parts and where on the animal they come from), roast duck, and soy sauce chicken. Park in the lot adjacent to the market. Note that as of this writing, the market and the kitchen share a phone number, so when phoning be sure to say you want the Asia Tea House.

Chinese Village
☎ (216) 228-0110

CITY: **Lakewood**   AREA: **West Side**
ATMOSPHERE: **Casual**   COST: $$$$$

ADDRESS: 13359 Madison Ave.
HOURS: Tue, Wed, Thu 11 a.m.–9 p.m., Fri & Sat 11 a.m.–10 p.m.   **RESERVATIONS:** Taken
PAYMENT: Cash only   **BAR:** None   **TAKEOUT:** Yes
SMOKING: Smoke-Free   **ACCESS:** ♿ Full access
OTHER ETHNIC SPECIALTIES: Chinese

More like eating in Mrs. Nguyen's dining room than in her restaurant, dining in this spotlessly clean seven-table restaurant is so intimate you can hear the oil sizzling in the kitchen. Van Nguyen does everything herself, cooking, managing, and sometimes serving, though she looks more like the glamorous classical opera singer she used to be in Vietnam than chief cook and bottle washer. When she came to America, Van Nguyen learned the restaurant business from her mother, who had opened the first Vietnamese eatery in Cleveland. Using her mother's traditional recipes, she prepares simple food with the tasty, nourishing feel of real home cooking, Vietnamese-style. There are 10 soups, and an order of any is big enough to feed two or as a meal in itself. Rice and rice noodle dishes are laced with various combinations of pork, chicken, beef, eggs, tofu, and vegetables; an unusual crepe is made with rice flour and coconut milk and stuffed with pork, shrimp, onions, and bean sprouts. Vietnamese style steak, grilled salmon, Pad Thai, and a large selection of vegetarian options have been added to menu since my first visit back in 1995. The menu also offers a selection of Chinese dishes that includes all the old standbys like fried rice, sweet-and-sour pork, and pepper steak, plus some less common dishes: boneless chicken Hong Kong–style, double-cooked pork, Szechuan bean curd, and hot and spicy kung po scallops. "We can prepare most Vietnamese and Chinese dishes without sugar, MSG, or even oil," says Mrs. Nguyen, "if customers request it." Reflecting the long-standing influence of French culture on Vietnam, French roast coffee is available to finish off the meal. On-street parking along this nicely rejuvenated section of Madison, with additional spaces at the rear of the building.

Jade Palace
☎ (330) 836-4300

CITY: **Akron**   AREA: **Farther South**
ATMOSPHERE: **Casual**   COST: $$$$$

ADDRESS: 1714 Meriman Rd.
HOURS: Mon–Thu 11 a.m.–10 p.m., Fri–Sat 11 a.m.–11 p.m., Sun noon–10 p.m.
RESERVATIONS: Taken   **PAYMENT:** MC, VS
BAR: Beer, wine, liquor   **TAKEOUT:** Yes
SMOKING: Smoking section   **ACCESS:** ♿ Full access

Things are really cooking in Akron, with new and different food choices appearing all the time. Now the Rubber City can claim its first Vietnamese restaurant. It opened in April 2003. Owners Li Feng Li and Yu Peng Zheng are from China, and both learned Vietnamese cooking in professional kitchens in New York City. They combine the best of the two worlds in their own place, with a menu that offers an appetizing and interesting selection of dishes representing the culinary traditions of both countries. The Chinese portion includes mild and spicy items that range from the well-known and generally well-loved moo shu pancake "wraps" to sweet and sour options; lo mein noodles; fried rice; orange beef; General Tso's chicken; and Happy Family, a mix of shrimp, scallops, beef, chicken, and vegetables. A few surprises on the menu got my attention—mushrooms in garlic sauce; Hong Kong shrimp; salmon with ginger and scallions; and Szechuan catfish. But it's the Vietnamese options—and there are many—that really offer a different kind of taste experience. The basics of chicken, beef, pork, seafood, and vegetables get sauced with curry and coconut milk; ginger and honey; lemon grass and red chili; tamrind dressing; or Nuoc Cham, a spicy lime-flavored condiment. Although they have some of the soups (pho) that have become so popular, they've chosen to concentrate on other types of foods such as bun, bun xao, and banh, noodle-based dishes with assorted toppings. Appetizers include grilled skewered beef, prawns, or vegetables; crystal dumplings; and cold chicken salad. The midsized dining room, with seating for 85, is pleasantly decorated, most notably with beautifully carved wooden chairs. There's ample parking in the lot that serves the Liberty Commons shopping area.

Khiem's Vietnamese Cuisine
☎ (216) 228-4414
CITY: **Lakewood**   AREA: **West Side**
ATMOSPHERE: **Relaxed**   COST: $$$$$

ADDRESS: 13735 Madison Ave.
HOURS: Mon–Sat 11 a.m.–8 p.m., Sun closed
RESERVATIONS: Not Taken   PAYMENT: Cash only

BAR: None   TAKEOUT: Yes   SMOKING: Smoke-Free
ACCESS: ♿ Limited

An odd little spot, this is a combination Vietnamese restaurant, coffee shop, and ice-cream parlor. It's set in a storefront with a decor that seems left over from something else: striped wallpaper with flowered borders, mix-and-match tables and chairs, a couple of very faux Tiffany lamp shades, with most everything a little worse for wear. It's small, only 15 seats plus a couple of stools at the counter, and much of the business is carryout. The menu is small too, but the food selection is interesting, the prices very reasonable, and it's a favorite with many who enjoy Vietnamese food. There's a dish made with marinated beef in garlic sauce, a chicken stew, and a "salad" made with rice noodles, pieces of egg roll, bean sprouts, vegetables, and a spicy vinegar dressing. Some dishes can be ordered in three sizes—small, medium, or large. The same person who takes your order for stir-fry can also make you an espresso, a milkshake, or a banana split. Metered parking on the street.

Minh Anh Vietnamese Restaurant & Market
☎ (216) 961-9671
CITY: **Cleveland**   AREA: **Near West Side**
ATMOSPHERE: **Casual**   COST: $$$$$

ADDRESS: 5428 Detroit Ave.
HOURS: Mon–Thu 11 a.m.–9:45 p.m., Fri 11 a.m.–10:45 p.m., Sat noon–10:45 p.m., Sun noon–8:45 p.m.   RESERVATIONS: Taken, recommended for large groups   PAYMENT: MC, VS, DIS   BAR: Beer, wine   TAKEOUT: Yes
SMOKING: Smoke-Free   ACCESS: ♿ None

This is a small family-style restaurant where children can feel free to get up and watch the fish in the aquarium. The walls are wood paneled, and the tables are covered in white oilcloth; there are a few green plants, and soft rock plays quietly on the radio. One waitress describes it as "a mellow little place." Vietnamese food makes use of many of the same ingredients as the cuisines of neighboring Thailand and Cambodia, so you'll find many dishes that use coconut milk, lemon grass, and peanuts. Owner Camla Wadsworth and her brother, the cook, are from Vietnam, but they use more familiar Chinese terms to help diners understand what they're ordering; so although the menu lists egg rolls, chow mein, and lo mein, you'll get the Vietnamese version. One of the most popular menu selections is a crepe, banh xeo, filled with bean sprouts, mushrooms, and chicken, pork, or shrimp. And there are some less common items as well: heo xao tuong (made with pork and spinach in a hot and sweet bean paste), tom rim (a dish of caramelized shrimp), and pho Saigon (beef and rice-noodle soup flavored with cinnamon). There is a decent selection of vegetarian dishes, and some surprises among the beverages: ginseng, jasmine, or sweet chrysanthemum tea, served hot or cold; mango or guava juice, soybean milk, and coconut or ginseng soda. Parking in the rear, enter from the front. A Vietnamese grocery store, now open in the space adjacent to the resturant. (See listing under markets in this chapter for more information.)

years ago when a fire damaged the old place. A first-time visitor may have difficulty finding this incarnation of Nam Wah; it's in a nondescript building in a small strip mall, behind McDonald's, near the Baldwin-Wallace campus. It's a real neighborhood place, nothing fancy, with seating for about 150 people. It seems to attract working couples who want to relax over an inexpensive meal and would be a nice place for a group of friends to meet and eat. The employees are all Chinese and Vietnamese, some newly arrived in the U.S., and though their English may not always be perfect, the service they provide is friendly without being, as one visitor put it, suffocating. The midsized menu features both Chinese and Vietnamese dishes. Some unusual dishes from the Chinese portion are bean cake with roast pork soup, Singapore-style rice noodles, and wild pepper chicken. The Vietnamese food is light yet surprisingly filling. Appetizers like grilled meatballs and shrimp on sugar cane are served with rice noodles and vegetables rolled up in rice paper with a sweet vinegar dipping sauce. Two diners told me they'd never tasted Vietnamese food before eating here. One ordered bun thit nuong (pork bowl), and the other scallops in lemon grass. "We have three words to describe the food," she told me, "yum, yum, yum."

Nam Wah
☎ **(440) 243-8181**

CITY: **Berea**   AREA: **Southwest**
ATMOSPHERE: **Casual**   COST: $$$$$

ADDRESS: 392 W. Bagley Rd.
HOURS: Mon–Thu 11:30 a.m.–10 p.m., Fri 11:30 a.m.–11 p.m., Sat noon–11 p.m., Sun noon–10 p.m. RESERVATIONS: Taken
PAYMENT: MC, VS, AX, DIS, checks BAR: Beer, wine, liquor TAKEOUT: Yes SMOKING: Smoking section ACCESS: ♿ Full access OTHER ETHNIC SPECIALTIES: Chinese

This family-owned and -operated restaurant has been around for 17 years but moved to its present location a few

Pho Hoa
☎ **(216) 781-7462**

CITY: **Cleveland**   AREA: **Near East Side**
ATMOSPHERE: **Relaxed**   COST: $$$$$

ADDRESS: 3030 Superior Ave., Golden Plaza
HOURS: Tue–Thu 11 a.m.–7 p.m., Fri & Sat 11 a.m.–8 p.m., Mon 11 a.m.–7 p.m.
RESERVATIONS: Not taken PAYMENT: MC, VS, DIS
BAR: None TAKEOUT: SMOKING: Smoke-Free
ACCESS: ♿ Full access

To express my enthusiasm about this place and encourage everyone to give it a try, I desperately wanted to write "Go Pho

It." Unfortunately, after I developed a literary attachment to this corny yet, to my mind, endearing pun, I learned that the correct pronunciation of the Vietnamese word for soup is "fuh," not "foe." Oh well, Pho-ged-aboud-it. The important thing is that this is Cleveland's one and only Vietnamese soup bar, a kind of simple, inexpensive fast-food eatery that's common on the coasts, and a very welcome addition to our local food community in 2002. Owner Manh Nguyen told me he knows he's taking a big risk trying this here. But his hopes are high, and with good reason. Pho Hoa, like all pho shops, makes one thing very, very well and then tweaks the basic dish to get variations, and serves them in two sizes—small (which was big enough for my lunch) and large. The soup begins with a light, clear but intensely flavorful beef broth. The intensity is the result of slow-cooking and a mix of herbs and spices. Rice noodles are part of every bowlful, which also comes with a side platter of fresh, crisp bean sprouts, hot peppers, Asian basil leaves, recao (a green herb similar in taste to cilantro), and a wedge of lime. Variations are about meat—beef and beef parts cut up and cooked all kinds of ways. Choose from thin slices of brisket, eye of round, flank steak, shank, tripe, and meatballs, alone or in combination with each other. Add all the crunchy stuff to the hot broth, squeeze in the lime's juice, and eat. You'll need chopsticks and a deep-bowled Asian soup spoon to get every last drop and sliver of this bargain-priced one-dish meal, and both are found on the table. If you need more zing to the thing, there are also bottled condiments within easy reach of each of the restaurant's 38 seats: red hot sauce; salty fish sauce; and thick soy paste. You can also order sides of steamed green onions or pickled onions, a dessert called marmalade on the menu that is more like canned fruit cocktail, and traditional drinks—soybean milk and pennywort, coconut juice, and hot or cold Vietnamese drip coffee. A wonderful French-bread sandwich made with pate and roast pork debuted in 2003. Also on the menu are: chicken cabbage salad; summer rolls; and bubble tea, a kind of Asian "shake" featuring black tapioca pearls. The place resembles a converted and spiffed-up garage, and decor is hyperminimalist. But the relaxed atmosphere, delicious, healthy food, and low cost more than compensate. Although picky young eaters are unlikely to find anything to their taste here, kids are welcome and booster seats are available. The restaurant is located at the rear of Golden Plaza, an urban mini-mall with an Asian essence. While you're there, check out the Chinese Golden Bakery (described elsewhere in this chapter). Parking on the street or in a lot behind the building, which has a back entrance.

Siam Cafe

☎ **(216) 361-2323**

CITY: **Cleveland**   AREA: **Near East Side**
ATMOSPHERE: **Casual**   COST: **$$$**$$

ADDRESS: 3951 St. Clair Ave.

HOURS: Daily 11 a.m.–midnight
RESERVATIONS: Taken PAYMENT: MC, VS, AX
BAR: Beer, wine, liquor TAKEOUT: Yes
SMOKING: Smoking section ACCESS: ♿ Full
access OTHER ETHNIC SPECIALTIES: Thai

Opened in 1994, this restaurant boasts a genuinely exotic, varied, and unusual menu, and eating here is an adventure. There are 18 choices of nonalcoholic hot and cold beverages, including da ba mau (made with palm sugar syrup, coconut juice, and tropical fruit), sinh to mang cau sim (a milkshake made with soursop nectar, ginger tea, and soybean milk), and richly flavored coffee made with sweetened condensed milk. The selection of soups, appetizers, noodle dishes, and other entrees that feature roasted duck, sea scallops, grilled pork, and marinated beef is equally varied. Many ingredients are common to Thai and Vietnamese cuisine—both kinds are featured here—though each is distinctive in its preparation. "Vietnamese cooking," explained owner Michael Hong, "has been influenced by the French and Chinese, and tends towards the sweet and salty. Thai food, which has incorporated Malaysian and Indian flavors, is much more spicy, or sour, or a combination of both." The kitchen will adjust the hot-and-spicy level to suit diners' tastes and can prepare most dishes vegetarian-style. The fish you order may be more than fresh—it's likely to be scooped right out of the tank where it's swimming and into the chef's pan. Portions on all dishes are large.

A hostess seats guests at booths or tables, and the ambience is pleasant and relaxed, a setting of light woods and polished brass with deep green accents. The restaurant's seating capacity doubled following renovations in 2002 that relocated the kitchen. Smoking and nonsmoking sections are well separated. Per person prices for preplanned banquet meals are very reasonable, and the selection of foods is stunning, visually and for the taste buds, too. I chose this option for 11 guests to celebrate my oldest son's graduation from high school and the twins' simultaneous completion of elementary school. We were able to sit in a booth, at a large round table, and food was placed on a lazy Susan that was in almost constant rotation, as everyone served themselves some of everything, and then some more. Because the kitchen stays open late, this is also a great place to get a meal at an unconventional hour—I like stopping here on the way home from the airport after a missed dinner and an evening flight that offered nothing but a handful of peanuts. A meal-in-a-bowl soup or a plate of pad Thai is perfect. And I have found that the later it gets, the more interesting the crowd. Be forewarned—there's something incongruous about the place from the outside until you realize that the Siam Cafe is housed in a converted Country Kitchen restaurant. The resulting exterior is a sort of barn with an Asian motif and neon highlights. Plenty of parking on the east and west sides of the building.

MARKETS

Asian Mix

Asia Food Company
☎ (216) 621-1681
CITY: **Cleveland**   AREA: **Near East Side**

ADDRESS: 3126 St. Clair Ave.

FOOD AVAIL.: meat (fresh, deli, frozen), fish (fresh, frozen), produce, grains, beans, flour, rice, baked goods, canned & packaged goods, spices, condiments, beverages, tea, coffee, wine, prepared frozen foods, takeout meals
HOURS: Daily 9 a.m.–7 p.m. **PAYMENT:** MC, VS, DIS, checks **ACCESS:** ♿ Limited **OTHER ETHNIC SPECIALTIES:** Chinese, Korean, Laotian, Thai, Vietnamese

The Duong family owns and operates this wholesale and retail business. They are from Vietnam and stock food products from their native country as well as Laos, Thailand, and Korea, but the emphasis is on Chinese imports. This a full-service neighborhood grocery, and the manager, Alex Duong, describes it as typical of those you'd find in any large city in Southeast Asia. Inside you'll find a butcher and a fresh-fish market; lots of prepared foods to go; an Asian pharmacy; and a Vietnamese restaurant (see listing earlier this chapter).

Asia Grocery & Gift
☎ (216) 459-8839
CITY: **Cleveland**   AREA: **Near West Side**

ADDRESS: 4825 Pearl Rd.

FOOD AVAIL.: Meat (frozen, dried), fish (frozen, dried), produce, grains, beans, flour, rice, canned & packaged goods, spices, condiments, tea, prepared frozen foods HOURS: Mon–Sat 11 a.m.–7 p.m., Sun 1–5 p.m. PAYMENT: Checks ACCESS: & Full access OTHER ETHNIC SPECIALTIES: Chinese, Korean, Japanese, Philippine, Thai

This small store specializes in food products for Korean cooking, including some fresh vegetables you aren't likely to find at your local supermarket and a small selection of prepared foods. Basic and essential ingredients for Chinese, Japanese, Thai, and Filipino cooking are also on the shelves. Most of the clientele are from the Pacific Rim nations. A large parking lot is adjacent to the store.

Asian Food Market
☎ (330) 928-1969
CITY: **Cuyahoga Falls**   AREA: **Farther South**

ADDRESS: 2603 State Rd.

FOOD AVAIL.: Fish (frozen), produce, grains, beans, flour, rice, canned & packaged goods, spices, condiments, beverages, tea, prepared frozen foods HOURS: Mon–Sat 10 a.m.–7 p.m., Sun closed PAYMENT: Checks ACCESS: & None OTHER ETHNIC SPECIALTIES: Japanese, Chinese, Korean, Thai

Korean-born Do So and his wife have been in the grocery business for 20 years. Their midsize market serves a clientele that by his estimate is 50% Asian and 50% American. All seem to know what to do with the Korean, Japanese, Chinese, and Thai ingredients he stocks. For those who don't want to start from scratch, the freezer case has prepared foods like dumplings and egg rolls. Among the produce you'll find gnarly chunks of ginger root, white radishes so big they look as if they were

raised with growth hormones (they weren't), a variety of hot and even hotter peppers, and purple Asian eggplants. If you want your table to be as authentic as your food, you can also purchase rice bowls and sushi plates here. In a small strip of stores with parking in front and in back.

Dong Duong Indochina Grocery
☎ (216) 651-8796
CITY: **Cleveland**   AREA: **Near West Side**

ADDRESS: 6406 Lorain Ave.

FOOD AVAIL.: Fish (frozen, dried), produce, grains, beans, flour, canned & packaged goods, spices, condiments, tea HOURS: Daily 9 a.m.–7 p.m. PAYMENT: Cash only ACCESS: & None OTHER ETHNIC SPECIALTIES: Cambodian, Chinese, Thai, Vietnamese

Open since 1987, this is another small family-owned store that carries a variety of food products imported from Thailand, Vietnam, China, Singapore, and Cambodia. They also sell electric rice cookers and woks. Store owners Srey Trinh and her husband, Phung, are from Cambodia but are well versed in all the products they sell and how to use them. They're happy to answer questions.

Hoan Nam Market
☎ (216) 281-0820
CITY: **Cleveland**   AREA: **Near West Side**

ADDRESS: 8401 Detroit Ave.

FOOD AVAIL.: Fish (frozen), produce, grains, beans, flour, rice, canned & packaged goods, prepared frozen foods HOURS: Daily 10 a.m.–7 p.m. PAYMENT: Checks ACCESS: & None

Phowe Souksavanh, who works behind the counter, is from Thailand. Her husband, who comes in to help out with the heavy lifting, is from Laos. Together with their son-in-law, they opened this store to serve the needs of Asian immigrants living in the neighborhood who needed a source of food products from their native lands. Though the emphasis is on the Thai kitchen, they stock an assortment that would be familiar to anyone from Vietnam, Laos, Cambodia, or China. Thai, Cambodian, and English are all spoken here, and if you want some cooking advice, Phowe is glad to help out, even going so far as to tell you exactly how to work with specific ingredients, and sharing her own recipes with anyone who asks. Though the interior shows its age, it is well organized and well stocked with a large selection of fresh and frozen produce and green herbs: papaya, long beans, bean sprouts, lemon leaves and lemon grass, galanga, hot and sweet basil, miniature eggplants, and peppers with kick. One entire wall is filled with a variety of noodles. Shoppers can expect to find jars of pickled mango; cans of the sweetened, condensed full-cream milk used in the preparation of Thai and Vietnamese coffee; chili sauces, fish powder, and curry pastes; sugar cane in syrup, tamarind leaves in brine, and jarred oyster mushrooms. The beige brick building sits on a corner. Don't be put off by the bars on the windows—it's a very friendly place inside. On-street parking out front or around the corner.

Kobawoo Oriental Food Market
☎ (216) 741-0688
CITY: **Cleveland**   AREA: **Near West Side**

ADDRESS: 4709 Pearl Rd.
FOOD AVAIL.: Meat (frozen), fish (frozen, dried), produce, grains, beans, flour, rice, canned & packaged goods, spices, condiments, tea, prepared frozen foods **HOURS:** Mon–Sat 10 a.m.–8 p.m., Sun noon–6 p.m. **PAYMENT:** MC, VS, DIS, checks **ACCESS:** ♿ None **OTHER ETHNIC SPECIALTIES:** Chinese, Korean, Japanese

Well stocked with products from Korea, plus a small selection of ingredients for Chinese and Japanese cookery, this store replaces Kim's Oriental Food Company, formerly at this location.

Though most of their clientele is Korean, the current owners, like their predecessors, also cater to the growing number of Americans interested in preparing Korean dishes in their own kitchens, and in using Asian flavorings to spice up American foods. You can find seasonings in both powder and liquid form here, as well as many varieties of canned and jarred pickled vegetables and kimchee. Though small, Kobawoo prides itself on its selection of fresh produce. The store has its own parking lot.

Oriental Food & Gifts
☎ (216) 291-1241
CITY: **South Euclid**   AREA: **East Side**

ADDRESS: 4271 Mayfield Rd.
FOOD AVAIL.: meat (fresh, frozen), fish (fresh, frozen), produce, grains, beans, flour, rice, canned & packaged goods, spices, condiments, beverages, tea, wine, prepared frozen foods, takeout meals **HOURS:** Mon–Sat 10 a.m.–9 p.m., Sun noon–7 p.m. **PAYMENT:** MC, VS, AX, DIS, checks **ACCESS:** ♿ Full access

Located at the corner of Belvoir and Mayfield in a strip mall that offers ample parking, this is a large, well-stocked supermarket with products from almost all the Pacific Rim nations. You can find tubes of Japanese wasabi (horseradish), Vietnamese hot sauce, cans of pennywort and sugar cane juice for Thai recipes, five-gallon jars of Korean bean paste, and dried Chinese mushrooms. Rice can be purchased in amounts ranging from 2- to 50-pound bags, soy sauce and sesame oil by the gallon, and exotic spices in 5-pound sacks. The selection is staggering: there are shelves and shelves of different sorts of cookies and crackers, noodles, flours, and teas of every type. In one visit I found yam noodles, acorn starch, and roasted barley tea. Freezer cases and refrigerators hold such specialties as duck and quail eggs, baby octopus and seasoned cuttlefish, fermented turnip greens and cabbage kimchee. Aisles are wide, lighting is bright, and staff are helpful. A deli-type display case features a variety of ready-to-eat noodle, fish, and vegetable dishes, and the produce section has most of the Asian vegetables you'd ever need, and some I've never seen before. They also carry all the ingredients needed to prepare Japanese sushi at home. You'll also find Asian-brand cosmetics, kitchen utensils, housewares, and even furniture. They even have Asian-language videos for rent. This place qualifies as an American-style superstore with a purely Asian flavor. They also do catering and restaurant supply services.

Sugarland Food Mart
☎ (440) 843-8646
CITY: **Parma**   AREA: **Southwest**

ADDRESS: 5790 Ridge Rd.
FOOD AVAIL.: Meat (frozen), fish (fresh, frozen, dried), beans, rice, baked goods, canned & packaged goods, spices, condiments, tea, prepared frozen foods HOURS: Mon–Sat 9 a.m.–6:30 p.m., Sun 11 a.m.–5:30 p.m.
PAYMENT: MC, VS, checks ACCESS: ♿ Limited

The emphasis at this small neighborhood store is on products from the Philippines, but this 16-year-old family operation also carries imported foods for all types of Asian cooking. There are many varieties of noodles, rice, and soy sauce. This is a good source for the kinds of specialized ingredients necessary for many Southeast Asian dishes: palm sugar, canned coconut, coconut and mango jellies, canned tropical fruits, and chili sauces. They even stock quail eggs.

Sun-Land Oriental Foods
☎ (440) 461-9966
CITY: **Mayfield Heights**   AREA: **East Side**

ADDRESS: 5888 Mayfield Rd.
FOOD AVAIL.: Meat (fresh, frozen), fish (fresh, frozen), produce, grains, beans, flour, rice, baked goods, canned & packaged goods, spices, condiments, beverages, tea, coffee, prepared frozen foods HOURS: Mon–Sat 10 a.m.–9 p.m., Sun 11 a.m.–7 p.m. PAYMENT: MC, VS, AX, checks
ACCESS: ♿ Full access

Japan may claim the official title "Land of the Rising Sun," but the sun also rises over Korea, China, and the Philippines at Sun-Land Oriental Foods. The small grocery store offers a selection of foods from all these Pacific Rim nations in every form: fresh, frozen, canned, jarred, wrapped, boxed, and bagged. They also stock kitchen tools needed for this type of cooking. Owner Iljae Ann, who came to the United States from Korea in 1988, is happy to note that most of his customers become regulars. In the Mayland Shopping Center, with plenty of parking.

Tink Hall Food Market
☎ (216) 696-1717
CITY: **Cleveland**   AREA: **Near East Side**

ADDRESS: 2999 Payne Ave.
FOOD AVAIL.: Meat (fresh, frozen, dried), fish (fresh, frozen, dried), produce, grains, beans, flour, rice, baked goods, canned & packaged goods, spices, condiments, beverages, tea, coffee, prepared frozen foods HOURS: Mon–Sat 9 a.m.–7 p.m., Sun 9 a.m.–6 p.m. PAYMENT: MC, VS, checks ACCESS: ♿ Full access OTHER ETHNIC SPECIALTIES: Chinese

Located in Asia Plaza, this place has the look and feel of a modern supermarket, but you won't find peanut butter and jelly on the shelves. One of the larger Chinese grocery stores in Ohio, it stocks strictly Asian products. The primary focus is on Chinese foods, but they have items imported from all over Southeast Asia, including traditional cooking and serving utensils. It's easy to make your way down the wide aisles, but hard to choose from among the many different types of noodles, sauces, oils, and frozen dumplings. This is the place to find bean paste, egg roll skins, five spice powder (a blend of anise, fennel, cinnamon, Szechuan pepper, and cloves), and tofu (a cheese-like curd made from soybeans). All sorts of fresh imported vegetables uncommon in America but typical for China are in good supply. It's no surprise that this is where many Asians shop. Ample parking in the lot that serves the entire plaza.

Chinese

Golden Bakery
☎ (216) 241-4418
CITY: **Cleveland**   AREA: **Near East Side**

ADDRESS: 3030 Superior Ave. (Golden Plaza)
FOOD AVAIL.: Baked goods HOURS: Tue–Fri 9 a.m.–7 p.m., Sat & Sun 10 a.m.–7 p.m., Mon closed PAYMENT: Cash only ACCESS: & Full access

Open since April 2002, this is the welcome reincarnation of the Superior Bakery, which closed a year earlier. Same address but now smaller in size, located farther back within the Golden Plaza, a blond-brick building that houses multiple businesses and eateries, Asian and otherwise. There are a couple of small tables in the bright red "mallway" for eating on the spot, but this is primarily a takeout and take-home operation and, according to owner Treeka Wong, just the sort of place you'd find in Hong Kong. Laid out on platters under clear, curved Plexiglas "hoods" is an array of Asian-style baked goods. The procedure is to use tongs to make your selection, place it on a tray, and carry it up to the sales counter, where the clerk rings it

up and packages it. The selection includes both main-meal and dessert foods. There are light, flaky pastries stuffed with curried beef, roast pork, preserved duck egg with ginger and lotus puree, and delicate Asian-style chicken "pot pie," and some that reflect Americanized tastes, featuring bacon, hot dogs, and ham and eggs. Moist miniature "breads" are filled with beef, chicken, red beans, or taro puree. Sweet buns are flavored with almonds, coconut, chestnut puree, or pineapple. Little egg custard tarts are a popular Chinese breakfast food. The kitchen, manned by Treeka's significant other, also turns out a Filipino-style sticky rice cake that has a soft custardy jello-textured consistency, and a sweet taste; an eggy sponge cake that is feather-light and less sweet than its American counterpart; a green tea roll with red bean cream; black sesame seed and sweet winter melon cakes; and cookies: Asian-inspired almond or sesame, and all-American chocolate chip. The bakery prepares beautifully decorated cakes to order, sized 8 inches to a full 16-by-24-inch sheet that serves 45 to 60, in a variety of flavors from mocha chocolate to taro fruit cocktail and chestnut puree. Park on the street in front of Golden Plaza and walk through this unusual little urban shopping center or park in the lot at the rear of the building and enter through the back door.

Good Harvest Foods
☎ (216) 861-8018
CITY: **Cleveland**   AREA: **Near East Side**

ADDRESS: 3038 Payne Ave.
FOOD AVAIL.: Meat (fresh, frozen, dried), fish (fresh, frozen, dried), produce, rice, canned & packaged goods, spices, condiments, beverages, tea, coffee, prepared frozen foods HOURS: Daily 9 a.m.–8 p.m. PAYMENT: MC, VS ACCESS: & Full access OTHER ETHNIC SPECIALTIES: Thai, Vietnamese, Korean, Japanese

Just a short block from Asia Plaza, in Cleveland's small but lively and growing

Asia Town, is a large white building with dragon heads flanking the front door. The sign above identifies this as the Hong Kong Supermarket, and the inside looks and sounds like a supermarket. The aisles are wide and brightly lit. Shelves, refrigerated coolers, and glass-doored freezers are well stocked, there's a produce section and a counter with fish kept cool on chopped ice, and the choices in every department are abundant. There are carts and baskets for your selections, and multiple cashiers at checkout lines are ready to take your money. Nondescript music is piped in by radio for your easy-listening pleasure. But here the resemblance between this place and where I generally go for my quart of milk and can of tuna ends. At 5' 7" I feel like a giant next to the elderly Chinese ladies who are shopping here. Signs are written in both English and Chinese, and most of the employees are more fluent in the latter than the former. There are pungent smells I can't identify, vegetables I don't recognize, cuts of meat I've never seen (and have reason to suspect come from parts of the animal I have never considered consuming), and products that represent an alternative universe of eating and drinking.

Among the teas are ginseng, roasted barley, jasmine, chrysanthemum, ginger, lichee black, and China green. There are medicinal teas and diet teas, teas in bags and loose leaves in lovely tins. For munching, perhaps carrot crackers, burdock, chili salt, or bamboo shoot biscuits, sweet-potato cookies, and prawn-flavored or cuttlefish chips. Making a fruit salad? Forget about the canned peaches—choose lychees, loquats, longan, sapota, or rambutan in heavy syrup. Add some spark to your meals with wasabi or curry paste. Dried shiitake mushrooms come in 5-pound bags as big as a couch pillow, and the cost is astonishingly reasonable. Jasmine rice from Thailand can be bought in a 1-pound or a 50-pound sack. Sauces, spices, herbs, condiments, oils, vinegars, noodles, and beans abound. Esoteric ingredients are available—almond powder, lotus seed

meal, red yeast, condensed plum syrup, grass jelly drink. So is everything and anything fresh, dried, pickled, and preserved, canned, bottled, bagged, and frozen that's likely to be called for in Chinese, Thai, Vietnamese, Korean, and Japanese cooking. Skip the cow juice—there's coconut and soy milk. Instead of cheese, there's a selection of tofu. Oddly, you'll also find anomalies like Ovaltine and cans of Campbell's pork and beans—who knew? Mundane apples, strawberries, and bananas sit side by side with exotic star squash, lotus root, bitter melon, opo, stalks of lemon grass, and miniature heads of baby choy. In the current American spirit of offering full-service, one-stop shopping, there's also a Chinese pharmacy, kitchen and cooking supplies, and housewares. The store's parking lot is on the 31st Street side of the building.

Filipino

Nipa Hut
☎ **(440) 842-7333**
CITY: **Parma Heights**   AREA: **Southwest**

ADDRESS: 6775 W. 130th St.

FOOD AVAIL.: meat (fresh, frozen), fish (fresh, frozen), produce, grains, beans, flour, rice, baked goods, canned & packaged goods, spices, condiments, beverages, tea, coffee, prepared frozen foods, takeout meals HOURS: Mon–Sat 8:30 a.m.–8 p.m., Sun closed PAYMENT: MC, VS, DIS, checks ACCESS: ♿ Full access OTHER ETHNIC SPECIALTIES: Thai, Korean, Chinese, Indian, Japanese

The market has the look and feel of a large convenience store. And it certainly is convenient if you're looking for a jar of Filipino Mang Tomas All Around Sarsa Sauce, papaya pickles, mango preserves, or tamarind concentrate. The brightly lit place is packed with products from virtually every nation in the Pacific Rim, stacked on industrial shelving, in refrigerator and freezer cases, and in boxes piled one on top of the other. But foodstuffs from the Philippines dominate, and you'll find things here that you are unlikely to find anywhere else. There are dried and frozen taro and hot pepper leaves; whole beef tongues; packaged hopia cakes laced with pineapple, red beans, or winter melon, and ginataan by the pint (a dessert made with sweet rice, coconut milk, sweet potatoes, taro root, and jackfruit). The fresh produce section offers upo (a green vegetable shaped like an eggplant), sitaw (long green beans), gabe (a leafy green), mangoes, and cassava and taro root. Milkfish, a favorite in the Philippines, is available fresh, frozen, dried, and fried, along with a nice selection of other types of fresh fish. If you want anchovy sauce, shrimp paste, pickled ginger, dried lily flowers, banana sauce, fried garlic crumbs, and agaragar this is the place. There is also a large selection of prepared foods that can be packaged for carryout or eaten in the store. (For information about the Nipa Hut as a restaurant, see listing earlier in this chapter).

Columbia Asian Food & Gift
☎ (440) 716-0808
CITY: **North Olmsted**   AREA: **West Side**

ADDRESS: 24529 Lorain Ave.
FOOD AVAIL.: Meat (frozen), fish (frozen, dried), produce, grains, beans, baked goods, canned & packaged goods, spices, condiments, beverages, tea, coffee, prepared frozen foods
HOURS: Mon–Sat 10 a.m.–8 p.m., Sun 1:30 p.m.–7 p.m. PAYMENT: MC, VS ACCESS: ♿ Full access

Thanks to a Cleveland Ethnic Eats reader for telling me about this market, which features a very good selection of Pacific Rim products that goes beyond the ordinary. This is the place if you're looking for a whole, frozen squid, a gallon jar of kimchee, dried sardines, roasted soybean powder, black vinegar, green tea ice cream,

or seaweed in three-foot strips. Freezer cases hold fish cakes and a selection of pot stickers and dumplings. There's a large variety of noodles, fresh and canned vegetables, and sauces. I was happy to find Ponzu, a citrus marinade that I like to keep on hand, and Hanayuki flakes, honey-sweetened bread crumbs that make a great coating for frying and baking. Lovely imported dishes and tableware, rice cookers, and specialized utensils fill an entire aisle. This market is in a brace of stores set back from the road by a huge parking lot. Aoeshi, a Japanese restaurant, is next door (see listing this chapter).

Korean

Kim's Oriental Food
☎ (216) 391-5485
CITY: **Cleveland**   AREA: **Near East Side**

ADDRESS: 3700 Superior Ave.
FOOD AVAIL.: Meat (frozen), fish (fresh, frozen), produce, grains, beans, flour, canned & packaged goods, spices, condiments, tea, prepared frozen foods HOURS: Mon, Wed–Sun 10 a.m.–9 p.m., Tue 10 a.m.–6 p.m. PAYMENT: Checks
ACCESS: ♿ Full access

This is one of the best sources for Korean foods in the area. It's located behind the Korea House restaurant, both in a remodeled commercial building, and the two establishments share a large, fenced-in parking lot. The store has a bright, clean, roomy look. Many varieties of rice are available in quantities ranging from 1 pound to 100 pounds, and there's also an extensive selection of noodles, different kinds of kimchee, and frozen dumplings. This is a place where the experienced cook can find obscure and unusual ingredients and a beginner can stock up on everything needed to get started in Korean cooking.

Bangkokville
☎ (330) 253-1444

CITY: **Akron**   AREA: **Farther South**

ADDRESS: 597 E. Market St.

FOOD AVAIL.: Fish (frozen, dried), produce, grains, beans, spices, condiments, beverages, tea, coffee
HOURS: Mon–Sat 10:30 a.m.–6 p.m., Sun closed
PAYMENT: Cash only ACCESS: ☖ None

The place looks closed even when it's open, and the yellow brick corner building is in serious need of a makeover. Inside, the small store's a veritable warren of narrow aisles, packed to the rafters in a fairly jumbled fashion with all sorts of foods. Who knows what you'll find—or if you'll find what you're looking for—but you're sure to leave with a culinary treasure such as sweet rice flour, red bean paste, taro chips, mung bean rice, or a can of pickled eggplant. English is definitely not spoken here, but it doesn't take much talk to buy a 50-pound sack of rice or a bag of tapioca pearls.

Southeast Asian Food Market
☎ (216) 281-5224

CITY: **Cleveland**   AREA: **Near West Side**

ADDRESS: 6108 Lorain Ave.

FOOD AVAIL.: Meat (frozen), fish (frozen, dried), rice, canned & packaged goods, spices, condiments, beverages, tea, prepared frozen foods HOURS: Mon–Sat 10 a.m.–6 p.m.; Sun 1–6 p.m. PAYMENT: Checks ACCESS: ☖ Limited
OTHER ETHNIC SPECIALTIES: Laotian, Vietnamese, Chinese

As the name indicates, this store, run by Brian and Thong Hook, features foods from many of the countries of the region. The couple live upstairs and either one of them or their daughter is always on hand to answer your questions, help you find what you're looking for, or find you something you've never even considered looking for, like tamarind leaves in brine; chili paste; bean curd sauce; or a remedy for prickly heat. To satisfy the needs of their mostly Asian clientele, they stock foreign-language videos as well. A sizable selection of noodles, rice, canned goods, pastes, and condiments of every description is neatly arranged in the two small carpeted rooms. The place is easy to miss, so drive slowly once you're near West 61st Street. Parking out front or on the side streets.

United Asia Market
☎ (330) 374-0584

CITY: **Akron**   AREA: **Farther South**

ADDRESS: 340 E. South St.

FOOD AVAIL.: Fish (fresh, frozen, dried), produce, grains, beans, spices, condiments, beverages, tea, coffee HOURS: Mon–Fri 9:30 a.m.–8:30 p.m.; Sat–Sun 9 a.m.–8:30 p.m. PAYMENT: MC, VS
ACCESS: ☖ Full access

Few are likely to describe this part of Akron as the best part of town, but this market offers the absolute best selection of Thai and Laotian food products I've seen anywhere in the region, from banana flowers to quail eggs. And there are some truly esoteric Pacific Rim finds—black sweet rice; red lime paste; pandam leaf extract; durian-coconut custard; Cambodian fried onion soup; straw mushrooms in brine; rambutan in syrup; taro ice cream; and my favorite curiosity, cans of pickled grey featherback fish in sauce. There are lots of choices when it comes to fresh produce, teas, rice, and noodles. The store is larger than it looks from the outside, and shelves are orderly. The owners, who are from Laos, expanded in summer 2003 to a second storefront, where they sell fresh fish.

Vietnamese

Saigon Trading USA
☎ (216) 252-3979

CITY: **Cleveland**   AREA: **West Side**

ADDRESS: 10246 Lorain Ave.

FOOD AVAIL.: Fish (frozen, dried), produce, rice, canned & packaged goods, spices, condiments, beverages, tea, prepared frozen foods
HOURS: Daily 11 a.m.–7 p.m. PAYMENT: Checks
ACCESS: & Limited OTHER ETHNIC SPECIALTIES: Chinese

Situated in a short strip of attached brick-fronted shops with apartments above, this very small store is run by the diminutive and friendly K. T. Nguyen. When I commented on the fact that she's open all day, seven days a week, she explained that it was her way of having fun. Apparently after her retirement, she found herself bored and lonely at home. So she opened this shop as her antidote. It's proven a great a way for her to keep busy and meet people. "No days off," she says, "because I like it here." She sits at the counter, with a small television set for company in between customers, surrounded by food products from her native Vietnam as well as from China. Considering the size of the space, it's no surprise that the selection of fresh fruits and vegetables is limited, but there's a surprising amount of food in cans, bags, and jars. She also sells vegetarian foods. Among all the things you'd expect to find, like fish sauce and egg roll wrappers, some less common things can be found, such as pickled mustard, dried turnips, tapioca flakes, and preserved radish tea.

Vietnam Market
☎ (216) 281-7724

CITY: **Cleveland**   AREA: **Near West Side**

ADDRESS: 5426 Detroit Ave.

FOOD AVAIL.: Fish (frozen, dried), produce, grains, beans, rice, canned & packaged goods, spices, condiments, beverages, tea, coffee, prepared frozen foods HOURS: Daily 9 a.m.–10 p.m.
PAYMENT: MC, VS ACCESS: & Limited OTHER ETHNIC SPECIALTIES: Chinese, Thai

---

When the fire-eater swallows a burning brand, the ringmaster always reminds the audience that they should not try this at home. But if you eat something you like at the Vietnamese restaurant Minh Anh, you really can try it at home by going next door to the Vietnam Market, buying the necessary ingredients, and preparing it yourself. Everything you'd need for virtually any Vietnamese dish, as well as a selection of essentials for Chinese and Thai cooking, can be found here. The store, which opened shortly after the second edition of this book went to press in 1998, can be accessed both from within the restaurant and through a separate street entrance. In addition to all the canned, bottled, and packaged foods you'd expect to see in a grocery catering to an Asian clientele, there is a small selection of fresh fruits and vegetables. You can shop every day, and much of the night—the store is open seven days a week until late. There's parking in a small lot behind the store and restaurant, or on the street.

{ *Chapter 2* }

MIDDLE EAST, AFRICA, INDIA

This chapter, a sort of patchwork quilt, pieces together an eclectic assortment of countries from two continents that share a kinship in matters of food.

Morocco, though sometimes considered a Mediterranean country, is an Arab nation in northwest Africa. Lebanon, too, is on the Mediterranean coast of the Islamic realm. And the cuisine that has developed in both countries has been clearly influenced by French culinary practices. I included India, though it is geographically closer to China, because its cuisine is unlike those of the rest of Asia. The use of lentils, flat breads, butter, and other dairy products relate it more to Middle Eastern cuisine. In addition, a significant portion of India's population is Moslem, which links them spiritually as well to that part of the globe. And though Ethiopia, situated on the east coast of Africa, is literally and figuratively worlds apart from India, its traditional wats, fiery hot stews served with injera, a pancake-like bread, bear a close resemblance to spicy Indian curries eaten with roti, an unleavened round bread. As in the Middle East, the Ethiopian tradition is to eat at low tables without utensils, scooping up food with pre-washed hands and pieces of bread. And in all these countries, meatless dishes are a major part of the daily diet.

What they also have in common: people from each of these countries have opened restaurants or markets in Greater Cleveland, which gives the rest of us a chance to be "table travelers" through these parts of the world.

There are no Ethiopian or Moroccan communities to speak of in Cleveland. The story of Ethiopian cuisine is probably best told by the one restaurant in town that serves it, for in the modern Western mind this country is profoundly linked only to images of famine and scarcity. It's difficult to imagine Ethiopia having a tasty and inviting food culture. But it does. Ethiopian food, reflecting a heritage that dates back thousands of years to the ancient Abyssinians, is especially interesting in that it has remained relatively free of European influences. It features a bread made with a form of millet called teff that grows only in Ethiopia. Berbere, a blend of ground chiles and other herbs and spices such as rue seed, ginger, cloves, bishop's weed, and cinnamon, is an often-used seasoning not unlike the spice blends of Morocco. Hot and hotter is to be expected. A typical main meal consists of some type of stewed legumes, vegetables, and sometimes meat or poultry. Dorowot is made with chicken and considered a national dish.

Until very recently, Cleveland had no Moroccan restaurants. But now, one on the Eaest Side offers a venue for "food journeying" to what has long been considered the most exotic outpost of the Middle East. Dishes show the effects of both the French and Spanish presence there, and hint at African and Middle Eastern influences, with the use of pungent spices like cumin, ginger, nutmeg, coriander, and cardamom. A blend of 35 spices, called ras el hanout, is used in the preparation of some tagines—slow-cooked sauces, soups, and stews made in an earthen pot. It includes juniper, paprika, and chiles, plus all the above-mentioned spices as well. Pumpkins, tomatoes, lentils, chickpeas, fava beans, carrots, and eggplants are present in many dishes. Couscous, made from semolina (a coarsely ground, starchy form of wheat—also known as farina), forms the basis for most meals. Sometimes referred to as Moroccan pasta, couscous is the country's national dish.

Currently there are approximately 100,000 Arab Americans in Northeast Ohio (half that number arrived in the last 15 years) representing Christians and Moslems from 23 different homelands. Historically the Arab world has not been a cohesive one, but in Cleveland all the different nationality groups and religious sects have formed an unprecedented working relationship. "We've been able to unite as Arab Americans," said Ed Farage, founder of CAMEO (Cleveland American Middle East Organization), an association dedicated to helping this constituency into the political mainstream. "We concentrate on what brings us together," Farage says, "and CAMEO, for example, is the only local group of its kind in the country. We don't define ourselves by religion or where we come from, but rather by our mutual concerns as American Arabs. Our membership is very diversified, from laborers to lawyers. Language is one thing we have in common, and another is food. We all eat the same things. The ingredients may be slightly different, but no matter where you go in the Arab world, you can get kibbee."

Lamb is the most popular meat throughout the Middle East and when mixed with bulgur, a nutty-flavored cracked wheat, it becomes kibbee. It may be prepared in countless ways: eaten raw, shaped into patties and baked, or stuffed and fried. Kibbee is the national dish of Lebanon, and it is Lebanese cooking that dominates our local Middle Eastern food scene. Like much of Arab cuisine, it is characterized by subtle, rich spicing, using fennel, mint, parsley, cardamom, ginger, nutmeg, saffron, and turmeric. This is as much about history as taste and tradition: Arabs controlled the spice trade between East and West throughout the Middle Ages. Lemons, onions, and garlic also play a significant role. Beans, fruit, vegetables (especially eggplant), and cereal grains are staples. Bulgur may be steamed and eaten on its own like rice or combined with tomatoes and chickpeas for tabouleh, a highly seasoned salad. Almonds and pine nuts are basic to the cuisine, and yogurt, as in Indian cuisine, is much more than the snack and breakfast food it is in this country, used as a marinade, in sauces and dressings, and as a side dish.

Many members of Cleveland's Indian community arrived in the 1960s. A second wave, often their relatives, followed over the next two decades. Many are highly educated, taking their place in this country as doctors, professors, engineers, and research scholars. Approximately 3,000 Indian families live in Greater Cleveland, and most try to maintain their Indian way of living, according to Mukund Mehta, former editor of *The Lotus*, an Indian community newspaper. "We want very much to keep our culture intact," explained Mehta, "and contribute its richness to American life. I am delighted when I see Americans enjoying the food in Indian restaurants."

Mehta and other members of the Indian community are justifiably proud of their cuisine. An ancient wisdom informs their cooking, and it is as much about a way of life as a way of eating. Rooted in a knowledge of how the body works, Indian cuisine is traditionally healthy, nutritious, and well balanced. Many of the spices were first used as medicines.

Ingredients such as onions, tomatoes, lentils, yogurt, rice, cauliflower, peas, and potatoes are typical. Many vegetables are pickled. Meat plays a minor role, though the food found in restaurants gives it a more prominent place to accommodate American tastes. The characteristic heat and complex flavor of Indian cuisine—and there are distinctive regional differences—is achieved by the use of masalas, which are aromatic blends of spices such as cardamom, mace, nutmeg, cumin, and coriander, mustard seed, chiles, pepper, and cloves. Curry powder is actually only one type of masala. Cooling fruit relishes called chutney, and yogurt side dishes, are served as a counterbalance.

"We are taught from the earliest age," said Sheela Sogal, former owner of the Saffron Patch restaurant, "that a cook should take no shortcuts. Care and love is the best spice of all. Everything in the kitchen should be done with heart and soul."

RESTAURANTS

Ethiopian

Empress Taytu Ethiopian Restaurant
☎ (216) 391-9400

CITY: **Cleveland**   AREA: **Near East Side**
ATMOSPHERE: **Casual**   COST: **$$$**$$

ADDRESS: 6125 St. Clair Ave.
HOURS: Tue–Thu 5–9 p.m., Fri 5–10 p.m., Sat 4:30–10 p.m., closed Sun & Mon
RESERVATIONS: Taken, recommended on weekends **PAYMENT:** MC, VS, AX **BAR:** Beer, wine, liquor **TAKEOUT:** Yes **SMOKING:** Smoke-free
ACCESS: ♿ Full access

Cleveland's only Ethiopian restaurant serves the traditional spicy cuisine of ancient Abyssinia, most of which is eaten sans silverware by scooping up stews and purees with pieces of injera, a soft flat bread that is made on the premises. Food arrives on large platters for sharing, and there are numerous combination plates on the menu that give newcomers to this cuisine a chance to sample a variety of dishes, which are primarily stews of meats, vegetables, or beans. Chicken in a sauce that resembles our barbecue is called dorowat and is made with onions, ginger, hot red peppers, rue, basil, cinnamon, cloves, and a flavoring called bishop's weed. T'ibs features small chunks of beef or lamb sauteed in spiced butter with herbs and onions. There are many completely vegetarian dishes. The decor is exotic, designed to du-

plicate native thatched-roof huts, and you can choose to eat at a regular table or from traditional low tables and stools—made comfortable by the addition of cushions and back rests. (If you want to sit at one of these traditional basket tables be sure to let them know when you make your reservation—they are very popular.) Warm, moist cloths for cleaning your hands are served before and after the meal by women in long white dresses. Enter through the back door from the restaurant's own parking lot. You pass by the kitchen and can look inside. There's an unusually comfortable area, near the thatched-roof bar, complete with couches and a coffee table where you can wait for your table or have a drink. Large photographs from Ethiopia are on the walls. For a very special experience, request the Ethiopian coffee ceremony. The green beans are roasted to order on the stove and brought to your table still hot; incense is lit, and the brew is made in a clay pot.

Bombay Sitar
☎ (330) 493-0671

CITY: **Canton**   AREA: **Farther South**
ATMOSPHERE: **Relaxed**   COST: **$$$**$$

ADDRESS: 4633 Belden Village St. NW
HOURS: Lunch daily 11 a.m.–2:30 p.m.; Dinner daily 5–10:30 p.m. **RESERVATIONS:** Taken, Recommended weekends **PAYMENT:** Cash only
BAR: None **TAKEOUT:** Yes **SMOKING:** Smoke-Free
ACCESS: ♿ Full access

I'm not a fan of sitar music—just ask my husband, who took up the instrument along with George Harrison back in the days—but I'm a big fan of the food served at Bombay Sitar, Canton's first and only Indian eatery. It's a real find out there in mallworld, where franchise food rules. The kitchen stakes out a unique culinary territory, producing an array of dishes seldom seen in these parts: a Bombay-style chicken and spinach soup; achar, spicy pickled vegetables; a pullao mix of rice, peas, and fruits; kofta lajawab, vegetable balls stuffed with cheese in a mild creamy sauce; black lentil dal; tandoori eggplant; chicken patta made with sweet and sour mangoes; Karachi lamb made in an iron skillet; and a sweet milk drink called falooda. Among the more commonly found items, the mulligatawny soup, vegetable korma, and lamb rogan josh are memorable. Two combination dinners provide a chance to sample many different things at a great price. Unlike any other Indian restaurant I've ever been to, servers brought complimentary munchies immediately after we were seated—a plate of crispy rice crackers, refilled after we quickly gobbled them all down, and two tasty dipping sauces. Basmati rice and mint chutney, which often must be ordered a la carte at other places, come with most entrees. Children's portions of some dishes are available by request at half price. Spicing is to order from mild to Indian hot (don't go there unless you're a pro). There are two dining areas, with the daily luncheon buffet set up in between. The location was once an Aladdin's, and their signature decor is still visible—in fact, the former tenants like to come back here to eat. The atmosphere is jeans casual. Located in a short brace of stores with a big red sign that makes it easy to spot from the road. They will cater parties of any size.

Cafe Tandoor
☎ (216) 371-8500

CITY: **Cleveland Heights**　AREA: **East Side**
ATMOSPHERE: **Casual**　COST: $$$$$

ADDRESS: 2096 S. Taylor Rd.
HOURS: Lunch Mon–Sat 11:30 a.m.–2 p.m.;
Dinner Mon–Sat 5:30–10 p.m., Sun 3–9 p.m.
RESERVATIONS: Taken, recommended
PAYMENT: MC, VS, AX, DIS　BAR: Beer, wine, liquor
TAKEOUT: Yes　SMOKING: Smoke-free
ACCESS: ♿ Full access

The smells that greet you at the door of this attractive, well-lit restaurant are exotic. You can pick up whiffs of cinnamon, cumin, ginger, and garlic. The second thing you notice upon entering is that many Indian families are eating here, a sure sign that the food is authentically prepared. Divided into two rooms, the place seats about 100 at cloth-covered tables. Storefront windows are filled with plants. The menu is all Indian, but that doesn't mean you'll only find curries or other dishes with over-the-top heat. Owner Raj Singh, who runs the restaurant along with his wife Beverly, is from the region of northern India near Nepal, and he did not grow up eating hot food. "Our food is intensely flavorful because of the spices and spice combinations we use," explains Raj. "People think all Indian food is spicy. It's not—but it is spiced." If you're not familiar with any of the dishes on the menu, the staff is knowledgeable and will graciously assist. Anything that does pack heat can be ordered mild, medium, or four-alarm. Typical of Indian cuisine, there are many vegetarian selections, but the menu includes a large choice of chicken, lamb, and shrimp entrees, too. When prepared in a clay tandoor oven, these are great choices for the fat- and weight-conscious, as the cooking method requires no oil. Traditional fried foods like pakora (batter-dipped meat or vegetables) are not at all greasy, and flavorful tandoori breads are made on the premises. Empty plates are brought warm from the kitchen, and food arrives beautifully arranged on large platters set in the middle of the table. Portions are generous, but desserts are worth saving room for. Cafe Tandoor has been ranked among the best Indian restaurants in the country by the Zagat guide, and *Northern Ohio Live* magazine readers have voted it the Best Indian Restaurant eight years running. Ample parking on the street and in back. The Singhs have opened additional locations; see following listings.

Cafe Tandoor
☎ (330) 562-5334

CITY: **Aurora**   AREA: **Farther East**
ATMOSPHERE: **Casual**   COST: $$$$$

ADDRESS: 96 Barrington Town Center
HOURS: Tue–Sat 11:30 a.m.–2 p.m. & 5:30–10 p.m., Sun 3–9 p.m., Mon closed
RESERVATIONS: Taken, Recommended
PAYMENT: MC, VS, AX, DIS BAR: Beer, wine, liquor
TAKEOUT: Yes SMOKING: Smoke-Free
ACCESS: ♿ Full access

The 70-seat Cafe Tandoor in Aurora is a twin of the restaurant in Cleveland Heights, and the place to go for Indian food in the area, which heretofore has been starved for vegetable samosas, marinated and charcoal-baked lamb chops, and pishori nan, a baked-to-order bread topped with ground pistachios and almonds. Plenty of free parking. For more information, see previous listing for the original restaurant.

Cafe Tandoor
☎ (440) 835-7999

CITY: **Westlake**   AREA: **West Side**
ATMOSPHERE: **Casual**   COST: $$$$$

ADDRESS: 30030 Detroit Rd.
HOURS: Mon–Sat 11:30 a.m.–2 p.m. & 5:30–10 p.m., Sun 3–9 p.m. RESERVATIONS: Taken, Recommended PAYMENT: MC, VS, AX, DIS
BAR: Beer, wine, liquor TAKEOUT: Yes
SMOKING: Smoke-Free ACCESS: ♿ Full access

The famous eastside location has expanded to the west at last, and taken up residence in Westbay Plaza. For more information see listing for Café Tandoor in Cleveland Heights.

Indigo Indian Bistro
☎ (216) 357-3308

CITY: **Cleveland**   AREA: **Downtown**
ATMOSPHERE: **Casual**   COST: $$$$$

ADDRESS: 503 Prospect Ave.
HOURS: Lunch Mon–Fri 11:30 a.m.–2 p.m.; Dinner Mon–Thu 5–10 p.m., Fri–Sat 5–11 p.m.; Sun closed RESERVATIONS: Taken, Suggested weekends and for large groups PAYMENT: Cash only BAR: Beer, wine, liquor TAKEOUT: Yes
SMOKING: Smoke-Free ACCESS: ♿ Full access

This is downtown Cleveland's first full-service Indian restaurant. It opened in August 2002, the brainchild of Amit Pandya, a banking man until he decided to switch to the restaurant game. The changeover grew out of his first career. He worked in a downtown office and often went out to lunch. Although he grew up in this country, his roots are in India, and he was raised in a vegetarian household. But there was nowhere to satisfy his taste for aloo gobi (a dish made with potatoes and cauliflower) or dal makhani (lentils with ginger, garlic, and onions) during the day. Nor could he introduce his coworkers to the culinary wonders of his culture. He saw a gap to be filled, and the next thing he knew he'd written a business plan and decided he was the one to put it in to action. The restaurant he's created is a good representative of the genre. The menu is primarily northern, with a few south Indian dishes and a nice selection of tandoori-roasted entrees, curries, and other classic preparations. Pandya is especially proud of his chef's versions of butter chicken and lamb curry. He also does some interesting things with swordfish, preparing it in a spiced tomato sauce; as a vindaloo with potatoes and dried red peppers; and in a rice biryani. Appetizers and sides include the popular samosas, pakoras, and freshly made flat breads, plus three soups—lentil, tomato, and chicken mulligatawny. A more unusual appetizer became available in fall 2003. Called aloo tikki, it's a potato pattie coated in a chick pea flour batter and deep fried. "Our many Indian customers," says Pandya, "are the best judges of the authenticity of our food, and they seem to be very happy with it." The lunch buffet offers a variety of tasting opportunities, but more unfamiliar and challenging dishes are unlikely to appear on it. It's set up at the back of the dining area that shares space with the bar, where three TVs are generally tuned to the news, unless one of the hometown teams is on a winning streak or there's a game that has the status of national obsession. Another, separate dining area has big windows that frame the scene on Prospect Avenue. In both, as well as a third room, natural wood defines the decor. The spacious restaurant is in Gateway country, a tenant of the Colonial Marketplace, and some booths beyond the bar let you watch the activity in the arcade. Parking in this neighborhood usually involves money—feeding the meters or paying the fees in nearby garages and surface lots. Indigo patrons with a validated ticket can get 50% off valet service provided by the Marketplace and adjacent Marriott Residence Inn.

Jaipur Junction
☎ (440) 842-3555

CITY: **North Royalton**   AREA: **Southwest**
ATMOSPHERE: **Relaxed**   COST: $$$$$

ADDRESS: 9377 Sprague Rd.
HOURS: Tue–Sat noon–10 p.m., Sun noon–9 p.m., closed Mon RESERVATIONS: Not taken PAYMENT: MC, VS, AX, DIS BAR: None TAKEOUT: Yes SMOKING: Smoke-free
ACCESS: ♿ Full access

Responding to the many requests she received to bring Indian food to the West Side (and make it fast, too, her customers told her), Sheela Sogal, former owner of the Saffron Patch (see listing further on in this chapter), opened what she calls a "gourmet-on-the-go" restaurant in the spring of 1997. Its listing in the Yellow Pages refers to

it as an oasis of vegetarian cuisine, which it is, and a "bhel-poori chat bar." What, I asked Ms. Sogal, does that mean? Bhel-poori is a crunchy mix of assorted fried foods, and chat are snacks and cold appetizers. The restaurant offers many of these foods, typically sold by the street vendors of Jaipur, India: lamb or fish kabobs; charbroiled chicken wrapped in fresh-baked naan (bread); masala dosa, rice crepes filled with potatoes and onions; tava-tikki, a potato pattie topped with vegetable chili; and kheema paratha, a grilled sandwich stuffed with seasoned ground lamb. There is also a selection of larger, heartier entrees similar to those on the menu at the Saffron Patch, including shrimp tandoor (baked in a special oven), nine different versions of curry, and three types of biryani (stew) made with either vegetables, chicken, or shrimp. If you're eating on the premises, you can try a sampler approach, selecting one dish at a time. There are also sides of relish, pickles, bread, and sauces, and a wonderful selection of hot and cold drinks (not available for carryout), including tea with cardamom; a minty milk tea; thandai, a mix of milk, fruit juice, and almond paste; lassi, made with yogurt and ginger; and a mango milkshake. You place your order at the counter; a server brings it to your table, one of about 10 four-tops. The food can be prepared mild, hot, or, in the words of one employee, "Indian hot, which makes most Americans wish they were somewhere else."

The restaurant is usually crowded with Indian customers who tend to beam on non-Indians eating there, as if to say, "Oh, how nice you like our food." The staff, who are all Indian, are also particularly warm and helpful. From the outside, this storefront restaurant, in the Timber Ridge Plaza behind a Blockbuster Video, appears rather ordinary. But inside there's a most unusual ambience created by original and large-scale artwork. There's a stunning full-wall mural, a detailed rendering of an early-20th-century Indian kitchen, complete with mud ovens, stacked baskets and pots, suitcase, a dresser, plates on shelves, and linens. A smiling woman in a sari can be seen in a doorway. A large window in the center of the scene looks down into a courtyard and out onto a desert village. In the distance, a train chugs along the tracks. Jaipur is a desert city on a heavily traveled route, and the painting, done by Ann Marie Place, an Australian woman living in Twinsburg, depicts a scene that one would see there. It's meant to make people feel as though they were in a country home in that part of India, and the response of first-time visitors is usually an emphatic "Wow." Elsewhere shelves display Indian dolls, colored bottles, and decorative clay pots. The wall to the right of the entrance is reserved for comments; patrons are encouraged to get a magic marker from the counter and leave messages either in words or pictures. Easily accessed from I-77 or I-71, with detailed directions from downtown, south, east, and west printed on the back of the takeout menu.

Kashmir Palace
☎ (440) 779-5774

CITY: **North Olmsted**   AREA: **West Side**
ATMOSPHERE: **Casual**   COST: **$$$**$$

ADDRESS: 26703 Brookpark Rd. Ext.
HOURS: Tue–Thu 11:30 a.m.–2:30 p.m. & 5–10 p.m., Fri 11:30 a.m.–2:30 p.m. & 5–11 p.m., Sat noon–3 p.m. & 5–11 p.m., Sun noon–3 p.m. & 5–9 p.m., Mon closed RESERVATIONS: Taken, recommended, especially on weekends and for parties of 5 or more PAYMENT: MC, VS, AX, DIS, checks BAR: Beer TAKEOUT: Yes
SMOKING: Smoke-free ACCESS: & Full access

Indian cooking is renowned for the great amount of time and labor that goes into each dish. Those of us who have neither the hours nor the expertise to invest in such a task need not, however, miss out on the pleasures of eating Indian food because people like Gurbux Singh Kala, his son Paul, and their talented kitchen staff do all the work for us, bringing the savory and aromatic cuisine of northern India to North Olmsted. Gurbux, who goes by the nickname Bakshi, writes on the menu that his home region of Kashmir, for which the restaurant is named, is known as the "garden of the Himalayas." The location of his restaurant could not be more at odds with the very notion of a garden—it's more like the asphalt jungle: an excess of busy, treeless streets, ugly shopping plazas surrounded by unsightly parking lots, and cookie-cutter chain stores lined up one after another. And then, suddenly, in this most unlikely strip mall of a spot there's Kashmir Palace, a little place serving the distinctive cuisine of a distant mountain region. Behind its bland facade is an attractive and inviting dining room that feels …and smells …a million miles away from the overdeveloped suburban landscape outside. This oasis is a labor of love for Kala, who started out in Cleveland as a chemist 25 years ago but gradually turned his attention from the Bunsen burner to the clay tandoori oven, transforming a hobby into a business. He partnered for a time with the former owner of the Saffron Patch, Sheela Sogal, but eventually decided to open his own place, and it has become his second home. Part of what he loves about the business is meeting new people and making new friends, so he is often to be found greeting, seating, and chatting with guests, who come from the surrounding towns, the East Side, and as far away as Oberlin (the restaurant is a special favorite of the college crowd).

The main dining area seats about 45 at tables draped in teal cloths topped with lovely paisley "scarves" under glass. A second, adjacent, smaller room seats 25 and can be reserved for private parties or meetings. A small serving area at the back is used for the lunchtime buffet. Intricate spicing characterizes every dish on the menu, which includes seafood and shellfish, lamb and mutton, chicken, vegetables, and rice in a large variety of styles and presentations. You'll find some dishes not found at other Indian restaurants: tandoori jheenga, a baked prawn appetizer; Kashmiri Dum Aloo (also known as the host's special), a vegetarian entree made with potatoes, fennel, and yogurt; machli dilruba (fish in a cashew sauce); and Kashmiri murgh (buttered chicken in a thick, rich red sauce spiked with fenugreek). There are also more familiar selections including samosas (appetizer pastries stuffed with potatoes and peas); pakoras (chickpea flour fritters); a variety of breads; tandoori dishes; and biryanis (basmati rice cooked with meat, fish, or vegetables, striped with saffron, the world's most costly spice, and topped with raisins and nuts). Desserts and drinks are worth a mention: there's a luscious mango milkshake and masala chai (spiced, milky tea); a small selection of beers that includes two Indian imports, King Fisher and the 22-ounce Taj Mahal; and kulfi, a traditional ice cream laced with pistachios, cardamom, and saffron, so thick it almost requires chewing. There are high chairs and booster seats available, and a roomy waiting area. On- and off-site catering services are available. Note, if you don't know the area, that Brookpark Road Extension can be hard to find—it's not even listed on some local maps. Brookpark and Lorain merge, and the Extension is a small side street near the merge also marked as "Sparky."

Maharaja Restaurant
☎ (440) 461-3737

CITY: **Richmond Heights**   AREA: **East Side**
ATMOSPHERE: **Casual**   COST: $$$$$

ADDRESS: 5156 Wilson Mills Rd.
HOURS: Mon–Fri 11 a.m.–2:30 p.m. & 5–10 p.m., Sat 11:30 a.m.–3:30 p.m. & 5–10:30 p.m., Sun noon–9 p.m. **RESERVATIONS:** Taken, suggested for large groups **PAYMENT:** MC, VS, AX, DIS **BAR:** Beer, wine, liquor **TAKEOUT:** Yes **SMOKING:** Smoking section **ACCESS:** ♿ Full access

This restaurant has been in the shopping plaza opposite Richmond Town Center since 1998. In July, 2002 Thakur Singh Yonzon, who is from Nepal, and his wife Madhu took it over. Formerly a chef at Café Tandoor, Thakur, who studied at the Royal School of Hotel and Restaurant Management in Katmandu, is thrilled to finally have a restaurant of his own. The front of the restaurant features a nine-stool bar and four tables for smokers. The spacious separate dining room seats about 100, with booths along each wall and tables down the center that can be pushed together to seat large groups. White cloths are spread out under glass, and green cloth napkins fan out from water glasses. Some images from India and Nepal grace the walls, and recorded Indian music plays in the background, providing the only traditional elements in a decor that is otherwise nondescript but pleasant enough. The emphasis is clearly on what happens behind the scenes—in the kitchen. Thakur and his staff have infused the menu with a new level of expertise. Their motto is: "We believe that the joy of eating lies in the art of cooking."

Northern Mughlai Indian cuisine is at the heart of what they do—it's a cooking style characterized by intricate blends of fresh and dry spices and herbs. You can taste the results in dishes like the creamy chicken makhani; Maharaja biryani made with rice, lamb, chicken, shrimp, and nuts; and channa masala, a dish of garbanzo beans and onions seasoned with a blend of roasted spices. Among the more unusual selections are their mango chicken; vegetable sangam, a combination of cauliflower, spinach, tomatoes, and potatoes; and karahi lamb prepared with onions, tomatoes, ginger, and garlic. Thakur is happy to prepare dishes with India-lite spicing or, on request, to increase the heat and aromatics to order. The lunch buffet, available Monday through Saturday and all day Sunday, provides an ever-changing array of dishes. A typical assortment might include lamb curry; tandoori chicken and butter chicken; palak paneer (cheese cubes in a spinach sauce); aloo gobi (cauliflower and potatoes cooked with ginger and tomatoes); bowls of spiced carrots and palate-cooling cucumber slices; five different condiments (perfect for dipping the fresh, warm naan and roti specialty breads that keep coming from the kitchen)—one made with coriander and mint, another with tamarind, a third with onions and tomatoes, a mango chutney, and a yogurt raita.

There are also desserts on the buffet: rice pudding, fresh fruit, gulab jaman (tiny fried cake "balls" infused with rosewater, a flavor that is at once sweet and flowery); little squares of semolina cake; and the Indian answer to fudge. Like most Indian restaurants, Maharaja offers specialty drinks: lassi (sweet, cold, sippable yogurt), mango shakes, and spiced milky tea. Three Indian beers are available, plus a small selection of imports and domestics and a short list of mostly California wines. The menu is not just for ordering, it's also educational, posing and answering what must be the two main FAQs on Indian eating: "What is curry?" and "What is tandoori?". And a third that I've never even known enough to wonder about: "What is makhni sauce?" . . . I'm not telling—you'll have to go there to find out. You'll also learn that they make their own yogurt and cheese, use only pure vegetable oil and fresh vegetables, and prepare poultry without the skin. Enough parking for a full battalion.

Mehak-e-Punjab
☎ (216) 581-5039

CITY: **Maple Heights**   AREA: **Southeast**
ATMOSPHERE: **Casual**   COST: **$$**$$

ADDRESS: 20940 Southgate Park Blvd.
HOURS: Mon–Sat 11 a.m.–9 p.m., Sun 11 a.m.–8 p.m. RESERVATIONS: Taken, suggested for large parties PAYMENT: MC, VS, AX, DIS
BAR: None TAKEOUT: Yes SMOKING: Smoke-Free
ACCESS: ♿ None

The Punjab region of India is in the northwest part of the country, and it has a distinctive identity in the same way New England or the Deep South does in the United States. One way its particular character is expressed is in its food, and that food is served at Mehak-e-Punjab. Though many of the dishes on the menu will be familiar to those who know Indian cuisine, preparation styles have their own special twist here, and there are some dishes I've never seen in a local restaurant. Among these are malai kofta, minced vegetables and cheese shaped into balls and simmered in a cream sauce spiked with cardamom, saffron, and garlic; baingan bhartha, sauteed eggplant with onions, tomatoes, and peas; a black bean dal; a masala made with okra; jalfarezi, vegetables cooked in cream; and ground meat baked in a clay oven (sheekh-kebab). Some special Punjabi-style dishes are available only on weekends. Drinks and desserts also hold some surprises from the North including thandal, a cold milk-based beverage made with almond paste and fruit juices (served seasonally) and warm carrot halwah, a pudding-like sweet. Owner Kuldip Pooni has a sense of humor that surfaces on the menu in his little asides: thandal, he writes, "cools your jets off"; Indian tea is "as good as a gentleman's handshake"; and methi palak paratha is described as "Popeye's favorite meal." He also shows his willingness to indulge the eat-and-run crowd, offering fast-food service on two thali (combination plates), one vegetarian, one not. There are also both lunch and dinner buffets (noon–2:30 p.m. and 6–9 p.m.). Pooni's catering service can meet needs large and small—from 15 to 700 people, he boasts—for only $8.99 per person. You have to make some effort to find this little place, as it cannot really be seen from the road. Located in a shopping plaza, it's actually part of the Saree Mahal Indian Grocery Store. Park in the plaza lot and look for a small neon sign. Once inside, you'll find seven tables covered with white cloths, plus a couple of booths, some decorative Indian artwork and photographs, an international clientele, and a pleasant, unpretentious atmosphere where you can enjoy Punjabi chicken and Punjabi kulcha, a baked-to-order bread made with white flour and potatoes.

Mughal Restaurant
☎ (440) 888-3700
CITY: **Parma Hts.**   AREA: **Southwest**
ATMOSPHERE: **Casual**   COST: $$$$$

ADDRESS: 6857 W. 130 St.
HOURS: Lunch: Tue–Fri 11:30 a.m.–2:30 p.m., Sat noon–3:30 p.m., Sun noon–4 p.m.; Dinner: Tue–Sat 5–11 p.m., Sun 5–9 p.m.; closed between meals; open Mon evening for vegetarian buffet **RESERVATIONS:** Taken, Suggested Fri & Sat nights **PAYMENT:** MC, VS, AX, DIS, checks **BAR:** Beer, wine, liquor **TAKEOUT:** Yes **SMOKING:** Smoke-Free **ACCESS:** ♿ Full access

The decor here is functional and forgettable, Middle-American generic. The food, however, is anything but, a memorable feast of aroma and flavor. A relatively new member of the area's restaurant community, Mughal opened in the fall of 2002. The menu features dishes from Bangladesh, favorites of the Moghul emperors who ruled from the 16th century to the 19th, and more familiar Indian fare, with a repertoire that spans the culinary styles of Kashmir in the north, Hyderabad in the south, Goa and Gujarat on the western coast, and Bengal to the east. This means that there's a large selection for those who love the classics—meats baked in a clay oven (the tandoori ovens are charcoal burning and not gas fueled, as are some of his competitors'), highly spiced curries, kabobs, and pilafs. But adventurers and explorers will also be rewarded by less common items: lamb achari made with yogurt and pickle spices; dal makhani, a combination of black and yellow lentils, kidney beans, garlic, tomatoes, and ginger root; Bombay balls, an appetizer of potatoes paired with sesame seeds

and curry leaves; scamber soup (lentils with vegetables); and shrimp and scallop Jal Farezi, an entree Syed swears he could eat every day. Everything is intricately seasoned. My son Nathan describes his dining experience here as a workout for his taste buds. Dishes can be ordered mild, medium, hot, and Indian hot but there are also options for those who want no heat at all, and a well-informed and friendly staff can point them out. As in most Indian restaurants, diners can expect a nice selection of roti (fresh-baked breads); traditional appetizers; and a veritable culinary playground for vegetarians. There are six dessert selections—rice pudding; kulfi, an ice cream made with pistachio nuts and saffron; a mango ice cream; sweetened cheese curds flavored with rose water, gajjar ka halwa (a combination of shredded carrot, cheese, and nuts), and cardamom; and gulub jamun, dumplings of flour and powdered milk soaked in sugar syrup. A 30-foot buffet is filled with assorted delicacies at lunchtime. The space accommodates large groups comfortably, and booths along the walls are just right for twosomes and foursomes. Takeout orders can be faxed to the restaurant, which is in a strip mall fronted by a large parking lot.

Raj Mahal Indian Cuisine
☎ (330) 926-0795
CITY: **Cuyahoga Falls**   AREA: **Farther South**
ATMOSPHERE: **Casual**   COST: $$$$$

ADDRESS: 2033 State Rd.
HOURS: Daily 11:30 a.m.–2:30 p.m. (lunch buffet) & 4:30–10 p.m. **RESERVATIONS:** Taken, suggested for large parties **PAYMENT:** MC, VS, DIS **BAR:** None **TAKEOUT:** Yes **SMOKING:** Smoke-Free **ACCESS:** ♿ Full access

My father, who has a certain meat-and-potatoes bent to his preferences, a lack of interest in all things legume, and little affection for spice-generated heat, ate his very first Indian meal here and came away with a newfound appreciation for this cuisine, saying he found the food "very tasty." He was especially enthusiastic about kulfee, a homemade ice cream flavored with almonds and rosewater (also with mango or pistachio), describing it as "absolutely delicious." When he and my mother visited the restaurant, they spoke with a couple who said they come almost every day for the luncheon buffet, a self-serve spread that features a changing assortment of dishes from the regular menu, and sometimes come back for dinner. These people seemed to be knowledgeable about Indian food and gave this restaurant high marks compared to other places they've eaten. All this should equal enough endorsement for connoisseurs of Indian food, hesitant novices, and everyone in between. The choice of entrees featuring chicken, beef, lamb, seafood, vegetables, and rice specialties is extensive, and the possibilities become almost dizzying when you mix and match appetizers (including soups, samosa, vegetable fritters, and potato pancakes), accompaniments like dal (spicy pureed lentils), homemade yogurt, mango chutney, spicy mixed pickles, and raita (yogurt with cucumbers and tomatoes), and freshly baked or fired Indian breads. The menu, which you can study online, offers a crash course in Indian cookery. From it you learn that makhani dishes are prepared in a butter and cream sauce with cashews and raisins; josh dishes include a yogurt-based sauce; masala-style dishes are made with tomatoes, ginger, onions, and bell peppers; anything done à la palak has curried spinach in it; rice is the central ingredient in a biryani; and if it's vindaloo, it's got to be floating in a tomato-based sauce. Indian drinks and desserts are a world unto themselves (a world, I might add, where dairy reigns supreme), and one I recommend you visit unless you are lactose intolerant. In addition to the kulfee my father liked so much, there's rice pudding (kheer), cheese in a sweet milk sauce (rasmalai), deep-fried milk balls in a sweetish syrup, and a yogurt drink called lassi. As with so many locations featured in

this book, these interesting and decidedly non-Ohio flavors are to be found in an uninteresting shopping plaza, behind an inconspicuous facade, in a place that puts more emphasis on food than decor. However, summer 2003 saw the restaurant close briefly while the interior got a complete facelift. The result is fresh and attractive, and more seating has been added. Tables are in two rooms, one with big storefront windows, the other with no windows at all. Some Indian artwork is on the walls. But great care is paid to the details: napkins may be paper, but they're carefully folded and placed in tall water glasses; place mats are paper, but underneath there's a real tablecloth. Servers are attentive and well dressed in white shirts, black pants, bow ties, and vests. A big eyesore of a sign makes the place easy to find, and a map on their website (http://go.to/rajmahal) also helps first-timers. The kitchen provides a full range of catering services.

Saffron Patch
☎ (216) 295-0400

CITY: **Shaker Heights**   AREA: **East Side**
ATMOSPHERE: **Dressy**   COST: $$$$$

ADDRESS: 20600 Chagrin Blvd. (Tower E Building)
HOURS: Lunch Mon–Fri 11:30 a.m.–2:30 p.m., Sat–Sun noon–3 p.m.; Dinner Mon–Thu 5–10 p.m., Fri & Sat 5–11 p.m., Sun 5–9 p.m.
RESERVATIONS: Taken, recommended
PAYMENT: MC, VS, AX, DIS   **BAR:** Beer, wine, liquor
TAKEOUT: Yes   **SMOKING:** Smoking section
ACCESS: ♿ Full access

Here you'll find exotic fare, and the aroma alone is an adventure. The luncheon buffet provides a great opportunity to sample a wide variety of foods: an okra curry, saffron rice, raita (a salad of cucumbers in yogurt sauce), chicken cooked in a stove-top tandoor oven, rice and lentil crepes filled with onions and potatoes, and naan (a flat bread). Each region of India has its own style of food preparation. The chefs here prepare some dishes from southern India but focus primarily on the cuisine of the north—spicy, pungent dishes, many vegetarian—and make it the traditional way, from scratch. They use authentic ingredients, even when they are costly or hard to obtain, like mangoes or what are called curry leaves. They make their own cheese, similar to our farmer cheese (a drier version of cottage cheese), in the kitchen too. Located in the basement of an office building, this is a large (capacity of about 110) and surprisingly lovely place to eat, with white-walled rooms adorned with fabric borders of blue elephants. Partitions divide the space into three sections, lighting is subdued, recorded sitar music plays softly in the background, and the overall effect is one of calm, comfort, and casual sophistication. They sometimes organize special eating events around American holidays, such as a Mother's Day champagne brunch buffet that was billed as a way to take your mom to India for only $12.95 and featured more than 15 different traditional dishes. Ample parking.

Lebanese

Amir's Marketplace Restaurant
☎ (216) 291-1878

CITY: **South Euclid**   AREA: **East Side**
ATMOSPHERE: **Relaxed**   COST: $$$$$

ADDRESS: 4422 Mayfield Rd.
HOURS: Mon–Thu 11 a.m.–9 p.m., Fri & Sat 11 a.m.– 10 p.m., Sun 11 a.m.–8 p.m.
RESERVATIONS: Not taken PAYMENT: MC, VS, AX, DIS BAR: Beer, wine, liquor TAKEOUT: Yes
SMOKING: Smoke-free ACCESS: & Full Access

As the name implies, this is both a place to shop and a place to eat. (For more information about the Middle Eastern groceries available, see the market listing for Amir's further on in this chapter.) The whole operation is run by the three Rassi brothers, and the staff are their sons and nephews. Much of the food offered is just the sort of thing their mother used to make for them back in Lebanon: thick lentil soup and a steamed lentil dish called mujadara; loubie bzeit (green beans made with tomatoes, onions, garlic, and olive oil); shish tawook (marinated, grilled chicken); and cheikh el mehshi (stuffed eggplant). Photos of many dishes (as well as a menu) hang in the restaurant's front window, so you can check out the offerings before going in. Displayed in glass cases are ready-made items available for immediate takeout, like fatayer (meat- or spinach-filled pies), hummus, and pickled beets, as well as a selection of traditional pastries, including baklawa (not quite the same as Greek baklava), bussma (made with farina and pistachios), and maamoul (bar-type cookies containing dates or pistachios). There's not much that's traditional about the ambience of the 90-seat restaurant, except the recorded music that plays softly in the background. It's strictly functional, with four-top tables that sport no cloths, paper napkins, and an overall sense of spic-and-span efficiency. Also breaking with tradition, the menu offers some American standbys like hamburgers, French fries, tuna salads, and grilled fish. An all-you-can-eat Sunday brunch from 11 to 3 with regular menu items, omelettes, fresh fruit, and vegeterian specialies. Catering information, a menu, and a map with driving directions on their website, www.amirfoods.com. Parking is available behind the storefront-type space located in a brick building.

Cedarland at the Clinic
☎ (216) 791-6606

CITY: **Cleveland**   AREA: **Near East Side**
ATMOSPHERE: **Casual**   COST: $$$$$

ADDRESS: 9491 Euclid Ave.
HOURS: Mon–Thu 7 a.m.–10 p.m., Fri 10 a.m.–9 p.m., Sat 11 a.m.–9 p.m., Sun closed
RESERVATIONS: Taken PAYMENT: MC, VS, DIS

MIDDLE EAST, AFRICA, INDIA

BAR: None **TAKEOUT:** Yes **SMOKING:** All sections
ACCESS: ♿ Full access

If you have a taste for kabab halabi (spiced ground beef with pine nuts) or mutabal (baked eggplant prepared with garlic, lemon, and olive oil) you're in luck. Serge Elias is cooking in Cleveland. His restaurant is an answer to the prayers of the many people from the Middle East who are at the Cleveland Clinic as staff, patients, and patients' families and entourages (if you are a member of a royal dynasty, like many who come to the Clinic for treatment, you don't leave home without an entourage), all of whom are happy to be able to get familiar foods. And they don't even have to walk across the street to the small mall where the 75-seat restaurant is located. Serge delivers—to the Clinic and to all the institutions in University Circle as well. If you're in a hurry, call or fax your order in, and it will be ready when you arrive. You can sit down inside, take it with you, or, in good weather, eat outside at the tables and benches that are part of the shopping strip. In a further attempt to be accommodating, Serge and his staff will make every effort to meet the needs of those with dietary restrictions (such as no-salt or low-spice diets) with one day's advance notice (some minimum charges apply).

The food is already ideally suited to a healthy diet: low fat, fresh, high in fiber, and prepared from scratch without additives, preservatives, or chemical flavor enhancers. The chicken noodle soup starts with a stock made on the premises. The menu includes Lebanese versions of vegetarian dishes such as hommus (chickpea dip), baba gannoj (baked eggplant dip), felafel (a batter of ground chickpeas and fava beans made into patties and fried), taboolee (salad made with bulghur wheat and parsley), meatless stuffed grape leaves, and fatoosh (salad topped with crunchy pieces of toasted pita bread). Among the entrees are lamb shish kabob, shish tawook (skewered grilled chicken in garlic sauce), kafta (a combination of freshly gound beef, onions, parsley, and spices), and the uncommon hommus barmaki (hommus topped with ground meat, pine nuts, onions, and the Lebanese equivalent of secret sauce). Elias also offers something he says is not found anywhere else around town, called arayiss—a pita stuffed with a choice of meat or vegetarian fillings and baked. There is also a selection of sandwiches, salads, and sides (Middle Eastern and the more familiar turkey, grilled cheese, coleslaw, French fries, and the like). For breakfast, you can go for a standard scrambled with home fries, or branch out and get right with the big health nut in the sky by choosing kamah (a Lebanese improvement on a boring bowl of oatmeal, made with boiled wheat, raisins, and walnuts). Formerly the Palmyra, the space retains some of the same furnishings, like the lovely wood and mother-of-pearl-inlaid tables, but the walls have a fresh coat of paint and the tired old carpeting is gone, replaced with attractive new tiling. Serge is a philosopher as well as a chef and a businessman, so on each menu he's printed a passage from Kahlil Gibran's book *The Prophet*. The restaurant is often crowded with men in kaftans and women in burkhas. For all you know, you may be sitting beside a foreign queen or prince, or a member of one of their retinues. You may not understand what they are talking about, but you can be sure you have something in common: the pleasure of eating the wonderful food that comes out of Serge Elias's kitchen. There are also some Middle Eastern grocery items available.

Continental Cuisine
☎ **(330) 864-1777**

CITY: **Fairlawn**   AREA: **Farther South**
ATMOSPHERE: **Casual**   COST: $$$$$

ADDRESS: 55 Ghent Rd.
HOURS: Mon–Thu 11 a.m.–9 p.m. (carryout until 10 p.m.), Fri & Sat 11 a.m.–9 p.m. (carryout until

11 p.m.), Sun closed **RESERVATIONS:** Taken, Suggested for large parties **PAYMENT:** MC, VS, AX, DIS **BAR:** Beer, wine **TAKEOUT:** Yes **SMOKING:** Smoke-Free **ACCESS:** & Full access

Summit Mall in Fairlawn is the quintessential all-American space, but the neighborhood's not quite as homogenized as it appears. Located just across the road is a small eatery that has some surprises in store for diners in search of an alternative to burgers and fries. In a bright, modern setting, Beshara Sabbagh and his family prepare and serve the classic dishes of Lebanon. You'll find spinach pies, felafel, shawarma, chicken and beef kebobs, and stuffed grape leaves. You can have them for lunch or dinner, eat-in or carryout. "All our food is fresh and very, very good," insists Sabbag, "and I'm not just saying that because it's my restaurant. I know it's true because we go to a lot of trouble to do everything right, the traditional way and with only the best ingredients. We use only lemon juice that we squeeze ourselves and extra virgin olive oil. We marinate our chicken and beef for hours. And we make each salad to order—we don't even slice tomatoes or chop lettuce in advance." The menu has grown beyond its Middle Eastern orientation to include hand tossed pizzas, more salads, gryos, fish, pasta, and filet mignon. A 2003 expansion has added more seating. Now there are places for 72 diners with full table service.

Middle Eastern

Aladdin's Eatery
☎ (216) 521-4005

CITY: **Lakewood**   AREA: **West Side**
ATMOSPHERE: **Casual**   COST: $$$$$

ADDRESS: 14536 Detroit Ave.
HOURS: Sun–Thu 11 a.m.–10:30 p.m., Fri & Sat 11 a.m.–11:30 p.m. **RESERVATIONS:** Not taken
PAYMENT: MC, VS, AX **BAR:** Beer, wine

TAKEOUT: Yes **SMOKING:** Smoke-free
ACCESS: & Full access

Aladdin's is bright, airy, and contemporary. It's located in a corner storefront in Lakewood, part of that city's restaurant renaissance. The decor is casual yet attractive—pale woods with pale green, yellow, and beige accents. The menu, featuring the healthy cuisine of Lebanon and the other countries of the Middle East, includes many vegetarian dishes. The kitchen prides itself on producing authentic dishes using only the freshest natural and preservative-free ingredients. There are a variety of soups, salads, and pita bread sandwiches that come stuffed or rolled. Traditional entrees include mujadara (steamed lentils and rice), sfiha (a meat pie), and shawarma (charbroiled beef and lamb). Some more contemporary variations on Middle Eastern themes can be sampled in the pita "pitzas" that make good use of tahini (sesame) sauce, feta cheese, eggplant puree, and falafel (mildly spiced chickpea-and-fava-bean patties). The menu does a good job of explaining what goes into every dish. A small but interesting wine and beer list. A parking lot in the rear.

Aladdin's Eatery
☎ (216) 932-4333

CITY: **Cleveland Heights**   AREA: **East Side**
ATMOSPHERE: **Casual**   COST: $$$$$

ADDRESS: 12447 Cedar Rd. at Fairmount Blvd.
HOURS: Sun–Thu 11 a.m.–10:30 p.m., Fri & Sat 11 a.m.–11:30 p.m. **RESERVATIONS:** Not taken
PAYMENT: MC, VS **BAR:** Beer, wine **TAKEOUT:** Yes
SMOKING: Smoke-free **ACCESS:** & Full access

The decor at this second, East Side incarnation of Aladdin's is colorful and cheerful. Banquettes are upholstered in a tapestry-like fabric with a palm-tree motif, and disks in a kaleidoscope of pastel hues hang inexplicably from the ceiling like deflated, renegade balloons. Like its Lakewood predecessor, this restaurant is a comfortable, congenial, and informal setting for a meal. Tables are packed fairly close together, but patrons seem to enjoy the sense of camaraderie, and many who eat here have told me they end up chatting with their neighbors, even though they have never met before. The menu duplicates some of the offerings of the Lakewood Aladdin's. Portions are generous, and vegetarians will have a field day. Some metered parking on the street and a city lot with meters around the corner. Parking also available in a tiny lot behind the building.

Aladdin's Eatery
☎ (330) 629-6450
CITY: **Boardman**   AREA: **Farther East**
ATMOSPHERE: **Casual**   COST: $$$$$

ADDRESS: 7325 South Ave.
HOURS: Sun–Thu 11 a.m.–10:30 p.m., Fri & Sat 11 a.m.–11:30 p.m. RESERVATIONS: Not taken
PAYMENT: MC, VS BAR: Beer, wine TAKEOUT: Yes
SMOKING: Smoke-free ACCESS: ᶘ Full access

Please see Aladdin's Eatery/Lakewood for description.

Aladdin's Eatery
☎ (216) 642-7550
CITY: **Independence**   AREA: **Southeast**
ATMOSPHERE: **Casual**   COST: $$$$$

ADDRESS: 6901 Rockside Rd.
HOURS: Sun–Thu 11 a.m.–10:30 p.m., Fri & Sat 11 a.m.–11:30 p.m. RESERVATIONS: Not taken
PAYMENT: MC, VS, AX BAR: Beer, wine
TAKEOUT: Yes SMOKING: Smoke-free
ACCESS: ᶘ Full access

Please see Aladdin's Eatery/Lakewood for description.

Ali Baba Restaurant
☎ (216) 251-2040
CITY: **Cleveland**   AREA: **Near West Side**
ATMOSPHERE: **Casual**   COST: $$$$$

ADDRESS: 12021 Lorain Ave.
HOURS: Tue–Sat 5–8:30 p.m. (will stay open later Fri & Sat if there are customers), closed Sun & Mon RESERVATIONS: Taken PAYMENT: Cash only
BAR: Byob TAKEOUT: Yes SMOKING: Smoke-free
ACCESS: ᶘ Limited

This is a tiny storefront restaurant with three booths and four tables. The chairs are wood, the tablecloths are pink, and even the menu is modestly small. But even so, people are willing to travel here from across town—especially those from the Middle East who are temporarily living and working in Cleveland—for a real taste of home. This casual, low-key restaurant has been around for more than a decade. The owner is from Lebanon, and many of the recipes come from his grandmother. In addition to the dishes we Americans have come to know well, like hummus and spinach pie, there are some other more unusual options here: labnee (a sort of cream cheese made from yogurt), moujaddara (a lentil stew), and loobi bzait (green beans simmered in a vegetable sauce and served over rice). They serve lamb and chicken shish kebabs and an interesting meat dish called soujook made from marinated ground beef. Everything is prepared without any artificial flavorings or colorings, and MSG is never used. They also offer some creative takeout options: 12- and 16-ounce containers of a variety of salads and dips, and little meat and vegetable pies and patties by the dozen. Metered on-street parking.

Desert Inn
☎ **(330) 456-1766**

CITY: **Canton**   AREA: **Farther South**
ATMOSPHERE: **Dressy**   COST: $$$$$

ADDRESS: 300 12th St. NW
HOURS: Mon–Thu 11 a.m.–2 p.m. &
5:30–10 p.m., Fri 11 a.m.–2 p.m. & 5:30–11 p.m.,
Sat 5:30–11 p.m., closed Sun
RESERVATIONS: Taken, required for dinner
PAYMENT: MC, VS, AX   **BAR:** Beer, wine, liquor
TAKEOUT: Yes   **SMOKING:** All sections
ACCESS: ♿ Full access

The Desert Inn is one of those restaurants so closely identified with the town where it's located that the two are almost inseparable. Everybody knows about the Desert Inn. It's a unique, funky hangout kind of place that attracts politicos, celebrities, and ordinary Joes … and Joans, and it's been a part of the Canton scene (is there a Canton scene?) for more than 40 years. John Shaheen, whose father started the business, now runs it with the help of his wife Sally, son Mark, and Mark's wife Tina. Hospitality has always been the family's specialty along with Middle Eastern–style food. They serve Syrian-style baba g'noush, tabooli, hummus, and baked or raw kibee. Shish kabobs are presented on a large platter atop mounds of rice, roasted potatoes, and salad. John's claim to fame is his Middle Eastern egg roll, which he says he invented: it consists of spiced ground lamb, pine nuts, and vegetables wrapped in an egg roll skin and fried. The kitchen also does standard sandwiches and steaks. The look, inside and out, is hard to describe. The place is a converted house with an add-on in front that doesn't quite match. Off to one side is a high, weathered wooden fence that shields the 40-seat patio from the street. The asphalt parking lot is cracked, and there's a slightly shabby air to the whole thing. The interior is divided into a series of small, dark, wood-paneled rooms on different levels (one is the bar decorated with photos of all the famous folks who've dropped in over the years). The chairs are comfortable, the atmosphere easygoing, and the service friendly. A belly dancer entertains most Thursdays and Fridays.

Felafel Cafe
☎ **(216) 297-0682**

CITY: **South Euclid**   AREA: **East Side**
ATMOSPHERE: **Relaxed**   COST: $$$$$

ADDRESS: 14421 Cedar Rd.
HOURS: Mon–Sat 10:30 a.m.–8 p.m.
RESERVATIONS: Taken   **PAYMENT:** MC, VS, AX, DIS
BAR: None   **TAKEOUT:** Yes   **SMOKING:** Smoke-Free
ACCESS: ♿ Full access

Walk into this 16-seat eatery, walk to the back to place your order, and walk out with very well made Middle Eastern food, either in a bag or in your belly. The kitchen offers few surprises, but the husband-and-wife team who run the place, as well as a second location in University Circle (see next listing), know what it takes to make perfect hummus, stuffed grape leaves, fatayer, falafel, which they serve with pickled turnips, and other familiar, healthy Middle Eastern fare made from scratch on the premises, including the baklava. No decor to speak of and not the sort of setting you'd select for a romantic dinner or leisurely meal, but rather a functional backdrop for the hungry. A few ethnic grocery items including olive oil, dates, and tahineh (sesame paste) are found on shelves that line one wall. Head-in parking in the lot that fronts the strip mall.

Felafel Cafe
☎ **(216) 297-9540**

CITY: **Cleveland**   AREA: **Near East Side**
ATMOSPHERE: **Relaxed**   COST: $$$$$

ADDRESS: 11365 Euclid Ave.
HOURS: Mon–Sat 10:30 a.m.–11 p.m., Sun
noon–7 p.m. (Sep–Jun)   **RESERVATIONS:** Taken

PAYMENT: MC, VS, AX, DIS BAR: None
TAKEOUT: Yes SMOKING: Smoke-Free
ACCESS: & Full access

This University Circle location at the corner of Ford and Euclid is the second for Mae and Heni. The menu's the same as the one at their original Cedar Road place, but there's more seating here and evening hours are later to accommodate the student crowd. Metered on-street parking, if you can find a spot, and a metered lot across the street. (For more information, see previous listing.)

Middle East Restaurant
☎ (216) 771-2647

CITY: **Cleveland**   AREA: **Downtown**
ATMOSPHERE: **Casual**   COST: $$$$$

ADDRESS: 1012 Prospect Ave.
HOURS: Mon–Thu 11:30 a.m.–4 p.m. (open until 7:30 p.m. during baseball games), Fri & Sat 11:30 a.m.–9 p.m.; closed Sun
RESERVATIONS: Taken, recommended Fri, Sat nights PAYMENT: MC, VS BAR: Beer, wine, liquor
TAKEOUT: Yes SMOKING: Smoking section
ACCESS: & Limited

I first began eating Josephine Abraham's fatiyar (meat- or spinach-filled turnovers), kibbee (lamb with cracked wheat and pine nuts), babaganoj (a dip of barbecued eggplant and sesame sauce), and rice pudding more than 25 years ago when the restaurant was located on Bolivar. My husband's mother treated us to a memorable meal there when he graduated from college. In 1974 the restaurant moved to a space in what's now called the Carter Manor and has been winning awards ever since, largely thanks to the fact that Josephine was still in the kitchen. She finally handed down the spoon to her sister, Margaret, shifting her own role to kitchen consultant and her tempo to semiretirement until her death in 2001. Margaret is no newcomer, though—she has 17 years' experience as a Middle Eastern chef. Restaurant owner Edward Khouri has also been known to lend a hand as well as advice. Whenever members of the Saudi royal family visit the Cleveland Clinic, Khouri sees to it that they get all their favorite dishes delivered. Menu selections include lamb and chicken kebabs, stuffed eggplant or cabbage, and lima beans or string beans simmered with ground meat in a tomato sauce, plus daily specials. The Turkish coffee is always perfectly thick and sweet. A blue-and-white Arabic motif decorates the walls, and music from the jukebox, which has only Middle Eastern selections, plays softly in the background. It's easy to get comfortable, make yourself at home, and take your time here, though they are used to accommodating the more hurried pace of lunchtime diners from area office buildings. Parking is not always easy, but there are a number of nearby lots and garages.

Nate's Deli & Restaurant
☎ (216) 696-7529

CITY: **Cleveland**   AREA: **Near West Side**
ATMOSPHERE: **Casual**   COST: $$$$$

ADDRESS: 1923 W. 25th St.
HOURS: Mon–Fri 10 a.m.–6 p.m., Sat 10 a.m.–5 p.m.; closed Sun RESERVATIONS: Taken, recommended for parties of 4 or more
PAYMENT: Cash only BAR: None TAKEOUT: Yes
SMOKING: Smoking section ACCESS: & Full access

Primarily a lunch place, Nate's is a casual, comfortable storefront restaurant near the West Side Market. Don't let the simple, unadorned look of the place lead you to believe the food is standard luncheonette fare. The menu is a most unusual combination: lunch and dinner entrees include both deli favorites and Middle Eastern specialties. You can get a kosher hot dog, a good corned beef sandwich, or a hot pastrami on rye. But you'll also find authentic, subtly seasoned hummus (a dip made with chickpeas, olive oil, sesame paste, and lemons), or a tabouleh salad (parsley, tomatoes, onions, wheat, and mint). Vegetarian and Middle Eastern entrees include falafel, foul medamas (fava beans with garlic, lemon, and olive oil), shish tawook (marinated, skewered cubes of chicken), and shawarma (strips of lean beef sauteed with onions and tomatoes and served with sesame sauce). Portions are generous, and a relish plate with tomatoes, hot peppers, and turnips pickled in beet juice arrives at every table, compliments of the house. The 50-seat restaurant is often crowded at midday with business people from downtown. Breakfast offerings are strictly American. There's some metered parking on the street, or use the municipal lot behind the market.

The Pyramid Restaurant
☎ (216) 671-9300

CITY: **Cleveland**   AREA: **Near West Side**
ATMOSPHERE: **Casual**   COST: $$$$

ADDRESS: 12657 Lorain Ave.
HOURS: Daily 11 a.m.–10:30 p.m.
RESERVATIONS: Taken PAYMENT: MC, VS, AX, DIS, checks BAR: None TAKEOUT: Yes
SMOKING: Smoking section ACCESS: ♿ Full access

It's obvious that a great deal of care went into decorating this restaurant, inside and out. The walls are done in an attractive, textured beige paper, there are many plants, and everything feels orderly, coordinated, and inviting. The 10 tables sit amidst interesting artwork, tapestries, and artifacts. There are photographs from Syria labeled "Sayda, Syria, where my friend Isa teaches school," or "Bedouins of the Syrian desert." Apparently they are for sale, taken by a man named Daniel Kirk while there on a Fulbright lectureship in the 1960s. The ambience quotient is high for such a small and inexpensive place. The menu offers a variety of Middle Eastern appetizers, sandwiches, two soups, salads, and dinner entrees featuring chicken, lamb, and beef. The Pyramids' combina-

tion plate includes shish tawook (a meat kebab), shish kafta (ground meat kebabs), shish kebab, grape leaves, fried kibbee, and hummus. The place is impossible to miss—without giving away the surprise completely to first-time visitors, I'll simply say that it's the only spot on Lorain that resembles the inside of a pharaoh's tomb.

Moroccan

Kasba
☎ (216) 371-1045

CITY: **Cleveland Heights**   AREA: **East Side**
ATMOSPHERE: **Dressy**   COST: $$$$

ADDRESS: 1932 S. Taylor Rd.
HOURS: Sun–Thu 5–10 p.m., Fri & Sat 5–11 p.m., Mon closed RESERVATIONS: Taken, Suggested on weekends for four or more and on belly-dancer nights PAYMENT: MC, VS, AX, DIS BAR: Beer, wine, liquor TAKEOUT: No SMOKING: Smoking section ACCESS: ♿ Full access

Agadir . . . Marrakesh . . . Tangier . . . Casablanca . . . Cleveland Heights. Cleveland Heights? What does this East Side community have to do with those other locales, cities in Morocco whose very names drip with a sense of the exotic and faraway? The suburb on the hill is the home of a Moroccan restaurant. And while the location is much tamer than anything you'd find in Casablanca, the food is an adventure in itself and a surprise to most people unfamiliar with this labor-intensive and intricately seasoned style of cookery. The place, which opened in the spring of 1998, provides a quiet, low-key backdrop to the food. The dining room is spacious and comfortable. Softly rounded North African–style arches frame the big storefront windows, are repeated in white plaster relief on the beige walls, and separate the main room from the bar area (where customers who like to smoke can also eat). Diners sit at low tables on cushions and benches, which heightens the experience of stepping into another world. Traditional music plays quietly in the background. All the attention and the action revolve around the plate, except for those special nights when a belly dancer makes an appearance—a performance sure to get the juices flowing. But even without her sultry charms, the smells and the menu descriptions should be sufficient to stimulate your appetite. Specialties include seven different kinds of tagines, beautifully presented in traditional-style crockery serving dishes. A tagine is a slow-simmered aromatic fruit or vegetable stew, spiced with combinations of garlic, turmeric, cumin, saffron, olives, and preserved lemons. At Casablanca there's Fez Chicken made with raisins and almonds or chicken in lemon sauce; classic beef or lamb tagines or a variation that is sweetened with honey and prunes; tagine slaoui that's made with beef, peas, and carrots in a red sauce and two other versions of it, one made with swordfish and the other with vegetables only. But that's not all—the kitchen also prepares shaaria, a dish of steamed noodles, chicken, tomatoes, and chickpeas; kefta kabobs, seasoned ground beef grilled on a skewer; brochettes, a choice of beef, lamb, or chicken, marinated and grilled; and the very special bastilla, a dish that is "usually reserved for special occasions and celebrations." For this creation, shredded chicken, onions, and parsley are layered with eggs and almonds, wrapped in a flaky pastry dough, baked, and served with a dusting of cinnamon and sugar. I was told by my server that bastilla and other entrees made with meat, fruit, and olives are called welcoming dishes because they are a way of telling your guests that they are very important and deserve something more than simple, ordinary meals of vegetables and couscous." If you really want to feel honored, treat yourself to the fixed-price, seven-course Sultan's Feast. And just like at home, everything here is made from scratch, even the stocks. Nothing comes out of a can, not even the chickpeas that are found in abundance in harira, the traditional soup that comes with every entree. On-street parking and spaces available across the street in a strip mall lot.

MARKETS

African

Barwulu/Hookes African Food Market
☎ **(216) 261-0553**
CITY: **Euclid**   AREA: **East Side**

ADDRESS: 917 E. 222 St.
FOOD AVAIL.: Meat (frozen), fish (frozen, dried), produce, grains, beans, spices, condiments, beverages, tea, coffee **HOURS:** Mon, Tue, Thu–Sat 10 a.m.–8 p.m., Wed 10 a.m.–6 p.m., Sun closed
PAYMENT: MC, VS **ACCESS:** ♿ Limited

William Barwulu Hookes is from Liberia and his wife, Ramona Hookes, is American born. He's been in this country for 20 years but never lost his taste for the foods of home, and he's banking on the fact that other people from Africa feel the same. That's why the couple decided to buy the business from its former owner in 2001, and are keeping the shelves stocked with African staples and delicacies: stockfish, cassava leaf, potato greens, palava sauce, fufu (plantain flour), fermented banku (flour of ground cassava and maize), and kenkey, a cereal from Ghana that's much like farina. But Barwulu is convinced that Americans will also like some of his products. "I get frozen free-range chickens flown in from Africa. And I tell you this—once a person has tasted this they will be running here to get some more. It is very special." In addition to all sorts of spices and condiments as well as the beans, grains, and frozen goat meat that are used in African cooking, shoppers will also find ingredients more familiar to those who prepare Jamaican food. This should come as no surprise if you know anything about the history of the Caribbean—the interplay of indigenous, European, Indian, and African cultures, the result of slavery, colonialism, and immigration, is vividly displayed in the region's cuisine. There are only two narrow aisles in this tiny store, but the floor-to-ceiling shelves and the boxes on the floor hold a whole world of food. Space for three cars to park head-in directly in front of the store, with additional parking on side streets.

Calabash African Market
☎ (216) 371-6641
CITY: **Cleveland Hts.**   AREA: **East Side**

ADDRESS: 1918 South Taylor Rd.
FOOD AVAIL.: Meat (frozen), fish (frozen, dried), produce, grains, beans, spices, condiments, beverages, tea, coffee **HOURS:** Tue–Sat 10 a.m.–8 p.m., Sun 2–6 p.m., Mon closed
PAYMENT: MC, VS, checks **ACCESS:** ♿ Full access

Sabina Smith opened her shop in November 2001. She came to Cleveland Heights from Ghana by way of New Jersey, where there were many African markets. When she realized there was a definite lack of places here to find zomi (palm oil), gari (cassava starch used for bread and porridge), and fufu (plantain flour), she decided to fill the void. She gets African customers, cooks in search of rare ingredients, and, in her words, "American who are very curious about what all these strange-looking foods are and how to use them." In fact she gets so many how-to questions, she's thinking of stocking African cookbooks and teaching some classes. She gave the small space a fresh coat of white paint, laid

new gray industrial-strength carpeting, put in simple metal shelves, and then filled the place with foods that make people from Ghana, Nigeria, and other parts of West Africa feel right at home. For most everyone else, it's a shopping adventure and an education. Huge, brown, prehistoric-looking tubers are yams. A vegetable labeled "garden eggs" turns out to be small eggplants. Beans as beautiful as beads come in a variety of colors and patterns. She stocks groundnut paste made from peanuts; egushie, a meal made from melon seeds that's used to thicken soups and stews; dried sorrel leaves; and ogbono, an herb from the baobab tree. There's frozen goat meat and pigs' feet, salted beef, smoked and dried fish, and an array of flours, canned condiments, and sauces. Long-handled wooden spoons, grinding rocks, clay mortars and pestles, and fabric printed with a wax-block technique in traditional colors and motifs give the two-aisle store a museum quality. CDs of African music, which play quietly in the background, are for sale, along with foreign-language videos, cosmetics, personal-care products, and home remedies. The Market is located in a strip of charming, older brick storefronts with metered parking in the street.

Asian Imports
☎ (440) 777-8101
CITY: **North Olmsted**   AREA: **West Side**

ADDRESS: 26885 Brookpark Ext.
FOOD AVAIL.: produce, baked goods, canned & packaged goods, spices, condiments, beverages, tea, coffee, prepared frozen foods, takeout meals
HOURS: Tue–Sun 11 a.m.–7 p.m., Mon closed
PAYMENT: MC, VS, DIS **ACCESS:** ♿ Limited

This small market is packed from floor to ceiling. Rice comes in many varieties and quantities. Freezer cases are filled with convenience foods, Indian-style prepared entrees and side dishes, and ready to cook naan, roti, and parantha (breads), plus samosa wrappers for do-it-yourselfers. You can also buy hot homemade samosas and pakoras to go. Also available are spices in abundance, nuts, dried fruit, esoteric ingredients like mango pulp and ginger paste, and fresh produce, including some vegetables with names that sent me to a culinary dictionary—karela (bitter gourd), gawar (a long green bean), and dudhi (white fleshed and pumpkin-like). Specialized cooking utensils, Indian-language videos, and personal care products complete the selection. Located in the same strip as Kashmir Palace (see listing in this chapter), with ample parking.

India Food & Spices
☎ (440) 845-0000
CITY: **Parma**   AREA: **Southwest**

ADDRESS: 5543 Ridge Rd.
FOOD AVAIL.: Meat (frozen), produce, grains, beans, flour, baked goods, canned & packaged goods, spices, condiments, beverages, tea, prepared frozen foods HOURS: Tue–Fri 1–7:30 p.m., Sat noon–7 p.m., Sun 1–6 p.m.; closed Mon PAYMENT: Checks ACCESS: ♿ None

Owner Bhavna Patel has moved her market across the street from its previous location. She takes pride in the fact that although this store is small it can supply customers with virtually any spice they ask for. She carries fruits and vegetables basic to Indian-style dishes, including bitter melon, okra, eggplant, long beans, mangoes, and guavas. A good selection of chutneys, Indian pickles (mango, gooseberry, ginger, lime), and flours made from ground beans—adoo besan, moong, dhokla, urad, and bajari. For an inexpensive weekend of armchair travel, you can stop in, buy some Indian ice cream and pastries, and rent an Indian video. There are a few basic, non-Indian grocery and household items available.

Indo-American Foods
☎ (216) 662-0072
CITY: **North Randall**   AREA: **Southeast**

ADDRESS: 4614 Warrensville Ctr. Rd.
FOOD AVAIL.: Produce, canned & packaged goods, spices, condiments, beverages, tea, prepared frozen foods HOURS: Mon–Sat 11 a.m.–8:30 p.m., Sun noon–6 p.m.
PAYMENT: MC, VS, AX, DIS, checks
ACCESS: ♿ None

A small convenience store that's best described as the Indian version of a 7-11. Dried, canned, and packaged staples include rice and spices, mango juice, and movies to rent (Indian and Pakistani with subtitles). Some seasonal produce. This is where local Indian families run when they need a jar of ghee (clarified butter), a can of ginger pickles, or a bottle of coconut oil.

Lakshmi Plaza
☎ (440) 460-4601
CITY: **Mayfield Hts.**   AREA: **East Side**

ADDRESS: 5850 Mayfield Rd.
FOOD AVAIL.: Produce, grains, beans, baked goods, spices, condiments, beverages, tea, coffee HOURS: Dail 10 a.m.–9 p.m. PAYMENT: MC, VS, checks ACCESS: ♿ Full access

Mayfield Road is becoming a veritable global marketplace, and this is the most recent addition. A full-service Indian grocery store in a small two-aisle space. Newly opened in mid-April 2002, the market carries fresh vegetables and every sort of spice, condiment, sauce, grain, bean, and flour used in Indian cooking. There are many short-cut mixes for curry, dal, kurma, and biryani; chapati and pappadums (breads) ready to fry; prepared ghee (clarified butter) and paneer (a farmer-type cheese); and some masalas (spice blends). Some of the more esoteric ingredients that caught my eye were green cardamom, mustard oil (a pungent fat from black mustard seeds), and ajwan seed (an herb with a strong thyme-like flavor). The store offers delivery service, a large selection of Indian-language movies, and some specialized cooking utensils. Located in a strip mall with ample parking both in front of and behind the store.

Patel Brothers
☎ (440) 885-4440
CITY: **Middleburg Heights**
AREA: **Southwest**

ADDRESS: 6876 Pearl Rd.
FOOD AVAIL.: Produce, grains, beans, flour, baked goods, canned & packaged goods, spices, condiments, tea, coffee, prepared frozen foods HOURS: Tue–Sat 11 a.m.–8 p.m., Sun 11 a.m.–6 p.m.; closed Mon PAYMENT: MC, VS, checks ACCESS: ♿ Full access

Tucked among the larger stores that are part of Southland Shopping Center is this small, family-owned shop offering Indian and Pakistani foods. Some basic household staples are shelved with the pickled mangoes, chutney, and chili paste. You'll find fresh items like bitter melon, squash, long beans, Chinese okra, eggplant, guava, mango, rotis (bread), and Indian pastries. A wide selection of masala (spice mixtures) and sambal (spicy condiments).

Raj Mahal Indian Foods
☎ (330) 926-0369
CITY: **Cuyahoga Falls**   AREA: **Farther South**

ADDRESS: 2037 State Rd.
FOOD AVAIL.: Produce, grains, beans, baked goods, canned & packaged goods, spices, condiments, beverages, tea, prepared frozen foods HOURS: Mon–Sun 11 a.m.–8 p.m. PAYMENT: MC, VS, DIS ACCESS: ♿ Limited

Owner Kala Chima, who also is the proprietor of the Raj Mahal Restaurant next door (see listing earlier in this chapter), has filled this three-aisle shop with a really great mix of foods. In addition to the standard Indian cooking ingredients, there are vegetables I do not recognize by sight with names I must come home and look up (and even then, I still don't know what they are or what to do with them): arbi (colocasia or elephant ears); karela (bittergourd); dudhi (bottle gourd); and turai (a relative of zucchini). Scanning the shelves for what's unusual, I zero in on mango pulp, gooseberries in sugar syrup, lime pickles, green and black cardamom, puffed rice, and dried tamarind. A freezer case holds breads—nan, roti, and parantha. I was entranced by 15-pound canvas sacks of basmati rice. The Royal brand graphics on the bag are charming, and the copy reads "from the foothills of the Himalayas to your table." Also a real eye-catcher are the traditional and brightly colored women's and children's clothing for sale. Busy commercial strip with easy head-in parking.

Saree Mahal
☎ (216) 581-9414
CITY: **Maple Heights**   AREA: **Southeast**

ADDRESS: 20940 Southgate Park Blvd.
FOOD AVAIL.: Fish (frozen), produce, grains, beans, flour, rice, baked goods, canned & packaged goods, spices, condiments, beverages, tea HOURS: Mon–Sat 11 a.m.–9 p.m., Sun 11 a.m.–7 p.m. PAYMENT: MC, VS, DIS
ACCESS: ♿ Limited

This market is part of Kuldip Pooni's expanding Indian food empire. He also owns the attached restaurant (see listing for Mehak-e-Punjab) and a second restaurant at Hilltop Plaza (see listing for Maharaja). It's 1,700 square feet of grocery store shelving filled with a wide variety of Indian cooking ingredients and a mix of foodstuffs that also meet the needs of his African and Middle Eastern customers. He boasts that he carries the largest selection of Indian snack foods—60 different ways to satisfy the munchies. Its mall location means parking is never a problem.

Spice Corner
☎ (330) 535-1033

CITY: **Akron**   AREA: **Farther South**

ADDRESS: 379 Spicer St.
FOOD AVAIL.: Produce, grains, beans, flour, canned & packaged goods, spices, condiments, beverages, tea HOURS: Tue–Sun 11 a.m.–7 p.m.
PAYMENT: MC, VS, checks ACCESS: ♿ Full access
OTHER ETHNIC SPECIALTIES: Malaysian, Pakistani

As its name suggests, this store specializes in spices and is a good source for hard-to-find flavorings essential to many traditional Indian, Pakistani, and Malaysian dishes. Their aroma mingles with the smell of incense, the only nonfood item available here, and the air is thick with the exotic scents. Produce available in season includes bitter melon, long squash, guavas, and Asian vegetables. There are jars of relishes and pickles from India, a variety of lentils and rice, and flour specially ground for making chapati (Indian flat bread) as well as ready-made frozen chapati. As so much Indian cuisine is meatless, this is a great source of food ideas and products for vegetarians.

Lebanese

Amir's Marketplace
☎ (216) 291-1878

CITY: **South Euclid**   AREA: **East Side**

ADDRESS: 4422 Mayfield Rd.
FOOD AVAIL.: grains, beans, flour, rice, baked goods, canned & packaged goods, spices, condiments, beverages, coffee, prepared frozen foods, takeout meals HOURS: Mon–Thu 11 a.m.–9 p.m., Fri & Sat 11 a.m.– 10 p.m., Sun 11 a.m.–8 p.m. PAYMENT: MC, VS, AX, DIS
ACCESS: ♿ Full access OTHER ETHNIC SPECIALTIES: Most other Middle East countries, Indian

Amir's Marketplace is at the same location as Amir's Marketplace Restaurant (see listing earlier in this chapter). If you plan to eat and shop, keep in mind that the store opens an hour and a half earlier than the restaurant. Separated from the dining area by a glass partition, the small grocery store displays its wares attractively. The proprietors manage to pack a sizable selection of typical Middle Eastern and Indian foods into the space and even carry some more unusual items like pomegranate molasses, ghee (clarified butter), honey with the comb, whole-wheat phyllo dough, sumac (a spice), and green cardamom pods. There's a large and tempting array of distinctive pastries, sweets made with such things as farina, pistachios, and dates. You can also buy prepared spinach and meat pies; with a salad, I call them dinner, and so do my kids. Meat pies iare great for school lunch bags (spinach evokes too many negative peer comments). They have added Indian and Pakistani products to their selection. The shop is actually just the retail end of a much larger wholesale operation; there's a warehouse in back, and they ship their products for sale in 18 states. A list of what's available, along with nutritional information, is on their website, www.amir-foods.com.

Jasmine Pita Bakery
☎ (216) 251-3838

CITY: **Cleveland**   AREA: **West Side**

ADDRESS: 16700 Lorain Rd.
FOOD AVAIL.: produce, grains, beans, flour, rice, baked goods, canned & packaged goods, spices, condiments, beverages, tea, coffee, prepared frozen foods, takeout meals HOURS: Mon–Sat 9 a.m.–9 p.m., Sun noon–6 p.m. PAYMENT: MC, VS, checks ACCESS: ♿ Full access OTHER ETHNIC SPECIALTIES: Middle Eastern

Take advantage of the head-in parking in front of the renovated business strip when you shop here. Large windows offer a sneak preview of the pleasant shopping and eating environment inside. You'll see a bright, spacious, uncluttered room, gleaming industrial shelving, large refrigerators, and sparkling glass cases, all filled with Middle Eastern delicacies. There's a good selection of prepared foods including hummus, baba ghannouj, kibbee, stuffed grape leaves, meat and spinach pies, felafel, and tabouli; a self-serve olive bar with at least six different varieties, plus turnip and cauliflower pickles; a bakery counter; cheeses and yogurt products; and a cooler stocked with drinks like guava and mango nectar. They carry pita, lavash (a thin, crepe-like bread), and seasoned breads. In addition to the ingredients you'd expect to find, such as tahini and olive oil, you'll also encounter some delightful specialties—fig marmalade, date honey, and large hunks of halvah (a candy made from crushed sesame seeds and honey). Four tables at the front of the store provide a place to dine on your counter purchases or to simply pause and enjoy the aroma.

Middle Eastern

Aladdin's Baking Company
☎ (216) 861-0317
CITY: **Cleveland**   AREA: **Downtown**

ADDRESS: 1301 Carnegie Ave.
FOOD AVAIL.: produce, grains, beans, flour, rice, baked goods, canned & packaged goods, spices, condiments, beverages, tea, coffee, prepared frozen foods, takeout meals   HOURS: Mon–Sat 7 a.m.–6 p.m., Sun 9 a.m.–1:30 p.m. (open Mon–Sat until 7 p.m. during baseball season)
PAYMENT: MC, VS, AX, DIS, checks
ACCESS: ♿ Limited

Freshly baked pita, a traditional flat bread made without sugar, oil, or fat, is the specialty here. A selection of Middle Eastern dishes is available daily, and you can purchase a full meal, already prepared. There's fatiyar (spinach or meat pies), beef

or chicken shawarma (meat formed into a loaf around a skewer and cooked by rotisserie), kafta (meatballs), and shish kabob. You can get containers of tabouli (a salad made with bulgur wheat, onions, mint, tomatoes, olive oil, and lemon juice), hummus (chickpea spread), and baba ghannouj (eggplant spread). For dessert, choose from Middle Eastern and Mediterranean-style pastries, including Beirut-style baklava, and pick up Turkish or Lebanese coffee. For use in your own recipes, they stock feta cheese, a wide variety of olives, olive oils, spices, and condiments.

Albelad Imported Food
☎ (216) 688-1219
CITY: **Cleveland**   AREA: **Near West Side**

ADDRESS: 3353 W. 117 St.
FOOD AVAIL.: meat (fresh, frozen), produce, grains, beans, baked goods, spices, condiments, beverages, tea, coffee, takeout meals
HOURS: Daily 8 a.m.–11 p.m.   PAYMENT: MC, VS
ACCESS: ♿ Full access

Full-service market takes on layers of meaning because the service includes providing foodstuffs to a variety of ethnic groups. Middle Eastern products dominate from bottles of laban (thick, cultured milk) and Egyptian molokhia leaves (a green herb), to frozen felafel; a large selection of Halal meats (Islamic approved) including beef, veal, goat, and lamb and less common lamb parts—kidneys, hearts, and livers; an olive bar; and freshly prepared hummus platters to go. In the dairy case, the selection of Middle Eastern cheeses is especially noteworthy: ackaw, Syrian, anari, halloumi. But those in need of Indian ingredients will also find what they need, and there is a limited but useful array of products for Greek and Hispanic dishes. The produce section offers some less usual items along with lemons and lettuce: a squash that looks similar to zucchini labeled casa; baby eggplants; and fresh green fava beans. The selection of prepared foods, ready to eat on the road or take home for later, is extensive and interesting, and the kitchen also does catering.

Almadina Imports
☎ (216) 671-4661
CITY: **Cleveland**   AREA: **Near West Side**

ADDRESS: 11550 Lorain Ave.
FOOD AVAIL.: meat (fresh, deli, frozen), fish (fresh, frozen), produce, grains, beans, baked goods, spices, condiments, beverages, tea, coffee, takeout meals HOURS: Daily 7–1 a.m.
PAYMENT: MC, VS, DIS, checks ACCESS: ⓺ Limited

This spacious full-service market, easily found by virtue of the big burgundy-colored awning over the front door, offers all things Middle Eastern from pomegranate juice to sesame paste, as well as a large variety of non-ethnic produce and household products. Halal meats, from animals slaughtered according to Islamic guidelines, are available fresh and frozen.

In addition to an olive bar, there's a nut bar—something I've never seen in any other Middle Eastern store in the region—with a large selection that includes spiced and flavored nuts and nut mixtures. They also carry the biggest rounds of fresh pita bread I've ever encountered—about 12 inches across. You could use one for a pizza or an edible platter. But the prepared foods really make this place stand out from the many other similar markets in town—definitely not your garden-variety takeout. Breakfast offerings include eggs with Halal beef bacon; eggs ageh made with parsley, mint, and spices; egg pies; and zatar (bread spread with sesame seeds, olive oil, herbs, and spices) with cheese. For later in the day and into the wee hours, in addition to typical entrees such as shish kabob, shish tawook (chicken) and shwarma (ground beef), hummus, salads, and rice pilaf, there are sandwiches made with lamb liver, lamb brains, lamb spleen, and lamb hearts.

Assad Bakery
☎ (216) 251-5777
CITY: **Cleveland**   AREA: **West Side**

ADDRESS: 12719 Lorain Ave.
FOOD AVAIL.: meat (fresh, deli), fish (dried), produce, grains, beans, flour, rice, baked goods, canned & packaged goods, spices, beverages, tea, coffee, prepared frozen foods, takeout meals
HOURS: Mon–Sat 9 a.m.–9 p.m., Sun 9 a.m.–8 p.m. PAYMENT: MC, VS, AX, checks
ACCESS: ⓺ Full access

Don't be misled by the name—this is much more than a bakery. Brothers Mike and Fred Assad founded the business in 1990 and employ almost all their extended family. They bake fresh pita on the premises and prepare meat and spinach pies as well as Middle Eastern pastries. Exotic fruits and vegetables such as raw dates, fresh figs, loquats, and cactus pears are available seasonally. There's an interesting selection of cheeses, olives, nuts, spices, and olive oils. They also stock some unusual cookware, Middle Eastern drums, and Arab clothing. Mike describes his clientele, many regulars who enjoy the friendly, personal service, as "like a United Nations."

Ellis Bakery
☎ (330) 376-5012
CITY: **Akron**   AREA: **Farther South**

ADDRESS: 577 Grant St.
FOOD AVAIL.: grains, rice, baked goods, canned & packaged goods, spices, condiments, beverages, coffee, takeout meals HOURS: Mon–Fri 9 a.m.–5 p.m., Sat 9 a.m.–4 p.m.; closed Sun
PAYMENT: Checks ACCESS: ⓺ Limited OTHER ETHNIC SPECIALTIES: Indian

Bill Ellis is supposed to be retired, but after about 50 years of baking pita bread and baklava he just can't bring himself to do anything else. But now he shares the job with his son, Jeff. Together they run a bakery and deli that offers fresh, made-on-the-premises Middle Eastern–style pastries and breads, hummus, tabouli, eggplant dip, and a selection of olives, cheeses, spices, nuts, and other Mideast and Indian grocery items. The business started in a garage and now fills 4,000 feet—a whole building—with about a fourth of the space devoted to retail sales and the rest used for food production.

Halal Meats
☎ (216) 281-1900
CITY: **Cleveland**   AREA: **Near East Side**

ADDRESS: 9418 Detroit Ave.
FOOD AVAIL.: Meat (fresh, deli, frozen), produce, grains, beans, baked goods, spices, condiments, beverages, tea, coffee **HOURS:** Mon–Sat 9 a.m.–9 p.m., Sun 10 a.m.–7 p.m.
PAYMENT: MC, VS **ACCESS:** ♿ Limited

Whether you're in search of dried Egyptian okra, tamarind syrup, a can of Moroccan sardines, labneh (a cream cheese made from yogurt-like cultured milk), or a footlong kebab skewer, this is the place. The selection of products used in Middle Eastern cookery is extensive and includes many esoteric ingredients and Halal meats (prepared according to Muslim law). Indian foods are also well represented: sauce mixes; chutney; tandoori paste; chili pickles; basmati rice; and mango jam. Rice, sugar, olive oil, and even pickled cucumbers are sold in large, cost-saving sizes. Some shelf space is devoted to Goya products, used in Latin American cooking, and the freezer case contains Goya frozen banana leaves alongside the filo dough and felafel. The only category of food not well represented is fresh produce—the variety and quantity are limited. Although I just discovered this market, it's been in operation since 1985, one of the first places in the state to sell Halal meats. The store, renovated in 2001, is brightly lit, and maneuvering around the aisles is easy.

Holyland Imports
☎ (216) 671-7736
CITY: **Cleveland**   AREA: **West Side**

ADDRESS: 12831 Lorain Ave.
FOOD AVAIL.: Meat (fresh), produce, grains, beans, flour, rice, baked goods, canned & packaged goods, spices, condiments, beverages, tea, coffee, prepared frozen foods **HOURS:** Mon–Sat 9 a.m.–9 p.m., Sun 9 a.m.–7 p.m. **PAYMENT:** MC, VS, AX, DIS, checks **ACCESS:** ♿ Full access **OTHER ETHNIC SPECIALTIES:** Indian, Greek

Arabic-language videos play on a television perched above the refrigerator case, and the sound adds to the sensation of having journeyed to another country. This store is cavernous, and neither modern nor showy. The linoleum's cracked, and many of the shelves are simply covered with fresh contact paper. Nonetheless the array of Middle Eastern food products and cookware is impressive, and you can find ingredients typically featured in Greek and Indian recipes as well. Large Rubbermaid bins hold almonds, pistachios, walnuts, and pine nuts, and the prices for these, which you scoop up yourself, are noticeably lower per pound than the packaged counterparts available at regular grocery or gourmet stores. Other bins are filled with olives, and delicacies like pickled turnips and pickled peppers. The place is run by the five Mohammad brothers. They all take turns behind the counter, keeping the store open seven days a week. It's easy to spot: there's a red shingle awning out front and a big black sign with lettering in both English and Arabic. On-street parking and additional spaces in a lot across the street.

DON'T FORGET: CALL AHEAD!

The Near East Market
☎ (330) 475-0538

CITY: **Cuyahoga Falls**　AREA: **Farther South**

ADDRESS: 3461 Hudson Dr.
FOOD AVAIL.: produce, grains, beans, baked goods, canned & packaged goods, beverages, tea, coffee, prepared frozen foods, takeout meals
HOURS: Mon–Sat 10 a.m.–9 p.m., Sun 10 a.m.–5 p.m.　**PAYMENT:** MC, VS, AX, DIS
ACCESS: ♿ Full access

Fan, ace librarian (Cleveland Heights-University Heights), and true food enthusiast Helene Stern tipped me off about this place. She and her husband Bud found it, shortly after it opened in June 2003, on their way home from the Akron Art Museum. Lucky thing, because they were hungry and looking for a place to get a late lunch. Unfortunately there were no tables, though plans are in the works to remedy that, but there was a great deal of great food to carry out, much of it prepared on the premises, including meat, cheese, and spinach pies; kibbeh balls (in meat and vegetarian versions); hummus; eggplant dip; stuffed grape leaves; lentils and rice; shwarma and felafel sandwiches; and fattoosh and tabouleh salads. Pastries are shipped in from commercial bakeries in Detroit and Toronto. The spacious modern market is situated at the corner of Graham Road and Hudson Drive, and offers a mix of ready-to-eat and groceries. Big self-serve buckets of olives sit on the floor, and store owner Moamar Mustafa cures some varieties himself. A refrigerator case features a large selection of Middle Eastern cheeses. Special finds among the fresh produce—fresh fava beans, green chickpeas, green almonds, and fresh figs Helene says are the best she's ever had. An aisle is devoted to spices and sauces. You can find all the canned, boxed, and jarred things you'd expect, plus some you wouldn't, like pickled wild cucumbers and Syrian sweets, pieces of nougat, and Turkish Delight candies. The big sign out front makes it easy to spot, and ample parking makes it hassle free.

Petra Food
☎ (330) 633-3830

CITY: **Tallmadge**　AREA: **Farther South**

ADDRESS: 57 Midway Plaza
FOOD AVAIL.: meat (fresh), produce, grains, beans, flour, rice, baked goods, canned & packaged goods, spices, condiments, beverages, tea, coffee, prepared frozen foods, takeout meals
HOURS: Mon–Sat 10 a.m.–8 p.m., Sun noon–5 p.m.　**PAYMENT:** MC, VS, DIS
ACCESS: ♿ Full access　**OTHER ETHNIC SPECIALTIES:** Greek, Italian, Indian

Mohammad Matar and his wife got tired of driving to Cleveland to purchase the food products they needed. They realized that if they wanted a store that sold Middle Eastern and North African groceries a little closer to where they lived, others probably did as well. So they started a business in 1994, along with a cousin, and now serve shoppers from Akron, Kent, and Canton. They like to think of their customers as friends, make an effort to learn shoppers' names and preferences, and miss them if they don't come in for a while. They also try to stay in touch by maintaining a mailing list and sending out news of in-store specials. The store stocks fresh lamb and goat meat; some hard-to-find fresh and frozen fruits and vegetables like baby eggplants, mikete (a sort of cucumber), and kseu (a type of zucchini); semolina, farina, and chickpea flour; basmati rice and bulgur wheat; dried fava beans and lentils; tahini (sesame paste) and jamid, dried yogurt used in the preparation of meats; and prepared felafel, kibbee (baked ground meat), and fresh pita bread. They also stock more than 60 different spices and spice blends, all in bulk, so you can purchase just the amount you need. Service is attentive and hospitable, and parking is plentiful in the plaza lot.

Sanabel Middle East Bakery

☎ (330) 253-4505

CITY: **Akron** AREA: **Farther South**

ADDRESS: 308 E. South St.

FOOD AVAIL.: grains, beans, baked goods, canned & packaged goods, spices, condiments, beverages, tea, coffee, takeout meals **HOURS:** Mon–Fri 9 a.m.–5:30 p.m., Sat 9 a.m.–5 p.m., Sun closed **PAYMENT:** MC, VS, checks **ACCESS:** ♿ Full access

The neighborhood's a little run down, with cracks in the sidewalk and weeds in the cracks, but the bakery space, in a World War II–era building, is nicely spiffed up. Since 1998, Shafik Zakahm's been preparing a selection of Middle Eastern favorites including stuffed grape leaves; hummus, felafel; kibbeh; and meat, spinach, cheese, and chicken pies. He's created a special sandwich using herbed zatar bread, tomatoes, onions, and his very own, and secret, version of special sauce. On Wednesdays and Fridays he does a vegetarian hot lunch of lentils and rice plus salad. For those who'd rather dine in than take out, there are a few tables set amidst shelves and cases of canned and jarred foods, dairy products, and spices. If you're in search of Egyptian tobacco for your hookah, you'll find it here too.

Vine Valley Mediterranean Market

☎ (330) 865-6777

CITY: **Akron** AREA: **Farther South**

ADDRESS: 1450 Portage Path

FOOD AVAIL.: grains, beans, baked goods, canned & packaged goods, spices, condiments, beverages, tea, coffee, takeout meals **HOURS:** Mon–Sat 10 a.m.–6 p.m., Sun closed **PAYMENT:** MC, VS **ACCESS:** ♿ Full access

The Merriman Valley is becoming a bit of an ethnic eats hub, and this little market is a standout for its freezer case stocked with quarts of Lebanese-style ice cream, made in Detroit. The most unusual is flavored with rosewater, but there's also mango, pistachio, and apricot. They prepare their own traditional Middle Eastern fare—meat and spinach pies, kibbeh, rolled grape leaves, zatar, and shawarma sandwiches. Shoppers will find an array of ingredients, from oils and spices to cheeses and fresh vegetables, in these two aisles and can even go home with their very own hookah. Located at one end of the strip in Parkway Plaza.

Chapter 3

MEDITERRANEAN

The term "Mediterranean" generally refers to the coastal regions of the countries surrounding the sea of that name. I've used it here rather cavalierly to provide a collective heading for a diverse group of countries and areas in Southern Europe. What ties them together in my mind is the robust, earthy flavor of their foods. Mediterranean cooking is characterized by its reliance on olives and olive oil, garlic, onions, lemons, grapes and the wines that can be made from them, capers (the pickled flower bud of a shrub that grows in the region), tomatoes, and green herbs like thyme, parsley, rosemary, basil, fennel, and bay leaves. Good bread and fresh fruit are seen as essential parts of every meal. With its emphasis on seafood and fresh garden vegetables, Mediterranean cuisine is considered to be one of the healthiest diets in the world. Both the tastes and simple techniques are well suited to the contemporary American lifestyle, and this approach to food has grown increasingly popular in recent years. In Cleveland, restaurants provide diners with a chance to explore Mediterranean cuisine as it is prepared in Greece, Italy, and southern France.

Between 1890 and 1920, 5,000 Greeks settled in Cleveland. They were mostly males intending to stay only long enough to make their fortunes and then return home. These *protporoi* (pioneers) took low-paying, menial jobs at first, but once they decided to remain and establish roots in the community many started their own small businesses. They sent for their wives or returned home to find a bride to bring back to Cleveland. By 1922 there were at least 137 Greek-owned businesses in town, among them coffeehouses, candy stores, and restaurants.

Much of Greek cultural and social life, even for second-, third-, and fourth-generation Greek Americans, centers around the city's four Greek Orthodox churches. "I have to travel far to get to church," said Debbie Alexandrou, who was born on the island of Samos but has lived in Cleveland since her marriage almost 40 years ago. "But I love it there, because it's just like being in Greece. I can pretend that I am back home."

Small in number and close knit, the Greek community of Cleveland is very dedicated not only to preserving their cultural heritage but to sharing it, and they sponsor many festivals around town. Food is always an important element. "All our events include food," said Penny Sikoutris, born here to Greek immigrant parents. "When Greeks get together, they eat. Years ago, the general public was not so familiar with our cuisine. Now that they've grown accustomed to it, they seem to like it as much as we do!"

Beyond its commonalities with all Mediterranean cooking, some ingredients are particular to Greek cuisine. Dill, sage (which seems to flourish in the sea air), oregano, and mint are used often. Lamb is the favored meat, and cheeses are made from goat's milk. Phyllo, thin sheets of pastry dough, goes into a variety of dishes. Honey is used with abandon in pastries.

I once attended a festival held at the Church of the Annunciation, the oldest Greek Orthodox church in the city. It was built on a parcel of land on West 14th, just across the river from "Greek Town," that was purchased in 1912. The array of food was staggering, as it always is at this annual celebration: there was pastitsio, moussaka, dolmathes, tiropeta, and spanakopeta, lamb shanks, baked fish, and souvlakia. And tray after tray of desserts, almost floating in a sea of golden sweetness: baklava, galaktoboureko, and kataife. To no one in particular I said, "What would Greeks do without honey?" The man behind me replied, "Not have a reason to live."

Italians have long been one of the largest ethnic groups in Cleveland. The earliest immigrants came from northern Italy after the Civil War, followed in the years just preceding World War I by people from the central and southern regions. Between 1889 and 1924, 25,000 Italians came to settle here. They were stonemasons, bootmakers, quarrymen, and produce sellers. They tended to live in close proximity to one another, build their own churches, and attend to all their needs through hometown societies. Big Italy, which no longer exists, was a downtown area that stretched from Ontario to East 40th Street. Little Italy was, and is, perched on Murray Hill along Mayfield Road, much like a little hill town in the old country. By 1911, 96 percent of the people who lived there were Italian born and most were from the Abruzzi region.

In 1919 an Italian immigrant named Vitantonio began making pasta machines in his Little Italy garage. He expanded, making the kinds of cookware Italians needed in their kitchens: tomato strainers, cavatelli and pizelli makers. His grandson, Louis, continues to run this local company under the family name, and it has become a large manufacturer and distributor of old-world kitchen tools. "Yesterday's ethnic customers," said Louis Vitantonio with obvious pride, "have been replaced by today's gourmet cooks. In spite of the trend towards convenience, there are still people who want food produced the traditional way."

Americans of Italian descent are for the most part fully assimilated into the mainstream of American life. Though Little Italy continues to be a densely populated Italian enclave and home to some of the city's best-known Italian restaurants and stores, Italian Americans are spread throughout Greater Cleveland now. But for many, no matter where they live, Italian-American clubs that promote cultural awareness and pride provide a link with their heritage. Local cookbook author Maria Volpe Paganini says much of this cultural legacy is expressed through food and family, the two basic and essential elements of the Italian soul.

"To Italians, family is what matters most and food is at the center of day-to-day family life. Food is more important to us than politics or money and we think about it a great deal. We gather around the table, and while we eat good food, we talk."

Italian cuisine has profoundly influenced how Americans eat, though the Italian dishes we're most accustomed to bear little resemblance to the real thing. Even the term Italian food is misleading. There are approximately twenty regions in that country, and every one has its own culinary heritage. In each, the unique foods produced there represent the area's distinctive style: Modena is the one true source for balsamic vinegar, Parma for prosciutto ham, and Emilia-Romagna for genuine Parmigiano-Reggiano cheese.

Pasta, however (and there are over 200 different types and shapes), is common to all. Cooks throughout the country also appreciate the qualities of Italian varieties of rice (arborio, vialone nano, carnaroli); polenta (a cornmeal mush); cannellini and other beans; and anchovies. And they do wondrous things with veal.

Though the cooks of southern France are a breed unto themselves, their culinary traditions are inextricably linked to their Italian neighbors. But as a group they have no real Cleveland history to speak of, for, as someone from Provence once said to me, "Why would they leave?" Which leaves me with only their cuisine to write about.

It's been described as full of gusto, passion, and vitality, imbued with the warm sunshine of their climate and the peasant's appreciation for nature's bounty. Their soups are said to have distinctive personality, and their lamb, which grazes on wild herbs, is like no other. In addition to the ingredients favored by all Mediterranean cooks, the kitchens of southern France are stocked with mushrooms, potatoes, shallots, and leeks. But it is not the type of ingredients so much as their freshness and the way in which they are combined to let the flavor of each shine through that characterizes this style of cooking. Ultimately it is the art of beautiful and savory simplicity.

MEDITERRANEAN

RESTAURANTS

Greek

Athens Restaurant
☎ (330) 453-6800

CITY: **Canton**   AREA: **Farther South**
ATMOSPHERE: **Relaxed**   COST: $$$$$

ADDRESS: 16 Harrison Ave. SW
HOURS: Mon–Sat 6:30 a.m.–3 p.m.
RESERVATIONS: Taken   **PAYMENT:** MC, VS, AX, DIS
BAR: None   **TAKEOUT:** Yes   **SMOKING:** All sections
ACCESS: ♿ Full access

Ted Karasarides opened this restaurant in 1976, and now his glamorous-looking daughter Dimitria (known to all as Dee), who has been helping out since she was 14, runs the place and her mom Maria still prepares the daily Greek specials. Most of the staff have been working here almost as long as Dee and Maria, some for 20 years, and they are all part of the family. Regular customers are part of the family too, and everybody calls each other by name. The early-morning hours bring retirees, folks getting off the night shift, police men and women, and bus drivers. At lunchtime, you see company people, both suits and non-suits, from nearby corporations like Timken and Diebold, hospital workers, plus men and women of unidentified occupation and age enjoying the increasingly rare opportunity to sit wherever they want and smoke as much as they want. There's a long lunch counter that stretches all the way from the front of the

restaurant to the kitchen, and the low stools have real wooden tops, burnished silky and golden by all the seats that have sat on them. Tables are covered in green vinyl, and white Christmas lights are strung up year round (or else they hadn't yet taken them down in June). Fake greenery and Greek scenes painted on the walls make up the decorative flourishes. It looks and feels like a cross between a truck stop and a workingman's club. Carryout business is always brisk. Breakfast is served until 11:30 on weekdays and all day Saturday. Saganaki (flaming cheese), Greek salads, mbefteki (chopped, spiced steak), gyros, soutsoukakia (sausages of northern Greece), rice pudding, Greek pastries, and Greek coffee are on the regular menu, along with standard American diner fare. Specials include roasted lamb shanks, sarmathes (stuffed cabbage leaves in egglemon sauce), yovecci (beef tips with rosemary and kasseri cheese), stifado (stew), pastitsio, mousaka, baked pork chops Thessalonika-style, and keftedes (meatballs with rice). A small bakery counter at the front offers baklava, cookies, and other traditional pastries for sale. A separate room called "The Athenian" is available for private gatherings or large groups. The restaurant is easy to spot as the lone white corner building is done in faux-Parthenon with distinctive white columns in front. Plenty of parking in a lot to the side and another across the street.

Casablanca
☎ (330) 735-3304

CITY: **Dellroy**   AREA: **Farther South**
ATMOSPHERE: **Relaxed**   COST: $$$$$

ADDRESS: 27 N. Smith St.
HOURS: Open daily anytime after 6 p.m., with reservations   **RESERVATIONS:** Required
PAYMENT: Checks   **BAR:** None   **TAKEOUT:** No
SMOKING: All sections   **ACCESS:** ♿ Full access
OTHER ETHNIC SPECIALTIES: Mediterranean mix

This is a truly unique dining destination, as unlike a restaurant as a restaurant could be. There are only four tables, and you can't get one unless you've got a reservation. The tables are in the dining room of a two-story house where owners Jim and Karen also live. There's a spectacular view of Atwood Lake from the dining room, and if you time your visit properly, you get to watch the sun set. Jim greets, seats, and serves while Karen handles the kitchen. You can see her at work because only a counter separates the two rooms in this century home that the couple gutted and renovated to function as both home and workplace. They've been in business since 1995 and have never advertised, relying instead on word-of-mouth recommendations. People come from all over the region, and they are usually booked well in advance on the weekends and every night throughout the summer. Jim generally wears a tuxedo and provides the kind of personal and attentive service found in high-end restaurants. The tables sport white linens and fresh flowers, and fine art decorates the walls. Even so, the atmosphere is informal, the pricing moderate, and the dress code casual—although if you want to put on your prom clothes and compete with Jim you won't feel out of place. The menu selection is not large, but it is interesting, and the inspiration is Mediterranean with Greek cuisine at the forefront. Among the appetizers are stuffed grape leaves, tiropita (cheese-filled triangles of phyllo dough), and keftedes (meatballs), and entrees include plaki (Greek-style fish), oregano chicken, and a slow-roasted Cretan pork done with rosemary and lemon. Writing for the *Canton Repository*, Saimi Rote Bergmann urged diners not to leave without trying the Greek coffee. They also do prime strip steak, crab cakes that everyone raves about, surf and turf, and some Italian-ish dishes. The nearby Whispering Pines Bed and Breakfast (read more about it in *Bed & Breakfast Getaways from Cleveland*) offers a weekend getaway package that includes a voucher for dinner here (330-735-2824, info@atwoodlake.com).

Fox & Crow Restaurant and Cafe

☎ **(440) 937-5078**

CITY: **Avon**   AREA: **Farther West**
ATMOSPHERE: **Casual**   COST: **$$$**$$

ADDRESS: 32045 Detroit Rd.
HOURS: Fox's Den: Mon–Thu 4–10 p.m., Fri & Sat 4–11 p.m.; Cafe Crow Kitchen: Mon–Thu 4–10 p.m., Fri & Sat 4 p.m.–midnight; Bar open until 2 a.m.   **RESERVATIONS:** Taken   **PAYMENT:** MC, VS, AX, DIS   **BAR:** Beer, wine, liquor   **TAKEOUT:** Yes   **SMOKING:** Smoking section   **ACCESS:** ♿ Limited

This attractive, sprawling place has been a stagecoach stop, an inn, and a speakeasy. Guy Lombardo played here, Gypsy Rose Lee once danced on the tables, and Eliot Ness came to eat. It's been a restaurant since the turn of the last century, and Mike Corpas has owned it since the '80s. He's responsible for adding Greek food to the classic American roadhouse menu, making food according to his mother and his grandmother's recipes. So in addition to prime rib, strip steak, and Caesar salad, you can get pastitsio, spanakopita, and dolmathes. The calamari, served with a spinach pie and wedge of feta, is Greek-style, and so is the sea bass, the Mediterranean grill, seafood Theasina, and Athenian pasta primavera. Your server will flame your saganaki (sharp kasseri cheese) tableside, and your chunky "village" salad is made traditionally with cucumbers, tomatoes, onions, and kalamata olives. There are a number of Greek imports on the wine list. A special multicourse meal is prepared to celebrate Greek Orthodox Easter in May, and recently Corpas has begun to schedule Greek Nights throughout the year featuring all-Greek food and music. But nobody would call this a Greek restaurant, and the menu defies definition. There's the bar food—wings, burgers, and ribs; the straight-ahead Ohio food—Lake Erie perch dinner,

MEDITERRANEAN

meatloaf, and grilled ribeye. Then there are the Italian entrees—chicken parmigiana, linguini with marinara sauce. and veal marsala. And still the description is not complete, because I'd also call this the menu that time forgot. The kitchen makes many dishes that once were associated with fine dining but have long been out of style: oysters Rockefeller, chicken cordon bleu, veal oscar, lobster tail with drawn butter, steak Diane, cherries jubilee, and bananas Foster. This something-for-everybody approach extends to the space itself. The historic building, which once housed a still and bottling factory in the sub-basement, has many different dining rooms, each with a distinctive style. Wood, wicker, and chintz dominate. These interconnected rooms, along with a large and gorgeous patio, comprise the Fox's Den. A chef grills lamb, beef, and kebabs outside in the summer months. Upstairs is Cafe Crow, a bar and more casual dining area. Live bands perform Thursday, Friday, and Saturday evenings, playing music for the over-40 set (or those with retro taste)—big band, swing, and disco, and there's a dance floor. A tree-shaded deck with tables and chairs runs the length of the room. In the back, a large tent is set up during the warm-weather months for private parties and special events.

The Greek Express
☎ (216) 589-0534

CITY: **Cleveland**   AREA: **Downtown**
ATMOSPHERE: **Casual**   COST: $$$$$

ADDRESS: 1026 Euclid Ave.
HOURS: Mon–Sat 10 a.m.–4 p.m.; closed Sun
RESERVATIONS: Not taken PAYMENT: MC, VS, DIS, checks BAR: None TAKEOUT: Yes
SMOKING: Smoke-free ACCESS: ಈ Full access

This small eatery in the Old Arcade caters to a busy business crowd. At first glance the cafeteria-style service, plastic tableware, and styrofoam plates give the impression that this is just another fast-food joint. But the quality, freshness, and authentic Greek taste convey a different message. You wouldn't choose this spot for a romantic tête-à-tête (though the charm of the landmark Arcade creates its own special atmosphere) or a leisurely meeting over lunch. But it is a good spot to stop for a quick, interesting meal. The menu offers an eclectic selection, including traditional Greek dishes like gyros, avgolemono (egg lemon) soup, and chicken kebobs plus curries, salads, and rice pilaf. The restaurant itself seats about 25, but there are additional tables available along the walkways of the Arcade. Phone orders are accepted for takeout.

The Mad Greek
☎ (216) 421-3333

CITY: **Cleveland Heights**   AREA: **East Side**
ATMOSPHERE: **Casual**   COST: $$$$$

ADDRESS: 2466 Fairmount Blvd.
HOURS: Lunch Mon–Sat 11:30 a.m.–4 p.m.; Dinner Sun–Tue 4–11 p.m., Wed & Thu 4 p.m.–midnight, Fri & Sat 4 p.m.–12:30 a.m.
RESERVATIONS: Taken, recommended Fri, Sat
PAYMENT: MC, VS, AX, DIS BAR: Beer, wine, liquor
TAKEOUT: Yes SMOKING: Smoking section
ACCESS: ಈ Limited OTHER ETHNIC SPECIALTIES: Indian

The Mad Greek is well known for serving a unique combination of Greek and Indian foods with a few Middle Eastern specialties like hummus and baba ghanouj thrown in for good measure. Owner Loki Chopra's mother came from Bombay to help create the Indian dishes on the menu, and his former wife supplied the Greek recipes, which she was taught by her mother. On the Greek side, entrees include gyros, shish kebob, moussaka, dolmades, and a sampler plate called mezedakia. The Indian half offers chicken marinated in yogurt sauce, lamb and spinach curry, and vegetable goa made with a creamy coconut sauce. Over the years, cooking techniques have been adjusted to reflect the current interest in reducing salt and fat consumption, and the portions have gotten noticeably smaller (which you may view as either a plus or a minus). There are also burgers, for the less adventurous palate. The original dining room is done with a classic Med decor—white walls accented with colorful ceramic tiles and lots of green plants. The newer bar and additional dining area feature more unusual black-and-silver accents with an Art Deco motif. A touch of European alfresco dining is provided here when the warm weather arrives; huge windows open to create a streetside cafe. There's live jazz on Friday and Saturday nights.

Mardi Gras Lounge & Grill
☎ (216) 566-9094

CITY: **Cleveland**   AREA: **Downtown**
ATMOSPHERE: **Casual**   COST: $$$$$

ADDRESS: 1423 E. 21st St.
HOURS: Mon–Wed 10:30 a.m.–2:30 a.m., Thu–Sat 10:30 a.m.–4 a.m.; closed Sun
RESERVATIONS: Taken **PAYMENT:** MC, VS, AX, DIS, checks **BAR:** Beer, wine, liquor **TAKEOUT:** Yes
SMOKING: Yes **ACCESS:** ♿ Full access
*Not recommended for children

You might come here for the food alone—the menu is peppered with Greek specialties such as pastitsio and moussaka, plus a few spicy Cajun dishes like shrimp Creole and blackened chicken. It's the only place in town you can get saganaki (flaming Greek kasseri cheese) or a souvlaki (marinated broiled lamb) at 3 a.m. on a Thursday. But this is no typical ethnic restaurant, and people are just as likely to find their way here because the bar is open late and the music is hot. Bands play at the front of the bar area that fills the center space. Tables on the mezzanine level (adjacent to the bar) and a few others parallel to the bar offer a good view of the performers. Another dining area is removed from the scene in a separate room. A favorite lunchtime hangout for *Plain Dealer*

employees, with a standard selection of salads and sandwiches, it also attracts enthusiastic jazz hounds three nights a week. Any time of the day or night, the clientele is a mix of white- and blue-collar folks, and the ambience is dark and funky. An ATM in the bar is handy, though I suppose it could easily lead some down the paths of overconsumption or overspending. There's a parking lot across the street.

Niko's
☎ (216) 226-7050

CITY: **Lakewood**   AREA: **West Side**
ATMOSPHERE: **Casual**   COST: $$$$$

ADDRESS: 15625 Detroit Ave.
HOURS: Mon–Sat 11 a.m.–11 p.m., Sun 11 a.m.–9 p.m. **RESERVATIONS:** Taken, Suggested Fri & Sat nights **PAYMENT:** MC, VS, AX, DIS
BAR: Beer, wine, liquor **TAKEOUT:** Yes
SMOKING: Smoking section **ACCESS:** ♿ Full access

From the outside, the restaurant, which opened in December 2002, looks like just another neighborhood burger joint. But inside it's a stunner and not like any other restaurant around. The unique interior was designed by owner and chef Niko Moulagianis—he says he's had the picture of this place in his head for years. He bought a building that had been a fur store ever since it was built in the 1940s. With the help of his father, who now serves as all-around helper and handyman, he gutted and renovated the space himself. The walls are a dramatic, textured blue-gray; chairs are brushed metal; and the big storefront windows are framed with looping folds of blue fabric. Blue cloth napery graces gray formica tabletops. Modern artwork with Greek themes and motifs adds visual interest. The bar is the real eye-catcher—a long granite top resting on a base of glass blocks illuminated by blue lights that cast an intriguing underwater glow. The net result is a gorgeous and sophisticated interior that manages to be

MEDITERRANEAN

both urbane and laid-back with an upscale look but a warmly welcoming atmosphere where everybody, and not just the young, the well-dressed, and the hip, can feel comfortable. Niko was delighted when I shared this observation with him—it is precisely the effect he was aiming to achieve. "I wanted to attract a real mix of people," he says. "Families, couples, singles, old and young. The only dress code is no backwards baseball caps. This is a place for birthday parties and dates, a neighborhood hangout, a good spot for a drink, where you go to get a sandwich and a salad or a fine Greek meal." And a fine Greek meal it will be, with "Mama Niko's Classics" defining the menu—mousaka (layers of eggplant, potato, and beef); pastitsio (macaroni and spiced beef); kokkinisto arni (braised lamb shank in tomato sauce); spanakopita (spinach and feta in filo dough); souvlaki; and gyros. Mama, who is from the island of Kos ("Dr. Hippocrates' hometown," as she calls it), is really in the kitchen, and these are her recipes, the food Niko grew up eating. "Every dish," she says, "has a secret, an ingredient or a way of preparing it that makes it perfect." She also makes traditional Greek pastries for dessert and a memorable rice pudding that is a favorite of Nicolas Cage. He first tasted it while filming Captain Corelli's Mandolin, and Niko's mom got the recipe from the folks who run the taverna in Greece where he ate it. There is a selection mezedes (appetizers), soupes (soup), and salate (salads) that includes saganaki (flaming cheese); tazatziki (cucumber yogurt dip); an outstanding meltzanosalata (eggplant spread); dolmades (grape leaves); avgolemono (egg and lemon soup); and horiatiki salad made with tomatoes, cucumbers, onions, and feta cheese. The restaurant fills a true need in this town, both because there are so few places to get this kind of food and because the kitchen is open late. It makes Niko happy because it is the fulfillment of a long-held dream, and it makes his parents proud that he is keeping their heritage alive. The rest of us can just be

happy it's here, an attractive place to dine where good food is the rule. The wine list offers plenty of selection with some interesting Greek vintages along with bottles from California, Italy, Australia, France, Germany, and Spain. In the daytime Niko can be found in chef's whites doing his part to make the back of the house run smoothly. By night, he's out front, the big guy in the suit making sure his customers are enjoying themselves. The presence of high chairs and booster seats is evidence that kids fit in, but I'd say they belong during mealtimes, and that in the latter part of the evening Niko's takes on a distinctly adult ambience. On-street parking and a metered lot in the rear of the restaurant, which does have a back entrance.

Italian

Affamato Italian Deli and Market
☎ (440) 892-1455
CITY: **Westlake**   AREA: **West Side**
ATMOSPHERE: **Relaxed**   COST: $$$$$

ADDRESS: 30610 Detroit Ave.
HOURS: Mon–Wed 10 a.m.–8 p.m., Thu & Fri 10 a.m.–9 p.m., Sat 10 a.m.–7 p.m., Sun closed
RESERVATIONS: Not taken **PAYMENT:** MC, VS, DIS, checks **BAR:** Beer, wine **TAKEOUT:** Yes
SMOKING: Smoke-Free **ACCESS:** ♿ Full access

The perfect marriage of cafe and market—a place to eat in, take out, and take stuff home to make your own. The love affair started, as so many do, over a drink . . . or three, according to partners Greg Grasso and Rick Molinari. Rick complained that he was tired of driving to Gallucci's to get real Italian ingredients; Greg, a skilled, self-taught chef with 30 years of professional experience, saw a need for high-quality, traditional prepared foods because fewer and fewer people had time to cook them at home anymore. The next thing they knew, or so the myth they like to cultivate goes, they were partners in Affamato. The word means "starving" in Italian, and it's what Rick's great-grandfather would say every night when he came home from work. And if you're affamato and on the west side, then this is where you want to be. At lunchtime, you can feed on calzone, stromboli, and pizza; sandwiches stuffed with Italian meats, meatballs, and cheeses plus goodies like grilled vegetables, roasted peppers, and fresh basil leaves; hot grilled pannini sandwiches; the pasta of the day; and salads. Dinner entrees, plated or boxed, include lasagna made with five different cheeses and three kinds of meat; chicken parmesan-ed or marsala-ed; fettucine alfredo; cracked-pepper tortellini stuffed with a blend of Asiago, ricotta, mozzarella, and provolone; smoked chicken ravioli with brown butter sauce; and pasta primavera. Dinners, available after 4 p.m., include a salad and roll, and meat entrees come with a side of pasta and a choice of marinara, tomato basil, vodka tomato cream, garlic and oil, or three meat sauce. They bake their own bread—available by the loaf and as a garlic bread side order. Their kitchen is the answer for noncooks, and all those who find themselves too busy, too tired, or too lazy to cook, and they do a brisk take-home business. Desserts are made by trained pastry chef Julie Lawler, who specializes in Italian treats such as cannoli, tiramisu, sfogliatelle, and pignoli nut and ricotta cheese tarts. There are tables and chairs for 35 plus an espresso bar, and the dining area is surprisingly attractive and inviting, considering the place is also a market. You can even enjoy wine or beer, imported and microbrews, with your dinner. The look is bright, modern, and sleek, and the food itself is part of the decor. There's a special catering menu. (For more information about the market, see second listing for Affamato later in this chapter.) Located in the same shopping strip as the Savannah. Parking in lots, front and back.

Agostino's Ristorante
☎ (216) 741-6522

CITY: **Brooklyn**   AREA: **Near West Side**
ATMOSPHERE: **Casual**   COST: $$$$$

ADDRESS: 4218 Ridge Rd.
HOURS: Mon–Thu 11 a.m.–10:30 p.m., Fri 11 a.m.–11 p.m., Sat 3–11 p.m., Sun noon–8:30 p.m. RESERVATIONS: Taken, weekdays for groups of 5 or more only, required weekends PAYMENT: MC, VS, AX, DIS BAR: Beer, wine, liquor TAKEOUT: Yes SMOKING: Smoking section ACCESS: ঙ Full access

The sign out front leads you to believe this is a typical Italian-American pizza-and-spaghetti place. But it's not. Joe Gallo, who has a friendly smile and a good word for every customer, is the owner, and his dad, who is from Calabria in southern Italy, is one of the chefs. Together they've created the kind of restaurant that attracts even "hard-core Italian eaters," as Joe describes them, who generally avoid food that's not prepared at home by a family member. They offer some well-loved, homestyle dishes that few area restaurants do, such as trippa (tripe, which, if you really must know, is made from the stomach lining of cattle or oxen, in a tomato and bell pepper broth); wedding soup; tortellini with ham and peas; and escarola (greens steamed in a garlic and oil broth). They also do more things with calamari, which they have shipped in directly, than any other single place I've visited: in addition to the usual frying, they marinate it and serve it cold in a salad, stuff it, grill it, saute it, use it in a seafood sauce for pasta, and make a zuppa di pesce (fish soup) with it. The bread is fresh and plentiful, the oil for dipping it in is herbed, the house dressing is a balsamic vinaigrette, and the menu also offers a nice selection of veal, chicken, and pasta dishes. For dessert there's tiramisu, spumoni, and real Italian lemon ice.

Joe takes great pride in his restaurant's level of hospitality and service. He and his

MEDITERRANEAN

staff never rush customers; everyone is welcome to sit, eat, and talk as long as they like, just as if they were in their own home. When a woman asked for "lotsa sauce," I heard the waiter reply, "No problem, I'll bring you a nice big bowlful on the side, you can eat what you want and take the rest with you." Agostino's has grown from the original 10-table place it was years ago to three rooms that can seat about 175 diners. That first room is now the smoking section, and it's a charming, darkish little brick and stucco space. Smoking is also permitted in the adjacent bar area, also part of the original place, with some tables and a television. The other two dining areas are for nonsmokers, and they are large, bright, and a bit more formal in appearance, comfortably accommodating large groups. Recorded singers crooning in Italian alternate with Frank Sinatra as soft background music, and on Wednesday, Saturday, and Sunday evenings a mandolin and guitar duo entertain. Periodically, the restaurant becomes a cabaret, and a special seven-course meal is offered along with a floor show. There's valet parking, and a convenient pickup window for take-out orders around the back. Easy to find, just north of I-480 and the intersection of Ridge and Memphis.

Alberini's

☎ (330) 652-5895

CITY: **Niles** AREA: **Farther South**
ATMOSPHERE: **Dressy** COST: $$$$$

ADDRESS: 1201 Youngstown-Warren Rd.
HOURS: Mon-thu 11:30 a.m.–10 p.m., Fri & Sat 11:30 a.m.–11 p.m.; Lunch menu available until 6 p.m. Mon–Fri, 4 p.m. Sat; Sun & holidays closed
RESERVATIONS: Taken, Suggested Fri & Sat
PAYMENT: MC, VS, AX, DIS **BAR:** Beer, wine, liquor
TAKEOUT: Yes **SMOKING:** Smoking section
ACCESS: ♿ Full access

"I'm an American Italian," says Richard Alberini, "and so's my wife Gilda. We were born knowing about good food.

When I got out of the navy, I learned about the restaurant business, and we opened this place together 40 years ago." Back then it was in a building about a mile away from their present location, and the rent was only $55 a month. The couple did everything from cooking to cleaning. In 1960, they built a place of their own, and kept adding to it over the years so it's now a sprawling collection of six distinctive dining rooms—and a local institution. Longtime customers bring their kids, and their kids' kids, and Richard, who continues to come to work every day even though he's handed over the management of kitchen and business to his two sons, always sees someone he knows. Although dining habits have changed since the restaurant opened, much about Alberini's hasn't, and that's part of its appeal. The decor is in the time-honored white-tablecloth style, where formality intersects with comfort. The heart of the menu is still classic, hearty Italian dishes like fried calamari, wedding soup, veal Parmigiana, spaghetti and meatballs, gnocchi with a Bolognese meat sauce, ravioli, linguini with clam sauce, and lasagna. And they still offer their own interpretation of dishes long associated with special occasions and deluxe dining: shrimp cocktail, escargots, Caesar salad, roast duck, rack of lamb, bananas Foster, and cherries jubilee. But the old pairs well with the new in traditional offerings with a contemporary flair: chicken with fresh artichokes and a tomatoes concasse in a balsamic sauce; roasted garlic risotto; baked oysters with spinach and anisette; a pork loin chop filled with taleggio cheese served over a cassoulet of Tuscan white beans, pancetta, and vegetables; osso bucco made with a gremolata of parsley, rosemary, lemon zest and garlic; and a filet of beef with portabella mushrooms in red barolo wine sauce accompanied by Parmigiano potato fritellas.

Wine is important here. The award-winning wine list features over 800 selections, and the cellar racks hold 10,000 bottles. Diners are encouraged to make their selection early on so it can be properly decanted, with time to breathe or chill. Thirty-eight different wines are available by the glass. But the large selection of alcoholic beverages doesn't end with wine: there are over 20 fine ports; 17 aged single-malt Scotches; 13 kinds of cognac and brandy; a rare armagnac; and 16 cordials, including Strega and Romano Sambuca. The spacious restaurant offers excellent party and banquet facilities and is a popular choice for large groups. Smaller rooms, such as the wine cellar, offer more intimate settings. Chooks (in honor of Chef "Chook" Alberini who runs the restaurant kitchen) is a wine bar and grill offering lighter fare and a casual atmosphere. Cigars are sold and can be smoked in this room. A retail shop called Cork and More Shoppé is also on the premises, selling wine and prepared gourmet foods. (For more information see listing in the market section of this chapter.) There's live piano music in the lounge Friday and Saturday evenings. Plenty of parking in the restaurant lot.

Aldo's
☎ (216) 749-7060

CITY: **Brooklyn** AREA: **Near West Side**
ATMOSPHERE: **Casual** COST: $$$$$

ADDRESS: 8459 Memphis Ave.
HOURS: Tue 4–9:30 p.m., Wed 11:30 a.m.–10 p.m., Thu 11:30 a.m.–10 p.m., Fri 11:30 a.m.–11 p.m., Sun 4–9 p.m.; closed Mon
RESERVATIONS: Not taken PAYMENT: MC, VS, checks BAR: Beer, wine, liquor TAKEOUT: Yes
SMOKING: Smoke-Free ACCESS: ♿ Full access
*Not recommended for children

The question is, how can Aldo's still be considered one of Cleveland's best-kept secrets when the restaurant has been enthusiastically reviewed by *Northern Ohio Live, Cleveland Magazine, The Plain Dealer, Currents,* and the *Akron Beacon Journal?* But that's how folks at nearby American Greetings corporate headquarters and food aficionados from all over

(some of whom say they come three or four times a month) describe this intimate little place. Tucked inconspicuously behind a nondescript facade in a six-store strip mall (part of the Memphis/Ridge business district), Aldo's serves traditional, but never standard, Italian fare. Each forkful is to be savored and every meal is really a celebration of the joys of good food. On any given night, specials could include bruschetta with roasted peppers and bocconcini, pasta fagiole, spezzatino di vitelle (veal stew), crepes stuffed with veal in basil sauce with escarole, and tripe in fresh tomato sauce. The decor is modern-looking, bold in turquoise and black, but the Zappa family photos on the wall lend a homey touch. It's painfully small, seating just 35, and not the best choice for large parties. If you have to wait for a table, your only option is to stand in the narrow entryway, but no one seems to mind, and newcomers chat with Aldo regulars. Customers, some in sweatshirts, some in suits and silk, call out greetings to Aldo, who often stops and visits, and everyone ends up feeling like a guest in his home rather than a customer. Service is impeccable and at the same time friendly. This is a place you'll want to remember. More than likely, they'll remember you, too.

Anthony's
☎ (216) 791-0700

CITY: **Cleveland** AREA: **Near East Side**
ATMOSPHERE: **Relaxed** COST: $$$$

ADDRESS: 12018 Mayfield Rd.
HOURS: Mon–Thu 10 a.m.–5 p.m., Fri 10 a.m.–8 p.m., Sat 10 a.m.–7 p.m.; Sun 9 a.m.–2 p.m. RESERVATIONS: Not Taken
PAYMENT: MC, VS, AX, DIS, checks BAR: None
TAKEOUT: Yes SMOKING: Smoke-Free
ACCESS: ♿ Full access

This really can't be classified as a full-scale restaurant. There are no servers—you order at the counter, help yourself to a beverage from the cooler (San

MEDITERRANEAN

Pellegrino, anyone?), pay, carry your food to the table, and throw away your place setting when you're done. And it is known as a market. But tables and chairs for 25, plus a counter with stools, and small tables outdoors on the sidewalk, weather permitting, leave little doubt that this is a place to eat. Virtually everything that's for sale by the pound can be ordered by the plate. You can take your time or get in and out in a hurry, linger over a hot lunch or inhale a slice or three of pizza. The lunch menu changes daily—there's always a special and a selection of veal, chicken, and sausage dishes, plus pasta, meatballs, subs, sandwiches, and salads. Try the grilled pesto chicken pannini: warm ciabatta bread stuffed with basil-dressed chicken that qualifies as a complete meal. Turn it into a multicourse event with an Italian pastry or some real gelato (Italian ice cream that packs more creamy flavor in every spoonful than its American cousin) for dessert and a cup of freshly brewed espresso or cappuccino. The atmosphere is grocery-store relaxed, so don't hesitate to bring young lunchers who haven't quite gotten up to speed in the table manners department. Expect to mingle with neighborhood regulars, CWRU students, and folks who work in University Circle.

Arrabiata's
☎ (440) 442-2600

CITY: **Mayfield Heights**	AREA: **East Side**
ATMOSPHERE: **Casual**	COST: **$$$**$$

ADDRESS: 6169 Mayfield Rd.
HOURS: Mon 11:30 a.m.–2:30 p.m. & 4:30–9 p.m., Tue–Thu 11:30 a.m.–2:30 p.m. & 4:30–10 p.m., Fri 11:30 a.m.–2:30 p.m. & 4:30–11 p.m., Sat 4:30–11 p.m., Sun 4–9 p.m.
RESERVATIONS: Taken, suggested for five or more
PAYMENT: MC, VS, AX, DIS **BAR:** Beer, liquor
TAKEOUT: Yes **SMOKING:** Smoking section
ACCESS: & Full access

What do you get when two sets of brothers with Italian roots go into the restaurant business together? Sibling rivalry? No. A food fight? Maybe, but if so, it's always after hours and nobody's 'fessing up. Escarola fagioli, fettucine alfredo, and zuppa di pesce? Yes. When the former owners of Arrabiata's put it up for sale in 1998, John and Nick D'Angelo and Joe and Paul Rini decided to buy. These guys have known each other since first grade (currently all are in their 20s); they grew up together, and each has worked here at one time or another. Nick got additional restaurant experience in Florida, while Joe honed his skills in New York, and they run the front of the house. Their younger brothers John and Paul (do they sing as well as cook? I ask myself) studied with Loretta Paganini at her cooking school in Hudson, and they man the kitchen. With Nick's fiance as their guide (she's an artist and student of interior design), they repainted and redecorated (she did the modern paintings on the walls, too, drawing her inspiration from a trip she and Nick made to Italy). The result is a sleek, modern-looking space done up in black, white, and eggplant purple, where people can expect to be comfortable and eat well.

The kitchen has a set of styles, culinary templates if you will, that are applied to a variety of pasta, meats, fish, and vegetables. If the veal or chicken is D'Agnese it's served in a lemon butter sauce with artichoke hearts, but if it's a cacciatore it will be in a plum tomato sauce with onions, green peppers, and mushrooms. Linguine, rigatoni, calamari, shrimp, a clam and mussel combination, and orange roughy get the "house special Arrabiata treatment"—a spicy marinara sauce studded with imported olives, cherry and banana peppers, and onions. Eggplant comes a la rollatini (rolled and stuffed), and so does chicken. Eggplant Parmigiana is a dish unto itself, but chicken and veal Sicilian style come with the stuff as a topping. You can get your beef (a filet mignon) done Arrabiata, D'Agnese, Cacciatore, or Pasqualina (with mushrooms, artichokes, roasted red peppers, and a marsala wine sauce; a boneless breast of chicken is done this way too). The guys are enthusiastic hosts. "We want to make sure all our customers leave with full stomachs and smiles on their faces," says Nick D'Angelo. Kids with small appetites or picky tastes can get a side order of pasta as their entree (with or without meatballs or sausage) or a couple of other child-friendly choices. The bar seats 12, and there's a nice selection of wines, domestic and imported, by the glass and the bottle. Private catering services are offered, and the restaurant is available for private parties when it is not open to the public. It's located in a shopping strip at the corner of Mayfield and Commonwealth, close to I-271, with ample parking.

Battuto Ristorante

☎ (216) 707-1055

CITY: **Cleveland**   AREA: **Near East Side**
ATMOSPHERE: **Casual**   COST: $$$$$

ADDRESS: 12405 Mayfield Rd.
HOURS: Dinner Tue–Sat 5:30 –10 p.m., Sun–Mon closed **RESERVATIONS:** Taken, Suggested
PAYMENT: MC, VS, AX, DIS **BAR:** Beer, wine, liquor
TAKEOUT: No **SMOKING:** Smoke-Free
ACCESS: & Full access

The first time I walked in, I was enthralled by the fabulous aroma. I asked the hostess what smelled so good. She sniffed with great concentration and replied, "I think you're getting the pan-seared scallops with butternut squash and hazelnuts, and the zuppa di pesce, a mix of mussels, clams, shrimp, and calamari in tomato broth, with a whiff of bucatini with Amatriciana sauce, that's our most popular pasta dish."

A quick glance at the menu, which changes constantly, instantly revealed the Daverios' range, creativity, and commitment to classical methods paired with Italian and Mediterranean traditions. "Our philosophy," says Mark, "is let each ingredient show itself." "We have a love and respect," adds Giovanna, "for every single thing we use, and we only use the best fresh and seasonal food. Our purveyors call, tell us what's good, and we plan around that." This commitment grows out of an approach pioneered by Alice Waters, and both Mark and Giovanna, who graduated from the Culinary Institute in Hyde Park, New York, worked under chefs in California who trained with her at Chez Panisse.

Battuto's fall menu might feature crispy risotto cakes with taleggio cheese; tagliatelle with prosciutto and asparagus; a grilled pork chop with Gorgonzola polenta and radicchio. In winter there's likely to be their popular roasted red and gold beets with olives, goat cheese, fennel, and oranges; a wild-mushroom risotto; veal piccata with rainbow chard or salmon with cannellini beans and tomato pancetta vinaigrette. Spring and summer bring a plethora of salads: arugula with radicchio, pancetta, hazelnuts, and Parmesan cheese in balsamic vinaigrette; Belgian endive with pears, spiced walnuts, and creamy Gorgonzola vinaigrette; butter lettuce, smoked trout, pink grapefruit, fava beans in a citrus vinaigrette. Entrees could be grilled steak with morel mushrooms; cioppino, a seafood stew; roasted duck breast with honey-lime couscous; pork scallopini; or swordfish with escarole and roasted red peppers. Creste de gallo (pasta in the shape of a cockscomb) with sausage and rapini, and strozzapreti (a wide noodle) with chicken and roasted garlic are menu regulars.

All pastas as well as breadsticks are made in-house daily. Mark butchers all his own meat and fish, and Giovanna does all the dolci (sweets), which are never the same from one week to the next: biscotti; gelato; sorbetto; panna cotta (a creamy pudding) with dried cherries in chianti, and blackberries, candied kumquats, or strawberries in limoncello liqueur; bocca nero, a flourless chocolate cake with blood oranges; and tarts like one with fig jam and another made with sweetened ricotta and lemon curd. These folks know their wine, too. Giovanna says, "We're all about wine,"

MEDITERRANEAN

and *Wine Spectator* magazine agrees, giving the Daverios their Award of Excellence two years in a row, which is almost as long as they've been open. They provide detailed descriptions of featured wines, and the cellar holds an impressive collection ranging from $24 bottles to some costing $100. Special multicourse dinners spotlighting wines and foods of a particular region are scheduled throughout the year. Service is impeccable, with attention to details that you find in the best restaurants anywhere in the country. Guests are encouraged to take their time and enjoy the food, the ambience, and the occasion. The intimate dining room seats 68 in a lovely space that blends contemporary design with timeless elegance. The couple always wanted to open their own restaurant, and after returning from a food tour of Italy, where they were married, they found the perfect spot in Little Italy. "And now," says Mark, " we're just trying to make a little food history."

toria perhaps, somewhere in southern Italy. The town of Bovalino, for which the restaurant was named, is in Calabria, at the southern tip of Italy. Owners Lori Williams and Chris Hass use some of their family recipes. The kitchen turns out more than 60 different Italian dishes that reflect southern and northern cuisine; two additional daily specials might be anything from chicken Milanese to lobster-filled ravioli. Lori is in there every morning, starting the sauces that will simmer all day, and she won't let anyone else prepare them. She also makes fresh pizza dough daily. Portions are huge, enough for the next day's lunch if you have an average appetite. The menu offers a hand-picked selection of imported and domestic wines, red and white, and an Italian beer. There's room for 40 diners and, in warm weather, additional seating outside in a small fenced-in courtyard adjacent to the parking lot.

Bovalino's Italian Ristorante
☎ (440) 892-9300
CITY: **Westlake**   AREA: **West Side**
ATMOSPHERE: **Casual**   COST: $$$$$

ADDRESS: 27828 Center Ridge Rd.
HOURS: Mon–Thu 4–9 p.m., Fri & Sat 4–10 p.m.; closed Sun   RESERVATIONS: Taken, Fri, Sat until 7 p.m. only   PAYMENT: MC, VS, checks   BAR: Beer, wine, liquor   TAKEOUT: Yes   SMOKING: Yes
ACCESS: ♿ Full access

A red-white-and-green awning helps you identify this freestanding brick building on a residential stretch of road as a restaurant and not a home. It is an utterly sweet little place, and driving up I had the same feeling I remember from years ago, in Italy, when we'd unexpectedly stumbled upon a delightful restaurant in the middle of nowhere. Inside, green plants hang in leafy profusion from latticework suspended from the ceiling, and it's as though you've come into a garden, an outdoor trat-

Bruno's Ristorante
☎ (216) 961-7087
CITY: **Cleveland**   AREA: **Near West Side**
ATMOSPHERE: **Casual**   COST: $$$$$

ADDRESS: 2644 W. 41st St.
HOURS: Mon–Thu 11 a.m.–10 p.m., Fri 11 a.m.–11 p.m., Sat 4–11 p.m., Sun closed (but available for private parties)
RESERVATIONS: Taken, suggested on weekends and for parties of four or more weekdays
PAYMENT: MC, VS, AX   BAR: Beer, wine
TAKEOUT: Yes   SMOKING: Smoking section
ACCESS: ♿ Full access

O wner Bruno DiSiena, former executive chef for the Cleveland Browns at their Berea facility, knows how to make patrons feel good about dining out and eating with gusto. His motto, printed on the menu, is "He who eats well is very close to God." His operating philosophy, also on the menu, reads "Make love to your stomach with these specials." How much more encouragement do you need? Bruno, an attentive host, can usually be found in the dining room, going from table to table to make sure people are happy and getting all they want. But he always has time to pause among those he knows—and he seems to know many of his customers—to offer handshakes to the men and kisses, on the cheeks of course, to the ladies. This friendly, welcoming atmosphere is echoed in the space itself, which achieves that special combination of cozy and classy. It's a small restaurant seating about 40 in a single room decorated in contemporary style, using an off-white and maroon color scheme, with dark wood furniture and subdued lighting. There's a beautiful old bar—a part of the original decor that thankfully did not fall victim to the renovation—that gleams with new life and a high gloss, with stools for 12; a comfortable waiting area; a private dining room under construction in 2002; and plans for an outdoor patio and installation of a brick oven.

Some of the dishes are familiar, although I must admit I think they sound more glamorous and enticing in Italian, which is how they appear on the menu (with translations and descriptions underneath): I'd rather eat Salciccia Pannini than a sausage sandwich, Zuppa di Sposa than wedding soup, and Pesce del Giorno than fish of the day. The kitchen offers a basic selection the classics: chicken, veal, and eggplant Parmesan, spaghetti, masticoli, ravioli, lasagna, gnocchi, calamari, and pizza plus some specialties such as vitello ala carciofi (veal and artichokes in marsala cream sauce); Bruno's Famous Fettucini ala Pescatore (pasta with seafood in a marinara sauce), and bistecca al funghetto (filet of beef in a wine sauce with mushrooms). The pepe al banana (a baked hot pepper stuffed with sausage) is a favorite appetizer, though I'd go for the more unusual baked mussels on the half shell every time. Portions are large enough to make every traditional Italian grandmother happy. Desserts to go along with your cappuccino and espresso don't appear on the menu, but don't let that fool you—just ask

your server. Many of the desserts are made by Bruno's mother, who is known for her tiramisu and cheesecake. The wine list offers an interesting variety of reds and whites, and the bar stocks three imported Italian beers. You can park across the street at a car wash owned by Bruno's brothers. At lunchtime, leave the keys and get your car cleaned while you clean your plate. In the evenings, the lot is guarded. Bruno's is located in a residential neighborhood, easy to spot by virtue of its brick facade and green awning sporting the place's name. There's a separate entrance near the back of the building for picking up carryout orders. Full service in-house, and off-premise catering is available.

MEDITERRANEAN

Bucci's
☎ (440) 331-5157

CITY: **Rocky River**   AREA: **West Side**
ATMOSPHERE: **Casual**   COST: $$$$$

ADDRESS: 19373 Hilliard Rd.

HOURS: Dinner Tue–Thu 4–10 p.m., Fri 4–11 p.m., Sat 4–11 p.m., Sun 4–9 p.m.; closed Mon **RESERVATIONS:** Not taken **PAYMENT:** MC, VS, AX, DIS **BAR:** Beer, wine **TAKEOUT:** Yes **SMOKING:** Smoking section **ACCESS:** ♿ Full access

This is the original Bucci's, opened 30 years ago. A small, homey, intimate restaurant seating between 50 and 60 people, Bucci's specializes in central and southern Italian food. The ceiling has exposed beams, there are hanging plants, and the pastel-toned wallpaper features classic scenes of Italian peasant life: vineyards, farms, and villages. The lighting is pleasantly soft, candles glow on each table, and linens are cloth. The bread basket brought to the table by servers who are both friendly and fast includes regular Italian bread, fat-free ciabatta bread, and freshly made garlic butter. Entrees, which are large, come to the table piping hot. There's always a homemade soup of the day, stuffed eggplant, pasta primavera made with angel hair and a light blush sauce, and beef funghetto (tenderloin in wine sauce). They also do pizza and all the classic pasta dishes (with smaller side orders available for children under 12), plus steak, chicken, veal, and seafood. And if you still have room, there's spumoni, homemade cannoli, and tiramisu.

Bucci's
☎ **(440) 826-4500**
CITY: **Berea**   AREA: **Southwest**
ATMOSPHERE: **Dressy**   COST: $$$$$

ADDRESS: One Berea Commons
HOURS: Mon–Sat 11:30 a.m.–11 p.m., Sun 3 p.m.–8 p.m. **RESERVATIONS:** Taken, recommended on weekends **PAYMENT:** MC, VS, AX, DIS **BAR:** Beer, wine, liquor **TAKEOUT:** Yes
SMOKING: Smoking section **ACCESS:** ☖ Limited
*Not recommended for children

Some of the windows of this comfortable, pleasant restaurant overlook the entrance to the Metroparks' Mill Stream Run Reservation. Others look out onto Berea's historic downtown triangle. Wherever the maitre d' seats you, you'll quickly realize that this is the sort of place where you settle back into the quiet, intimate reading-room atmosphere and enjoy the view. Shortly after you're seated, fresh bread and rolls and flavored butter will arrive at the table. The kitchen consistently turns out a good selection of Italian favorites. The ravioli, cavatelli, and gnocchi are homemade. Some of their more unusual offerings include angel hair pasta with baby squid and tricolored peppers, and chicken sauteed with capers and fresh herbs in a brown sauce with balsamic vinegar and lemon. This second Bucci's is more formal than the original. Think of eating here as an occasion, even if you don't have anything special to celebrate. Dress up a bit, let the subdued lighting set the mood, and take your time, because this is a place you choose when you want to ap-

preciate a well-served, well-prepared meal eaten in good company.

Ferrante Winery & Ristorante
☎ **(440) 466-8466**
CITY: **Geneva**   AREA: **Farther East**
ATMOSPHERE: **Casual**   COST: $$$$$

ADDRESS: 5585 SR 307
HOURS: Wed–Thu noon–8 p.m., Fri & Sat noon–10 p.m., Sun 1–6 p.m., Mon–Tue closed
RESERVATIONS: Not Taken **PAYMENT:** MC, VS, AX, DIS, checks **BAR:** Wine **TAKEOUT:** Yes
SMOKING: Smoking section **ACCESS:** ☖ Full access

This is the story of a family, and it begins with a woman. Great-grandma Ferrante bought land in Geneva to grow grapes on in the early years of the 20th century. The next generation started the winery in Collinwood in 1937, trucking the grapes in from the country. In the '70s, Nicholas and Anna Ferrante's sons, Peter and Anthony, moved the winery out to the family's Geneva vineyards. It was a small operation, with only about 2,000 gallons of wine bottled each year and everything from harvesting to labeling done by hand. By the 1980s, the family had a little restaurant there too, with a simple menu that featured Italian-style appetizers, pizza, and of course, their wine. Over time, most of Peter's eight kids got involved, learning the art of grape-growing and winemaking while growing the business and running the restaurant. In 1994 they suffered a major setback when a fire destroyed the restaurant. But they turned a disaster into an opportunity, They built a new, bigger and better restaurant, expanded their menu, and transformed their winery into one of the most beautiful and popular dining destinations in Harpersfield Township. The spacious, modern building with its stone facade has high, cathedral-style wooden ceilings, a multilevel design, and huge windows that look out over the vineyards and flood the space with natural light, augmented by clerestory windows on the second floor. At sunset, the dining room is filled with a golden glow. An earth-tone color scheme enhances the sense of connection to the outdoors, where much of the restaurant's activity takes place in good weather. There are three covered pavilions, a small lake with a spray of water gushing in the center, and tables and chairs for about 80. Wine is always served; weekdays full lunch and dinner menus are available; on Fridays and Saturdays, selected items are offered on the patio. Bands play in the summer, and there's room for dancing. Another, more intimate garden space is located at the front of the building. It's connected to the gift shop, where wine is sold by the bottle and case (they now produce about 80,000 gallons annually), and the wine bar, a tasting room equipped with a fireplace, small tables, and comfortable chairs.

The restaurant is designed with families in mind, just like you'd find in Italy; it's comfortable, casual, welcoming to people of all ages, and affordable. With seating for 200 and numerous semiprivate areas, it's an ideal place for birthdays, anniversaries, reunions, and special events. The Ferrantes treat regulars as members of their own extended family. Acting as hostess, Carmel Ferrante often greets guests with hugs, kisses, and questions about kids and parents. The food is also family-style—huge portions of Italian classics such as lasagna; spaghetti and meatballs; linguine with clam sauce; seafood alfredo; pasta primavera; capellini with pesto; veal with wine and mushrooms; and chicken in a red wine marinara sauce with peppers and cappicola. The tomato sauce was so good that one of my sons, who's old enough to know better, couldn't resist using his fingers to get the last drops out of his bowl and into his mouth. But it's a friendly, forgiving place—even the kinds of messes kids make are cleaned up with good humor and speedy efficiency. Specials reflect a more creative approach, especially with fresh fish—salmon, for example, in a raspberry

sauce with garlic mashed potatoes. Pizza, antimisto plates (Italian meats, cheeses, and bread), and salads are always available. There is a children's menu. Most diners are too full for dessert, but the Italian bread pudding with Riesling wine sauce is too good to pass up—quit eating before you've finished and box it up to take home, so you can enjoy the *dolce*. A wine suggestion for every entree is part of the menu, and a separate wine list gives detailed descriptions of each of their whites, blush wines, reds, and specialty wines. Sampler trays are a way to explore a variety of vintages. Reservations are not accepted (except, of course, for private parties) because people tend to take their time. "Customers," she says, "often come from more than 30 miles away. They're in no hurry to leave because they enjoy themselves so much." Visit yourself, and you'll understand why. The winery and restaurant have a website with more information and directions: www.ferrantewinery.com.

Frankie's Italian Cuisine
☎ (440) 734-8646

CITY: **North Olmsted**   AREA: **West Side**
ATMOSPHERE: **Casual**   COST: **$$**$$

ADDRESS: 4641 Great Northern Blvd.
HOURS: Mon–Thu 11 a.m.–11 p.m., Fri & Sat 11 a.m.–midnight, Sun 1–10 p.m.
RESERVATIONS: Taken, for groups of 6 or more only   PAYMENT: MC, VS, AX, DIS   BAR: Beer, liquor
TAKEOUT: Yes   SMOKING: Smoking section
ACCESS: ⑤ Full access

Established in 1967, Frankie's is a mid-sized restaurant that families flock to because the atmosphere is casual, and the food, served in generous quantities, is the kind almost nobody can resist: veal Parmesan, lasagna, spaghetti with marinara sauce, meatball and sausage sandwiches, and hand-tossed pizza. The garlic bread is worth a special mention. The dishes on this menu are meant to satisfy rather than surprise, and food is prepared and presented "mamma's kitchen–style" without flash or nouveau anything. But the sauce is so popular they sell it by the quart, meatballs by the dozen, lasagna by the tray, and pizzas by the sheet for takeout. The restaurant seats about 95 in a pleasant, modern setting, and the kitchen will cook for private parties in the restaurant in a room that can easily accommodate 10–30. They do off-site catering as well. Jeans are acceptable here, but you wouldn't feel out of place if you dressed up a bit to make your own out-to-eat occasion special. A six-item kids' menu for the under-10 set and some entrees like chicken piccata and veal à la Frankie are geared to those who'd rather eat light.

Frankie's Italian Cuisine
☎ **(440) 892-0064**

CITY: **Westlake**   AREA: **West Side**
ATMOSPHERE: **Casual**   COST: $$$$$

ADDRESS: 25939 Detroit Rd.
HOURS: Mon 5–10 p.m., Tue–Fri 11 a.m.–10 p.m., Sat noon–10 p.m., Sun closed
RESERVATIONS: Taken, for groups of 6 or more only   PAYMENT: MC, VS, AX, DIS   BAR: Beer, wine, liquor   TAKEOUT: Yes   SMOKING: Smoking section
ACCESS: ♿ Full access

The first Frankie's, in North Olmsted, was so successful that in 1986 this second incarnation opened in Westlake's Williamsburg Square Center. (It's a strip mall, so parking is never a problem.) Easy to reach via I-90 (Columbia Road exit), this Frankie's is a bit larger than the other, comfortably seating up to 150 in a pleasant, well-lit dining room decorated in a contemporary style with plants and wooden ceiling fans. (For more information, see the previous entry for the original Frankie's, North Olmsted.)

Gavi's
☎ **(440) 942-8008**

CITY: **Willoughby**   AREA: **East Side**
ATMOSPHERE: **Dressy**   COST: $$$$$

ADDRESS: 38257 Glenn Ave.
HOURS: Lunch Tue–Fri 11:30 a.m.–2 p.m.; Dinner Tue–Thu 4:30–10 p.m., Fri & Sat 4:30–11 p.m.; closed Sun & Mon to general public, but open for private parties   RESERVATIONS: Taken
PAYMENT: MC, VS, AX, DIS   BAR: Beer, wine, liquor
TAKEOUT: Yes   SMOKING: Smoking section
ACCESS: ♿ Full access   *Not recommended for children

The setting is a great example of the current architectural aesthetic that favors recycling. Once a powerhouse, the 100-year-old building has taken on a new identity as an elegant, upscale 80-seat restaurant on a side street in the center of downtown. The original interior brick walls and high, wood-beamed ceiling remain, complemented by track lighting, floral carpeting, potted plants, and a pastel color scheme of salmon pink and mint green. Napkins are cloth, upholstered chairs designed for comfort have an opulent look, and ornate pieces of antique furniture function as service stations. All these design elements work together to create a sumptuous backdrop suitable for fine dining. The kitchen strikes an impressive first note by sending out hot, crusty, homemade bread after you're seated, along with pinzimonio, a bowl of beautifully arranged fresh vegetables. The focus is on country-style cooking, but peasants never had it this good.

The offerings, some of which change seasonally, can include imported rack of Australian lamb, a filet mignon of milk-fed veal tenderloin, halibut cheeks, and calamari steaks. If you select a seafood entree, the fish is likely to have been flown in from Seattle and brought to the restaurant from the airport by courier. If you select pasta, it will be handmade. Two of the most popular versions are caramelle al mascarpone, in which candy-shaped pasta is filled with

MEDITERRANEAN

a mix of veal, spinach, and mascarpone cheese (a thick, rich, moist cow's milk cream cheese with a consistency that ranges from that of clotted or sour cream to butter) and served with a roasted tomato mascarpone sauce; and cavatelli in a tomato sauce made with ground mortadella and veal. Mozzarella is made in-house and served in a variety of dishes: as part of the antipasto plate, which also includes different salads and imported meats; rolled with prosciutto and served with roasted red peppers; stuffed and drizzled in herbed olive oil. The chef likes to alter the menu periodically to keep things interesting, but when the polenta e portobello alla gorgonzola, a marinated mushroom cap appetizer, was eliminated, customers protested and after a week's absence, it reappeared. You can check out what's happening in the kitchen from a seat at the bar, where you can also order a glass of wine, choosing from the tremendous selection that restaurant owners Mary and David Gromelski have assembled. If you're not schooled in the wine arts, David, a graduate of a sommelier training program, will be glad to advise. In fact, his enthusiasm for wine is the basis of the restaurant's name: Gavi is a major wine-producing town in Italy. The bar area is also a good spot for taking a peek at the desserts, displayed in a refrigerated case located here. A display tray is also brought to your table. Mary's mother, Adele Busetto, who is from Venice, makes the cannoli and the tiramisu, always available, and there's a rotating selection of other lavish pastry confections. Service is accommodating; you can ask for half-size portions or half-and-half combinations of two items that call to your taste buds.

Guarino's Restaurant
☎ **(216) 231-3100**

CITY: **Cleveland**   AREA: **Near East Side**
ATMOSPHERE: **Dressy**   COST: $$$$$

ADDRESS: 12309 Mayfield Rd.
HOURS: Mon–Wed 11:30 a.m.–10 p.m., Thu 11:30 a.m.–11 p.m., Fri 11:30 a.m.–11:30 p.m., Sat 12:30–11:30 p.m., Sun 1–8 p.m.
RESERVATIONS: Taken, recommended weekends
PAYMENT: MC, VS, AX, DIS   **BAR:** Beer, wine, liquor
TAKEOUT: Yes   **SMOKING:** Smoking section
ACCESS: ♿ Full access

MEDITERRANEAN

According to Marilyn Guarino, the restaurant established in 1918 by her father-in-law, Vincenzo Guarino, now claims the honor of being the oldest continuously operating Italian restaurant in town—it celebrated its 50th anniversary in November 1997. It's not unusual for tour buses to stop here. The family used to live above the restaurant; now one floor has become a bed and breakfast, and another is a series of Victorian-style parlors where dinner is served to private parties of 2 to 50 people. For reservations, contact Nancy Phillips, Marilyn Guarino's business partner. Downstairs, the restaurant, which seats between 75 and 90, also has an antique Victorian motif. The food is primarily southern Italian with some northern influence. In addition to the standard selection of pasta dishes with a variety of sauces, the menu includes wedding soup, lumache (snails), saltimbocca (veal with prosciutto ham and cheese), and brasciole (a thin steak stuffed and rolled). The wine list offers a comprehensive selection. In warm weather, there's outdoor dining amidst the grape and trumpet-flower vines that Vincenzo Guarino originally brought with him from Sicily. Valet parking available on weekends; otherwise use their lot adjacent to the restaurant.

MEDITERRANEAN

Jimmy Daddona's
☎ (440) 248-2444

CITY: **Solon**   AREA: **Southeast**
ATMOSPHERE: **Casual**   COST: $$$$$

ADDRESS: 6200 Enterprise Pkwy.
HOURS: Mon–Thu 11 a.m.–10 p.m., Fri
11 a.m.–11 p.m., Sat 4–11 p.m.; closed Sun
RESERVATIONS: Not taken **PAYMENT:** MC, VS
BAR: Beer, wine **TAKEOUT:** Yes
SMOKING: Smoking section **ACCESS:** ♿ Full
access

One *Cleveland Ethnic Eats* reader who
recommended this place wrote, "It's a
very small restaurant—no reservations
accepted. Expect a long wait on weekend
evenings, but what better testimony?! Sin-
fully good." But there's more to this "long
wait" remark. The waiting area is cramped,
with only seven or eight chairs, but so determined are so many to get their turn at
the table that they're willing to sit in their
cars or go to the bar at the restaurant next
door until the hostess, who's happy to
oblige, comes to get them. The big attraction is the food. The choice is interesting,
the flavors as authentic as you can get, and
the portions so huge that plates resemble
serving dishes and everyone—those who
go beyond full to stuffed, the large-sized,
and even self-proclaimed starving
teenagers—takes leftovers home. There
are all the Italian standards like spaghetti,
ravioli, lasagna, veal and eggplant Parmigiana, pizza, and chicken Marsala, plus
some less common dishes: chicken car-
dinel, made with shrimp, scallops, and a
white-wine butter sauce; veal aglio e olio,
breaded medallions of meat sauteed in
olive oil with garlic, artichoke hearts,
mushrooms, roasted red peppers, and
spinach; pasta arrabiata, which is linguine
topped with fresh tomatoes, capers, and
basil; mussels or calamari marinara; and
two or three different specials every night.
They make their own bread, using their
pizza dough, and "twisting" it before baking with garlic, olive oil, and spices.

The brightly lit dining room, a simple
brick-floored space with a combination of
wood paneling and stucco, decorated with
pictures of Italy, contains mostly tables for
four (two seat six), all covered in gold-and-
green plastic cloths. This is a simple, unpretentious place favored by families, and
the kitchen accommodates children with
half portions. Service is quick and efficient
but nonetheless attentive. The restaurant is
named for the owner and chef, and most of
his staff have been here as long as he has,
since 1988. Expect it to be busy, even on
weeknights, during the dinner hours. Close
to what passes for downtown in Solon, the
restaurant is located in a small shopping
plaza, west of Route 91.

Johnny's Bar
☎ (216) 281-0055

CITY: **Cleveland**   AREA: **Near West Side**
ATMOSPHERE: **Formal**   COST: $$$$$

ADDRESS: 3164 Fulton Rd.
HOURS: Lunch Thu & Fri 11:30 a.m.–2:30 p.m.;
Dinner Mon–Thu 5–10 p.m., Fri 5–11 p.m., Sat
5–11 p.m.; dining room closed between lunch &
dinner; closed Sun **RESERVATIONS:** Taken, for
parties of 4 or more on Fri, Sat **PAYMENT:** MC, VS,
AX **BAR:** Beer, wine, liquor **TAKEOUT:** Yes
SMOKING: Smoking section **ACCESS:** ♿ Limited
*Not recommended for children

The Zagat survey described Johnny's, a
sumptuous, upscale restaurant that sits
inconspicuously on a corner in an aging
blue-collar neighborhood, as "outstanding
in every way." Cleveland's own food experts
and cookbook authors Fred and Linda
Griffith rank it among the best in town.
The place has a genial, private-club ambience, a unique and stunning decor, and un-
forgettable northern Italian food prepared
with an innovative, continental flair. When
the three Santosuosso brothers took over
the place from their parents, they decided
to re-create a bygone era; entering their
restaurant is like going back to the 1930s.
"We wanted a restaurant that looked like a
real restaurant from the old days," said Joe
Santosuosso, "when food service was at its

height and eating out was an experience. The look is post-Deco, pre-streamline, the same as New York's Radio City Music Hall, and we reproduced everything exactly, down to the last detail of aging the color of the wood." Those details include faux-leopardskin carpeting, crisp linens, fine china, wood paneling, original murals painted on the walls, black leather banquettes, and a mahogany bar. There is both a sense of humor and an elegance in it all. The food, however, is serious business, made for people who appreciate and understand fine dining. The menu is large, and there are a number of specials each day featuring fish, veal, and pasta. The potato gnocchi are made according to Mamma Santosuosso's original recipe by Joe's aunt, and all the other pasta is made fresh on the premises too. In their book *The Best of the Midwest,* the Griffiths describe these pastas as "light as air" and name the pasta puttanesca, the angel hair with escargot, the mussels marinara, the baked calamari, and the veal tenderloin as standouts. In true Old World style, tomatoes and fresh herbs are grown out back. The walled-in garden also contains a patio with seven tables and a bocce ball court.

Johnny's Downtown
☎ (216) 623-0055
CITY: **Cleveland**   AREA: **Downtown**
ATMOSPHERE: **Dressy**   COST: **$$$$$**

ADDRESS: 1406 W. 6th St.
HOURS: Lunch Mon–Fri 11:30 a.m.–3 p.m.; Dinner Mon–Thu 5–10:30 p.m., Fri & Sat 5–11:30 p.m., Sun 4–9 p.m.; closed between lunch & dinner RESERVATIONS: Taken, recommended; required for parties of 4 or more on Fri, Sat PAYMENT: MC, VS, AX BAR: Beer, wine, liquor TAKEOUT: Yes SMOKING: Smoking section ACCESS: ♿ Full access *Not recommended for children

The menu at this second Johnny's, opened in 1993, is close to that at the original Johnny's on Fulton Avenue (see

previous description), featuring pasta, veal, and fish. The main difference here is that preparation is less refined, more reminiscent of the rustic cuisine of Tuscany. The setting, however, is not a duplicate of the old place, though it is equally special, evoking images of the once-famous and stately Oak Room in New York's Plaza Hotel. There's plenty of highly polished mahogany; leather; heavy, high-backed, upholstered chairs; and snowy table linens. The handsome barroom, which is often crowded and lively, is separate from the dining room, and meals are served there, too. The dining area is lighter, brighter, and more spacious, offering panoramic views of downtown. The entire setting is sophisticated and chic, and attracts a very urbane sort of clientele who come to see and be seen, enjoy the food, and listen to the music. A great place to bring out-of-towners and suburban visitors to give them a taste of just how suave this city can be.

La Gelateria
☎ (216) 229-2637
CITY: **Cleveland Hts.**   AREA: **East Side**
ATMOSPHERE: **Relaxed**   COST: **$$**$$$

ADDRESS: 12421 Cedar Rd.
HOURS: Mon–Thu noon–11 p.m., Fri noon–midnight, Sat 11 a.m.–midnight, Sun 11 a.m.–11 p.m. RESERVATIONS: Not taken PAYMENT: MC, VS BAR: None TAKEOUT: Yes SMOKING: Smoke-Free ACCESS: ♿ None

Ice cream is featured here, but not your ordinary frozen-milk sweet. This is the Italian version, and to my taste buds a far superior rendition of cool and luscious smoothness. And consider this comforting factoid—it's got less fat than its American counterpart. Less air, too. Hence the dense texture and intense flavor. Valerio Iorio, owner and chef at Valerio's in Little Italy and co-owner of Osteria di Valerio & Al downtown (see listings earlier in this chapter), is the man who's made this indulgence available—late into the night, I'm happy to add. He imported the machinery, set up a gelato-making operation in the basement, and opened for business at the top of Cedar Hill in August 2002. He also makes delectable dairy-free sorbet. The changing array of flavors, in both gelato and sorbet, is large and eclectic: fruits dominate, but are kept in their place by the likes of tiramasu, tartuffo (chocolate and hazelnut), zuppa inglese (English trifle), pistachio, rum crunch, espresso, and stracciatella (think cookies-'n-cream). It's an utterly charming—and very blue (you'll see what I mean when you get there)—little spot, and unlike anyplace else around. Seating for about 50, with tables opposite the counter and upstairs in a loft. Unfortunately there's no outdoor seating—it would be the perfect touch and so European—unless you count standing around in a crowd on the sidewalk, or hunkering down on the steps, which is exactly what many people do. Weekend nights in the summer often mean lines out the door, but service is swift and the wait never too long. It seems lots of people have been yearning for this Italian treat and didn't even know it. And they're willing to pay—these dips cost more than your average scoop, but as the marketing mantra goes, "You're worth it." More importantly, so's the gelato. Metered parking on the street, if you can find it, and more metered spots in a small garage around the corner.

Leo's Ristorante
☎ (330) 856-5291

CITY: **Warren**   AREA: **Farther South**
ATMOSPHERE: **Casual**   COST: $$$$$

ADDRESS: 7042 E. Market St.
HOURS: Mon–Fri 11 a.m.–11 p.m., Sat 4–11 p.m., Sun closed RESERVATIONS: Taken, Suggested for eight or more PAYMENT: MC, VS, AX, DIS
BAR: Beer, wine, liquor TAKEOUT: Yes
SMOKING: Smoking section ACCESS: ♿ Full access

To those of us who don't live there, Warren may seem like the middle of nowhere, and its location, an hour from both Cleveland and Akron, definitely qualifies as off the beaten path. But Warren is home to Leo's, and that makes it very much a destination town for those food enthusiasts who will let neither rain, sleet, snow, nor miles get in the way of a good meal. Your efforts will be well rewarded because owner and chef Leo Delgarbino Jr. knows what to do with escarole and artichokes, prosciutto and provolone. He can take the lowly fava bean and turn it into pesto, transform ordinary tomato sauce with the addition of brandy and cream, or basil and vodka. It's true he's a graduate of the Culinary Institute of America, but he also has cooking in his blood on both his mother's and his father's side, and the kitchen know-how goes back at least three generations. So it's no surprise that he works wonders with a veal chop, topping it with eggplant and a three-wine sauce; makes a wedding soup that will likely be a contender for the "best you've ever had" award; and redefines traditional lasagna by layering the noodles with leeks, portobello mushrooms, spinach, roasted red peppers, and a tomato basil sauce. The menu changes seasonally, with a mix of pasta, poultry, meat, and seafood dishes. Expect creativity with an Italian flourish—an olive-and-sun-dried-tomato stuffing for a filet of beef paired with oven-roasted polenta; linguine and clams in a lemon wine broth. There are also simpler, more familiar entrees: spaghetti and meatballs in a marinara sauce, chicken Parmigiana, and cavatelli. Salads show the same range, from a straightforward tossed version made with a variety of greens to a mesclun and endive combination, or strawberries with fresh mozzarella dressed in extra-virgin olive oil and balsamic syrup. All of the luscious desserts are made in their own kitchens. The wine list offers many options, including some of those rare vintages that are kept under lock and key.

With the help of his wife, Lisa, siblings,

and a cousin, Chef Leo has built up a loyal and enthusiastic following, and the restaurant is something of a local legend. (He still makes the pizzas that made the family's Parkman Road Dairy famous.) Ask anyone in Warren for directions, and they'll point the way. "Everybody knows Leo's," said a young woman filling her tank at an area gas station. A large, modern facility designed by Leo's uncle, Larry Strollo, was built from the ground up to replace his parents' original little eatery and pizza parlor on the other side of town, where he started his kitchen career. It seats 225 in the dining room: the space is two stories high with balcony seating available on weekends. There's a three-table area enclosed by glass walls toward the back of the main floor, and a small bar. The decor is tasteful, with paintings, hangings, and shelves holding candlesticks, small pieces of pottery, and antiques. Paper place mats at lunch, linens at dinnertime. Although the place has a classy feel and the menu includes some upscale-type dishes, children are always welcome here, and even the pickiest are likely to find something they like (there's a children's menu for those 12 and under). Outside, a canopy-covered patio has room for 60 diners in good weather, and jazz bands play here on Friday and Saturday nights. There's also a banquet center with its own entrance that can handle up to 500 people, or be divided into three smaller spaces. Photos of the facilities, as well as menus, prices, directions, and information about booking private events can all be found at www.leosristorante.com.

Mama Guzzardi's
☎ (330) 499-1247

CITY: **North Canton**   AREA: **Farther South**
ATMOSPHERE: **Relaxed**   COST: $$$$

ADDRESS: 1107 N. Main St.

HOURS: Mon & Wed–Sat 11 a.m.–9 p.m., Sun noon–7 p.m. RESERVATIONS: Taken, suggested for 6 or more PAYMENT: MC, VS, DIS, checks

BAR: None TAKEOUT: Yes SMOKING: Smoking section ACCESS: ♿ None

Family-style, no-nonsense Italian food in a "rec room"–style setting. The tablecloths and curtains are regulation red-and-white checkerboard, the walls sport fake wood paneling, and the only artwork is photographs documenting the lives, loves, weddings, christenings, graduations, and other celebrations of three generations of Guzzardis. Frank Sinatra sings softly in the background, and customers call the waitresses by name. It's been like this since 1986, when Mama opened the place. Though she's handed control over to younger members of the clan, "she still comes in," says granddaughter Kathy, "to keep us on our toes and be sure we're doing everything right." Right means Mama's way, which translates into good food, made from scratch using her recipes and served up in generous portions at a reasonable price in a homey atmosphere where people of all ages feel welcome. I ended up in conversation with a group of guys when I was there for lunch, and when they found out I was gathering information for this book, they assured me I'd come to the right place. And they expressed pride that the little North Canton place they've patronized for years is attracting notice. The waitress, listening in, added that when she wears her Mama Guzzardi's T-shirt out in public, people always stop her to talk about how long they've been eating here and how much they love the food.

At the top of the menu are two classic, heartwarming Italian soups, wedding and pasta fagioli. They do pasta all the ways you'd expect, with cheese, alla marinara, with meatballs, and aglio e olio (garlic and olive oil). Their lasagna, manicotti, and stuffed shells are not for the lactose intolerant. Each day has its own dinner special, from chicken or eggplant Parmigiana to chicken cacciatore and seafood cannelloni. Half portions are available, and garlic bread comes with every entree. Even the salad dressings are homemade. They also

MEDITERRANEAN

mention that they'll cut up the meatballs in your meatball sub if it's too hard to handle. Can a restaurant get any more friendly and accommodating than that? The restaurant seats about 90 in two rooms, one for smokers. In a small, three-store strip with parking.

Mamma Santa's
☎ (216) 231-9567

CITY: **Cleveland**   AREA: **Near East Side**
ATMOSPHERE: **Casual**   COST: **$$**$$

ADDRESS: 12305 Mayfield Rd.
HOURS: Mon–Thu 11 a.m.–11:45 p.m., Fri & Sat 11 a.m.–12:45 p.m.; closed Sun
RESERVATIONS: Taken, only for large groups
PAYMENT: MC, VS **BAR:** Beer, wine **TAKEOUT:** Yes
SMOKING: Smoking section **ACCESS:** ♿ Full access

My husband and I have been eating here since 1971, when we were students down the hill at CWRU and the restaurant was only 10 years old. We liked the casual, friendly, relaxed atmosphere, affordable prices, good taste, and plentiful portions. Thirty years later, Mamma Santa's still offers all those some qualities, and now we take our kids there. The restaurant attracts a steady crowd of students, couples, families, and workers whose collars come white, blue, pink, and just about every other color, too—many from the institutions of nearby University Circle. Many have been eating here for years. When it's full, and it often is, the restaurant can serve pizza and pasta to about 120 at booths and tables spread among three rooms. The cooking is Sicilian-style, and the noodles are all homemade. When you want to try something different from spaghetti with meatballs, order noodles with fagioli (beans), lenticchie (lentils), or ceci (chickpeas). Pizzas are baked to order, so it can take 20 minutes, but you can get an antipasto plate and garlic toast or a side of fried green peppers to hold you. Lights are low, and old wine bottles and pictures

of Italy are all the decor you'll find. Seniors get a discount. A limited number of parking spaces in the rear, otherwise you're on your own on the street.

Maria's
☎ (216) 226-5875

CITY: **Lakewood**   AREA: **West Side**
ATMOSPHERE: **Casual**   COST: **$$$**$$

ADDRESS: 11822 Detroit Ave.
HOURS: Mon–Thu 11 a.m.–10 p.m., Fri 11 a.m.–11 p.m., Sat 5–11 p.m., Sun 4–9 p.m. (5–10 p.m. in the summer)
RESERVATIONS: Taken, for groups of 5 or more
PAYMENT: MC, VS, AX **BAR:** Beer, wine, liquor
TAKEOUT: Yes **SMOKING:** Smoking section
ACCESS: ♿ Limited

Maria's has been around more than 40 years, by owner Maria Bastulli's reckoning. It's easy to spot—there's a neon version of their logo, a fork and spaghetti-filled pasta bowl, that can be seen from two blocks away. Inside are a pleasant bar and three dining rooms, two handsomely decorated with a flower motif on curtains and wallpaper, one featuring a red-white-and-green awning stretched across the ceiling. Lots of framed photographs of Italy on the walls, with booths and tables for up to 150. Dressings, sauces, and pasta are all made on the premises. Servings are generous, and when the menu says clam sauce it means *clam* sauce: huge meaty chunks plus some still in the shell grace an order here. They serve their own tasty version of garlic bread, called cucina bread, toasted with Parmesan cheese. Pizza, calzone, lasagna, and ravioli are available in addition to classic veal and chicken dishes. There's a two-item children's menu. Try to leave room for Maria's signature confections, which include white chocolate cheesecake served with raspberry sauce and chocolate salami made with pistachios—voted one of Cleveland's best chocolate desserts by *The Plain Dealer*.

Molinari's
☎ (440) 974-2750

CITY: **Mentor**   AREA: **Farther East**
ATMOSPHERE: **Casual**   COST: $$$$$

ADDRESS: 8900 Mentor Ave.
HOURS: Lunch Mon–Sat 11:30 a.m.–2 p.m.;
Dinner Tue–Thu 5:30–10 p.m., Fri & Sat
5:30–11 p.m.; closed for dinner on Mon
RESERVATIONS: Taken, recommended
PAYMENT: MC, VS, AX, DIS, checks **BAR:** Beer,
wine, liquor **TAKEOUT:** Yes **SMOKING:** Smoking
section **ACCESS:** & Full access

Molinari's has grown from a small dining area in a market to a 150-seat restaurant set in the midst of a wine shop. The look is sophisticated New York contemporary, and the view into the kitchen from the dining room is a source of entertainment and interest. The menu, which changes seasonally, is northern Italian and northern California. The wine list is not only extensive but full of great values, reflecting retail rather than restaurant pricing. Owner and chef Randal Johnson specializes in bold flavors and unique, creative presentations: calamari with three-pepper relish; veal slices tossed in a lemon vodka cream sauce; pancetta shrimp; hot peppers stuffed with four cheeses and herbs; balsamic and brown sugar marinated pork tenderloin; and beef tenderloin risotto. He's also venturing further afield in the world of food and flavor—the current menu includes a Japanese style yellowfin tuna preparaed with daikon radish slaw and wasabi and a globe-trotting array of sauce choices: chipotle butter, roquefort cream sauce; and orange bourbon BBQ. On Mondays, when the restaurant itself is closed, Molinari's hosts special events open to the public, such as wine tastings and cooking classes. The website, www.molinaris.com, includes announcements for these events along with the season's new menu and a separate catering menu. There is a private room suitable for business meetings and parties.

Nino's
☎ (440) 353-9580

CITY: **North Ridgeville**   AREA: **West Side**
ATMOSPHERE: **Casual**   COST: $$$$$

ADDRESS: 32652 Center Ridge Rd.
HOURS: Mon–Sat 4–10 p.m., Sun 1–7:30 p.m.
RESERVATIONS: Not taken **PAYMENT:** Cash only
BAR: Beer, wine, liquor **TAKEOUT:** Yes
SMOKING: All sections **ACCESS:** & Full access

A clue that this isn't just another run-of-the-mill Italian restaurant is the appetizer listing for Nana's pork neck bones: when's the last time you saw neck bones on a menu—Nana's or anybody else's? For an ethnic food writer, that traditional, unglamorous dish and its attribution to Grandma are a dead giveaway that the food here is the real lasagna. That's why Chip Kullik, news director of WMJI, recommended it to me, describing it as a small, hole-in-the-wall kind of place with incredible food. Other menu items that get my authenticity meter going are smelts, baccala (dried salt cod), bread pudding, and aglio e olio sauce. The recipes for many dishes are family treasures. The food is homestyle, not fancy, so you'll find pasta e fagioli (pasta and beans), fried escarole, fresh (not fried and frozen) calamari in homemade marinara sauce, and sausage they make on the premises. Other, more elaborate offerings include pasta Florentine with spinach cream clam sauce; veal scallopini with wine sauce and capers; white cavatelli with chicken in alfredo basil sauce; and Asiago cheese–stuffed gnocchi. Some of their house specialties are so popular they prepare and sell them by the pound, pint, and the quart, including sausage, salad dressing, wedding soup, and clam sauce. They also do pizzas and a few sandwiches. There are no high chairs, and the intimate space is suitable for well-behaved kids old enough to hold still for the length of a meal and control their personal volume. The restaurant has only 13 tables, with seating for 60: six are booths, but the

MEDITERRANEAN

others can be pushed together for larger parties. There's a view into the kitchen from the dining room, and a lobby waiting area—essential as seating is always first come, first serve—that's equipped with an ATM machine for those who don't arrive prepared with cash or check. Family photos and pictures of famous Italian-Americans grace the walls. In a strip mall with plenty of parking.

Osteria

☎ (216) 685-9491

CITY: **Cleveland** AREA: **Downtown**
ATMOSPHERE: **Casual** COST: **$$$$$**

ADDRESS: 408 St. Clair Ave.
HOURS: Mon–Thu 5–10 p.m., Fri & Sat 5–11:30 p.m., Sun 4–8 p.m.
RESERVATIONS: Taken, Suggested always—especially Fri & Sat **PAYMENT:** MC, VS, AX, DIS
BAR: Beer, wine, liquor **TAKEOUT:** No
SMOKING: Smoking section **ACCESS:** ♿ Full access

Chef Michael Annadono spent three years learning his craft in the northern Piedmont region of Italy. His boss (and Osteria's owner) Al Cefaratti describes him as strictly "old school," a traditionalist although he's not yet 30, with a passion for cooking and a respect for food. In fact, Annadono has such strong feelings about what he prepares that he insisted, over Cefaratti's objections, on eliminating salt shakers from the restaurant's 13 tables. Salt is available on request, but only after you've tasted what's on your plate. Annadono likes to play in the kitchen, so his modest-sized menu of classic Italian dishes is augmented with 15 to 20 specials every day that allow him to take advantage of whatever ingredients are freshest, best, and most intriguing. You can always get carpaccio (raw sirloin), ribollita Toscana (Tuscan vegetable soup), saltimbocca (veal and prosciutto), osso bucco (slow-roasted veal shank), seafood risotto, and pasta with a genuine deep-flavored Bolognese sauce made with duck and veal. The zucchini flan served with vegetable-filled crepe appetizers and the cappelletti in cream sauce with peas, also menu fixtures, are signature creations, along with coniglio arrosto al timo (roasted rabbit), an entree not often found on area menus. Specials might include squid ink ravioli filled with lobster meat, seared halibut with porcini mushrooms and asparagus, veal scallopini with artichokes, or a long-bone veal chop Milanese that's pounded, breaded, pan fried, and served with lemon truffle oil. Desserts too feature a few regular items, such as fruity sorbets, and specials that give Annadono a chance to show off his skills as a pastry chef—cassata cake, hazelnut torte, chocolate cappucino mousse, and a flourless mint chocolate cake. Service is European-style—once your maitre d has made you comfortable and told you all about what the kitchen has to offer, he turns your table over to the wait staff, all of whom are available to help you—no waiting for "your" server. The restaurant opened in late 2001. It represents a partnership between Valerio Iorio, chef and owner of Valerio's in Little Italy, and Cefaratti, who formerly tended bar there. The two believe in running very hands-on operations with high standards for food and service. The result, here in the Warehouse District location, is a restaurant that is upscale and stylish yet retains the warm, friendly atmosphere of a neighborhood hangout. Cefaratti is a nightly presence, backslapping regulars, personally welcoming newcomers, and making sure customers who have to wait longer than expected for their table get a drink on the house. The wine list is extensive, focusing on Italian vintages that range in price from $20–$72. Wine bottles are integral to the decor, displayed on shelves lining one wall, in a wine rack on another, and in a glass-fronted cabinet near the entrance. The dining room is actually below street level, and this adds to the "wine cellar" feel of this pleasantly intimate and cozy space. Subdued lighting, a black-and-white color scheme with maroon accents, and background music that features timeless classics and Sinatra-style crooners augment the sense that you've stumbled on a lovely little secret hideaway. A head count on a typical Thursday night reveals a romantic tête-à-tête in progress at one table, a business meeting at another, a two-couple get together at a third, and four women celebrating at the back. At the bar men and women in suits sit beside folks in jeans, and the comfortable high-backed stools clearly make it easy to linger.

Personally, I would not choose to bring young kids here, but for those who think otherwise there is a high chair stashed in the ladies' room. The front entrance has steps and is not handicapped accessible, but there is a rear entrance with a ramp. Parking does not come easily or cheaply in this part of downtown—you can drive around endlessly in hopes of finding a meter on the street or pay to put your car in one of the numerous lots that dot the area.

The Palazzo
☎ (216) 651-3900

CITY: **Cleveland** AREA: **Near West Side**
ATMOSPHERE: **Dressy** COST: $$$$$

ADDRESS: 10031 Detroit Ave.
HOURS: Thu–Sat 5–10 p.m.; closed Sun–Wed
RESERVATIONS: Required, recommended
PAYMENT: MC, VS, AX **BAR:** Beer, wine, liquor
TAKEOUT: Yes **SMOKING:** Smoking section
ACCESS: & None *Not recommended for children

They call their place a restaurant and they even have a menu to prove it, but what Gilda and Carla Carnicelli do at the Palazzo bears little resemblance to anything I've ever encountered. Though they prepare and serve food to people, there's nothing very businesslike about it. The two women treat diners as honored guests, not customers. Those who come regularly are friends. Everyone gets special treatment. You don't just walk in, you're ushered in,

with Carla welcoming you as though into her own home. In fact it is a home, in every sense of the word. The sisters agree that they spend more time here than anywhere else, and always have. They grew up in the apartment above the restaurant and have worked here, in one way or another, all their lives. The Palazzo is the modern incarnation of Palmina's, a restaurant started by their grandmother in the very same building in 1947 (though it was, at that time, on the other side of the street . . . but that's another story—ask Carla about it). And it looks like a house, too, both inside and out, a Tuscan villa to be exact. The exterior is yellow brick and fieldstone, with a brick-paved courtyard out front surrounded by a wrought-iron fence, a lovely setting for a meal alfresco or an after-dinner espresso. The dining area has a charming, Old World opulence, replete with statuary, fountains, gilt-framed oil paintings, sumptuous draperies, and thick carpeting. The colors are rich and warm: red, mauve, burnt umber, ochre. The scale is intimate, seating for just 40 or so, and this allows them to pay extraordinary attention to every table, each person. You can have your favorite wine open and waiting for you; your favorite dish, whether it's on the menu that week or not, made just the way you like it. If you want Gilda to come out of the kitchen so you can tell her exactly how you want your veal done, just ask. Many customers who come often just say, "You know my tastes... make me something good," and she does. If there was something on the menu last time you were in that you want again, let her know when you make your reservation, and she'll be sure it's ready for you. Feel free to drop off a recipe you'd like her to try, and let her know when you'll be back to taste the results.

Gilda, who has expanded on all she learned about cooking from her mother and her grandmother by studying with Marcella Hazan, and at schools in Bologna and Venice, is a food artist and likes nothing better than to experiment and create new dishes. She goes to the market herself to select fresh fish, meat, and produce, transforming them into Italian-inspired dishes that are never the same from one day to the next. You might encounter scampi made with lemon and peppercorns; chicken with sun-dried tomatoes and a porcini mushroom cream sauce; roasted quail with sage and pancetta (smoked Italian bacon); swordfish with a fresh tomato and basil sauce; salciccia, fennel-seasoned sausage with peppers, onions, and mushrooms in wine; or a braised pork loin in balsamic vinegar with roasted rosemary potatoes. There are always a variety of pasta entrees: paglio e fieno, a combination of penne pasta, broccoli, and provolone cheese; pasta fagioli with anncellini beans, onions, and pancetta; an aglio e olio that's made with sauteed fennel, portobello mushrooms, olive oil, and garlic. But Grandma Palmina's classic renditions of minestrone soup, antipasto, spaghetti and meatballs, and veal Marsala, and her seafood stew of calamari, shrimp, and mussels in a marinara sauce are still part of what comes out of the kitchen. Bread is baked there, too, in a stone oven—if you order bruschetta and tapenade, you'll get it with a pesto and caper crust and an olive and tomato spread.

When the restaurant is closed to the public, it's available for private parties with customized menus. The Carnicellis also host some of their own unique events: cigar parties, wine tastings, and a traditional medieval feast during the winter holiday season. But their most remarkable undertaking is the Big Night dinner party, which occurs periodically throughout the year. In the movie Big Night, two Italian brothers in the restaurant business make a lavish seven-course meal for a select group of guests. Carla and Gilda do the same, re-creating each and every extraordinary dish in the film including a Parmesan risotto with seafood and spinach, a baked sea bass with fennel, a whole roast suckling pig, and il timpano, a pasta "drum" with a filling composed of five different dishes, which takes two to three days to prepare. All is laid out banquet style and served with an almost endless stream of champagne and wine. And there's more: they show the film (sound down), play the same music, and incite a duplication of the riotous conga dancing that happens on screen.

Eating here anytime is a singular experience, one meant for adults, not children. There's a cozy marble-floored lounge, a 1982 addition to the house, and an extensive and eclectic wine list; labels for each vintage appear on individual pages of a spiral-bound book. The building has its own parking lot, which can be accessed either from Detroit or 101st Street.

Piatto
☎ (330) 255-1140
CITY: Akron   AREA: Farther South
ATMOSPHERE: Casual   COST: $$$$$

ADDRESS: 326 South Main St.
HOURS: Lunch: Mon–Fri 11 a.m.–3 p.m.; Dinner: Mon–Thu 5:30–10:30 p.m., Fri & Sat 5:30–11:30 p.m., Sun closed
RESERVATIONS: Taken, Suggested Fri & Sat nights
PAYMENT: MC, VS, AX, DIS **BAR:** Beer, wine, liquor
TAKEOUT: Yes **SMOKING:** Smoking section
ACCESS: ♿ Full access

"Piatto was born when this building, built as a bank in 1947, became available," says owner and chef Roger Thomas. "I had wanted to open a glamorous, upscale restaurant serving the traditional Italian food I loved for a long time. I saw an opportunity and I took it." Before opening he did a true cook's tour, visiting northern and southern Italy to fire up his creative juices and inspire his menu. In Tuscany, Thomas worked in the kitchen of a small hotel near Cortona (made famous in Frances Mayes's book Under the Tuscan Sun) for a month. "From the chef there," he says, "I learned how to get foods to give up their flavors. We became good friends, and 10 days before Piatto was scheduled to open, this chef surprised me by coming to

Akron and working in my kitchen for two weeks." The place opened in June 2000, and in its first year Northern Ohio Live magazine readers voted it the best Italian restaurant in the region and the best in Akron. Food critic and editor Joe Crea of The Plain Dealer has raved about it in print, calling it a "contender" for one of his favorites, and a spot he'd go back to "in a heartbeat," even if his meal weren't on the paper's tab. The allure is both in the food and the stunning decor—the rustic simplicity of the first contrasting with the sleek, "mode moderne" post-Deco look. The kitchen turns out some classic dishes like a tomato and bread soup and another made with white beans and pancetta; a caprese salad composed of fresh tomatoes, mozzarella made in-house, red onions, and basil; the very popular Bolognese tomato sauce for linguini made with simmered beef, veal, and pork; penne pasta with tomato basil sauce and sausage; and vitello Florentine, a thin veal cutlet in an egg batter. Other dishes have a contemporary flair: ravioli filled with roasted butternut squash; lobster risotto fritters; a lasagna that includes smoked chicken; toasted walnuts with Gorgonzola cream sauce; pork tenderloin in Chianti sauce; a wood-grilled sliced sirloin served atop arugula and Roma tomatoes with a garlic and red wine dressing. The dessert menu features the same mix—wonderful standards such as tiramasu, gelati, and sorbetti, as well as surprising pairings like panna cotta (the Italian eggless custard) with balsamic marinated strawberries; a cold Arborio rice pudding with roasted pears and orange syrup; and the intriguing mignardises, an array of little "chocolate surprises." Olive oil is treated like wine here. There is an oil menu with Italian regional specialties, estate-bottled varieties, one from France, and another made from a very particular type of olive. The flavor of each is vividly, almost poetically, described. The oils are offered as appetizers, sprinkled with freshly grated cheese, and served with fresh and scrumptious bread for dipping.

The wine list is extensive and impressive, running the gamut from reasonably priced good-quality bottles to some very costly and select vintages. You can choose a glass of California zinfandel for $4.24, a bottle of Italian Valpolicella for $30, or, from the Limited Availability List, a $200 1994 Far Niente "Estate" Cabernet Sauvignon, plus some very nice Italian, French, and California sparkling and dessert wines and four different brands of port. The 12-stool bar stays open between lunch and dinner, and appetizers are available during these hours. Service is excellent: professional and attentive without being unctuous, and those extra touches that make a restaurant experience memorable are standard here. One friend recalls that on a rainy night Thomas himself, who regularly gets out of the kitchen nowadays to meet and greet his guests, carried an umbrella and walked customers to their cars. Now, that's going beyond the call of duty. The restaurant is surprisingly spacious, exceptionally comfortable, and beautifully appointed. Few sharp angles anywhere in sight—everything curves sensuously: walls, leather banquettes, chair backs, light fixtures, railings, and pillars. Natural light-colored wood and moss-green upholstery set off white table linens. There are two dining rooms front and back, a raised platform area for smokers, and a separate room that seats up to 70 for private parties. During the warm-weather months, except for game nights, diners can also enjoy the outdoor patio, which overlooks the Aeros' Stadium. Younger patrons are welcome, and the kitchen will accommodate those with a less adventurous palate by whipping up a plate of plain spaghetti or a humble pizza on request. A jazz trio plays dinner music on Monday nights. Piatto is an ideal choice any day of the week, for a special occasion, or a meal meant to wow friends, family, a date, or a client. Valet parking is available in the evenings. There are also public lots that charge for parking and meters on the street.

MEDITERRANEAN

MEDITERRANEAN

Pileggi's
☎ (330) 497-0309
CITY: **Canton**   AREA: **Farther South**
ATMOSPHERE: **Relaxed**   COST: $$$$$

ADDRESS: 5808 Fulton Dr.
HOURS: Mon–Fri 11 a.m.–7:30 p.m., Sat 11 a.m.–4 p.m., Sun closed **RESERVATIONS:** Not Taken **PAYMENT:** MC, VS **BAR:** None
TAKEOUT: Yes **SMOKING:** Smoke-Free
ACCESS: ♿ Full access

Mostly a carryout place, but there are five tables with plastic covers and folding chairs for eating in, so this Canton fixture is entitled to restaurant status. The Pileggi family has been serving home-cooked Italian lunches and dinners to area residents since the 1960s, but they've only been at their current location near the little community of Lake Cable since 1999. Whether you eat here or take it with you, your order comes in Styrofoam, but they will ante up real silverware if you sit down. Workmen dig in knowing they're not out of place in grimy pants and mud-caked boots, and nobody bats an eye when little kids are noisy or messy. They do catering and prepare party trays. Each day Silvio Pileggi and his wife Ferna make something different: it might be smoked sausage and rigatoni, chicken Milano, vegetable lasagna, sausage, pepper, and onions over pasta, veal Parmigiana, spaghetti and meatballs, or flounder stuffed with crabmeat. Silvio slow-cooks something he calls "Godfather Sauce," and he proudly tells me he's sold over 9,000 quarts of this special blend that he makes with tomatoes, wine, and a number of secret ingredients. They also prepare soups; subs; big sandwiches on Italian bread, including the Prosciutto Supreme, the "Calabrese" (with eggplant), and Bruschetta Coto, made with sweet roasted red peppers and fresh mozzarella; pizzas (topped with the regular red stuff or a white garlic sauce); pepperoni rolls; and salads like antipasto and Sicilian. The double-crust stuffed antipasto pizza is many good things rolled into one, and you can get it by the slice (really more of a hunk). A customer, seeing me taking notes, asks what I'm doing. When I tell him, he says, "You should write down that the food here is the best Italian in Stark County." Ferna reciprocates by adding, "We're very lucky because we have wonderful, loyal customers." Everyone seems to know everyone else, and they ask after each other's families, gardens, jobs, and health. (For more information about the deli, see listing under the same name in the market section of this chapter.) The building has its own convenient parking lot. During the good weather months, there are tables, chairs, and umbrellas out front.

Players on Madison
☎ (216) 226-5200
CITY: **Lakewood**   AREA: **West Side**
ATMOSPHERE: **Casual**   COST: $$$$$

ADDRESS: 14527 Madison Ave. (at Belle)
HOURS: Sun & Mon 5–9 p.m., Tue–Thu 5–10 p.m., Fri & Sat 5 p.m.–midnight
RESERVATIONS: Taken, between 5 p.m.–7 p.m.
PAYMENT: MC, VS, AX, DIS **BAR:** Beer, wine, liquor
TAKEOUT: Yes **SMOKING:** Smoking section
ACCESS: ♿ Full access

The building's old pressed-tin ceiling, painted white, is still in evidence, and the old wood floors have been sanded to gleaming perfection, but everything else about Players is sleek and contemporary, that uncanny blend of minimal and glamorous. The most interesting illumination I've ever seen in a restaurant, oddly shaped bits of glimmering light hang clothesline-style across the two dining areas. Tables are white cloth under glass; hand-painted ceramic plates and beautiful bottles of herb vinegar decorate the walls. The menu reflects that same panache. Traditional Italian dishes are updated and pizza or pasta can be ordered with a large selection of toppings including roasted garlic, arugula, herbed chicken, smoked mussels, or shiitake mushrooms. But lest you think it's all just too trendy, on one visit I saw two kids happily tucking into platefuls of spaghetti with tomato sauce, with milk chasers.

Porcelli's
☎ (216) 791-9900

CITY: **Cleveland**   AREA: **Near East Side**
ATMOSPHERE: **Dressy**   COST: $$$$$

ADDRESS: 12022 Mayfield Rd.
HOURS: Sun 5–9 p.m., Mon–Thu 5:30–9 p.m., Fri & Sat 5–11 p.m. **RESERVATIONS:** Taken, recommended on weekends **PAYMENT:** MC, VS, AX, DIS **BAR:** Beer, wine, liquor **TAKEOUT:** Yes
SMOKING: Smoking section **ACCESS:** ♿ None
*Not recommended for children

Originally, this restaurant was quite small, but an expansion into the space next door added a second dining room. But the larger size has not changed the intimate feel of the place. The decor has a chic, understated artistic elegance. Owner Robert Porcelli, who studied painting in Rome, hangs his own works on the walls. The black plates with a beautiful border design make a gorgeous backdrop for the food. The overall effect of the crisp, snowy table linens, glowing candles, and servers dressed in classic black and white is reminiscent of the fine little restaurants that abound in Rome and Florence. Most diners look like they're on their way to the symphony or coming from the theater, and just being here makes you feel a bit glamorous and oh-so-interesting. You won't find the familiar American renditions of Italian food here, so don't come with an appetite for meatballs. What you can sample is fresh pasta in light cream sauces that are laced with brandy and garlic or infused with fresh green herbs. Dishes on this menu and five daily specials make optimal use of veal and seafood, fresh tomatoes, exotic mushrooms, imported full-flavored cheeses like bocconcini and Parmigiano-Reggiano, and smoked meats such as pancetta and prosciutto. Cappuccino, espresso, and desserts made from family recipes are available for a perfect ending.

Portofino Ristorante
☎ (440) 572-3466

CITY: **Strongsville**   AREA: **Southwest**
ATMOSPHERE: **Formal**   COST: $$$$$

ADDRESS: 12214 Pearl Rd.
HOURS: Mon–Fri 5:30–9 p.m., Sat 5:30–9:30 p.m.; closed Sun **RESERVATIONS:** Taken, recommended **PAYMENT:** MC, VS, AX, DIS
BAR: Beer, wine, liquor **TAKEOUT:** No
SMOKING: Smoking section **ACCESS:** ♿ Full access *Not recommended for children

The restaurant, located in a small, fairly new shopping plaza, has a formal air. The waiters, well dressed in white shirts and colorful ties, are professionals: they know how to use their crumb combs, pronounce the Italian name of each dish correctly, and pay meticulous attention to the details of fine service. Tables are dressed in white linens with fresh flowers on each. This is definitely not a place for the kids when they're still in the throes of the terrible twos (or threes, fours, and fives). Decor in this intimate 75-seat restaurant is contemporary, with black marble accents, and even the faucets in the restrooms are stylish. While waiting for your table you can relax on plush couches and leaf through *Wine Spectator* or drink at the five-seat bar in the back. Once you are seated, your waiter will bring bread and mix a dipping dish of extra-virgin olive oil and balsamic vinegar tableside for you. Food preparation and presentation are decidedly artistic. The cuisine is a blend of northern and southern influences; dishes are classic but in no way ordinary. Fusilli pasta is dressed in a rose cream sauce with pancetta (Italian bacon), onions, and vodka; capelli puttanesca is made with angel hair pasta, anchovies, capers, olives, and chile peppers; and the manicotti, stuffed with ricotta and spinach, comes in a tomato sauce bechamel. There's an interesting selection

MEDITERRANEAN

of antipasto and salads, chicken, and veal dishes, and a fabulous-looking dessert tray.

Presti Bakery
☎ (216) 421-3060

CITY: **Cleveland**　AREA: **Near East Side**
ATMOSPHERE: **Relaxed**　COST: $$$$$

ADDRESS: 12101 Mayfield Rd.
HOURS: Mon–Thu 7 a.m.–7 p.m., Fri & Sat 7 a.m.–10 p.m., Sun 7 a.m.–6 p.m.
RESERVATIONS: **PAYMENT:** MC, VS, AX, checks
BAR: None **TAKEOUT:** Yes **SMOKING:** Smoke-Free
ACCESS: ♿ Full access

It's a bakery. It's a cafe. It's Presti's. New and improved, this Presti's, just one door down from the old one, is a place to sit as well as shop. Claudia Presti Di Bartolo and Sheila Presti Gentile, who took over the business from their father, oversaw a two-year renovation project that transformed the long-empty storefront adjacent to the old bakery from an eyesore to a showpiece. Working with local architect Steven Bucchieri, who has made it his personal mission to preserve the historical integrity of the Murray Hill neighborhood, they have managed to strike a balance between tradition and innovation. The result is something timeless and wonderful. The aim was to save as much of the original building and fittings as possible. Behind the counter is a large mahogany cabinet that was once used to display and stack clothes, back when this was Two Sisters Variety Store. The glass doors were removed, the finish restored, and new mahogany shelves were built to show off the bread. The pressed-tin ceiling, much of which had been destroyed by years of leaking and neglect, was pieced together like a patchwork quilt, and old-fashioned schoolhouse-style lights hang down from it. The wood paneling on the walls was left in place but given a fresh coat of paint. Water damage had marred the maple floor beyond repair, but it was replaced with a new one. Tables now sit in the big windows, perfect for watching the street life that is a distinctive feature of this community. Small glass- and marble-topped tables with wrought-iron and bentwood chairs seat about 70, and in good weather tables appear outside on the sidewalk, European-style. The mix of clientele, from the neighborhood and beyond, reinforces this blend of Old World and new. Consider this grouping spotted one afternoon: at one table a mom with two kids out for a treat orders dishes of spumoni with a cookie, while she chooses coffee and cannoli; youngish arty and college types—their membership in these groups suggested by their affinity for tattoos, piercings, black clothes, and backpacks—fill the window seats and talk with animation and intensity; a lone middle-aged woman in a back corner enjoys a book and a cappuccino; and at another table a large elderly man, his pants held up over his ample belly by suspenders, a 1940s-style felt fedora on his head, reads an Italian-language newspaper while he sips his espresso.

This is an ideal spot for meeting friends, hanging out, catching up, and taking time to enjoy good talk and good eats. Come for breakfast, lunch, a light dinner, and anything in between. There's a soup each day, salads, pasta, sandwiches, pizza by the piece, bruschetta (bread topped with slices of fresh-grilled tomatoes and melted cheese), and meat, vegetable, or spinach-and-cheese stromboli, and spinach or pepperoni bread. The glass-fronted cases of pastry are a feast for the eyes, and the effect is to make any thought of calorie control seem like yesterday's dumb idea. All things good, sweet, and Italian are to be found here (for a more detailed description see the listing for Presti's in the market section of this chapter). Since there's a real shortage of parking around here, consider walking, even if you live a few miles away or have to leave your car somewhere in Cleveland Heights or University Circle. The exercise will make you feel much better about all the cookies and cakes you will feel compelled to consume.

Ristorante Di Gianni
☎ **(330) 678-1931**

CITY: **Kent**   AREA: **Farther South**
ATMOSPHERE: **Casual**   COST: **$$$**$$

ADDRESS: 4624 SR 43
HOURS: Tue–Sat 5–9 p.m. **RESERVATIONS:** Taken, Always suggested **PAYMENT:** MC, VS, AX
BAR: None **TAKEOUT:** No **SMOKING:** Smoking section **ACCESS:** ♿ Limited

I had to work hard to find Judy and Gianni Filippone's restaurant. It's far off the "eaten" path, in a small house by the side of a road that's called S. Water Street at one end and State Route 43 at the other, in a small town just outside the Kent city limits. But I was highly motivated by a Cleveland Ethnic Eats reader's recommendation. He had told me that Gianni's serves incredibly good, authentic Italian cuisine that reminded him and his wife of meals eaten in Italy. And then there was this entrancing detail in his e-mail. "Gianni's reaches its zenith in late summer. He grows his own basil and salad greens in back of the restaurant. The pesto is often made fresh the same day." In August, the response to my question, "Anything in the salad from out back?" was "Everything but the tomatoes. We grow our own but they're not quite ready yet." A passion for freshness and quality characterizes the Old World approach to good eating that sets the tone here. Only the freshest vegetables and herbs are used and the kitchen prefers locally raised meat and poultry. Everything—from minestrone soup to meat sauce—is prepared from scratch and to order. The Filippiones cook together on a five-burner stove. There's just one oven in the kitchen and no microwave or fryer. The short menu is a log of simple dishes that are well made. Chicken and veal come al marsala (in red wine); al vinco (white wine); alla parmigiana; and alla milanese (breaded with lemon). Pasta can be had with olive oil, garlic, and hot peppers; olive oil, garlic, and anchovies; and marinara.

Linguine con le cozze features mussels, and linguine con gamberoni has shrimp. Cod and trout are served baked in a sauce of white wine and herbs. Scotto filleto is a strip steak sauteed in Burgundy.

In America, food like this usually comes with a hefty price tag and an upscale atmosphere that makes ordinary people feel underdressed and out of place. Not here. The relaxed ambience and leisurely pacing are very much as they would be in a country trattoria in the Aosta Valley, east of Milan, where Gianni grew up, and the prices are reasonable. It's a lace-curtained oasis of European charm in a place where fast-food chains abound, and it welcomes children but caters to adults. Each table has a white cloth and fresh flowers. Most tables are for two or four, but large groups are easily accommodated by pushing tables together.

The restaurant does no advertising. It doesn't need to because its reputation travels by word of mouth, and people have been finding their way here, just like I did, since 1987. Judy says they have many longtime regulars, including a couple who come three times a week because he's Italian and his wife doesn't cook. It's always best to make a reservation—not only is seating limited, but if nobody's expected after 8 p.m. and no one's left in the dining room, they close early. They're happy to host private parties on site during nonbusiness hours. Plenty of parking in a lot that wraps around the restaurant. The converted house is not wheelchair friendly and handicapped guests should be aware that there are a couple of very small steps at the entrance.

Ristorante Giovanni's
☎ **(216) 831-8625**

CITY: **Beachwood**   AREA: **East Side**
ATMOSPHERE: **Formal**   COST: **$$$$$**

ADDRESS: 25550 Chagrin Blvd.
HOURS: Lunch Mon–Fri 11:30 a.m.–2:30 p.m.; Dinner Mon–Fri 5:30–9:30 p.m. (lounge open

MEDITERRANEAN

between lunch & dinner), Sat 5:30–10:30 p.m.; closed Sun **RESERVATIONS:** Taken, recommended **PAYMENT:** MC, VS, AX, DIS **BAR:** Beer, wine, liquor **TAKEOUT:** Yes **SMOKING:** Smoking section **ACCESS:** ♿ Full access *Not recommended for children

Established in 1976, Giovanni's specializes in fine northern Italian cuisine and has earned a reputation as one of Northeast Ohio's best restaurants. The wall of the lobby is peppered with awards: the Chefs of America named it one of the nation's finest, *Cleveland Magazine* gave it Silver Spoons for both best Italian and best service, the American Automobile Association honored it with four diamonds for exceptional cuisine and service, and *Wine Spectator* called its wine list one of the most outstanding in the world. Located in a stark, modern concrete office building that gives no hint of the plush and sparkling elegance inside, this is a place to enjoy leisurely, sumptuous five-course meals, an appropriate setting for celebrations and special occasions. The dining area is roomy, seating about 90, and the appointments are luxurious; wood gleams, linens are crisp, the copper-and-brass espresso machine is polished to a high shine, and champagne buckets are ready and waiting. The menu features traditional cuisine prepared with a contemporary sensibility: river mussels in roasted tomato broth, fusilli pasta with braised veal, swordfish and calamari diavolo, or a Parmesan-crusted veal chop with tomato concasse.

This restaurant began life as a very tiny eatery with cosmopolitan big-city panache. It functioned primarily as a take-out place, and a very popular one, judging by the size of the crowds that regularly lined up at the counter to collect their orders of Agostino ('Stino) Iacullo's Neapolitan specialties. But the original eight-table space has been expanded, and now there's seating for 50. Whether you choose to take out or eat there, it's an opportunity to sample the fresh, flavorful cuisine of southern Italy: dishes like spaghetti al fumo del Vesuvio (featuring a tomato sauce lightly smoothed with cream and studded with smoked bacon and onions); penne all' Arrabiata (tube-shaped pasta in a spicy tomato sauce); or gnocchi alla Napoletana (hand-rolled potato dumplings baked with mozzarella, ricotta, and Parmigiano cheese). Patrons get so into the food that the servers even have some special stuff on hand for spot-cleaning olive oil and tomato sauce from shirtfronts and cuffs. Cappuccino and espresso are available, as well as Italian desserts like tiramisu and cannoli. Toddlers are as comfortable here as their well-dressed parents, and although it's literally elbow to elbow, with knees touching under the table, everyone seems to manage to make themselves at home. This is, however, probably not the best choice for groups larger than eight. For bigger gatherings, you can always order a full pan of lasagna alla meridionale 24 hours in advance and serve it at home.

'Stino da Napoli
☎ (440) 331-3944
CITY: **Rocky River**   AREA: **West Side**
ATMOSPHERE: **Casual**   COST: $$$$$

ADDRESS: 19070 Detroit Rd.
HOURS: Tue–Fri 5–9:30 p.m., Sat noon–10 p.m., Sun–Mon closed **RESERVATIONS:** Taken, recommended **PAYMENT:** Checks **BAR:** Beer, wine **TAKEOUT:** Yes **SMOKING:** Smoke-free **ACCESS:** ♿ Full access

Trattoria Roman Gardens
☎ (216) 421-2700
CITY: **Cleveland**   AREA: **Near East Side**
ATMOSPHERE: **Casual**   COST: $$$$$

ADDRESS: 12207 Mayfield Rd.
HOURS: Sun–Thu 11:30 a.m.–9:00 p.m., Fri–Sat 11:30 a.m.–11 p.m. **RESERVATIONS:** Taken, recommended **PAYMENT:** MC, VS, AX **BAR:** Beer, wine, liquor **TAKEOUT:** Yes **SMOKING:** Smoking section **ACCESS:** ♿ Limited

A host will seat you, and shortly thereafter you'll be presented with a basket of fresh, crusty Italian bread. The menu features such classic entrees as veal Marsala, chicken piccata, lamb chops Calabrian, cavatelli, ravioli, and gnocchi. There are also pan pizzas and a fair number of choices for vegetarians. Sauces are homemade, as are all the pastas except for the linguine, which is imported from Italy. Cappuccino and espresso are available. The decor is simple but sophisticated: black-and-white checkerboard floor tiles, white walls, white table linens, wood accents, muted lighting, and potted plants. Unspoken convention keeps attire to the casual side of dressy, the ambience is subdued, and the impression is that this would be a good spot for a romantic dinner. At lunchtime, the restaurant attracts businesspeople and hospital staff from University Circle, and the atmosphere is a bit louder and livelier. Although there's a nonsmoking section, most of the tables are in a single room, and the separation is not really effective. The bar in front has a few additional tables where food is also served. A basement room, which can be reserved, is ideal for private parties and meetings. If you're not already familiar with the place and its location, beware—there seems to be a bit of an identity crisis going on here. On one exterior wall, the restaurant bills itself as Trattoria on the Hill. The front window, however, flashes the name Trattoria Roman Gardens. I guess you just can't believe everything you read. The restaurant has its own parking lot around back.

Tuscany
☎ (216) 464-6220

CITY: **Woodmere Village**   AREA: **East Side**
ATMOSPHERE: **Casual**   COST: $$$$$

ADDRESS: 28601 Chagrin Blvd.
HOURS: Mon–Sat: Breakfast 8:30 a.m.–11:30 a.m.; Lunch 11:30 a.m.–5 p.m.; Dinner 5–10 p.m.; closed Sun RESERVATIONS: Not taken PAYMENT: MC, VS, AX, DIS, checks

BAR: Beer, wine TAKEOUT: Yes SMOKING: Smoke-free ACCESS: ♿ Full access

Like the Eton Collection shopping center where it is located, this place radiates trendiness. Everything is chic, from the moms who wheel their babies in strollers directly up to the tables and the dapper, silk-tied business types who do lunch here, to the requisite black-and-white decor. There are only 16 close-together tables to seat the regional-Italian food lovers who flock here. Pasta is made on the premises, and pizzas are baked in a brick oven. Lunch and dinner menus feature a large selection of traditional chicken, veal, and pasta dishes, and soups, salads, and desserts. Breakfast is self-serve—muffins, bagels, and danish only. Tuscany also does catering and is as much a gourmet grocery and bakery as a trattoria. (See their market listing in this chapter for more information.)

Vaccaro's Trattoria
☎ (330) 666-6158

CITY: **Bath**   AREA: **Farther South**
ATMOSPHERE: **Casual**   COST: $$$$$

ADDRESS: 1000 Ghent Rd.
HOURS: Mon–Thu 11 a.m.–9:30 p.m., Friday 11 a.m.–11 p.m., Sat noon–11 p.m., Sun closed
RESERVATIONS: Taken, recommended
PAYMENT: MC, VS, AX, DIS BAR: Beer, wine, liquor
TAKEOUT: Yes SMOKING: Smoke-free
ACCESS: ♿ Full access

The minute you walk in, a large photo of Great-grandma Vaccaro greets you. Scattered on the walls are photos of the "our trip to Italy" variety. The front of the menu features a mom-dad-and-the-kids-in-chef-hats photo that's captioned "From our family to yours!" And on the back of the menu, the Vaccaros include a personal *grazie* for dining with them. Together, these are a tip-off that this is a family-run place that caters to families. In fact, I saw many three-generation groups dining together on a weekend evening, as well as

MEDITERRANEAN

couples young, older, and in between. Though the food is elegantly prepared and served and the atmosphere is classy, children are welcome to draw on the white butcher paper that tops the cloth-covered tables, and neither guests nor staff seem uncomfortable when the kids do creative things with spaghetti. The close-together tables mean there's not much privacy, and it's actually amazing how skillfully the white-aproned servers make their way through, but rather than feel crowded it feels friendly, a big, boisterous party where everyone is welcome. Newly arrived guests are quickly served a basket of salted, crusty rolls redolent of garlic and accompanied by herbed olive oil. The food is festive, too—edible artwork that is as colorful and dramatic as it is appetizing. The menu features primarily pasta, veal, chicken, and seafood dishes. Some of the interesting selections include mussels in white wine broth; wedding soup; Sicilian citrus salad made with baby greens, oranges, olives, and mozzarella; Tuscan scallops in lemon wine sauce; osso bucco (veal shanks and root vegetables herbed and braised); spinach tortellini in a creamy tomato basil sauce; and farfalle (bowtie pasta) with broccoli. There are also pizzas with a large selection of toppings; meatballs made with ground turkey rather than beef; risotto, polenta, and potato gnocchi; and some more contemporary-style entrees such as black bean ravioli; feta-stuffed eggplant; and veal portabella. Be forewarned—some of the appetizers are as big as entrees. Desserts, which I can only describe as a carnival on a plate, are made on the premises and are a blend of traditional Italian favorites and some creative variations: tiramisu; warm bread pudding; and cannoli plus pizza fritta (fried dough with sugar, caramel, and chocolate); semifreddo (layers of custard and sponge cake with chocolate sauce); what they call an "Italian creamsicle," made with vanilla ice cream and oranges; and exclusive gelato flavors from Italy. The selection of beers is outstanding, including the unusual along with the predictable: Peroni and Moretti, which are Italian brews, Corsendok from Belgium, Younger's Tartan, and Newcastle Brown Ale. Vaccaro's is a *Wine Spectator* award winner; the wine list offers mostly Italian labels plus some French, Australian, and popular American vintages, with 22 different glass wine pours. There are two dining rooms, which can easily accommodate large groups, done up in shades of grey, white, and mauve with mahogany accents, and a 10-stool bar in the middle, all together seating about 150. The Vaccaros periodically host wine events that include a six-to-eight-course Italian feast. They also run a full catering service with its own phone number: (330) 990-6158. The restaurant, in a newly built shopping plaza, is visible from I-77 and is easily accessed via the Ghent Road exit, exit #138.

Valerio's Ristorante Cafe & Bar
☎ (216) 421-8049

CITY: **Cleveland**   AREA: **Near East Side**
ATMOSPHERE: **Casual**   COST: **$$$$$**

ADDRESS: 11919 Mayfield Rd.
HOURS: Dinner only, Tue–Sun 5:30–late; As long as people are there who want to eat, Valerio's kitchen is open. RESERVATIONS: Taken, required Fri, Sat PAYMENT: MC, VS, AX, checks BAR: Beer, wine, liquor TAKEOUT: No SMOKING: Smoke-free ACCESS: ♿ Limited

Valerio Iorio, trained at the Culinary School of Florence in Italy, where he was born and raised, is more than the owner of this restaurant, more than the chef. He is the quintessential host, devoted to making sure all the guests in this very small establishment (only 36 seats) are comfortable, well fed, and enjoying themselves. That's why his hours read "til late": he won't close as long as someone wants to eat. He likes to emerge from the kitchen and go table to table, meeting his customers and finding out for himself if they're happy. The sense of being a guest in his home is reinforced by his staff. There's none of the typical restaurant pecking order among employees, and you can't tell the maitre d' from the busboy. Everyone, it seems, takes orders, brings bread, refills water glasses, serves food, wishes you "Buon apetito," stops by to ask if you need anything, and clears tables. I overheard one server teaching a child a few words of Italian, and another jokingly chiding a customer for not cleaning their plate. The overall impression is that this group of friends has decided to give a dinner party and you've been invited. And what a dinner it will be. Valerio is a passionate, principled chef who creates unique dishes inspired by the rich-flavored, herb-scented cuisine of Tuscany, using only the freshest, top-quality ingredients, such as whole sides of genuine Provimi veal and New Zealand lamb that he cuts by hand himself, extra-virgin olive oil and balsamic vinegar, the best imported cheeses, and pasta made locally to his specifications. The presentation is elegant without being pretentious: generous portions of food look beautiful on simple white dinnerware. The decor, too, echoes that sense of elegant simplicity. The place has retained the homey look of the neighborhood tavern–type eatery it once was (there's still a cozy eight-stool bar), but tables are now dressed in crisp white linens and sparkling glassware. For those who know wines, he carries a handpicked selection of some very fine and hard-to-get vintages. For those who don't, his menu includes wine recommendations for every entree. Dinner offerings include nodino al fungo (a grilled veal chop prepared with portobello mushrooms and sun-dried tomatoes); pollo al limon (a lemon chicken in a white wine sauce); risotto; gnocchi with Gorgonzola; and frutti di mare that includes mussels, clams, shrimp, and scallops. The tiramisu dessert is not to be missed.

Mediterranean Mix

Sans Souci
☎ (216) 696-5600

CITY: **Cleveland**   AREA: **Downtown**
ATMOSPHERE: **Dressy**   COST: $$$$$

ADDRESS: Renaissance Cleveland Hotel, 24 Public Square
HOURS: Lunch Mon–Fri 11:30 a.m.–2:30 p.m.; Dinner Mon–Thu 5:30–10 p.m., Fri–Sat 5:30–11 p.m., Sun 5:30–10 p.m.; special hours for holidays **RESERVATIONS:** Taken, recommended **PAYMENT:** MC, VS, AX, DIS, checks **BAR:** Beer, wine, liquor **TAKEOUT:** No **SMOKING:** Smoking section **ACCESS:** craccess **OTHER ETHNIC SPECIALTIES:** French, Italian, Spanish, Moroccan, Greek

MEDITERRANEAN

Diners feel like pampered hotel guests here, with attentive service in an elegant yet relaxed atmosphere; a meal can feel like a short vacation. The menu, which features contemporary renditions of traditional recipes, changes often and bears the stamp of the many different national cuisines found in the Mediterranean region, including southern French, Italian, Spanish, Moroccan, and Greek. Special events throughout the year feature unique fare from each of these countries. Diners might encounter a goat cheese and eggplant terrine (the name comes from the dish in which this layered pate is prepared); chicken spiced with saffron; a sauce made of crushed fresh tomatoes, citrus, and capers; a side of roasted red-pepper couscous; or vegetables in a vermouth cream sauce. Count yourself especially lucky when the bouillabaisse is available. A selection of freshly baked breads is served with olive tapenade (a flavorful spread with the consistency of soft butter)—a meal in itself. The kitchen draws much of its inspiration from the foods of Provence, often called the "cuisine of the sun," and the decor echoes that bent. The place glows with the sunny warmth of southern

MEDITERRANEAN

France, and stunning, panoramic, hand-painted wall murals depicting flower-filled country landscapes are so vivid you can almost hear the bees buzzing. Like the French country style it emulates, it is both homey and opulent; all at once charming, comfortable, and gracious. The effect is enhanced by the plaster walls with earth-tone wash, oak floors, rough-hewn exposed beams, and large hearth accented with copper pots, bunches of dried herbs, and baskets. Yet in other areas, there's no shortage of carpeting, marble, and tapestry fabrics. All conspire to create a wonderful setting for celebrating a special event or doing business. The selection of wines is extensive, and a paneled wine room, which is also a dining area, is located at the front of the restaurant. Just a few words about the dessert cart: don't let it pass you by. The fruit tarts, chocolate confections, and other sweets taste as wonderful as they look. Hotel parking is complimentary for patrons.

Spanish

Mallorca Restaurant
☎ (216) 687-9494

CITY: **Cleveland**   AREA: **Downtown**
ATMOSPHERE: **Dressy**   COST: **$$$$$**

ADDRESS: 1390 W. 9th St.
HOURS: Lunch Mon–Sat 11:30 a.m.–3 p.m.; Dinner Mon–Thu 3–10:30 p.m., Fri & Sat 3–11:30 p.m., Sunday 1–10 p.m.
RESERVATIONS: Taken, recommended Sun-Thu, accepted only for parties of 5 or more Fri and Sat
PAYMENT: MC, VS, AX   BAR: Beer, wine, liquor
TAKEOUT: Yes   SMOKING: Smoking section
ACCESS: ♿ Full access   *Not recommended for children   OTHER ETHNIC SPECIALTIES: Portuguese

Downtown dining took on an entirely new flavor when this 150-seat restaurant opened in March 1997 in a beautifully remodeled space in the historic Warehouse District. Now you can sample classic Spanish dishes such as broiled chorizo sausage, sopa de ajo (garlic soup), paella (a mix of saffron-seasoned rice, seafood, sausage, and chicken), and flan (an egg custard dessert), as well as Portuguese specialties like baby goat in red wine sauce, roast suckling pig, and rabbit prepared with white wine and sherry. On a Saturday night there may be as many as 30 specials, and the regular menu includes a mix of veal, chicken, beef, and pork. There's also an array of seafood dishes, so popular in those regions around the Mediterranean, prepared here with a variety of traditional sauces (green, wine, garlic, and spicy tomato), and squid is done in a broth made with its own ink. Portions are huge, and entrees come with rice, vegetables, and potatoes sliced thin and fried like a chip, all served family-style. They don't stint on service either, and it's executed with artful showmanship in the best European style, where waitering is a profession, not just a job. You'll have not one waiter in black tie but a well-trained troop of six or seven organized to attend to your every need. Upon request, they will even go so far as to gather together around a table and sing "Happy Birthday" in Spanish or Portuguese.

If you order wine or anything from the bar (thus cueing staff that you consume alcoholic beverages), they will serve you a glass of Portuguese almond-flavored after-dinner liqueur, on the house. If they don't bring it and you want it, just ask. Speaking of ordering from the bar, there's an inviting 12-seater in the front room (with a TV), which also includes a dining area for smokers. The bartender mixes up pitchers of sangria (wine and fresh fruit), poured tableside with a special flourish that makes it an event. The wine list is large, with many reasonably priced bottles, and there's also a port and sherry list. At night there's a lovely view of lights twinkling on the Main Avenue Bridge from the big picture window at the back of the main dining room, which is done up in a mix of exposed white-painted brick, earth and flesh tones, and a few pieces of contemporary artwork. All is bathed in the kind of subdued lighting that makes everyone look a bit glamorous. Customers tend to dress not in their party best but well and stylishly. This is a great place for a celebration, an occasion that mixes business with pleasure, or a romantic rendezvous. There are both private and city lots nearby as well as on-street parking.

Marbella Restaurant
☎ (216) 464-9939
CITY: **Pepper Pike**   AREA: **East Side**
ATMOSPHERE: **Dressy**   COST: $$$$$

ADDRESS: 29425 Chagrin Blvd.
HOURS: Lunch Mon–Sat 11:30 a.m.–3 p.m.; Dinner Mon–Thu 3–10:30 p.m., Fri & Sat 3–11:30 p.m., Sunday 1–10 p.m.
RESERVATIONS: Taken, recommended Sun-Thu, accepted only for parties of 5 or more Fri and Sat
PAYMENT: MC, VS, AX **BAR:** Beer, wine, liquor
TAKEOUT: Yes **SMOKING:** Smoking section
ACCESS: ♿ Full access *Not recommended for children **OTHER ETHNIC SPECIALTIES:** Portuguese

This is Mallorca's sister restaurant. See above listing for details.

Viva Barcelona
☎ (440) 892-8700
CITY: **Westlake**   AREA: **West Side**
ATMOSPHERE: **Casual**   COST: $$$$$

ADDRESS: 24600 Detroit Rd.
HOURS: Mon–Thu 11:30 a.m.–10 p.m., Fri 11:30 a.m.–11 p.m., Sat 3–11 p.m., Sun 1–9 p.m.
RESERVATIONS: Taken, suggested at all times
PAYMENT: MC, VS, AX, DIS **BAR:** Beer, wine, liquor
TAKEOUT: Yes **SMOKING:** Smoking section
ACCESS: ♿ Full access

Westlake, home of numerous gastronomically dull, brand-name, cookie-cutter restaurant chains, is getting a culinary wake-up call. First there was the French invasion (see entry for Bistro Beaujolais). Now the Spanish have arrived, armed with garlic, saffron, and wine. Fernando Nuñez wanted to bring the flavors of Spain, where he was born and raised, to this little corner of Northeast Ohio, and the crowds who pack his place nightly to eat dishes that reflect regional specialties are evidence that his efforts have been enthusiastically received.

Many appetizers and entrees feature seafood and fish—extra-large shrimp, sea scallops, clams, mussels, lobster tails, salmon fillet, tilapia, and Chilean sea bass enhanced with Basque-style green sauce, garlic sauce, white or red wine sauce, or their trademark Viva Barcelona suquet, a sauce made with wine, brandy, and dried fruit. Those who prefer *carnes* (meat) have plenty to choose from too. There's medallones de solomillo al cabrales (filet mignon in cheese sauce); chuletas de cerdo con mostaza granulada (pork chops made with granulated mustard); and suprema de pollo al azafrán (chicken in saffron sauce). Or get the best of both worlds with paella Valenciana, saffron rice studded with pieces of chicken and Spanish sausage, plus shrimp, scallops, and clams and mussels in their shells. Two dinner-sized salads are intriguing: there's one made with field greens and pickled chicken (ensalada verde con pollo escabechado) and another with garlic-crusted scallops (ensalada de vieiras en costron de ajo). The daily list of specials may be longer than the menu, including game such as rabbit and quail, and Barcelona's versions of goat, veal, suckling pig, lamb shanks, and catch of the day. All main courses come with soup or salad, saffron rice, steamed vegetables, and potatoes sliced paper-thin and fried to chip-crisp perfection—served family-style. So you start with, say, chorizo salteado a la Andaluza (broiled sausage with black olives), followed by sopa Castellana (garlic soup), move on to an entree of perhaps lenguado a la nyoca con acceite de arbequina (fillet of sole with dried fruits) or solomillo de buey al oloroso (filet mignon with sherry and mushrooms), plus all those sides that are on the house, and you're likely to end up with leftovers for the next day, especially if you're trying to leave room for a dessert

MEDITERRANEAN

flan or fruit sorbet. The lunch menu is an abbreviated version of the evening's, with smaller portions and the addition of five bocadillos (sandwiches).

Although the food is the obvious draw, the service and the ambience surely are a big part of what brings people back. A veritable bevy of tuxedoed waiters and busboys are constantly at your beck and call, there to pull out your chair and place a white cloth napkin in your lap, and later to replace silverware as needed for each course, refill wine and water glasses, and transfer food from platter to plate with a deft and very professional flourish. These guys are so skilled that each can manage five large, full dinner plates, and carry away as many as (I counted) 14 empties at once. There are so many staff members available that you'll never have to wait long to get what you need. All this attention doesn't seem frenzied or overzealous. The atmosphere is relaxed, and it's a house policy that no one is ever hurried. You're made to feel important and pampered, and it's pleasant to linger . . . and linger . . . and linger, long after the meal has been eaten. This has become a bit of a problem for Nuñez and his partner, Jesus DeManuel. "Nobody wants to leave," says Nuñez. "People are so comfortable here and enjoy themselves so much that it's not uncommon for our guests to sit at the table for four hours." Perhaps another reason tables don't empty quickly is that the bar has so much to offer. According to Nuñez, they stock the area's largest selection of port wines, single malts, and tequilas, and boast a cellar of 250 different wines. The sangria, by the glass, half-pitcher, or a go-for-the-gold whole pitcher, is made, I was told, from a secret family recipe. The bar area is a handsome space dominated by an unusual wall relief with a seashore motif. There are 22 seats, 14 at the counter plus a few high tables and stools, the TV's tuned to sports, and a humidor is filled with cigars sold for your puffing pleasure. The dining area is divided into a number of smaller spaces—some by low walls, another by large folding French doors that can be left open or closed, and one small room is completely separate and private, so large groups and private parties have a number of options. It's also a great place to celebrate a birthday because the staff willingly gathers round to sing the happy-day song in full-throated Spanish. The color scheme is earthy and easy on the eye: shades of brown, taupe, and gray with wine-red accents. Lighting and decoration are very contemporary and understated, with a dash of Mediterranean style. There is dining outside on a secluded patio in good weather. The restaurant is located on the ground floor of a large, eye-catching black-and-white office building surrounded by parking spaces, off I-90, between the Clague Road and Columbia Road exits, on the north side of Detroit. A bright red-and-yellow illuminated sign close to the road makes it easy to find.

MARKETS

Greek

Athens Pastries & Imported Foods
☎ (216) 861-8149

CITY: **Cleveland**   AREA: **Near West Side**

ADDRESS: 2545 Lorain Ave.

FOOD AVAIL.: meat (fresh, frozen), fish (fresh, frozen, dried), grains, beans, flour, rice, baked goods, canned & packaged goods, spices, condiments, beverages, tea, wine, prepared frozen foods, takeout meals **HOURS:** Mon–Thu 8:30 a.m.–6:00 p.m., Fri & Sat 8 a.m.–6 p.m.; closed Sun **PAYMENT:** MC, VS **ACCESS:** ♿ Limited

Recorded Greek music is almost always playing softly in the background. Dark roasted coffee beans, spices, and golden baklava pastry dripping honey syrup give off a heady and decidedly non-Midwestern scent. The overall effect upon entering the store is to feel as though you've left Cleveland far behind. You'll find every sort of Greek delicacy imaginable here—feta cheese, many different kinds of olives, fresh phyllo dough, pastries, and spinach and meat pies, and many brands of olive oil. You'll also find toiletries imported from Greece, kitchenware, religious icons, music tapes, and Greek greeting cards. A 2003 remodeling brought more space, bright lights, wider aisles, and new merchandise. The new owner is Serbian and has added some food items from his homeland— sausage, bacon, and salami—plus a world of beers: Dutch, Czech, Jamaican, English, German, Mexican, Italian, Scotch, and of course, Greek. All the Greek specialities still dominate. On-street parking plus a lot parallel to the building.

Canton Importing Company
☎ **(330) 452-9351**
CITY: **Canton**　AREA: **Farther South**

ADDRESS: 1136 Wertz Ave. NW
FOOD AVAIL.: Meat (deli), baked goods, canned & packaged goods, spices, condiments, beverages, tea, coffee, prepared frozen foods
HOURS: Mon–Fri 9 a.m.–6 p.m., Sat 9 a.m.–5 p.m., Sun closed **PAYMENT:** MC, VS, checks **ACCESS:** ♿ Full access **OTHER ETHNIC SPECIALTIES:** Italian

Mom and Pop Regas started out in downtown Canton in 1960 in a shop that sold only Greek foods. They moved to their present location in 1972, and as the place had formerly been an Italian import store they combined the two cultures and product lines, many of which overlap anyway. Nick Regas, their son, studied to be a lawyer but found his true calling behind the counter and has been running the family business, which is both wholesale and retail, since 1994. Years ago, he explains, when his parents started out, their customers were mostly Greek and then later Italian immigrants, but now everybody wants to eat a Mediterranean diet because it's both healthy and delicious. All kinds of people come in to get things like fresh mozzarella, never-frozen phyllo dough, arborio rice, and polenta. They stock 15 different brands and types of olive oil, Italian cold cuts, pasta, Italian breads, Greek pastries, and some kitchen equipment, including espresso pots, garlic presses, pizelle makers, and an old-style rocking mincer. Cheese and olives are a specialty. There are 12 varieties of olives and four types of feta: domestic (which, I learned from Nick is made from cow's milk and hence does not have the sharp, tangy flavor of the real thing), Bulgarian, French, and Greek, which is kept in a real wood barrel in the back (only old-timers and connoisseurs can appreciate this). Some of the more unusual and interesting products to be found here are preserves made from quince, sour cherries, rose petals, and figs; wild Greek onions in brine; frozen smelts; a traditional Greek cereal, trahanas, cooked and served like Cream of Wheat; and krithr, a tiny little pasta shaped like orzo. Plenty of free parking on all sides of the blue-and-white building with the eye-catching mural on one side.

Western Fruit Basket and Beverage
☎ **(330) 376-3917**
CITY: **Akron**　AREA: **Farther South**

ADDRESS: 121 E. Market St.
FOOD AVAIL.: Produce, beans, baked goods, canned & packaged goods, spices, condiments, beverages, tea, coffee, prepared frozen foods
HOURS: Mon–Sat 9 a.m.–6 p.m.; closed Sun

MEDITERRANEAN

PAYMENT: MC, VS, DIS, checks **ACCESS:** ♿ Full Access **OTHER ETHNIC SPECIALTIES:** Many Eastern European countries

MEDITERRANEAN

This has been a family-run business since 1989. Mike Detorakis is responsible for the wine selection and the on-site state store that stocks ouzo, a licorice-flavored drink, and metaxa, a Greek brandy. Mom's in charge of the baking, turning out specialties like Greek wedding cookies, baklava, and kataife (sweet shredded wheat dough and nuts), and Dad does the customized fruit baskets. And everybody works together to keep the shelves stocked with imported grocery products like grape leaves, feta cheese, and phyllo dough, used to prepare homemade Greek entrees such as spanakopeta (spinach rolls) and tiropeta (cheese rolls), plus pastitsio (similar to lasagna), and moussaka (eggplant casserole). All of these dishes are also sold frozen and ready to bake. They also offer fresh, as distinct from cured, olives. The Detorakis family wants everyone to know that they'll always get a warm, friendly, personal welcome here, and immediate help. Since the store is across the street from the Akron Art Museum, consider making your shopping trip into a full-blown cultural outing by also stopping in there and checking out what's on display. Western Fruit is on a corner in an architecturally interesting older building. Parking available in back.

Italian

Affamato Italian Deli and Market
☎ (440) 892-1455
CITY: **Westlake**   AREA: **West Side**

ADDRESS: 30610 Detroit Ave.
FOOD AVAIL.: meat (deli), baked goods, spices, condiments, beverages, tea, coffee, takeout meals **HOURS:** Mon–Wed 10 a.m.–8 p.m.,
Thu–Fri 10 a.m.–9 p.m., Sat 10 a.m.-7 p.m., Sun closed **PAYMENT:** MC, VS, AX, DIS, checks **ACCESS:** ♿ Full access

A gourmet market and more. You can take a cooking class here, attend a wine tasting, book the place for a private party, hire them to cook for a party at your house, and order a custom-made gift basket for a very lucky someone. There's a small selection of Italian basics and specialty condiments like jarred pesto and sun-dried-tomato spread, plus a variety of prepared foods; traditional breads and desserts baked on the premises; and hand-painted pasta bowls from Italy. By their own reckoning, owners Greg Grasso and Rick Molinari offer one of the best selections of Mediterranean wines in the area, along with quality vintages from California, Chile, France, and Australia. Helpful descriptions and recommendations are posted on the racks. Imported meats and cheeses crowd the deli counter cases, with Italian varieties dominating. Along with the standards there are some less common choices—Asiago, taleggio, and ricotta salata cheeses; mortadella, ham, and porkette made by Leoncini, a family in the business of curing meats since 1918. But there are representatives of other countries too: English Stilton, Dutch Gouda, French Brie, Danish Havarti. Management has thoughtfully printed up cheese facts brochures with a wealth of helpful information. The kitchen turns out fresh sausage, made Naples style. In a stone-lined oven imported from Italy they bake traditional Italian white bread, a round Tuscan loaf, focaccia, ciabatta, Pugliese breads, and a soft Pane Abrussze. The trained pastry chef does Italian eclairs, butter cookies, cannoli, tiramisu, biscotti, and cassata cakes. The 6,000 square feet of space is colorful and pleasant, with an inviting espresso bar and cafe/restaurant in front. (For more information about the menu of sandwiches and entrees, available for eating in or taking out, see Affamato's restaurant listing earlier in this chapter).

Located in the Savannah Commons strip mall, there's ample free parking.

Alesci's of South Euclid
☎ (216) 382-5100
CITY: **South Euclid**   AREA: **East Side**

ADDRESS: 4333 Mayfield Rd.
FOOD AVAIL.: meat (deli), grains, beans, flour, baked goods, canned & packaged goods, spices, condiments, beverages, tea, coffee, wine, prepared frozen foods, takeout meals
HOURS: Mon–Sat 9 a.m.–6 p.m., Sun 9 a.m.–2 p.m. PAYMENT: MC, VS, AX, DIS, checks ACCESS: ♿ Full access

This is a 7,000-square-foot gourmet Italian food superstore. Alesci's opened in 1943 and has been at this location since 1957. The selection of prepared foods is just this side of awesome: Italian meatballs, lasagna, subs (one favorite is the "grinder," made of hard-crust Italian bread, salami, cappicola, provolone, and roasted pimientos), and more than 15 different types of pizza sold by the slice, ranging from standard pepperoni to less conventional ones like crabmeat pizza, broccoli pizza, spinach pizza, and pizza bianco (white pizza). There are more than 30 types of salads in the deli, including pasta salads and olive salads, and fresh Italian sausage is available at the deli counter too. Alesci's prepares 13 varieties of homemade pasta sauces, sold fresh and frozen by the pint or quart. They are famous for their Italian bread and also bake pepperoni bread, strawberry whipped-cream cakes, sfogliatelli, and breadsticks. Spices, grated Romano cheese, and coffee (38 kinds) are available in bulk. Many brands of olive oils and balsamic vinegar are available in either quart or gallon sizes. They also carry imported pastas, pignoli nuts, confetti candy, polenta, semolina, and couscous. Delivery service and catering are available. Nonfood items include pasta machines, pizza stones, ravioli plates, and kitchen accessories. Parking lot.

Anthony's
☎ (216) 791-0700
CITY: **Cleveland**   AREA: **Near East Side**

ADDRESS: 12018 Mayfield Rd.
FOOD AVAIL.: meat (deli), grains, beans, flour, rice, baked goods, canned & packaged goods, spices, condiments, coffee, wine, beer, prepared frozen foods, takeout meals HOURS: Mon–Thu 10 a.m.–5 p.m., Fri 10 a.m.–8 p.m., Sat 10 a.m.–7 p.m.; Sun 9 a.m.–2 p.m. PAYMENT: MC, VS, AX, DIS, checks ACCESS: ♿ Full access

When I first started shopping at this Italian food market in the heart of Little Italy in the 1970s, it was called Mayfield Italian Imports. When my husband and I lived in University Circle, with no car and little disposable income, this was where we went when we wanted to treat ourselves well. I always felt I was getting more than my money's worth in atmosphere, friendly personal service, and foods that turned our meals into Italian feasts. The name has changed, and the place has gradually become less of an Italian grocery and more of an Italian eatery. (For more information about dining options, see listing for Anthony's in the restaurant section of this chapter.)

There is still a selection of packaged pastas, canned sauces, olive oil, imported wines and beers on the shelves; the glass-fronted cases are still stocked with fresh Italian sausage, domestic and imported prosciutto, Genoa salami, mortadella, cappicola, and bocconcini (the sweet, fresh version of mozzarella cheese), big hunks of Parmesan and Romano cheese that the counterman (or woman) will grate for you, plus a large selection of other deli meats and cheeses, sliced to order, many types of olives, roasted red peppers, marinated artichoke hearts, sun-dried tomatoes, salads, and fresh pastries and cookies. There are steaming trays of meatballs, lasagna, manicotti, and pizza, all available for takeout, just as there were 25 years ago, along with a variety of subs and cold sandwiches. And

MEDITERRANEAN

it's still a real neighborhood kind of a place where a guy can walk in and expect a personal greeting. The dining area is set off from the rest of the store by wrought-iron shelves displaying imported kitchenware for sale: pasta makers, pizzelle bakers, cheese graters, and olive oil dipping sets. There are gift baskets with packaged foods and Little Italy souvenir coffee mugs, and if you're so inclined you can pick up a Mario Lanza or Louis Prima CD along with everything you need to create an antipasto platter. The catering end of the business has expanded, and there's a special menu of party trays and entrees to choose from, including chicken Marsala, cavatelli, and garlic-roasted potatoes with sausage and peppers. Whole sheet pizzas are available but must be ordered 2 to 3 days in advance. When you plan a shopping trip here, my advice is to make it a lunch stop, too, or at least leave time for a cup of espresso and a biscotti. And remember, parking is always tricky in this old and densely populated neighborhood.

Baraona's Baking Co., Inc.
☎ (216) 662-8383
CITY: **Maple Heights**   AREA: **Southeast**

ADDRESS: 15842 Libby Rd.
FOOD AVAIL.: Baked goods HOURS: Mon 8 a.m.–4 p.m., Tue–Fri 8 a.m.–5:30 p.m., Sat 8 a.m.–5 p.m., Sun 8 a.m.–1 p.m. PAYMENT: Cash only ACCESS: ⚫ Full access

Family owned and operated since 1949, Baraona's has built a solid reputation—reaching as far as Mentor and Brunswick—based on their spumoni, gelati, and lemon ice, home made the Old World way, as well as their large, beautifully decorated cakes, including cassata, for all occasions. They bake a variety of cookies that includes both Italian and other ethnic specialties like kolachies. No bread.

Colozza's Cakes & Pastries
☎ (440) 885-0453
CITY: **Parma**   AREA: **Southwest**

ADDRESS: 5880 Ridge Rd.
FOOD AVAIL.: baked goods, coffee, takeout meals HOURS: Wed–Sat 7:30 a.m.–5:30 p.m., Sun 8 a.m.–3 p.m.; closed Mon & Tue PAYMENT: MC, VS, DIS, checks ACCESS: ⚫ Full access

Because Angelo Colozza bakes every day, Clevelanders can take home some very special Italian desserts. There's Santa Lorenzo, alternating layers of puff pastry, raspberry filling, amaretto-soaked sponge cake, and whipped cream topped with shaved chocolate; three-layer glazed fruit tortes; and rum-babas. His traditional cassata cake is rum-soaked, ricotta-filled, and studded with chocolate chips and diced fruit. He also makes what he refers to as "American" cassata cake with strawberries and whipped cream; cannoli; and sfogliatelli, a sweet ricotta-filled pastry that looks like a clam shell. Colozza will decorate any of his 30 varieties of tortes (some of which he'll sell by the slice) and cakes to suit any occasion. There's a second store at 5600 Wallings Road in North Royalton; telephone (440) 230-0770, same hours.

Corbo's Dolceria
☎ (216) 421-8181
CITY: **Cleveland**   AREA: **Near East Side**

ADDRESS: 12200 Mayfield Rd.
FOOD AVAIL.: baked goods, prepared frozen foods, takeout meals HOURS: Tue–Sat 8 a.m.–6 p.m., Sun 8 a.m.–1 p.m.; closed Mon PAYMENT: MC, VS, checks ACCESS: ⚫ Full access

Family owned and operated for over 30 years, this is a landmark in Little Italy. Though every day brings in regular customers from the neighborhood, people from all over the state also stop in to buy one of their famous cassata cakes (a strawberry-and-cream-filled yellow layer cake) and cannoli. They bake Italian-style cookies, breads, and sheet pizzas as well. Spumoni (Italian ice cream) and Italian ices are available, too.

Cork & More Shoppe

☎ (330) 652-5895

CITY: **Niles** AREA: **Farther South**

ADDRESS: 1201 Youngstown-Warren Rd. (US 422)
FOOD AVAIL.: baked goods, canned & packaged goods, spices, condiments, beverages, coffee, prepared frozen foods, takeout meals
HOURS: Mon–Thu 11:30 a.m.–10 p.m., Fri–Sat 11:30 a.m.–11 p.m.; lunch Mon–Fri until 6 p.m., Sat until 4 p.m.; Sun closed **PAYMENT:** MC, VS, AX, DIS **ACCESS:** ♿ Full access

The Shoppe is really just another room in the complex of additions that has become Alberini's. Many of the most popular dishes served in the restaurant—including made-from-scratch tomato sauce, wedding soup by the quart, stuffed peppers, meatballs, and pasta dishes—are available in take-home, heat-and-eat versions here. The "halls" are also decked with pepperoni and spinach breads, quiche, pizza, a selection of freshly baked desserts, and a large and stellar array of wines. Gift baskets are a specialty, and gift certificates are available. (For more information about the restaurant, see listing for Alberini's that appears earlier in this chapter.) Ample, convenient parking.

DeVitis & Sons

☎ (330) 535-2626

CITY: **Akron** AREA: **Farther South**

ADDRESS: 560 E. Tallmadge Ave.
FOOD AVAIL.: meat (deli), produce, grains, beans, flour, rice, baked goods, canned & packaged goods, spices, condiments, beverages, tea, coffee, prepared frozen foods, takeout meals
HOURS: Mon–Fri 9 a.m.–6 p.m., Saturday 9 a.m.–6 p.m., Sunday 9 a.m.–1 p.m.
PAYMENT: MC, VS, checks **ACCESS:** ♿ Limited
OTHER ETHNIC SPECIALTIES: Greek

Robert DeVitis likes to say that "Columbus discovered America, Marco Polo discovered spaghetti, and the DeVitis family discovered a way to bring Italy (and spaghetti) to Northeast Ohio." Frank DeVitis, born in 1900, emigrated here from Italy and opened the store (which sold only produce) in 1940; it's remained a family business. But it's expanded both in size and scope, now offering a large variety of imported Italian staples, deli meats, cheeses, homemade sausage, and Italian salads and entrees in addition to top-quality fresh produce. Heat-and-eat meatballs, lasagna, veal patties, and breaded eggplant are always available, and staff estimate they prepare 300–400 sandwiches to order daily. Sausage comes regular, hot, and Sicilian-style, and to satisfy their customers' changing tastes they now make another version using turkey. Their customers are a loyal band and often know each other. According to Robert, they use the store as a meeting place, so there's a kind of sociable atmosphere. "People come in, see folks they haven't seen in a while, and it's like a reunion or a celebration."

DiStefano's Authentic Italian Foods

☎ (440) 442-7775

CITY: **Highland Heights** AREA: **East Side**

ADDRESS: 5600 Highland Rd.
FOOD AVAIL.: flour, baked goods, canned & packaged goods, spices, condiments, beverages, tea, wine, prepared frozen foods, takeout meals
HOURS: Mon–Fri 9 a.m.–8 p.m., Sat 9 a.m.–6 p.m., Sun 9 a.m.–1 p.m. **PAYMENT:** MC, VS, checks **ACCESS:** ♿ Full access

This is what most grocery stores were like just a generation ago: a family-owned, friendly neighborhood place, not too big or too small, with a regular and familiar clientele. Shoppers will find homemade (on the premises) sausage, meatballs, lasagna, and chicken cutlets prepared for takeout or heat-at-home, and freshly baked breads, pastries, biscotti, and other cookies. Their Calabrese breads are served in many fine restaurants throughout Northeast Ohio. Made-from-scratch pizzas can be ordered. There's a large selection of imported olive oils, spices, packaged pasta, imported and domestic wines, plus a few basic household items.

Dougardi's Italian Foods
☎ (330) 492-3777
CITY: **Canton**   AREA: **Farther South**

ADDRESS: 3116 Market Ave.
FOOD AVAIL.: meat (deli), baked goods, canned & packaged goods, spices, condiments, beverages, tea, coffee, prepared frozen foods, takeout meals HOURS: Mon–Fri 8 a.m.–6 p.m., Sat 8:30 a.m.–5 p.m., Sun 8:30 a.m.–1 p.m.
PAYMENT: MC, VS, DIS ACCESS: ♿ Full access

A red-white-and-green awning makes this Italian market easy to find for those who don't already know about the place. In the old days, the Dougardis lived across the street from their shop, but this is no longer much of a residential neighborhood and a busy four-lane road now runs in front of the small brick building they put up in 1920. They sell Italian salads, olives, cold cuts, and cheeses, including Calabrese salami, mascarpone (thick, rich, moist cow's milk cream cream cheese with a consistency that ranges from that of clotted or sour cream to butter), and scamorze (a hard, distinctively flavored cheese). They make their own sausages, sauces, and meatballs. Also on hand are Moretti beer, a large selection of wines, pasta (dried and frozen), spices, and jars of traditional products like peppers in sauce, lupini beans, and marinated mussels. You can get sandwiches to go here, party trays, or everything you need to put together a meal at home. Gourmet cooks like this place because the owners are willing to track down whatever special ingredients customers request.

Fragapane Bakery & Deli
☎ (440) 779-6050
CITY: **North Olmsted**   AREA: **West Side**

ADDRESS: 28625 Lorain Rd.
FOOD AVAIL.: meat (fresh, deli), baked goods, canned & packaged goods, condiments, beverages, tea, coffee, wine, prepared frozen foods, takeout meals HOURS: Tue–Thu 6 a.m.–6:30 p.m., Fri & Sat 6 a.m.–7 p.m., Sun 9 a.m.–3 p.m.; closed Mon PAYMENT: MC, VS, AX, DIS, checks ACCESS: ♿ Full access

This is a bakery, an Italian deli, and an import store. They make the usual Italian-style breads, cakes, cookies, and pastries; pans of lasagna and sheets of pizza; and frozen homemade sauces, garlic bread, sausage, and pasta. They also stock a selection of wines, sauces, peppers, and pasta from Italy. There's a large variety of non-Italian baked goods, too, from croissants to strudel. They have two other locations: in Bay Village and Middleburg Heights (see separate listings for details).

Fragapane Bakery & Deli
☎ (440) 871-6340
CITY: **Bay Village**   AREA: **West Side**

ADDRESS: 650 Dover Center Rd.
FOOD AVAIL.: meat (fresh, deli), baked goods, condiments, beverages, tea, coffee, prepared frozen foods, takeout meals HOURS: Tue–Sat 6 a.m.–6 p.m., Sun 6 a.m.–2 p.m.; closed Mon PAYMENT: MC, VS, AX, DIS, checks ACCESS: ♿ Full access

All the baking is done at the North Olmsted store and delivered fresh to this location each morning. For a description of their stock, see previous listing for Fragapane on Lorain, but be aware that the selection here is smaller.

MEDITERRANEAN

Fragapane Bakery & Deli

☎ (216) 234-1434

CITY: **Middleburg Heights**
AREA: **Southwest**

ADDRESS: 7523 Pearl Rd.
FOOD AVAIL.: Meat (fresh, deli), baked goods, canned & packaged goods, condiments, beverages, tea, coffee, prepared frozen foods
HOURS: Tue–Sat 7 a.m.–6 p.m., Sun 8 a.m.–4 p.m.; closed Mon **PAYMENT:** MC, VS, AX, DIS, checks **ACCESS:** ♿ Full access

See Bay Village store entry for details.

Gallucci Italian Food

☎ (216) 881-0045

CITY: **Cleveland**   AREA: **Near East Side**

ADDRESS: 6610 Euclid Ave.
FOOD AVAIL.: meat (fresh, frozen), grains, beans, flour, baked goods, canned & packaged goods, spices, condiments, beverages, tea, wine, prepared frozen foods, takeout meals
HOURS: Mon–Fri 8 a.m.–6 p.m., Sat 8 a.m.–5 p.m.; closed Sun **PAYMENT:** MC, VS, DIS, checks **ACCESS:** ♿ Full access

The Gallucci family has been selling Clevelanders Italian specialty foods since 1912. Current manager Ray Gallucci Jr., the third generation to be involved in this importing and retailing business, goes "shopping" in Italy every year. Because they buy directly from producers themselves, they're able to pass the cost savings on to their customers, a loyal and devoted breed. It's not uncommon for second- and third-generation customers to frequent Gallucci's, following them from the original downtown location to the newer Euclid Avenue store. The space is large, modern, and convenient, and the selection of everything Italian is huge. I've never seen so many different kinds of canned and jarred roasted red peppers in one place. Some of the pasta and olive oils are packaged so attractively that I buy them to give as gifts. Gallucci's offers customers a number of noteworthy products: a grilled artichoke that comes from Italy in a large vacuum-sealed tray; mascarpone, a thick, rich, moist cow's milk cream cheese used in traditional desserts like tiramisu; polenta prepared in a refrigerated roll; their own brand of extra virgin olive oil; and a ham from Parma, only recently allowed into this country, called Parmacotto, that is cooked instead of cured like the famous prosciutto from the same region. They have their own baker on staff who makes a very special little clamshell-shaped pastry filled with sweet ricotta cheese, called sfogliatelli. The store is often packed on Saturdays with many shoppers driving in from distant suburbs, but it's a congenial kind of crowd. You might have to take a number and wait in line at the counter if you want a hunk of Parmigiano-Reggiano, antipasto salad, or some pancetta (an herb-flavored smoked bacon). The prepared food counter offers a variety of hot and cold Italian dishes, pizza, and sandwiches. The wine department was expanded in 2002; it now features an even larger selection of imported and domestic bottles than before—many not available elsewhere in the state—and several wines imported by Gallucci's directly from Italy and France. The store has its own parking lot, and staff will even help shoppers get their purchases packed into the car. Their website, www.tasteitaly.com, offers online shopping, recipes, party tray descriptions and prices, the lunch menu, and a chance to sign up for the monthly newsletter so you can find out about new products and special offers.

Giganti's Imported Foods

☎ (440) 546-4455

CITY: **Broadview Heights**   AREA: **Southeast**

ADDRESS: 9200 Broadview Rd.
FOOD AVAIL.: meat (fresh, deli), grains, beans, flour, baked goods, canned & packaged goods, spices, condiments, wine, takeout meals
HOURS: Mon–Thu 9 a.m.–6 p.m., Fri & Sat 8 a.m.–6 p.m., Sun 9 a.m.–1:30 p.m.

MEDITERRANEAN

PAYMENT: MC, VS, AX, DIS, checks **ACCESS:** ♿ Full access

In September 1996 the old Giganti's on Broadway, in Maple Heights, closed, and in March 1997, a new and better Giganti's opened in The Center, a new retail complex. The Giganti family continues to bake bread as well as Italian-style pastries seven days a week. They've added a deli counter in the middle of the store and feature, as they always have, a very large selection of olive oils and vinegars. The shelves are filled with a variety of canned imports, including tuna, sardines, olives, and peppers. They have coffee from Italy, too. Specialty takeout items available daily include Italian subs, cavatelli, rigatoni, stuffed mushrooms, and marinated artichokes. They will gladly prepare party trays and order spices in bulk.

Giovanni's Meats & Deli
☎ (440) 442-8440
CITY: **Lyndhurst**   AREA: **East Side**

ADDRESS: 5716 Mayfield Rd.
FOOD AVAIL.: meat (fresh, deli, frozen), fish (fresh, frozen), canned & packaged goods, spices, condiments, beverages, tea, coffee, takeout meals **HOURS:** Mon, Tue, Thu & Fri 9 a.m.–6 p.m., Sat 8 a.m.–6 p.m., Wed & Sun closed
PAYMENT: MC, VS, AX, DIS, checks **ACCESS:** ♿ Full access

Joseph Castrataro came from Italy, started this business in 1968, and his son John took over when Joseph retired in 1980. He's managed to keep a sense of neighborliness and European style that makes shopping here a pleasure. That leads to this riddle: How can a butcher shop be like a bar? Or why is Giovanni's like *Cheers*, of TV fame? Answer: because everybody knows your name. Once you're a regular like I am, expect to walk in the door and be greeted with a warm, friendly, and very personal hello from John (Giovanni, in Italian) and all his staff. You can chitchat about the kids and the weather if you've got the time, get good advice about how best to prepare the pork scallopini or veal brisket, and have one of the guys help you carry your packages to the car. You can phone your order in, just like in the good old days gone by, and it will be ready for pickup when you arrive. You may have to take a number on Saturdays and before holidays because this market is a popular stop for those who care about what they put on the table. I buy all my meat and poultry here—not just Italian specialties—because once I tasted the fresh Amish-raised chickens, milk-fed veal, Black Angus beef, and spring lamb John stocks, I was no longer willing to eat the stuff they wrap in plastic and keep on the shelves of the supermarket. But it is a great source of things Italian. They're known for their fresh, homemade sausage (hot and mild), but many customers—the older, the old-fashioned, and the culinarily intrepid—prefer to prepare their own, and it's not unusual to wait in line behind someone requesting 50 pounds of ground pork and a quantity of sausage casings. John carries fresh pasta, frozen homemade meatballs and sauce, frozen pizza dough, a variety of olives, mortadella, Genoa salami, prosciutto, and pancetta. There's a good selection of cheeses imported from Italy, including some uncommon and delicious ones made from sheep's milk, and they'll grind Romano and Parmesan to order. These are also mounds of fresh ricotta. Floor-to-ceiling shelves—and all available floor space—are filled with imported olive oil, wines, tomato products, dried pasta, spices and herbs, breadcrumbs, cornmeal for polenta, canned products like tuna in olive oil, caponata, marinated artichoke hearts, and roasted red peppers, espresso, and household essentials (if you're a make-it-from-scratch type) like meat grinders, tomato strainers, and pizelle irons. Party trays and custom cutting are available. The shop is located in a little strip beside the larger plaza known as the Greens of Lyndhurst, just east of Brainard Road, with ample parking.

Molisana Italian Foods
☎ (440) 526-4141
CITY: **Broadview Heights**   AREA: **Southwest**

ADDRESS: 8037 Broadview Rd.
FOOD AVAIL.: Meat (deli), beans, flour, baked goods, canned & packaged goods, spices, condiments, beverages, tea, coffee, wine
HOURS: Tue–Fri 9 a.m.–6 p.m., Sat 8:30 a.m.–4:30 p.m.; closed Sun & Mon
PAYMENT: MC, VS   **ACCESS:** ♿ Full access

The two women who started this business took its name (though they feminized it) from the Molise region of Italy on the Adriatic coast. They aim to offer traditional Italian foods in a modern, upscale European-style setting, complete with marble countertops, custom-made cabinetry, and ceramic floor tiles. There's a varied and interesting selection of deli meats and cheeses, which they use for made-to-order sandwiches on their freshly baked breads and authentic crusty little bread rolls called panini. They prepare gourmet pizzas and party trays. Lots of interesting imports available, including Italian wines and apertifs, and they'll assemble unusual food gift baskets, incorporating some of the kitchenware they carry. Use their cookware catalog to special order products, too. And while you're trying to decide what to buy, you can sample a cup of their espresso or cappuccino from the coffee bar.

Ninni's Bakery
☎ (330) 634-0060
CITY: **Akron**   AREA: **Farther South**

ADDRESS: 1155 East Tallmadge Ave.
FOOD AVAIL.: meat (deli), baked goods, beverages, tea, coffee, takeout meals
HOURS: Tue–Sat 8 a.m.–6 p.m., Sun 8 a.m.–2 p.m.   **PAYMENT:** MC, VS, DIS
ACCESS: ♿ Full access

MEDITERRANEAN

Anthony Ninni and his son Aric are proud that their family has been seeing to it that Akronites have cannoli since 1926. On my visit here with fellow food writer Jane Snow, we discovered that we share a passion for them. Our nonstop conversation went on pause while we gobbled up every last delicious crumb and licked the perfectly sweet ricotta cream from our fingertips. Using family recipes that came to this country at the turn of the century with Antonio Ninni, who had a bakery in New York City, they prepare Italian tortes; traditional cookies like fig bars, tadole, biscotti, pisselli, and pignoli, which are available by mail order for shipping anywhere in the country; pasticciotti, a pastry "cup" filled with custard; neopolitans; sfogliatelle; rum baba sponge cakes; and torroni nougat candy. They also bake crusty breads and are famous for their beautiful and tasty wedding cakes.

A deli counter offers Italian-style cold cuts, cold pasta, and salads. There are three tables inside where you can sip cappuccino, lick lemon ice, or dig into a piece of tiramisu. A few shelves display Italian-themed gift items, like a sign that reads "Parking for Italians Only," T-shirts, imported candies, and pretty bottles of olive oil. This isn't the original location of the family's business, but the old sign still hangs in the window. A nice place to shop or hang out with no-problem parking.

Pileggi's
☎ (330) 497-0309
CITY: **Canton**   AREA: **Farther South**

ADDRESS: 5808 Fulton Dr.
FOOD AVAIL.: meat (deli), canned & packaged goods, spices, condiments, takeout meals
HOURS: Mon–Fri 11 a.m.–7:30 p.m., Sat 11 a.m.–4 p.m., Sun closed   **PAYMENT:** MC, VS
ACCESS: ♿ Full access

This Italian deli has a long track record in the area. The business's roots go back to the New York of the 1930s. Silvio

Pileggi's grandfather and father had on olive oil importing business in Brooklyn, and Ohio was on their delivery route. Silvio decided to set up shop out here permanently, and his homemade Italian foods and imported specialties have earned him local renown. He stocks Italian cold cuts like prosciutto, soppressata, pancetta, capicolla, and mortadella; cheeses; pasta; olive oil, of course; olives; and vegetable salads like marinated mushrooms, artichoke hearts, and roasted red peppers. The store's list of prepared foods available for catering or carryout (as well as eat-in) says, "Let us do the cooking for you!" Pileggi's sauces are sold by the quart. (For more information about the prepared foods available, see listing for Pileggi's in the restaurant section of this chapter.)

Presti Bakery
☎ (216) 421-3060
CITY: **Cleveland**   AREA: **Near East Side**

ADDRESS: 12111 Mayfield Rd.
FOOD AVAIL.: baked goods, beverages, tea, coffee, takeout meals **HOURS:** Mon–Thu 7 a.m.–7 p.m., Fri & Sat 7 a.m.–10 p.m., Sun 7 a.m.–6 p.m.
PAYMENT: MC, VS, AX, checks **ACCESS:** ♿ Full access .

In its third generation as a family business, Presti's is a Little Italy fixture, but the bakery relocated to bigger, better quarters next door just as we were about to slip into the new century. Much has changed along with the address, but the crusty preservative-free Italian breads for which they have long been known are still baked fresh daily. They come in many shapes—some are still molded by hand, just as they were when Grandma and Grandpa Presti were doing the baking at the original place on Coltman Road back in the 1920s. Their granddaughters, Sheila Presti Gentile and Claudia Presti Di Bartolo, run the place now, and Claudia's son Michael does much of the specialty baking, after having been trained by a New York pastry chef flown in

for the purpose, who shared some of his own traditional Italian recipes. The large new kitchen and storefront have allowed them to go beyond bread, and they now offer a mouthwatering array of cakes and pastries. There are Italian classics like tiramisu (sponge cake soaked in coffee and Marsala wine combined with sweet mascarpone cheese and chocolate); cannoli, mini-cannoli, and chocolate-dipped cannoli; a veritable army of biscotti flavored with cinnamon, almond, lemon, anise, and hazelnut; sweet ricotta–filled sfogliatelle; and cassata cake. You'll also find some more unusual but nonetheless traditional desserts: casatini (a little sponge cake with cannoli filling wrapped in almond paste); buccelati (once you taste these fig-filled cookies you'll never be happy with a Fig Newton again); pignoli (an almond paste and pine nut cookie) and pizzicotti (an almond paste and cinnamon-flavored cookie); and ricotta pie. They also prepare pizza, which is sold by the slice, pepperoni and spinach breads, focaccia, stromboli (stuffed breads) and bruschetta: all can be purchased ready to eat or for heat-and-eat at home. Gelato and Italian ices are also on the menu and my must have list. The lines get long around lunchtime on Saturday and Sunday after Mass.

Rito's Italian Bakery
☎ (440) 845-9414
CITY: **Parma**   AREA: **Southwest**

ADDRESS: 10551 W. Pleasant Valley Rd.
FOOD AVAIL.: meat (deli), fish (frozen), baked goods, canned & packaged goods, coffee, wine, prepared frozen foods, takeout meals
HOURS: Mon–Fri 8 a.m.–7 p.m., Sat 8 a.m.–6 p.m., Sun 8 a.m.–3 p.m. **PAYMENT:** MC, VS, checks **ACCESS:** ♿ Full access

A family business for 30 years, Rito's specializes in Sicilian- and Neapolitan-style foods. They are especially proud of their almond paste cookies and sfogliatelli, a cheese-filled pastry. They also prepare lasagna and eggplant Parmesan, sheet pizzas, and homemade breads and rolls. The deli counter maintains a nice selection of meats and cheeses, and sandwiches are made to order. They also carry a selection of non-Italian cookies and donuts, and bake cakes for all occasions.

The Stone Oven Bakery Cafe
☎ (216) 932-3003
CITY: **Cleveland Heights**   AREA: **East Side**

ADDRESS: 2245 Lee Rd.
FOOD AVAIL.: meat (deli), baked goods, beverages, tea, coffee, takeout meals
HOURS: Mon–Thu 7 a.m.–10 p.m., Fri & Sat 7 a.m.–11 p.m., Sun 8 a.m.–10 p.m.
PAYMENT: MC, VS, AX, checks ACCESS: ⅃ Full access

Opened in January 1995 in a converted bank, Stone Oven is the brainchild of Tatyana Rehn, a Russian immigrant and former engineer. But it's traditional Italian, not Russian breads, that she hand shapes and bakes in small batches in stone-lined ovens that give the place its name and the bread its distinctive crust. It all began when she tasted bread freshly made by an Italian chef at her brother-in-law's New York restaurant. It was, she recalls, the first good bread she'd had since leaving Russia, and she decided to perfect her own baking skills at home. At her bakery, where the only piece of kitchen machinery she'll allow is a mixer, she and her staff prepare traditional focaccia loaves, Siciliano and Pugliese bread, and others scented with rosemary or flavored with olives, cheese, or nuts. She does a large wholesale business, supplying many area restaurants and grocery stores. Italian desserts like tiramisu and biscotti are also available along with bread pudding, tea biscuits, fruit tarts, and European style cakes. There are about 10 tables in this spacious cafe, plus more outside in good weather where you can enjoy homemade soups, salads, sandwiches, or a piece of gourmet pizza, as well as espresso,

cappuccino, and dessert. On-street parking and additional parking in a city lot at the back.

Tuscany Gourmet Foods
☎ (216) 464-6220
CITY: **Woodmere Village**   AREA: **East Side**

ADDRESS: 28601 Chagrin Blvd.
FOOD AVAIL.: meat (fresh, deli, dried), fish (fresh), grains, beans, flour, rice, baked goods, canned & packaged goods, spices, condiments, beverages, tea, coffee, wine, prepared frozen foods, takeout meals HOURS: Mon–Sat 9:30 a.m.–10 p.m.
PAYMENT: MC, VS, AX, DIS, checks ACCESS: ⅃ Full access

Located in the upscale Eton Collection shopping center, this is both a sophisticated gourmet shop and a small, urbane cafe. Whether you're sitting down or stocking up, this place is all about eating, and food is even used to decorate. Salted hams, dried peppers, and strands of garlic hang over sleek glass cases filled with a huge variety of pasta and vegetable salads, take-home veal and chicken entrees, and hunks of prosciutto, mortadella, and Genoa salami. Another case displays a large and mouthwatering array of traditional pastries, cakes, and cookies. Fresh breads are stacked on shelves suspended from the ceiling. The food looks so tempting you might decide to just buy all you need for a meal ready made. But if you still are inspired to cook, there's an extensive selection of imported Italian flavored vinegars, olive oils, sauces, and pasta, plus candies, tins of biscuits, and bottled waters. Staff will assemble gift baskets.

Chapter 4

EUROPE EAST OF THE DANUBE

Europe east of the Danube River includes newly emerging and re-emerging nations, groups engaged in fierce struggles to redefine both their borders and their identities. Some of the countries whose names I learned in grade school no longer exist, and places I never knew existed, long lost in the no-man's-land of the Soviet bloc, now proclaim themselves nations. So it is problematical even to begin with a simple list of countries whose heritage is reflected in this chapter. Perhaps it is more accurate to focus on the people rather than the places, for it is through their lives that traditions endure. Czech, Slovak, Lithuanian, Croatian, Polish, Slovenian, Serb, Hungarian, Byelorussian, and Ukrainian immigrants all left the land they knew for a new start in Cleveland, transplanting their cultural and food traditions in the process.

A local newspaper editorial written in 1851 urged immigrants to immediately become "Americanized" by "casting off" their European "skins." It was advice few could really follow, needing that sense of national identity to see them through the hardships of being strangers in a strange land, often engaged in grueling, mind-numbing labor. Most stuck close to their own kind, finding comfort and protection in the proximity of their countrymen.

This was especially true for those of Eastern European descent, and they formed distinct ethnic corridors throughout the city, with nationality neighborhoods growing around the various industries and factories where the men earned their hourly wage.

As the century came to an end, each of the various Slavic groups had formed its own self-help societies, social clubs, schools, and religious congregations based on ethnic affiliations. Singing societies, sports clubs, and dance groups created a sense of solidarity that has endured, even as following generations left the old neighborhoods, moved to the suburbs, and became fully assimilated into an American lifestyle.

These are heritages difficult for an outsider to fully understand, and I admit my shortcomings here. There are at least 12 different so-called Slavic nationality groups. "Historically, as well as in the present," explains Algis Ruksenas, executive director of Cleveland's International Services Center, "there has been a tendency to homogenize the various Eastern European peoples, to bunch them together and see them as a single entity. Immigration officials used to mistakenly log newcomers in as Russians when in fact they may have been from Poland, Lithuania, Latvia, or Estonia. Each nationality is a distinct cultural group, as different as an Italian from a Frenchman though both are from what's called Western Europe."

Czechoslovakia as a state was a modern political entity representing an affiliation of Czechs and Slovaks. Cleveland's Czech community is one of its oldest and largest. The Slovaks are a separate immigrant group, and in the early 1900s the Cleveland area was home to the largest number of Slovaks in the world. Poles, too, came in great numbers. The Association of Polish Women in the USA chose Cleveland as the site for their first annual convention in February 1913. In a 1930 census, 32,688 people named Poland as their country of origin.

At one time, only Hungary itself had more Hungarians than Cleveland, and we still rank fourth in this country in the number of Croatians living here. There are approximately 16,000 Lithuanians in Greater Cleveland, and they are one of the most active Lithuanian communities outside of Lithuania itself. It's hard to identify the numbers of Russians who have come here because there has always been a question about what the word actually means. Under that umbrella might be included Byelorussians, Carpatho-Russians, Great Russians, and Ukrainians. And Jews from all these Eastern European homelands formed yet another separate, distinctive subset of immigrant Americans (see Chapter 7, American Regional).

What all this really means is that, collectively, the people of Eastern Europe have had a profound effect on the development of Cleveland, significantly impacting what this city has become. Ruksenas, himself an immigrant from Lithuania, calls them "the quiet influence," for they interacted with the city from the bottom up. They were the muscle that provided the infrastructure for a growing Cleveland.

Years ago there were countless restaurants and boardinghouses all around the city where the foods beloved by these Slavic groups could be had. Now there are relatively few. But there remain a surprisingly large number of shops, bakeries, and butchers that cater to these ethnic groups—tangible evidence of their long-standing presence and deep roots in the community. Many of the stores have been run by one family for generations or have been in the same location for half a century or more. There a visitor today will encounter the timeless aroma of pickles and paprika, kielbasa and kraut. The sight of mounds of potato-filled pierogies, slices of liver sausage, and strips of flaky strudel tell a story of day-to-day life that perennially unfolds around the table. In their own way, these stores are windows looking back into the lives of all those Eastern European immigrant families. Though culturally diverse, they have always shared a taste for many of the same foods and a common style of preparing them.

Eastern and Central European cooks traditionally make hearty, filling food rich with the taste of butter, cottage cheese, and sour cream. The cuisine depends upon potatoes, cabbage, beets, mushrooms, peppers, noodles, and dumplings seasoned with dill, caraway seeds, onions, garlic, and parsley as well as paprika.

All varieties of meat and poultry are used in soups and stews laced with root vegetables. Pickling is the favored way to handle garden produce. Sausage-making is an art, and the variety is almost endless; the same could be said of their traditional pastries, cakes, and cookies, many made with fruit such as apples, cherries, and plums.

"People who have Americanized," said Ruksenas, who was seven when he arrived in Cleveland with his parents as a World War II refugee, "can recapture their heritage with a recipe, which is literally and figuratively palatable. Often that's all that remains of their cultural legacy. While I think it's terribly important to understand that the sum and substance of each of these old-world cultures is much more than sausage and sauerkraut, food is without a doubt a basic, concrete connection to one's own history, and menus hearken back to a deeper, more abstract cultural wealth."

Every Clevelander with Eastern European roots I've ever spoken with insists that nobody makes dishes as good as their own grandmother's, but nonetheless they can all be depended upon to do justice to a plateful of stuffed cabbage or a brimming bowl of goulash, no matter who prepared it. "For Eastern Europeans," explained Chris Jagelewski, whose grandparents came from Poland, "eating is a social occasion, and social occasions always include eating. When I was growing up, friends and relatives regularly gathered around the kitchen table to eat, talk, and laugh. My mother and my grandmother always had something extra ready to serve to unexpected guests. There's an old Polish housewives' saying that goes, 'If you have no leftovers, tomorrow will be a beautiful day.' I think it means that when people come together and enjoy your food, it's a good thing."

RESTAURANTS

Croatian

Dubrovnik Garden Restaurant

☎ (440) 946-3366

CITY: **Eastlake**   AREA: **Farther East**
ATMOSPHERE: **Casual**   COST: **$$$**$$

ADDRESS: 34900 Lakeshore Blvd.
HOURS: Lunch daily 11 a.m.–2:30 p.m.; Dinner daily 4:30–10 p.m.; closed between lunch & dinner **RESERVATIONS:** Taken, recommended
PAYMENT: MC, VS, AX, checks **BAR:** Beer, wine, liquor **TAKEOUT:** Yes **SMOKING:** Smoking section
ACCESS: ♿ Full access

Coming here is more than going out to eat—it's a cultural event. That's because this restaurant is located inside the American Croatian Lodge, which also houses the Croatian Heritage Museum, Library, and Gift Shop (usually open on Friday and Saturday nights, Sunday afternoons, and by appointment). The lobby, too, always has some interesting historical or craft exhibits on display. The restaurant itself feels like a private club, but all are welcome. You step up into the dining room, which has tables down the center and booths on the sides, and step down to the bar. The walls feature paintings of Croatian cities done by a local artist, as well as carved wooden plates and other pieces of folk art and craft. The back of the menu is a full-page history of the ancient seaside town of Dubrovnik. There are four traditional Croatian entrees: the Dubrovnik

Grill, which includes raznici (pork and veal kebabs) and cevapcici (a blend of beef, pork, and veal); the Croatian Dish, made with raznici, cevapcici, pork chops, and chicken; and the Chef's Specialty of sauerkraut, sausage, smoked pork chop, and bratwurst. The rest of the menu is pure Ohio, an eclectic mix of spaghetti, steak, and a dish called Chicken American. Whatever you choose to eat for your main course, try to leave room for their palacinke, a light and delicate dessert.

Czech

John's Cafe

☎ (216) 641-3671

CITY: **Cleveland**   AREA: **Near East Side**
ATMOSPHERE: **Casual**   COST: **$$**$$

ADDRESS: 3658 E. 52nd St.
HOURS: Tue–Sat 11:30 a.m.–7 p.m., Sun noon–6 p.m.; bar open later; closed Mon
RESERVATIONS: Taken, recommended
PAYMENT: Checks **BAR:** Beer, wine, liquor
TAKEOUT: Yes **SMOKING:** Smoking section
ACCESS: ♿ Full access

The unimposing two-story frame building that has housed John's for more than 20 years blends right in with the surrounding neighborhood. You won't even see it until you're right in front of it. Inside, it looks like almost any tavern; the only clues that this place has ties to the Old Country are the accent of owner George Radler, the Czech beers available at the bar (which takes up half the space), and recorded Czech music playing softly in the background. Everything looks old and well used, from the wood-paneled walls to the eight plastic-covered tables and the nine bar stools. The waitress *cum* barmaid, who's been here since 1976, says John's is the first place she ate when she came to America, and she stayed. Ordering here is simple; there's always Czech beef or liver dumpling soup, roast pork and roast duck, and one special entree each day, like ptacky (rolled beef), chicken paprikash, goulash, svickova (pickled beef), and Wiener schnitzel. I've been told by quite a few folks that the duck made with caraway seeds is just this side of heaven. The dumplings are unusual—they look like slices from a loaf of soft bread, and, like the sauerkraut, have an intriguing sweetness. Roast goose is available on request, by ordering in advance. There seem to be a lot of regulars, folks from the neighborhood who come to relax, and I've spoken with people from all over Cleveland who think of this as their own little secret find. Depending on business, the bar sometimes stays open after the kitchen closes.

Marta's
☎ (216) 731-9596
CITY: **Euclid**   AREA: **East Side**
ATMOSPHERE: **Relaxed**   COST: $$$$$

ADDRESS: 800 E. 222nd St.
HOURS: Mon–Thu 9 a.m.–9 p.m., Fri 9 a.m.–10 p.m., Sat 4–10 p.m.; closed Sun
RESERVATIONS: Taken, for parties of more than 6 only **PAYMENT:** MC, VS, AX, DIS **BAR:** Beer, wine, liquor **TAKEOUT:** Yes **SMOKING:** Smoking section
ACCESS: ♿ Limited **OTHER ETHNIC SPECIALTIES:** Polish, Hungarian, German

Located in a neighborhood of small shops and neat little houses fronted by carefully tended lawns, Marta's offers real home cooking, if your home or your ethnic roots are Bohemian. In this country just 16 years, Marta Runza calls herself a newborn American. She perfected her traditional cooking skills before emigrating from Prague, learning to cook by watching her mother, and as a young bride. The first inkling she had that she enjoyed feeding a crowd was when she prepared meals for all the workmen who helped her and her husband build a house. That experience led her to jobs in restaurant kitchens in Cleveland, including the Czech Inn, and finally to owning her own restaurant, which she runs with the help of her family. "Business has been good, knock on wood," she says. In the first weeks after the *Plain Dealer* review came out, she and her daughter Lenka served about 300 meals a day … quite a lot for a restaurant with just eight tables and 18 bar stools.

It's what they serve that makes their customers so happy: roast pork loin so tender you can cut it with a fork; tangy sauerbraten; Wiener schnitzel; crispy-on-the-outside, tender-on-the inside roast duck; beef goulash; chicken paprikash; Czech bread dumplings; and spaetzle, those little noodly drops that are good gravy's perfect mate. One story she tells is of a 94-year-old man who came in looking for kidney stew. He was quite disappointed when he discovered this dish was not on the menu, but when told that she does make liver dumpling soup, he visibly brightened and announced, "I'll be back!" And he has been, along with a host of other regulars from nearby and as far away as Bay Village and Akron. Dinner portions must be described as huge; younger children could easily share an entree. There are also a few kid-sized meals on the menu and a choice of American-style breakfasts, appetizers, salads, sandwiches, and burgers. Virtually everything they serve, including the salad dressings, the real mashed potatoes, and the strudel, is made from scratch in their own kitchen. Marta also prepares palacinka, a crepe filled with fresh fruit and topped with whipped cream; you can order it as dessert or for breakfast. There's a simple sweetness to the place, which still maintains the feel of the cozy tavern it once was, despite the lace curtains at the windows, the cloth flowers on the tables, the white paper napkins banded with burgundy paper rings, and the Czech folk music playing softly in the background. Czech beer is available. Marta's is easy to find: the place has a distinctive black-and-white diner-style exterior, with an awning. Parking in back.

EUROPE, EAST

Old Prague Restaurant
☎ (440) 967-7182

CITY: **Vermilion**   AREA: **Farther West**
ATMOSPHERE: **Dressy**   COST: $$$$$

ADDRESS: 5586 Liberty Ave.

HOURS: Jun–Oct: Mon–Fri 4–10 p.m., Sat & Sun noon–10 p.m.; Nov–Feb: Fri 4–10 p.m., Sat noon–10 p.m., Sun noon–9 p.m.; Mar–May: Wed–Fri 4–10 p.m., Sat & Sun noon–10 p.m.
RESERVATIONS: Taken, recommended on weekends PAYMENT: MC, VS, DIS BAR: Beer, wine, liquor TAKEOUT: Yes SMOKING: Smoking section ACCESS: ♿ Full access

Set in the heart of Vermilion's historic harbor district, the place looks like a European mountain chalet. It's definitely a "destination restaurant," and patrons consider it well worth the 45-minute trip from downtown Cleveland, a drive many of the area's Czech Americans make regularly. The cook is from the former Czechoslovakia, as is Vera Lich, who owns and operates the restaurant, which has been in her family for 30 years. Del Donahue has visited here, and Dick Feagler's a regular. The most popular dishes are shishki, a spicy meat-stick appetizer; roast duck with sauerkraut and dumplings; roast pork; Wiener schnitzel; chicken paprikash; Bohemian goulash; and Moravian beef, made with lean filets in a creamy sauce. It's the kind of food you keep on eating even when you know you're full. They bake all their own pastries, including melt-in-your-mouth strudel. There are also some simple American items on the menu, like steak and seafood (including fresh Lake Erie perch). There is a meatless paprikash entree option for vegetarians, plus some other vegetarian dishes. They carry wines and beers made in the Czech Republic, including the famous Pilsner Urquell. The size of the place is modest, the ambience warm and comfortable in the Old World style, with Czech crystal and folk art on display.

Al's Corner Restaurant
☎ (330) 753-7216

CITY: **Barberton**   AREA: **Farther South**
ATMOSPHERE: **Relaxed**   COST: $$$$$

ADDRESS: 545 W. Tuscarawas Ave.

HOURS: Mon–Fri 11 a.m.–2 p.m.
RESERVATIONS: Not taken PAYMENT: Checks
BAR: None TAKEOUT: Yes SMOKING: Smoke-Free
ACCESS: ♿ Full access

Barberton is a working-class town with strong Eastern European roots, so it's surprising that no local restaurant was dishing up ethnic food on a daily basis. People had such a craving for it that they begged Tim and Jeanette Eberhardt, who sold homemade sausages and fresh heat-'n-eat cabbage rolls at their butcher shop, to start offering hot lunches. (For more information about the butcher shop, see listing for Al's Quality Market in the market section of this chapter). Jeanette heeded the call and decided to open a restaurant, but her mantra is "Keep It Simple." She makes only five different entrees, and serves them on disposable plates that customers carry to the tables themselves. Here "simple" also means delicious. There's chicken paprikash with fluffy, melt-in-your mouth dumplings that are also paired up with cabbage; stuffed cabbage rolls with a dense meat filling that you can order with a side of real mashed potatoes; potato and cheese pierogies sauteed in butter with onions; and Slovenian and Hungarian sausages, made by the Eberhardts themselves, with sauerkraut. And if that doesn't leave you feeling full, they make their own strudel and cheesecake. The restaurant is located in a building Tim already owned, a few doors away from the butcher shop. He and his father did the remodeling themselves, leaving the old tin ceiling intact, and re-creating the look of a '50s luncheonette, using a counter and red swivel stools from an old Woolworth's store and booths from a long-gone restaurant on Portage Lake. The interior is painted a sunny yellow. At the end of July when I visited they still hadn't put a sign up out front, but that didn't seem to keep the hungry customers from finding them. The midweek lunch line was out the door, and Jeanette told me that the day before she'd served 144 meals in three hours. Not bad for a little place that doesn't even have a phone. (If you must reach the restaurant, use the number for the butcher shop, 330-753-7216, and Tim will walk over there the first chance he gets to deliver the message. Likewise, although credit cards are not accepted at the restaurant, in a pinch, or for very large orders, Jeanette will run over to the butcher shop and use the machine there.) Apparently there was a need—or should I say an appetite—for a place like this, and Jeanette's happy to serve up a hearty, home-style solution.

Marie's Restaurant
☎ (216) 361-1816

CITY: **Cleveland**   AREA: **Near East Side**
ATMOSPHERE: **Casual**   COST: $$$$$

ADDRESS: 4502 St. Clair Ave.
HOURS: Mon–Sat 11 a.m.–9 p.m.; closed Sun
RESERVATIONS: Taken, recommended
PAYMENT: Checks **BAR:** Beer, wine, liquor
TAKEOUT: Yes **SMOKING:** Smoking section
ACCESS: ♿ Full access **OTHER ETHNIC SPECIALTIES:** Croatian

Marie's is definitely the sort of place you'd have to know about before choosing it. A storefront amidst mostly commercial buildings, it offers little to attract a passerby (the area would never be mistaken for a restaurant row). But once you do know about it, there's every reason to get yourself there because of the made-from-scratch food Mila Sabljic prepares each day. Born and raised in the former Yugoslavia, Mila makes stuffed cabbage, chicken paprikash, stuffed peppers, beef goulash, schnitzel, and dumplings the Old World way. She also prepares cevapi (a grilled Croatian sausage), and if you call a few days in advance she'll make roast lamb

or pork for a large group. The effort here is on the food and not the atmosphere. There are two small rooms; the front section handles the takeout business. The rooms have high, old-fashioned ceilings of pressed tin, wood paneling, and fresh carpeting. Tables wear white cloths. One patron described the place as 15 degrees shy of comfortable but nonetheless a good place to eat, and regulars call it warm and welcoming. I'd have to agree, and so would my three sons, who found the hefty portions and informal, friendly atmosphere much to their liking. The prices make it possible for a family like mine to eat well without having to take out a second mortgage on the house. The place is often busy at lunch with a downtown business crowd, but the dinner hour seems to draw fewer people, mostly folks from the neighborhood.

New Era Cafe
☎ (330) 784-0087

CITY: **Akron**   AREA: **Farther South**
ATMOSPHERE: **Relaxed**   COST: $$$$$

ADDRESS: 10 Massillon Rd.
HOURS: Mon–Thu 10 a.m.–9 p.m., Fri & Sat 7 a.m.–9 p.m.; closed Sun **RESERVATIONS:** Not taken **PAYMENT:** Cash only **BAR:** Beer, wine, liquor **TAKEOUT:** Yes **SMOKING:** Smoking section
ACCESS: ♿ Full access

This homey old tavern has been in operation since 1937. These days Mary Lekic is in charge, along with her husband Milos, aka Mitch, who mans the bar, and her mother, Lucija Strebick, who cooks everything herself, from scratch, six days a week, no small accomplishment for a woman in her seventies. She's been doing it for almost 40 years. Her cousin, who was the restaurant and bar's original owner, brought her over from the former Yugoslavia to help in the kitchen because she'd heard that Lucija was a really hard worker. That's an understatement. I overheard this small, grey-haired dynamo, who still stretches her strudel dough by hand daily (no premade sheets of filo dough allowed here), tell a customer that she was just beginning to feel her age. So she goes home for a few hours between the lunch and dinner hours to give her tired legs a little rest. The rest of the time she has plenty to do. There's chicken paprikash and dumplings to make daily; the dinner includes a side dish and a piece of her strudel at a steal of a price, with a smaller portion at an even lower price for kids. The meat is so fall-off-the-bone tender that the only thing you need a knife for is to push it onto the fork. Her version, however, is a dish best eaten with a spoon, in my opinion, so you can scoop up all the good paprika-red gravy and onions, too. The paprikash and the strudel, served warm, are the only obviously ethnic item on the regular menu. The rest is standard bar food and Ohio tavern fare, but Mrs. Strebick, who is originally from a region near the Adriatic Sea, has her own distinctive way of preparing things like chicken noodle, potato, vegetable, or bean soup; pork chops; and meatloaf. She also proclaims with great pride that there's no microwave in her kitchen. Specials that change daily, listed on the board behind the bar, give her a chance to show off her heritage in the form of entrees like stuffed cabbage, stuffed peppers, ham and cabbage, or chicken livers. Her soups are so popular that they're available by the quart for carryout, and whole and half sizes of her strudel can be ordered in advance.

The cafe is a combination bar and dining room, brighter than such establishments usually are, due to some glass block windows, and people are as likely to stop by for a beer as a meal. The long wooden counter is lined with the kind of '50s-style round, Naugahyde-and-chrome stools I loved as a kid, and a television on the wall behind it murmurs scores and news. Tables are brown plastic, quickly cleaned by a swipe of Mary's cloth, place mats are white paper, booths are orange, and the floor tile is reminiscent of schools and hospitals. The place, though modest in appearance, is a real Akron fixture, frequented by politicians, professionals, and celebrities, as well as everybody else. T-shirts, jeans, and work-stained coveralls predominate, but nobody will look twice if you're wearing a suit. It's a stand-alone brick building surrounded by an unpaved gravel parking lot, in a not-so-pretty industrial part of town, easily accessed from I-76 or East Market Street.

Hungarian

Balaton Restaurant

☎ (216) 921-9691

CITY: **Shaker Heights** AREA: **East Side**
ATMOSPHERE: **Dressy** COST: **$$$$$**

ADDRESS: 13133 Shaker Square
HOURS: Tue–Thu 11:30 a.m.–9:30 p.m., Fri 11:30 a.m.–10:30 p.m., Sat 12:30–10:30 p.m., Sun 12:30–8:30 p.m., Mon closed; closes an hour earlier each day Jan–Mar **RESERVATIONS:** Taken, Suggested and preferred **PAYMENT:** MC, VS
BAR: Beer, wine **TAKEOUT:** Yes
SMOKING: Smoking section **ACCESS:** ♿ Full access

Originally located in an aging building on Buckeye Road, this is Cleveland's oldest Hungarian restaurant. The kitchen's gift with classic entrees like becsi-szelet (a thin boneless breaded veal cutlet), goulash, chicken paprikash with dumplings, stuffed cabbage, and palacsinta (crepes) has received high marks and praise from *Where to Eat in America, Bon Appétit, Gourmet, Cleveland Magazine, Northern Ohio Live, Ohio Magazine, The Balaton Cincinnati Enquirer,* and out-of-state newspapers as far afield as Florida, New Jersey, and Kansas. Despite the fact that the walls were fake wood and the decor consisted of little more than paper place mats, people who enjoyed good food had long raved about this place. Owner Louis Olah closed the old place down after 33 years, only to re-open a larger, lovelier version on Shaker Square in the fall of 1997 with the help of new partners George and Christina Ponti, who are proud and happy to be continuing the tradition. Olah's mother, Theresa, used to do all the cooking herself, but she's been training Erika Nagy, who was born and raised in Budapest, since 1992 and can now leave the kitchen in her more than capable hands. "But Grandma Olah," George Ponti assured me, "is still our official taster and critic."

The food is as fine as ever, most served in huge portions (half portions are available on many entrees), and for a moderate price. The menu has expanded and the new additions include a seasoned Hungarian feta cheese appetizer called korozott; lecso, a tomato-based stew made with peppers and smoked sausage (also available in a vegetarian version); a pork cutlet gypsy-style served in a paprika cream sauce with fried onion rings; skewers of cubed pork, Hungarian bacon, and sausage; tenderloin of Budapest, a fillet mignon made according to a recipe that's several hundred years old; and roast duck with red cabbage on the first Saturday of each month and on certain selected holidays. The Wood Platter for two offers a selection of different entrees and side dishes served on a beautiful hand-carved serving dish, a feast that just "begs" for a good Hungarian wine, says George Ponti, to accompany it—which Balaton now offers by the glass and the bottle. To cater to a wider variety of tastes and needs, they also offer three lighter entrees of broiled or grilled fish and chicken. Every day has its own soup and special, and non–meat eaters can make a great meal out of side orders of potato pancakes or dumplings paired with a cucumber, beet, or tomato pepper salad. It is this eater's considered opinion that the wise diner will leave room for dessert: strudel, a napolean (layers of flaky pastry alternating with custard and whipped cream), rum raisin cake, or Dobos torte (a multi-layer cake). The two spacious and nicely appointed dining areas offer more in the way of comfort and ambience than the Balaton

of before. The Pontis have re-created the look and feel of a Budapest restaurant circa 1920–1930, and they had the perfect space—the building first opened for business in 1928 as a men's clothing store. They tried to restore as much of the original structure and fittings as possible and replaced, when necessary, with reproduction-quality materials and fixtures. The ceilings are high, the floors are natural wood, and the walls are white. The curtains on the large storefront windows are made with fabric imported from Hungary. The lights, which are reminiscent of gas fixtures from the 19th century, give off a soft, pleasant glow. There are fresh flowers on the tables and soft music in the background. Parking on the Square, or follow the signs to a municipal lot.

Budapest Hungarian Cafe
☎ (216) 371-2280

CITY: **University Heights**   AREA: **East Side**
ATMOSPHERE: **Casual**   COST: $$$$$

ADDRESS: 13968 Cedar Rd.
HOURS: Daily 11 a.m.–9 p.m.
RESERVATIONS: Taken, recommended for dinner Fri, Sat PAYMENT: MC, VS BAR: Beer, wine, liquor
TAKEOUT: Yes SMOKING: Smoking section
ACCESS: ♿ Full access

Once there were numerous Hungarian restaurants in Cleveland, and plenty of boardinghouse kitchens that served up plates of paprikash, jokai (a bean soup), and goulash. But tastes changed, immigrants moved away or became Americanized, and few Hungarian eateries remained. But Jozsef Lacza, who arrived in the United States from Hungary in the 1980s, is determined to revive local interest in his native cuisine and provide us with an opportunity to sample the best that it has to offer. He opened his restaurant in the Cedar Center strip mall in 1997, and many of the dishes he prepares, using only fresh meat and vegetables he hand-picks himself at the Food Terminal six

EUROPE, EAST

mornings a week, are unavailable anywhere else in the area. They are identified on the menu as being "chef's recipes," "Hungarian recipes," or "very old Hungarian recipes," and the selection is impressive. There are four appetizers, including csekonits (a mix of vegetables, marinated scallops, shrimp, and smoked oysters) and hortobagyi husos palacsinta, which is a chicken crepe in paprikash sauce; six different soups, among them halaszle, a fish soup, and hideg barackleves, a cold peach soup; six kinds of salad; nine side dishes such as lentils and smoked meat, vegetable pate, and burgonya fozelek (creamy potatoes); and six desserts, including a crepe stuffed with walnut cream and chocolate sauce and topped with whipped cream, a rum-laden sponge cake, and turo gomboc, a sweet cheese confection. Among the more unusual of the 15 entrees—which of course include schnitzel, chicken and veal paprikash, and cabbage rolls—are roasted duck in red wine; bakonyi beef Tokany prepared with white wine, garlic, onions, peppers, and sour cream; a gypsy-style fish fillet, baked smoked salmon served with caviar, and szekely kaposzta, a Transylvanian dish of sauteed sauerkraut and stewed beef.

Regular portions are so generous that every entree can also be ordered in a smaller size (for a smaller price). There's an interesting, though small, selection of red and white Hungarian wines, available by the glass or the bottle. The dining area, which seats about 95, is a longish rectangle. The room is a miscellany of wood, wicker, wallpaper, plastic flowers, mirrors, chandeliers, scenic paintings and photos, "dressed up" wine bottles for table centerpieces, and mismatched silverware that has a quirky, Old World sort of charm all its own. Often on Friday nights there's some live music, and the kitchen will stay open later than the published hours if the "party" is going strong. Parking both in front and in the rear of the building. If you park in back, however, you must walk around to the front entrance.

Clara's European Restaurant and Bakery
☎ **(216) 481-7776**

CITY: **Cleveland**   AREA: **East Side**
ATMOSPHERE: **Relaxed**   COST: $$$$

ADDRESS: 644 E. 185 St.

HOURS: Tue–Sat 8 a.m.–8 p.m., Sun 9 a.m.–3 p.m.; Mon closed RESERVATIONS: Not taken, Except for groups of 6 or more
PAYMENT: Cash only BAR: None TAKEOUT: Yes
SMOKING: Smoke-Free ACCESS: ♿ Full access

The date was April 23, 2002, and it was only the second day this small, sweet place had been open. And I was there, happily forking up fluffy dumplings, chicken paprikash, and dobos torte. I overheard first-time customers gush with excitement over the bakery cases filled with strudel, zerbo (here presented as a layered chocolate square), and chestnut cream torte. The owner, chef, and force of nature behind this 20-seat restaurant is Clara Nemeth, a small gray-haired Hungarian lady who looks rather like Santa's wife. At 65, when most people are retiring, she decided to start a new business. "My friends told me I must be crazy, but I like to work, I've worked hard all my life," she says, "and I love to cook and bake." She's proud of the fact that everything she serves is made from scratch. Her menu features a mix of classic Hungarian dishes and American comfort standards: chicken soup, fried pork with mushroom sauce, beef goulash, chicken paprikash, stuffed cabbage and peppers, baked fish, and a salad of pickled peppers, cabbage, and mixed vegetables, plus chili, meatloaf, and roast chicken. Breakfast is straight-ahead eggs, plus croissant, muffins, and Danish pastries (she makes those too), and there are sandwiches at lunchtime. Other special and uncommon Hungarian treats on her bakery list are sweet rice in vanilla sauce, herb-flavored cottage cheese squares, and crackling biscuits. Portions of everything are substantial, and desserts can be purchased by the piece, the slice, or the pound, or as a whole cake. She offers extremely inexpensive senior specials for lunch and dinner: perhaps her age and status as grandmother four times over motivates this consideration, but it fits in naturally with her philosophy, printed on the menu page, "Like wine, we all get better with age." The storefront dining space is family-room quaint with dried flower arrangements everywhere, souvenir plates on the walls, and homey green-and-white-checked tablecloths and curtains. Standard issue for the waitresses is charmingly—but, I am convinced, unintentionally—retro fifties style: a green-and-white-checked half-apron with a bow at the back, and a pert little matching fabric tiara. Headgear is important here—Clara wears Old World–style kitchen whites, complete with a topper that looks like a 19th-century nightcap, and her assistant has a white head scarf that hides every strand of hair. In good weather, Clara puts a couple of tables out front. Free on-street parking.

Helen's Kitchen
☎ (440) 934-5194

CITY: **Avon**   AREA: **Farther West**
ATMOSPHERE: **Relaxed**   COST: $$$$$

ADDRESS: 36795 Detroit Rd.
HOURS: Tue–Sat 11 a.m.–8 p.m.; closed Sun & Mon   RESERVATIONS: Not taken   PAYMENT: MC, VS, AX, checks   BAR: Beer   TAKEOUT: Yes   SMOKING: Smoking section   ACCESS: & Full access   OTHER ETHNIC SPECIALTIES: German

H elen Birkas left Hungary with her parents in 1956. If you're still here after the dinner rush has died down, she may come out of the kitchen to say hello. And if you ask the right questions, she'll tell you about her experiences as a child during World War II, describe life under Communist rule, and give you the story of her family's escape to America. You can also get her talking about the delights of Hungarian food. Helen, who learned to cook from her

mother, likes to say, "You have to eat what your mother cooked for you." But if your mother was neither Hungarian nor a good cook, you can dip into the Birkas tradition instead. In the kitchen of her small storefront restaurant, which she runs with her son, Kal, she prepares homemade soups, beef goulash, dumplings, stuffed cabbage, veal and chicken paprikash, and Wiener schnitzel. But hers is by no means a strictly ethnic restaurant. She also turns out simple, American-style staples: ribs, breaded fish, steaks and burgers, sandwiches, spaghetti and meatballs. This is a homey place, decorated with knickknacks, curios, paintings. Located in the French Creek district, in a shopping strip across from the Avon fire department and the city hall, it's a popular stop-in spot for the antique hunters who frequent the area on Saturdays and during festivals held three or four times a year.

House of Nagy
☎ (440) 548-5757

CITY: **Burton**   AREA: **Farther East**
ATMOSPHERE: **Casual**   COST: $$$$$

ADDRESS: 15186 Main Market
HOURS: Tue–Thu 4–9 p.m., Fri 4–11 p.m., Sat 5 p.m.–1 a.m., Sun & Mon closed
RESERVATIONS: Taken, suggested on weekends
PAYMENT: MC, VS, AX, DIS   BAR: Beer, wine, liquor
TAKEOUT: Yes   SMOKING: All sections   ACCESS: &

C urrent owners Terry and Bonnie Nagy are the third generation of family to run the restaurant at this location (in a building that was a dance hall and roadhouse in the 1940s). Back then, the place had a reputation for being pretty wild, but the Nagy family made some changes in the '50s and did some remodeling. As the years have passed, it has definitely taken on a more reputable identity. There's a glass-fronted cupboard in the foyer filled with family mementos, baby pictures of various Nagys, and artwork from the Old Country. The main dining area looks like a cozy and comfortable family room complete with drapes, plants, and a stone-faced, wood-burning fireplace. Servers wear white shirts and black ties, but don't get the idea that this suggests either formality or trendiness. By way of illustration, the waitress announces her name very matter-of-factly—without any of that cloying, artificial manner observed in chic, upscale spots—adding that the only reason she mentions it is "it beats being called 'Hey you.'" This the sort of place you can dress up for if you feel like it—as one gray-haired couple did, he in jacket and tie, she in a nice dress—or not, like the two women who opted for sweatshirts and jeans. But if truth be told, this lodge-style setting hasn't totally lost its former uninhibited tavern tone. One winter night, the bar (a completely separate room on the opposite side of the entryway with stools for 12 and tables for about 20 patrons) was filled with a lively group of snowmobilers. These guys had parked their vehicles out front in the big lot and had come inside to eat and make merry, a boisterous bunch in brightly colored, wind-resistant thermal wear.

The same menu serves both sides of the establishment, and while it has a nice selection of steaks, chops, chicken, and fish, it's the Hungarian dinners that stand out, and many are made using Grandma Nagy's original recipes. There's chicken paprikash, schnitzel, gulyas (beef stew), pork with sauerkraut, and stuffed cabbage. One word of culinary caution about the cabbage rolls—the Hungarian version made here tastes quite different from the Polish and Slovenian varieties that may be more familiar to many people. Of course, there are dumplings—the kitchen makes 70–100 pounds of them each week. For the egregiously gastronomic, and for those who simply can't or won't choose, there's a combination plate of paprikas, gulyas, and stuffed cabbage, or side-order portions of dumplings, cabbage rolls, gulyas, and pork with kraut to accompany your entree of choice. For dessert, expect strudel and a

multi-layer Dobos torte. The wine list is very limited but does offer five Hungarian vintages, including a dry red called Egri Bikauer, which means Bull's Blood of Eger. Terry Nagy can usually be found on-site doing everything from stoking the fireplace and bussing tables to greeting guests at the front door. He's glad to be doing whatever it takes because he grew up in the restaurant and is determined to keep the family business alive to preserve the tradition, started by his grandparents, of serving real Hungarian food in Northeast Ohio. If getting there is a bit of a drive for you, make it even more worth your while by combining a meal with a visit to one of the nearby state parks or nature preserves.

Hungarian Business and Tradesman Club
☎ (216) 587-3773

CITY: **Maple Heights**   AREA: **Southeast**
ATMOSPHERE: **Relaxed**   COST: $$$$$

ADDRESS: 15805 Libby Rd.
HOURS: Tue–Fri 11:30 a.m.–2 p.m.
RESERVATIONS: Not Taken   PAYMENT: Cash only
BAR: None   TAKEOUT: No   SMOKING: All sections
ACCESS: ♿ Full access

There's no better food deal in town. This is a private club, originally formed in the 1920s and still going strong, but they open the dining room to the public four days a week for lunch. Don't expect a menu—each day features a single soup and an entree—but count on large portions of traditional Hungarian fare at the bargain price of $6. Your money buys you a bowl of thick, hearty soup (chicken noodle, mushroom, vegetable, potato, or perhaps liver dumpling) and a plate of roast pork or duck, chicken or veal paprikash, Wiener schnitzel, or goulash—all of which are likely to come with a side of those little, melt-in-your-mouth dumplings that do such an admirable job of soaking up gravy, pierogies, stuffed peppers, or stuffed cabbage. The bread is from a bag, and the salad is a chunk of iceberg with a few carrot shreds soaked in bottled dressing, but it's hard to care about those shortcomings when the rest of the food is so satisfying. "Lunch to go" can be dinner at home—one man told me he comes in a few days a week, eats just the soup, and takes home the rest of his meal along with a second one that he buys for his wife because they both work and have no time to cook. "And the food here," he says, "is just one step away from your own grandma's kitchen." Tables are large, and strangers, as well as friends, sit together. It's a big space with a party-room atmosphere, because it *is* a party room—the club's an all-purpose social hall, complete with a dance floor and a small, raised platform for the band—and it can be rented. The club offers a catering service, too. Nothing fancy here (this is a hangout, not a destination)—it's a place where members come to see friends, play cards, shoot pool, and celebrate milestones. And all the rest of us are welcome to join them for lunch. Find it next to a bowling alley, between Lee and Broadway, with plenty of parking in an adjacent lot.

Little Budapest
☎ **(440) 617-0404**

CITY: **Westlake**   AREA: **West Side**
ATMOSPHERE: **Casual**   COST: $$$$$

ADDRESS: 25125 Center Ridge Rd.
HOURS: Mon–Sun 11 a.m.–10 p.m.
RESERVATIONS: Not Taken **PAYMENT:** MC, VS, AX, DIS **BAR:** Beer, wine, liquor **TAKEOUT:** Yes
SMOKING: Smoking section **ACCESS:** ♿ Full access

This is a second location for restaurateur Jozsef Lacza. It's on the west side of town, in King James Plaza. Opened in late spring of 2001, it's a cozy place, with seating for 52 and a bar that keeps on pouring six days a week, long after the kitchen closes at 10 p.m. (until 2:30 a.m. Monday through Saturday). It has the same menu as the University Heights location. For more information, see the listing for Budapest Hungarian Cafe.

Marinko's Firehouse
☎ **(440) 943-4983**

CITY: **Willoughby Hills**   AREA: **East Side**
ATMOSPHERE: **Casual**   COST: $$$$$

ADDRESS: 2768 Stark Dr.
HOURS: Mon–Thu 11:30 a.m.–10 p.m., Fri & Sat 11:30 a.m.–midnight; closed Sun
RESERVATIONS: Taken, required on weekends and for large groups **PAYMENT:** MC, VS, AX, DIS
BAR: Beer, wine, liquor **TAKEOUT:** Yes
SMOKING: Yes **ACCESS:** ♿ Full access

Here you can enjoy Hungarian specialties in a restored fire station. The building is the former Willoughby Hills firehouse, and it's decorated with firehouse memorabilia, firefighting equipment, and antiques. There are six separate dining areas, including the room with the bar, a banquet room, and a 60-seat outdoor patio with vine-covered gazebo and fountain. The way the space is broken up, even when the place is busy it doesn't feel too large or crowded. Although the menu is weighted toward standard American fare, the szekely goulash, chicken paprikash, potato pancakes, sausage with cabbage and noodles, and stuffed peppers insure that the restaurant keeps one foot firmly planted on the side of ethnic cooking. Traditional dumplings called spaetzle are available with all the Hungarian entrees. The chef creates an ever-changing Hungarian combination plate daily for those who want to try grazing Eastern European-style. They draw clientele of all ages, including family groups, from the surrounding counties. Some come for the food, others for the casual, friendly tavern-like atmosphere, and still others for the fun of the nostalgic setting. Plenty of convenient parking.

EUROPE, EAST

Lithuanian

Gintaras Dining Room
☎ (216) 531-2131

CITY: **Cleveland**   AREA: **East Side**
ATMOSPHERE: **Casual**   COST: $$$$$

ADDRESS: 877 E. 185th St.
HOURS: Open only on Sun for brunch
11:30 a.m.–2 p.m.   **RESERVATIONS:** Taken,
recommended on weekends   **PAYMENT:** MC, VS,
DIS, checks   **BAR:** Beer, wine, liquor   **TAKEOUT:** Yes
SMOKING: Smoke-free   **ACCESS:** ♿ Full access

This was once a private restaurant reserved for members of the Lithuanian
American Club, but it is now open to the
public. The entrance is at the back of the
building. There's not much to look at outside, but inside it's pleasant, with wood
paneling and details carved in the Old
World tradition—much as a living and
dining room might be in a home in the
Lithuanian countryside. Eating here was
described by one patron as "the total
Lithuanian dining experience." Here's a
place to taste bulvinai blynai (potato pancakes), koldunai (another version of
pierogi), naliesnikai (crepes), and balan-
deliai (stuffed cabbage), with the possibil-
ity of falling into conversation with some
Clevelanders of Lithuanian descent, and
learning a bit of their history, too. There are
many American items on the menu, too,
from shrimp cocktail to charbroiled
chicken, and the selection of desserts includes both traditional treats like homemade strudel and tortes, and American-
style carrot cake. Rooms are available for
private parties, banquets, and meetings.

Polish

Ewa's Family Restaurant
☎ (216) 441-7040

CITY: **Cleveland**   AREA: **Near East Side**
ATMOSPHERE: **Relaxed**   COST: $$$$$

ADDRESS: 4069 E. 71st St.
HOURS: Tue–Sat 11 a.m.–8 p.m., Sun 8
a.m.–8 p.m., breakfast served Sun only until
8 a.m.–11 a.m., closed Mon   **RESERVATIONS:** Taken
PAYMENT: Checks   **BAR:** Beer, wine, liquor
TAKEOUT: Yes   **SMOKING:** Smoking section
ACCESS: ♿ Limited

Many *Cleveland Ethnic Eats* readers
mailed in the form at the back of the
book to tell me about Ewa's. A look at the
menu and the list of daily specials explains
why so many people are enthusiastic.
There's czernina (duck's blood) soup; pyzy
(a combination of ground beef, veal, and
pork served with onions, bacon, and melt-
in-your-mouth sauerkraut that comes to
the table warm and speckled with bits of
carrot); stuffed cabbage; flaki (tripe soup);
goulash; chicken paprikash with spaetzle;
pierogies; bigos (pork and sauerkraut);
krokiety (blintzes); what they call a War-
saw sandwich, made with fresh kielbasa,
ham, and poledwica (Polish-style bacon);
and Okocim, a Polish beer. It's all served in
a friendly, homey setting where children
are welcome and guys can feel free to leave
their hats on. The large, bright dining area,
which seats about 80 people, is furnished
with laminated wood tables, metal chairs
with vinyl seats, and cloth flowers. Tableware is strictly utilitarian: plastic drinking
glasses, paper placemats, and thick white
china that is almost unbreakable. But there
are lace curtains at the windows and a gas-
burning fireplace, and polka music plays in
the background. The waitresses, some of
whom chat in Polish with their customers,
are adept at handling the always heaping
platefuls and quick to offer free refills on
soft drinks. The main dining room easily
accommodates large groups, and there's

also a party room downstairs that seats 50–60. Although the restaurant has been in operation since 1994, everything is shiny and new here because owners Wesley Ostrowski and Ewa Golebiewski relocated to this space in 1998. Polish food is their specialty, but the kitchen tries to please a wider audience by also turning out more American fare as well—meatloaf, liver, ribs, walleye, burgers, grilled chicken, and steaks. Breakfast, served on Saturdays and Sundays only, includes all the morning standards plus cheese- and fruit-filled blintzes, and a Polish omelette made with kielbasa, ham, onions, and mushrooms. Seniors get special treatment Monday through Thursday, between 1:30 p.m. and 5:30 p.m., when they can get all the specials 10% off. The freestanding brick building, located on the outer edge of Slavic Village, has its own parking lot.

Polish American Cultural Center
☎ (216) 883-2828

CITY: **Cleveland**   AREA: **Near West Side**
ATMOSPHERE: **Relaxed**   COST: $$$$$

ADDRESS: 6501 Lansing Ave.
HOURS: Oct–Jun Sun only 11 a.m.–1 p.m.
RESERVATIONS: Not taken PAYMENT: Checks
BAR: None TAKEOUT: No SMOKING: Smoke-Free
ACCESS: 占 None

Real Polish food made by real Polish, and Polish-American, people. In keeping with this private club's mission to preserve and promote their cultural heritage, members prepare traditional dishes and serve them buffet style once a week, nine months of the year, in the social room of their facility, located in the heart of Cleveland's Slavic Village. Each Sunday lunch features a soup; two different main dishes; potatoes, noodles, dumplings, or pierogies; salad; and dessert. Expect large portions of things like kielbasa and other varieties of Polish sausage, stuffed cabbage, bigos (stew), goulash, and paprikash. It's always fixed price and always inexpensive. The atmosphere is friendly, welcoming, and clubby. Many diners will know each other, but newcomers quickly feel at home. A step at the entrance, another down into the hall, and short few leading to the restrooms make this a poor choice for the handicapped or elderly who may have difficulty going up and down.

Sokolowski's University Inn
☎ (216) 771-9236

CITY: **Cleveland**   AREA: **Near West Side**
ATMOSPHERE: **Casual**   COST: $$$$$

ADDRESS: 1201 University Rd.
HOURS: Lunch Mon–Fri 11 a.m.–3 p.m.; Dinner Fri 5–9 p.m., Sat 4–9 p.m.; closed between lunch & dinner; open for private parties & catering on Sat, Sun & weeknights RESERVATIONS: Taken, for large parties only PAYMENT: MC, VS, checks
BAR: Beer, wine, liquor TAKEOUT: Yes
SMOKING: Smoking section ACCESS: 占 Full access

EUROPE, EAST

This cafeteria, popular with the downtown business crowd for lunch, began as a tavern that Mike and Bernie Sokolowski's grandfather opened in 1923. In the 1950s, their parents turned it into a restaurant, and Mrs. Sokolowski cooked hearty meals for the men who worked at the nearby steel mills. Now the restaurant has expanded and serves a group that includes judges, truckers, and everybody in between. It fills three rooms and a kitchen, added on in 1979. One room has a woodburning fireplace, old trestle tables, and gorgeous copper pots that were used long ago at Cleveland's Leisy Brewery. An expansion connected and converted the garage next door, a huge place where dragsters were once built. They offer live piano music here all day on Fridays and on Saturday evenings. In a 2002 remodeling of the landmark, the small wood-paneled bar at the back was turned into a dining area, and a new 23 seat bar with a spectacular view of downtown was installed where it had originally been located back in the

20's, at the front of the building. The food line offers homestyle Ohio cooking plus the same Polish specialties they've been serving up for more than 40 years: stuffed cabbage with mashed potatoes, stuffed peppers, award-winning pierogies, fresh bratwurst, smoked kielbasa, Salisbury steaks, grilled rainbow trout, and fresh Lake Erie perch.

Globe Cafe
☎ **(330) 864-1000**
CITY: **Akron**   AREA: **Farther South**
ATMOSPHERE: **Relaxed**   COST: $$$$$

ADDRESS: 1375 N. Portage Path
HOURS: Mon–Thu 11:30 a.m.–9 p.m., Fri–Sat 11:30 a.m.–10 p.m. **RESERVATIONS:** Taken
PAYMENT: MC, VS, AX **BAR:** None **TAKEOUT:** Yes
SMOKING: Smoking section **ACCESS:** ♿ Full access

The Globe Cafe is a world apart from its all-American strip mall surroundings. The bill of fare offers a rare opportunity to sample Ukrainian, Georgian, Siberian, and Russian dishes. That translates into bowls of borscht and beet salad, and generous portions of cabbage rolls, stuffed peppers, meat-filled blintzes and others with caviar, stuffed and breaded chicken cutlets, perojok (a meat turnover), and pelmeni (ravioli). Back home in Russia owner Elizabeth Olefir, who came here in 1991, was a doctor with no medicine for her patients. Here she's a restauranteur with wonderful food to serve to her customers, and she says she's never been happier. She opened in May 2003, and the place is more than just a way to make a living. It's a tribute to her father, who had a restaurant in Ukraine. She uses his recipe to make her Odessa eggplant appetizer—the vegetable is buttery soft and wrapped around a filling of red peppers and carrots seasoned with garlic and dill. She grew up in the restaurant business, and always wanted to have one of her own. But that's not easy to do in Russia, especially for a woman. "This is symbol of

my independence," explains Olefir. "I didn't need a man to help me because in America a person can achieve anything if they're willing to work hard." She and her staff certainly work hard to please their customers, and it's not unusual to hear happy, satisfied patrons say they'll definitely be back. Everything's made from scratch, including the Napoleans, honey cake, and poppy seed rolls on her dessert tray. Much effort was put into decorating the space, which has the color scheme of an eternal purplish dusk. The ceiling was hand painted with fluffy clouds, and original folk art paintings hang on the walls. A liquor license is pending as of this writing. When she gets it, Olefir will serve Georgian and Moldavian wines and Russian beers and vodkas. Tables are on two levels. Those with any mobility problems should reserve a table on the lower level. Plenty of parking in a lot.

Slovenian

Fanny's
☎ **(216) 531-1231**
CITY: **Cleveland**   AREA: **East Side**
ATMOSPHERE: **Casual**   COST: $$$$$

ADDRESS: 353 E. 156th St.
HOURS: Mon–Sat 7 a.m.–8 p.m., Sun 11:30 a.m.–7 p.m. **RESERVATIONS:** Taken, for groups of 6 or more only **PAYMENT:** MC, VS, AX, DIS, checks **BAR:** None **TAKEOUT:** Yes
SMOKING: Smoking section **ACCESS:** ♿ None

This friendly place has been a neighborhood fixture for more than 50 years. Started by the current owners' mother and grandmother, its menu still features Slovenian specialties like beef goulash served over spaetzle, ajmont soup (chicken soup made Slovenian-style with a dash of vinegar), and pork-and-kraut goulash. "Our customers don't want us to change," said owner Terry Kollar. Many items on the menu are not ethnic at all, just simple, home-cooked food like liver and onions or roast chicken. You can't miss this big blue building with brown-and-red trim located in an old residential neighborhood, not far from Raddell's Slovenian Sausage Shop (see market listings for more information). Inside, it feels like walking into someone's home: dining areas are a series of small, cozy rooms with flowered wallpaper. Patrons dress up or down depending on how they feel, what occasion brings them out to eat, and whether they went home after work or not. This is the kind of place to bring children, knowing they'll find foods they like in low-key, family-oriented surroundings. There's a large enclosed porch where you can wait for a table or wait for friends, and plenty of parking in the restaurant's own lot.

Frank Sterle's Slovenian Country House
☎ (216) 881-4181

CITY: **Cleveland**   AREA: **Near East Side**
ATMOSPHERE: **Casual**   COST: $$$$$

ADDRESS: 1401 E. 55th St.
HOURS: Mon–Wed 11:30 a.m.–2:30 p.m. (also open for dinner if they have a party of 45 or more), Thu & Fri 11:30 a.m.–9 p.m., Sat 4:30–9 p.m., Sun 11:30–7 p.m.
RESERVATIONS: Taken, recommended for parties of five or more   **PAYMENT:** MC, VS, AX, checks
BAR: Beer, wine, liquor   **TAKEOUT:** Yes
SMOKING: Smoking section   **ACCESS:** ♿ Full access

Sterle's began life as the Bonner Cafe, a bar with some food that opened for business 40 years ago. When Frank Sterle bought the place it was just one small room, but like Topsy, it just grew and grew. Now, the huge space, which can handle as many as 300 people, is a tourist destination, attracting suburban visitors and out-of-town guests who want to get a taste of Cleveland's ethnic past. It begins at the parking lot, a large enclosed area that you enter through an impressive, decorative gateway, like the entrance to a castle. The

leitmotif, inside and out, is a European mountain chalet, with all the accompanying Old World warmth and hospitality. Waitresses wear a version of Slovenian traditional dress, much like a German dirndl, and many have worked here for years. And they're adept at managing the heaping plates full of roast pork, stuffed cabbage, Wiener schnitzel, and paprikash. There's always a selection of American standbys, like meat loaf and roast chicken, and some so-called European favorites (mostly Italian-style), but the really interesting part of the menu is Slovenian: kidney or tripe stew, jeterca (liver with onions), klobase and zelje (sausage and sauerkraut), and segedin goulash. Family-style dinners offer a combination of entree items and side dishes. There's a large bar in front and a separate room for meetings and private parties. Live music on Friday nights, from 6 to 9 p.m., and Saturday from 8 p.m. to midnight. The kitchen closes at 9 p.m.

MARKETS
• • • • • • • • • • •

Czech

Bohemian Hall
☎ (216) 641-9777

CITY: **Cleveland**   AREA: **Near East Side**

ADDRESS: 4939 Broadway Ave.
FOOD AVAIL.: Baked goods, prepared frozen foods   **HOURS:** n/a   **PAYMENT:** Checks
ACCESS: ♿ Full access

The female members of the Sokol Greater Cleveland (a Czech athletic club) raise money by preparing traditional Czech dumplings, which they sell frozen year-round on Wednesdays and Saturdays. They also hold a Christmas bake sale featuring homemade strudel and raisin-and-almond bread, and another at Easter when they offer raisin-filled sweet breads. Prices are always reasonable. Caraway seed, barley, Czech mushrooms (when available), and imported gifts are also available for purchase by the general public. They have a new edition of their cookbook for sale that contains tried-and-true Czech recipes for breads, soups, dumplings, and main course dishes. Call for information. You can ask to be put on their mailing list.

Al's Quality Market
☎ (330) 753-7216
CITY: **Barberton**   AREA: **Farther South**

ADDRESS: 563 Tuscarawas Ave.
FOOD AVAIL.: Meat (fresh, deli), canned & packaged goods, spices, condiments, beverages
HOURS: Mon–Fri 9 a.m.–5:30 p.m., Sat 8 a.m.–5 p.m. PAYMENT: MC, VS ACCESS: 占 Limited

There once was an Al, and he opened this butcher shop when he came back to Cleveland after serving in World War II. Tim and Jeanette Eberhardt have owned it since March 2003, and they're committed to continuing what he started, making traditional Hungarian, Slovenian, Slovakian, Polish, and Italian sausages by hand, the old-fashioned way. They also smoke their own hams, and prepare head cheese, cabbage rolls, Hungarian bacon, and salami. In addition, this is a full-service butcher shop offering fresh meat, hand-cut steaks, plus lard and suet, both hard to find and essential in some recipes. He also grinds his own paprika. The wood-floored shop was also once home to one of the earliest Acme grocery stores, and a few shelves remain stocked with homemade noodles from Richfield, hot pickled peppers from a Suffield, Ohio, company, and convenience items like chips, napkins, sugar, and ketchup. There's an out-of-time feel in here, a sense of small town friendliness and personal service that's getting harder and harder to find. Tim, a man with a quick and ready smile, is usually behind the counter, and a chat with him is sure to make shopping more fun.

Buettner's Bakery
☎ (216) 531-0650
CITY: **Cleveland**   AREA: **Near East Side**

ADDRESS: 704 E. 185th St.
FOOD AVAIL.: Baked goods HOURS: Tue–Fri 9 a.m.–4:30 p.m., Sat 8 a.m.–5 p.m., Sun 9 a.m.–12:30 p.m.; closed Mon PAYMENT: Checks ACCESS: 占 Full access OTHER ETHNIC SPECIALTIES: Croatian, Hungarian, Polish

There's been a family-owned bakery at this spot for 70 years or so, according to the current manager, who has been there over 30 years herself. They still use old-fashioned gas ovens with rotating shelves, and the products they turn out are not quite like their counterparts made in more modern stoves. In fact, in a tradition that hearkens back to a time when the baker's oven was used by the entire community, Buettner's makes these special ovens available to the public at holidays and roasts whole pigs and lambs for various ethnic celebrations. Swedish limpa bread is available at Christmastime and Irish soda bread around St. Patrick's Day. The rest of the year they make a variety of Polish, Slovenian, Hungarian, and Croatian specialties, including kuchens, strudels, nut and poppyseed rolls, and kolachy plus a variety of non-ethnic breads, danish, pies, and donuts.

C & H Gertrude Bakery
☎ (216) 641-7582
CITY: **Cleveland**   AREA: **Near East Side**

ADDRESS: 6506 Gertrude Ave.

FOOD AVAIL.: baked goods, takeout meals
HOURS: Wed–Sun 7:30 a.m.–4 p.m.; closed Mon & Tue   PAYMENT: Checks   ACCESS: ⚬ Limited

This bakery's been in existence for more than 80 years. The present owner has been there for nearly 11 years, and has been baking traditional homemade baked goods for nearly 25 years. The change in management has not meant a change in product or process. The bakery continues to turn out homemade Eastern European specialties like Polish sweet breads, paczki, strudel, and kolaczki. They also bake loaves of rye, Vienna, and pumpernickel bread daily, as well as cookies, danish, donuts, and cakes.

International Foods
☎ (216) 932-5000
CITY: **Cleveland Heights**   AREA: **East Side**

ADDRESS: 2078 S. Taylor Rd.

FOOD AVAIL.: meat (deli), fish (deli, dried), grains, baked goods, canned & packaged goods, beverages, tea, wine, prepared frozen foods, takeout meals   HOURS: Mon 11 a.m.–4 p.m., Wed–Fri 10 a.m.–7 p.m., Sat 10 a.m.–5 p.m., closed Sun & Tue   PAYMENT: Checks
ACCESS: ⚬ None   OTHER ETHNIC SPECIALTIES: Polish, Russian

This small store is part deli, part grocery, and the best of what they have to offer is in the glass case filled with one of the biggest selections of smoked fish anywhere in town, including sable and lox, and both black and red caviar. Prepared Jewish and Eastern European specialties are available for takeout: gefilte fish, blintzes, pierogies, and pelmeni (a Russian dumpling stuffed with meat, potato, or cheese). They also stock 20 varieties of herring, 60 different kinds of Old World prepackaged cakes and cookies, and 25 different types of chocolate candy. Beer, wine, and mineral water available. Party trays made to order with meats, fish and fish salads, and baked goods.

K & K Meat Shoppe
☎ (216) 662-2644
CITY: **Maple Heights**   AREA: **Southeast**

ADDRESS: 6172 Dunham Rd.

FOOD AVAIL.: meat (fresh, deli, frozen), fish (frozen), baked goods, canned & packaged goods, condiments, beverages, tea, takeout meals   HOURS: Mon–Fri 9 a.m.–6 p.m., Sat 8 a.m.–5 p.m., Sun 9 a.m.–2 p.m.   PAYMENT: MC, VS, DIS, checks   ACCESS: ⚬ Full access   OTHER ETHNIC SPECIALTIES: Polish, Slovenian, many Western European countries

The claim to ethnic fame at this full-service meat market is their homemade fresh and smoked sausages, including Polish-style hurka (with rice), Bohemian weiners, and Slovenian links. Family owned and operated for three generations, they also offer offer an array of ethnic specialties including stuffed cabbage, roast pork and sauerkraut, chicken paprikash, Bohemian sekanice (Easter loaf), and various types and cuts of meats. Made-to-order sandwiches are available along with a selection of imported items that complement their meats, such as pickles and mustards.

K & K Meat Shoppe
☎ (330) 274-5322
CITY: **Mantua**   AREA: **Farther East**

ADDRESS: 10682 Main Street

FOOD AVAIL.: meat (fresh, deli, frozen), fish (frozen), baked goods, canned & packaged goods, condiments, beverages, tea, takeout meals   HOURS: Mon–Fri 9 a.m.–6 p.m., Sat 8 a.m.–5 p.m., Sun 9 a.m.–2 p.m.   PAYMENT: MC, VS, DIS, checks   ACCESS: ⚬ Full access   OTHER ETHNIC SPECIALTIES: Polish, Slovenian, many Western European countries

EUROPE, EAST

See description for K & K Meat Shop in Maple Heights.

Kathy's Kolacke & Pastry Shop
☎ **(440) 835-6570**
CITY: **Westlake**   AREA: **West Side**

ADDRESS: 25076 Center Ridge Rd.
FOOD AVAIL.: Baked goods, beverages, coffee
HOURS: Tue–Thu, & Fri 10 a.m.–4 p.m., Sat
9 a.m.–4 p.m.; closed Sun & Mon
PAYMENT: Checks ACCESS: ♿ Full access OTHER
ETHNIC SPECIALTIES: Hungarian, Polish

Located in King James Plaza, this bakery is best known for its kolacke. The Polish version of this traditional pastry is light, flaky, and filled with fruit and nuts. The Czech form is soft, sweet, and stuffed with meat. Kathy Schreiner runs this one-woman business that was named "Best Ethnic Bakery" in the Cleveland Sweet Revenge contest. She also makes Hungarian nut and poppyseed rolls, a cheesecake that's been featured on Del Donahoo's television show, and a large variety of non-ethnic cookies, cakes and cupcakes, brownies, and muffins.

Kenmore Market Place
☎ **(330) 848-9202**
CITY: **Akron**   AREA: **Farther South**

ADDRESS: 1472 Kenmore Blvd.
FOOD AVAIL.: Meat (fresh), produce, canned &
packaged goods HOURS: Mon–Sat 9 a.m.–6
p.m., Sun closed PAYMENT: Checks
ACCESS: ♿ None

No window-shopping here. This old-fashioned butcher is located in a large, forbidding industrial building that's also home to the wholesale end of the sausage-making operation. Without the tip from the Beacon's food editor, Jane Snow, I'd never have suspected that it was worth stopping in. But it is, because if sausage is your thing, you'll find Balkan/Serbian stuff here you're not likely to come upon anywhere else—pljeskavica (minced meat patties), ground veal and pork cevapcici, and fresh srpske kobacice, plus a selection of fresh and smoked Hungarian and Polish varieties. They also cure their own hams and brine their own cabbage. Pull up to the loading dock to park.

Raddell's Sausage Shop, Inc.
☎ **(216) 486-1944**
CITY: **Cleveland**   AREA: **East Side**

ADDRESS: 478 E. 152nd St.
FOOD AVAIL.: Meat (fresh), grains, baked goods,
canned & packaged goods, spices, condiments,
tea, coffee HOURS: Mon–Sat 8 a.m.–5 p.m.;
closed Sun PAYMENT: MC, VS, DIS, checks
ACCESS: ♿ Full access OTHER ETHNIC SPECIALTIES:
German, Lithuanian, Slovenian

Specializing in the traditional foods of Slovenia, Lithuania, Croatia, and Germany, Raddell's is in its third generation of family ownership. It's best known for the large variety and Old World quality of its meats and sausages. "People come from all over just to buy our sausage," said partner Mark Tichar. "The homemade rice-and-blood sausage and the Slovenian smoked sausage are among our best sellers, and customers even ask us to UPS our ethnic specialties out of state." They also offer imported chocolates, noodles, jams and jellies, pickles, cookies, and European mineral waters. Located in a freestanding building with its own parking area.

DON'T FORGET: CALL AHEAD!

EUROPE, EAST

Russian

Smokehouse Deli
☎ (216) 371-3066
CITY: **University Hts.**   AREA: **East Side**

ADDRESS: 13891 Cedar Rd.
FOOD AVAIL.: Meat (fresh, deli, frozen), grains, beans, baked goods, spices, condiments, beverages, tea, coffee **HOURS:** Mon–Sat 10 a.m.–8 p.m., Sun 10 a.m.–5 p.m.
PAYMENT: MC, VS **ACCESS:** ♿ Limited **OTHER ETHNIC SPECIALTIES:** Greek, Israeli, Eastern European

World flavors can be found in Cedar Center. This place is a hotbed of international tastes. Here, two wide, brightly lit aisles are filled with an intriguing array of meats, cheeses, and tasty condiments that can jazz up any meal. Siberian horseradish? Israeli mushroom salad? How about gypsy-style salami from Russia? Or try some walnut jam, taramosalata (fish egg spread), sunflower tea, or real European-style butter. The meat counter displays a large variety of sausages, hams, bacon, and smoked meats. There are packaged breads, spices, imported candy, and all sorts of canned and bottled pickled vegetables, plus Russian-language newspapers. Park for free in back or at metered spaces in front.

Hungarian

Farkas Pastry
☎ (216) 281-6200
CITY: **Cleveland**   AREA: **Near West Side**

ADDRESS: 1983 W. 28th St.
FOOD AVAIL.: baked goods, takeout meals
HOURS: Fri 9 a.m.–4 p.m., Sat 9 a.m.–2 p.m.; closed Sun–Thu PAYMENT: Checks
ACCESS: ♿ None

Attila Farkas and his wife have been baking and selling Hungarian pastry in this tiny shop near the West Side Market for more than 30 years, and the only advertising they've ever needed is the reputation of their products. The word "shop," in this case, is a euphemism. The store is in fact the kitchen itself, and on the two days they're open for retail sales, the line spills out onto the sidewalk, and the doorway is almost always crowded with people. Hungarians, Germans, Serbians, and Slovaks as well as generic Clevelanders gossip in a babble of languages while patiently waiting to buy some of whatever is still left. Farkas bakes traditional dobos, hazelnut, and chocolate tortes; nut, poppyseed, and fruit rolls; napoleons; and zserbo. Get there early if you want to have a selection, or call to place an order in advance. And leave enough time to engage Farkas in conversation; it's always an interesting experience.

EUROPE, EAST

Laurinda's
☎ (216) 267-4622
CITY: **Middleburg Heights**
AREA: **Southwest**

ADDRESS: 13637 Pineview Ct.
FOOD AVAIL.: Baked goods **HOURS:** Daily 8 a.m.–5 p.m. **PAYMENT:** Checks
ACCESS: ♿ Limited

Laurinda's is not really a store at all. They bake to order only and deliver your goodies right to your door. While they specialize in Hungarian strudel, kolacke, nut horns, and a cheesecake made from a closely guarded and very old family recipe, they're unique in that they'll also custom bake items using your own recipes. Since everything is made to order, there are no shortcuts taken or commercial techniques used; everything is made from scratch, with no preservatives, using only the freshest and best ingredients. Place orders by phone during business hours.

EUROPE, EAST

Lucy's Sweet Surrender
☎ (216) 752-0828
CITY: **Cleveland**   AREA: **East Side**

ADDRESS: 12516 Buckeye Rd.
FOOD AVAIL.: Baked goods, spices, condiments, coffee HOURS: Mon–Fri 7 a.m.–4 p.m., Sat 7 a.m.–4 p.m., also open by appointment.
PAYMENT: MC, VS, AX, checks ACCESS: ♿ Limited

Michael Feigenbaum and his wife, Marika, who is from Transylvania, are the current owners of this 50-year-old bakery (formerly known as Lucy's Hungarian Strudel), and they are dedicated to continuing the tradition of making unique, authentic Eastern European specialties. The women who prepare the strudel dough each morning have been stretching it by hand the old-fashioned way for just a few years less than the shop's been open, and this is still a cut-no-corners, everything-from-scratch operation. Michael even buys the apples they use for strudels and pies fresh from local growers. This is one of the few places that still bakes zserbo, layers of crisp dough alternating with raspberry preserves, hazelnuts, and chocolate; grillazs, a "lace" cookie filled with chocolate cake and chocolate buttercream and decorated with chocolate sprinkles; pogacsa, a flaky layered biscuit seeded with bits of bacon that's like a meal you can hold in your hand; and krupli, yellow cake with chocolate cream inside, a marzipan coating on the outside, and a dusting of powdered sugar and cocoa that leaves it looking a bit like a potato, only better. Lucy's also offers kolac, a braided yeast bread with golden raisins, Dobos torte, cream cheese and sour cream cookies filled with fruit, and nut and poppyseed rolls. Also available are other types of European-style cakes and pastries, muffins, bread, doughnuts, and pies. Michael also specializes in creating unusual customized, made-to-order chocolate mousse, cassata, and Dobos torte wedding cakes. The couple of tables and chairs, plus the availability of coffee by the cup and Hungarian-Language newspapers, makes this an informal, impromptu gathering place for Hungarians from all around town, as well as anyone else interested in soaking up the atmosphere and the goodies. Parking lot adjacent to the store.

Mertie's Hungarian Strudel Shop
☎ (216) 362-0012
CITY: **Middleburg Heights**
AREA: **Southwest**

ADDRESS: 6606 Smith Rd.
FOOD AVAIL.: Baked goods HOURS: Tue–Fri 8 a.m.–5 p.m., Sat 8 a.m.–4 p.m.; closed Sun & Mon PAYMENT: Checks ACCESS: ♿ Limited

Mertie Rakosi has done all the baking herself, from scratch, for 23 years—and for many more before that at a bakery on Buckeye. The variety of strudels is almost endless: apple, cherry, cheese, apricot, blueberry, poppyseed, lemon, raspberry, and peach. She also prepares sugar-free versions of her apple, cherry, and blueberry strudels. Ethnic goodie seekers will also find dobos, double chocolate, Black Forest, strawberry, and lemon tortes here, as well as ladylocks, potica (nut roll), and homemade noodles.

R. Kaczur Meats
☎ (440) 232-6556
CITY: **Bedford**   AREA: **Southeast**

ADDRESS: 712 Broadway Ave.
FOOD AVAIL.: Meat (fresh, deli), baked goods, canned & packaged goods, spices, condiments, beverages HOURS: Wed 9 a.m.–1 p.m., Thu & Fri 9 a.m.–5 p.m., Sat 9 a.m.–3 p.m.; closed Sun–Tue
PAYMENT: Checks ACCESS: ♿ Full Access

Robert Kaczur has customers from all around the state and the country, and he's even had some international visitors from as far away as Australia. They come for the Hungarian meat products he makes on the premises, using traditional techniques and ingredients. "The Hungarian 'old-timers' like what I do," says Kaczur, "and they've given me their seal of approval. To them, I'm a person who's keeping alive a dying art, and even though making things the way I do is time-consuming and labor-intensive, I won't compromise because I personally don't want these traditions to be lost. And besides, it's what makes me and my business so special." Robert learned his trade from his uncle and his father. He makes his own cottage hams using a dry cure method with no water added; fresh 100%-pork Hungarian kolbasz sausage, a smoked version and another spicy-hot variety; hurka, a rice-and-liver sausage and veres hurka (blood sausage); kocsonya, pigs' feet in their own gel (available from October until Easter); and head cheese. *Szalonna* means bacon in Hungarian, and Kaczur prepares a number of different kinds: garlic-flavored; garlic and paprika; a fattier version used in a Hungarian specialty made with drippings, bread, and grilled vegetables; and abalt szalonna, a boiled bacon with the rib bones attached that can be sliced and used without further cooking. He also makes his own cracklings, some of which go into the pogacsa (buns) he sells. The store, which Robert describes as an old-fashioned butcher shop without the sawdust on the floor, also carries Hungarian-style salamis, imported pickles, noodles, and a small selection of spices and seasonings. When the store is closed, you can use the answering machine to place an order. Tell Robert when you'll be in to pick it up, and he'll have it ready for you.

Tommy's Pastries
☎ (216) 521-4778
CITY: **Lakewood**   AREA: **West Side**

ADDRESS: 14205 Madison Ave.
FOOD AVAIL.: Baked goods, beverages

HOURS: Mon–Sat 5 a.m.–3 p.m., closed Sun
PAYMENT: Cash only   ACCESS: ♿ Full Access
OTHER ETHNIC SPECIALTIES: Many Eastern and Western European countries

The owners and the baker are from Hungary, and when you taste their strudel, Dobos torte, pogacsa (a bun made with bacon), and kolache, you can be sure you're eating the real thing. They also offer Linzer tortes, croissants, a variety of muffins, and European-style pastries, scones, and pies. Staff can chat and answer your questions comfortably in English or Hungarian. It's a little shop, with easy access from I-90 using the Bunts Road exit. Metered parking available out front.

Polish

Europa Deli
☎ (216) 271-5822
CITY: **Cleveland**   AREA: **Near East Side**

ADDRESS: 6308 Fleet Ave.
FOOD AVAIL.: meat (fresh, deli, frozen), fish (dried), grains, beans, baked goods, spices, condiments, beverages, tea, coffee, takeout meals   HOURS: Mon–Fri 9 a.m.–8 p.m., Sat 9 a.m.–7 p.m., Sun 10 a.m.–3 p.m.
PAYMENT: Checks   ACCESS: ♿ Limited

WCPN Radio's April Baer sent me here, and I'm glad she did. She offered her personal and enthusiastic endorsement of their pierogi, filled with sauerkraut, mushrooms, cheese, or cheese and potatoes, and prepared in the big white-tiled kitchen at the back of the store by Maria and Kizimierz Chruscik. The husband and wife also make gozabki (stuffed cabbage), czarnina (duck-blood soup), flaczki (tripe soup), kapusta (sauerkraut and kielbasa slow-baked together), potato pancakes, and salatka jarzynowa (potato salad). They don't speak English very well and although their customers may, many seem equally at ease chatting in Polish, and it is clearly for them that the store stocks Polish-language newspapers and magazines. There's a very large selection of Polish foods—cookies and candy; noodles; mixes for cakes, dumplings, sauces, and soups; jars of pickles, peppers, beets, sauerkraut, and jam; tins of fish, pate, and fruit compote; boxes of tea and juice concentrates; and fresh bread, rolls, and pastries. The refrigerated case is filled with jars of herring, horseradish, cultured milk, and white borscht. A section of the glass-fronted meat case is devoted to fresh pork, beef, and veal; the rest is filled with a variety of sausages, cured meats, and imported cheeses. Technically a market, with prepared foods ready to take home, the place does have eight tables for eating on the spot, and in good weather two tables with umbrellas appear on the sidewalk out front. The store is spacious, bright, and cheery with plants in the windows and fresh flowers and dried arrangements atop the meat case. Mostly modern in appearance, the place retains some older, original fixtures that lend a special charm. Free on-street parking and small lot at the side of the building.

Jaworski's Meat Market & Deli
☎ (216) 271-4575
CITY: **Cleveland**   AREA: **Near East Side**

ADDRESS: 5324 Fleet Ave.
FOOD AVAIL.: meat (fresh, frozen), produce, beans, flour, baked goods, canned & packaged goods, spices, condiments, beverages, tea, prepared frozen foods, takeout meals
HOURS: Tue–Fri 8:30 a.m.–6 p.m., Sat 8 a.m.–5 p.m., closed Sun & Mon **PAYMENT:** MC, VS, DIS, checks **ACCESS:** ♿ Full access

The Jaworski family has been making fresh and smoked kielbasa sausage here for more than 65 years. Stuffed cabbage and pierogies as well as hard-to-find Polish delicacies are also prepared on the premises, including flaczki (tripe) and czarnina (duck) soups; bigos, a stew of sauerkraut, kielbasa, tomatoes, and mush-

rooms; head cheese; and kabanose, a dried smoked sausage made with pork and garlic. Shelves are stocked with imported pickles, sauces, jarred peppers, and canned cabbage. There's a full deli with pierogies, cold cuts, and salads. Over-stuffed sandwiches are made to order. The meat cases hold cuts of fresh beef, pork, chicken, and hard-to-find Muscovy ducks (a breed many gourmet chefs prefer because it's less fatty).

Krusinski Finest Meat Products
☎ (216) 441-0100
CITY: **Cleveland**   AREA: **Near East Side**

ADDRESS: 6300 Heisley Ave.
FOOD AVAIL.: meat (fresh), beverages, tea, wine, takeout meals **HOURS:** Mon, Tue, Thu, Fri, Sat 8 a.m.–5:30 p.m.; closed Wed & Sun (open Wed the week before a major holiday)
PAYMENT: Cash only **ACCESS:** ♿ None

This classic old-fashioned butcher shop in the heart of Slavic Village has been around for over 40 years, and is still owned and operated by the Krusinski family, who prepare their own flavorful garlic-laced sauerkraut. A wide variety of pierogies are made fresh daily, including potato, cheese, kraut, and fruit. Helen Krusinski and her staff also prepare smoked and fresh kielbasa, potato pancakes, blintzes, stuffed cabbage, and stuffed peppers. Other Polish specialty items include jeternice (liver puddings); hurka, a rice and liver ring; and krakowska, a lean-meat cold cut similar to salami. They also sell all types and cuts of meat, deli meats, and cheeses.

Peter's Market
☎ (216) 341-5910
CITY: **Garfield Heights**   AREA: **Southeast**

ADDRESS: 4617 Turney Rd.
FOOD AVAIL.: meat (fresh), produce, grains, beans, flour, baked goods, canned & packaged goods, condiments, beverages, tea, coffee, wine, beer,

prepared frozen foods, takeout meals
HOURS: Mon–Wed 8:30 a.m.–6 p.m., Thu
8:30 a.m.–6 p.m., Fri 8 a.m.–6:30 p.m., Sat
8 a.m.–6:00 p.m.; closed Sun **PAYMENT:** Checks
ACCESS: & Full access

Peter's is a neighborhood meat market and grocery, with an emphasis on Eastern European foods and a good reputation that's grown by word of mouth. They carry cottage hams, head cheese, a variety of sausages and kielbasa, and canned and packaged products from Poland. There's a small selection of kitchen staples, plus deli meats. But the pierogies are the real specialty here. The little dough pockets come filled with potatoes, potatoes and cheese, sauerkraut, mushrooms, vegetables, apples, apricots, and prunes. They are prepared fresh on Friday only (from 11 a.m. to 6:30 p.m.) at Sophie's Cafe, a carryout food operation located within the market. Yes, there is a real Sophie, and she also makes traditional Polish homemade favorites to go, including soups, dumplings, blintzes, stuffed cabbage, potato pancakes, and fruit and vegetable crepes.

Samosky Home Bakery
☎ (440) 845-3377
CITY: **Parma Heights**   AREA: **Southwest**

ADDRESS: 6641 Pearl Rd.
FOOD AVAIL.: Baked goods, beverages, coffee
HOURS: Tue–Sat 7 a.m.–4 p.m.; closed Sun &
Mon **PAYMENT:** MC, VS, AX, DIS, checks
ACCESS: & Full access

Decorated to resemble an Old World bake shop with antique display cases, Samosky's has been in existence since 1910. And during that time they've continuously done what they do best: make traditional Polish baked goods, including hoska (a Polish bread traditionally served at Easter), paczki (donuts), and kolacky. They also make a variety of cookies, cakes, and pies, strudel, Hungarian nut and poppyseed rolls, angel wings, plus brownies, dan-

ish, ladylocks, and Russian tea biscuits. They also carry old-fashioned jellies, candies, and novelty gift items.

T & T Sausage Market
☎ (216) 441-4022
CITY: **Cleveland**   AREA: **Near East Side**

ADDRESS: 5901 Fleet Ave.
FOOD AVAIL.: meat (fresh), baked goods, canned
& packaged goods, spices, condiments, takeout
meals **HOURS:** Tue–Thu 9 a.m.–6 p.m., Fri
9 a.m.–7 p.m., Sat 9 a.m.–5 p.m.; closed Sun &
Mon **PAYMENT:** Checks **ACCESS:** & None

Another Slavic Village establishment, this one specializes in homemade products, made fresh daily. "We cater in the old-country style," says Irene Chybowski, "to an ethnic, European clientele." With her father-in-law, Irene prepares everything from scratch on the premises including kiszka (blood sausage); krakowska (ham sausage); pasztet (liver pate); garaleta (pigs' feet in gelatin); kotleciki (little meat loaves); and four different types of kielbasa. They also sell heat-and-eat stuffed cabbage and pierogies.

Russian

Gorby Grocery Store
☎ (216) 382-3006
CITY: **South Euclid**   AREA: **East Side**

ADDRESS: 4004 Mayfield Rd.
FOOD AVAIL.: Meat (deli), fish (deli), produce,
grains, beans, flour, baked goods, canned &
packaged goods, spices, condiments, beverages,
tea, prepared frozen foods **HOURS:** Mon–Fri
10 a.m.–8 p.m., Sat 10 a.m.–7 p.m., Sun
10 a.m.–4 p.m. **PAYMENT:** Checks
ACCESS: & None **OTHER ETHNIC SPECIALTIES:**
most other Eastern European countries

This mini-market at the corner of Mayfield and Warrensville is almost invisible; it shares an entryway with the bar next door, and it's beside a fast-food franchise. But there's a lot of food packed in this small space, a veritable cornucopia of Russian delicacies and imports from other parts of Eastern Europe. There are bags of pelmeni (a potato-filled "ravioli") and blintzes in the freezer; soft white farmer cheese with raisins, and a large variety of pickles, mustard, and horseradish in the refrigerator case; smoked fish, sausages, and salami at the deli counter; and big bowls full of candy on every available surface. On the shelves, you might find jars of vegetable spread from Bulgaria, sweet pepper relish from Slovenia, fruit jam from Poland, and seven different kinds of honey. There are bags of poppy seeds, buckwheat groats, millet, and barley, and a limited selection of fresh vegetables and fruits. If you're not fluent in Russian, you probably won't be interested in the Russian-language newspapers for sale or all the announcements posted on the bulletin board, but it's clear that the Russian immigrants who shop here find these worth their attention. Convenient parking in front of the store.

Odessa European Market
☎ (330) 836-2380
CITY: **Akron**   AREA: **Farther South**

ADDRESS: 71 Westgate Circle
FOOD AVAIL.: meat (deli), grains, beans, baked goods, canned & packaged goods, spices, condiments, beverages, tea, coffee, prepared frozen foods, takeout meals   HOURS: Mon–Fri 11 a.m.–8 p.m., Sat 10 a.m.–8 p.m., Sun noon–6 p.m.   PAYMENT: MC, VS, checks
ACCESS: ♿ Full access

Natalie and Bogdan Butriy emigrated from the Ukraine and, in December 2002, opened this market tucked at the back of Westgate Plaza. Back home, he was an oral surgeon, and he hopes, with some additional schooling, to be one again in this country. The well-stocked, attractive, and brightly lit market is a way for the cou-

ple to earn a living now, and fill a gap they saw in the area's shopping options. They stock an international array of products with an emphasis on Russian foods. There's fresh caviar, smoked fish, salamis, and sausages; jars of walnuts floating in Siberian honey; cans of sour cabbage soup, Ukrainian borscht, and vegetable spread; and frozen pelmeni (similar to ravioli) and blintzes. Hungarian and Bulgarian cheeses, German ham, Polish chocolates, Slovenian sausage, and Israeli-style salads can also be found here, along with imported juices, teas, noodles, condiments, and packaged breads, crackers, and cookies. They're also preparing food that can be boxed for takeout or eaten at one of the four tables inside the store (plus a couple outside in good weather). In addition to gourmet sandwiches and salads, there are some Russian specialties: eggplant rolls, cabbage rolls, stuffed peppers, pelmeni, blintzes, and fried cabbage. Ample and convenient parking.

Yeleseyevsky Deli
☎ (440) 605-0907
CITY: **Mayfield Heights**   AREA: **East Side**

ADDRESS: 5832 Mayfield Rd.
FOOD AVAIL.: meat (deli), fish (deli), produce, grains, beans, flour, baked goods, canned & packaged goods, condiments, beverages, tea, coffee, prepared frozen foods, takeout meals
HOURS: Mon–Sat 10 a.m.–8 p.m., Sun 10 a.m.–4 p.m.   PAYMENT: Checks   ACCESS: ♿ Full access   OTHER ETHNIC SPECIALTIES: many Eastern European countries

Tucked back in a strip mall behind the Mayland Shopping Center, this store is clearly meant to serve the Russian immigrant community. The front windows display posters in Russian announcing, I was told, upcoming events. There's the requisite small table with a few chairs, which provides a place for Russian men, who always seem to be wearing black leather jackets no matter what the weather, to gather, smoke, talk, and observe. Open bins are filled with the brightly wrapped hard candies and chocolates Russians favor. And the shelves and refrigerated cases are stocked with the foods they were familiar with back home—pickles and pickled vegetables, barley, buckwheat groats, pear preserves and gooseberry jam, sunflower seeds, smoked fish, and farmers' butter. There are usually at least seven versions of salamis, and the labels, in Russian and English, reveal regional preferences, historical influences, and the sometimes humorous realities of modern life: there's Estonsky salami (think Estonia) and others called, respectively, Kievsky, Minsky, Vienskaya, Hungarian, German, and the one I personally find intriguing—Tourist salami. They also offer caviar in white, red, and black, homemade dumplings, Russian-style cakes, and prepared salads.

Slovenian

Malensek's Meat Market
☎ (216) 361-1037
CITY: **Cleveland**   AREA: **Near East Side**

ADDRESS: 1217 Norwood Rd.
FOOD AVAIL.: Meat (fresh) HOURS: Mon 11 a.m.–3 p.m., Tue 9:30 a.m.–3 p.m., Thu–Fri 9:30 a.m.–4 p.m., sat 9 a.m.–3 p.m., closed Wed & Sun PAYMENT: Cash only ACCESS: & None

This small, old-fashioned butcher shop almost qualifies as an official Cleveland landmark. The Malensek family has been in business at this same location since 1917, and the third generation is currently on hand to answer all your questions about Slovenian sausage, their specialty, including the traditional rice-and-blood versions. They prepare smoked and fresh sausage, and a unique smoked sausage loaf that can be sliced and used as lunch meat. They also cure and smoke a large variety of pork cuts. According to Ken Malensek,

their customers are a mix of people who hear about the store by word of mouth and those whose families have been shopping here for years. "Even people who have moved away to other communities come back here to stock up two or three times a year. And folks who never lived here themselves come in, especially around the holiday times, to buy the traditional meats they grew up eating."

Patria Imports
☎ (216) 531-6720
CITY: **Cleveland**   AREA: **East Side**

ADDRESS: 794 E. 185th St.
FOOD AVAIL.: Meat (deli), canned & packaged goods, beverages, wine, beer HOURS: Mon–Sat 9 a.m.–5 p.m., Sun closed PAYMENT: Checks ACCESS: & Full access OTHER ETHNIC SPECIALTIES: Croatian

This is a fairly small store located in Cleveland's Old World Plaza shopping district. They carry imported cheeses, canned fish, sprats (a smoked fish similar to sardines), chocolates, cookies, jams, and preserves. Some household products and convenience items. Parking lot in back.

Rudy's Quality Meats
☎ (440) 943-5490
CITY: **Willowick**   AREA: **East Side**

ADDRESS: 31728 Vine St.
FOOD AVAIL.: Meat (fresh), fish (frozen), canned & packaged goods, spices, condiments, prepared frozen foods HOURS: Mon–Thu 9 a.m.–6 p.m., Fri 9 a.m.–7 p.m., Sat 8 a.m.–6 p.m., Sun closed PAYMENT: Checks ACCESS: & Full access OTHER ETHNIC SPECIALTIES: Polish, Hungarian, Italian

Rudy came to America from Slovenia just as the First World War ended, and in 1928 he opened a butcher shop on Superior Avenue in Cleveland. In 1937, he died in a car accident, and his wife Agnes took over the business with the help of their three sons. By 1955, there was a second store on East 67th and St. Clair, and a third opened in Willowick in 1963. The family sold the two Cleveland locations, and now Rudy and Agnes's youngest son, Karl Bukovec, and grandson, David, run the remaining suburban store with the help of Karl's nephew Tom. Father and son are convinced that the success of the family business is tied to the uniqueness and quality of their products and the personal service they provide. "A supermarket can't offer what we do," says Dave, "and our customers know it." They prepare zelodec (a rarely found type of large-sized cooked Slovenian sausage that can be sliced and used like lunch meat), regular Slovenian smoked sausage, blood sausage, and rice sausage using their own cherished recipes; they also offer Polish, Hungarian, and Italian sausage, Mexican chorizo, and hot Cajun Andouille sausage. Nothing is prepackaged—meat is cut fresh every day, and cut to order—and the staff is friendly and knowledgeable. The shop is in a four-store strip with plenty of parking.

Wojtilas Bakery
☎ (216) 731-7080
CITY: **Euclid**   AREA: **East Side**

ADDRESS: 897 E. 222nd St.
FOOD AVAIL.: baked goods, beverages, coffee, takeout meals HOURS: Tue–Sat 6 a.m.–3 p.m., Sun 7 a.m.–noon, Mon closed PAYMENT: Checks
ACCESS: ♿ Full access

Using family recipes his father brought over from Czechoslovakia, Donny Wojtilas and his wife Barb prepare a variety of traditional Slovenian pastries daily, including potica (a nut bread), flancete (often called angel wings), and krofe (a sort of donut). They also offer a selection of non-Slovenian fresh breads, muffins, cookies, cakes, wedding cakes, and party trays. They opened the bakery with the idea of re-creating the kind of neighborhood shop Donny recalled from his childhood.

Wojtilas Bakery
☎ (216) 361-0499
CITY: **Cleveland**   AREA: **East Side**

ADDRESS: 6413 St. Clair Ave.
FOOD AVAIL.: baked goods, beverages, coffee, takeout meals HOURS: Tue–Sat 6 a.m.–12:30 p.m., closed Sun–Mon
PAYMENT: Checks ACCESS: ♿ Full access

See listing for Wojtilas Bakery on 222nd Street in Euclid for more information.

EUROPE, EAST

{ *Chapter 5* }

EUROPE WEST OF THE DANUBE

For the purposes of this book, Western Europe includes Ireland and the United Kingdom, France, Germany, and Scandinavia. Grouping these countries together, even from a culinary point of view, is problematical, for they are all as different as the languages they speak. But one thing they hold in common is a connection to Cleveland, both past and present.

It has been estimated that by 1860, 45 percent of the city's population was foreign born, with the majority of immigrants coming from Germany, Ireland, England, Scotland, and Wales. They were poor, usually uneducated, and forced to accept backbreaking jobs at the bottom of the economic pyramid. So they labored to build canals and railroads, worked in the quarries, the steel mills, and at the docks, and manned the growing number of factories that transformed Cleveland from a rural outpost to an industrial metropolis.

Swedes followed in the 1870s, and then the Danes and Finns. The French, however, came one by one, as traders in the 1700s, nuns in the 1850s, and the brides of American servicemen after World War II. While the flow of immigrants from most other Western European nations tapered off, Germans continued to settle here in significant numbers well into the 20th century. Many were skilled craftsmen: jewelers, tailors, musical instrument and cabinet makers, and machinists.

Over the years, these nationality groups quietly transformed themselves from immigrant outsiders to mainstream Americans. The Irish, especially, were eager to put aside all that reminded them of the poverty and despair that most had left behind. But what was kept by all were the rich folk traditions of their homelands, traditions that lived on in music, dance, storytelling, and, of course, food.

Though Ireland is renowned more for starvation than feasting, and for a cuisine of potatoes and boiled meat, those who know the food well insist that it is in its own way memorable. "I grew up on a little farm in County Mayo," said Celine O'Leary, who came here in 1952 at the age of 20. "Vegetables grew in our garden, and my grandfather was a butcher, so we always had some meat. There were griddle cakes made over an open fire, soda bread, and scones with whole milk and fresh butter. We'd roast lamb or beef in a cast-iron pot oven. It would cook on hot peat coals in the hearth. And of course we ate plenty of potatoes and turnips. Our food was plain and nourishing, but now when I think of the things we ate, I think how good they were."

The British and the Irish eat much the same way. Bacon, oats, root vegetables and cabbage, dairy products and seafood are basic, along with tea, toast, and marmalade. Traditionally, cooking is done simply, and food is seasoned with a light hand. Pies filled with meat, rolls stuffed with sausage, and eggs with bacon may not be haute cuisine, but they are invariably satisfying.

Equally satisfying are the substantial dishes of old-fashioned German cooking, a genuine meat-and-potatoes cuisine. Good, hearty breads, cheeses, wurst (cold cuts), sausages of all kinds, sauerkraut, and pickles are characteristic. Braten (roasted meat) is the national dish, and pork, both cured and fresh, is the favored meat. "Our food," explained Dr. Robert Ward, a third-generation German American, "is so much a part of the American way of eating, that most people don't even know they're enjoying German food. It was Germans, for example, who introduced Americans to sauerkraut and beer. In the 1850s, Germans started brewing beer in Cleveland. The Hofbrau Haus Restaurant is located in what was once a German neighborhood full of gasthauses (taverns) and outdoor beer gardens like those in Europe, and each one made their own brew."

The cuisine of the Scandinavian countries warrants little exposition here because there are no longer any restaurants that serve it; only a few stores sell some of their imported products or bake traditional breads. Like the other nationalities that make up this chapter, they use potatoes and pork extensively. Fish and cheese also dominate their table. Dill is the herb of choice, as it is for the Germans.

And then, at last, there is French food, a cuisine that has had an influence on fine dining far out of proportion to the number of French people who have come to America. "The French live their food," said Marcie Barker, who, with her husband—chef Ali Barker—owned and operated Cleveland's French-inspired restaurant, Piperade, now closed. "They are passionate about cooking and eating."

French cooking at the professional level has long set the standard for chefs and gourmets in this country, and the precise techniques and methods of preparation they've perfected form the foundation of a good culinary education.

"French cuisine is organized and unified with a great respect for the character of each ingredient," said chef and teacher Donna Adams. "Once you've got the basics, they can be expanded in so many ways."

A well-stocked French larder includes butter, wine, cream, mustard, onions, garlic, shallots, leeks, potatoes, and wild mushrooms. Bay leaves, chervil, bouquet garni, tarragon, and parsley are favored herbs. Root vegetables, green beans and peas, fresh fruit, nuts, and cheeses are also important.

"Real French cooking," said Jeanine Mihallek, who came here from Paris in 1946, "is about the art of beautiful simplicity. We like to know what we are eating, and waste nothing. Even leftovers can look and taste like a feast. But we need our bread; good bread is everything."

Luckily for Jeanine and the rest of us, good French bread is indeed available in Cleveland, along with some other authentic examples of the French culinary art of beautiful simplicity.

DON'T FORGET: CALL AHEAD!

RESTAURANTS

Austrian

Mozart Restaurant

☎ **(330) 493-8664**

CITY: **Canton**   AREA: **Farther South**
ATMOSPHERE: **Relaxed**   COST: **$$$**$$

ADDRESS: 3522 Cleveland Ave., NW
HOURS: Tue–Sat 4–11 p.m., Sun & Mon closed
RESERVATIONS: Taken, Suggested for five or more
PAYMENT: MC, VS, AX, DIS **BAR:** Beer, wine
TAKEOUT: Yes **SMOKING:** Smoking section
ACCESS: ♿ Full access **OTHER ETHNIC SPECIALTIES:**
German

This very European restaurant, voted the most romantic dining spot in Stark County, is located in a very non-European, non-romantic section of Canton, an oasis of fine food and soft lights in a fast-food desert. It's here because in 1992 Kara Karasarides, a local girl, met Alois Maierhofer, who was born in a small village in Austria. He was the chef on a cruise ship, she was on vacation. Love bloomed, marriage followed, and the couple settled in her hometown with the idea of creating a restaurant unlike anything in the area. He's a master chef, one of only two in Ohio, and that means he's trained to teach as well as cook. He is remarkably knowledgeable about food history and speaks passionately about ingredients and techniques. Alois learned his craft at culinary school in Vienna—he studied for five years and then served as an apprentice for another six.

Kara, who grew up in a restaurant family, manages the front of the house and the business end of things. She is a one-woman cheerleading squad for her husband, their restaurant, the charming little beer garden they have created out back, and the difference between the authentic food they serve and everybody else's. If food like spaetzle and sauerkraut are part of your heritage, or if you've traveled extensively, as I have, in those parts of Europe where these are among the basic food groups, then you'll know after one bite that you're in the presence of the Real Thing.

In the world of food, Germany and Austria are one nation, and Hungary is a kissing cousin. Selections on the menu blend the tastes and styles of all three, in dishes from the kartoffel suppe (creamy potato soup) and the apple-and-red-cabbage slaw to the Wiener saftgulasch (otherwise known as goulash) and Rheinischer sauerbraten. There are potato pancakes and German potato salad laced with crispy crumbled bits of bacon, nockeri (homemade noodles with cheese and onions), stuffed cabbage, and Schweinsbraten (oven-roasted pork loin). Schnitzel comes in veal, pork, or chicken versions, and it's done in a mouthwatering variety of ways: the simple breaded and pan-fried version; with raspberry schnapps cream sauce; grilled with paprika cream sauce; with onions, peppers, mushrooms, and bacon; Swiss-style on a bed of cabbage with melted cheese; with wild mushrooms and burgundy sauce; in a zinfandel cream sauce; and . . . (yes, there are more choices). Bratwurst, those lovely sausages that are the German equivalent of a burger, are made up specially for the restaurant according to their own recipe, and the kitchen adds a beer sauce. You might find another sausage, like Munich weisswurst, on the list of daily specials. A pot of German mustard is essential, and they supply the good imported stuff. The Bavarian and Oktoberfest combo platters are just the ticket for those who can't make up their minds. Backtracking to the start of your meal, I must mention the German sourdough bread and homemade seasoned cream butter (really a butter spread made with cheese, garlic, paprika, and other top-secret ingredients) that comes to the table first—it's very tempting to eat so much of this stuff that there's no room left for all the rest. And that includes dessert, too. The Viennese are known for their pastry, and Alois carries on the tradition. He makes Black Forest torte, strudel, sweet crepes, and Bavarian custard torte.

The wine list features European reds and whites, as well as bottles from California, Italy, France, and Spain. For a memorable experience try the Gluhwein, a traditional Austrian favorite of spiced and flaming red wine. As you'd expect, the selection of German and Austrian beers is awesome: there are Pilsners, Bocks, Doppelbocks, and lagers with brand names like Stiegel, Paulaner, Bischofshof, Allgauer, Augustiner, Warsteiner, and Spaten. The restaurant's name reflects the fact that Kara and Alois consider food and music two of life's best pleasures. A strolling musician plays on Friday and Saturday evenings. Get on Kara's mailing list (2,000 people already have) to receive notice of special events so you can make reservations early for things like their big Oktoberfest, periodic wine tastings, the Schnitzel Festival (held in honor of a visit by Alois's mother—the two cooked together for the first time), and the weeklong celebration of Mozart's birthday at the end of January. They have a private room and will cater your celebration or meeting. The white stucco building is next to a church and surrounded by a parking lot. It's decorated with scenes of medieval castles, a suit of armor, and a picture (or at least a reasonable likeness) of the restaurant's namesake. A bright red awning and a big sign near the street make it easy to find. Don't hesitate to bring the whole family: although many find it a romantic spot, kids—who are, after all, often the end result of romance—are quite welcome.

British

His Majesty's Tea Room
☎ (440) 417-0220

CITY: **Madison**   AREA: **Farther East**
ATMOSPHERE: **Dressy**   COST: $$$$$

ADDRESS: 63 W. Main St.
HOURS: Reservations taken for Wed–Sat 11 a.m.–3 p.m.   RESERVATIONS: Taken, highly suggested   PAYMENT: MC, VS, AX, DIS, checks
BAR: None   TAKEOUT: Yes   SMOKING: Smoke-Free
ACCESS: ♿ Full access

In 1875, the brick building at 63 West Main Street was a bank. Since 1996, it's been His Majesty's Tea Room. The bank vault is now the coatroom. The location is Madison Village, a small town on the eastern edge of Lake County, a few minutes' drive from I-90, but the ambience and the attitude are pure English. Inside, the 121 years that have passed between these two dates and the distance between the two countries seem irrelevant. Owner Michael Loparo and her partner and husband Vincent have gone to great lengths to create a stately, elegant Victorian parlor where afternoon tea is served British-style in the leisurely, aristocratic fashion of a bygone era. The five narrow, 10-foot-tall windows looking out on the village square are draped in lace. The original wood paneling has been restored to a gleaming shine. The dominant color is royal blue. Tables are set with good silver, fine china, lace runners, and flowers. The Victorians were great lovers of knickknacks, souvenirs, and curios, and in that spirit, every available bit of space here is filled with a charming clutter of decorative 19th-century collectibles, both antiques and reproductions, most of which are for sale, as well as teas and tea-making accessories, and His Majesty's own line of salad dressings, flavored honeys, preserves, and dessert mixes.

All of this provides the perfect backdrop for a "proper" English afternoon tea

EUROPE, WEST

EUROPE, WEST

served by staff that understands that an essential element of the experience is to make each guest feel like pampered royalty. The menu changes monthly but typically includes finger sandwiches (chicken salad, cucumber, ham, and roast beef), cheese tartlets, and a light appetizer; scones or crumpets with lemon curd, preserves, and Devon cream; some combination of muffins, tea bread, cookies, shortbread, and chocolates; cake (two of the house specialties, baked on the premises like everything else, are macaroon cake and coconut rose cake); and of course a bottomless pot of tea that arrives with its own cozy (a quilted cover to keep the contents warm). No bland and characterless Lipton's brew here—the selection of tea is extensive: rich, black darjeelings, orange pekoes, and specialty blends like English Breakfast and Earl Grey; oolong and green teas; and fruit, flower, and herbal tisanes (the correct term for what results when these ingredients are steeped in hot water). Throughout the year there are special-event teas, like the Dickens Dinner Tea in December (think Yorkshire pudding, game hens, and trifle), with even more elaborate menus and decorations: there's also a Victorian Strawberry Festival, Spring High Teas, Garden Talk and Tea, and Teddy Bear and Doll Teas. The facilities are available, by reservation, for your own private celebrations such as bridal and baby showers, wedding party dinners, birthdays, anniversaries, and group luncheons. For information, get on the mailing list and you'll receive copies of the newsletter *His Majesty's Quill*. The place is a bit like a 19th-century stage set, and you get to be the star of the show. A mostly female crowd is attracted to the opportunity to exchange their jeans for something nicer, slow down, and utter phrases like "I beg your pardon" and "Excuse me?" rather than "My bad" and "Say what?" I'm also convinced that a large number of women may be genetically predisposed to respond with pleasure to Victorian excess and the old-fashioned aura of doilies, chintz, cherubs, and lace

swags. But men are made comfortable too (the luncheon menu has some hearty and substantial offerings that can satisfy a macho appetite), and for those who think the only hot beverage should be coffee, an herbal tea offers a java taste.

In addition to being a popular destination for friends who want to sit and have a long talk-filled visit and sweethearts in search of a romantic setting, the tearoom, which seats about 44, has appeal for cross-generational get-togethers. Mothers and daughters like to dress up and take tea. "But don't," urges Loparo, "leave out the boys." Grandparents, some of whom find the place and the service reminiscent of their own youth, bring their grandchildren to give them a taste of the past. The ambience is the antithesis of the fast-food, fast-paced world most are familiar with, and it seems to encourage good manners (or at least a discussion of what the term means). Michael Loparo considers this atmosphere of civilized gentility a big part of the secret of her success. "People crave this. It represents a way of living that has mostly disappeared. Some remember it, others want to experience what they've only read about, and many want to bring their children to a place that both welcomes them but at the same time requires ladylike and gentlemanly behavior." Prince and princess teas are offered to the under-12 set. Food is also served outside on the patio in good weather (table seating for about 20), and visitors are invited to walk through and enjoy the traditional English garden Michael has created behind His Majesty's. Reservations, though not required, are essential as the place is small and almost always busy. Ample parking on the street. The Tea Room closes for one month in mid-December so Michael and her husband can spend the holiday season with their large family.

The Lobby Lounge at the Ritz-Carlton Hotel
☎ (216) 902-5255

CITY: **Cleveland**   AREA: **Downtown**
ATMOSPHERE: **Casual**   COST: $$$$$

ADDRESS: 1515 W. 3rd St.
HOURS: Tea: Mon–Sun noon–4 p.m.
RESERVATIONS: Taken, suggested PAYMENT: MC,
VS, AX, DIS BAR: Beer, wine, liquor TAKEOUT: No
SMOKING: Smoke-Free ACCESS: ♿ Full access

This is a place you choose when you want a setting for a very special occasion. I took my friend Jean—a dedicated Anglophile—there for her birthday. We felt quite grand, sitting in comfortable, high-backed chairs, sipping Earl Grey tea poured from a bottomless silver pot by an attentive server, and nibbling little finger sandwiches and cakes. It was just like the game "Ladies" I used to play with my younger sister, only better because the food was real. It's a beautiful room, with large windows, a fireplace, and consistently stunning arrangements of fresh flowers on a table in the center. The full afternoon tea includes elegant finger sandwiches and a three-tiered dessert tray that comes with a bowl of thick, sweet Devonshire cream. Light tea is the same, without the sandwiches. On Sundays, they offer a children's tea at which hot chocolate and Shirley Temples are also available. It's a great opportunity to make the kids dress up and experience what it's like to eat in a civilized manner. Tell them to think of it as a sort of off-season Halloween. For Americans, it's pretend, but English folk would probably feel at home, recognizing this as the best part of an almost bygone era. There's a small full-service bar for those not thoroughly into the etiquette of tea, and, on request, the bartender will produce a special gadget for trimming cigars. Before arriving, practice crooking your little finger while holding a tea cup. You can park in Tower City's lot and walk through the mall to the entrance on the upper level, or drive to the front entrance of the hotel on West Third, and have your car parked by a valet.

French

Chez Francois
☎ (440) 967-0630

CITY: **Vermilion**   AREA: **Farther West**
ATMOSPHERE: **Formal**   COST: $$$$$

ADDRESS: 555 Main St.
HOURS: Tue–Thu 5–9 p.m., Fri & Sat 5–10 p.m.,
Sun 4–8 p.m. In warm weather months, patio
opens at 2 p.m. on Sat & Sun; Restaurant closed
December 31–March 14 RESERVATIONS: Taken,
recommended, required for Fri, Sat evenings and
patio PAYMENT: MC, VS, AX, checks BAR: Beer,
wine, liquor TAKEOUT: No SMOKING: Yes
ACCESS: ♿ Limited *Not recommended for
children

Vermilion was once a fishing port, and long ago sails were made and nets were stored in the building that now houses this restaurant. The original hand-carved beams and exposed-brick floors and walls create a rustic ambience countered by coral-colored table linens and a classic French menu. Chef John D'Amico, who owns the place along with partner and maitre d' Matthew Mars, uses reduction sauces made with cream, butter, and stock and tends toward grilling and poaching his meat, poultry, and seafood. "In keeping with contemporary tastes," he explained, "I try to make my sauces lighter than the traditional version, and flavor with fresh herbs that I buy from local farmers along with their fresh produce. Much of what I use is organically grown." At a customer's request, John will gladly prepare dishes with no saucing at all, and can compose interesting offerings for vegetarians with some advance notice. All the desserts, from napoleons to sorbets, are made in his kitchen too. In business since 1987, Chez Francois relies primarily on word of mouth to attract diners, many of whom willingly

EUROPE, WEST

travel over an hour (it's a 45-minute trip from downtown Cleveland) for the experience. The patio garden overlooks the Vermilion River, and diners here sit amidst greenery under an awning. A few tables inside share this lovely view. At least eight times a year there are scheduled events, such as wine tastings, Mother's Day celebrations, and a cigar party—the only time cigar smoking is permitted in the restaurant. Get on the mailing list to receive newsletters announcing these special activities.

Johnny's Bistro
☎ **(216) 774-0055**

CITY: **Cleveland**   AREA: **Downtown**
ATMOSPHERE: **Dressy**   COST: **$$$$$**

ADDRESS: 1400 W. 6th St.
HOURS: Mon–Thu 5–10 p.m., Fri & Sat 5–11 p.m., Sun closed **RESERVATIONS:** Taken, Suggested on weekends and for parties of six or more
PAYMENT: MC, VS, AX, DIS, checks **BAR:** Beer, wine, liquor **TAKEOUT:** Yes **SMOKING:** Smoking section **ACCESS:** ♿ Full access

"Brutes feed," wrote a 19th-century observer of American life. "The best barbarian only eats. Only the cultured man can dine." By that definition, you will encounter no brutes or barbarians here. This elegant bistro is meant for the gastronome who sips and sups, not for those who tend toward grabbing, gulping, or gobbling, and thus must surely attract the cultured man. It's the third such place for owners Joe Santosuosso and Paul Anthony, and as in their other two venues, the food, setting, and service are geared for those who appreciate fine dining and all the elements associated with it dishes crafted for the connoisseur. (See listings for Johnny's Bar and Johnny's Downtown.) Here, they've shifted the focus from Italian food to French cuisine, naming the place after a 14th-century French saint, whose picture is featured on the menu (oddly, they chose one who found himself forced to live in the woods surviv-

ing on loaves of bread brought to him by a dog—hardly evocative of good meals in a deluxe setting. The restaurant has claimed bistro status since its opening, but only moved closer to meeting that description in the past year, lowering the prices a bit, simplifying the food, and getting rid of the coats and ties dress code. But it's still no neighborhood tavern- even if the neighborhood is in Paris. There's seating for 75, plus additional rooms for private parties, and decor that features imported marble, highly polished wood, crystal chandeliers, and thick carpeting. Tables are adorned with fresh roses in silver vases, crisp white linens, fine china, and glassware. Music comes from a baby grand piano. The seasonal menu, with fewer French terms, is built around hearty, classic main courses such as braised short ribs, rack of lamb, roast chicken, and crispy duck in orange sauce, plus French kitchen standards— onion tart, croque monsieur (think high-end grilled cheese and ham), mussels Provencal, chateaubriand, bouillabaisse, and papillote (fish and vegetables baked in parchment). In the cold weather months expect more stews, soups, and peasant style dishes like cassoulet, a layered, slow-cooked casserole made with duck, pork, garlic sausage, beans, and tomatoes. You can enjoy eating here even if it represents your first encounter with truffles, frogs' legs, or escargot (snails) but for those who know the difference between a Bearnaise and Bordelaise sauce or recognize a duxelle (a paste made from mushrooms, shallots, and herbs cooked in butter) when they taste it, it will be a special pleasure. Desserts range from the simplicity of perfectly poached pears to a sweet soufflé topped with crème Anglaise custard. An open kitchen design means chefs work in full view of patrons, and for those who want an even better view than what's available from the tables, there is also some close-up counter seating. A separate bar area, where smoking is allowed (it's not permitted in the rest of the restaurant), is equipped with couches and chairs, as is the lobby (smokers welcome here, too). Waiters and waitresses are well trained and make every effort to be both gracious and unobtrusive, providing a level of service in keeping with the cost and the atmosphere. The wine list, as you would expect, is extensive, selective, and expensive, with a variety that includes the best of California cabernets and chardonnays, merlots, meritages, pinot noirs, zinfandels, French and Italian reds and whites, champagne and other sparkling wines, and dessert wines. Valet parking is free.

Parker's New American Bistro
☎ (216) 771-7130

CITY: **Cleveland**   AREA: **Near West Side**
ATMOSPHERE: **Casual**   COST: $$$$$

ADDRESS: 2801 Bridge Ave.
HOURS: Mon–Sat 5 p.m.–no closing time
RESERVATIONS: Taken, always suggested;
required Sat **PAYMENT:** MC, VS, AX, DIS, checks
BAR: Beer, wine, liquor **TAKEOUT:** No
SMOKING: Smoking section **ACCESS:** ♿ Limited
*Not recommended for children

After his successful, elegant, high-end restaurant, Parker's, was named one of the nation's top 50 restaurants by Gourmet Magazine, Parker Bosley changed everything. In February 2002, he renamed it, redecorated, changed the menu, lowered the prices, and created a less formal and truly unique place to eat—a place that more completely represents his approach to the art and craft of making food. Almost anybody can take an expensive cut of meat and make something good to eat. The test of a truly great chef is what he or she can do with what is normally considered a humble and less desirable selection. By this standard, Parker Bosley proves himself a master six nights a week at his Ohio City restaurant where he turns things like pork belly, short ribs, beef liver, and sweetbreads into extraordinary fare. He draws inspiration from the traditional homestyle cuisine of France (as well as other cultures), where recipes of economy have developed over centuries that, in his words, "elevate the lowliest foods to new heights of taste." But the simple components he favors are far from ordinary. Dishes are created around the idea that truly good food is the result of simplicity married to fresh, seasonal, locally produced ingredients. He works in partnership with a network of nearly 20 area farmers, ranchers, and dairymen committed to organic and sustainable agricultural practices to get the products he needs. Often the menu lists the source of what's used: roasted young chicken from Tea Hills Poultry in Ashland County; all natural beef filet from Knox County; cream of mushroom soup garnished with Killbuck Valley Mushrooms. He personally visits every place he buys from.

The selections from his kitchen are constantly changing. Winter offerings might feature kohlrabi, fennel, cabbage, and apple slaw; pork strudel; braised rabbit with celery root puree; vegetable stew with fennel flan; and duck leg confit with parsnip mashed potatoes. Warmer weather brings spring onion or cream of asparagus soup; baked goat cheese on mixed greens; sauteed pork loin with rhubarb sauce; and a grilled hangar steak with shallot sauce and seasonal vegetables. Desserts feature seasonal fruits as well as pastries, creams, and custards made with organic dairy products; apple tarts baked to order and served with vanilla ice cream; chocolate souffle tart with crème fraiche ice cream; creme brulee; almond angel food cake with crème anglaise; and bittersweet chocolate ice cream. The wine list is considered outstanding and reasonably priced. Beyond food and drink, there is the setting and the service. The well-trained serving staff understands their role in making the evening complete. The space, remodeled in 2002, capitalizes on the special qualities of the 1860s-era building featuring exposed brickwork and hardwood plank floors. The décor is comfortable, attractive, and understated. Patrons enter each of the two

EUROPE, WEST

dining rooms through the bar area, where they can also be seated for dinner. Private rooms, special menus, and off premise catering are available.

German

Der Braumeister
☎ (216) 671-6220

CITY: **Cleveland** AREA: **Near West Side**
ATMOSPHERE: **Casual** COST: $$$$$

ADDRESS: 13046 Lorain Ave.
HOURS: Mon–Fri 11 a.m.–9 p.m., Sat 3–10 p.m.; bar open until 1 a.m.; closed Sun
RESERVATIONS: Taken PAYMENT: MC, VS, AX, DIS
BAR: Beer, wine, liquor TAKEOUT: Yes
SMOKING: Smoking section ACCESS: ♿ Full access

The decor is German *gasthaus* cum American rustic, and the atmosphere is warm, comfortable, and friendly. It was recently updated and spiffed up. Many patrons are regulars and address each other, as well as the servers, by name. The 100-seat dining room works as a setting for a drink and a quick, light meal or a place to linger over a four-course dinner, and the Castle Room, which seats up to 75, is a popular venue for club meetings or private parties. The menu is a mix of German specialties like rouladen (filet of beef rolled around a stuffing laced with pickles, onions, and bacon), schnitzel (a thin veal cutlet), and schweinsbraten (braised pork roast), and American-style dishes such as pan-fried walleye and roast duck. Portions are large. Appetizers, soups, salads, and snacks also reflect the blend of traditional German and thoroughly American favorites. There is a selection of German sausages and cold cuts for sandwiches, and side dishes like pickled cucumber salad and potato dumplings. German beers are on tap, and imported wines are available by the glass or bottle. Easy to find with convenient parking on the well-lit side

street and in the rear. A small German deli operates under the same name and roof (see market listings in this chapter for more information).

Donauschwaben German American Cultural Center
☎ (440) 235-2646

CITY: **Olmsted Twp.** AREA: **West Side**
ATMOSPHERE: **Relaxed** COST: $$$$$

ADDRESS: 7370 Columbia Rd.
HOURS: Tue–Sat 11 a.m.–2:30 p.m., Sun closed
RESERVATIONS: Taken, only for groups of 6 or more PAYMENT: Checks BAR: Beer, wine
TAKEOUT: Yes SMOKING: Smoking section
ACCESS: ♿ Full access

Go German for lunch at Leanu Park. Following a talk I gave at Fairview Park Library, a member of the audience (you know who you are…unfortunately, I don't. But I owe you a thank-you) told me about it. In the summer of 2002, this private club decided to open up to the public in a small way. Executive chef Steve Weiss prepares a variety of traditional entrees and side dishes including sauerbraten, wiener schnitzel, kassler rippchen (smoked pork chops), bratwurst, potato pancakes, and sauerkraut, with the menu changing every few months. Food is served in the small bar area and outdoors on the patio overlooking a lake in the warm weather. Large groups and private parties can be accommodated in the main dining room. It's very informal, kids are welcome, and casual attire is fine, although the Sunday-after-church crowd is generally well dressed.

Heimatland Inn
☎ (330) 220-8671

CITY: **Brunswick**   AREA: **Farther South**
ATMOSPHERE: **Casual**   COST: $$$$$

ADDRESS: 3511 Center Rd.
HOURS: Summer: Tue–Thu 11 a.m.–8 p.m., Fri 11 a.m.–9 p.m., Sat 8 a.m.–9 p.m., Sun 8 a.m.–7 p.m., closed Mon; Fall & Winter: Mon–Thu 11 a.m.–8 p.m., Fri 11 a.m.–9 p.m., Sat 8 a.m.–9 p.m., Sun 8 a.m.–7 p.m.
RESERVATIONS: Taken, for parties of 6 or more
PAYMENT: MC, VS, DIS **BAR:** Beer, wine, liquor
TAKEOUT: Yes **SMOKING:** Smoking section
ACCESS: ♿ Full access

"This," said one diner, "is some serious grub. I left the table in a delightful food coma." He went with a friend, whose father is from Germany, and his official word was that the *deutsche* part of the menu is the genuine article. Evelyn Rowerstein, who opened the restaurant in mid-1994, learned to cook from her German mother, who now helps run the place, along with Rowerstein's husband. They prepare spaetzle, potato salad, and dumplings from scratch to serve with sauerbraten, rouladen, knockwurst, bratwurst, and schnitzel. The marinated herring appetizer served with sour cream, raw onions, and cucumbers rates high on the ethnic Richter scale, as does the red cabbage side dish. There are other European dishes on the menu, many of which are featured on the buffet, a section for kids, and numerous non-German dishes that range from grilled chicken breast to chef salad. An ever-varied selection of European-style desserts is available. Breakfast is straight bacon and eggs. The building is made to resemble a mountain chalet. The main dining room is narrow and deep, decorated with handpainted murals that depict various Bavarian cities, European scenes, and distinctive town crests. The restaurant seats about 60. They offer an authentic European buffet every Sunday from 1 p.m. to 6 p.m. Service is that nice combination of friendly and efficient, and many employees are members of the owners' families. *"Herzlich willkommen,"* they write on the menu: "With a warm heart, we welcome you."

Henry Wahner's Restaurant & Lounge
☎ (330) 678-4055

CITY: **Kent**   AREA: **Farther South**
ATMOSPHERE: **Casual**   COST: $$$$$

ADDRESS: 1609 E. Main St.
HOURS: Mon–Thu 4–9 p.m., Fri & Sat 4–10 p.m.; closed Sun **RESERVATIONS:** Not taken
PAYMENT: Checks **BAR:** Beer, wine, liquor
TAKEOUT: Yes **SMOKING:** Smoking section
ACCESS: ♿ Full access

This family restaurant is well known and loved by the German-American community. The two sisters who own the place will often stop by tables to chat with diners, comfortable in either English or German. Many people have been coming here for years to celebrate their high-water marks—birthdays, anniversaries, and graduations—and the staff, too, have almost all worked here for a long time. Mixed in with a standard selection of steaks, chops, and seafood are some German classics: sauerbraten, rouladen, schnitzel, and kassler rippchen (smoked pork chops). Spaetzle, potato pancakes, German potato salad, and sauerkraut are also available, and the "Deutsche combination plate" offers a selection of German house specialties including homemade sausage. Portions are enormous. There is a children's menu, and half portions (which still tend to fill the plates to overflowing) are available during the early-bird-special hours between 4 and 6 p.m. The dining room is wood paneled, the carpeting looks well used, and the place doesn't offer much in the way of ambience or decor. Nonetheless, it attracts a crowd and it's easy to find, a freestanding building surrounded by a parking lot just past the Kent State University campus.

EUROPE, WEST

Kuhar's
☎ (216) 731-0888

CITY: **Euclid**   AREA: **East Side**
ATMOSPHERE: **Relaxed**   COST: $$$$$

ADDRESS: 823 E. 222nd St.

HOURS: Mon–Fri 11 a.m.–8:30 p.m., Sat 11 a.m.–8 p.m., Sun closed **RESERVATIONS:** Not taken **PAYMENT:** Cash only **BAR:** None
TAKEOUT: Yes **SMOKING:** All sections
ACCESS: ♿ Full access

You can't sit down here, but you can take home a complete German lunch or dinner and hardly notice the cost. Very reasonable prices and very traditional recipes lend appeal to this otherwise inconspicuous and informal takeout and catering operation. If you're a fan of things like sauerbraten, rindsrouladen (stuffed and rolled steak), roast pork, and stuffed cabbage you'll be tempted to call in an order often. They prepare veal schnitzel four different ways—in wine sauce with peppers, onions, and mushrooms (natur); sauteed in butter (Paris); breaded and fried (Wiener); and stuffed with ham and Emmenthaler cheese (St. Moritz). All just beg for sides like cucumber salad, potato pancakes, or dumplings, and should be followed by German chocolate cake, strudel, or Black Forest torte. The kitchen also does Hungarian goulash, chicken paprikash, and a Slovenian smoked sausage sandwich. The Old World meets the new here because the menu includes fried chicken, burgers, and assorted sandwiches. They bake their own bread and offer a daily soup special. Phone ahead to have your food ready when you arrive. The shop is located next to Euclid Meat and Sausage, so you can pick up some supplies for cooking at home another day.

Irish

Flannery's Pub
☎ (216) 781-7782

CITY: **Cleveland**   AREA: **Downtown**
ATMOSPHERE: **Casual**   COST: $$$$$

ADDRESS: 323 Prospect Ave.

HOURS: Mon–Tue 11:30 a.m.–9, Wed 11:30 a.m.–9 p.m., Thu 11:30 a.m.–11 p.m., Fri 11 a.m.–midnight, Sat noon–midnight, Sun closed; bar open daily until 2 a.m. **RESERVATIONS:** Taken
PAYMENT: MC, VS, AX **BAR:** Beer, wine, liquor
TAKEOUT: Yes **SMOKING:** Smoking section
ACCESS: ♿ Full access *Not recommended for children **OTHER ETHNIC SPECIALTIES:** British

It's a bar, it's a restaurant, it's a concert hall; it's all three rolled into one. The bar is long, 24 seats with the requisite wall-mounted televisions that are always tuned to people chasing various sorts of balls. Nearby are four round, tall tables with stools and a ledge along the front window that's at just the right height for resting a beer or an elbow. In addition to all your common brews, they have a selection of Irish and British Isle ales, lagers, and stouts including Guinness, Beamish, Harp, English Old Speckled Hen, Newcastle Brown, and Old Speckled Hen—my personal favorite for both name and taste. When it comes to "sippin" whiskey, the choice of single-malt scotches is large and the brand names lilting: Glenfiddich, Bunnahabain, Glenmorangie, Craggamore, Glenronach, Dalwhinnie, Glenkinchie. The restaurant serves up some traditional pub food and Irish fare including fish and chips; Irish stew; poached salmon; potato and cheese soup; fish cakes; and a specialty rarely served outside Ireland or an Irish mom's kitchen: colcannon, a flavorful, stick-to-your-ribs portion of mashed potatoes with cabbage, carrots, and scallions. The menu also offers a selection of sandwiches, steaks, and salads. Desserts include bread pudding, and fruit and cream. There is seating for about 360 people, divided into three main dining areas (two are completely separate rooms, one with a fireplace, and both can be reserved for private parties), plus some absolutely intriguing secluded little rooms just big enough for a couple or a foursome that want to sit up close and personal. The place has a true pub look, though on a somewhat grander and larger scale, all done up in pool-table green, rich red woods, and well-polished brass. The bands, who make music Thursday, Friday, and Saturday nights between 9:30 p.m. and 1 a.m. on a built-in stage specially designed to accommodate them, are mostly Irish, but there's also some jazz, folk, and rock groups. Saturdays, however, are always reserved for the sounds of Ireland. The Pub is housed in a beautifully restored brick building on the corner of East Fourth and Prospect, across from the Gund Arena.

The Harp
☎ (216) 939-0200

CITY: **Cleveland**   AREA: **Near West Side**
ATMOSPHERE: **Casual**   COST: $$$$$

ADDRESS: 4408 Detroit Ave.
HOURS: Mon–Thu 11 a.m.–10 p.m., Fri & Sat 11 a.m.–11 p.m., Sun 11 a.m.–9 p.m.
RESERVATIONS: Taken **PAYMENT:** MC, VS, AX
BAR: Beer, wine, liquor **TAKEOUT:** Yes
SMOKING: Smoking section **ACCESS:** ♿ Full access

The question for today's geo-quiz is: where are you if the signpost reads Carr Chlos, Oilean Acla, Dueige (pronounced Dooega), but your feet are firmly planted on Detroit Avenue? The answer is the Harp, a place to eat and drink that is so thoroughly Irish you might think the Emerald Isles had been relocated to the Erie shores. Those signs out front are the real thing, and once pointed the way to the small village in County Mayo where Mike O'Malley, the father of Harp owner Karen O'Malley, was born and raised, and to Achill Island, which is near it. (Carr Chlos,

in case you're curious, is where you park your car.) Mike O'Malley built this brick-and-stucco building for his daughter from the ground up. "It was," says Karen, "a labor of love for him, and he's very proud of it." He should be. The careful attention to detail and the fine craftsmanship, visible especially in the wooden moldings and millwork, has resulted in something fine, lovely, and rare. The Harp was designed by a prominent Irish architectural firm, Frank Ennis and Associates, to resemble the pubs found in Dublin and Galway. There's a stone hearth, hardwood floors, inviting nooks, and comfy benches. All the furniture's from Ireland too, and the beautiful murals were painted by a Dublin artist. At the center of the coffered ceiling is a Celtic knot, ancient symbol of love and friendship, and on one wall is a rendering of the view from the front gate of Mike O'Malley's childhood home. The soda bread, dense without being heavy, rich-flavored and studded with raisins, is made from Grandma's recipe, and it's so popular that they sell it by the loaf. A family recipe is also used for the Irish coffee. The 20-ounce imperial pints of Guinness and Murphy's Stout, Harp Lager, Caffrey's Cream Ale, and Murphy's Amber are as Irish as you can get when it comes to slaking your thirst. Unless of course you prefer Irish whiskey: you can ask the barkeep for Jameson, Bushmills, Tullamore Dew, Midleton Rare, or a potion called James Joyce Hot Whiskey, made with sugar, cloves, and lemon. There are also nonalcoholic, but nonetheless authentic, liquid options including and Barry Irish Teas by the pot, which Karen describes on the menu as "just like back home." The music's Irish on Wednesday, Friday, and Saturday nights.

The atmosphere is as relaxed and sociable as you'd find in a real pub, too. Friends gossip and play cards here, groups celebrate, families gather knowing that children of all ages are made welcome, and couples hold hands. And then there's the food. Although the menu does not limit itself to Irish fare, there is a selection of

Emerald Isle dishes that would surely please any traditionalist: Achill Island smoked salmon with brown bread; country potato and root vegetable chowder; and scones for a lavish Sunday brunch. The colcannon, a smooth flavorful combination of mashed potatoes and cabbage, prompts clean-your-plate behavior. The boxty (potato pancakes) can be ordered with chicken, salmon, or vegetables. The shepherd's pie is first-class comfort food. Other choices include chicken pot pie, "Dublin lawyer" (lobster in Irish whiskey sauce), and fish and chips. For those not inclined toward Irish cuisine, there are salads, a soup of the day, sandwiches, and all sorts of appealing appetizers, plus beef tenderloin, steak, chicken, salmon fillet, and pork chop entrees. The menu does change seasonally. My description of the kitchen's accomplishments would not be complete without a mention of a truly inspired dessert creation called the Guinness ice-cream sundae. I don't understand exactly how the stout is married to the vanilla bean ice cream, chocolate, honey-roasted pecans, butterscotch, caramel, and whipped cream, but for my taste, it's a match made in heaven. There's a kids' menu; on- and off-site catering services; and special dinners, cooking classes, and monthlong festivities in honor of St. Patrick's Day. To keep informed, get on their mailing list and receive copies of the *Harp News.* A few final words about the space and the place. Big windows frame a stunning view of the lake and the city skyline. A deck that seats 80 is open during good weather. The bar is a beauty, backed by stained-glass windows from an old Woodland Avenue church that was demolished. Karen is usually found at the front door greeting her customers and making them feel like they've just arrived at her house for a party.

Nighttown

☎ (216) 795-0550

CITY: **Cleveland Heights** AREA: **East Side**
ATMOSPHERE: **Casual** COST: **$$$$$**

ADDRESS: 12383 Cedar Rd.

HOURS: Daily 11 a.m.–midnight; bar open nightly until 1 a.m. **RESERVATIONS:** Taken, recommended Fri, Sat nights, especially before Cleveland Orchestra concerts **PAYMENT:** MC, VS, AX, DIS **BAR:** Beer, wine, liquor **TAKEOUT:** Yes **SMOKING:** Smoking section **ACCESS:** ♿ Full access *Not recommended for children **OTHER ETHNIC SPECIALTIES:** British

A literary education lets you in on the meaning of the name and logo, explaining why this place looks like a cross between an early-20th-century bawdy house, a British Isles pub, and a piano bar. In his book *Ulysses,* James Joyce calls the district in Dublin frequented by women of ill repute and their customers Nighttown, the after-dark world of food, drink, music, and other assorted entertainments. But knowing this is not an essential prerequisite to enjoying either the atmosphere or the food here. It's a clubby sort of restaurant, much frequented by a loyal coterie of regulars, darkish, comfortable, and eccentric. Busy during lunch and dinner, the place has a special late-night charm, and real appeal when it's cold and wet outside. Typically it's packed before and after Cleveland Orchestra performances. The decor, which is distinctly different in each of the two bar and four dining areas, is an eclectic, tongue-in-cheek mix. An altar and pews make up one of the bars, and a marble slab that once graced a public men's room is used for the other. There are mounted elk heads; assorted bits of memorabilia from the days of trolley cars, straw boaters, and bustles; an odd assortment of vintage photos, portraits (most notably one of Joyce himself), posters, and prints, including one of a creature that's half naked woman, half chicken; a tavern clock made by Joseph Clark of London in the

1700s; and, on the wall in the men's room (don't ask how I know), an old, framed menu from the Blazes Boylan Grill Room in Bloom's Hotel, Ireland. There's an abundance of gleaming wood, stained and etched glass, mirrors, and dim lighting from gas lamp look-alikes. There are spaces for large groups and very private twosomes, and the smoking room is completely separate from those reserved for nonsmokers. In 2002, a lovely and delightful outdoor bar and dining area was added. It's called Stephen's Green (another reference to Joyce).

The menu is a mix, too, of standard upscale favorites like shrimp cocktail, Caesar salad, steaks and prime rib (all beef is certified Angus), and some classic Irish and English dishes, among them bangers and mash, a platter of sausages, cabbage, and mashed potatoes; Mayo lamb stew; poached salmon; fish and chips; and Irish whiskey-bread pudding. One of the kitchen's specialties is "Dublin Lawyer," a combination of lobster meat, mushrooms, and scallions in cream sauce spiked with cayenne pepper and Irish whiskey. To quench that specific kind of thirst: Harp and Guinness are on tap; there are 10 classic single-malt whiskeys between 8 and 12 years old, and 9 premium single-malts 10–18 years old; 7 brands of port; and Cafe Ulysses, a drink that blends coffee with Jameson's Irish Whiskey, Bailey's Irish Cream, Frangelico liqueur, and whipped cream. The regular wine list is comprehensive in both choice and cost, and well organized to make selection easier. (Bottles are available for sale to go at carryout prices.) The cellar reserve or "Captain's List" offers additional extraordinary vintages that go for anywhere from $83 to $133 a bottle. A brunch, offering five specials like eggs Benedict and quiche, plus the regular lunch menu, is served every Sunday from 10 a.m. to 3 p.m. The last Sunday night of each month is reserved for the Irish, a regular event that features a special menu and live Irish folk music, everything from lyric ballads to lewd bar tunes: make reservations, it's always a sell-out. On every other night jazz performers entertain; on any given evening you might encounter a piano soloist playing old standards on the baby grand, a locally renowned singer, or a nationally known quartet. Get on the mailing list to stay up to date about visiting artists as well as scheduled wine tastings, champagne brunches, and cigar dinners. Private rooms for parties and meetings can be reserved. This is really an "adults only" sort of place, a spot to eat and drink with gusto, laugh loudly, make confessions, hold hands, celebrate, and do business.

MARKETS

French

French Street Cafe
☎ (330) 609-5100
CITY: **Warren**   AREA: **Farther South**

ADDRESS: 1195 Niles Cortland Rd.
FOOD AVAIL.: baked goods, canned & packaged goods, tea, coffee, takeout meals
HOURS: Mon–Sat 7 a.m.–6 p.m., Sun closed
PAYMENT: MC, VS, AX, DIS ACCESS: ⑁ Full access

The name reveals the concept behind this unusual spot. Alain Pisan, who was born and raised near St. Tropez in France, where his parents had a pastry shop, and his wife, Renee, who was born and raised in the Warren area, wanted to create a facsimile of the little shops found on a single street in a small French town, where residents would go to get the basics of the good life—wine, cheese, bread, pastry, and a well-brewed cup of coffee. This Ohio "French Street" is all under one roof, in a quaint old house with hardwood floors and rooms decorated Provençal-style, complete with imported fabrics. A little dining room, with table service only at lunchtime, offers light meals and coffee-shop fare. They roast their own coffee beans and bake their own traditional French breads, rolls, and, of course, cakes and pastries galore including brioche filled with custard, vanilla sponge cake layered with strawberries and cream, chocolate croissants, fresh fruit tarts, napoleans, and flaky puff pastry. Other rooms are filled with imported wines and French cheeses, most from small proprietors who do not generally distribute in this country. The Pisans are filling a huge void in this part of the region. You'd be hard pressed to find products like those they offer any closer than Cleveland, which is more than an hour away. The one exception is in Canfield, home of Renee's French Bakery (see next listing), where the new owners, who bought the business from Alain and Renee, bake many of the same breads and pastries.

it's their son Gavin hanging out in his playpen while his parents make scones, biscotti, and fruit tarts. It's the bread, however, that defines their mission and their passion. "The ingredients are simple," says Adam, "but are made special by process and time—the unique flavor and texture come from slow fermentation." The entire place smells yeasty, and the air in the bakery, which also has a few tables and chairs, is warm. Bread comes out of the oven twice a day, as it does in France, so the loaf you take home at 5 p.m. is truly fresh—baked in the afternoon and not the early morning hours. French baguettes and epi loaves that are shaped like a stalk of wheat; pain de mie (Pullman sandwich loaves); sourdough; and rustic Italian, focaccia, and Italian olive bread are always available. Daily specials include scali (a white Italian bread with sesame seeds), fougasse (a French-style flat focaccia), and challah. It's worth a visit for the setting alone—makes you feel like you've had a lovely outing and not merely run a food errand. The place is charming—walls are bright yellow and peach, a small marble-topped antique buffet holds self-serve hot coffee and tea, and the counter is an old, stripped wooden sideboard; free samples are always offered on a tasting board.

On The Rise— Artisan Breads and Pastries
☎ (216) 320-9923
CITY: **Cleveland Hts.**   AREA: **East Side**

ADDRESS: 3471 Fairmount Blvd.
FOOD AVAIL.: Baked goods, tea, coffee
HOURS: Tue–Fri 7 a.m.–6 p.m., Sat 8 a.m.–5 p.m., Sun 8 a.m.–2 p.m., Mon closed
PAYMENT: Checks **ACCESS:** ♿ Full access

The old world meets the new at this bakery specializing in handcrafted European baked goods, which opened in December 2001. Husband and wife Adam and Jennifer Gidlow are owners and bakers, and if you hear baby sounds from the back,

Renee's French Bakery
☎ (330) 533-2668
CITY: **Canfield**   AREA: **Farther South**

ADDRESS: 584 E. Main St. (SR 11)
FOOD AVAIL.: baked goods, beverages, tea, coffee, takeout meals **HOURS:** Mon–Fri 7 a.m.–6 p.m., Sat 8 a.m.–5 p.m., Sun closed **PAYMENT:** MC, VS, AX, checks **ACCESS:** ♿ Full access

The French baker who originally opened this shop named the place after his wife. Five years ago he decided to return to France and sold the business; the new owners decided to keep the name, as well his recipes. But before he left, Alain Pisan taught them how to prepare his napoleans, eclairs, fruit tarts, palmier, chocolate truffle, fraisier cakes, cream puffs, petits fours, loaves of crusty bread, and buttery croissants. (Pisan and his wife, Renee, have since returned to the U.S. and started another store in Warren. See previous listing for French Street Cafe). There is a small cafe in the shop where coffee, tea, all their baked goodies, sandwiches (only the bread is French), and soups (also not particularly French) are served.

German

Der Braumeister Deli
☎ **(216) 671-6220**
CITY: **Cleveland**   AREA: **Near West Side**

ADDRESS: 13046 Lorain Ave.
FOOD AVAIL.: Baked goods, canned & packaged goods, spices, condiments, beverages, tea, wine
HOURS: Mon–Fri 11 a.m.–6 p.m.; Sat 3–8 p.m.; closed Sun **PAYMENT:** MC, VS, AX, DIS
ACCESS: ♿ Full access

This well-stocked deli is located inside Der Braumeister restaurant. It carries a variety of German food imports and many of the most popular German brands and products. Imported biscuits and cookies, mustards, jelly and jam, and pickles can be found here. There's a good selection of German wines and beers and a deli counter with traditional favorites such as head cheese, leberwurst, blood tongue, and other cold cuts. (See restaurant listing under same name in this chapter.)

Hansa Import Haus
☎ **(216) 281-3177**
CITY: **Cleveland**   AREA: **Near West Side**

ADDRESS: 2701 Lorain Ave.
FOOD AVAIL.: Meat (deli), baked goods, canned & packaged goods, spices, condiments, beverages, tea, coffee, wine, beer **HOURS:** Mon–Sat 9 a.m.–5:30 p.m.; open Sun in December only,

1–4 p.m. **PAYMENT:** MC, VS, checks
ACCESS: ♿ Full access

You can't miss this place. Built to resemble a Bavarian mountain chalet complete with white stucco and exposed wood beams, it's a standout in its West Side neighborhood. The Hanseatic League, from which this store gets its name, was a medieval trading association of merchants from northern Germany and neighboring areas, and like its namesake this store does a brisk business buying and selling German imports. They stock a variety of packaged breads, cakes, cookies, and Swiss as well as German chocolates, and maintain a good selection of beers and wines; and the deli counter offers traditional German cold cuts, sausages, and cheeses. In addition to food products, the store has a large number of German-language magazines and tapes, toiletries, and gift items such as nutcrackers, beer steins, and wall plaques. At Christmastime, they also stock traditional German tree ornaments.

Meat Mart
☎ **(440) 845-4935**
CITY: **Parma**   AREA: **Southwest**

ADDRESS: 10405 W. Pleasant Valley Rd.
FOOD AVAIL.: Meat (fresh, deli, frozen), fish (deli), baked goods, canned & packaged goods, spices, condiments, beverages **HOURS:** Mon noon–6 p.m., Tue–Wed 10 a.m.–6 p.m., Thu–Sat 9 a.m.–5 p.m., Sun closed **PAYMENT:** Checks
ACCESS: ♿ Limited

Much like a an old-fashioned butcher shop from days gone by, the Mart offers an assortment of cuts and deli meats. The many varieties of smoked and fresh sausage made on the premises are their real specialty. But this large store also has a selection of imported foods, including honey, packaged German breads, cookies, chocolates, and biscuits, plus bottled and canned foods like pickles and sauerkraut.

Michael's Bakery
☎ (216) 351-7530
CITY: **Cleveland**   AREA: **Near West Side**

ADDRESS: 4478 Broadview Rd.
FOOD AVAIL.: meat (fresh, deli), baked goods, beverages, tea, takeout meals **HOURS:** Mon–Sat 7 a.m.–6 p.m., Sun closed **PAYMENT:** MC, VS, checks **ACCESS:** ♿ Limited

Best known for the past 20 years for their baked goods made from authentic Old World recipes, Michael's also offers a nice selection of other foods, imported primarily from Germany, including soups, pickles, peppers, and juices. They ship their heavy dark rye, German rye, crusty Vienna, and other old-fashioned European breads all over the country. The deli counter prepares sandwiches to order on this same freshly baked bread. A variety of tortes like mocha, chocolate, and rum are available as well as cookies, poppyseed and nut rolls, danish, and donuts. Michael's has a second location at the West Side Market that's open Wednesdays, Fridays, and Saturdays; for further information, call 216-351-7530. (Also see listing for West Side Market in chapter 8.)

Old Country Sausage
☎ (216) 662-5988
CITY: **Maple Heights**   AREA: **Southeast**

ADDRESS: 15711 Libby Rd.
FOOD AVAIL.: Meat (fresh), baked goods, canned & packaged goods **HOURS:** Tue & Wed 9 a.m.–5 p.m., Thu 9 a.m.–6 p.m., Fri 9 a.m.–7 p.m., Sat 9 a.m.–5 p.m.; closed Sun & Mon **PAYMENT:** Checks **ACCESS:** ♿ Limited

Some of their customers come from the other end of the state—or another state altogether—just to get their genuine German-style meats and sausages. When the Neiden family took over the business in 1982, they brought in a German *metzger* (butcher) to teach George Neiden how to make sausages the Old World way. Now one of only a few stores left in Cleveland that actually prepare these products themselves, Old Country offers 40 different kinds of sausage and wursts including bratwurst, liver pate, mettwurst (a spread made with smoked meats), and rohschinken (a smoked, aged ham similar to Italian prosciuto). They also stock a selection of cheeses, candies, packaged cookies and pickles from Germany, imported sauerkraut and red cabbage, and mixes for potato pancakes, dumplings, and spaetzle. "We're considered an authentic source of German food," says George, "even by people visiting Cleveland from Germany. Our spicings and flavorings are just like what you'd find there." Their products can also be found at the West Side Market at Stand G8, (216) 579-0233. (For information about the West Side Market see listing in the market section of Chapter 8).

Pearce Provisions
☎ (440) 543-4287
CITY: **Bainbridge**   AREA: **Farther East**

ADDRESS: 17800 Chillicothe Rd.
FOOD AVAIL.: Meat (fresh, frozen), fish (fresh, frozen), canned & packaged goods, spices, condiments, beverages, tea, coffee, prepared frozen foods **HOURS:** Tue–Sat 10 a.m.–6 p.m., Sun 10 a.m.–2 p.m. **PAYMENT:** MC, VS, DIS, checks **ACCESS:** ♿ Full access **OTHER ETHNIC SPECIALTIES:** Hungarian, Polish, Slovenian

What used to be Wisch's Old World Butcher Shop is now Pearce Provisions, but former owner Fred Wisch still makes his German and Hungarian meat products. Sausage is made on the premises, and they also have their own smokehouse. Though primarily a butcher shop, the store stocks an array of specialty grocery items, fresh seafood, and lots of imported food products. The small place with a big sign out front is located next to the firehouse. Party trays, catering services, and outdoor BBQs.

EUROPE, WEST

Reinecker's Bakery
☎ **(330) 467-2221**
CITY: **Macedonia**   AREA: **Southeast**

ADDRESS: 8575 Freeway Dr.
FOOD AVAIL.: Baked goods **HOURS:** Mon–Fri
4 a.m.–5:30 p.m.; closed Sat & Sun
PAYMENT: MC, VS, checks **ACCESS:** & Full access

Seven members of the Reinecker family run this business, which is primarily a wholesale operation. They've been supplying area grocery stores with German-style baked goods for almost 40 years. But if you're willing to make the trip to their place, they're happy to sell smaller quantities to individuals, too. They specialize in breads—rye is their particular triumph— and all five types of bread that they bake are natural whole-grain products with little sugar or fat. They are preservative-free, and most are made from recipes the family says are over 300 years old. Reinecker's is one of the only bakeries in the country to make these types of bread, and even their baking equipment is from Germany. They also make Christmas stollen, nut and poppyseed potica, and a variety of tortes. Note: there's no storefront to speak of. Heidi Reinecker, who says the casual, family-like atmosphere of the place means that most of their retail customers feel like old friends, suggests people use the back door.

Sachsenheim Hall
☎ **(216) 651-0888**
CITY: **Cleveland**   AREA: **Near West Side**

ADDRESS: 7001 Denison Ave.
FOOD AVAIL.: Meat (fresh) **HOURS:** Three times a year (one day in Nov, Dec, & Feb), 11 a.m.–7 p.m.
PAYMENT: Cash only **ACCESS:** & Full access

The exact date varies from year to year, but annually in November and December traditional bratwurst, made with and without garlic, is offered for sale. In February, there's liver sausage as well. They're prepared by hand by members of the Alliance of Transylvanian Saxons on a Wednesday and sold the next day. Call about one month in advance to find out the precise date. Orders must be placed about two weeks ahead. The freshly made sausages can be purchased in bulk and frozen. Enter the Hall from the side door. There's a 300-car parking lot adjacent to the building.

The Sausage Shoppe
☎ **(216) 351-5213**
CITY: **Cleveland**   AREA: **Near West Side**

ADDRESS: 4501 Memphis Ave.
FOOD AVAIL.: Meat (fresh, deli), baked goods, canned & packaged goods, beverages
HOURS: Tue–Thu 10 a.m.–5 p.m., Fri 9 a.m.–6 p.m., Sat 8:30 a.m.–4 p.m.; closed Sun and Mon **PAYMENT:** MC, VS, checks
ACCESS: & Full access

The *Cleveland Ethnic Eats* reader who brought this establishment to my attention told me that the liverwurst made here is the best she's ever tasted. And no wonder: master sausage maker Norm Heinle, who owns and operates the market with his wife Carol, has been practicing and perfecting his craft for 40 years. The shop was originally opened by Hans Kirchberger, a German immigrant who brought with him many of the Old World recipes still used here today. Norm was 13 when he started working for Herr Kirchberger, and since then he's added a few recipes of his own to the shop's repertoire. Like his predecessor, Norm does not use any MSG, preservatives, additives, or fillers in the meat products he makes, which include a large selection of fresh sausages; 15 varieties of bratwurst; regular kielbasa plus a special holiday version made with wine and garlic, available now at Christmas, New Years, Easter, Memorial Day, Fourth of July, Labor Day, and Thanksgiving; proski (a garlic-flavored pork-based cold cut); and leberkasse (literally translated as

EUROPE, WEST

"liver cheese"). Irish potato sausage, made from the original Kirchberger recipe is a March special. Chef Parker Bosley has described Norm's award winning paté as "customer friendly" because it's sold in containers rather than unappetizing casings and attractively topped with chives, peppercorns, or five other garnishes. Bosley calls the shop " ...a one-stop sandwich-maker's paradise." Bread from four different bakeries is also sold, three made locally and one from Canada. There are lunchmeats and cheeses, and a small selection of imported pickles, sauerkraut, and candy. Their catalog and information about seasonal specials are available on their website, www.sausageshoppe.com The store is one block south of the Cleveland Zoo in Old Brooklyn and close to three major highways—I-71, I-90, and I-480—and parking is convenient. During the summer months, Norm and Carol fire up a grill on the front patio and cook weiners and "the brat of the day." For those who want to dig right in, there are picnic tables in the backyard. If you're in a hurry, call ten minutes before you get there and your food will be ready for pick-up. Call or check the Web site for grill hours.

Irish

Casey's Irish Imports
☎ (440) 333-8383
CITY: **Rocky River**   AREA: **West Side**

ADDRESS: 19626 Center Ridge Rd.
FOOD AVAIL.: Meat (frozen), baked goods, canned & packaged goods, condiments, beverages, tea
HOURS: Mon–Wed & Fri 10 a.m.–6 p.m., Thu 10 a.m.–8 p.m.; Sat 10 a.m.–5 p.m., Sun closed; extended hours during the Christmas holiday season and for St. Patrick's Day   PAYMENT: MC, VS, AX, DIS, checks   ACCESS: & Full access

Vera Casey, who hails from County Mayo, and husband Tom, of County Galway, emigrated from Ireland with their three young daughters and one son in the '70s. Every time they went home for a visit, friends here asked them to bring things back. Eventually these "favors" turned into a business, one that involves the entire family. Now both friends and strangers can easily get Irish teas, cookies, biscuits, oatmeal, jams, black/white pudding, packaged soups and cake mixes, and steak sauces. "Some people come in daily," says Patricia Casey-Lowery, "for their bit of Irish candy. It's a taste of home for them." Freshly baked Irish soda bread is available by special order and on Saturdays. The shop, which is easily identified by the large attractive window displays of Irish china, crystal, and gifts, also stocks silver and gold Irish theme jewelry, Aran knit sweaters, tapes, and books. They now offer online shopping at www.caseysirishimports.com.

Gaelic Imports
☎ (216) 398-1548
CITY: **Cleveland**   AREA: **Near West Side**

ADDRESS: 4882 Pearl Rd.
FOOD AVAIL.: Meat (frozen), baked goods, canned & packaged goods, condiments, tea, prepared frozen foods   HOURS: Tues–Fri 10 a.m.–6 p.m.; Sat 10 a.m.–5 p.m., Sun 1–5 p.m., closed Mon
PAYMENT: MC, VS, DIS, checks   ACCESS: & Limited
OTHER ETHNIC SPECIALTIES: British

The shelves here are well stocked with foods imported from Scotland, Ireland, Wales, and England. Products whose brand names are music to the ears of those who know them well include Bovril, Marmite, Branston Pickles, H.P. Sauce, and Cadbury Candies. There's a good selection of marmalades and teas. The store's own sausage is available frozen. Homemade meat pies, Cornish pasties, and sausage rolls are available, too. Also made on the premises are black-and-mealy pudding, and haggis (a dish you must have grown up with to fully appreciate, as it consists of minced or calf innards mixed with barley and oatmeal boiled together). Baked goods are fresh, too, and include tarts, shortbread, scones, and biscuits. Some gift items are available, including tartan accessories, made-to-order kilts, music, and jewelry. Parking is available in the rear or on the street.

Irish Cottage
☎ (216) 221-6412
CITY: **Lakewood**   AREA: **West Side**

ADDRESS: 18828 Sloane Ave.
FOOD AVAIL.: Meat (fresh, frozen), baked goods, canned & packaged goods, condiments, tea, coffee HOURS: Mon, Tue, Fri & Sat 10 a.m.–6 p.m., Wed & Thu 10 a.m.–8 p.m., Sun noon–5 p.m.; extended winter holiday hours
PAYMENT: MC, VS, checks ACCESS: ♿ None

Three greenhouse rooms make up the Cottage, and its owners describe this shop as "filled to the gills" with unique items from Ireland. Children love the wishing pond. The store stocks jellies, jams, and marmalades, packaged crackers and cookies, oatmeal, Irish sausage and bacon, and locally baked scones and soda bread, which arrive fresh from the oven on Mondays, Wednesdays, and Fridays. The focus, however, is more on nonfood items: there's imported crystal and china, clothing, dolls, books, and Blarney stones.

Swedish

Swedish Pastry Shop
☎ (440) 993-6702
CITY: **Ashtabula**   AREA: **Farther East**

ADDRESS: 5713 Main Ave.
FOOD AVAIL.: Baked goods HOURS: Mon–Fri 6 a.m.–5:30 p.m., Sat 6 a.m.–5 p.m., Sun closed
PAYMENT: Cash only ACCESS: ♿ Full access

Fans of Scandinavian baked goods have been asking me where to go for years. I didn't have anyplace to send them until 2002, when a reader told me about this 51-year-old shop in Ashtabula. Owner and baker Bill Murphy continues the business his father started. It may strike you, as it did me, that Murphy doesn't sound like much of a Swedish name, and lead you to doubt the authenticity of his product. But have no fear. Murphy's mother was from Sweden, and she supplied the recipes for skorper (toasted sweet bread), apple cake, nissua (cardamom braid), and limpfa (rye bread) that are the bakery's specialty. Bill, who starts his day at midnight, bakes till dawn, and makes deliveries in the afternoon, also prepares Finnish rye bread and Danish pastries. The shop is a popular stop for area tours; 20 to 30 groups a year come by the busload to meet Bill, get a walkthrough, a talk, and a taste.

Swiss

Zoss The Swiss Baker
☎ (216) 368-4055
CITY: **Cleveland Heights**   AREA: **East Side**

ADDRESS: 12397 Cedar Rd.
FOOD AVAIL.: Baked goods, beverages, coffee
HOURS: Tue–Fri 7:30 a.m.–6:30 p.m., Sat 8 a.m.–4 p.m.; closed Sun & Mon
PAYMENT: Checks ACCESS: ♿ Full access OTHER ETHNIC SPECIALTIES: French, Italian

We're very lucky that Barbara Zoss is from Cleveland Heights. Because when she and her husband, Kurt, a baker from a family of Swiss bakers, decided to leave Zurich and come to America with their children, they also decided to open their bakery in her hometown. That's provided us with a unique opportunity to sample the kinds of breads and pastries the Swiss have traditionally enjoyed. With skills honed over more than 20 years, starting with an apprenticeship that began when he was a teenager in Zurich and augmented by a stint on the West Coast, where he learned about San Francisco sourdough techniques, Kurt creates an array of Swiss/European specialties rarely, if ever, available in this area. Since the spring of 1996, the shop has been offering Zurcherbrot, a crusty loaf with a chewy interior texture; Tessiner, a softer crusted bread typically found in the Italian region of Switzerland; Zopf, an egg bread often eaten for Sunday breakfast in Switzerland; and Swiss farmer bread. There are also a variety of baguettes, some laced with herbs or flavored with roasted garlic, brioche (slightly sweet and egg-yellow), and all sorts of flavorful little rolls. Some of the more unusual and outstanding sweets include zimtblatt, a chocolate-frosted cookie; hollandertortes made with either apples or apricots and almonds; and flaky prussiens (we'd recognize them as angel wings). Only unbleached flour, filtered water, and fresh best-quality ingredients are used. You can watch Kurt at work through a small window in the shop that looks into the large work room, with the kneading table, cooling racks, and steam-injected stone-deck oven. Many items are available every day the bakery's open, others only when posted on a board or as listed in their product handout sheet. The shop is set back from the street, with limited parking in front but more in the back, which can be accessed via a driveway that is just past Night Town.

Western European Mix

Bavarian Pastry Shop
☎ (216) 521-1344
CITY: **Lakewood**   AREA: **West Side**

ADDRESS: 17004 Madison Ave.
FOOD AVAIL.: Baked goods HOURS: Mon–Fri 7 a.m.–7 p.m., Sat 8 a.m.–6 p.m.; closed Sun
PAYMENT: MC, VS, AX, checks ACCESS: & None

The scope of this bakery goes way beyond what its name indicates, and it has to be among the most uncommon shops in the region. Owner Caron Von Carlowitz draws on the baking traditions of all Europe and combines them with his own determination to offer healthy, high-quality baked goods. One-of-a-kind foods are the result. Eschewing the use of all chemical additives and preservatives, he bakes nutritious breads that are full of Old World flavor and goodness, and the variety is large: Vienna, white, flax seed, buckwheat, five grain, sunflower millet, rye, and amaranth. He does 25 different kinds of cookies, plus a special line for the holidays. He also prepares sausage rolls, pies, pastries, a large variety of European tortes, special-occasion cakes, and party trays.

Charles Peters Bake Shop
☎ (216) 641-6887
CITY: **Garfield Heights**   AREA: **Southeast**

ADDRESS: 4608 Turney Rd.
FOOD AVAIL.: Baked goods HOURS: Tue–Fri 8 a.m.–5 p.m., Sat 7:30 a.m.–2 p.m.; closed Sun & Mon PAYMENT: Checks ACCESS: & None OTHER ETHNIC SPECIALTIES: many Eastern European countries

Only three different owners have run this bakery since it opened in 1929. The shop features specialties that span the European continent: Slavic sweet bread, Polish paczki (donuts), Hungarian nut or poppyseed rolls, and Italian eclairs. A large variety of breads, including Bohemian rye, Viennese seedless rye, and potato bread, plus salt sticks and hard rolls topped with caraway seeds and salt are baked in a brick oven. Professional baker Jeff Stadnik prepares authentic, made-from-scratch danish, strudel, kuchens, cookies, and pastries daily.

Puritan Bakery
☎ **(440) 354-3851**

CITY: **Painesville** AREA: **Farther East**

ADDRESS: 15 S. St. Clair St.
FOOD AVAIL.: Baked goods, coffee
HOURS: Tue–Fri 6 a.m.–6 p.m., Sat 6 a.m.–5 p.m.; closed Sun & Mon **PAYMENT:** Checks
ACCESS: ♿ Full access **OTHER ETHNIC SPECIALTIES:** Finnish, Hungarian, British, many Eastern European countries

This place is hard to classify. You couldn't go so far as to call Puritan a Scandinavian bakery, but they're the only ones in the area to carry some unusual Scandinavian specialties, including a Finnish round bread, Finnish coffee cake, and Finnish toast. Manager Margaret McCormick is sure that each of these items has a Finnish name, but admits she has no idea how to spell them! It seems a baker previously employed there brought the Finnish recipes with him and taught the Puritan staff how to prepare them. You couldn't rightfully describe it as a Scottish bakery, either, but three or four times per year they have Scottish Week. The store is decorated with Scottish calendars and tapestries, and they feature Scottish specialties such as meat pies, sausage rolls, and scones. These can also be ordered at any other time, in large quantities, by calling in advance. Nor could you say this is an Eastern European bakery though they regularly bake Hungarian pastries filled with nuts, apricots, raspberries, and cheese. Non-ethnic muffins, donuts, and assorted cakes are regularly available, too. Many neighborhood regulars shop here, but some people make a special trip for Finnish products, especially around the holidays, and for the Scottish items. Everything is made on the premises, and has been for more than 30 years.

Rudy's Strudel & Bakery
☎ **(440) 886-4430**

CITY: **Parma** AREA: **Southwest**

ADDRESS: 5580 Ridge Rd.
FOOD AVAIL.: baked goods, coffee, prepared frozen foods, takeout meals **HOURS:** Tue–Fri 7 a.m.–6 p.m., Sat 8 a.m.–5 p.m.; closed Sun & Mon **PAYMENT:** MC, VS, checks **ACCESS:** ♿ Full access

Dessert strudel, fresh and frozen, is their signature item, and fillings are apple, cherry, cheese, poppyseed, nut, pineapple, blueberry, apricot, and peach. They also prepare gourmet dinner strudels—layers of flaky dough alternating with cabbage, broccoli and cheddar cheese, spinach and mozzarella, mushroom and onion, or potato, onion, and bacon. Dobos, Sacher, and Black Forest tortes are also available, and everything is all-natural and preservative-free. The business turned 45 years old in 1994, and to celebrate, the owners added a takeout line called "Flavor of Europe," featuring ready-to-eat ethnic dishes like goulash, paprikash, and 15 varieties of pierogi. Muffins, breads, danish pastry, crepes, and a variety of cakes are made fresh daily.

EUROPE, WEST

{ *Chapter 6* }

LATIN AMERICA

Culinary practices form a living historical record, reflecting the political and economic events that have generated cultural exchange. Nowhere is this more apparent than in Latin America and the island nations of the Caribbean, represented in the Cleveland food community by Mexico, Brazil, and the countries of Central America, as well as Jamaica, Puerto Rico, and Cuba. For centuries these countries played host to pirate brigs and trading ships, slaves from Africa, conquistadors and explorers, expatriates from the far reaches of the British Empire, and immigrants from the war-torn nations of Western Europe. Over time, the foods of indigenous tribal peoples merged with the products and techniques these outsiders brought with them.

"How we Mexicans eat," explains Maria Galindo, a member of Cleveland's Hispanic Cultural Center, "reflects much of our history. You cannot separate the two. We were invaded, conquered, and colonized. And these people gave us language, religion, and culture. But behind that are the influences of our ancient ancestors which we never gave up, and it is from them we got the tortilla, the tostada, and our taste for hot and spicy food made with the hundreds of different types of chiles that grow here."

Chris McLaughlin, who is from Jamaica, tells the same story about her own country. "Our food is a mix of cultures and flavors, telling all about the people who've come to the islands. You can taste Africa, India, and China, mixed in with what is native to the region."

So Jamaicans use ackee, a fruit first brought by a slave ship from West Africa; allspice and Scotch Bonnet chiles, which grow there in abundance; and curry, which they think of as their own national dish. Mexicans eat flan, a custard dessert that came with the Spanish, and make moles using cocoa, an ingredient rooted in their Aztec past, which they serve with rice, a food that was introduced to them by Asian sailors and merchant ships.

Most of the Caribbean island nations work with similar ingredients, which appear in the cuisines of Central and South America, too. Rice, beans, garlic, onions, citrus fruits, thyme, and both sweet and hot peppers are widely used throughout these regions. Where seafood is plentiful, it is an important part of the cuisine. Fruits like papaw (another name for papaya), mangoes, bananas, and coconuts are important ingredients in many dishes.

But there are obvious differences, too. Jamaicans tend to cook with allspice, curry powder, and ginger, while Mexicans more often use cilantro, cinnamon, and cacao. For Brazilians, manioc flour made from cassava is a staple and, seasoned, it's a standard table condiment. Jerked meat is a strictly Caribbean specialty. A rich, fiery version of barbecue, it's said to have originated when escaped slaves, hiding in the jungle, survived by pit-roasting wild pigs and flavoring the smoked meat with the herbs and spices they learned to use from the local Arawak Indians. The addition of salt helped preserve the meat for long periods.

The people of Mexico and South America use tomatoes and corn in much of their cooking. According to Salvador Gonzalez, a Mexican of Indian descent who has lived here for 15 years, each area of his country has its own way of preparing tostadas, tamales, and tortillas. "Tortilla making by hand is an art," he says, "and they taste nothing like the packaged variety available in this country. In my family, they were made fresh every day."

The largest group of Spanish-speaking people for whom Cleveland is home are Puerto Ricans, followed by those from Mexico. Many make their home on Cleveland's West Side, where numerous Hispanic restaurants and markets are to be found. Like other immigrant groups past and present, people from Latin America have come to Northeast Ohio to escape political instability and pursue economic advancement. They have filled the ranks of industrial and agricultural workers, and increasingly in recent years have been attracted here by the wealth of educational opportunities.

The Club Azteca, a local Mexican social organization begun in 1923, now includes members from 21 different Latin American nations. "We try not to focus so much on where we've come from," explained Zulema Carreon, an active member for many years, "but on the fact that we all want to work together to share our cultures with Cleveland. We are proud of our pasts and don't want to lose what is our own. But it's also important to learn about one another. I get so excited when I have a chance to experience other people's ethnic customs, and I want them to feel the same about my heritage."

RESTAURANTS

D'Ici de Là
☎ (216) 763-3636
CITY: **Beachwood** AREA: **East Side**
ATMOSPHERE: **Relaxed** COST: $$$$$

ADDRESS: 2101 Richmond Rd.
HOURS: Mon–thu 10 a.m.–8 p.m., Fri–Sat
10 a.m.–7 p.m., Sun closed **RESERVATIONS:** Not
taken **PAYMENT:** MC, VS, AX, DIS, checks
BAR: Beer, wine **TAKEOUT:** Yes **SMOKING:** Smoke-
Free **ACCESS:** & Full access

Owner and chef Patricia Cornejo likes to describe this as a food boutique.
Part cafe, part gourmet market and bakery, plus a kitchen that's set up to turn out meals to go for one or 21, it offers a unique, eclectic collection of good things to eat. There's seating for 25 amidst the shelves of imported wines and glass-fronted display cases featuring pastries, salads, wraps, and the house specialties. (For more information about the market, see the listing in Chapter 8). Carnejo, who is from Argentina, prepares foods from her homeland. There are meat- or vegetable-filled turnovers called empanadas; tarta pascualina, a sort of quiche; albóndigas (meatballs in white wine sauce); and matambre arrollado, stuffed, rolled veal slow cooked, sliced, and served cold on Fridays and Saturdays (except during the warm-weather months). Her menu also includes what she calls "cowboy stews and country food," dishes favored by the famous gauchos of the pampas: locro, a com-

bination of vegetables, beans, sweet potatoes, and sausage; picante de panza, made with tripe, beans, and tomatoes; and cazuela de pollo, which features chicken, butternut squash, and corn. None are available anywhere else in town, and they can also be purchased here frozen in 8- and 16-ounce portions. Sandwiches and simple chicken breasts get Latinized with chimichurri sauce, a marinade and dressing made with oil, vinegar, lemons, parsley, garlic, and mild Argentine chile pepper. But Cornejo doesn't want to be limited by a single cuisine. So she chose a French name—it means from here and there—and samples from a more worldly palette to extend the options, favoring hummus, stuffed grape leaves, couscous, salad niçoise, and paté. The bakery combines the best of French and South American patisserie: expect croissants; palmiers; alfajores, a sandwich cookie; pasta frola, little cakes filled with quince, sweet potato, or dulce de leche (caramel) paste; and pan madrileño, sweet dough with custard. Coffee, together with all its more sophisticated sisters including café con leche and cortado (the Argentine version), is served along with tea, hot chocolate, and maté, a caffeinated beverage that's said to pack an energizing punch without any side effects. There are cookies, muffins, and cheesecake, vegetarian burgers, pasta, and simple cheese plates, and a couple of high chairs, so people of diverse ages and tastes are likely to find something that pleases. Tucked away on the lower level of La Place, it's an attractive and cozy spot for a bite any time of day, and it gives takeout a whole new flavor. An extensive catering menu offers even more selection. Gift certificates available.

LATIN AMERICA

Central American

La Tortilla Feliz
☎ (216) 241-8385

CITY: **Cleveland**   AREA: **Near West Side**
ATMOSPHERE: **Relaxed**   COST: $$$$$

ADDRESS: 2661 W. 14th St.
HOURS: Lunch: Mon–Fri 11:30 a.m.–3 p.m.;
Dinner Tue–Thu 4:30 p.m.–10 p.m., Fri & Sat
4:30 p.m.–11 p.m; bar open until midnight,
serving appetizers; Sun & Mon closed
RESERVATIONS: Taken, suggested for parties of 4
or more **PAYMENT:** MC, VS, AX, DIS **BAR:** Beer,
wine, liquor **TAKEOUT:** Yes **SMOKING:** Smoking
section **ACCESS:** ♿ Full access

It took a while for this place to find and define itself, but there's no doubt now that it has become a restaurant success story and a valuable addition to the area's dining scene. La Tortilla Feliz serves expertly prepared Latin American dishes of Central and South America. It began as a bare-bones cooperative-style venture in 1996, struggled to keep going against a variety of obstacles, closed at the end of 2001for five months of remodeling and reorganization, and reopened in the spring of 2002. The setting is a wonderful backdrop for the foods of Central and South America that incorporate ingredients and cooking styles from the region's coastal lowlands, the area of the Sierra Madre range, and the Andean highlands. Some dishes trace their culinary roots back to the ancient Aztec, Inca, and Mayan civilizations. Though many of the basic elements are similar to those used in Mexican cuisine, the results are quite different. The freshly baked, handmade tortillas here resemble fluffy pancakes. The steamed corn-dough tamale is stuffed with chicken, vegetables, and a sauce made from ground seeds, spices, and tomatoes. Avocados appear not only in gaucamole, but also as part of a salad made with capers and jalapenos marinated in wine vinegar, and in a cold soup called sopa de palta. The dessert flan is more like cheesecake than custard.

The staff play a major role in crafting the menu, which changes seasonally. Customer favorites, such as ejotes empanizadas (cheese covered with green beans, dipped in an egg batter and fried), have a permanent place, but the kitchen is also eager to provide opportunities for trying new things. Many of these "opportunities" are dishes rarely found in restaurants in this part of the country: sopa de cebollas y almendras (almond and onion soup); pollo a la mostaza (chicken in a savory mustard sauce); pescado en salsa picante (fish in a spicy sauce made from mountain grown peppers and served with yampi, a potato-like root from the coastal jungles of the Caribbean); lomo de cerdo en salsa de tamarindo (pork loin marinated in tamarind sauce); and a vegetable stew from the Andes. At lunchtime there's a selection of unusual sandwiches such as choripan, made with Argentinean sausage, and del mar, creamy lobster with bread soaked in egg and fried. Every dish is described in detail. Some write-ups also include a little culinary history or geographic information: pepian rojo (chicken in a spicy sauce), the menu explains, is made from a recipe that originated in Huehuetenango, an ancient Mayan city in Guatemala's Antigua region Other descriptions are almost poetic. This may be intentional or merely the result of shifting from one language to another. Either way, it's an art form, as far as I'm concerned: "From the mountains of Peru to the three hills of Tremont comes this Peruvian delicacy of chicken and red peppers. The tender shredded flank steak known as ropa vieja is served floating on a plate of rice and is so flavorful that it jumps off the plate." They promise that their gazpacho "takes you to a fragrant summer world of fresh vegetables touched with garlic." In camarones in salsa blanca, made with shrimp in pepper-laced white sauce, "the folk flavors of Central America meet black-tie elegance." Cheese-filled empanadas are "a pastry delicacy that will conquer your palate."

There are always at least two completely vegetarian selections available. (Call ahead to request vegan modifications.) Rice, tortillas, and salad come with each main dish. A small plate of tasty bean dip with fried potato "fingers" for dipping comes to your table shortly after you do. Wines from Central America are available by the bottle and the glass, and beers from El Salvador, Guatemala, and Brazil, plus a few domestics. The house-made sangria is extraordinary. The bar whips up tequila martinis and a variety of very cool, tropically inspired cocktails. There are some standout nonalcoholic drinks—agua de sandia (with watermelon), horchata (with rice water and cinnamon), and tamarindo (with tamarind fruit).

The two connected dining rooms, which can hold up to 95, are lovely. The wood and tile floors, golden textured walls, arched doorways, brightly colored napkins, artwork, and craft items combine to create an informal, Latin folkways setting. An original mural painted by local artist Hector Castellanos graces an entire wall—look closely at the faces, and you will recognize such famous figures Emiliano Zapata, Frida Kahlo, and Che Guevara. A bar in the front room has seating for nine, and appetizers are available here until midnight. Occaisionally local bands play traditional music on Saturday nights (call for schedule). Weather permitting, there's sidewalk dining for about 20 on the 14th Street side. On-street parking, and more in the lot across the street. If you're planning a party, ask about their catering services.

Dominican

El Manantial
☎ (216) 685-9550

CITY: **Cleveland**   AREA: **Near West Side**
ATMOSPHERE: **Relaxed**   COST: $$$$

ADDRESS: 2998 W. 25 St.

HOURS: Mon–Sat 9 a.m.–10 p.m., Sun closed
RESERVATIONS: Not taken **PAYMENT:** Cash only
BAR: None **TAKEOUT:** Yes **SMOKING:** Smoke-Free
ACCESS: ♿ Limited

Bob Smith, reporter for The Plain Dealer, sent me here, and I'm glad he did. Owner Doña Leonor and her staff may not have mastered the English language yet, but they know how to feed people very well. The simple, bare-bones place—sparkling clean and with a few homey touches like flowered curtains at the window—offers a large variety of Dominican dishes, which are similar to those of Puerto Rico. There is octopus salad, baked fish, fried chicken with plantains, roast pork, chicken stew, marinated steak, rice with pigeon beans, and shrimp with garlic. For breakfast, announces the menu, you can get "scrambled eggs with anything you like," and that includes smoked pork chops, green bananas, and chicken gizzards. Every day features a special: it could be goat, rabbit, mofongo rellenos de camarrones ô langosta (banana balls stuffed with shrimp and lobster), cangrejo guizado (crab stew), or sopa de pata de vaca (cow-leg soup). Food is ordered at the counter, and drinks are self-serve from the cooler. Tables sport bottles of salsa picante along with ketchup, mustard, oil, and vinegar. You can't miss this little 48-seat place on the corner of Clark—the exterior is painted a vivid neon green, a bright spot on an otherwise cheerless block of buildings.

LATIN AMERICA

LATIN AMERICA

Let's Mango Tea Garden Restaurant
☎ (330) 854-1111

CITY: **Canal Fulton**   AREA: **Farther South**
ATMOSPHERE: **Relaxed**   COST: **$$**$$

ADDRESS: 239 N. Canal St.
HOURS: Tue–Sat 11 a.m.–3 p.m.
RESERVATIONS: Taken, Suggested for 4 or more
PAYMENT: MC, VS, DIS   BAR: None   TAKEOUT: Yes
SMOKING: Smoke-Free   ACCESS: ♿ Full access

Canal Fulton is not the sort of place you'd expect to find Latin food and Latin flair. But Margarita Roberts, who is from the Dominican Republic, and her husband, Ken, think it's a perfect location to do "the mango," and introduce people to the tropical tastes of her homeland. They opened for business in the spring of 2003, and they've committed to the project in a big way, importing two special machines found nowhere else in Ohio: one to make guarapo (sugar cane juice) and the other for canawlers, a long, cream-filled pastry that's deep-fried and dusted with cinnamon–sugar that collects in the distinctive ridges that run from top to bottom. They're always made fresh to order. After eating one, I'd have to say that no matter how far you drive to get here, this alone makes it worth the trip. But there are so many more delicious reasons to get yourself to this 40-seat tearoom tucked away at the back of the Warehouse on Canal, where vendors sell art, antiques, and collectibles. Let me list some of them: meat-filled yucca rolls; sweet fried plantains with barbecued pork; corn patties stuffed with cheese; the Cuban pork and turkey sandwich; croquetas (croquettes), crispy on the outside and creamy on the inside, made with chicken or ham; potato puffs; flan; and 11 astonishingly refreshing drinks squeezed from coconuts, pineapples, papayas, guanabana, and other fruits, plus mango and guava floats. Before visitors taste anything, Margarita likes to do a little show-and-tell, arriving at each table with a stalk of sugar cane, a plantain, and a yucca. She gives a short presentation about each to, in her words, "put a face on the food and maybe encourage people to try something new." That's because she's what I'd call a food evangelist, a zealous preacher of the gospel of Caribbean cuisine. For those "not ready to step out of the box," she also offers conventional teahouse fare: 33 teas, scones with Devonshire cream, dessert bars, cookies, little sandwiches, and wraps. But don't expect to order Coke or Pepsi. "It's so boring," she says with laugh, "why bother! If you're here, you have it my way." This is such a charming and unique spot that words can hardly do it justice. Ken and Margarita, who own the building, have done a lovely restoration, leaving the pressed-tin ceiling, exposed brickwork, and hardwood floors intact. Each table in Let's Mango is dressed in colorful cloth topped with lace and pretty flowered china. There are lots of live plants. Speaking of live, they sometimes have live Latin music too, and Margarita is always willing to sing "HappyBirthday." They do meetings and private parties in the tearoom before and after regular operating hours, by reservation. There is outdoor seating beside the Canal, weather permitting. Some packaged Caribbean products are for sale—guava jelly, mango jam, plantain chips, and sweet, milky cajeta paste.

Jamaican

Dailey's West Indian Food Mart
☎ (216) 721-7240

CITY: **Cleveland**   AREA: **East Side**
ATMOSPHERE: **Relaxed**   COST: **$$**$$

ADDRESS: 3019 E. 116th St.
HOURS: Mon–Thu 8 p.m.–midnight, Fri–Sat 8 p.m.–2:30 a.m., Sun 8 p.m.–midnight
RESERVATIONS: Not taken   PAYMENT: Cash only
BAR: Beer, wine, liquor   TAKEOUT: Yes
SMOKING: Yes   ACCESS: ♿ Full access
*Not recommended for children

This come-as-you-are Jamaican eatery does not have a particularly inviting exterior, and even after you enter you'll think you made a wrong turn somewhere and ended up in a mini-mart. Orders are placed at the takeout counter in the rear of the store, where you can see the food that's been freshly prepared that day by Chris McLaughlin, who learned the art of Caribbean cooking from her grandmother when she was a girl living on a farm in Clarendon Parish on the island of Jamaica. Then you take a seat in a dining area at the back that looks rather like a windowless family rec room, usually populated with West Indians who are eating, visiting, hanging out at the small bar, or watching television. The menu is surprisingly varied, each day featuring a different mix of selections. Some dishes are quite alien to the American palate: cowfoot and tripe, salt fish and ackee (cod stewed with fruit, onions, and other vegetables), beef skin, and oxtail (they're just what the name implies). But those who grew up on this food say it's got the real taste of home. More popular with native Clevelanders are jerk (spicy barbecued) chicken wings, curried chicken, fried snapper, rice with gungo (pigeon) peas, and peppered shrimp. There's a soup a day, and the variety is wide—from chicken and beef to conch, red pea, and mutton. One diner reports that this is not a place for the timid: unless you're West Indian or live in the neighborhood, both the food and the location demand a certain adventuresome spirit.

This little out-of-time luncheonette harkens back to the fifties: a couple of booths, a short counter with cakes on display under glass domes, four low stools, fluorescent lighting, and white walls. A TV blares in back for the entertainment of staff, not patrons. The dinnerware is sturdy and the service perfunctory. This is the real deal and not a nostalgic re-creation, the kind of place immortalized in the Saturday Night Live sketches about the Olympia Cafe with Dan Aykroyd and John Belushi, and their now-famous line, "Cheeseburger, cheeseburger, cheeseburger." You can get a cheeseburger here too along with other standard American dinner fare, but what caught my interest— and the attention of "the fat traveler," the code name of the reader who recommended it to me—are the Jamaican dishes. There's curry goat, curry chicken, oxtail stew, jerk chicken, jerk pork (both in a milder version than I've encountered before), red snapper, fried plantains, and meat patties (a stuffed and fried dough pocket, what my husband calls Caribbean knishes). All dinner entrees come with beans and rice, and portions are generous. As at most Jamaican eateries, traditional "tonic" health drinks are also available: Irish moss (a sort of eggnog made with a seaweed extract that's reputed to give men who drink it an added performance advantage), carrot juice, and sorrel juice, plus less beneficial but equally Jamaican ginger beer and kola champagne soda. With seating for only 12, consider takeout as a possible option. With at least a week's advance notice, you can enlist the kitchen to cater Jamaican-style. Parking is on the street and free.

Enterpride Restaurant
☎ (216) 481-8788

CITY: **Cleveland**   AREA: **East Side**
ATMOSPHERE: **Relaxed**   COST: $$$$$

ADDRESS: 621 E. 185th St.
HOURS: Mon–Thu 9:30 a.m.–9 p.m., Fri & Sat 9:30 a.m.–midnight, Sun closed
RESERVATIONS: Not taken **PAYMENT:** Cash only
BAR: None **TAKEOUT:** Yes **SMOKING:** Smoke-Free
ACCESS: ♿ Limited

Island Style Jamaican Cuisine
☎ (216) 851-4500

CITY: **East Cleveland**   AREA: **East Side**
ATMOSPHERE: **Relaxed**   COST: $$$$$

ADDRESS: 2144 Noble Rd.
HOURS: Tue–Thu 11:30 a.m.–8 p.m.; Fri–Sat 11:30 a.m.–9 p.m., closed Sun–Mon

RESERVATIONS: Not taken **PAYMENT:** Checks
BAR: None **TAKEOUT:** Yes **SMOKING:** Smoke-free
ACCESS: ♿ Full access

Isolene Burke opened her tiny eatery in March 1997, in the same location as the L & R Tropical Food Store listed in the first edition of *Cleveland Ethnic Eats*. She gave the place a fresh coat of paint, took out the old counter and stools and put in a steam table, installed new shelving for the bottles of imported pepper and jerk sauce she carries, and remodeled the kitchen and the bathroom. It's still a simple, laid-back place where connoisseurs of Caribbean cookery can indulge their taste for jerk chicken, curried goat, and rum cake. With the help of her daughter, Ms. Burke, who is from Kingston, Jamaica, also prepares her version of stewed beef and stewed chicken, beans and rice, dumplings, fried plantains, and banana bread according to treasured family recipes. They also make gingery coconut drops, a special candy from home, and roti, a pita-like bread that came to the Jamaican table by way of India with the immigrants from the subcontinent who ended up on the islands. Packing up takeout orders is a big part of her operation because the restaurant only seats 15–20 diners. Though she has plans to expand the line of Caribbean groceries and produce she stocks and sells, Ms. Burke wants her business to stay small and feel friendly. She likes getting to know her customers and says, "People seem to like us just the way we are, so why change when things are going good!" Because the space itself is so tiny, she tries to keep the place smoke free out of consideration for those who hate the stuff, but if a smoker requests permission to light up and there are no other customers present, or none who object, she lifts that ban.

Rachel's Caribbean Cuisine
☎ **(216) 382-6952**

CITY: **South Euclid**   AREA: **East Side**
ATMOSPHERE: **Relaxed**   COST: $$$$$

ADDRESS: 14417 Cedar Rd.
HOURS: Mon–Thu 11 a.m.–10 p.m., Fri 11 a.m.–11 p.m., Sat 5–11 p.m., Sun closed
RESERVATIONS: Taken, Suggested for large parties
PAYMENT: MC, VS, AX, checks **BAR:** Beer, wine, liquor **TAKEOUT:** Yes **SMOKING:** Smoking section
ACCESS: ♿ Full access

Like the old song says, "If I ruled the world, every day would be the first day of spring." And in my version I'd add, "every chef would be as inspired as David Sterling." He's come to Cleveland and to the opening of his own place in November 2000 by way of Jamaica (the Caribbean island, not the neighborhood in New York), culinary school, and years spent in the kitchens of cruise ships and area restaurants. And everything he learned along the way comes together here in food that is wonderful to look at and to eat, and a dining room that is low key, welcoming, and pleasant. The menu is concentrated: it features six appetizers, two soups, three salads, four sandwiches, 12 entrees, six sides that could be meals unto themselves, especially for vegetarians, and three desserts labeled Rachel's Finale that just might bring you to your feet for a standing ovation. Amongst these choices are some Caribbean-style, Caribbean-influenced dishes that are rare finds in this area: conch fritters served with a punchy, chunky version of cocktail sauce; seafood chowder; rice and beans; fried plantains; Jamaican honey biscuits that come with all the house specialties; jerked marinated halibut crowned with pineapple mango salsa; jerk chicken and chicken curry; coconut bread pudding; and David's Island Touch carrot cake with spiced rum cream-cheese frosting. The other dishes, like grilled salmon in a lobster cream sauce, cilantro shrimp, hickory-smoked baby back ribs, a marinated, aged New York strip steak, and garlic mashed potatoes, are not, strictly speaking, Caribbean, but they are made with the same distinctive care and flair.

The presentation is meticulous, lovely, and dramatic—not what you'd expect in a reasonably priced and relaxed place like this. Even something as simple as a club sandwich gets upgraded with cilantro aioli in place of mayonnaise, and a Caesar salad goes tropical with the addition of jerk chicken breast, grilled shrimp, or blackened salmon. Because he loves to cook and to create, I would not be surprised if Sterling's menu grows and changes, with new dishes added and others disappearing. That's part of the excitement of eating at a one-of-a-kind place like this rather than a chain. The owner is not some faceless corporation focused on the bottom line, but a real person who takes pride in delivering something special to his customers even if that requires long hours and hard work, which David is quick to admit is the price of having his own place and doing everything the way he thinks it should be done. At least he has his family to keep him company. His wife Rachel, in whose honor the restaurant is named, runs the front of the house, and the couple's two older daughters, Madia and Nikki, pitch in on weekends along with Rachel's sister and niece. Rachel makes it her business to court and coddle the customers, and she's very good at it, convincing one to try a Shandy Caribe (lager beer spiked with ginger) from the bar and getting another to say to her companion, "I just order whatever Rachel tells me to because I know she knows what she's talking about." They've done a nice job of sprucing up the interior of this small, narrow space, painting the upper half of the wall area a shade of blue that seems to be a reflection of sea and sky, and bleaching the wood paneling on the lower half to sandy white. Tables are covered in white cloths under glass. There's an eight-stool bar near the entrance that pours Jamaican Red Stripe beer, and a waist-high partition down the center separates the booths on one side from the tables and chairs (which can be pushed together for groups of more than four) on the other. Recorded reggae is likely to be playing softly in the background. The combination of food, atmosphere, and location attracts a laid-back, interracial, intergenerational crowd. None of this ambience is even hinted at from the outside: the restaurant is located behind an uninviting facade in an equally uninviting strip that's an unlikely home for a place such as this (the best that can be said about it is that there is plenty of free parking). But now that you know, there's no excuse not to go. Or have David bring his culinary magic to your house or event—he does catering.

Tab West Indian American Restaurant

☎ **(216) 295-2272**

CITY: **Warrensville Heights**   AREA: **East Side**
ATMOSPHERE: **Relaxed**   COST: $$$$$

ADDRESS: 20019 Harvard Rd.
HOURS: Mon–Sat 9 a.m.–10 p.m.; closed Sun.
RESERVATIONS: Not taken PAYMENT: Checks
BAR: None TAKEOUT: Yes SMOKING: Smoke-free
ACCESS: ♿ Full access

Much of Tab's trade comes via the West Indian grapevine. While you may run into a few folks from the neighborhood, most of the customers who eat and order out from here are clearly from the islands, and the food is meant to please their taste buds. Offerings include curried goat, cow feet, jerk chicken, codfish and ackee (salt fish cooked with a popular Jamaican fruit), mackerel and bananas, and Jamaican beef patties. Jamaican movies and reggae music videos are available for rental. Beyond that, there's not much to this little storefront eatery located in a short strip mall at Warrensville. Just nine plastic-covered tables, fake flowers, and a television—plus a kitchen.

LATIN AMERICA

Mexican

Cancun Family Mexican Restaurant

☎ (330) 723-2555

CITY: **Medina**   AREA: **Farther South**
ATMOSPHERE: **Relaxed**   COST: $$$$$

ADDRESS: 126 N. Court St.

HOURS: Mon–Thu 11 a.m.–10 p.m., Fri & Sat 11 a.m.–11 p.m., Sun noon–9 p.m.

RESERVATIONS: Not Taken   **PAYMENT:** MC, VS, AX, DIS   **BAR:** Beer, wine, liquor   **TAKEOUT:** Yes

SMOKING: **ACCESS:** ♿ Limited

On a corner just off the town square, in a colorful stucco building, is a restaurant that does all it can to make sure diners get what they want. The concept of having it your way reaches a new customer-pleasing level here. Many popular items can be ordered as side dishes, so you can have your chalupa and eat it too—along with a taco, burrito, or tamale. Nachos come 10 different ways—with shrimp; with spicy Mexican chorizo sausage; with just cheese, or cheese plus chicken, ground beef, or shredded beef; or the house special version made with refried beans, jalapenos, cheddar cheese, onions, tomatoes, sour cream, and guacamole. If all that's not enough, you have the option of chicken, ground beef, or shredded beef. Paul Simon sings of 50 ways to leave your lover; the theme at Cancun is eight ways to eat your camarones (shrimp): rancheros (sauteed with sweet peppers, onions, and carrots); "Al Mojo" (with mushrooms in a butter, wine, and garlic sauce); a la Diabla (with prawns in a spicy red sauce); cabo blanco (featuring a wine and cheese sauce); arroz-style (served over a bed of rice); as part of a seafood mix with crab, scallops, and vegetables; or as a botonas del mar (appetizer of the sea), a combination of sauteed shrimp, mushrooms, onions, spices, wine, avocado, tomatoes, and lemon, in either a half-pound or a full-pound portion. Chicken,

pork, and beef get their own variety of treatments. Most Mexican restaurants allow you to choose the filling you want in your tortilla wraps, but here a section of the menu titled "Combinations" allows for a frenzy of mixing and matching. Pick one, two, or three items from two lists and fill them with your choice of meat, poultry, or cheese: one list includes enchiladas, tostadas, tamales, and tacos; the other, burritos, chimichangas, chiles rellenos, and chalupas. And if that doesn't satisfy your need for variety, you can do a crossover, choosing one item from the first list and another from the second. Get your tostadas made with corn or with flour, Northern-style. Vegetarians find out-of-the-ordinary options: enchiladas, fajitas, and burritos are made Verdura- or Acapulco-style with an assortment of vegetables (broccoli, cauliflower, zucchini, celery, onions, bell peppers, tomatoes, mushrooms); and a chimichanga is available with a potato stuffing. And there's still more evidence of Fernando and Veronica Ganindo's desire to accommodate every taste and appetite. Sangria, that divine wine punch made with fruit, comes by the glass, half carafe, and carafe. Fernando learned the restaurant business working for his family in Seattle, helped his cousin with a restaurant in North Olmsted, and opened his own place in partnership with another cousin before relocating to Medina. He and his wife were attracted to the town as a good place to raise their five children. Their choice is a boon to the southwestern suburbs, where good ethnic eateries are few and far between. The spacious dining area is divided into three sections: the main room , which has comfortable booths and tables; a smaller side room that's perfect for meetings, groups, and private parties; and the cantina, where smokers can eat, drink, and be merry as they inhale to their heart's content. Mexican arts and crafts provide touches of color and an out-of-Ohio mood. Parking area in the rear with a back entrance.

Cancun Restaurant & Lounge
☎ **(440) 888-8900**

CITY: **Parma**   AREA: **Southwest**
ATMOSPHERE: **Casual**   COST: $$$$$

ADDRESS: 6855 Ridge Rd.
HOURS: Mon–Thu 3:30–10 p.m., Fri & Sat 3:30–11 p.m.; Sun 3:30–9 p.m.
RESERVATIONS: Taken, for parties of 5 or more only   **PAYMENT:** MC, VS, AX, DIS   **BAR:** Beer, wine, liquor   **TAKEOUT:** Yes   **SMOKING:** Smoking section
ACCESS: ♿ Full access   **OTHER ETHNIC SPECIALTIES:** German

One half of the husband-and-wife team that owns and operates the Cancun is from Germany; the other is Hungarian. Eight years ago they decided to open a Mexican restaurant, and no, this is not a misprint. Georgie and Peter Mueritz simply loved Mexican food, as well as what's usually referred to as Tex-Mex. For fun, in their first year in business they decided to celebrate Oktoberfest by occasionally slipping a few traditional German dishes into their list of daily specials. The move was so successful, with customers clamoring for more, that a German-Mexican restaurant was born. According to Peter, Mexico actually has a large German immigrant population, and it's not unusual for restaurants there to have a menu that includes dishes from both cuisines. And to make it even more interesting, when Georgie is in the mood, she whips up something Hungarian that reminds her of home. So when they claim that the restaurant has something for everyone, they really mean it. Is there any other place in Cleveland where you can get a spicy chorizo sausage burrito while your tablemates enjoy bratwurst, goulash, and barbecued baby back ribs? Portions are large, and the chips and salsa are plentiful. There's also a selection of both German and Mexican beers. The atmosphere is casual, homey, and unpretentious, attracting customers who readily admit they come back regularly. They can handle about 112 diners at once, and seating is primarily in booths. The decor, which features dark wood and a red, orange, and cream-color scheme, has a mostly Mexican motif. The Cancun is located in a strip mall with nothing in its exterior appearance to indicate what a unique and pleasant place is inside. A good choice for families and groups of friends.

Cozumel
☎ **(440) 717-1080**

CITY: **Broadview Heights**   AREA: **West Side**
ATMOSPHERE: **Casual**   COST: $$$$$

ADDRESS: 9180 Broadview Rd.
HOURS: Mon–Thu 11 a.m.–9:30 p.m., Fri 11 a.m.–10:30 p.m., Sat noon–10 p.m., Sun noon–8:30 p.m.   **RESERVATIONS:** Taken, not accepted Fri–Sat nights   **PAYMENT:** MC, VS, AX, DIS, checks   **BAR:** Beer, wine, liquor   **TAKEOUT:** Yes
SMOKING: Smoking section   **ACCESS:** ♿ Full access

Cozumel fills a definite void when it comes to ethnic eateries in general, and Mexican in particular, in this southwestern suburb. So it's no surprise that business has been booming since the doors opened in January 2001. The restaurant is part of the Center, a new shopping plaza, and parking is a breeze. (Giganti's Imports is only a few doors away, if you want a little something Italian to take home for tomorrow—see listing for this market in Chapter 3.) Indoor and outdoor seating is available. Inside, the theme is tropical—walls are a lush shade of green and a golden yellow that glows like real sunshine even on the gloomiest Cleveland day. Big windows let in plenty of natural light, and wooden blinds help block it out when it overwhelms (and hide the less-than-attractive parked cars from view). Regulation serapes, sombreros, and some pieces of folk art provide decoration, and a TV mounted on the wall in the smoking section provides distraction—either welcome or not, depending on your point of view. But the real entertainment is at the tables. The cuisine of central Mexico provides the kitchen's in-

LATIN AMERICA

spiration, and a glossary of Spanish food words is found on the back of the menu. Among the notable house specials are chilaquiles (fried tortilla chips in a ranchero sauce with chicken or beef, cheese, lettuce, guacamole, and pico de gallo); pollo con crema, a dish of chicken cooked in sour cream with three kinds of peppers; the burrito de la roqueta, filled with pork and onions; and Mexican tacos made with steak, chorizo sausage, onions, and cilantro. Burritos, quesadillas, enchiladas, tacos both crispy and soft, tostados, taquitos, and tostaguac, each with a variety of fillings and toppings, can be ordered a la carte or in combination platters. For those who prefer big hunks of meat to the ground version or to dainty little strips gussied up with vegetables, there's the grilled rib eye steak ranchero or pollo loco (a whole marinated chicken breast). Two can get what's too much for one—the Fajita Grande is meant for sharing, with enough beef, chicken, shrimp, and chorizo sausage plus rice, beans, salad, and tortillas for a pair of hungry diners. Fried eggs get upgraded from breakfast fare to real meal status—huevos rancheros are served here any time of the day or night with rice, beans, tortillas, and a possible sausage add-on. There are seven items on the menu strictly for vegetarians and six different child-sized plates. Portions are generous, and sides of yellow rice and refried beans make them even more so. Margaritas and daiquiris are mixed in small, medium, jumbo, half-pitcher, and pitcher portions. There's a large selection of Mexican beers to keep your throat wet as you nibble on nachos: Corona, Dos Equis, Tecate, Negra Modelo, Pacifico, and Desperados.

El Charrito
☎ (440) 585-2530

CITY: **Wickliffe**   AREA: **East Side**
ATMOSPHERE: **Casual**   COST: $$$$$

ADDRESS: 30560 Euclid Ave.

HOURS: Mon–Thu 11 a.m.–9 p.m., Fri 11 a.m.–10:30 p.m., Sat 2–10:30 p.m.; closed Sun
RESERVATIONS: Not taken   **PAYMENT:** MC, VS, AX, DIS   **BAR:** Beer, wine   **TAKEOUT:** Yes   **SMOKING:** Yes
ACCESS: ♿ Full access

This doesn't look like much of a restaurant from the outside, with a neon sign advertising Mexican beer glowing in the window, but inside it has the pleasant feel of a south-of-the-border cantina. A family business, it was established in 1968 and has been at its present location since 1980. The small, cozy place seats about 48, and owners Olivia Costilla Jones and husband Bill or one of their employees greet guests at the door and serve as well. The homemade chips are so popular that they sell them for takeout by the bagful along with orders of their salsa. Many of their recipes, says Olivia, have been passed down among family members for generations, and in addition to tacos, burritos, and enchiladas, the menu features some very hot and spicy pescado (red snapper fillet), carne guisada (steak chunks), and pollo con mole (chicken). Some entrees include a generous dollop of sour cream and guacamole. The menu, which has a dictionary of Mexican food terms and dishes, also offers American sandwiches and special child-sized dinners. They prepare a special dessert that consists of a deep-fried tortilla folded over ice cream, and they also offer Mexican coffee and coffee con leche (coffee with hot milk). There's only one table large enough to accommodate six; the rest seat four or two, but bigger groups can be accommodated.

El Charro Restaurante

☎ (440) 237-6040

CITY: **North Royalton** AREA: **Southwest**
ATMOSPHERE: **Casual** COST: $$$$$

ADDRESS: 13570 Ridge Rd.

HOURS: Tue–Thu 11 a.m.–10 p.m., Fri 11
a.m.–11 p.m., Sat 2–11 p.m., Sun 3–9 p.m.;
closed Mon **RESERVATIONS:** Taken, for parties of
6 or more **PAYMENT:** MC, VS, AX, DIS, checks
BAR: Beer, wine, liquor **TAKEOUT:** Yes
SMOKING: Smoking section **ACCESS:** ♿ Full
access

No one could accuse this place of being trendy. It's just an easygoing neighborhood restaurant with a timeless quality, run by a family for families. The interior is a bit of mixed-metaphor pseudo-Southwestern, with sombreros and bullfighting posters, but that's part of its charm. Patrons can sit at booths, tables, or the bar at the back. The menu has no big surprises but offers a broad and crowd-pleasing selection: Tex-Mex favorites plus classic Mexican combination plates and popular dishes like quesadillas (flour tortillas with cheese and onions) and chiles rellenos. The menu explains that foods are prepared with flavorful spices and are never hot unless you add the heat yourself. Service is fast and friendly, portions are substantial, and nachos with hot and mild sauce are complimentary. The bunuelo (light, fried dessert pastries with cinnamon and sugar) are a special after-dinner treat, because they are traditionally served only at New Year's. There's an all-you-can-eat lunch buffet daily and a Sunday brunch buffet. Park in the small lot out front or in the additional spaces in the rear. Hope Nedelec runs the restaurant with the help of her brother, Tito Rocha.

DON'T FORGET: CALL AHEAD!

El Rincon Mexican Restaurant

☎ (330) 497-2229

CITY: **North Canton** AREA: **Farther South**
ATMOSPHERE: **Casual** COST: $$$$$

ADDRESS: 720 South Main St.

HOURS: Mon–Thu 11 a.m.–10 p.m., Fri
11 a.m.–10:30 p.m., Sat 11:30 a.m.–10:30 p.m.,
Sun 11:30 a.m.–9 p.m. **RESERVATIONS:** Taken
PAYMENT: MC, VS, DIS **BAR:** None **TAKEOUT:** Yes
SMOKING: Smoking section **ACCESS:** ♿ Full
access

Mexican knickknacks provide the visual theme, inside and out. In front of the building, which looks like it was once home to a pancake- or steakhouse, are ceramic burros and little guys in sombreros and serapes. The walls in the dining room are decorated with scenes from Mexico, and festive piñatas hang from the ceiling. The food is straight-ahead Mexican with no surprises—tacos, enchiladas, burritos, tostadas, fajitas, quezadilla (their spelling), chalupas, chiles rellenos, and carne asada. The menu is chatty and shows a sense of humor, with the following announcement from "The Boss": "Due to inflation and everything else you already know, we are not allowed to accept Mexican pesos" (probably a lot of those floating around North Canton). He also promises that "brave amigos" who want their food hot need only ask. There's also a description of Mexican dishes, but I must admit they go a bit overboard as I doubt there's anyone around who needs a definition of nachos. Chips and salsa are available in take-home portions. They have a bonus plan—eat nine meals with them, get your card punched each time, and the 10th lunch or dinner is free (sort of, since the card's value is up to $10, but then again, the most expensive entree is $9.50, so you can stay within budget if you skip appetizer and dessert and stick with water as your beverage). A second El Rincon is located in Akron, at 1485 South Arlington Street (330-785-3724).

LATIN AMERICA

LATIN AMERICA

El Tango Taqueria
☎ **(216) 226-9999**

CITY: **Lakewood**   AREA: **West Side**
ATMOSPHERE: **Relaxed**   COST: $$$$$

ADDRESS: 14224 Madison Ave.
HOURS: Daily 11 a.m.–10 p.m.
RESERVATIONS: Not Taken PAYMENT: MC, VS, AX, DIS BAR: None TAKEOUT: Yes SMOKING: Smoke-Free ACCESS: & Full access

Antonio Carafelli is not a modest guy. In his menu he declares that his tacos and burritos are the best in the world! How's that for confidence? Bite into one created by him or his partner, Heidi Springer, and decide for yourself. They are certainly among the largest I've run across—the burrito might be considered a piece of carry-on luggage if you were to trying to board a plane with it in your hand. As their names suggest, neither Carafelli nor Springer has Mexican roots, but Antonio has had a long-standing passion for all things Mexican and edible. He has studied Mexican cooking, lived in Santa Fe, New Mexico, and San Antonio, Texas, where he learned how good Mexican food should taste, and honed his skills at a number of other restaurants. My own internal taco tester tells me Antonio knows what he's doing. Daily specials like pollo con pina (tostadas with chicken, cheese, grilled pineapple, and green chile sauce) and enchiladas rojas (beef with a red chile sauce) are outside the box of standard Mexican fare. There are four versions of salsa, all made on the premises: two mild blends, ranchera and poblano verde; a medium-hot cinnamon chipotle combination; and hot mexicana. The outstanding tamale pie, rarely found in these parts, is made with layers of chicken, cheese, and corn tortillas baked together with a spicy chili cascabel sauce and salsa. Nachos go beyond the ordinary—they come in a "grande" portion topped with beans, poblano sauce, cheese, and fresh salsa. Since I first visited, the menu has been expanded to include dishes

from Brazil, Argentina, Cuba, and Puerto Rico. The place itself has expanded too. The new dining room seats 25, and paper and plastic have been replaced with real china and silverware. Custom-made wooden tables, a warm red-and-yellow color scheme, and Antonio's paintings set a tone evoking a country hacienda in central Mexico or Spain. The original storefront space, geared for takeout, is still there, with a low, tiled counter and four stools in the window. The kitchen, wide open and visible from the customer side of the counter, dominates the room. It's also become a classroom; the owner's began to offer cooking classes in the fall of 2002. Call for information about upcoming sessions. El Tango is located in a brick building with plenty of on-street parking in front.

La Fiesta
☎ **(440) 442-1445**

CITY: **Richmond Heights**   AREA: **East Side**
ATMOSPHERE: **Casual**   COST: $$$$$

ADDRESS: 5115 Wilson Mills Rd.
HOURS: Lunch Mon–Fri 11:30 a.m.–2:30 p.m.; Dinner Mon–Sat 5–10 p.m.; closed Sun & most holidays RESERVATIONS: Taken, recommended for parties of more than 5 PAYMENT: MC, VS, AX, DIS BAR: Beer, wine, liquor TAKEOUT: Yes SMOKING: Smoking section ACCESS: & Full access

Antonia Valle began serving Mexican food to Clevelanders in 1952. Using many of the same family recipes, Antonia's children and grandchildren continue the tradition in a restaurant that features the cuisine of the central Mexican region of Michoacan, the area south of Guadalajara where Antonia came from. Diners will find many familiar Mexican dishes on the menu, including tacos, enchiladas, burritos, and tamales, but the flavor is different from the Tex-Mex most Americans are used to. There are also some more unusual offerings like lomo de cerdo con chipotles y ciruelas (roast pork loin stuffed with chipotle peppers and prunes and topped with orange gravy) and chilaquiles (a mixture of beaten eggs, corn tortilla strips, cheese, and salsa). Servers, who are knowledgeable about the food, are glad to explain and advise. There's a large selection of items for vegetarians and special children's platters, too. The walls are peach-colored stucco, the floors are clay tile, and the overall effect is attractive and comfortable. Located in a retail strip adjacent to Richmond Mall, this is a relaxing place to eat and socialize.

La Posadita
☎ 330-733-3174

CITY: **Akron**   AREA: **Farther South**
ATMOSPHERE: **Relaxed**   COST: $$$$$

ADDRESS: 886 Canton Rd.
HOURS: Tue–Thu 11 a.m.–7:30 p.m., Fri–Sat 11 a.m.–9 p.m., Sun 11 a.m.–5 p.m., Mon closed
RESERVATIONS: Not taken **PAYMENT:** Cash only
BAR: None **TAKEOUT:** Yes **SMOKING:** All sections
ACCESS: ⅇ Full access

In her weekly Akron Beacon Journal column, Jane Snow wrote that this the only spot serving truly authentic Mexican food in Akron. Her readers let her know there was one other—see the listing for Rancheros Taqueria in this chapter. What's important is the fact that the food here is indeed bona-fide Mexico City, working-class traditional, and very, very good.

A friend of Snow's told her he was becoming addicted to the salsa here. I love his description: "It is so perfectly spiced—not hot in the mouth, but it keeps on warming in the tummy." This is a family place run by Silvia Rubio Mendez, her two daughters, and her mother that attracts other Hispanic families who often fill the little 20 seat, no frills spot. The two older women honed their already significant culinary skills cooking lunches one day a week at St. Bernard's Church in the company of other Latina women for 10 years.

They opened the restaurant in December, 2002, and the recipes they use for things like mole, pozole (shredded pork and hominy), chile relleno, menudo (tripe soup), caldo mariscos (seafood and rice), and bisteak a la Mexicana (beef in tomato-based sauce) are generations old. The little corn tortillas are handmade and prepared to order. Beans and rice feature the legumes slow-cooked with pork. With their reputation growing fast, Mendez wonders if expansion is in her future. But one thing she's sure of is that no matter how big or how busy the restaurant becomes, quality and tradition will always come first.

Luchita's Mexican Restaurant
☎ (216) 252-1169

CITY: **Cleveland**   AREA: **Near West Side**
ATMOSPHERE: **Casual**   COST: $$$$$

ADDRESS: 3456 W. 117th St.
HOURS: Lunch Tue–Fri 11 a.m.–2 p.m.; Dinner Tue–Thu 5–10 p.m., Fri & Sat 4–11 p.m., Sun 4–9 p.m.; closed between lunch & dinner; closed Mon **RESERVATIONS:** Not taken **PAYMENT:** MC, VS, AX **BAR:** Beer, wine, liquor **TAKEOUT:** Yes **SMOKING:** Smoking section **ACCESS:** ⅇ Full access

A friend who has spent considerable time in Mexico says that a bite of Luchita's food transports her back there. The Galindo family has been preparing authentic regional dishes from central Mexico since 1981, and the only modification they make to traditional recipes is to substitute vegetable oil for lard. The menu, with glossary, explains what goes into each dish. There are some rarely encountered sauces such as mole (rich with cocoa), suiza (tomatillos and cheese or sour cream), and pico de gallo (a sweet and sour salsa made with sugar and vinegar); unusual appetizers like ceviche (a tomato dish made with lime-flavored shrimp, onions, and cilantro), corn masa turnovers stuffed with chicken and chihuahua cheese and topped with marinated cabbage, and sopes de chorizo ("boats" made of corn masa filled with black beans, spicy sausage, anejo cheese, and guacamole). Specialties offered change every three months both to take advantage of what's in season and to feature specific regional cuisines. So you might find puerco potosino, a simmered pork; pollo sinaloa, a stew of chicken, potatoes, onions, and cactus; pescado pibil, a fish fillet marinated in achiote orange salsa and wrapped in banana leaves; empanadas con mole Amarillo, a filled flour-dough turnover in a mole typically made in Oaxaca; or tinga de pollo, shredded chicken prepared with homemade Mexican cream and a tomato-based salsa of chipotle peppers and tomatillos. Of course, there are always burritos, enchiladas, tacos, and flautas (a stuffed tortilla rolled and deep fried). There is a good selection for vegetarians. The world beyond Cleveland is more familiar with this place than locals; its praises have been sung in airline magazines and international dining guides. But despite its fame, the atmosphere here is low key, friendly, and comfortable. Both the bar, which serves Bohemia beer, a brand popular in Mexico, plus top-shelf tequilas, and the 80-seat dining room are often populated by regulars. The building is vintage 1930s, and, inside, the simple stucco walls accented with Mexican ceramics, artwork, and figurines form an ideal backdrop for the food, which is the real attraction here.

Luchita's Mexican Restaurant
☎ (216) 241-8200
CITY: **Cleveland**   AREA: **Downtown**
ATMOSPHERE: **Casual**   COST: $$$$$

ADDRESS: 740 W. Superior Ave.
HOURS: Lunch Tue–Fri 11:30 a.m.–2:30 p.m.; Dinner Tue–Thu 5–10 p.m., Fri & Sat 11:30 a.m.–11 p.m., Sun 4–9 p.m.; closed between lunch & dinner; closed Mon
RESERVATIONS: Taken, for groups of 6 or more
PAYMENT: MC, VS, AX   BAR: Beer, wine, liquor
TAKEOUT: Yes   SMOKING: Smoking section
ACCESS: ♿ Full access

Located inside House of Cues. See listing for Luchita's on Cleveland's West Side.

Luchita's Mexican Restaurant
☎ (440) 205-5966
CITY: **Mentor**   AREA: **East Side**
ATMOSPHERE: **Casual**   COST: $$$$$

ADDRESS: 8870 Mentor Ave.
HOURS: Lunch Tue–Fri 11:30 a.m.–2:30 p.m.; Dinner Tue–Thu 5–10 p.m., Fri & Sat 11:30 a.m.–11 p.m., Sun 4–9 p.m.; closed between lunch & dinner; closed Mon
RESERVATIONS: Taken, for groups of 6 or more
PAYMENT: MC, VS, AX   BAR: Beer, wine, liquor
TAKEOUT: Yes   SMOKING: Smoking section
ACCESS: ♿ Full access

See listing for Luchita's on Cleveland's West Side.

Luchita's on the Square
☎ (216) 561-8537
CITY: **Cleveland**   AREA: **East Side**
ATMOSPHERE: **Casual**   COST: $$$$$

ADDRESS: 13112 Shaker Square
HOURS: Tue–Thu 11:30 a.m.–10 p.m., Fri 11:30 a.m.–11 p.m., Sat 5–11 p.m., Sun 5–9 p.m., closed Mon   RESERVATIONS: Taken
PAYMENT: MC, VS, AX   BAR: Beer, wine, liquor
TAKEOUT: Yes   SMOKING: Smoke-free
ACCESS: ♿ Full access

Same owners, same menu, same prices, same atmosphere as the original Luchita's on the West Side, this 92-seat restaurant opened its doors to the public in January 1998.

Marcelita's Mexican Restaurant
☎ (330) 656-2129
CITY: **Hudson**   AREA: **Farther South**
ATMOSPHERE: **Casual**   COST: $$$$$

ADDRESS: 7774 Darrow Rd. (SR 91)
HOURS: Tue–Thu 11 a.m.–9:30 p.m., Fri & Sat 11 a.m.–10:30 p.m.; closed Sun and Mon; Happy

Hours in "La Cantina" Tue–Fri 3–6 p.m., Sat 11 a.m.–4 p.m. **RESERVATIONS:** Not taken, except for parties of 6 or more (excluding prime time on weekends and holidays) **PAYMENT:** MC, VS, AX, DIS **BAR:** Beer, wine, liquor **TAKEOUT:** Yes **SMOKING:** Smoking section **ACCESS:** & Full access

---

Marcelita, who hails from Mexico City, husband Jack, and sister-in-law Jeanne have been helping, in their own words, "to stamp out gringo food" since 1978. The crowds have grown larger every year, so they've had to keep breaking through walls and adding space. First the original one-room restaurant got a new kitchen, foyer, and spacious cantina (bar) plus greenhouse. In 1992 came the garden room, a bright, cheery, tropical-feeling place, even in the dead of an Ohio winter. The restaurant can now accommodate about 200 diners, in four rooms, each one with a different color theme and distinctively decorated with traditional pottery and pieces of whimsical folk art the family has brought back from their many trips to Mexico. The two-section middle room is composed of the original low-ceilinged dining area and foyer. It has a darkish intimacy, brightened by candles on the tables and a mural of a window with flowers on the sill. The former kitchen is now a small, separate dining area perfect for private parties. The sunny, yellow garden room is all blond wood, big windows, plants, and ceramic birds. The 75-seat cantina is reminiscent of a log cabin, and is usually filled with people who are easing the wait for a table (typically 15-30 minutes on the weekend) by enjoying complimentary chips and sauces and sipping one of the many types of "Marvelous Margaritas" the restaurant is famous for, a Mexican or microbrewed beer, or a shot of tequila. The menu offers enchiladas; burritos; tostadas; tacos; chiles rellenos; chimichangas; steak, chicken, and vegetarian fajitas; and a traditional "pepita" salad made with roasted pumpkin seeds. Desserts include homemade flan, ice cream nachos, and arroz con leche (rice pudding). This is a family restaurant in every sense—it's run by a family, much of the wait staff is like family (many having been with Marcelita's for 10 or more years), and it's genuinely kid friendly with a fleet of boosters and high chairs. A room is available for private parties. There's a large parking lot surrounded by a thick backdrop of trees.

Mexican Village Restaurante y Cantinas
☎ (216) 661-3800

CITY: **Parma**   AREA: **Southwest**
ATMOSPHERE: **Casual**   COST: $$$$$

ADDRESS: 1409 Brookpark Rd.
HOURS: Mon–Thu 11:30 a.m.–10 p.m., Fri 11:30 a.m.–10 p.m.; Sat 4–10 p.m., Sun closed **RESERVATIONS:** Taken, recommended on weekends **PAYMENT:** MC, VS, AX, DIS **BAR:** Beer, wine, liquor **TAKEOUT:** Yes **SMOKING:** Smoking section **ACCESS:** & Full access

---

The building appears small from the outside, but inside there's actually room for up to 200 diners. The decor is traditional and attractive: tile floors, stucco walls decorated with masks, pottery, and blankets from Mexico, and arched tile-trimmed doorways. There's a separate bar-room with a few tables. Established in 1962 and still family owned, the Village features both traditional northern Mexican specialties and those Mexican-style dishes, like fajitas and chimichangas, found only on this side of the border. They offer tacos American-style or a more Mexican version. There's something to please those who crave Tex-Mex or those in search of truly regional dishes—like enchiladas in a mole or a tomatillo sauce, chorizo con huevos (sausage and eggs served with beans, rice, and tortillas), and chiles rellenos (poblano peppers stuffed with Mexican cheese). There are three classic desserts: flan, fried ice cream, and sopapillas (fried dough flavored with honey, sugar, and cinnamon). Downstairs, the Latin

LATIN AMERICA

LATIN AMERICA

Club is open for drinking and dancing on Friday, Saturday, and Sunday nights from 9 p.m. to 2:30 a.m. A disc jockey plays strictly Latin music, and the place is usually packed with people who know how to do the salsa, merengue, cumbia, and lambada, and those who want to watch. There's a small cover charge, and no food is served in the cantina. It is also available for private parties of 50 to 150 guests. The exterior of the building was recently remodeled to give it a Spanish/Mediterranean look that features a red clay tile roof with real beams protruding from the building, stucco walls with arches, and ornate Spanish lanterns.

Mi Pueblo
☎ (216) 671-6661

CITY: **Cleveland**   AREA: **West Side**
ATMOSPHERE: **Relaxed**   COST: $$$$$

ADDRESS: 12207 Lorain Ave.
HOURS: Mon–Thu 9 a.m.–11 p.m., Fri 9 a.m.–midnight, Sat 8 a.m.–midnight, Sun 8 a.m.–11 p.m. **RESERVATIONS:** Taken
PAYMENT: MC, VS, DIS **BAR:** None **TAKEOUT:** Yes
SMOKING: Smoking section **ACCESS:** & Full access

This combination restaurant and market is a convenience concept whose time has come, and one sure way to avoid the well-known dangers of grocery shopping on an empty stomach. (For more information about the market, see Mi Pueblo's market listing further on in this chapter.) Informal simplicity is the standard here—food is served in plastic baskets, napkins are found in table dispensers. But there's no scrimping on quality or quantity. Portions are huge and just as big on taste. The menu offers a choice of tacos, burritos, and tortas (sandwiches) with a variety of fillings, and all are so big and overstuffed that an average appetite is challenged. And the fillings bear no resemblance to the bland ground beef or beans that most Americans expect: there's spicy Mexican sausage, diced skirt steak, roasted

barbecued pork, steamed beef, avocado, and lengua (artfully translated on the menu as "Mexican delicacy" to avoid the off-putting reality of tongue, which is what it is). Daily specials might be chiles rellenos, chicken mole, or tamales. On Saturdays and Sundays only, because they are so time-consuming to prepare, menudo (tripe soup) and birria (goat stew) are added to the menu, and the demand for these flavorful and rarely encountered dishes is so great that they're available in take-home gallons. A complimentary relish tray of pickled carrots and jalapeno peppers, red tomato pepper sauce, and green tomatillo sauce arrives at your table shortly after you sit down. From your booth or table you can see the open kitchen and grill where pork cooks slowly on a spit. Entrees can be accompanied by an intriguing array of drinks: orchata (rice water, a concoction that is like a liquid version of rice pudding); tamarindo (a soft drink made from tamarind fruit); freshly made natural fruit juices; and malteadas, malts so thick, sweet, and special that they can double as dessert, made by blending milk, ice, sugar, and fresh fruit. For breakfast, consider huevos rancheros, a combination of eggs and salsa, warm tortillas, beans, and chorizo sausage.

Though the four owners—two sets of brothers—and staff are originally from Mexico, and much of the taqueria's clientele is Spanish-speaking, the menu is easy for everyone to read, with English-language descriptions to accompany dishes listed by their Spanish names. The CD jukebox contains only Spanish and Mexican selections, from traditional folk music to popular singers, and a disc is almost always playing. Sometimes staff sing along. On a wall near the entrance is a large hand-painted mural of a Mexican village scene. Carved wooden miniatures depicting traditional 19th-century Mexican kitchens and some wooden plates of the type used in Mexico in the 1800s decorate the other walls. There is a lightness and brightness here that adds to the tropical, far-from-the-steel-mills feel; walls are orange, floor tiles are red, and light pours in from the big plate-glass storefront windows. The atmosphere, as well as the food, is so decidedly un-Cleveland that coming here is like taking a trip out of town. In addition, the place is very kid friendly, so a visit can serve double duty as a family outing—throw in a stop at the grocery and you've accomplished three things at once!

Mi Pueblo
☎ (216) 791-8226

CITY: **Cleveland** AREA: **Near East Side**
ATMOSPHERE: **Casual** COST: $$$$$

ADDRESS: 11611 Euclid Ave.
HOURS: Sun–Thu 10 a.m.–10:30 p.m., Fri & Sat 10 a.m.–2:30 a.m. RESERVATIONS: Taken, Suggested for four or more on weekends
PAYMENT: MC, VS, AX, DIS BAR: Beer, wine, liquor
TAKEOUT: SMOKING: Smoking section
ACCESS: ♿ Full access

Mi Pueblo took on a whole new identity when it migrated east. This location, which opened late in 1998, is a larger, prettier, dressed-up version of the original West Side taqueria, but the food has retained all its authenticity and flavor. Plates of chiles rellenos (stuffed poblano peppers), enchiladas, and shredded beef tortas prepared in the culinary tradition of the central regions provide a taste-bud ticket to the heartland of Mexico. You get the same ride when you spoon up some caldo de pollo (cilantro-spiked chicken soup) or take a mouthful of guacamole con tostaditas. There's a good selection of dishes familiar to fans of the burrito and the taco, and some more unusual preparations made from seafood, beef, chicken, and pork. Portions are always generous, and most entrees come with rice and beans. It's unlikely you'll leave with that empty feeling, especially if you freely indulge in the on-the-house corn chips (freshly made and served in a basket that is constantly refilled), salsa (red and green), and pickled

carrots before your meal. The margaritas, prepared in the cantina at the front of the restaurant, can also fill you up as they come in various sizes, one as big as a punch bowl (42 ounces of liquor-laced liquid), and the same is true for the luscious tropical fruit milkshakes and the glasses of sweet orchata. (For more information about food and drinks, see previous listing for the original Mi Pueblo).

Like the food, the decor honors tradition. At the entrance are a 100-year-old wooden butcher's block and a stone grinder. Stucco walls, tilework, masks, murals, and brightly colored paper flowers all evoke a sense of place . . . and that place is Mexico, not Cleveland. The same care and attention that go into preparing each dish are evident in the imported hand-carved chairs. On Friday, Saturday, and Sunday from 6 to 9 p.m., a pair of strolling musicians sings Mexican favorites—if you're with that special someone and the time is right, request a love song (and don't hesitate to show your appreciation with both applause and cash). Although I'd say this is a fine choice for the romantically inclined, the place draws diners of all ages and types. Part of its charm is the mix—AARP members and those almost old enough to vote; the well-dressed and the should-have-dressed-better; students and staff from Case Western Reserve University, the Art Institute, and the Cleveland Institute of Music; families from Cleveland and Shaker Heights with kids ranging from the high-chair set to the body-pierced; Latinos who talk to the servers in Spanish; and a varied assortment of folks who could be on their way to or from the Art Museum, University Hospitals, the Garden Center, the oh-so-funky Euclid Tavern next door, the Food Co-op, or the laundromat across the street. A separate, semi-enclosed dining area at the back offers seating for smokers, and it has its own ventilation system. With space for about 30, it's also available by reservation for private parties. The restaurant also does off-site catering, but heed this word of caution—my husband and his partner had them prepare the food for a party at their photography studio, and it was so good that nobody wanted to leave, nor were they content to nibble politely, and halfway through the event I had to make a run to the restaurant for more! Two very small lots in front of and behind the restaurant, and on-street parking.

Nuevo Acapulco
☎ (440) 734-3100

CITY: **North Olmsted**   AREA: **West Side**
ATMOSPHERE: **Casual**   COST: $$$$$

ADDRESS: 24409 Lorain Rd.
HOURS: Mon–Thu 11 a.m.–10 p.m., Fri & Sat 11 a.m.–11 p.m., Sun noon–10 p.m.
RESERVATIONS: Not taken PAYMENT: MC, VS, AX, DIS BAR: Beer, wine, liquor TAKEOUT: Yes
SMOKING: Smoking section ACCESS: ♿ Full access

Opened in 1994, Nuevo Acapulco, located close to Great Northern Mall, bills itself as a Mexican restaurant for families. There are American steaks, hamburgers, and chicken dishes on the menu for those family members who'd rather not come face to face with a plate of camarones a la diabla (prawns and mushrooms in a spicy red sauce) or quesadillas (flour tortillas stuffed with cheese, tomatoes, and chiles). Entree choices reflect cuisine from many regions of the country, and the explanations on the menu will help even novices to understand what they're choosing. Staff, who greet guests in Spanish, are friendly and helpful. A dish of complimentary salsa arrives at the table before diners even place their order, and rice and beans (your choice of refried or cholesterol-free beans) come with most main dishes. The large, bright, colorful, open space seats about 130 and features beautiful murals and artwork with a Mexican motif.

Rancheros Taqueria
☎ (330) 510-2110

CITY: **Akron**   AREA: **Farther South**
ATMOSPHERE: **Relaxed**   COST: $$$$$

ADDRESS: 286 E. Cuyahoga Falls Ave.
HOURS: Mon–Thu 11 a.m.–9 p.m., Fri–Sun 11 a.m.–10 p.m. RESERVATIONS: Not taken
PAYMENT: Cash only BAR: None TAKEOUT: Yes
SMOKING: Smoke-Free ACCESS: ♿ None

This is a joint, in the best sense of the word—small, inexpensive, and with a no-fuss, no-frills atmosphere that comes from being itself with no apologies or excuses. "You pays your money" (cash only)—and you get really good, really authentic Mexican food in return. That's it. Places like this are a dime a dozen in Austin, Texas, but rare in these parts. When Beacon food editor Jane Snow and I walked in, early in the day before the lunchtime crowd appeared, chef, owner, and some-time server David Soreque already had a pot of stock simmering, evidence that everything here is made from scratch, just as his mother taught him back in Michoaca, a little town east of Mexico City where he has born. Although there are some Tex-Mex items available, what makes his menu special is the more traditional preparation of things like tamales, enchiladas, and quesadillas. Tortillas are top quality. Tacos, filled with cubes of spiced pork, chicken, steak, chorizo sausage, or tongue, are fried twice and topped with grilled onions, a squeeze of lime, and a sprinkling of cilantro. According to David, the Mexican dishes most popular in the U.S. would be considered merely appetizers in a proper meal. So on the weekends, he cooks more complicated, time- and labor-intensive specials—mole, chiles rellenos, or a dish made with pork and nopales (cactus)—because he wants to give Americans a taste of what he describes as "the true Mexican cuisine," adding, "that's why lots of Mexicans come here. It's real home cooking to them." Seating is limited to an eight-stool counter and three four-top tables, plus a couple more outside in good weather. The no-smoking policy is flexible. If a patron wants to smoke, and nobody else is there, or nobody objects, it's okay with management. But much of their business is takeout, which means you can do what you want after you take your food home. Delivery is available in North Hill and to downtown.

Tlaquepaque Restaurant
☎ (330) 649-9109

CITY: **Canton**   AREA: **Farther South**
ATMOSPHERE: **Relaxed**   COST: $$$$$

ADDRESS: 4460 Dressler Rd.
HOURS: Sun–Thu 11 a.m.–10 p.m., Fri & Sat 11 a.m.–11 p.m. RESERVATIONS: Taken, Suggested for large parties PAYMENT: MC, VS, AX, DIS BAR: Beer, wine, liquor TAKEOUT: Yes
SMOKING: Smoking section ACCESS: ♿ Full access

As I pulled into the big parking lot of this newish stand-alone stucco building, my first thought was that I'd arrived in the Mexican neighborhood at Disney World. The place has a look that is loosely (very loosely) connected to pueblo-style architecture, but it's a cartoon fantasy version of the real thing. I didn't have high hopes for what I'd find on the other side of the door, but although the look is still kitschy, it's also pleasant, and the large dining area (seats 200) is divided by half walls into cozy, comfortable sections with a mix of tables and booths. Owner Rafel Madragal and his family opened the restaurant in 1998 and have already garnered many regulars. Standard, familiar Mexican dishes fill the menu, with variations coming mostly in the form of fillings, combinations, and quantity, but the preparation, according to Madragal, is rooted in old family recipes. The kitchen does like to play with beef tips (you may like to eat them, but how many of you actually know just where the cow's tips are?): you'll find

them in chile Colorado; Tlaquepaque (with rice and beans); and the Special La Casa (with burritos and melted cheese). The menu includes a pronunciation guide as well as a glossary, so you can perfect your ability to order correctly: say, "Chelays Rayya-nos" and "En-chie-lah-das." I left humming that great old tune, "I say Tah-mahlays and you say . . ." The bar at the front near the entrance pours Mexican beer, sangria, and margaritas. There's a patio with seating for about 70 that is relatively sheltered from the parking area.

Puerto Rican

El Taino Restaurant
☎ (216) 621-4888

CITY: **Cleveland**   AREA: **Near West Side**
ATMOSPHERE: **Relaxed**   COST: $$$$$

ADDRESS: 3038 Scranton Rd.
HOURS: Mon–Sat 10 a.m.–9 p.m., Sun noon–7 p.m. RESERVATIONS: Taken
PAYMENT: MC, VS, AX BAR: None TAKEOUT: Yes
SMOKING: Smoke-Free ACCESS: ♿ None

I learned about this place, formerly called Lincoln Deli, in my favorite way—from a satisfied customer and fan. I was sitting in another small West Side ethnic restaurant and fell into conversation with the man at the next table. I told him about my ongoing search for authentic ethnic eateries, and he told me to visit El Taino. It's not the sort of place that advertises, but even so, it attracts a crowd, and not just people who have grown up eating tostones (plantains) and bacalaito (dried, salted cod). According to manager Vivian Sanchez, their clientele is international. "Americans, Irish, Italians, even Oriental people," she says, "they come here, and they seem to really like our food. We get families, policemen, all kinds of city workers. We're a real neighborhood place, a place for everybody." That may be true, but Spanish is the first language here. The list of daily specials required translation. Our

LATIN AMERICA

server, afraid her English wasn't good enough for us, sent Vivian over, and the background music featured Latin beats and lyrics. The small storefront restaurant, which takes its name from the island's indigenous people, offers home cooking Puerto Rican–style. There's goat stew (cabro en fricasse), fried pork (chicharrones), chicken stew (pollo guisado), chuleta (pork chops), and pescadilla (fish). Most dishes include arroz (rice) and habichuelas (beans) or gandules (pigeon peas). Green bananas are a staple—combined with shrimp you get mofongo con camarones; with octopus, mofongo con pulpo; and with lobster, mofongo con langosta. Stuff them with ground beef, and they become alcapurria; with a pork filling, they're pasteles. Not every item on the menu is available every day. Expect a relaxed, congenial atmosphere in a plain and simple setting. Parking is on the street.

Lelolai Bakery & Cafe
☎ (216) 771-9956

CITY: **Cleveland**   AREA: **Near West Side**
ATMOSPHERE: **Relaxed**   COST: $$$$$

ADDRESS: 1889 W. 25th St.
HOURS: Mon–Wed 7:45 a.m.–5 p.m., Thu–Sat 7:45 a.m.–6 p.m., Sun closed   **RESERVATIONS:** Not Taken   **PAYMENT:** MC, VS   **BAR:** None
TAKEOUT: Yes   **SMOKING:** Smoke-Free
ACCESS: ♿ Full access   **OTHER ETHNIC SPECIALTIES:** Spanish

Another contender in the bakery-cafe combo category. Come to shop, come to eat, or stop trying to choose and do both. Caribbean is the culinary theme and carries over into the ambience—the walls are white with bright, bold color accents. Seating for about 22 at small tables of wrought-iron and glass—the sort you'd find in a garden—that fill up the front half of the store. More tables and chairs appear outside when the weather is inviting. This is especially nice as the city has recently invested in an overhaul of the street to make

it more pedestrian friendly. The menu is short and mostly sweet. In addition to sandwiches, cake, pastries, and flans, you can also order cups of gourmet coffee, espresso, latte, cappuccino, tea, hot chocolate, and cold drinks. (For more information see Lelolai's listing under markets.)

Lozada's Restaurant
☎ (216) 621-2954

CITY: **Cleveland**   AREA: **Near West Side**
ATMOSPHERE: **Relaxed**   COST: $$$$

ADDRESS: 1909 W. 25th St.
HOURS: Mon–Thu 10 a.m.–8 p.m., Fri & Sat 10 a.m.–9 p.m.; closed Sun   **RESERVATIONS:** Taken
PAYMENT: MC, VS, AX   **BAR:** None   **TAKEOUT:** Yes
SMOKING: Smoking section   **ACCESS:** ♿ Limited

This is the place where bacalao (dried salted cod) and baseball meet. Former Cleveland Indians Carlos Baerga, Sandy Alomar Jr., and Manny Ramirez have been regular patrons. Current members of the Tribe with Latin American roots and pro players from visiting teams love to come and enjoy the Puerto Rican and Latin house specialties. Owners Santos Lozada Senior and Junior honored these famous patrons by decorating their restaurant, now a few doors north of their former location, with every form of baseball memorabilia: trophies, bats, posters, uniforms, and pennants. The family has been serving Puerto Rican food for 28 years. The new place is bigger than the old one but still casual and comfortable, with a mix of tables and booths that seat groups of two, four, six, or more. Nothing fancy here: it looks like a typical neighborhood joint complete with reasonable prices—a great place to bring the kids or hang out with your friends. But you won't be ordering a grilled cheese sandwich; the dishes are unlike what you'll find most anywhere else in town. The menu, in both English and Spanish, offers such items as pateles (a meat-and- green-banana pie), biste (a T-bone steak Puerto Rican–style with plantains), and bacalao arroz y habichuelas (codfish with rice and beans). There are soups (including one outstanding version made with conch), seafood salads, and unusual imported juices from South America. Fried banana balls with meat are available as an appetizer, and daily specials might include goat or beef stew. Metered on-street parking and a lot at the rear with a back entrance to the restaurant. In the spring of 2001, this stretch of West 25th, near the West Side Market, was upgraded with new lighting, brick sidewalks, and trees.

Rincon Criollo
☎ (216) 939-0992

CITY: **Cleveland**   AREA: **Near West Side**
ATMOSPHERE: **Relaxed**   COST: $$$$$

ADDRESS: 6504 Detroit Ave.
HOURS: Mon–Thu 11 a.m.º8 p.m., Fri–Sat 11 a.m.–9 p.m., Sun closed **RESERVATIONS:** Taken
PAYMENT: Cash only **BAR:** None **TAKEOUT:** Yes
SMOKING: Smoke-Free **ACCESS:** ♿ Full access

Same name, different location. Rincon Criollo, listed in the 2002 edition of Cleveland Ethnic Eats, disappeared from the 2003 volume while they were moving from the old space on St. Clair to their current home in a double storefront in the Detroit-Shoreway neighborhood. It's still the same laid-back, family-run place with a friendly atmosphere and Caribbean accents. The menu is a short list of Latin comfort foods—meat pies, chicken and vegetable soup, stewed pork chops, banana and potato balls, crispy chicarrones (fried pork), rice, and beans. Specialty of the house is the Jibarito sandwich, Rincon's equivalent of a hamburger, made with steak tips served between two slices of plantain. Owner Felix Ocasio told my son Nathan, who had never tasted one, that he'd love it. Felix was right, as evidenced by the purring sound, punctuated by words like "wow" and "yum," that escaped from Nathan between bites. For dessert, he had flan, and he commented, "This alone is worth the trip across town. If we weren't out in public, I'd be licking the bowl." I felt the same about my pescao encebollado en salsa (fish in red sauce). Puerto Ricans call their cuisine "cocina criollo." Like the restaurant's name, which translates as "Creole corner," it refers to the blend of foodstuffs and cooking cultures that characterizes their dishes. Each of the different nationality groups that have populated the island has left its culinary mark, including the native Taino Indians, the Spanish and other Europeans, Africans, Asians, and Cubans. That mix is reflected in the highly spiced, but not spicy, dishes that Rincon Criollo has to offer: Ensalada de Pulpo (octopus salad); stews made with beef, goat meat, or tripe; steak in an onion and vinegar sauce; vianda con bacalao (cod with root vegetables); and Monfongo, "bowls" made with mashed plantain that can be filled with shrimp, pork, octopus, or fish. Not every dish is available every day—one or two are featured as specials each weekday, with a larger selection on Fridays and Saturdays. Plants in the windows, soothing colors, tablecloths under glass, and photos of Puerto Rico combine to create a pleasant setting. Rincon Criollo does a brisk takeout business, and there are two counter seats where you can wait for your order. Kids are more than welcome, and high chairs are available. Judging from all the Spanish-language notices on the bulletin board, I'd say much of the clientele is Hispanic. Easy to find—look for the green awning.

LATIN AMERICA

MARKETS

D'Ici de Là
☎ (216) 763-3636
CITY: **Beachwood**   AREA: **East Side**

ADDRESS: 2101 Richmond Rd.
FOOD AVAIL.: baked goods, spices, condiments, beverages, tea, coffee, prepared frozen foods, takeout meals **HOURS:** Mon–thu 10 a.m.–8 p.m., Fri–Sat 10 a.m.–7 p.m., Sun closed **PAYMENT:** MC, VS, AX, DIS, checks **ACCESS:** ♿ Full access

Not the spot to pick up staples, but definitely where you want to be if you're throwing together an elegant picnic or your own version of tapas for two made up of specialty foods. Browse jars pf guava jelly, sweet potato paste, white and wild asparagus, snails, imported crackers, and caper-stuffed olives. There's an array of oils and vinegars, biscotti, and chocolate. But the largest selection is liquid, what Argentine owner Patricia Cornejo calls "Spanish-speaking wines" and beers from around the world. This is reputed to be the largest collection of South American wines in the region, with some labels unlikely to be found in any other store. Periodically Cornejo, who opened her cafe and gourmet shop in May 2002, hosts wine tastings here to familiarize the public with some of her collection. There's a large selection of prepared foods to go. (For more information see listing in Chapter 6). Located on the lower level of La Place.

Jamaican

Dailey's West Indian Food Mart
☎ (216) 721-7240
CITY: **Cleveland**   AREA: **East Side**

ADDRESS: 3019 E. 116th St.
FOOD AVAIL.: meat (fresh, frozen), fish (fresh, frozen), produce, grains, beans, flour, baked goods, canned & packaged goods, spices, condiments, beverages, tea, wine, prepared frozen foods, takeout meals **HOURS:** Daily 8 a.m.–midnight **PAYMENT:** Checks **ACCESS:** ♿ Full access

From the outside, this looks like a typical little neighborhood grocery. But inside it's filled with exotic, imported Caribbean foods, such as cans of pigeon peas or callalou (a Jamaican spinach), jars of guava jelly, soursop nectar (a fruit pulp), pickapeppa sauce, and many varieties of bottled jerk (a spicy barbecue sauce). Dailey's also stocks many different types of hot peppers, including the hard-to-find fiery Scotch Bonnets; unusual species of fish like conch and Caribbean snapper, plus dried salted codfish; and a large selection of fresh specialty produce, including chocho (a root vegetable that resembles a turnip), huge yams, coconuts (as well as canned coconut milk), and plantains, those hard green bananas so good for cooking. Traditional Jamaican foods like fried plantains, mutton soup, spiced shrimp, and jerk chicken are prepared fresh every day, and you can purchase a complete meal or just a single item ready to eat on the spot or take home. Irish moss, a seaweed used to make a sweet, invigorating drink that's reputed to be especially good for giving a guy's engine a jump start, is sold dried in bags. There are also tropical fruit drinks and Jamaican sodas, and freshly baked rum cake.

Latin American Mix

Dave's Supermarkets
☎ (216) 961-2000

CITY: **Cleveland**   AREA: **Southwest**

ADDRESS: 3565 Ridge Rd.

FOOD AVAIL.: Meat (fresh, frozen), fish (fresh, frozen), produce, grains, beans, flour, rice, baked goods, canned & packaged goods, spices, condiments, beverages, tea, wine, prepared frozen foods **HOURS:** Mon–Sat 7 a.m.–10 p.m., Sun 7 a.m.–8 p.m. **PAYMENT:** MC, VS, checks **ACCESS:** ♿ Full access

This full-service grocery store caters to the Hispanic community, and just about anything you need for Latin cookery can be found here. They stock Goya, La Proferita, and Iberia brand canned goods; rice in 25-pound bags; salted codfish; Mexican cheeses like panela, manchego, ranchero, anejo, asadero, and chihuahua; chipotle chiles en adobo (dried smoked jalapenos in sauce); and a large selection of fresh produce, including plantains, fresh chiles, tomatillos, and uncommon root vegetables. Produce specifically from the West Indies, such as malanga and breadfruit, is also in evidence, and there are unusual colas and fruit drinks from the Islands. If you don't see what you want, ask for it; if they don't have it, they'll try to get it. Renovation on the building that now houses the store was completed in 1993. It's spacious, modern, and convenient, with plenty of free parking. Dave's on Carroll in Ohio City and Dave's on Payne also carry these products. For more information on the Payne Avenue store, see listing in chapter 7. For more information about Dave's in Ohio City, see next listing.

Dave's Supermarkets
☎ (216) 274-2940

CITY: **Cleveland**   AREA: **Near West Side**

ADDRESS: 2700 Carroll Rd.

FOOD AVAIL.: meat (fresh, deli, frozen), fish (fresh, frozen), produce, grains, beans, flour, rice, baked goods, canned & packaged goods, spices, condiments, beverages, tea, coffee, prepared frozen foods, takeout meals **HOURS:** Mon–Sat 7 a.m.–9 p.m., Sun 7 a.m.–8 p.m. **PAYMENT:** MC, VS, DIS, checks **ACCESS:** ♿ Full access **OTHER ETHNIC SPECIALTIES:** African-American, many Mediterranean countries

This 35,000-square-foot full-service store opened in the summer of 1997 in Ohio City. For information about products stocked, see listing for Dave's on Ridge Road (above), and Dave's on Payne Avenue (see chapter 7). They also carry some ethnic foods that are considered more gourmet than traditional, including imported cheeses, Italian-style hams and salami, and Greek olives.

La Borincana Foods
☎ (216) 651-2351

CITY: **Cleveland**   AREA: **Near West Side**

ADDRESS: 2127 Fulton Rd.

FOOD AVAIL.: meat (fresh, frozen), fish (fresh, frozen), produce, grains, beans, flour, rice, baked goods, canned & packaged goods, spices, condiments, beverages, tea, coffee, wine, prepared frozen foods, takeout meals **HOURS:** Mon–Sat 9 a.m.–7 p.m., Sun 9 a.m.–3 p.m. **PAYMENT:** MC, VS, checks **ACCESS:** ♿ Full access **OTHER ETHNIC SPECIALTIES:** Caribbean, Mexico, Puerto Rico, El Salvador, Guatemala, Guyana

This is where to find a large selection of meats and sausages used in Caribbean cookery, and hard-to-find fresh produce like plantains, Scotch peppers, and mountain parsley. There are also some food products from Trinidad and Tobago, Barbados, and other countries in the West In-

LATIN AMERICA

dies. Owner Ricky Muniz Jr. calls it "the home of Caribbean food in Cleveland; one-stop shopping for all your Caribbean recipes." He also carries a wide variety of ingredients essential for preparing dishes from Jamaica, Puerto Rico, Mexico, Columbia, Venezuela, and Peru. Since the publication of the first edition of *Cleveland Ethnic Eats*, he's added a large variety of products from Africa. If he doesn't have it, insists the proprietor of this Ohio City market, he will find it for you and order it. The place has the feel of a neighborhood "corner store," also stocking Spanish-language newspapers, magazines, tapes, and some American grocery items.

La Michoacana
☎ (330) 864-0565
CITY: **Akron**   AREA: **Farther South**

ADDRESS: 1448 Copley Rd.
FOOD AVAIL.: Produce, grains, beans, baked goods, canned & packaged goods, spices, condiments, beverages, tea, coffee
HOURS: Mon–Sat 10 a.m.≠9 p.m., Sun 10 a.m.–7 p.m. PAYMENT: MC, VS, AX, DIS
ACCESS: ⅃ Full access

This is the only Mexican grocery store in the Akron area, and it's easy to spot. The exterior of the building is decorated with a mural painted in bright colors. The images of food on the outside only hint at the wealth of stuff on the inside. The market is spacious, well organized, and full of surprises. This is a Mexican cook's paradise. In addition to all the predictable items from tortillas to tomatillos, there's a really impressive assortment of more esoteric ingredients—Mexican-style sour cream, dried tamarinds, pasilla and arbol peppers, guajillo paste, masa, dried corn husks for wrapping tamales, fresh chayote squash, cans of cajeta, a thick syrup made from caramelized sugar and milk, and a crate filled with the green cactus "pads" called nopales. For those in search of culinary shortcuts, there's a good selection of

jarred mole and adobo sauces, and owner Evelia Gudino, who opened for business in September 2002, makes her own tamales and sells them by the dozen. Easy parking right in front.

Mi Pueblo
☎ (216) 671-6661
CITY: **Cleveland**   AREA: **West Side**

ADDRESS: 12207 Lorain Ave.
FOOD AVAIL.: meat (fresh), fish (fresh), produce, grains, beans, flour, rice, baked goods, canned & packaged goods, spices, condiments, beverages, coffee, takeout meals HOURS: Daily 9 a.m.–9 p.m. PAYMENT: MC, VS, AX, DIS
ACCESS: ⅃ Full access OTHER ETHNIC SPECIALTIES: Puerto Rican, other Latin American countries

This is a combination taqueria (a place for tacos) and supermercado (supermarket). I love the idea of a single location where you can eat and then stock up for the rest of week; you can even get some shopping done while waiting for your food to be served. The combination is a popular one in Chicago, and the Loera and Ortega families brought it with them when they relocated here from the Windy City. You enter the market and the restaurant through the same door leading into a vestibule. Turn right, and you're a diner; left, and you're a shopper. The market and the restaurant are mutually visible through a large glass wall, and if you're inspired to try preparing the food you eat there, the store sells all the ingredients they use. (For more information about the restaurant see Mi Pueblo's other listings in this chapter.) The market also offers a large variety of salsas, moles (a type of sauce), butcher-prepared beef and pork featuring the types of cuts necessary for preparation of traditional Mexican and Latin dishes, fresh produce of both the American and the more tropical South American variety, and ready-made specialties like guacamole; ensalada de nopales (made with cactus, peppers, and tomatoes); carnitas (cooked pork) on

LATIN AMERICA

weekends; and pan dulce (Mexican sweet bread). The owners, originally from Mexico, pride themselves on being a source for Latin American products not typically found in other markets. Parking available on the street and across the street in a lot with 20–25 spaces.

Puerto Rican

Caribe Bake Shop
☎ (216) 281-8194
CITY: **Cleveland**   AREA: **Near West Side**

ADDRESS: 2906 Fulton Rd.
FOOD AVAIL.: meat (deli), grains, beans, flour, baked goods, canned & packaged goods, spices, beverages, tea, takeout meals   HOURS: Mon–Sun 7 a.m.–6 p.m.   PAYMENT: Checks   ACCESS: ♿ Full access

This Puerto Rican bakery, first opened in 1969, has new owners. Luis and Sandra Burgos took over from the Morales family. They continue to offer freshly baked breads and traditional sweets such as bread pudding, coconut candy, flan, and guava-filled turnovers but have expanded the menu to include a variety of other prepared Caribbean specialties, and added a few tables so if you can't wait until you get home (or at least into your car) to dig into your empanada (a meat-filled pastry they describe as a "Caribbean pierogi"), fried plantain, Cuban sandwich, or potato balls, you can sit down and eat it on the spot. Chicken is available by the piece and by the pound, fried, roasted, and barbecued, and roast pork can also be purchased as a single serving or in quantity. Green bananas or yucca come stuffed with meat, or you can go for the yucca with escabeche (poached or fried fish in a flavorful marinade). Different rice, meat, and bean combinations are available daily. There are also some grocery items: canned products, seasonings, and packaged goods to stock an

authentic Puerto Rican pantry. Catering service.

Lelolai Bakery & Cafe
☎ (216) 771-9956
CITY: **Cleveland**   AREA: **Near West Side**

ADDRESS: 1889 W. 25th St.
FOOD AVAIL.: baked goods, takeout meals
HOURS: Mon–Wed 7:45 a.m.–5 p.m., Thu–Sat 7:45 a.m.–6 p.m., Sun closed   PAYMENT: MC, VS
ACCESS: ♿ Full access

Maria Sapia and Alma Alfonzo are sisters, born and raised in Puerto Rico. They've lived in Cleveland for more than 20 years, and for much of that time Maria had a small home-based baking business, preparing made-to-order Caribbean- and European-style cakes and pastries. With the help of Alma's husband Francisco, they decided to grow the operation to the next level, and in March 2001 they opened a bakery near the West Side Market. It's a lovely place to shop—light, bright, and spacious. The wonderful Hispanic– and Spanish–inspired desserts that come out of the kitchen are attractively displayed in glass-front cases. Choose from pastelillos (flaky crust turnovers) with fillings of mango, strawberry, apple, and pineapple; tropical fruit cheesecakes; flans flavored with almonds, coconut, or vanilla; and mallorcas, warm buttered buns made of sweetened bread dough that are a popular breakfast food on the island. Cakes can be purchased whole or by the slice. Everything is prepared from scratch daily using fresh fruits and quality ingredients. A small selection of sandwiches is available, prepared Carribean–style: after they pile on combos like ham and cheese or turkey and Swiss and add a special, well-seasoned sauce, the sandwich is put in a hot press that's like a waffle iron with a smooth rather than a ridged surface. The bakery will do special custom orders and prepare party trays of bite-size portions. I went to an opening that featured a variety of sweet eats, and Lelolai's flan was the first to disappear! I heard some guests whimpering for more. (There is some seating. For more information see Lelolai's listing under restaurants.)

Reposteria Mana Homemade Bakery
☎ (216) 651-3819
CITY: **Cleveland**   AREA: **Near West Side**

ADDRESS: 3466 W. 41st St.
FOOD AVAIL.: produce, grains, beans, flour, rice, baked goods, canned & packaged goods, spices, condiments, beverages, takeout meals
HOURS: Mon 7 a.m.–1 p.m., Tue–Sat 7 a.m.–6 p.m., Sun 7 a.m.–3 p.m. **PAYMENT:** Cash only **ACCESS:** ♿ Full access **OTHER ETHNIC SPECIALTIES:** Mexican

It takes a village, we've heard, to raise a child; it takes a family, according to Miguel Rodriguez, to keep his store open seven days a week and stocked with traditional Puerto Rican foods. His father, Jose, does the baking, turning out almendrados (sticky almond-paste cookies), cornbread, polvorones (sugar cookies), and fruit-filled pastries. A host of brothers, sisters, cousins, nieces, and nephews help him serve customers, prepare delicacies like green banana salad (a favorite for special occasions), yellow rice with green pigeon peas, potato balls, and roast pork, and fill the shelves with produce and groceries. They also do catering and prepare wedding cakes to order. Located in the Tremont area, just three blocks from I-71, the little bakery is easily identified by the big sign out front with a baker holding a cake aloft. Parking lot on the left side of the building.

Supermercado Rico
☎ (216) 631-1156
CITY: **Cleveland**   AREA: **Near West Side**

ADDRESS: 4506 Lorain Ave.
FOOD AVAIL.: Meat (frozen), fish (frozen), produce, grains, beans, flour, rice, canned & packaged goods, spices, condiments, beverages, coffee, prepared frozen foods **HOURS:** Mon–Sat 9 a.m.–8 p.m., Sun 9 a.m.–5 p.m.
PAYMENT: Checks **ACCESS:** ♿ Full access **OTHER ETHNIC SPECIALTIES:** Mexican, many Central and South American countries

Those 40 and older, as well as folks from small towns, will find the scale of this market familiar. It hearkens back to the time before grocery shopping meant places as big as warehouses with carts large enough to hold a steamer trunk, and to stores that could be staffed by just two or three people. There's nothing fancy or flashy here, either. The decor is strictly utilitarian, and there are no carefully calculated displays aimed at promoting sales. The result is a shopping environment that has a sort of sweetness to it, a simplicity and human appeal. The store is well stocked despite the fact that the shelves are not mile high. The selection of fresh produce, including plantains, bito (sweet potatoes), and malaga (a potato-like vegetable), is displayed in cardboard boxes rather than sleek metal crisper cases. There are interesting products imported from all over Latin America and the Caribbean: soursop syrup, pounded yam flakes, red and yellow hot pepper sauce, chorizo sausage, dried chiles, plantain chips, coconut water, tamarind soda, passionfruit nectar, and bacalao (salt fish). Of course, you'll also find a large variety of rice, beans, and cornmeal. Spanish is spoken here by staff who also speak English, and by most of the clientele as well. A fenced parking lot is adjacent to the brick building, which is easily identified by the wood-shingle awning out front.

Chapter 7

AMERICAN REGIONAL

This is a short chapter, and the title is somewhat misleading. There are just three distinct food cultures included in this section, and only two, Louisiana Cajun/Creole and Southern soul, are actually tied to a specific geographic section of this country. The third, Jewish-style, is as placeless as, historically, the people who claim it as their own. But each represents a way of eating that has become identifiably American, a blend of regionalism and ethnic roots, combined with a hodgepodge of influences from around the world that could only happen in the United States. You could say that they are the best of what was once called, before it became politically incorrect, the melting pot.

The idea of one homogenous blend has been put aside. Now the dominant motif is a mosaic. Diversity is the buzzword, and celebrating it has become the new American way. Acknowledging our social and historical singularities is a way to express enthusiasm about one's own particular way of fitting into the big picture, and it's more than just fashionable. It speaks of how we are redefining who we are as a culture and a country.

The word "ethnic" evokes images of folksy people in quaint costumes from a bygone era. And even though that view is outmoded, it does not seem out of place when applied to the cultures of other countries. It makes sense to us to go to restaurants and see waitresses in Tyrolean dirndls or Japanese kimonos. But in fact, the word really connotes any racial, religious, or social group with a common culture. So while they are neither exotic nor old-fashioned, existing very much in this time and place, the three groups assembled under this heading are also very definite and distinct ethnic entities. And their food, whether you view it as what comes from the melting pot or the tossed salad result of diversity, contributes to this city's cultural and culinary wealth.

The terminology can be perplexing. Should hoppin' John (black- eyed peas with rice) and sweet potato pie be called African American, Southern, or soul? As far as many people are concerned, when you're talking about food, there's not much difference. "Compare what are called soul food cookbooks with Southern cookbooks, and you'll find that they are pretty much the same," said Dr. Lolly McDavid. "White women of means didn't do their own cooking, and many cherished southern recipes were actually created by the black women who cooked for them. And while the two races were segregated in their lives and lifestyles, they both ate the same things for Sunday dinners and celebrations. Even for blacks like me who have lived our entire lives in the North, home food, traditional food, is still what you'd call Southern food."

"My father grew up on a farm where all the women cooked," she continued. "He met my mother at college, and he had no idea she didn't know her way around the kitchen. It never even occurred to him. When he discovered that she couldn't cook, he sent her down to his family in Alabama so she could learn. The story goes that she followed the women around with a notebook, wanting to write down all their recipes."

But there were no recipes to write down. And an old expression explains why: "Frying pork chops is like drinking water—you either know how or you don't."

But Southern cooking is much more than fried chops and chicken. Cooks in the coastal states have countless ways to prepare seafood. Beaten biscuits, country ham, pan gravy, and stewed tomatoes are dinnertime favorites, along with cornbread and corn cooked any other way you can think of. Grits, greens, beans, and yams are staples. Echoes of a long-forgotten African past crop up in the way many dishes are prepared, and some scholars suspect that seeds of okra and sesame, which are not native to the area, came here with the slaves.

Much of what came out of the black kitchens of the South is inextricably linked to a culture of slavery and discrimination. Rice was originally viewed as poor folks' food, unfit for higher society, and chitterlings, which have now acquired a certain down-home panache, were used because they were the leftovers that nobody else wanted. Once, you could get them by the bucketful for free. Now, even people who can afford prime rib eat them because they are a treasured taste from childhood.

Black families have been a presence in Cleveland since the settlement's earliest days, increasing in numbers gradually over the years: 1,300 in 1870, 3,000 in 1890, 8,500 in 1910. Most came from the South, and by 1930 they accounted for the majority of the population in many of the inner-city neighborhoods once filled with immigrants from Europe. During the World War II years, many more came, lured by the opportunities in the city's expanding industrial economy.

As people migrated north, their cooking style was transformed in the context of an urban and often poverty-stricken environment. It came to be associated with salty, greasy dishes, but true African-American cooking is neither. "Real Southern cooking is both healthy and economical," explained Curtis English, owner of Fins and Feathers Catering. "It's about playing with what's available, figuring out how to make it pleasing with spices, and how to make a little bit of meat 'stretch' by using grains, beans, and vegetables. Many dishes were meant to be baked or simmered all day, and every meal included lots of fresh natural foods from the garden like tomatoes, onions, sweet peppers, and cucumbers. As a child, visiting family in Georgia, I remember eating slow cooked smothered chicken, yams, green beans, and okra. When I talk with my grandmother now, she tells me they used to eat stuff white folks didn't even know was edible."

Whether it's called Cajun, Creole, or New Orleans–style, the purely Louisiana way of eating is a kissing cousin to Southern cuisine. Cajun food is actually a very old form of French country cooking that came to the region with the Acadians of Canada, adapted to make use of all the game and wild foods indigenous to the area, like alligator and tabasco peppers. The result is étouffe (a sort of stew), jambalaya, and boudin (pepper hot sausage). Creole cooking is more citified, the New Orleans version of Cajun with its own unique accent that came from the variety of people who gathered there. Gumbo, for example, is an African word, and the file it's made with (the powdered leaves of the sassafras tree) was introduced to the Acadians by Choctaw Indians. After the Civil War, Greek, German, and Italian immigrants added to the culinary mix. So you can get a mufalletta (an Italian-inspired sandwich unique to New Orleans), oyster loaves and shrimp po' boys, bouillabaisse and crawfish bisque, and praline pudding.

You can find a few of these dishes on some Cleveland restaurant menus, but it must be understood up front that little of it can hold a candle to what you might encounter—if you were lucky—down in Bayou Lafourche or the French Quarter. That said, it's still an experience worth having if you want to learn something about hot sauce, 'gator, or red beans and rice.

In his book about Southern food, which explores the particularities of African-American and Louisiana kitchens, writer John Egerton sums up the heart and soul of it all this way: "Fix plenty, make it good, share it around."

As a motto, that's too homespun and folksy to be a good fit for the Cleveland Jewish community of today, but the same sentiments still apply. That sense of plenty coupled with a voluble sociability characterizes the Jewish-style delis listed in the following pages. All serve sandwiches almost too big to get your mouth around, a smear of cream cheese equals a mountainous slather, and the bowls of pickles on the tables seem bottomless.

What most of us think of as Jewish-style is actually very European. Jews from Morocco eat quite differently from those whose roots are in Hungary. The Jews of Europe didn't eat bagels and lox, but we think of that as typically

AMER. REGIONAL

Jewish. The kind of deli food familiar to Clevelanders is actually Eastern European Jewish by way of New York. So how to define Jewish food?

"There's really no such thing as Jewish cooking," insists Rabbi Daniel Schur of the Heights Jewish Center. "Jews have lived in various countries, a minority among a majority, and historically, we have always adapted, and adopted new ways of cooking. What makes food Jewish is the fact that it's kosher, prepared according to precise and ancient dietary laws."

In the early part of the 19th century, the largest number of Jews arriving in Cleveland were from Germany. But by 1870, they were emigrating from Poland, Hungry, Rumania, and Russia. Between 1905 and World War I, the flow became a flood as Jews from other parts of the area known as the Pale—Latvia, Lithuania, and Estonia—struggled to escape the pogroms. In recent years, there has been another flurry of immigration by Jews from the former Soviet Union. Though they may have come from different countries, Jews have always been, and to a great extent continue to be, an ethnically cohesive community because of their shared values, ideas, and practices, which spring from their religious traditions.

"We Jews are an interesting people," said Eva Cohen, who runs Personal Touch Catering. "There's a huge world contained in our history and customs. Jews from Poland eat Polish. Jews from Russia eat Russian. Each country where Jews have made their home has influenced what we call Jewish cuisine. We've always taken on something of the food culture where we live, and then taken it with us, wherever we go. In Cleveland, most Jewish people are of Eastern European descent, so pickled herring, matzo ball soup, kugels and kreplach, borscht and blintzes are what reminds us of our past, and that's the kind of Jewish food you'll find here in the delis and stores that cater to a Jewish clientele."

AMER. REGIONAL

RESTAURANTS

Alexandria's on Main
☎ (216) 344-4500

CITY: **Cleveland** AREA: **Downtown**
ATMOSPHERE: **Casual** COST: $$$$$

ADDRESS: 1275 Main Ave.
HOURS: Lunch Mon–Fro 11 a.m.–3 p.m.; Dinner Sun–Thu 5–11 p.m., Fri–Sat 5 p.m.–1 a.m.; Brunch Sun 11 a.m.–3 p.m.
RESERVATIONS: Taken, Always preferred; essential on weekends **PAYMENT:** MC, VS, AX, DIS, checks
BAR: Beer, wine, liquor **TAKEOUT:** Yes
SMOKING: Smoking section **ACCESS:** & Full access

This places oozes big-city cool, urban style, and real Southern hospitality. It's a revelation for people who may not associate down-home cooking and uptown chic. And it's the only restaurant of its kind in Cleveland. The combination has such appeal and works so well that it's a wonder no one thought of doing it before. Jim Buchanan, who opened for business in October 2002, deserves all the credit. He had the idea, a vision for the renovation of the brick building in the Flats on the west side of the river, and the smarts to bring in terrifically talented and knowledgeable chefs. They've crafted a menu that features updated and expertly prepared "soul-full" comfort foods: collard greens, grits, catfish, smothered pork chops, mac-and-cheese, Louisiana gumbo and etouffee, fried chicken, ribs, candied yams, and peach cobbler. Manager Jeremy Thompson says a rumor's been circulating that they keep three grandmas in the kitchen to do the cooking. The perfectly moist and crumbling corn bread and sweet potato muffins that arrive at the table soon after you do give credence to the story. Everything's made from scratch, and made to order—from the mashed potatoes and the melt-in-your-mouth fried oysters to the pineapple chutney that keeps the blackened catfish company on the plate. If you want a floor show and a nightcap for a finish, order Alexandria's Coffee, a Buchanan invention prepared tableside. It's a memorable experience. Come in a T-shirt if you choose—plenty of people do—but be forewarned that the servers will then be better dressed than you in black pants, white shirts, and red ties. Don't be surprised if you spot a well-known athlete across the room. Alexandria's is popular with players for the Cavaliers and the Browns. The main dining room is located on the second floor, and an elevator takes you there. You enter a room with terra cotta–colored walls, black wooden tables and chairs, and a 15-stool bar. Decor is industrial chic with original support columns and steel beams visible. Lots of windows let in the daylight, and candles set the tone after dark. Though the look of the place says adult, the availability of high chairs and a kid's menu makes it clear that children are welcome. But they're more likely to be in evidence early in the evening and at the Sunday buffet brunch. Weekday lunch hours draw the business crowd. There are also private rooms available on the ground floor for meetings, and downtown delivery service. The club and party crowds take advantage of the fact that the kitchen stays open late. A word about handicapped accessibility—there is a small step up at the entrance. But if you call ahead, you can make arrangements for someone to let your party in through a side door. They cater on and off site and there's a large party room with full bar and dance floor available for rent. There's ample parking in a lot adjacent to the restaurant, which was named after the Louisiana town where Buchanan's mother was born.

Big Mary's

☎ (330) 252-1647

CITY: **Akron**   AREA: **Farther South**
ATMOSPHERE: **Relaxed**   COST: $$$$$

ADDRESS: 243 Tallmadge Ave.
HOURS: Tue–Sat 11 a.m.–8:30 p.m., Sun noon–6 p.m., Mon closed RESERVATIONS: Not taken PAYMENT: MC, VS, AX, DIS BAR: None
TAKEOUT: Yes SMOKING: All sections
ACCESS: & Full access

A sign on the wall of this homely little spot explains the ruling point of view. "This is not fast food. This is soul food. So please be patient." And your patience, promises Jane Snow, food editor for the Akron Beacon Journal, will be rewarded with some very, very good eating. Mary McCall, her daughter Laberta, and her son-in-law Maurice work together. It's primarily a carryout operation, with only a few booths, and you can take home their fried chicken or turkey, hot wings, smothered porkchops, barbecued ribs, and red beans with rice, plus sides of greens, yams, mac-and-cheese, black-eyed peas, and fried green tomatoes. The kitchen also makes chitterlings, pig feet, sweet rolls, and peach cobbler. You can order a complete Sunday dinner 48 hours in advance (deposit required) and/or have Big Mary cater your event.

Bradford Restaurant

☎ (216) 991-0181

CITY: **Cleveland**   AREA: **Near East Side**
ATMOSPHERE: **Relaxed**   COST: $$$$$

ADDRESS: 17415 Harvard Ave.
HOURS: Tue–Sat 12:30 p.m.–9 p.m., Sun 12:30 p.m.–6 p.m.; closed Mon RESERVATIONS: Not taken PAYMENT: Cash only BAR: None
TAKEOUT: Yes SMOKING: Smoking section
ACCESS: & Full access

The restaurant seats 70, but most of the business here is takeout. Many neighborhood families are regulars, stopping in throughout the week to pick up orders of fried chicken, pork chops, barbecue, fried fish, black-eyed peas, macaroni and cheese, collard greens, mashed potatoes, and pinto beans. On Sunday there is baked chicken, plus sweet potato, apple, and peach pies. There isn't any decor to speak of, and Linda Bradford is the first to admit it. "People come here for the food, and that's what keeps everybody coming back."

The Lancer Steak House

☎ (216) 881-0080

CITY: **Cleveland**   AREA: **Near East Side**
ATMOSPHERE: **Casual**   COST: $$$$$

ADDRESS: 7707 Carnegie Ave.
HOURS: Daily 11 a.m.–2 a.m.
RESERVATIONS: Taken PAYMENT: MC, VS, AX, DIS
BAR: Beer, wine, liquor TAKEOUT: Yes
SMOKING: Yes ACCESS: & Limited

The city's oldest black-owned and -operated restaurant, Lancer's is tantamount to a landmark. The original restaurant started by Fleet Slaughter more than 50 years ago at this location had another name. Back in those days, when every black celebrity who came to town came to Lancer's to see and be seen, the waiters wore tuxedos. Over the years, the place has grown considerably more casual. The restaurant is still a watering hole for well-known athletes, performers, and politicians, but the not-so-rich-and-famous are right at home here too. Everybody table hops, glad-handing and backslapping friends and making new ones. The place feels like a private club, though if you're not a "member," you can still drop by for a heaping plateful of perch, catfish, or pork chops and cole slaw. In the South, frogs are abundant in the freshwater ponds and rivers, and frogs' legs are considered by some to be a true delicacy. Which must be why they appear on Lancer's menu. Mr.

AMER. REGIONAL

Dixon, whom I overheard hailed by patrons as "King George," regally presides over his boisterous domain. Sometimes he's the host, other times you'll find him in cook's whites manning the kitchen. His operating philosophy is "I do whatever it takes to make it all work." The round-the-clock party atmosphere must mean he's doing it right. Parking available in the rear.

Phil the Fire
☎ **(216) 458-3473**

CITY: **Cleveland**   AREA: **East Side**
ATMOSPHERE: **Relaxed**   COST: **$$**$$

ADDRESS: 2775 S. Moreland Blvd.
HOURS: Sun–Thu 7 a.m.–9 p.m., Fri & Sat 7 a.m.–midnight **RESERVATIONS:** Not taken
PAYMENT: MC, VS, DIS **BAR:** None **TAKEOUT:** Yes
SMOKING: Smoke-Free **ACCESS:** ♿ Full access

One door closes, goes the old saying, and another opens, and so it is at this small eatery on South Moreland. Lucy's on the Square closed in December 2002, and Phil the Fire opened for business in January. It didn't take long for the word to spread that the man who had been serving the chicken-and-waffle brunch at the Civic was offering the unique combo seven days a week, three meals a day. The 100 seats are almost always filled, and there's often a wait for a table, which suggests that Cleveland has taken to Phil's menu in a big way. Legend has it that the unlikely pairing of crisp, sweet, fresh-off-the-iron waffles with crisp, juicy, just-out-of-the-fryer chicken originated at a renowned joint in Harlem back in the 1940s. The dish showed up in Hollywood, California, at Roscoe's House of Chicken and Waffles in 1975. Phil "The Fire" Davis visited one of Roscoe's restaurants while a student at Stanford. His initial doubts about eating the two foods together disappeared after the first forkful. Phil became an instant fan and proselytizer. Opening this restaurant is a dream come true, a chance for him to connect his University of Virginia MBA with his self-described "passion for good food" and his enthusiasm for the batter-n-bird. As if the two together aren't odd enough, diners are advised to top them with both hot sauce and maple syrup…and all who try it agree it's a heavenly match. But there's more. No place else in the surrounding Heights area offers Southern comfort food—or, as Davis calls it, "comfort food for the soul"— grits, greens, fried catfish, chicken wings, red beans and rice, mac and cheese, sweet-potato pie, banana pudding, and butter-milk pound cake. Phil was raised on good food and brings two family recipes to his kitchen: Dad's Famous Potato Salad, and Mom's Double Butter Peach Cobbler. Exactly what makes them famous and special is a secret. A retired Browns player, who prefers anonymity, confessed to eating here so often and in such quantity while his wife was out of town that he gained nine pounds in a week. That's not surprising, considering that Phil's philosophy of cooking is as follows: "I want each of my customers to put a forkful of food in their mouth and say, "That's good, that's really good." This means the first bite will surely be followed by another and another. Everything can be prepared for takeout, and the desserts can also be purchased as a whole pie or cake. Phil's is close to the Shaker Square Cinema, perfect for before or after eating. Or use it as a pit stop before or after making your purchases from the many local growers and producers of the North Union Farmer's Market who set up shop in the Square each Saturday, May through November, from 8 a.m. to noon. There will be a few outdoor tables during the warm-weather months. The place is available for private parties during non-business hours, and Phil and his staff will be happy to cater the food for events on site and off. Metered parking directly across the street and around the Square, which underwent a major redevelopment in 2000, and ample free parking in a lot in the back. The entrance is on South Moreland Street.

AMER. REGIONAL

Vivian's Restaurant
☎ (216) 751-8002

CITY: **Cleveland**   AREA: **Near East Side**
ATMOSPHERE: **Relaxed**   COST: $$$$$

ADDRESS: 14222 Kinsman Rd.
HOURS: Tue–Sat 11 a.m.–5 p.m., Sun noon–5 p.m., Mon closed **RESERVATIONS:** Not taken **PAYMENT:** Cash only **BAR:** None
TAKEOUT: Yes **SMOKING:** Smoking section
ACCESS: ♿ None

Located on a commercial block on a busy stretch of Kinsman, Vivian's presents a less than welcoming appearance from the outside. There are metal grates over the windows and door, and the white paint has seen better days. Truth is, you're not likely to stop in unless you're familiar with the neighborhood or the restaurant. But the menu is all Southern comfort foods, portions are large, and conversation is always lively, with everybody jumping in to give their two cents' worth, whether they're sitting at your table or not. The menu changes daily, so you might get ham hocks and black-eyed peas, beef tips and rice, and chicken done every which way one day, and meat loaf, salisbury steak, pigs' feet, and greens on another.

Cajun

Crawdad's
☎ (330) 630-1386

CITY: **Akron**   AREA: **Farther South**
ATMOSPHERE: **Casual**   COST: $$$$$

ADDRESS: 1099 East Tallmadge Ave.
HOURS: Mon–Fri 11:30–2:15 a.m., Sat noon–2:15 a.m., Sun noon–2:15 a.m.
RESERVATIONS: Taken, for parties of 5 or more
PAYMENT: MC, VS, DIS **BAR:** Beer, wine, liquor
TAKEOUT: Yes **SMOKING:** All sections
ACCESS: ♿ Full access

AMER. REGIONAL

If you like your fun loud, your food spicy, and your music funky, you'll like this place. If, however, you get hinky about smoke, aren't the type to drink your beer from the bottle, want your tunes soft and in the background, and think a bucket on the table (for shells) is sort of crude, I suggest you choose a different destination. This is a bar first, though, it must be said, one with tall chairs as well as televisions, a pool table, dartboard, and video golf. It's a rollicking music venue: the jukebox is stocked with Santana, Clapton, Vaughn, Otis Redding, James Brown, and the Grateful Dead, and live blues bands play on Saturday nights. There's even a small dance floor. And it's a Louisiana Cajun restaurant whenever the kitchen's open—until midnight every night.

You can get your pickles, crab cakes, and catfish fried Southern-style and served with Creole sauce. For those who can handle the wallop packed by Andouille sausage, there's gumbo and jambalaya. And then there's crawfish. Get it as an appetizer, or go for a 3-pound platter that's big enough to qualify as a party tray. The little red devils are cooked in highly seasoned court-bouillon and come with boiled red-skin potatoes and drawn butter. Eating them is both play and art, as messy as fingerpainting but demanding the dexterity of a master. My teenage son was not technically proficient, but our server was more than willing to give instruction and then go beyond the call of duty and provide a hands-on demonstration. She boldly reached right into the pile of critters piled in front of him, grabbed one, and did a show and tell: " First pull the head off and suck out the juice like this." She popped the severed head into her mouth, antenna and beady little eyes protruding from between her lips, and (presumably) drained it. "Then shove the tail up in the body like this, pull the shell off, and don't worry about this little dark thing, it's nothing disgusting, just a vein, you can pluck it right off if you want, and dip what you've got left in your hand into that pool of butter and eat it. Now isn't that great?" This represented the first (and thus far the only) time in my restaurant dining experience that food was shared with the person who brought it to the table. But it is this very friendly, very relaxed, very uninhibited attitude that makes Crawdad's special. The Cajun seafood platter, a mix of mussels, crawfish, and crab legs, requires the same forkless down-and-dirty, shell-cracking, slurping and sucking technique demonstrated by our server. Decor is tavern classic. The dim interior gets some party sparkle from Christmas lights twinkling above the large rectangular bar year round. The exterior is painted an odd purplish mauve, there are almost no windows, and it sits in the middle of a big cracked asphalt parking lot, on a particularly ugly overdeveloped stretch of road. But take my word for it, this place is really cooking inside.

Fat Fish Blue
☎ (216) 875-6000

CITY: **Cleveland**   AREA: **Downtown**
ATMOSPHERE: **Casual**   COST: $$$$$

ADDRESS: 21 Prospect Ave.
HOURS: Mon 11:30 a.m.–10 p.m., Tue–Thu 11:30 a.m.–midnight, Fri 11:30 a.m.–2 a.m., Sat noon–2 a.m., Sun noon–10 p.m.
RESERVATIONS: Taken, for parties of 8 or more
PAYMENT: MC, VS, AX, DIS **BAR:** Beer, wine, liquor
TAKEOUT: Yes **SMOKING:** Smoking section
ACCESS: &. Full access

Come for the food and stay for the music. Or come for the music, but be sure you have an appetite. Their motto is "food, fun, and music," and owner Steven Zamborsky and his staff like to think that a visit here is a total experience, more than just eating a meal or listening to some music. They work with a year-round Mardi Gras mentality, Northern Ohio–style. The crowds and the energy help make it so. It all happens downtown, at the corner of Prospect and Ontario, within shouting distance of Jacobs Field and the Gund Arena,

in a former tire store and parking garage that's been rehabbed, retooled, and redecorated with warehouse chic and Cajun accents (and parking still available in the garage above the restaurant). Windows dominate the large space, and inspirational concepts like "Laissez les bons temps rouler" are part of the wall art, along with their signature fish graphics. Eye-pleasing curves and multiple levels break up the big room, and a large bar opposite the small stage is the centerpiece. Some tables are ideal for watching the performers, while others put you out of the way and at a distance that brings with it fewer decibels. The tunes tend to be blues, jazz, Latin licks, and zydeco, and swing blues.

Wherever you sit, you need to give some of your attention to the menu—a mouthwatering mix of Louisiana Creole artistry and Southern charm. Choosing is no easy thing. The appetizers alone are enough to overwhelm: honey-grilled Cajun shrimp and sausage, fried green tomatoes with collard greens, crawdaddy tails in hot sauce or crawfish in shrimp sauce, crab and bluefish fritters fried crispy and doused with New Orleans–style cream sauce, praline duck tenders that are made with ground pecans in place of breadcrumbs, shrimp remoulade, and oysters either fried Delta-style or swimming in shrimp sauce. Jambalaya and gumbo are available in both appetizer and entree portions. If it's a sandwich you want, there's muffaleta, made with olive paste, cheese, meats, lettuce, and tomatoes; pulled pork; and po-boys in fried oyster, shrimp, catfish, chicken, or Andouille sausage versions. Main courses bring you Southern-fried chicken; étouffé made with crawfish, chicken, or shrimp cooked in brown gravy and served over rice; pecan chicken juiced with Jack Daniels; boiled crawfish; catfish, pan-fried, beer battered, broiled, or blackened; and specials like 'Nawlins barbecued shrimp, soft shell crabs, and a blackened Delmonico steak. Sides stay true to the theme too: grits, cornbread, and rice and beans. They've earned a following for their

AMER. REGIONAL

coffee, made with chicory, and their desserts: Mississippi mud pie, bread pudding with Jack Daniels cream sauce, pecan pie, beignets (otherwise known as fried dough), and bananas Foster (the lowly fruit raised to new heights with caramelized butter and sugar, rum, and vanilla ice cream). Lunch is strictly "bidness"—the business of eating that is. Music is served up in the evenings, every night except Mondays. Tuesday through Thursday there's usually no cover, and local acts are featured, with Wednesdays reserved for Cleveland's king of the blues, Robert Lockwood Jr.—from now 'til the Grammy-nominated guitar man quits doing what he does. Fridays and Saturdays you pay at the door to see big names and nationally touring artists. The restaurant hosts its own parties to celebrate holidays and CD releases, and they'll be glad to host your party too. They'll give you a room (holds around 40), and you can use their standard menu or customize your selections. Information about planning an event, plus directions, a calendar of events, and menu are available on their website, www.fatfish-blue.com.

The Savannah
☎ (440) 892-2266
CITY: **Westlake**   AREA: **West Side**
ATMOSPHERE: **Casual**   COST: $$$$$

ADDRESS: 30676 Detroit Rd.
HOURS: Mon–Fri 11 a.m.–2 a.m., Sat & Sun 8 a.m.–2 a.m. RESERVATIONS: Taken, Suggested on Tue nights PAYMENT: MC, VS, AX, DIS
BAR: Beer, wine, liquor TAKEOUT: Yes
SMOKING: All sections ACCESS: ♿ Full access

This place warrants an ethnic food category all its own; let's call it blues cuisine. Bands play seven nights a week with a heavy emphasis on eight-bar and 12-bar groans, moans, and wails, and the standard bar-food menu is highlighted by some dishes deeply connected to places that nurtured this music: New Orleans, St. Louis, and Delta juke joints. There's gumbo, so thick you can stand a spoon in it; Cajun catfish and Cajun spiced fries; blackened fish and blackened prime rib; barbecued ribs St. Louis–style; some serious Southern-fried delicacies that include the unlikely but amazing fried dill pickles; steamed mussels with French bread; garlic shrimp with rice; and for dessert, pecan pie. But we are, after all, in Cleveland, where polka was once king, and the restaurant does try to showcase local and regional talent. So in a nod to the hometown, they also offer potato/cheese pierogies daily and the occasional Eastern European–style special. On a less ethnic note, there are always assorted sandwiches; pasta, steak, and chicken entrees; salads; and a pint-size kids' menu. Drinking is as important as eating and listening here, so the beer list—featuring reasonably priced domestics and more pricey microbrews, imports, and seasonal varieties—is long. This is the kind of place where you can feel comfortable quaffing it straight from the bottle, though wine sippers are also welcome and get their beverage of choice served in a proper, stemmed glass.

The Savannah attracts a truly eclectic crowd that morphs nightly depending on the music, which is a mix of blues, jazz, R&B, and Motown. You're just as likely to find guys in golf shirts and black leather jackets, women in jeans or straight-from-work dress-for-success suits. There are folks with walkers and crowds of college kids, all-female groups and families celebrating birthdays. You are, goes a New Age adage, what you eat. You are also what you wear, especially if you favor clothes featuring slogans, endorsements, logos, and words of wisdom. To get a good read on the Savannah crowd, check out the variety of messages emblazoned on T-shirts. On a single night, I saw the following: "Joe Boxer," "Go Tribe," "Blues Project," "Phunk Junkeez," "Ameritech," "Rock Your World," "Ohio State," and "Calvin and Hobbes." Even when the band's not playing on the stage up front, the place is lively and buzzing, full of talk, laughter, and high-fiving. Tuesday nights are special. Ernie Krivda and the Fat Tuesday Big Band play classic swing, and the miniature dance floor is filled with those who want to boogie their woogie—those who remember how, a younger set who have taken it up as a hobby, and those who can't but do it anyway—and the result is an excellent, interactive floor show. There are tables—good for four and easily pushed together for more—booths, a bar, and some small, high pedestal tables with stools. All this action lurks behind a staid exterior in a newish, generic-looking shopping plaza that gives no hint of how pleasant and almost old-fashioned the place is inside. If you're squeamish about being exposed to smoke, you're going to have to miss out on the fun here because there is no designated smoking section. The kitchen does on- and off-premises catering. Breakfast—served Saturday and Sunday morning starting at 8 a.m., a perfect way to finish off an all-night revel—includes real Southern-style biscuits and gravy, and flapjacks with Cajun sausage. Parking lot in front is large and well lit after dark. Visit www.thesavannah.com, for detailed information about everything they've got going on.

Za Za

☎ **(216) 320-1300**

CITY: **South Euclid**   AREA: **East Side**
ATMOSPHERE: **Casual**   COST: **$$$$**$

ADDRESS: 13897 Cedar Rd., Cedar Center
HOURS: Mon–Sat 5 p.m.–2:30 a.m., Sun closed
RESERVATIONS: Taken, Suggested Fri & Sat
PAYMENT: MC, VS, AX, DIS BAR: None
TAKEOUT: Yes SMOKING: All sections
ACCESS: ⚹ Limited

The walls are deep red, the velvet couches and armchairs are equipped with big, fat, sink-into-me pillows, the atmosphere is dark, smoky, and sexy, and I keep saying to myself, "Dorothy, you're not in the Heights anymore." But I am, and Cedar Center will never be same. Open since November 2001, this hip eatery and watering hole offers club ambience, white-tablecloth sophistication, and dining fun. And it's the only place like it this side of downtown. The decor reminds me of descriptions of turn-of-the-century Storyville bordellos: I'd call this neo–urban brothel. The menu's got its own special mojo, drawing inspiration from Louisiana kitchens where cooks have a way with food. There's cornmeal-crusted catfish with remoulade; pork loin with pecan gravy; shrimp etouffe; gumbo (different every night); jambalaya; red beans and rice; a variety of po' boy sandwiches; a New Orleans–style muffaletta (a large sourdough roll stuffed with cold cuts, cheese, and olive salad); and sides of cheddar grit-cakes, hoppin john, cornbread, macaroni and cheese, and sweet-potato fries. "Southern" is just another word for fried, and so the menu features fried stuffed olives, fried oysters, fried chicken with andouille gravy, and fried catfish. I don't know what ethnic group can lay claim to the spinach-and-artichoke bread pudding, but it is what I call a moan-and-groan food—so good you make sounds when you eat it. Other nonethnic options include steak, tuna, a blackened burger finished with blue cheese (endearingly called a black and blue); and a Mexico-meets-"N'awlins" oyster burrito. Entrees come with a plate of Za Za bread: fresh, crusty slices accompanied by four dipping sauces and spreads—pistachio pesto, red-pepper cream, virgin olive oil, and a zingy tomato sauce. Like most food writers I hold the ordinary iceberg salad in great disdain, but the wedge here is dressed in an outstanding Bloody Mary vinaigrette and topped with marinated green beans, and I am happy to eat my words along with my lettuce. Portions of appetizers and entrees are large, but the shiny black Za Za takeout boxes turn your leftovers into a fashion accessory. And then there are the martinis. These glamour drinks come in a variety of flavors, colors, and levels of alcoholic intensity. Sipping

AMER. REGIONAL

the one made with vodka, espresso, and Bailey's Irish Cream is like eating dessert. Another, made with vodka and Cointreau and a slice of fruit, gives new meaning to the words "orange drink." This is not a place to bring the kids…unless your kids are old enough to order their own martinis. It is a great spot for romance, or for those who hope to find some, and perfect for a girls' night out.

Jewish

Corky and Lenny's
☎ (216) 464-3838

CITY: **Woodmere Village**　　AREA: **East Side**
ATMOSPHERE: **Casual**　　COST: $$$$$

ADDRESS: 27091 Chagrin Blvd.
HOURS: Sun–Thu 7 a.m.–11 p.m., Fri & Sat 7 a.m.–midnight **RESERVATIONS:** Taken, for parties of 8 or more only. **PAYMENT:** MC, VS, AX, DIS **BAR:** Beer, wine, liquor **TAKEOUT:** Yes **SMOKING:** Smoke-Free **ACCESS:** ⟨ Full access

The first thing you see when you walk in is the mouthwatering display of brownies, cheesecakes, and rugelach (little pastries). Then the eye moves on to the deli counter packed with pickled herring, gefilte fish, huge hunks of corned beef, and long salamis. Behind this counter are the deli men, trained professionals who understand that making a real sandwich is an art. The menu here is almost big enough to be a room divider and features every kind and combination of deli food ever imagined. You can eat light—a bagel with lox and cream cheese or a fruit platter; indulge in house specials like beef and latkas (corned beef stacked on potato pancakes), or "Three Little Tootsies" (corned beef, chopped liver, and hot pastrami on small rolls); or go the whole nine yards with beef flanken (potted short ribs) or roast stuffed kishkas (don't ask what it is, you're better off not knowing, and as any traditional Jewish grandma would say, "Just taste it").

Northern Ohio Live magazine readers rated this the best deli in 1996. It has an intergenerational mink-coat-to-jeans clientele—sometimes mink coats *with* jeans. Grateful parents will find an ample supply of boosters, pull-up-to-the-table high chairs, and even hook-onto-the-table seats for the very youngest diners. There is a kids' menu, dairy specials, daily specials, seafood, and burgers. Located in the Village Square shopping plaza.

Goodman's Sandwich Inn
☎ (216) 398-6885

CITY: **Old Brooklyn**　　AREA: **Near West Side**
ATMOSPHERE: **Casual**　　COST: $$$$$

ADDRESS: 5164 Pearl Rd. (at Brookpark)
HOURS: Mon–Sat 8:30 a.m.–4:30 p.m.; closed Sun **RESERVATIONS:** Not taken **PAYMENT:** Checks **BAR:** Beer **TAKEOUT:** Yes **SMOKING:** Yes **ACCESS:** ⟨ Limited

Goodman's, which opened in 1950 and is still owned and operated by the Goodman family, may be one of the few delis left in town that still hand cuts its corned beef. Though its small, narrow space seats only 31, and its menu is equally abbreviated, the place draws those in the know who visit Cleveland, including movie and sports stars, and it's not unusual to see a limo or a motorcade parked out front. Adult patrons often tell Dennis Goodman they remember coming in as kids with their parents. The lure is the corned beef, brisket, and pastrami sandwiches (hot or cold), which, according to one patron who's been a regular for 40 years, ". . . are the finest deli sandwiches, bar none, anywhere in this city, even the country." Worth a mention, too, are the egg specials: they're prepared, pancake-style, with corned beef, pastrami, or salami. The biggest part of the business is takeout. Located in the Pearl-Brookpark Shopping Center, so parking is easy.

Jack's Deli & Restaurant
☎ (216) 382-5350

CITY: **University Heights**   AREA: **East Side**
ATMOSPHERE: **Casual**   COST: $$$$$

ADDRESS: 2175 S. Green Rd.
HOURS: Mon–Fri 6:30 a.m.–9 p.m., Sat & Sun
7 a.m.–9 p.m. **RESERVATIONS:** Not taken
PAYMENT: MC, VS, DIS, checks **BAR:** Beer, wine
TAKEOUT: Yes **SMOKING:** Smoke-free
ACCESS: ♿ Full access

The 1980s Jack's got a facelift in the '90s to update the original look to something more contemporary. The result is a comfortable, pleasant, unpretentious restaurant. Black-and-white caricatures of classically famous Hollywood personalities adorn the walls, and if you look closely you'll also find the faces of owners Alvie Markowitz and his father, Jack. Though the decor has changed, the waitresses still call you "Dear," and the many regulars who frequent this place continue to feel at home. Happily for them and the rest of us, the menu remains the same, loaded with traditional Jewish dishes of the Eastern European school. There's borscht (beet soup) with sour cream, blintzes (thin pancakes rolled around a cheese, fruit, or potato filling), potato pancakes, noodle kugel (pudding), and deli sandwiches packed with steak pastrami, turkey (roasted in-house and sliced off the bone), and pickled tongue. You can even order your already-thick sandwiches extra large. A bowl of pickles and pickled tomatoes is part of the standard table setting, like napkins and forks. Breakfast is served anytime, and they also serve up standard fare like hamburgers, onion rings, and salads. There's a kids' menu for those under 12 who can't handle the regular hefty portions. Alvie says they also make the best-looking deli trays in town, but admits he may not be totally objective on this point since he assembles them himself. Located in a small strip mall off Cedar Road, so parking is easy.

Max's Deli
☎ (440) 356-2226

CITY: **Rocky River**   AREA: **West Side**
ATMOSPHERE: **Casual**   COST: $$$$$

ADDRESS: 19337 Detroit Rd.
HOURS: Mon–Thu 11 a.m.–11 p.m., Fri
11 a.m.–midnight, Sat 11 a.m.–midnight, Sun
brunch buffet 10 a.m.–9 p.m.
RESERVATIONS: Not taken **PAYMENT:** MC, VS
BAR: Beer, wine **TAKEOUT:** Yes **SMOKING:** Smoke-free **ACCESS:** ♿ Full access

Owner Michele Anter-Kotoch describes her place as "a traditional New York–style deli with a California flair." So there's food for those who think watching cholesterol is just a fad that will soon blow over, and more health-conscious options for those who don't. You'll find your corned beef on rye, blintzes, potato pancakes, and chopped liver, but you can also choose from a large list of salads, pasta dishes, low-calorie plates, and vegetarian sandwiches. This is the West Side source for true cure-what-ails-you Jewish chicken soup with matzo balls. Breads come from the Jewish bakeries on the East Side, but everything else is made on the premises from scratch, including a truly awesome selection of desserts that range from a classic cheesecake to brownies, truffles, and fruit tarts. Max's has consistently won *Cleveland Magazine* "Silver Spoon" awards for their desserts and sandwiches, and *Northern Ohio Live* readers have given it their votes for Best Desserts and Best Deli again and again. Clients are an eclectic mix, giving Max's an urbane and cosmopolitan feel, and it seems that almost everybody from families to dating couples, seniors to babes-in-arms, artists to accountants, feels at home here, and the place buzzes with lively conversation and energy. Artist James Longs used one long wall as his "canvas," creating a mural of abstract design that vibrates with lush, hot tropical colors.

AMER. REGIONAL

Slyman's Deli
☎ (216) 621-3760

CITY: **Cleveland**   AREA: **Downtown**
ATMOSPHERE: **Casual**   COST: $$$$$

ADDRESS: 3106 St. Clair Ave.
HOURS: Mon–Fri 6 a.m.–2:30 p.m., Sat & Sun closed **RESERVATIONS:** Not taken **PAYMENT:** Cash only **BAR:** None **TAKEOUT:** Yes **SMOKING:** Yes **ACCESS:** ♿ Full access

This is not a place you'd choose for either the decor or the ambience. But even so, the line is usually out the door between 11 a.m. and 1 p.m., both for tables and takeout, because the deli-style sandwiches are awesome. A Slyman's sandwich is so big that average eaters simply cannot get their mouths around one, and the place is best known for its unbelievably huge corned beef on rye. This small luncheonette, located in an industrial area near the Inner Belt, has a counter and tables that seat only about 46, and serves a clientele that runs the gamut from be-suited business folks to the truck drivers who like to come in early for their eggs and coffee.

MARKETS
• • • • • • • • • • • • • •
African-American/ Southern

Dave's Supermarkets
☎ (216) 361-5130

CITY: **Cleveland**   AREA: **Near East Side**

ADDRESS: 3301 Payne Ave.
FOOD AVAIL.: Meat (fresh, frozen), fish (fresh, frozen), produce, rice, baked goods, canned & packaged goods, spices, condiments, beverages, tea, coffee, wine, prepared frozen foods **HOURS:** Daily 7 a.m.–9 p.m. **PAYMENT:** MC, VS, AX, DIS, checks **ACCESS:** ♿ Full access

This is one of the few really large supermarkets within the city limits, and it's been around for 70 years. About 10 years ago they expanded to stretch the entire block and can now provide plenty of parking, too. Over the years their stock has changed to serve the needs of the changing ethnic makeup of the community. Currently they carry everything for Southern and soul food cooking, including a large selection of smoked meats and hams; fresh salted ham hocks, pigs' feet, hog maws, pork brains, neck bones, and chitterlings; fresh greens; and a variety of barbecue and hot sauces. They carry the full line of Glory Foods, canned and packaged Southern soul-food products. The heat-and-eat dishes, created to make it quick and easy to serve traditional (and labor-intensive) favorites, include the following: kale; collard, mustard, turnip, and mixed greens; field and black-eyed peas; beans; sweet potatoes; and okra. There are also mixes for homestyle cornbread and corn muffins. The store used to have many items used in Latin American and Caribbean cooking and still maintains a small selection at this location, but since the store on Ridge Road was opened, and another in Ohio City, most of those products are stocked there. The result has been that this Dave's is less crowded and cramped than it used to be, and there's a shorter wait in the checkout lines.

Dave's Supermarkets
☎ (216) 441-0034
CITY: **Cleveland**   AREA: **East Side**

ADDRESS: 7422 Harvard Ave.
FOOD AVAIL.: meat (fresh, deli, frozen), fish (fresh, frozen), produce, baked goods, canned & packaged goods, spices, condiments, beverages, tea, coffee, prepared frozen foods, takeout meals
HOURS: Mon–Sat 7 a.m.–9 p.m., Sun 7 a.m.–8 p.m.   PAYMENT: MC, VS, DIS, checks
ACCESS: ♿ Full access

For information about the Southern-style and African-American products stocked, see description for Dave's on Payne.

Dave's Supermarkets
☎ (216) 486-6458
CITY: **Euclid**   AREA: **East Side**

ADDRESS: 15900 Lake Shore Blvd.
FOOD AVAIL.: meat (fresh, deli, frozen), fish (fresh, frozen), produce, baked goods, canned & packaged goods, spices, condiments, prepared frozen foods, takeout meals   HOURS: Mon–Sat 7 a.m.–9 p.m., Sun 7 a.m.–8 p.m.   PAYMENT: MC, VS, DIS   ACCESS: ♿ Full access

See description for Dave's on Payne.

Old Country Smokehouse
☎ (216) 361-0276
CITY: **Cleveland**   AREA: **Near East Side**

ADDRESS: 4041 Payne Ave.
FOOD AVAIL.: Meat (dried), flour, canned & packaged goods, spices, condiments
HOURS: Mon noon–6 p.m., Tue–Sat 9 a.m.–6 p.m.; closed Sun   PAYMENT: MC, VS, checks   ACCESS: ♿ None

"It smells like a smokehouse," says owner Gloria Carruthers, "and looks like an honest-to-goodness country store. You step in that door and feel like you've gone down South." Slabs of smoked meat are hanging from hooks, and the shelves here are filled with products like cornmeal, hoop cheese, and sausages. She carries not only the famous Smithfield hams but others from Kentucky, Virginia, Tennessee, and North Carolina, each made with a distinctive signature flavoring. She's got other smoked meat, too, including bacon, ham hocks, jowl, and pig tails. The store's been around for 30 years, and Carruthers has been in charge since 1987. She ships her products all around the country and makes up specialized gift baskets full of her own version of Southern comfort. To thank her customers, Carruthers, who is as gracious a hostess as ever there was, sponsors a pig roast once a year, in the summer. She sets up a "big top" tent, long tables, and chairs, and gets a genuine Alabama chef to handle the barbecue, while she keeps the outdoor party going, complete with live bands. You pay a nominal fee for what you eat—the music, the dancing, and the good times are on the house.

Jewish

Boris's Kosher Meat
☎ (216) 382-5330
CITY: **University Heights**   AREA: **East Side**

ADDRESS: 14406 Cedar Rd.
FOOD AVAIL.: meat (fresh, frozen), fish (fresh, frozen), baked goods, canned & packaged goods, beverages, wine, beer, prepared frozen foods, takeout meals   HOURS: Mon–Wed 8 a.m.–6 p.m., Thu 8 a.m.–7 p.m., Fri 8 a.m.–2 p.m., Sun 8 a.m.–1 p.m.; closed Sat
PAYMENT: MC, VS, checks   ACCESS: ♿ Full access

Boris's is primarily a meat market but does carry some of its own prepared Jewish-style specialties. Take home chicken or mushroom barley soup, stuffed cabbage, matzo balls, potato kugel, kreplach, and chicken roasted and stuffed or cut up into cutlets, breaded, and fried. Salami, smoked turkey, and Rumanian-style pastrami are made on the premises.

In the freezer you'll find gefilte fish and blintzes. They also stock a small line of canned and packaged goods—basics that you might pick up to complete a meal, plus wine and beer, mostly imports, including some from Israel. They also have some baked goods from Unger's. (See entry for Unger's in this section.) Convenient parking in the strip.

Lax & Mandel Kosher Bakery
☎ (216) 932-6445

CITY: **Cleveland Heights**   AREA: **East Side**

ADDRESS: 2070 S. Taylor Rd.
FOOD AVAIL.: Baked goods, beverages
HOURS: Very limited hours. Call ahead.
PAYMENT: Checks ACCESS: ♿ Full access

Lax & Mandel offers Jewish rye (which happens to be fat- and cholesterol-free), French, garlic, and potato breads, Russian raisin pumpernickel, challah (including one that's cholesterol-free), and dense, chewy corn rye, available only on Sunday. They also bake rugelach, Russian tea biscuits, tortes, custom-made cakes, and a variety of cookies, donuts, and danish. Metered parking on the street and in a municipal lot to the rear of the building.

Lax & Mandel Kosher Bakery
☎ (216) 382-8877

CITY: **University Hts.**   AREA: **East Side**

ADDRESS: 14441 Cedar Rd.
FOOD AVAIL.: Baked goods, beverages
HOURS: Mon–Wed 5:30 a.m.–9 p.m., Thu 5:30 a.m.–midnight, Fri open 5:30 a.m., closing time varies (call for information), Sat a half hour after Shabbos (sunset) to midnight (bakery only), Sun 5:30 a.m.–8 p.m. PAYMENT: Checks
ACCESS: ♿ Full access

Please see listing for Cleveland Hts. location.

Pincus Bakery
☎ (216) 382-5120

CITY: **University Heights**   AREA: **East Side**

ADDRESS: 2181 S. Green Rd.
FOOD AVAIL.: Baked goods, beverages, coffee
HOURS: Daily 6 a.m.–8 p.m. PAYMENT: Checks
ACCESS: ♿ Full access OTHER ETHNIC SPECIALTIES: French, German, Italian, Hungarian, British

This is the kind of Jewish bakery I grew up with in New York City and its environs. Though it's located in a thoroughly contemporary strip mall (the Cedar-Green Shopping Center), there's something timeless about this place. Customers are typically greeted by name, totals are figured by adding up columns of figures penciled on bags or boxes, and the egg kichel (sweet little biscuits), mandelbrot (almond cookies), and large loaves of dark, raisin-studded pumpernickel bread look exactly as I remember them from my childhood. Owner and baker Steven Pincus is a member of the Bread Bakers Guild of America, and a sign above the counter identifies him as The Artisan Baker. What all this means is that bread, cake, and pastry are taken seriously here and handcrafted the Old World way. Traditional Jewish products such as egg and water challah bread, corn rye, and honey cakes are available as well as European-style specialties such as Linzer torte, Hungarian strudel, baguettes, biscotti, scones, and focaccia bread.

Tibor's Quality Kosher Meat Market
☎ (216) 381-7615

CITY: **University Heights**   AREA: **East Side**

ADDRESS: 2185 S. Green Rd.
FOOD AVAIL.: meat (fresh), grains, beans, baked goods, canned & packaged goods, spices, condiments, wine, prepared frozen foods, takeout meals HOURS: Mon–Wed 8 a.m.–6 p.m., Thu 8 a.m.–7 p.m., Fri 8 a.m.–3 p.m., Sun 8 a.m.–1 p.m.; closed Sat PAYMENT: MC, VS, checks
ACCESS: ♿ Full access

Tibor Rosenberg, once an Altman's employee, is now the owner of what used to be Altman's Quality Kosher Meat Market. Originally located on Chagrin Boulevard, Altman's was in business 45 years, and at the present location since 1968. The new owner has given the place a new name but continues to offer all the same items, including many Jewish-style foods prepared on the premises according to old Eastern European recipes. One longtime customer, now in his 70s, told me that going here takes him back 60 years, because the food tastes just like the kind he grew up eating. There's chicken soup, matzo ball soup, kreplach (the Jewish version of ravioli) in soup, mushroom barley soup, roast chicken, brisket, potato and noodle kugels (puddings), stuffed cabbage, and potato latkes (pancakes). Among the cold items are chopped liver, gefilte fish, potato salad, cole slaw, and pickles. They make their own salamis and hot dogs, including unusual veal and turkey dogs. Zucchini kugels and zucchini latkes are two of their own modern versions of traditional delicacies. The baked goods are from Unger's, and challah is delivered every Friday. The store has its own parking lot. Jack's deli is only a few doors away, so before you head home with dinner in a bag, you might want to stop off there for a "nosh."

Unger's Kosher Bakery & Food Shop
☎ **(216) 321-7176**
CITY: **Cleveland Heights**   AREA: **East Side**

ADDRESS: 1831 S. Taylor Rd.

FOOD AVAIL.: meat (fresh, deli, frozen), fish (fresh, deli, frozen), produce, baked goods, canned & packaged goods, spices, condiments, beverages, tea, coffee, wine, beer, prepared frozen foods, takeout meals **HOURS:** Sun–Wed 6 a.m.–10 p.m., Thu 6 a.m.–11 p.m., Fri open 6 a.m., closing time varies (call for information); closed Sat (sometimes open Sat night, after sunset; call to confirm) **PAYMENT:** MC, VS, AX, DIS **ACCESS:** & Full access

Unger's is a bakery and a supermarket, with a deli counter that also features a selection of ready-to-eat entrees like kishka, roast chicken, and stuffed cabbage, plus cole slaw and other salads. I like to buy pickles, an essential part of a deli meal, here because they have both sour and half-sour, and pickled red peppers like those found on New York's Lower East Side. Fresh-baked breads include Jewish rye, challah, and pumpernickel, plus onion rolls and bagels, cinnamon-raisin bread, and croissants. A variety of cakes, pies, danish, donuts, and cookies are available, but Unger's is known mainly for true Jewish-style treats (some of which bear a strong resemblance to those of Eastern Europe) such as Dobos torte, kichel, honey and sponge cakes, Russian tea biscuits, cinnamon-, nut-, or chocolate-laced coffee cakes called babkas, and Hungarian nut slices. On the shelves, along with regular grocery store items, are food imports from Israel and packaged Israeli-style salads. The store is bright and modern. They've got their own parking lot.

AMER. REGIONAL

{ *Chapter 8* }

INTERNATIONAL

There is no historical lead-in appropriate for this chapter, no groups of people to write about or "palette" of ingredients to explain. This section is devoted to restaurants and markets that defy a single, simple ethnic definition yet still have some definite ethnic characteristics.

Included are restaurants that successfully prepare a variety of dishes from many different food traditions, while staying true to the origins of each. There are only a few, but they do what they do so well that they deserve a place of their own in this book.

Interest in ethnic ingredients is growing rapidly, and those ingredients are assuming an increasingly prominent role in contemporary American cooking. The markets listed in this section are important resources. They offer convenience, variety, and a global array of choices so busy shoppers can get what they need to stock a multicultural kitchen at a single location.

Restaurants and markets with an international flair reveal our current preoccupation with diversity, pluralism, and what has been called our "tossed salad" society, a recently coined term meant to replace the old "melting pot" concept. The idea is that as a society we no longer want to see ourselves as a bland, homogenized American whole but instead wish to keep what is our own and strive for an interesting, eclectic, all-inclusive mix.

At a time when borders are changing rapidly and national allegiance can be a highly charged issue, restaurants and markets whose offerings transcend the divisions of geopolitics are a sort of cultural oasis, a metaphor for peaceful coexistence.

RESTAURANTS

International

Johnny Mango
☎ **(216) 575-1919**

CITY: **Cleveland**   AREA: **Near West Side**
ATMOSPHERE: **Relaxed**   COST: **$$$**$$

ADDRESS: 3120 Bridge Ave.

HOURS: Mon–Thu 11 a.m.–10 p.m., Fri
11 a.m.–11 p.m., Sat & Sun 9 a.m.–11 p.m.; the
bar is open Mon–Sat until 1 a.m., Sun until
midnight **RESERVATIONS:** Taken, for groups of 8
or more only **PAYMENT:** MC, VS, AX **BAR:** Beer,
wine, liquor **TAKEOUT:** Yes **SMOKING:** Smoking
section **ACCESS:** ♿ Limited **OTHER ETHNIC
SPECIALTIES:** Thai, Mexican, Jamaican

Owners Shelly Underwood and Gary
Richmond refer to their place as a
world cafe and juice bar. They offer a small
but eclectic selection of dishes, drawing
their inspiration from the Pacific Rim, the
Caribbean, and Central America, which
have cuisines that traditionally emphasize
grains and vegetables. They also feature
New Age–style drinks made from the likes
of carrots, cucumbers, apples, melons, yogurt, and soy milk. If this makes you think
it's a health food restaurant, you're right,
but that's only half the story. It's a health
food restaurant that goes the extra mile to
try to make everybody happy. So you can
get a burrito filled with beef or grilled veg-
gies; a cup of coffee or a "morning after" (a
blend of freshly juiced tomatoes, carrots,
celery, scallions, green peppers, and garlic); fried tofu or French fries (made, it

should be noted, with plantains rather
than potatoes). The ethnic menu mix includes Jamaican jerk chicken and Bangkok
barbecued chicken, Cambodian-style fried
rice, Thai noodles, and Mexican black bean
quesadillas. Produce comes fresh from the
nearby West Side Market, and when it's
available Underwood and Richmond favor
organically grown stuff.

Depending on your point of view, some
aspects of the Mango modus operandi are
either too cute for comfort or tongue-in-
cheek amusing: legumes are dubbed
"Happy Beans" (presentation changes
daily); extras for the burritos are listed
under the heading "Merry Add-ins"; and
the carrot and apple juice combo is known
as a "Fruity Wabbit." The decor is equally
whimsical—colors are tropical; artwork
on the walls, done by local Tremont artist
Chris Demkow, has a "primitive" look; the
pressed-tin ceiling is painted sky blue and
dotted with clouds and glow-in-the-dark
stars; and wood-slatted window blinds
draped with ragged-edge fabric and rope
seem meant to create a beach shack ambience. Servers dress to express themselves
and tend to be the sort who favor combat
boots with shorts. It's a hip sort of hangout
with a decidedly youngish feel that can accommodate vegans and unrepentant carnivores; light eaters and self-described
gluttons; clean-living food purists and the
persistently sinful who still indulge in animal flesh, alcohol, and sugar. The restaurant is not large, accommodating about 35
diners. Tables have tile tops and each one
displays a different design. The blond
wood bar seats 10. It's located at the corner
of Bridge, Fulton, and West 32rd, in an unusual triangular-shaped building of or-
ange-yellow brick. Brunch is served on Saturday and Sunday from 9 a.m. to 2 p.m.
and includes Vietnamese rice crepes,
huevos rancheros, whole-wheat waffles,
and omelettes. The regular menu kicks in
at 11 a.m. Plenty of free parking on the adjacent streets.

INTERNATIONAL

Loretta Paganini
School of Cooking
☎ (440) 729-1110

CITY: **Chester Township**   AREA: **Farther East**
ATMOSPHERE: **Casual**   COST: **n/a**

ADDRESS: 8613 Mayfield Rd.
HOURS: Mon–Sat 9 a.m.–5 p.m. (open until
9 p.m. if there's an evening session); closed Sun
RESERVATIONS: Required **PAYMENT:** MC, VS, DIS,
checks **BAR:** None **TAKEOUT:** No
SMOKING: Smoke-free **ACCESS:** ♿ Full access
*Not recommended for children

Technically speaking, Paganini's is a cooking school, not a restaurant, but each year the school sponsors a series of ethnic dinners prepared both by staff and visiting chefs. One calendar, for example, highlighted the foods of Bohemia in Central Europe, Brazil, Italy, the American Southwest, Poland, Scandinavia, and Japan. The dinners are not exactly workshops, but they're definitely not your regular out-to-eat experience, either. Each features the cuisine of a different country or region, and diners learn a bit about the area, discuss recipes, and actually watch the meal being prepared. Although it is not really meant to be a hands-on event, sometimes the chef invites participation. The evening takes place in the school's large and comfortable classroom *cum* dining area. The room is brightly lit, and a mirror hangs over the stove and work area so that no matter where you sit you can see what's going on. Long tables seat six or more. To attend, you must sign up beforehand and pay in advance. Call for more information.

A second building has been added that includes a large kitchen and a wood-paneled dining area with a fireplace. The space is used for "cooking with a partner" classes—couples prepare a meal with a chef's supervision and then eat what they've made.

Ruthie & Moe's Diner
☎ (216) 881-6637

CITY: **Cleveland**   AREA: **Near East Side**
ATMOSPHERE: **Casual**   COST: **$$**$$$

ADDRESS: 4002 Prospect Ave.
HOURS: Mon–Fri 6 a.m.–3 p.m.; closed Sat & Sun
RESERVATIONS: Not taken **PAYMENT:** MC, VS, AX,
DIS **BAR:** None **TAKEOUT:** Yes **SMOKING:** Smoke-
free **ACCESS:** ♿ Full access

I knew that this unique restaurant deserved a place in this book, but for a long time I couldn't decide exactly where it belonged. Ruthie Helman, who owns the place in partnership with her son Josh, and does the cooking, is self taught, with a natural flair for flavor that asserts itself no matter what culinary tradition she tackles. In true diner spirit, she promotes the real home-cooked quality of her food. The key word here is home, and the question is, whose home? Because whatever ethnic dish Ruthie puts a spoon to turns out to be the real thing: her matzo ball soup is as good or better than anybody's Jewish bubbe (grandma) ever made, and her wedding soup is as Italian as it gets. The same is true of her Greek salad, Indian mulligatawny, Hungarian beef goulash, Creole chicken gumbo and cornbread, and Thai noodles in peanut sauce—any of which might be the daily special. Then again, she'll blend the best of two worlds and make something with a contemporary twist, like white chicken chile or turkey burritos with jalapeno sauce. Or, she might just bake pans of simple, creamy macaroni and cheese. It's all served up by friendly waitresses who are quick to refill your coffee cup. The fact that the restaurant is here is a little bit of a miracle. Ruthie and her husband, Moe, opened the restaurant in 1989 but a fire in May, 2001, left much devastation in its wake and closed this beloved spot down for a year. The cost of bringing it back has been indescribably high, and in the interim we lost Moe, a man who lit the place up and made everybody feel wel-

INTERNATIONAL

come. His family, his friends, and the Diner's loyal, longtime customers miss him, and always will. But Josh is there to greet you now, and that's it own special thing.

The original diner car, circa 1930, was saved, but the 1995 second-car addition, a vintage 1950s model brought in from Pennsylvania, was damaged beyond repair. The new structure, however, successfully mimics the old one, and an 11-seat counter has been added. The only way to classify this popular restaurant is to view it as an international, cross-cultural, down-home joint. Many people regard it as their own private club, stopping by daily for food and friendly conversation. The Plain Dealer's Steven Litt once called it "a social landmark as well as an architectural one." American-style breakfasts are served until 11 a.m. The regular lunch menu also offers hamburgers, sandwiches with a variety of flavored spreads, soups, salads, and homemade desserts that are in a class all their own. You might have to wait your turn for a table during peak lunch hours but it's always worth your time. The diner floats like an island in a sea of parking spaces.

Sergio's in University Circle
☎ (216) 231-1234

CITY: **Cleveland**   AREA: **Near East Side**
ATMOSPHERE: **Casual**   COST: $$$$$

ADDRESS: 1903 Ford Dr.
HOURS: Lunch Mon–Fri 11:30 a.m.–2:30 p.m.; Dinner Mon–Thu 5:30–9:30 p.m., Fri 5:30–11 p.m., Sat 5:30–11 p.m.; Sun 4–9 p.m.
RESERVATIONS: Taken, strongly recommended
PAYMENT: MC, VS, AX, DIS   BAR: Beer, wine, liquor
TAKEOUT: Yes   SMOKING: Smoke-Free
ACCESS: ♿ Limited   OTHER ETHNIC SPECIALTIES: Brazilian

INTERNATIONAL

This is surely one of Cleveland's most interesting places to eat. It opened, in a historic carriage house in University Circle, in January 1995, and these days it's next to impossible to get a table during peak weekend hours if you haven't booked one in advance. Chef Sergio Abramof, who owns the restaurant with his wife Susan, draws upon a truly international culinary palate for his inspired cross-cultural offerings, which reflect both his own personal history and his philosophy of cooking. His grandparents were Russian Jews, his father a French citizen, his mother Brazilian. Born in Brazil himself, Sergio lived in America for much of his life after age seven. A graduate of Cleveland Heights High School, for 14 years he served as executive chef at Ristorante Giovanni's. All these influences come into play in his kitchen, but he aims for uncomplicated dishes prepared so that the flavors stay true to the culinary tradition they spring from. And while there are some decidedly Italian interpretations, with a variety of unusual pasta dishes, some bursts of the Asian, and even mashed potatoes, the dominant theme here is Brazilian. Camarao baiana is made with shrimp, coconut milk, fresh tomatoes, and hot malaguetta pepper. There's Amazon River fish, and the beef tenderloin is served with black beans and rice and farofa (a flavorful topping made with flour from the cassava, sauteed in butter with onions, olives, and parsley). Frango passarinho (small pieces of chicken marinated and grilled on a stick) is served with a hot green sauce or carioca relish for dipping. They prepare Brazil's national drink, caipirinha, made of sugar cane liquor with lime and sugar and a nonalcoholic tropical drink called guarana. Sergio's is child friendly and has a children's menu designed by the owners' son Julian. The decor echoes the gaiety and zest of the tropics with splashes of bold, primary color, and clean modern lines. The place is small, seating just 46 in close quarters. During warm weather, there's a 60-seat tropical garden patio for outdoor dining. Seating here is on a first-come, first-serve basis. Created with the help of Don Vanderbrook of D. K. Vanderbrook Florist, it reproduces some of the ambience of a seaside resort, complete with palm trees and gaily colored umbrellas, and live Brazilian jazz. Take your chances finding a parking spot or use their valet service.

West Point Market
☎ (330) 864-2151
CITY: **Akron** AREA: **Farther South**
ATMOSPHERE: **Casual** COST: $$$$$

ADDRESS: 1711 W. Market St.
HOURS: Mon–Fri 8 a.m.–8 p.m., Sat 8 a.m.–7 p.m.; closed Sun **RESERVATIONS:** Not taken **PAYMENT:** MC, VS, AX, DIS, checks
BAR: Wine **TAKEOUT:** Yes **SMOKING:** Smoke-free
ACCESS: & Full access

The cafe expanded and an atrium was added in Spring 2001. The result is a spacious, bright, informal in-store eatery with seating for 75. Diners can look into the kitchen and watch the chefs at work. The menu changes seasonally, and diners choose from a selection of sandwiches, salads, and soups, plus specials the chefs are preparing that day. Items are also available to heat-and-eat at home. Making use of the array of international ingredients featured in the store, offerings are an eclectic mix of regional cuisines and flavors. Meals are served at tall, round butcher block tables, and diners sit on high stools. There are a few lower tables to accommodate patrons in wheelchairs and high chairs. It's a popular spot with busy executives, harried shoppers, and parents with children. In addition, there's a 45 seat British style tearoom called Mrs. Ticklemore's offering teas, cakes, and savouries.

DON'T FORGET: CALL AHEAD!

MARKETS
• • • • • • • • • • • • • •
International

Chandler and Rudd
☎ (216) 991-1300
CITY: **Shaker Heights** AREA: **East Side**

ADDRESS: 20314 Chagrin Blvd.
FOOD AVAIL.: meat (fresh, deli, frozen), fish (fresh, deli, frozen, dried), produce, grains, beans, flour, rice, baked goods, canned & packaged goods, spices, condiments, beverages, tea, coffee, prepared frozen foods, takeout meals
HOURS: Mon–Sat 9 a.m.–6:30 p.m.; closed Sun
PAYMENT: MC, VS, checks **ACCESS:** & Full access

The almost windowless brick facade of this market facing Chagrin at Warrensville is less than eye-catching and gives no hint of what's inside. Parking is in a lot off Lomond (a side street), at the rear, and entering through that back door is a revelation. The supermarket is large, with wide, easy-to-negotiate aisles, well lit and well organized, and loaded with attractively displayed food products from around the world. Whether you're hankering for digestive biscuits from England, Swedish gingersnaps, Dutch cocoa, Indian chutney, or Southern-style chow chow relish, you'll find it here. There are many popular brand-name packaged products from Europe, and the ingredients for almost any cuisine you care, or dare, to prepare. Under this one roof you can find such specialty items as vanilla sugar; Euro-style butter (which contains less water than what we're used to); almond paste; handmade pastry

INTERNATIONAL

shells from Belgium; French chestnut puree; the short-grain sticky rice used in Japanese sushi preparation; Chinese cellophane noodles; and jars of nopalitos, the cactus plant called for in Mexican recipes. There's also a large selection of mixes that make international cookery simple, everything from Scottish oat scones, Italian risotto, and German cakes to New Orleans–style dirty rice and Moroccan couscous. The array of specialized imported condiments, sauces, mustards, vinegars, oils, jams, and jellies is huge, perfect for spicing up ordinary dishes. Imagine a simple roast chicken made new with mango chutney; done-in-a-minute Uncle Ben's transformed by a topping of peanut sauce; a relish tray saved from mediocrity by the addition of okra pickles and piccalilli. This is a great place to buy food gifts—there are a variety of wines to choose from, imported chocolates in lovely tins, specialty candies like licorice drops and butter rum toffees, and many unique, prettily packaged gourmet items. Of interest to vegetarians, and anyone else who cares to eat something different and tasty, are a number of meatless vegetable pates. Also, this is a full-service market, so there is a selection of non-ethnic foods and prepared meals. Shopping here combines all the advantages of a global perspective on eating, modern convenience, and the cozy, intimate feel of an almost extinct type of market that existed before mega-retailing was the norm.

Cleveland Food Co-op
☎ (216) 791-3890

CITY: **Cleveland**   AREA: **Near East Side**

ADDRESS: 11702 Euclid Ave.
FOOD AVAIL.: meat (fresh, frozen), fish (fresh, dried), produce, grains, beans, flour, rice, baked goods, canned & packaged goods, spices, condiments, beverages, tea, coffee, prepared frozen foods, takeout meals **HOURS:** Mon–Sat 9 a.m.–8 p.m., Sun 10 a.m.–6 p.m.
PAYMENT: MC, VS, DIS, checks **ACCESS:** ♿ Full access

It all started on our front porch, and in bad weather in our living room, on Hessler Road in University Circle, in the '70s. My husband and I were among the founding members of the Food Co-op, a bunch of people, many with neither cars nor much cash, looking for a source of wholesome, interesting, and inexpensive food. So we banded together, as folks so readily did back in those days, with others of our kind and formed a buying club. Members would take orders over the phone all week, then take turns going down to the Food Terminal in the dawn hours, using a borrowed and barely running old van, to pick up crates of fresh produce, wheels of cheese, and 50-pound bags of rice and flour. The demand kept growing, and the operation expanded and became more sophisticated, moving first to a church basement, then a small leased storefront, and finally to its current home in a commercial garage space that has been completely renovated and remodeled. The result is a large, bright, pleasant, full-line, full-service grocery store. The Co-op is a nonprofit operation, just as it was when it began, owned and staffed by members. It now provides all the convenience of a modern supermarket but none of the sprawl or the impersonal commercialism.

The focus is on natural, healthy foods. Vegetarians form an important subset of the store's clientele. Much traditional ethnic food is also good for you and ideal for those who don't eat meat, so it should come as no surprise that the Co-op is a wonderful source of products from around the world and a good place to find the unusual ingredients used in a wide variety of distinctive regional cuisines. They are especially well stocked with Indian, Asian, and Middle Eastern items, such as the following: curry pastes, ghee (clarified butter), chutney, canned Indian dishes like saag (mustard spinach), chole (hot and spicy chickpeas), matar paneer (peas and cheese), and heat-and-eat curry entrees; Japanese miso soup, sheets of dried seaweed, umeboshi plum paste, and noodles made from buckwheat, lotus root, or wild yams; Chinese rice sticks, tamari soy, hoisin, and sweet and sour sauces, fresh bean sprouts, sesame oil, and egg-roll skins; coconut milk for Thai cooking, noodles for pad Thai, and peanut sauce; pita bread and spinach pies, containers of hummus or, for making it yourself, cans of chickpeas and jars of tahini (sesame paste), goat's milk cheese, and freshly prepared tabbouleh salad and baba ghanouj. For those who want to eat well and eat ethnic without hours invested in cooking, there are mixes for everything from pilaf and felafel to polenta and risotto. They also give a nod to American regional specialties, providing Jewish holiday foods, and black-eyed peas, greens, and grits for Southern-style dishes. To add ethnic flair to just about anything you serve, they offer jars of Greek kalamata olives and roasted red peppers; pickles and sauerkraut from Poland and Hungary; Mexican green and red salsas, jalapeno peppers, and green chiles. Spices and herbs of every description, as well as teas, are available in bulk, so you can measure out as much or as little as you need. Grains like buckwheat groats and bulgur wheat, as well as many different types of rice, barley, and pasta are available the same way. There's probably not a variety of bean, nut, or seed you might need for any recipe that's not on the shelf. Everyone, whether they are a Co-op member or not, is welcome to shop here, but membership, which comes with payment of a fee, brings special benefits and extra cost savings. Volunteer workers are an important part of the operation, and although there is no work requirement for members, those who choose to put in some hours earn additional discounts on their purchases. You can get information about joining and working at the information desk. Parking is available both in front of and behind the building.

Euclid Meat & Sausage Shop
☎ (216) 261-9006

CITY: **Euclid**   AREA: **East Side**

ADDRESS: 821 E. 222nd St.
FOOD AVAIL.: Meat (fresh), spices, condiments
HOURS: Mon–Fri 9 a.m.–5:30 p.m., Sat 9 a.m.–4:30 p.m., Sun closed **PAYMENT:** MC, VS, checks **ACCESS:** ♿ None

This is a full-service meat market offering all the regular meats and cuts, plus custom cutting. They are also a virtual sausage boutique, and that's their claim to ethnic fame. They carry traditional Italian, Mexican, Hungarian, Lithuanian, and German links; Slovenian smoked sausage, and rice-and-blood rings made with a combination of beef, pork, and rice stuffed in a casing and tied in a circle; fully cooked Irish-style potato-pork-veal sausage; and Andouille, which is a must for Louisiana cooking. They also have a small selection of meat-related products such as barbecue sauces, marinades, and steak sauces. This is a family business, open for 15 years; the family also operates a stand at the West Side Market called the Euclid Sausage Shop.

Hot Prospects
☎ (440) 779-5099

CITY: **North Olmsted**   AREA: **West Side**

ADDRESS: 4860-A Dover Center Rd.
FOOD AVAIL.: Spices, condiments
HOURS: Tue–Thu noon–8 p.m., Fri noon–6 p.m., Sat 11 a.m.–6 p.m., Sun noon-5 p.m.
PAYMENT: MC, VS, checks **ACCESS:** ♿ Full access

This heat boutique treats hot sauce and seasonings like wine, stocking an eclectic handpicked selection from around the world that reflects the personal taste and expert judgment of owners Rick and Irish Blankenburg. Chile peppers speak many languages, and the bottles of sauces and condiments made from them are organized according to ethnic group: Cajun and Caribbean; Mexican and Tex-Mex; Chinese, Vietnamese, and other Asian groups are all represented. There are many varieties of salsa, too. For do-it-yourselfers there are incredibly high-quality, fresh herbs and spices, including 12 varieties of ground peppers, sold in bulk that will surely inspire home cooks to new heights when it comes to blending their own curry powder, dry barbecue rubs, hot mustard, and Jamaican jerk. In addition, shoppers will find such unusual but nonetheless desirable items as garlic juice and top-of-the-line Mexican chocolate for making mole, as well as frozen tortillas flown in from New Mexico, and a jalapeno seeder. Call to find out when the Blankenburgs are scheduling tasting days or cooking demonstrations. Advice is available every day, and Rick assured me it's always free. This unique shop is located in a small strip with easy, head-in parking out front.

Lake Road Market
☎ (440) 331-9326
CITY: **Rocky River**   AREA: **West Side**

ADDRESS: 20267 Lake Rd.
FOOD AVAIL.: meat (fresh, frozen), fish (fresh, frozen), produce, grains, beans, flour, baked goods, canned & packaged goods, spices, condiments, beverages, tea, coffee, wine, takeout meals HOURS: Mon–Fri 9 a.m.–9 p.m., Sat 9 a.m.–7 p.m., Sun 9 a.m.–6 p.m.
PAYMENT: Checks ACCESS: ＆ Full access

This gourmet specialty grocery store is owned and operated by three brothers, Jim, Alan, and Sal Rego, who grew up in the food business. They've made it a source for unique foods from around the world, as well as a quality full-service food market. Shoppers can find one of the area's largest selections of sauces and seasonings from the island nations of the Caribbean; pastas, cheeses, and olive oils from Italy; and products from France, England, Germany, Greece, and the Middle East, such as mustard from Provence, Devon cream, and European butters. They bake their own French bread, which has gotten rave reviews from French visitors.

Leach's Meats and Sweets
☎ (330) 825-6400
CITY: **Barberton**   AREA: **Farther South**

ADDRESS: 256 31st St. SW
FOOD AVAIL.: meat (fresh, deli), produce, grains, beans, baked goods, canned & packaged goods, spices, condiments, beverages, tea, coffee, takeout meals HOURS: Mon–Fri 9 a.m.–6 p.m., Sat 9 a.m.–5 p.m., Sun closed PAYMENT: MC, VS, DIS ACCESS: ＆ Full access

The name is charming, the place is not—but that doesn't make it any less popular with shoppers. Don't be surprised if you have to take a number on Saturday to get service. The low-slung stand-alone building houses a grocery, full-service butcher, deli where sandwiches and salads are sold, and bakery counter. Akron Beacon Journal food writer Jane Snow says they have the area's largest selection of homemade ethnic sausages including Italian hots, Mexican chorizo, Cajun andouille, Hungarian smoked, German bratwurst, Polish kielbasa, and Slovenian zelodec. The bakery offers European-style pumpernickel, Jewish rye, kolachi cookies, and sweet paska loaves at Easter. Leach's also does catering. Being unfamiliar with greater Akron, I had a hard time finding the store until I discovered that Cleveland-Massillon Road turns into 31st Street. A big, tall sign makes it easy to spot from the road. The big lot makes it easy to park.

Loretta Paganini School of Cooking
☎ (440) 729-1110
CITY: **Chester Township**   AREA: **Farther East**

ADDRESS: 8613 Mayfield Rd.

INTERNATIONAL

FOOD AVAIL.: Grains, canned & packaged goods, spices, condiments, tea, coffee **HOURS:** Mon–Fri 10 a.m.–5 p.m., Sat 10 a.m.–4 p.m., also during class; closed Sun **PAYMENT:** MC, VS, DIS, checks **ACCESS:** & Full access

This is an all-gourmet specialty store housed in a cozy, converted old home fondly known as the Gingerbread House. It offers a large and eclectic selection of imports and hard-to-find items. The stock of merchandise changes regularly: you might find vanilla sugar and almond paste from Germany, cannoli forms from Italy, and cloves from Madagascar on the shelves one month and pickled ginger, chestnut honey, and a tortilla press the next. A selection of gourmet oils, vinegars, spices, pastry supplies, and professional quality cookware and utensils are always on hand. Everything is personally selected by owner, chef, and cooking-school teacher Loretta Paganini. There are also many ethnic and international cookbooks for sale, and sometimes authors visit and the shop hosts book signings. Everything is neatly crammed together in a very small but nonetheless delightful space at the front of the Paganinis' cooking school, with lace curtains at the window, an Oriental rug on the floor, a stereo in the fireplace, and china from England gracing the old wooden mantel. For more information about this location see listing under the same name in the restaurant section of this chapter.

Mediterranean Imported Foods
☎ (216) 771-4479
CITY: **Cleveland**   AREA: **Near West Side**

ADDRESS: 1975 W. 25th St.
FOOD AVAIL.: Grains, beans, flour, rice, baked goods, canned & packaged goods, spices, condiments, beverages, tea, coffee, prepared frozen foods **HOURS:** Mon 9 a.m.–4 p.m., Wed 8 a.m.–4 p.m., Fri 8 a.m.–6 p.m., Sat 7 a.m.–6 p.m.; closed Sun, Tue, Thu **PAYMENT:** MC, VS, checks **ACCESS:** & Full access

Your first impression on entering Maria and Costa Mougianis's store is that they've tried to stock this small place with everything from everywhere, and that's not too far from the truth. This tiny corner shop, which can be entered either from within the West Side Market building itself or off West 25th Street, is crammed with an almost all-world selection of food: there's candy from England, chocolate from Belgium, saffron from Spain, coffee from Turkey, beans from Jamaica, rice from India, and tinned fish from Norway. A deli case is packed with a variety of Greek and Italian cheeses and olives. Shoppers will find imported mustard, jam, sauces, and honey; black, blossom, and herbal teas; a wide selection of gourmet oils, including walnut, hazelnut, almond, and rapeseed, as well as safflower and olive, and almost as many vinegars; dried fruits and mushrooms; pasta; canned salmon, caviar, and herring; crackers, biscuits, breads, and cookies. Rice, bulgur wheat, buckwheat groats, barley, chickpeas, and oatmeal are available in bulk quantities. And still, that's not all. There are meat grinders, tomato strainers, cheese graters, and coffeemakers too. A visit here isn't just a shopping trip, it's an education. Metered parking on the street or use the market lot, which is a good city block away at the opposite end of the market building.

Miles Farmers Market
☎ (440) 248-5222
CITY: **Solon**   AREA: **Southeast**

ADDRESS: 28560 Miles Rd.
FOOD AVAIL.: meat (fresh, deli), fish (fresh), produce, grains, beans, flour, rice, baked goods, canned & packaged goods, spices, condiments, beverages, tea, coffee, wine, prepared frozen foods, takeout meals **HOURS:** Mon–Fri 9 a.m.–8 p.m., Sat & Sun 9 a.m.–6 p.m. **PAYMENT:** MC, VS, DIS, checks **ACCESS:** & Full access

Known among the cooking cognoscenti as "The Place to Shop" if you're searching for the freshest, most exotic gourmet foods or hard-to-find imported ingredients, Miles Farmers Market is a huge, bright, noisy specialty grocery store packed with products from around the world.

It's a place with a history. The store began as an open-air roadside produce stand in 1971, run by the Cangemi family. It's still family owned and operated, and Frank Cangemi, the man who started the business, runs things now. His VP and general manager, David Rondini, who used to cut the grass for Frank's dad, has been involved in the business since 1972. Produce manager Joe DeGeatano has been overseeing the gorgeous displays of fruit and vegetables since 1985. Many people come here for an outing, and the notion that shopping is a leisure-time activity is reinforced by the freshly-ground serve-yourself coffee that's just inside the door.

The selection of produce is vast, and it's not uncommon to see such exotica as Asian pears, starfruit, or papayas, morels, and fiddlehead ferns. An olive, pickle, and salsa bar, set up like a salad bar, allows shoppers to select and package their own combinations. The variety of beans is staggering: French falgeolet, calypso, tongues of fire, giant limas, five different kinds of lentils, plus all the more standard sorts like garbanzo, fava, pinto, and black. There's an equally large variety of nuts and dried fruits. The cheese department has a stunning selection of almost 400 varieties. The full-service bakery offers a country Italian loaf, a French pain au levain, a Jewish rye, an Italian chocolate bread with the musical name of pane alla cioccolata, and much more. In Miles Hidden Cellars, shoppers will find wines and beers from around the world. There are at least 100 different brands and types of salsa, 40 versions of hot sauce, and 30 different kinds of barbecue sauce. It's impossible to list all the products Miles stocks, but rest assured that whether you need crumpets or grape leaves, pickled peppers or pasta, an estate-bottled olive oil, balsamic vinegar or butter from Europe, sausage or salsa, you'll surely find it here. For take-home meals, the prepared food department also features an international selection: each day has a special, and it could be anything from bruschetta pasta salad or chicken marsala to roast pork with dumplings and sauerkraut, fried chicken, ribs, and freshly made sushi. And if your salivary glands just can't take all the stimulation, there are even a few booths available where you can sit down and eat some of their prepared foods. The Market does catering and assembles gift baskets, a new service developed by Frank's son Sebastian. For more information, check out the store's website www.MilesFarmersMarket.com

Pat O'Brien's of Landerwood
☎ (216) 831-8680
CITY: **Pepper Pike**   AREA: **East Side**

ADDRESS: 30800 Pinetree Rd.
FOOD AVAIL.: Meat (fresh, deli, frozen, dried), fish (frozen), beans, flour, rice, baked goods, canned & packaged goods, spices, condiments, beverages, tea, coffee, wine, beer, prepared frozen foods
HOURS: Mon–Sat 9:30 a.m.–6 p.m.; closed Sun
PAYMENT: MC, VS, AX, DIS, checks   **ACCESS:** ♿ Full access

Pat O'Brien has been in business for more than 30 years as a supplier of unusual, exotic, imported gourmet foods and wines. The store received Cleveland Magazine's Silver Spoon Award in 1998, 1999, 2000, and 2002. Shoppers will find a large and interesting selection of cheeses, many air-shipped from France; olive oils; vinegars; pasta; sauces; caviar; Scottish smoked salmon; tapenades; bottled pickles, olives, peppers, and steaks. There are many brands of jam and jelly from around the world plus cookies, crackers, biscuits, imported chocolates, and candy. They also carry an extensive selection of teas and fresh-roasted coffees. Food items can be selected and assembled into custom-made gift baskets. Some nonfood items, such as French wine accessories, Reidel glassware, Spiegelau crystal, wine racks, and pretty-to-look-at napkins are also sold. Delivery available nationwide.

Rego's Lake Road Market

☎ (440) 878-9466

CITY: **Strongsville** AREA: **Farther South**

ADDRESS: 19600 W. 130th St.

FOOD AVAIL.: meat (fresh, frozen), fish (fresh, frozen), produce, grains, beans, flour, baked goods, canned & packaged goods, spices, condiments, beverages, tea, coffee, wine, takeout meals **HOURS:** Mon–Sat 8 a.m.–9 p.m., Sun 8 a.m.–7 p.m. **PAYMENT:** Checks **ACCESS:** ♿ Full access

See listing for Lake Road Market.

West Point Market

☎ (330) 864-2151

CITY: **Akron** AREA: **Farther South**

ADDRESS: 1711 W. Market St.

FOOD AVAIL.: meat (fresh), fish (fresh), produce, grains, beans, flour, baked goods, canned & packaged goods, spices, condiments, beverages, tea, coffee, wine, prepared frozen foods, takeout meals **HOURS:** Mon–Fri 8 a.m.–8 p.m., Sat 8 a.m.–7 p.m.; closed Sun **PAYMENT:** MC, VS, AX, DIS, checks **ACCESS:** ♿ Full access

This is a full-service grocery store for adventurous cooks. The focus is on specialty gourmet products from all over the country and the world. Shoppers will find most everything available in a regular grocery store—and then some. So when looking for rice you can choose from white, wild jasmine, or Indian basmati rice. There may be only one brand of paper towels on the shelves but 50 different olive oils from France, Italy, Greece, and Spain. The market hosts international food fairs throughout the year that highlight a country and its cuisine with lectures, cooking demonstrations, and tastings. They regularly stock hard-to-find products like Devonshire clotted cream, piccalilli, and treacle from England; Swedish crispbreads and Scandinavian lingonberries; wine kraut from Germany; and the rose and orange waters used in Greek and Middle Eastern cookery. Uncommon produce is common here, and fresh herbs are available year round. Bakers come in at midnight to prepare made-from-scratch Old World breads. With over 4,000 labels in stock, they boast the largest selection of premium imported wines in the state, and the choice of cheeses is equally impressive: imports like Italian Parmigiano-Reggiano, French triple Brie, Dutch Gouda, Greek feta, and English Lancashire, plus products from small American regional cheesemakers. Using an international array of ingredients, the kitchen, staffed by eight chefs, prepares a variety of entrees to take home or enjoy in the market cafe. (For more information about dining in, see West Point's listing in the restaurant section of this chapter.) There are always samples of new and unusual food products for tasting, and a newsletter, published monthly, lets you know about upcoming events. Visit their website, www.westpoint-market.com, to find out more about tastings, cooking demonstrations, and special buys. The site also lets you shop online, read recipes and cookbook reviews, and get directions to the market.

The West Side Bakery

☎ (330) 836-4101

CITY: **Akron** AREA: **Farther South**

ADDRESS: 2303 W. Market St.

FOOD AVAIL.: baked goods, beverages, tea, coffee, takeout meals **HOURS:** Mon–Fri 7 a.m.–7 p.m., Sat 8 a.m.–5 p.m., Sun closed **PAYMENT:** MC, VS, AX, checks **ACCESS:** ♿ Limited

The husband-and-wife team of Barbara and Steve Talevich whip up a whole world of sweet things here at Pilgrim

Square. The pretty little bake shop produces long, crusty French baguettes and buttery croissants; Hungarian walnut tortes and slabs of strudel ; Italian cassata cakes and crunchy biscotti; English-style scones; and traditional German, Greek, and Eastern European cookies. A few tables and counter service make it possible to enjoy a coffee and a crème brûlée or slice of poppy seed roll on the spot, along with a small selection of sandwiches and other light foods. They're also known for their colorful and beautifully decorated cakes.

West Side Market

☎ **(216) 664-3387**

CITY: **Cleveland**   AREA: **Near West Side**

ADDRESS: 1979 W. 25th St.
FOOD AVAIL.: meat (fresh, deli, frozen, dried), fish (fresh, frozen, dried), produce, grains, beans, flour, rice, baked goods, canned & packaged goods, spices, condiments, beverages, tea, coffee, wine, takeout meals   **HOURS:** Mon & Wed 7 a.m.–4 p.m., Fri & Sat 7 a.m.–6 p.m.
PAYMENT: Cash only   **ACCESS:** & Limited

Back in the 1860s, this corner was known as Market Square, a place where farmers brought their produce and city dwellers came to shop. The present building on this spot, dedicated in 1912, is an architectural landmark, and the West Side Market is one of the few remaining municipal markets of its kind in the country. An 18-month, $6.5 million renovation began in August 2000. The 115 tenants and 80 stands in the outdoor fruit and vegetable arcade include families who trace their ethnic roots back to 22 different nationalities. Many of the stands have been operated by the same family for three or four generations, serving customers whose own families have been shopping there just as long. Specialty produce items for many types of cuisine, from pomegranates and star fruit to bean sprouts and green bananas, will be found outside, along with just about any other fresh fruit or vegetable

you can imagine. The same huge variety is available inside along the main concourse.

The following list highlights the merchants (with their stand numbers) who offer ethnic products. Inside the Market— Rhonda Raidel, Pierogi Palace (E-5), homemade pierogies; Jerry Czuchraj, Czuchraj Meats (B-10 & B-6), Eastern European–style cured meats and sausage; Pat Delaney (C-2), Slovenian–style cured meats; Hans Meister, Meister's Meats, (C-5), German style cured meats; Scott Kindt (C-9), Mexican chorizo sausage; Dion Tsevdos, Urban Herbs (C-13), exotic spices, small quantities or bulk; Michael Mitterholzer (D-2), Eastern European Bakery; John Bistricky (D-11), lamb, goat, Halal meats; Tracey Januska, Orale (E-2), prepared Mexican and Puerto Rican specialties; Angela J. Dohar Szucs (F-1 & F-2), homemade Hungarian sausage; Frank Ratschki (G-3, H-3), bratwurst; Freddy Graewe (G-10), German sauerkraut; Stamatios E. Vasdekis (H-12), gyros; Husam Zayed (Grocery Department #1, 2), Middle Eastern foods; Hoeun Khin (E-11), Asian spices, sauces, and condiments; Judy's Oasis (A-5), Middle Eastern foods; Reilly's (C-11), Irish goodies; Ohio City Pasta (E-3); Old Country Sausage (G-8), an international array of sausages; and Sam's International Grocery (H-13). There is free parking in a lot east of the building. There's information about the market online, including a map and directions for getting there, hours, pictures, a vendor directory with direct phone numbers, and instructions for buying gift certificates, at www.westsidemarket.com.

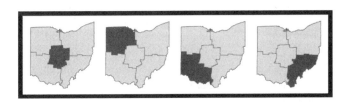

Chapter 9

ALL OHIO

Would you like to take a trip around the world? Unfortunately, not everyone has the time or the money for international travel, but you can still get a real "taste" of faraway places. You won't need a passport and you don't even have to cross state lines. All that's required is an appetite because Ohio is home to restaurants, bakeries, and markets representing fifty different nationality groups. Visiting them is a way to encounter a transcontinental array of interesting sights, sounds, smells, and flavors.

For two centuries, immigrants have been propelled here by famine, poverty, war, oppression, and of course, hopes for a better tomorrow. Some have arrived recently, others trace their roots back to immigrant grandparents and great grandparents. In the years between 1800 and 1850, most immigrants to Ohio came from northern and western Europe, and in the second half of the century from southern and eastern Europe. Conflicts in the Middle East following WWII sparked a large influx of people from that region. In the 1950's students from India, Pakistan, Korea, and Taiwan began to attend U.S. colleges in large numbers and many who came to study stayed. Following the U.S. withdrawal from Vietnam in the '70's, many refugees from Southeast Asia found their way to America and to Ohio. In the past few decades, Hispanics have become the state's newest and one of its largest immigrant groups.

Food memories, recipes, and cooking styles migrate too. Preparing traditional dishes that reflect their heritage is a way for people to celebrate their national identity, feel connected to home and family, and link their foreign past with their American present. Luckily for those of us who enjoy eating from a global grocery cart, many immigrants have gone into business preparing and selling the foods of their native lands. Many newcomers are excited about introducing Americans to the cuisine of their homelands, and even more pleased when their customers love it. It is not uncommon for American-born children to operate places first opened by parents or grandparents.

I've spent years doing what I call fork-in-hand research in Northeast Ohio. Now I've put together a culinary road map for the entire Buckeye state. Use it to plan your own food adventures. Cleveland and Cuyahoga County have Ohio's largest foreign born population, Columbus and Franklin County are in second place, and Cincinnati and Hamilton County are third. In general newcomers have tended to settle in the larger cities and adjacent suburbs so most ethnic restaurants are in the state's larger cities but there are some real "finds" in Ohio's small towns too.

You may discover that there's a very special little jewel of a place you never heard of in your own hometown or find a restaurant so unique it's worth a cross-state drive. Some authentic ethnic restaurants are small, humble, and plain. But the outstanding food at such eateries as well as the reasonable prices more than make up for the unpretentious decor and cramped quarters. But don't think that all restaurants offering authentic ethnic foods are little mom-and-pop type 'shops'. Some are quite elegant and upscale. You can use my All Ohio Ethnic Eats Guide to help you find the place that's right for every occasion.

Foods from Mexico, Italy, Germany, France, and the countries East of the Danube have become national staples and need no introduction. But each cuisine has much more to offer than the few dishes that have become part of how America eats. There are plenty of opportunities to sample the real thing in Ohio. You may be hesitant to try dishes of other, less familiar cultures. Think of eating as a quest, a way to expand your horizons and find things to eat you didn't even know you liked . . . in fact things you didn't even know existed. Experiment with new foods by ordering sampler plates, appetizer portions, or dining out at lunchtime when portions are smaller and prices lower.

Whether you're in search of food like your grandmother made or curious about what somebody else's grandma whips up in her kitchen, Ohio's a good place to be. There are many more authentic ethnic restaurants, markets, and bakeries than I could include, but these suggestions will get you started on your all-Ohio culinary trip around-the-world. Bon Apetit.

DON'T FORGET: CALL AHEAD!

CENTRAL

ARLINGTON
MIDDLE EASTERN

Niko's
☎ (614) 442-5555

ADDRESS: 3145 Kingsdale Center
HOURS: Daily 11 a.m.–10 p.m. **PAYMENT:** MC, VS, AX, DIS, checks **ACCESS:** ♿ Limited

High-quality, moderately priced Middle Eastern food in a 100% smoke-free setting. A thicker, fluffier form of pita bread than usual is baked on the premises daily. Spit-roasted lamb and beef. Marble-topped tables and countertops plus high ceilings give the dining room a bright, clean, spacious feeling. No alcohol.

BEXLEY
ITALIAN

Giuseppe's Ritrovo Italian Cafe
☎ (614) 235-4300

ADDRESS: 2268 E. Main St.
HOURS: Mon–Thu 4:30–9:30 p.m., Fri & Sat 4:30–11 p.m., Sun closed **PAYMENT:** MC, VS
ACCESS: ♿ Full access

A small family-run trattoria where care and quality are the rule. Giuseppe, who is from Calabria, learned to cook from his mother. He's in the kitchen preparing the dishes of central and southern Italy, while his wife runs the front of the house. Absolutely everything is made from scratch. The wine list is small but choice, and bottles are reasonably priced.

COLUMBUS
AMERICAN REGIONAL

Katzinger's
☎ (614) 228-3354

ADDRESS: 475 S. 3rd St.
HOURS: Mon–Fri 8:30 a.m.–8:30 p.m., Sat & Sun 9 a.m.–8:30 p.m. **PAYMENT:** MC, VS, AX, DIS
ACCESS: ♿ Limited

Breakfast, lunch, and dinner, seven days a week. New York–style Jewish deli foods in German Village. The original deed holder to this property was Thomas Jefferson, circa 1782. The place has been modernized but still retains an out-of-time feel, and the dining room features old wooden tables and chairs. They prepare 60 different kinds of sandwiches on bread they bake fresh daily. They cook their own corned beef, roast their own roast beef (and turkey, too), and make soup, salads, latkes, and kugel from scratch just like a bubby (grandma) would. Most of the cheeses they use are all made from raw milk, and many are imported. They do catering and also have a specialty food store at the same address. The restaurant is a nonsmoking facility, and only beer is available in the alcohol department.

AUSTRIAN/GERMAN

Cafe Mozart
☎ (888) 669-2787

ADDRESS: 4490 Indianola Ave.
HOURS: Tue–Sat 7:30 a.m.–10 p.m., Sun 8:30 a.m.–4:30 p.m., Mon closed **PAYMENT:** MC, VS, DIS, checks **ACCESS:** ♿ Full access

See description under High St. location.

Mozart's Pastries & Cafe
☎ (614) 268-3687

ADDRESS: 2885 N. High St.
HOURS: Tue–Sat 7 a.m.–10 p.m., Sun 8 a.m.–5:30 p.m., Mon closed **PAYMENT:** MC, VS, DIS, checks **ACCESS:** ♿ Full access

Breakfast, lunch, and dinner served. Live performances of classical music with your traditional Austrian tortes and tartlets. Known for their outstanding and authentic cakes and pastries, such as cream horns, napoleans, Sacher torte, Black Forester, and their famous "Austrian Peach"—a pastry shell filled with butter cream and coated in marzipan. What started as a bakery in 1995 quickly expanded to a cafe that serves some of the favorite foods of Germany, Hungary, and Austria. Outdoor seating in good weather.

ALL OHIO

CHINESE

Fortune Chinese Restaurant
☎ (614) 263-1991

ADDRESS: 2869 Olentangy River Rd.

HOURS: Mon–Sat 11 a.m.–10 p.m., Sun 11 a.m.–9 p.m. PAYMENT: MC, VS, AX, DIS ACCESS: ⟨ Full access

Authentic food in a strip mall storefront popular with Chinese diners, near the Ohio State University campus. Known for their dim sum, which literally means "a little bit of whatever your heart desires." It's a rolling buffet of assorted sweet and savory Chinese pastries such as dumplings filled with steamed pork, shrimp, or parsley, beef balls, egg-crusted tofu, lotus seed buns, and custard tarts. Order by selecting items from carts that are wheeled to your table.

Pho Little Saigon
☎ (614) 231-1810

ADDRESS: 885 S. Hamilton Rd.

HOURS: Mon–Thu 11 a.m.–9 p.m., Fri & Sat 11 a.m.–10 p.m., Sun closed PAYMENT: MC, VS, AX, DIS ACCESS: ⟨ Full access OTHER ETHNIC SPECIALTIES: Vietnamese

This midsized restaurant serves Chinese and Vietnamese cuisine at very reasonable prices. Reservations accepted only for groups of eight or more. No alcohol.

Sunflower Chinese Restaurant
☎ (614) 764-7888

ADDRESS: 7370 Sawmill Rd.

HOURS: Mon–Thu 11:30 a.m.–11 p.m., Fri & Sat 11:30 a.m.–midnight, Sun noon–10 p.m. PAYMENT: MC, VS, AX, DIS ACCESS: ⟨ Full access

A very friendly Chinese eatery that goes the extra step to make their customers happy by letting them "create" their own dishes. If diners don't find the exact combination of ingredients and seasonings they want on the menu, they can ask the chef to prepare something to their specifications. If it's possible for the kitchen to do it, they will. Great for people on special and restricted diets.

ETHIOPIAN

Blue Nile Ethiopian Restaurant
☎ (614) 421-2323

ADDRESS: 2361 N. High St.

HOURS: Tue–Fri 11:30 a.m.–3 p.m. & 5–10 p.m., Sat noon–3 p.m. & 5–10 p.m., Sun noon–3 p.m. & 5–9 p.m., Mon closed PAYMENT: MC, VS, AX, DIS, checks ACCESS: ⟨ Full access

Husband and wife Mequanent and Meaza Berihun serve up the flavorful cuisine of Ethiopia—chicken, lamb, beef, and lots of vegetarian dishes— on large edible "plates" of *injera,* freshly baked soft flatbread.

FRENCH

Alex's Bistro
☎ (614) 457-8887

ADDRESS: 4681 Reed Rd.

HOURS: Mon–Fri 11:30 a.m.–2 p.m. & 5:30 p.m.–last customer is finished, Sat 5:30 p.m.–last customer is finished, Sun closed PAYMENT: MC, VS, AX, DIS ACCESS: ⟨ Full access

A surprising find in a strip mall. Very authentic French cuisine in an upscale setting. Less than formal and suits are not *de rigueur,* but jeans are definitely a no-no.

L'Antibes
☎ (614) 291-1666

ADDRESS: 772 N. High St.

HOURS: Tue–Sat 5 p.m.–closing, Sun & Mon closed PAYMENT: MC, VS, AX, DIS ACCESS: ⟨ Full access

Small, intimate, and romantic. Genuine French food prepared by the chef/owner, Dale Gussett. Reservations recommended. Valet parking.

Refectory
☎ (614) 451-9774

ADDRESS: 1092 Bethel Rd.

HOURS: Mon–Thu 5:30–9:30 p.m., Fri & Sat 5–10 p.m., Sun closed PAYMENT: MC, VS, AX, DIS ACCESS: ⟨ Limited

A spacious, elegant, and upscale restaurant with seating for 150, plus two private rooms. Chef Richard Blondin, from Lyon, France, prepares classic and contemporary French dishes, and the menu changes seasonally. The restaurant's wine list has been the winner of *Wine Spectator*'s Grand Award every year since 1990—the only restaurant in Ohio to earn such recognition, and one of only 94 worldwide. AAA gives the Refectory four diamonds, and *Columbus Monthly* gives it five stars. It is housed in two connected buildings from the 1850s that once were a church sanctuary and Sunday school. A beautiful setting features exposed wooden rafters, original brick walls, stained glass, white linen, fine china and crystal, and thick carpets. Reservations suggested at all times.

GERMAN

Juergen's Bakery and Restaurant
☎ (614) 224-6858

ADDRESS: 525 4th St.
HOURS: Tue–Thu 8 a.m.–8 p.m., Fri & Sat 8 a.m.–9 p.m., Sun 10 a.m.–6 p.m.
PAYMENT: MC, VS, AX ACCESS: ♿ Limited

Located in German Village in a charming brick building that's more than 100 years old, with German food and baked goods served for breakfast, lunch, dinner, and in between. And you can even sleep here, too, because there's a three-room bed and breakfast. The restaurant has real Old World charm, and your host, Rosemarie Keidel, boasts that her place is "the next best thing to being in Germany." The menu is full of hearty classics like gulaschsuppe, bratwurst, chicken and dumplings, sauerbraten, jägerschnitzel, and freshly baked bread. The pastry counter will make you lose any resolve you may have to count calories, and the Black Forest coffee is not to be missed. Imported beers and wines. A gift shop is also on the premises, stocked with packaged foods from Germany and hand-crafted Christmas ornaments year round.

Resch's Bakery
☎ (614) 237-7421

ADDRESS: 4061 E. Livingston St.
HOURS: Mon–Fri 7 a.m.–7 p.m., Sat 6:30 a.m.–6 p.m., Sun closed PAYMENT: Checks
ACCESS: ♿ Full access

The fourth generation of the Resch family runs this bakery famous for such German delights as springerle and stollen.

Schmidt's Restaurant and Sausage Haus
☎ (614) 444-6808

ADDRESS: 240 Kossuth St.
HOURS: Sun & Mon 11 a.m.–9 p.m., Tue –Thu 11 a.m.–10 p.m., Fri & Sat 11 a.m.–11 p.m.
PAYMENT: MC, VS, AX, DIS ACCESS: ♿ Full access

A German restaurant in Columbus's German Village. Located since 1967 in a building that has been in the family since 1886. Traditional German favorites including bratwurst, Wiener schnitzel, braised red cabbage, and warm sauerkraut in a beer hall setting.

INDIAN

Annapurna
☎ (614) 523-3640

ADDRESS: 5657 Emporium Sq.
HOURS: Tue–Sun 11 a.m.–9 p.m., Mon closed
PAYMENT: MC, VS, AX, DIS ACCESS: ♿ Full access

This is the only 100% vegetarian ethnic restaurant I've found in the state, which makes it a prime destination for those who want plenty of choice but no body parts. The menu is based on the meatless cuisine of southern India, in which no animal products, including eggs, are used. New owner Kamal Panchal, himself a vegetarian, is very excited to be offering such a wide selection and has plans to expand beyond Indian cooking, preparing meat-free entrees from other countries and cultures.

ALL OHIO

Bombay Grille
☎ (614) 336-2610

ADDRESS: 6665 Dublin Center Dr.

HOURS: Mon–Fri 11 a.m.–2 p.m. & 5:30–10 p.m., Sat & Sun 11:30 am.–2:30 p.m. & 5:30–10:30 p.m. PAYMENT: MC, VS, AX, DIS ACCESS: ♿ Full access

Serving Indian cuisine. Buffet available at lunch seven days a week, and for dinner Monday, Tuesday, and Thursday. Menu offers specialties from all regions of the country. *Columbus Monthly* and Zagat give the restaurant a definitive thumbs up.

The Indian Oven
☎ (614) 220-9390

ADDRESS: 427 E. Main St.

HOURS: Mon–Thu 11:30 a.m.–3 p.m. & 5–10 p.m., Fri 5–10 p.m., Sat 1–10 p.m., Sun closed PAYMENT: MC, VS, AX, DIS ACCESS: ♿ Full access

Formerly on North High Street, this popular Indian restaurant relocated here in July 2001. They are proud of their new, modern look with big windows and a beautiful plant-filled patio. They take an equal or greater measure of pride in their northern and Bengali-style food. According to owner Murad Hossain, "Once you eat here, you never forget it, and you always come back." Reservations suggested for groups of six or more. Full bar. Private room that seats 30 available.

Taj Mahal
☎ (614) 294-0208

ADDRESS: 2247 N. High St.

HOURS: Tue–Thu 11:30 a.m.–2 p.m. & 4:30–9:30 p.m., Fri & Sat 11:30 a.m.–2 p.m. & 4:30–10 p.m., Sun 11:30 a.m.–2 p.m. & 4:30–10 p.m. PAYMENT: MC, VS, AX, DIS ACCESS: ♿ Full access OTHER ETHNIC SPECIALTIES: Pakistani

Indian and Pakistani cuisine in the university area. Reservations suggested but not required. All nonsmoking. Beer and wine.

DaVinci's Ristorante
☎ (614) 451-5147

ADDRESS: 4740 Reed Rd.

HOURS: Mon–Thu 11 a.m.–10 p.m., Fri 11 a.m.–11 p.m., Sat 5–11 p.m. PAYMENT: MC, VS, AX, DIS, checks ACCESS: ♿ Full access

Lunch buffet Monday–Friday. Domenico Ciotola came to this country from Italy in 1968 and opened his restaurant in 1974. He's still using the family recipes he brought with him, making his own sausage, pasta, sauces, and rum cake from scratch. The gnocchi is always hand rolled. A member of his family is always on hand to help you. A white-linen atmosphere in a dining room that is spacious and attractive. Banquet and meeting rooms available for as many as 350.

TAT Ristorante di Famiglia
☎ (614) 236-1392

ADDRESS: 1210 S. James Rd.

HOURS: Tues–Sun 11 a.m.–9 p.m. PAYMENT: MC, VS, AX, DIS, checks ACCESS: ♿ Full access

The oldest Italian restaurant in Columbus, in business and family owned by the Corrovas since 1929. Good food is a tradition here. A party room can accommodate up to 125, and there is no extra charge for either the room or the service of a bartender.

Kihachi
☎ (614) 764-9040

ADDRESS: 2667 Federated Blvd.

HOURS: Mon–Sat 6–10 p.m. PAYMENT: MC, VS, AX ACCESS: ♿ Full access

Known for their traditional 10-course Japanese dinner. No sushi, but an interesting selection of Japanese dishes with a 50-seat dining room, bar, and private tatami mat rooms, this restaurant has earned a large and loyal following strictly on word-of-mouth recommendations. An unlikely "find" in a strip mall location. Reservations suggested. All nonsmoking.

Kikyo

☎ (614) 457-5277

ADDRESS: 3706 Riverside Dr.

HOURS: Tue–Sun 5:30–10:30 p.m. **PAYMENT:** MC, VS, AX, DIS **ACCESS:** & Full access

Traditional Japanese cooking. Known for seafood and the freshness of their fish. All ingredients are very fresh, delivered daily from their own market, Koyama Shoten, just 10 minutes away at 5857 Saw Mill Road in Dublin (614-761-8118).

Restaurant Japan

☎ (614) 451-5411

ADDRESS: 1173 Old Henderson Rd., Kenny Center

HOURS: Mon–Sat lunch & dinner, Sun dinner only **PAYMENT:** MC, VS, AX, DIS **ACCESS:** & Full access

Very popular, often crowded. Reservations suggested.

Sapporo Wind

☎ (614) 895-7575

ADDRESS: 6188 Cleveland Ave.

HOURS: Mon–Fri 11:30 a.m.–1:30 p.m. & 4:30–10 p.m., Sat 4:30–10 p.m., Sun 5–9 p.m. **PAYMENT:** MC, VS, AX, DIS **ACCESS:** & Full access

Japanese cuisine with sushi their biggest attraction. Reservations suggested but never required. All nonsmoking, full bar.

Shoku

☎ (614) 485-9490

ADDRESS: 1312 Grandview Ave.

HOURS: Mon–Thu 11:30 a.m.–2 p.m. & 5–10 p.m., Fri 11:30 a.m.–2 p.m. & 5–10 p.m., Sat 5–11 p.m., Sun 5–10 p.m. **PAYMENT:** MC, VS, AX, DIS **ACCESS:** & Full access **OTHER ETHNIC SPECIALTIES:** Thai

Japanese and Thai food in a stunning modern setting. An upscale place with a dressy atmosphere. Reservations recommended, especially on Friday and Saturday nights, when a DJ spins the vinyl. One room has pillows and low tables for traditional floor seating. To accommodate Westerners who may find it difficult to get comfortable, the tables are positioned over an opening cut into the floor. Diners sit on the floor in an upright position as if on a chair, and their feet dangle underneath the table.

KOREAN

Korean Restaurant

☎ (614) 294-5096

ADDRESS: 2155 N. High St.

HOURS: Tue–Sun 11 a.m.–9 p.m., Mon closed **PAYMENT:** MC, VS **ACCESS:** & None

Korean dishes served for lunch and dinner in the university area. Reservations not accepted at this reasonably priced, unprententious place. It's all nonsmoking, and there's no alcohol.

Min-Go Korean Restaurant

☎ (614) 457-7331

ADDRESS: 800 Bethel Rd.

HOURS: Wed, Thu & Sun 4 p.m.–midnight, Fri & sat 11 :30 a.m.– 1 a.m., Mon & Thu closed **PAYMENT:** MC, VS, DIS **ACCESS:** & None

Located in the northwest part of the city, this place offers moderately priced Korean food. Reservations are not accepted, and that's a good thing because most of the staff have only the barest command of English and phone conversations are difficult at best. Full bar.

LATIN AMERICAN

Tapatio

☎ (614) 221-1085

ADDRESS: 491 N. Park St.

HOURS: Mon–Thu 11:30 a.m.–3:30 p.m. & 5–10 p.m., Fri & Sat 11:30 a.m.–3:30 p.m. & 5–11 p.m., Sun 5–10 p.m. **PAYMENT:** MC, VS, AX, DIS **ACCESS:** & Full access **OTHER ETHNIC SPECIALTIES:** Carribean

Latin American and Caribbean mix in a casual upscale environment more suited to adults than kids. It's a midsized restaurant with decor that fuses Art Deco with tropical colors and L.A. flair, and ever-changing exhibits of works by local artists adorn the walls. There's a large, attractive patio that

ALL OHIO

overlooks the cityscape, with both a cocktail and a dining section. A smoker's bar, where food is served, is completely separate from the main eating area. A private room for parties and meetings, which holds up to 40, is available by special arrangement Sunday through Thursday nights and during the day. In the heartland of white bread and lily-livered seasoning, the kitchen knows what to do with hot peppers and an array of other spices. Jon Christensen, restaurant reviewer for the *Columbus Dispatch,* called this "an enduring destination for flavor." Think Jamaican jerk chicken with pineapple salsa; fresh fish Vera Cruz–style with olives, capers, onions, tomatoes, chiles, and garlic; and salt cod fritters. Renowned for their margaritas, which are available at bargain happy-hour prices on Wednesdays from 4 p.m. until 7 p.m. Reservations are always suggested.

MIDDLE EASTERN

Aladdin's
☎ (614) 262-2414

ADDRESS: 2931 N. High St.

HOURS: Mon–Thu 11 a.m.–10 p.m., Fri & Sat 11 a.m.–11 p.m., Sun 11 a.m.–9 p.m.

PAYMENT: MC, VS, AX, DIS ACCESS: & Full access

Favorite menu items are schwarma, (a blend of ground beef and lamb that has been marinated and grilled); felafel (a fried patty made from chickpeas); and loubie (green beans slow-cooked with tomatoes and garlic). The color scheme is bright, the decor is cheerful, and the place is very kid friendly with plenty of crayons and high chairs on hand.

SPANISH

Spain Restaurant
☎ (614) 840-9100

ADDRESS: 888 E. Dublin-Granville Rd.

HOURS: Mon–Thu 11:30 a.m.–2 p.m. & 5–10 p.m., Fri 11:30 a.m.–2 p.m. & 5–11 p.m., Sat 5–11 p.m., Sun 4–10 p.m. PAYMENT: MC, VS, AX, DIS ACCESS: & Full access

Surprisingly, this truly authentic Spanish restaurant is located in a Best Western hotel, a venue not generally associated with fine food. Owner George Jorge is from northern Spain, and he and his chefs have created a menu that features the flavors of Galicia: garlic, lemon, and wine are key ingredients. The most popular dish is paella Valencia, but the kitchen does wonders with fresh fish like grouper, halibut, salmon, and trout as well as shrimp, veal, and chicken. Fridays and Saturdays are Latino nights, when a DJ spins in the bar area, dancers dance, and the place is packed. A banquet room is available (50 to 200 guests), and the restaurant will open during Saturday and Sunday lunch hours for private parties (minimum 30 guests). Reservations always accepted, recommended for weekends.

THAI

Thai Orchid
☎ (614) 792-1112

ADDRESS: 7654 Sawmill Rd.

HOURS: Mon–Fri 11 a.m.–2:30 p.m. & 4:30–9:45 p.m. (carryout until 10 p.m.), Sun 4:30–8:45 p.m. (carryout until 9 p.m.)

PAYMENT: MC, VS, AX ACCESS: & Full access

Thai cuisine on the city's northwest side. Reservations suggested. All nonsmoking.

VIETNAMESE

Saigon Palace
☎ (614) 464-3325

ADDRESS: 114 N. Front St.

HOURS: Mon–Fri 11 a.m.–3 p.m. & 5–9 p.m., Sat 5–9 p.m., Sun closed PAYMENT: MC, VS, AX, DIS ACCESS: & None

Specializes in Vietnamese cuisine. Small, unadorned restaurant with only 11 tables offers real dining-out bargains. The food is light, with almost no fat used in the cooking, and very tasty. Reservations suggested, especially for large groups. Beer served; all nonsmoking.

ALL OHIO

HILLIARD
CHINESE

Hunan Lion
☎ (614) 777-0550

ADDRESS: 3799 Ridge Mill Dr.

HOURS: Mon–Thu 11:30 a.m.–10 p.m., Fri 11:30 a.m.–10:30 p.m., Sat 4:30–10:30 p.m., Sun noon–9 p.m. **PAYMENT:** MC, VS, AX, DIS **ACCESS:** ঙ None

Lunch menu available Mon–Fri and Sun until 4 p.m. Chinese cooking that features seasonal ingredients, upscale atmosphere and service, plus European wines. A popular place, so reservations are suggested.

INDIAN

Taj Palace
☎ (614) 771-3870

ADDRESS: 3794 Fishinger Blvd.

HOURS: Mon–Thu 11 a.m.–2 p.m. & 5:30–10 p.m., Fri 11 a.m.–2 p.m. & 5:30–10:30 p.m., Sat 11:30 a.m.–2:30 p.m. & 5:30–10:30 p.m., Sun 11:30 a.m.–2:30 p.m. & 5:30–9:30 p.m. **PAYMENT:** MC, VS, AX, DIS **ACCESS:** ঙ Full access

Northern Indian cuisine with some unusual specialties, including Indian "wok" stir-frying, char-grilling, black lentil dal, cheese and vegetable dumplings, and pickled potatoes. Reservations suggested. All nonsmoking. Delivery service available, catering, and private parties.

LATIN AMERICAN

Starliner Diner
☎ (614) 529-1198

ADDRESS: 5240 Cemetery Rd.

HOURS: Tue–Thu 9 a.m.–3 p.m. & 5–9:30 p.m., Fri & Sat 9 a.m.–3 p.m. & 5–10 p.m., Sun 9 a.m.–3 p.m. **PAYMENT:** MC, VS, AX, DIS **ACCESS:** ঙ Full access **OTHER ETHNIC SPECIALTIES:** Caribbean

Latin American and Caribbean mix in what's been described as a fun and funky setting.

REYNOLDSBURG
CHINESE

Sun Tong Luck Tea House and Restaurant
☎ (614) 863-2828

ADDRESS: 6517 E. Livingstone Ave.

HOURS: Mon–Thu 11 am–9 p.m., Fri & Sat 11 a.m.–10 p.m., Sun noon–9 p.m. **PAYMENT:** MC, VS, DIS **ACCESS:** ঙ Full access

What makes this place unusual is that they serve Hong Kong–style Chinese cuisine and also do dim sum, and the prices for everything on the menu are reasonable. The 74-seat place has been run by the Lei family for more than 20 years. Reservations suggested on weekends and for groups of six or more. All nonsmoking and no alcohol.

ITALIAN

Scali Ristorante
☎ (614) 759-7764

ADDRESS: 1901 SR 256

HOURS: Tue–Thu 11:30 a.m.–2:30 p.m. & 5–9 p.m., Fri 11:30 a.m.–2:30 p.m. & 5–10 p.m., Sat 5–10 p.m., Sun & Mon closed **PAYMENT:** MC, VS, AX, DIS **ACCESS:** ঙ Full access

On the far east side of the city, this is the place for those who know the difference between real Italian food and the Americanized version, and those who want to learn what lies beyond meatballs and spaghetti. It's a family business: Francesco Scali is the chef; his wife, Judy, runs the front of the house; his mother bakes the bread from scratch daily; and his father makes the ravioli by hand. Combining upscale service, atmosphere, preparation, and presentation with a welcoming, friendly attitude and affordable prices, the restaurant aims to be a place where folks can indulge in the art of fine dining without any of the pretension or expense that usually comes with it. They may be located in the fast-food capital of the country, but the Scalis want their clientele to slow down, taste, and enjoy themselves, and they do all they can to make it happen. There's an open kitchen so you can watch Francesco work, and you're free to walk in for a closer look, much as you would in someone's home. A very good wine list features reasonably priced Italian imports. All nonsmoking. Reservations always suggested, highly recommended on Friday and Saturday.

NORTHWEST

FINDLAY

JAPANESE

Japan West
☎ (419) 424-1007

ADDRESS: 406 S. Main St.

HOURS: Mon–Fri 11 a.m.–2 p.m. & 5–10 p.m., Sat 5–10 p.m. **PAYMENT:** MC, VS, AX, DIS
ACCESS: ♿ Full access

Food preparation becomes a floor show when chefs cook your order of hibachi chicken or shiitake sirloin at one of five teppan (grilling) tables while you watch, or prepare rolls of fish, rice, and seaweed at the sushi bar. Both owner and manager are from Japan and take pride in the authenticity of their food. The daily presence of many Japanese diners—corporate visitors from that country and employees of area companies—confirm that this food offers a real taste of home.

TOLEDO

GERMAN

Wixey Bakery
☎ (419) 382-6684

ADDRESS: 2017 Glendale Ave.

HOURS: Tue–Sat 6 a.m.–6 p.m., Sun & Mon closed **PAYMENT:** MC, VS **ACCESS:** ♿

A family business for more than 50 years, the bakery is known for German cookies like springerle, lebkuchen, pfeffernuse, and stollen, as well as Polish and Hungarian specialties.

GREEK

Manos Greek Restaurant
☎ (419) 244-4479

ADDRESS: 1701 Adams St.

HOURS: Mon–Fri 11 a.m.–11 p.m., Sat 5–11 p.m.
PAYMENT: MC, VS, AX, DIS **ACCESS:** ♿ Full access

This place prides itself on its Old World hospitality. Kids are always welcome, and the patio is a perfect spot for enjoying sunny days and balmy nights.

HUNGARIAN

Budapest
☎ (419) 241-1513

ADDRESS: 3314 Monroe St.

HOURS: Tue–Fri 11 a.m.–2 p.m. & 4–8:30 p.m., Sat 4–8:30 p.m., Sun 11 a.m.–6:30 p.m., Mon closed (often closed month of August)
PAYMENT: Cash only **ACCESS:** ♿ Full access

Hungarian specialties at reasonable prices in a small, unassuming, and very informal restaurant that cannot claim an interior decorator's influence. Portions are large, and only real imported paprika is used in the kitchen. The mashed potatoes are the real thing, the Hungarian noodles have their own devotees who come specifically to eat them, and the strudel dough is hand pulled.

INDIAN

Indian Jewel
☎ (419) 269-1122

ADDRESS: 325 W. Alexis Rd.

HOURS: Tue–Thu 11:30 a.m.–2:30 p.m. and 5–9 p.m., Fri–Sat 11:30 a.m.–2:30 p.m. and 5–10 p.m., Sun 1 p.m.–3 p.m. and 5–9 p.m., Mon closed **PAYMENT:** MC, VS, AX, DIS
ACCESS: ♿ Limited

One of Toledo's culinary jewels, offering an interesting selection of "Curry Bowls," vegetarian dinners, grilled entrees, and rice dishes.

IRISH

Mickey Finn's Pub
☎ (419) 246-3466

ADDRESS: 602 Lagrange
HOURS: Mon–Sun 4 p.m.–2:30 a.m.
PAYMENT: MC, VS ACCESS: ♿

Table treats from the Emerald Isle including shepherd's pie, fish & chips, and potato soup, plus burgers and sandwiches. Irish beers on tap. St. Patrick's Day is celebrated on the 17th of every month with live music and dance. Independent Film Showcase every Monday and live music Tuesday through Sunday.

JAPANESE

Fujiyama
☎ (419) 537-0700

ADDRESS: 1208 N. Reynolds Rd.
HOURS: Mon–Thu 11:30 a.m.–10 p.m., Fri –Sun 11:30 a.m.–11 p.m. PAYMENT: MC, VS, AX, DIS
ACCESS: ♿ Full access

A tiny Japanese restaurant where 18 equals a full house.

LATIN AMERICAN / GERMAN

Fritz and Alfredo's
☎ (419) 729-9775

ADDRESS: 3025 North Summit St.
HOURS: Mon–Thu 11 a.m.–10 p.m., Fri & Sat 11 a.m.–11 p.m. PAYMENT: MC, VS, AX, DIS
ACCESS: ♿ Limited

German and Mexican under one roof on the north side of town.

LEBANESE

The Beirut
☎ (419) 473-0885

ADDRESS: 4082 Monroe
HOURS: Mon–Fri 4–10:30 p.m., Sat 4–11:30 p.m., Sun closed PAYMENT: MC, VS, AX, DIS
ACCESS: ♿ Full access

A popular spot for Lebanese food for more than 20 years.

Tiger Lebanese Bakery and Restaurant
☎ (419) 473-8942

ADDRESS: 4215 Monroe St.
HOURS: Mon–Sat 9 a.m.–7 p.m., Sun 10 a.m.–4 p.m. PAYMENT: MC, VS, AX, DIS
ACCESS: ♿ Full access

A small grocery store and cafe (eight tables) near Toledo Hospital and Toledo Children's Hospital. Eat in or carry out. Food is served on disposable plates with plastic tableware. The selection is large: Lebanese favorites such as tabouleh (parsley and bulgur wheat salad), hummus (chickpea dip), fatayer (spinach and meat pies), kibbee (seasoned ground beef with pine nuts), shish tawook (grilled chicken), and shish kafta (grilled beef); Moroccan-style dishes including spinach rice, couscous with vegetables, and a tajeen (stew) of potatoes and eggplant in a garlic tomato sauce. All food can be purchased by weight or scoop as well as in individual portions. Pita bread made fresh daily on the premises. A full line of Middle Eastern ingredients, including olives and spices.

LEBANON

Tiger Lebanese Bakery and Restaurant
☎ 419-842-0047

ADDRESS: 6720 Central Ave.
HOURS: Mon–Sat 9 a.m.–7 p.m., Sun 10 a.m.–4 p.m. PAYMENT: MC, VS, AX, DIS
ACCESS: ♿ Full access

Please see Tiger Lebanese / Monroe St. location for description.

MEXICAN

El Tipico Restaurant
☎ (419) 382-0661

ADDRESS: 1444 South St.
HOURS: Mon–Sat 11 a.m.–10 p.m., Sun 4–10 p.m. PAYMENT: MC, VS, AX
ACCESS: ♿ Limited

The Villa family has been preparing Mexican food here since 1968, and they run

Toledo's oldest Mexican restaurant. Ezekiel Villa and his wife Consuela use recipes that have been in their families for generations. They also grow some of the produce and herbs they use in their own garden and make everything from scratch. In 1999, readers of *El Tiempo* voted this their favorite Mexican restaurant. Located in a charming white stucco building with a red clay tile roof.

MEXICAN

Loma-Linda's Restaurant
☎ (419) 865-5455

ADDRESS: 10400 Airport Highway
HOURS: Mon 11 a.m.–11 p.m., Tue–Sat 11 a.m.–midnight, Sun closed PAYMENT: MC, VS, AX, DIS ACCESS: ♿ Full access

They must be doing something right because this Mexican eatery has been serving tacos and burritos since 1955. No reservations but plenty of room, with 275 seats. Kid and family friendly, liquor license, and mostly nonsmoking.

MIDDLE EASTERN

Ferdos Restaurant
☎ (419) 535-9494

ADDRESS: 3065 W. Bancroft St.
HOURS: Mon–Thu 11 a.m.–9 p.m., Fri 11 a.m.–11 p.m., Sat 4–11 p.m., Sun closed
PAYMENT: MC, VS, AX, DIS ACCESS: ♿ Full access

Midsized 30-table restaurant serving traditional Middle Eastern dishes.

Grape Leaf
☎ (419) 868-9099

ADDRESS: 909 S. McCord Rd.
HOURS: Mon–Thu 11:30 a.m.–9 p.m., Fri & Sat 11:30 a.m.–10 p.m. PAYMENT: MC, VS, AX, DIS
ACCESS: ♿ Full access

Known for their many vegetarian dishes and healthy beverages made from fruits and vegetables. A full array of Middle Eastern specialties. Portions are always generous and prices reasonable. Located in a

shopping strip, the dining room is small and plain.

SYRIAN

Barada
☎ (419) 843-2080

ADDRESS: 5215 Monroe St.
HOURS: Mon–Fri 11 a.m.–10 p.m., Sat 4–11 p.m.
PAYMENT: Cash only ACCESS: ♿ OTHER ETHNIC SPECIALTIES: Lebanese

Considered by many to be one of the area's hidden culinary treasures, serving Syrian and Lebanese dishes. Lunch specials, child-size portions for those under 12, and a banquet room.

MEXICAN

Casa Nueva
☎ (740) 592-2016

ADDRESS: 4 W. State St.
HOURS: Mon–Thu 8 a.m.–2:30 p.m. & 5–9 p.m., Fri 8 a.m.–2:30 p.m. & 5–10 p.m., Sat 9 a.m.–10 p.m., Sun 9 a.m.–9 p.m.
PAYMENT: MC, VS ACCESS: ♿ Full access

Serving breakfast, lunch, and dinner. Established in 1985, this is the oldest continuously operating worker-owned restaurant cooperative in the country. Purchases locally grown and produced products whenever possible. Mexican dishes plus seasonal American options with the emphasis on healthy eating. Their salsa, guacamole, and meatless Mexican-style spicy sausage available by the jar, the pint, and the pound. A large selection of beers.

Tomatia's
☎ (740) 594-8118

ADDRESS: 20 W. Stimson Ave.
HOURS: Mon–Thu 11 a.m.–9 p.m., Fri & Sat 11 a.m.–10 p.m., Sun noon–9 p.m., Mon closed
PAYMENT: MC, VS, DIS ACCESS: ♿ Full access

In an area that's deprived when it comes ethnic eating, this Mexican restaurant is a rarity. Laid back, comfortable, and family friendly with seating for about 60 at tables and booths. Domestic and imported beers, wine, and margaritas. All nonsmoking.

Tampico
☎ (740) 374-8623

ADDRESS: 221 Second St.

HOURS: Mon–Thu 11 a.m.–10 p.m., Fri 11 a.m.–10:30 p.m., Sat 11:30 a.m.–10:30 p.m., Sun 11:30 a.m.–9 p.m. PAYMENT: MC, VS, AX, DIS ACCESS: ♿ Full access

Owner Luis Salas and his partner Simon Banda serve traditional Mexican favorites plus house specials such as black bean soup, mole poblano, and chile verde in a room decorated with colorful hand-painted murals and tabletops by artist Alberto Villfanna. This restaurant is located in the town's restored historic district. A nice place to celebrate—margaritas by the pitcher, tequila shots, fried ice cream for dessert, and a huge sombrero you can wear for photos.

SOUTHEAST

SOMERSET
GERMAN

Clay Haus Restaurant
☎ (740) 743-1326

ADDRESS: 123 West Main St.

HOURS: Tue–Thu 11 a.m.–2 p.m. & 4–8 p.m., Fri & Sat 11 a.m.–2 p.m. & 4–9 p.m., Sun 11 a.m.–3 p.m. (buffet), Mon closed PAYMENT: Checks ACCESS: ♿ Limited

Located on the Zane Trace (Route 22), one of the state's earliest highways, in a historic Federal-style 1812 building filled with antiques. Dining areas on three floors. Kitchen serves German specialties and hearty country dishes.

ZANESVILLE
MEXICAN

Zak's
☎ (740) 453-2227

ADDRESS: 32 N. Third St.

HOURS: Tue–Thu 5–10 p.m., Fri & Sat 5 p.m.–11 p.m., Sun & Mon closed PAYMENT: MC, VS, AX, DIS ACCESS: ♿ Limited

The restaurant used to have lunch hours but discontinued them in the spring of 2001. At press time, they were still undecided about whether or not to do lunches in the fall and winter—call for more information. A Mexican restaurant located in an old stylishly renovated warehouse space that features an Art Deco look. Owner Al Zakany's father, from whom he gets his very non-Hispanic last name, was Hungarian, but the recipes he uses are from his Mexican mother. The food is top-drawer; the margaritas are memorable. Zagat reviewers give it a unanimous thumbs up.

SOUTHWEST

BEAVERCREEK
CHINESE

China House
☎ (937) 426-8532

ADDRESS: 4492 Indian Ripple Rd.

HOURS: Mon–Sun 11 a.m.–10 p.m. PAYMENT: MC, VS, AX, DIS ACCESS: ♿ Full access

For the real thing rather than the American version, avoid the regular menu and ask staff to help you choose from the Chinese-language one or ask about off-the-menu specials.

CENTERVILLE
INDIAN

Amar India
☎ (937) 439-9005

ADDRESS: 2759 Miamisburg-Centerville Rd.

HOURS: Mon–Sat 11:30 a.m.–2 p.m. & 5–10 p.m., Sun noon–9 p.m. PAYMENT: MC, VS, AX, DIS ACCESS: ♿ Full access

Lunch buffet daily. Northern Indian cuisine—which means that spicy hot dishes are blistering to the typical American palate. Considered a good choice for those

ALL OHIO

on a budget or in search of vegetarian selections. A totally nonsmoking restaurant.

MEXICAN

Las Piramides Mexican Restaurant
☎ (937) 291-0900

ADDRESS: 101 W. Franklin St.
HOURS: Mon–Fri 11 a.m.–10 p.m., Sat noon–11 p.m., Sun noon–9 p.m. PAYMENT: MC, VS, AX, DIS ACCESS: ♿ Full access

The atmosphere here is so relaxed that Alfredo Leon, who owns the place along with his brothers Jesus and Lorenzo, says "anything but a bikini is fine." The name of the restaurant honors the pyramids of Mexico built by the ancient Mayans. The food honors the cooking traditions of the west-central state of Jalisco and its capital, Guadalajara. Smokers and nonsmokers get their own individual rooms. Full bar.

CINCINNATI
FRENCH

La Petite France
☎ (513) 733-8383

ADDRESS: 3177 Glendale-Milford Rd.
HOURS: Mon–Sat 11 a.m.–2 p.m. & 5–10 p.m., Sun closed PAYMENT: MC, VS, AX, DIS
ACCESS: ♿ Full access

Actually located in an Evendale shopping plaza, where it's easy to miss, this place has been serving authentic French food for 20 years. Zagat reviewers have called it an "undiscovered gem." Owner Daniele Crandall is from northern France, and she does much of the cooking, using family recipes for some house specialties like veal sweetbreads. Also on her menu are canard (duck), beef filet with morel (mushrooms), and bouillabaisse. A major expansion and renovation in 2002 added a 40-foot bar, two party rooms, and a separate bistro dining room. Atmosphere is dressy in the main part of the restaurant, more casual in the bistro, and reservations for both are always suggested.

Maisonette
☎ (513) 721-2260

ADDRESS: 114 E. 6th St.
HOURS: Mon 6 p.m.–9:30 p.m., Tue–Fri 11:30 a.m.–2 p.m. & 6–9:30 p.m., Sat 5:30–10:30 p.m., Sun & holidays closed
PAYMENT: MC, VS, AX, DIS ACCESS: ♿ Full access

The only restaurant in North America to win five stars from the *Mobil Travel Guide* for 39 consecutive years. Reservations required. Jackets required, ties preferred. This formal, white-linen dining room has been offering classic French presentations for more than 50 years. Private dining and meeting rooms available.

GERMAN

Mecklenberg Gardens
☎ (513) 221-5353

ADDRESS: 302 East University
HOURS: Mon–Tue 11 a.m.–9 p.m., Wed & Thu 11 a.m.–9 p.m., Fri & Sat 11 a.m.–11 p.m.
PAYMENT: MC, VS, AX, DIS ACCESS: ♿ Full access

Offering German favorites since 1865. The original 19th-century mahogany bar lends old-time charm, and a vine-covered arbor offers lovely outdoor dining April through October.

INDIAN

Akash India
☎ (513) 723-1300

ADDRESS: 24 E. 6th St.
HOURS: Mon–Fri 11 a.m.–2:15 p.m. & 5–10 p.m., Sat noon–2:30 p.m. & 5–10 p.m., Sun noon–2:30 p.m. & 5–9 p.m. PAYMENT: MC, VS, AX, DIS ACCESS: ♿ Full access

Northern Indian cuisine featuring foods baked in a traditional clay tandoori oven and a variety of curries. Buffet available at lunchtime. A large, pleasant dining room in the heart of downtown. Many vegetarian specialties and unusual beverages such as lassi (a sweet yogurt drink), spiced tea, and Indian beers.

ITALIAN

Nicola's Ristorante
☎ (513) 721-6200

ADDRESS: 1420 Sycamore St.
HOURS: Mon–Thu 11:30 a.m.–2 p.m. &
5:30–10 p.m., Fri 11:30 a.m.–2 p.m. &
5:30–10 p.m., Sat 5:30–11 p.m., Sun closed
PAYMENT: MC, VS, AX, DIS **ACCESS:** & Full access

Fine Italian dining courtesy of chef and owner Nicola Pietoso, who learned his art at the Culinary School of Florence. He came to America in 1990. This is his first restaurant in Cincinnati, and it's in an unusual setting. It's housed in an old building called an incline house, once used as a storage area for streetcars. The renovated space is airy and attractive—the ceilings are high, the windows are big, the room spacious. There's also a beautiful outdoor dining area. Pietoso has his own way with veal, chicken, chops, and seafood. "Each of the pasta dishes," he says, "has its own personality that makes it different from what you find at most other Italian restaurants here." One of the most popular is his lobster ravioli. Another specialty his customers love is a three-course fish meal that is prepared tableside. A big fish such as char, walleye, or snapper is cut into serving-size portions and prepped to order while you watch, then taken back to the kitchen for cooking. By the time you're done with your salad and pasta, it's ready. There's an excellent wine list with many interesting Italian imports. At lunchtime, the restaurant draws a business crowd, and coats and ties are common. In the evening, people still treat it as a special place and dress well. During the week a few tables are reserved for smokers, but on weekends smoking is permitted only at the bar.

Pane E Vino
☎ (513) 321-7100

ADDRESS: 2724 Erie Ave., Hyde Park Square
HOURS: Tue–Thu 5:30–10 p.m., Fri & Sat
5:30–11 p.m., Sun 5:30–9:30 p.m. **PAYMENT:** MC,
VS, AX, DIS **ACCESS:** & Full access

Northern Italian cuisine is featured, but owner and chef John Leonard likes to expand the boundaries of this traditional cooking style to include a more comprehensive Mediterranean approach to ingredients and preparation. Fresh buffalo mozzarella is made from scratch in the kitchen, and fresh fish—like steamed sea bass over capellini with lobster—is a house specialty. The restaurant is done in warm shades of brown, yellow, and blue, and there's a large saltwater fish tank. The wine list features bottles from Spain, France, and Italy, as well as California. Reservations recommended. Full bar. Easy to find—look for the pig out front, a souvenir of the Big Pig Gig.

Primavista
☎ (513) 251-6467

ADDRESS: 810 Matson Place
HOURS: Mon–Thu 5:30–9:30 p.m., Fri
5:30–10 p.m., Sat 5–11 p.m., Sun 5–9 p.m.
PAYMENT: MC, VS, AX, DIS, checks **ACCESS:** & Full
access

Five minutes west of downtown, the restaurant gets rave reviews for both food and view. Locals have voted it "Best Italian" for seven straight years, earning it a place in *Cincinnati Magazine*'s Hall of Fame. Specializing in veal and fresh fish and also offering steak, lamb, poultry, and pasta. Windows offer stunning panoramic vistas of the city skyline and the Ohio River.

JAPANESE

Ko-Sho
☎ (513) 665-4950

ADDRESS: 215 E. 9th St.
HOURS: Mon–Thu 11:30 a.m.–2 p.m. &
5–10 p.m., Fri 11:30 a.m.–2 p.m. & 5–11 p.m., Sat
5–11 p.m., Sun 5–9 p.m. **PAYMENT:** MC, VS, AX,
DIS **ACCESS:** & Full access

Opened in June 1999. The name means "My Place" in Japanese, and here at his place owner Yukio Fukunaga combines a sushi bar with a kitchen that prepares a variety of traditional Japanese cooked fish, noodle, vegetable, chicken, and beef dishes. Cook your own sukiyaki (poached beef and vegetables) tableside on a portable stove.

MEXICAN

Rincon Mexicano
☎ (513) 943-9923

ADDRESS: Biggs Place Mall, 4450 Eastgate Blvd.
HOURS: Mon–Thu 11 a.m.–10 p.m., Fri & Sat 11 a.m.–11 p.m., Sun noon–9 p.m.
PAYMENT: MC, VS, DIS **ACCESS:** ⅃ Full access

Despite its shopping mall setting, the Zagat guide has described it as "the real enchilada," and it was voted "Best Mexican" in Cincinnati by the locals. The restaurant is spacious, festively decorated, and attractive, and includes a cantina and a private meeting/party room. Family owned and serving homestyle Mexican food. Live mariachi band plays on Tuesdays from 6 to 9 p.m. Twenty flavors of margaritas.

SCOTTISH

Nicholson's Pub and Tavern
☎ (513) 564-9111

ADDRESS: 625 Walnut St.
HOURS: Mon–Thu 11 a.m.–10 p.m., Fri & Sat 11 a.m.–11:30 p.m., Sun 4–9 p.m. **PAYMENT:** MC, VS, AX, DIS **ACCESS:** ⅃ Full access

A rarity in Ohio (or anywhere in the U.S.)—a Scottish eatery and bar complete with staff decked out in tartan—Nicholson's is located in what's called the Backstage area of downtown, across from the Arnoff Center for the Arts. Dine in any one of a number of small "clubby" rooms, each with its own distinctive character, or sit at the 80-foot-long mahogany bar. Enjoy shepherd's pie, Atlantic salmon, fish and chips, finnan haddie, bangers and mash, or a ploughman's lunch. Scottish beers on tap plus a large variety of bottled beers from Scotland, England, and Ireland, and American microbrews. They claim the largest selection of fine single-malt scotches in the region—I've counted at least 60.

CLIFTON
INDIAN

Ambar India
☎ (513) 281-7000

ADDRESS: 350 Ludlow Ave.
HOURS: Mon–Thu 11:30 a.m.–2:30 p.m. & 5–10 p.m., Fri & Sat 11:30 a.m.–2:30 p.m. & 5–10:30 p.m., Sun 11:30 a.m.–2:30 p.m.
PAYMENT: MC, VS, AX, DIS **ACCESS:** ⅃ Full access

Setting is ordinary, food is extraordinary.

Amol India
☎ (513) 961-3600

ADDRESS: 354 Ludlow Ave.
HOURS: Mon–Thu 11:30 a.m.–2:30 p.m. & 5–10 p.m., Fri 11:30 a.m.–2:30 p.m. & 5–10:30 p.m., Sat 11:30 a.m.–4 p.m. & 5–10:30 p.m., Sun 11:30 a.m.–4 p.m. **PAYMENT:** MC, VS, AX, DIS
ACCESS: ⅃ None

To help diners get just as little or as much heat as they want in their food, there is a spice scale with ratings from 1 to 10 to use when ordering. Guests are especially enthusiastic about their homemade mango ice cream, mango milkshakes, and mango lassi drink.

CLIFTON HEIGHTS
GERMAN

Lenhardt's & Christy's
☎ (513) 281-3600

ADDRESS: 151 W. McMillan St.
HOURS: Mon 4 p.m.–2 a.m., Tue–Fri 11 a.m.–2 a.m., Sat 4–2 a.m., Sun closed
PAYMENT: MC, VS, AX, DIS **ACCESS:** ⅃ Limited
OTHER ETHNIC SPECIALTIES: Hungarian

Family owned and operated since 1955, the restaurant serves a mix of classic German and Hungarian dishes. They have seating in an outdoor biergarten during the warm-weather months and a cozy rathskeller where European wines are served.

LITHUANIAN

Elinor's Amber Rose
☎ (937) 228-2511
ADDRESS: 1400 Valley St.

HOURS: Mon 11 a.m.–2 p.m., Tue–Sat 11 a.m.–9 p.m., Sun closed PAYMENT: MC, VS, AX, DIS ACCESS: ♿ Full access OTHER ETHNIC SPECIALTIES: Hungarian, Russian, German

Serving Lithuanian, Hungarian, Russian, and German dishes in what was once a general store, built in the early 1900s. Building retains the original hardwood floors and pressed tin ceiling.

ITALIAN

Dominic's Restaurant
☎ (937) 222-3667
ADDRESS: 1066 S. Main St.

HOURS: Tue–Thu 11 a.m.–10:45 p.m., Fri 11 a.m.–11:45 p.m., Sat 4–11:45 p.m., Sun 4–10 p.m., Mon closed PAYMENT: MC, VS, AX ACCESS: ♿ Full access

This place has been a local fixture since 1957. Their motto—and not every restaurant has one—reflects their long-standing and deep-rooted reputation: "Dominic's—Isn't That Where Dayton Is?" Dominic Mantea started his business in a little house at this address, with room for about 15 tables. Business boomed, so he continued to expand every few years, buying up surrounding buildings and empty lots, connecting each new wing with the others, and redoing the front—now the place can seat up to 275 diners. His son Richard now runs the place, located near Victoria Hall, the University of Dayton, the Memorial Theater, and the Montgomery County fairgrounds. Anybody famous who comes to Dayton usually ends up here for a meal of traditional Italian food with sauces and sausage made from scratch. One of the kitchen's basic operating principles is that you can never use too much garlic, and their house salad dressing laced with bits of the pungent little bulb is renowned far and wide. Reservations not accepted for Friday and Saturday, and only for five or more Monday–Thursday and Sunday. The only exception is for parties of 25 or more, and they can have their own room (holds 35) at no extra cost.

JAPANESE

I-ZU
☎ (937) 277-9596
ADDRESS: 5252 N. Dixie Dr.

HOURS: Tue–Sun 11 a.m.–2 p.m. & 5–9:30 p.m., Mon closed PAYMENT: MC, VS, AX, DIS ACCESS: ♿ Full access

Sushi and bento box meals (small portions of different dishes, each in a separate compartment). Daily specials offer an opportunity for the adventurous to try some more unusual Japanese dishes. The restaurant seats 45 at traditional low tables or tables at regulation Western height. A separate party/meeting room available for up to 50 guests.

VIETNAMESE

Little Saigon
☎ (937) 258-8010
ADDRESS: 1718 Woodman Dr.

HOURS: Mon–Thu 11 a.m.–2 p.m. & 4:30–9 p.m., Fri 11 a.m.–2 p.m. & 4:30–10 p.m., Sat 11 a.m.–2 p.m. & 4:30–9:30 p.m., Sun closed PAYMENT: MC, VS ACCESS: ♿ Full access

The food tastes so much like home that Vietnamese families come from all over the area to eat here on the weekends. This small, very casual place seats 40.

CHINESE

Grand Oriental
☎ (513) 677-3388
ADDRESS: 4800 Fields-Ertel Rd.

HOURS: daily 11:30 a.m.–10:30 p.m. PAYMENT: MC, VS, AX, DIS ACCESS: ♿ Full access

Specialty of the house is weekend dim sum.

ALL OHIO

EVENDALE
INDIAN

Anand India
☎ (513) 554-4040

ADDRESS: 10890 Reading Rd.
HOURS: Mon–Sat 11:30 a.m.–2 p.m. & 5–10 p.m.,
Sun noon–3 p.m. PAYMENT: MC, VS, AX, DIS
ACCESS: ♿ Full access

A totally nonsmoking restaurant serving northern Indian cuisine. Tali sampler platters are a house favorite. Located in a large modern building with seating for about 100.

FAIRBORN
LEBANESE

Greek Islands Deli
☎ (937) 429-2598

ADDRESS: 2642 Colonel Glenn Hgwy.
HOURS: Mon–Fri 11 a.m.–8 p.m., Sat
11 a.m.–4 p.m., Sun closed PAYMENT: Checks
ACCESS: ♿ Full access

The name is misleading because the food is more Lebanese than Greek. Although stuffed grape leaves, gyros, and Greek salad are on the menu, the majority of offerings focus on the cuisine of the Middle East—hummus, tabouleh, felafel, and fatoosh. This is mostly a carryout business with seating for only about 40.

HYDE PARK
THAI

Bangkok Bistro
☎ (513) 871-0707

ADDRESS: 3506 Erie Ave.
HOURS: Mon–Thu 11 a.m.–10 p.m., Fri
11 a.m.–10:30 p.m., Sat 4:30–10:30 p.m., Sun
4:30–10 p.m. PAYMENT: MC, VS ACCESS: ♿ Full access

Sushi available during dinner hours only, Tuesday through Sunday. This family-run restaurant specializes in Thai food and also offers Japanese sushi. It began as a single room with only 10 seats in 1994 but now boasts seating for 120, plus some tables and chairs outside in good weather

and full bar service. A completely nonsmoking eatery and very popular, so reservations are recommended for weekends and large groups.

Lemon Grass
☎ (513) 321-2882

ADDRESS: 2666 Madison Rd.
HOURS: Mon–Thu 11 a.m.–3 p.m. & 5–10 p.m.,
Fri 11 a.m.–3 p.m. & 5–10 p.m., Sat 4–10:30 p.m.,
Sun 4–9:30 p.m. PAYMENT: MC, VS
ACCESS: ♿ Limited

The Yee family serves Thai food, and loyal customers who love it come back regularly. Reservations are recommended on Friday and Saturday evenings. Beer and wine only at this casual little 15-table place. It's all nonsmoking.

KETTERING
FRENCH

L'Auberge
☎ (937) 299-5536

ADDRESS: 4120 Far Hills Ave.
HOURS: Mon–Thu 11:30 a.m.–2 p.m. &
5:30–10 p.m., Fri & Sat 11:30 a.m.–2 p.m. &
5:30–11 p.m. PAYMENT: MC, VS, AX, DIS
ACCESS: ♿ Full access

Two restaurants in one, both serving French food. The Bistro is a small, casual, and moderately priced place to eat. The main dining room is quite elegant and formal, the food more elaborate and expensive. Mobil gives this Dayton-area restaurant, which has been in business for more than 20 years, a four-star rating. Reservations required for the main dining room, suggested for the Bistro.

ITALIAN

Mamma DiSalvo's Ristorante
☎ (937) 299-5831

ADDRESS: 1375 E. Stroop Rd.
HOURS: Tue–Thu 11 a.m.–10 p.m., Fri
11 a.m.–11 p.m., Sat 4–11 p.m., Mon closed
PAYMENT: MC, VS, AX, DIS ACCESS: ♿ Full access

Elena and Rinaldo DiSalvo emigrated from the small southern town of Duronia in

Italy in the 1940s. In 1979 they opened a little restaurant, and everything is still made from scratch, using Elena's recipes. The restaurant, now located in an office building, has grown bigger and more popular since then, but it's still a family business with Elena (known to all as Mamma), her husband, sons Roberto and Nicholas, and their aunt and uncle involved in the day-to-day operations. The restaurant's famous sauce and salad dressing are now bottled and available in Dayton-area markets as well as through their website: www.mammadisalvo.com. It's not a formal place, but it's no fast-food joint either; people dress nicely, though comfortably, to dine here. Kids are always welcome. Reservations are accepted weekdays and on Fridays and Saturdays for dining times before 6 p.m. and for large groups.

MIDDLE EASTERN

Middle Eastern Deli
☎ (937) 254-3509
ADDRESS: 1050 Patterson Blvd.
HOURS: Mon–Sat 10:30 a.m.–8 p.m., Sun 11:30 a.m.–5 p.m., Fri closed from 1–2:30 p.m.
PAYMENT: MC, VS, AX, DIS, checks ACCESS: & Full access

A combination grocery store, carryout place, and tiny 10-seat restaurant featuring Lebanese and Egyptian food.

MASON
THAI

Arloi Dee
☎ (513) 229-3997
ADDRESS: 4920 Socialville Foster Rd.
HOURS: Mon–Fri 11 a.m.–3 p.m. & 5–10 p.m., Sat noon–3 p.m. & 5–11 p.m., Sun 5–10 p.m.
PAYMENT: MC, VS, AX, DIS ACCESS: & Full access
OTHER ETHNIC SPECIALTIES: Chinese, Japanese

Locals have given this place their Top 10 rating for Thai, Chinese, and Japanese food, but Thai dishes are the house specialty. "When you eat here," says owner Mali Lamsun, "you eat as you would in Bangkok, where I come from. You will find

dishes that you do not see on the menus of other Thai restaurants." Mali runs the restaurant, which has won high praise from the *Cincinnati Post,* the *Cincinnati Enquirer, City Beat,* and *Nation's Restaurant News,* with the help of her husband, Preecha, their daughters, Pat and Chanida, and her mother, Sanom Hunsuwan.

MONTGOMERY
CHINESE

Pacific Moon Cafe
☎ (513) 891-0091
ADDRESS: 8300 Market Place Ln.
HOURS: Sun–Thu 11 a.m.–10 p.m., Fri 11 a.m.–11 p.m., Sat 10 a.m.–midnight
PAYMENT: MC, VS, AX, DIS ACCESS: & Full access

Critics sing its praises in the *Cincinnati Post* and *Cincinnati Magazine.* It's a consistent winner of readers' polls for "Best Chinese" in the city and always wins awards at the "Taste of Cincinnati." The menu is large and creative, and features a special section with "light" entrees. Worth mention is the dim sum, served on Saturday and Sunday from 10 a.m. to 3 p.m.: the selection includes both the familiar and the unusual. Located across from Montgomery Square, with delivery service to some areas during lunch and dinner hours. Live jazz on Saturday nights.

INDIAN

Tandoor India
☎ (513) 793-7484
ADDRESS: 8702 Market Place Ln.
HOURS: Mon–Thu 5:30–9:30 p.m., Fri & Sat 5:30–10:30 p.m., Closed Sun; Mon–Sat lunch buffet 11:30 a.m.–2 p.m. PAYMENT: MC, VS, AX, checks ACCESS: & Full access

Lunch buffet daily, and the selections change each day. Established in 1985, this restaurant has earned praise from Zagat's, the *Cincinnati Post, Cincinnati Magazine,* and the *Cincinnati Enquirer,* and won awards at the "Taste of Cincinnati." As the name suggests, the specialty of the house is

ALL OHIO

tandoori clay oven preparation of meat, fish, poultry, and bread.

MOUNT ADAMS
THAI

Teak Thai Restaurant
☎ (513) 665-9800

ADDRESS: 1049 St. Gregory St.

HOURS: Mon–Fri 11:30 a.m.–3 p.m. & 5–9:30 p.m., Sat 4:30–10:30 p.m., Sun 4:30–9:30 p.m. **PAYMENT:** MC, VS, AX, DIS
ACCESS: & Full access

Large, pretty dining room (seating for 300), good selection of Thai dishes, and patio dining in good weather. Reservations suggested for weekends. Full bar.

NEWTOWN
HUNGARIAN

Iron Skillet
☎ (513) 561-6776

ADDRESS: 6900 Valley Ave.

HOURS: Tue–Fri 11 a.m.–2 p.m. and 4:30–9 p.m., Fri–Sat 11 a.m.–2 p.m. and 4:30–9:30 p.m., Sun 3–8 p.m. **PAYMENT:** MC, VS, DIS **ACCESS:** & Full access

Laszlo Molnar Jr. and his sister, Monica Lippmeier, run the restaurant started by their parents, who left Hungary in 1956 and started their business in 1973. Hungarian and German dishes are their specialty. Three small rooms, with a completely separate one set aside for smokers, are decorated with an Old World touch using folk art and traditional costumes. In addition to their chicken paprikash, schnitzel, and potatoes made six different ways, they're famous for their Gundel crepes: filled with walnuts and topped with a warm chocolate sauce, it's a dessert big enough for two.

PIQUA
MEXICAN

El Sombrero
☎ (937) 778-2100

ADDRESS: 902 Scot Dr.

HOURS: Sun–Thu 11 a.m.–10 p.m., Fri & Sat 11 a.m.–11 p.m. **PAYMENT:** MC, VS, DIS
ACCESS: & Full access

Cooks are all from Mexico, and everything here is made from scratch. Especially popular is their arroz con pollo (chicken and rice). Outdoor patio. No reservations accepted on Friday and Saturday nights.

PLEASANT RIDGE
AFRICAN-AMERICAN/SOUTHERN

Manhattan West (soul food)
☎ (513) 531-7222

ADDRESS: 6041 Montgomery Rd.

HOURS: Wed–Fri noon–9 p.m., Sat 2 p.m.–9 p.m., Sun 1 p.m.–6 p.m., Mon & Tue closed
PAYMENT: MC, VS, AX **ACCESS:** & Full access

Call it soul food or Southern food, it's still comfort food. This family-friendly place dishes up macaroni and cheese, real mashed potatoes, ribs, pork chops, real fried chicken, catfish, greens, cornbread, and sweet potato pie in pleasant surroundings.

IRISH

Dubliner
☎ (513) 531-6111

ADDRESS: 6111 Montgomery Rd.

HOURS: Sun–Thu 11 a.m.–10 p.m., Fri & Sat 11 a.m.–midnight **PAYMENT:** MC, VS, AX, DIS
ACCESS: & Full access

Celtic music played by local and touring bands four nights a week, Wednesday through Saturday. Guinness on tap, and paired with beef in one of the house specials that the manager boasts "is good and good for you." Other Irish edibles include Celtic stew, boxty, shepherd's pie, and salmon. Owner Mike Kull married into an Irish family and learned his stuff from his wife, his in-laws, and visits to Eire. The pub side, where smoking is allowed and the bands play, seats 100, and a completely separate dining room, with another 100 seats, is for nonsmokers and those who want a bit of quiet. There's also a small outdoor patio with tables.

ROSELAWN
VIETNAMESE

Song Long
☎ (513) 351-7631

ADDRESS: 1737 Section Rd.

HOURS: Mon–Thu 11 a.m.–9 p.m., Fri & Sat 11 a.m.–10 p.m., Sun noon–9 p.m.

PAYMENT: MC, VS **ACCESS:** & Limited

This modest, inexpensive, family-run place serves a large selection of absolutely authentic Vietnamese food.

TROY
JAPANESE

Arang
☎ (937) 335-3411

ADDRESS: 439 N. Elm St.

HOURS: Mon–Fri 11 a.m.–2 p.m. & 5–10:30 p.m., Sat 5–10:30 p.m., Sun closed **PAYMENT:** MC, VS, AX **ACCESS:** & Limited **OTHER ETHNIC SPECIALTIES:** Korean

Japanese sushi and Korean food authentic enough to satisfy the Asian executives who do business with corporations along I-75.

MEXICAN

El Sombrero
☎ (937) 339-2100

ADDRESS: 1700 N. County 25 A

HOURS: Sun–Thu 11 a.m.–10 p.m., Fri & Sat 11 a.m.–11 p.m. **PAYMENT:** MC, VS, DIS **ACCESS:** & Full access

See descripion under location in Piqua.

WEST CARROLLTON
MEXICAN

El Meson
☎ (937) 859-8229

ADDRESS: 903 E. Dixie Dr.

HOURS: Tue–Thu 11 a.m.–2 p.m. & 5–9 p.m., Fri 11 a.m.–2 p.m. & 5–9 p.m., Sat 5–9 p.m., Sun & Mon closed **PAYMENT:** MC, VS, AX, DIS **ACCESS:** & Full access

Gourmet Hispanic food highlighting many different Hispanic regional styles plus the cuisines of Central America, South America, and Spain. Tapas (a variety of "tasting" portions) is a specialty. An inviting place created and run by the Castro family, serving dishes found nowhere else in the area. They are also known for their attractive bar and a wine list featuring imports from Chile, Spain, Argentina, and Portugal.

WEST CHESTER
GERMAN

Black Forest
☎ (513) 777-7600

ADDRESS: 8675 Cincinnati-Columbus Rd.

HOURS: Mon–Fri 11:30 a.m.–2:30 p.m. and 4:30–10 p.m., Sat 4:30–10 p.m. **PAYMENT:** MC, VS, AX, DIS **ACCESS:** & Full access

Bavaria comes to southern Ohio in this traditional-style gasthaus where German beers are on tap and real German food is on the menu. Famous for huge portions and a good selection of wines. Spaetzle is homemade and "Oktoberfest Chicken" is available year round.

MEXICAN

Amigos
☎ (513) 777-9424

ADDRESS: 8111 Cincinnati-Dayton Rd.

HOURS: Mon–Fri 11 a.m.–2 p.m. & 5–10 p.m., Sat & Sun noon–10 p.m. **PAYMENT:** MC, VS, AX **ACCESS:** & Full access

The Leal and Rodriguez families have run this business since 1990, and they take great pride in their food because it is prepared not to meet American tastes but just as it would be back home in southern Mexico. They call the place "The 100% Authentic Mexican Restaurant," and food writers for the Cincinnati papers agree. A mariachi band plays Sundays from 12:30 to 3:30. Twenty-seven different brands and types of tequila, and nine Mexican beers. Kids' menu. A second location at 11711 Princeton Pike, Springdale, (513) 671-5985.

ALL OHIO

Ethnic Festivals

The ethnic festivals listed below are annual events—dates and locations vary from year to year. Whenever possible, I've supplied a phone number where you can get more information. But please note: many of the sponsoring organizations are small and lack permanent offices. Often, when new officers are elected, phone numbers change. Contact the Nationalities Service Center (216-781-4560) for listings of groups and officers. The Mayor's Office of Cultural Affairs also keeps track of various ethnic events. Call (216) 664-3405 for more information. Local newspapers and magazines usually carry festival announcements, too.

PACIFIC RIM

Chinese New Year Celebration, contact various Chinese restaurants directly, late February (see also restaurant listing for Li Wah)

MIDDLE EAST, NORTH AFRICA AND INDIA

Republic of India Celebration (India Community Center, 216-791-8640), late January

Indian Republic Day (India Community Center, 216-791-8640), late August

Egyptian Festival (St. Mark Coptic Church, 216-642-7691), late August, early September

Middle East Festival (St. Elias Church, 216-661-1155), Labor Day weekend

MEDITERRANEAN

Greek Heritage Festival at Annunciation Church (216-861-0116), late May

National Greek Festival (Cuyahoga County Fairgrounds), mid September

Our Lady of Mt. Carmel Italian Festival (216-651-5043), July

Feast of the Assumption in Little Italy (Holy Rosary, 216-421-2995), mid August

EUROPE EAST OF THE DANUBE

Slavic Village Harvest Festival (Slavic Village Association, 216-271-5591), mid August

Slovak Heritage Festival (St. Anthony's, 440-842-2666), Labor Day weekend

Slovenian Polka Festival (216-692-1000), late November

Czech St. Wenceslaus Celebration (Karlin Hall, 216-341-9867), late September

Polish Heritage Festival (St. John's Cantius, 216-781-9095), early September

St. Stanislaus Polish Festival (216-341-9091), early October

Baltic Freedom Day Celebration (Lithuanian Hall, 216-531-8318), June

EUROPE WEST OF THE DANUBE

Ohio Irish Festival (West Side Irish-American Club, 440-235-5868), late June

Irish Cultural Festival (Cuyahoga Co. Fairgrounds, 216-251-0711), late July

Ohio Scottish Games (Oberlin, 440-442-2147), late June

Celtic Heritage Fair (Warren City Hall, 330-856-3432), mid July

Celtic Feis (Geneva-on-the-Lake, 440-466-9300), late August

German Heritage Day (Donauschwaben Club, 440-235-2646), early June

Sommer Oktoberfest (Donauschwaben Club, 440-235-2646), mid August

LATIN AMERICA

La Sagrada Familia Parish Festival (216-631-2888), late June

Puerto Rican Coffee Festival (Club Amla Yaucana, 216-241-7641), late July

Our Lady of Guadaloupe Feast (San Juan Bautista Church, 216-631-2888), early December

AMERICAN REGIONAL

Afro-American Festival (Elyria, 440-366-3244, or Lorain County Visitor's Bureau, 440-245-5282), early July

Glenville Community Festival (Luke Easter Park, 216-268-3378), Labor Day

INTERNATIONAL

Lorain International Festival (Centre of Sheffield, 440-277-5244), late June

East 185th Street Festival (216-481-3220), early August

One World Day in Cleveland Cultural Gardens (City Hall, 216-664-3405), mid-Sept.

Indexes

Index by Name *(Markets in italic)*

#1 Pho, 52

A

Affamato Italian Deli and Market, 138
Affamato Italian Deli and Market, 104
Agostino's Ristorante, 105
Akash India, 272
Akira Sushi & Hibachi, 36
Al's Corner Restaurant, 154
Al's Quality Market, 166
Aladdin's, 266
Aladdin's Baking Company, 91
Aladdin's Eatery, 82
Albelad Imported Food, 91
Alberini's, 106
Aldo's, 107
Alesci's of South Euclid, 139
Alex's Bistro, 262
Alexandria's on Main, 233
Ali Baba Restaurant, 82
Almadina Imports, 92
Amar India, 271
Ambar India, 274
Amigos, 279
Amir's Marketplace, 90
Amir's Marketplace Restaurant, 79
Amol India, 274
Anand India, 276
Annapurna, 263
Anthony's, 139
Anthony's, 107
Aoeshi, 37
Arang, 279
Arloi Dee, 277
Arrabiata's, 108
Asia Food Company, 57
Asia Grocery & Gift, 58
Asia Tea House, 52
Asian Food Market, 58
Asian Imports, 87
Assad Bakery, 92
Athens Pastries & Imported Foods, 136
Athens Restaurant, 100

B

Balaton Restaurant, 156
Bangkok Bistro, 276
Bangkok Gourmet, 46
Bangkokville, 64
Barada, 270
Baraona's Baking Co., Inc., 140
Barwulu/Hookes African Food Market, 86
Battuto Ristorante, 109
Bavarian Pastry Shop, 198
Beirut, 269
Big Mary's, 234

Black Forest, 279
Blue Nile Ethiopian Restaurant, 262
Bo Loong, 23
Bohemian Hall, 165
Bombay Grille, 264
Bombay Sitar, 70
Boris's Kosher Meat, 243
Bovalino's Italian Ristorante, 110
Bradford Restaurant, 234
Bruno's Ristorante, 110
Bucci's, 112
Budapest, 268
Budapest Hungarian Cafe, 157
Buettner's Bakery, 166

C

C & H Gertrude Bakery, 167
Cafe Mozart, 261
Cafe Tandoor, 72
Calabash African Market, 87
Cancun Family Mexican Restaurant, 210
Cancun Restaurant & Lounge, 211
Canton Importing Company, 137
Caribe Bake Shop, 227
Casa Nueva, 270
Casey's Irish Imports, 196
Cedarland at the Clinic, 79
Chandler and Rudd, 251
Charles Peters Bake Shop, 198
Chez Francois, 183
China House, 271
Chinese Village, 53
Clara's European Restaurant and Bakery, 158
Clay Haus Restaurant, 271
Cleveland Food Co-op, 252
Colozza's Cakes & Pastries, 140
Columbia Asian Food & Gift, 63
Continental Cuisine, 80
Corbo's Dolceria, 140
Cork & More Shoppe, 141
Corky and Lenny's, 240
Cozumel, 211
Crawdad's, 236

D

D'Ici de Là, 224
D'Ici de Là, 203
Dailey's West Indian Food Mart, 224
Dailey's West Indian Food Mart, 206
Daishin, 37
Daishin Hibachi Steak House, 38
Dave's Supermarkets, 225
DaVinci's Ristorante, 264
Der Braumeister, 186

Der Braumeister Deli, 193
Desert Inn, 83
DeVitis & Sons, 141
DiStefano's Authentic Italian Foods, 141
Dominic's Restaurant, 275
Donauschwaben German American Cultural Center, 186
Dong Duong Indochina Grocery, 58
Dougardi's Italian Foods, 142
Dubliner, 278
Dubrovnik Garden Restaurant, 152

E

El Charrito, 212
El Charro Restaurante, 213
El Manantial, 205
El Meson, 279
El Rincon Mexican Restaurant, 213
El Sombrero, 278
El Taino Restaurant, 221
El Tango Taqueria, 214
El Tipico Restaurant, 269
Elinor's Amber Rose, 275
Ellis Bakery, 92
Empress Taytu Ethiopian Restaurant, 70
Enterpride Restaurant, 207
Euclid Meat & Sausage Shop, 253
Europa Deli, 171
Ewa's Family Restaurant, 162

F

Fanny's, 164
Farkas Pastry, 169
Fat Fish Blue, 237
Felafel Cafe, 83
Ferdos Restaurant, 270
Ferrante Winery & Ristorante, 112
Flannery's Pub, 188
Fortune Chinese Restaurant, 262
Fox & Crow Restaurant and Cafe, 101
Fragapane Bakery & Deli, 142
Frank Sterle's Slovenian Country House, 165
Frankie's Italian Cuisine, 113
French Street Cafe, 191
Fritz and Alfredo's, 269
Fujiyama, 269

G

Gaelic Imports, 196
Gallucci Italian Food, 143
Gavi's, 114
Giganti's Imported Foods, 143
Gintaras Dining Room, 162
Ginza Sushi House, 38
Giovanni's Meats & Deli, 144

Giuseppe's Ritrovo Italian Cafe, 261
Globe Cafe, 164
Golden Bakery, 61
Golden Dragon, 24
Golden Swan, 25
Good Harvest Foods, 61
Goodman's Sandwich Inn, 240
Gorby Grocery Store, 173
Grand Oriental, 275
Grape Leaf, 270
Greek Express, 102
Greek Islands Deli, 276
Guarino's Restaurant, 115

H
Halal Meats, 93
Hansa Import Haus, 193
Harp, 189
Heimatland Inn, 187
Helen's Kitchen, 159
Henry Wahner's Restaurant & Lounge, 187
His Majesty's Tea Room, 181
Hoan Nam Market, 58
Holyland Imports, 93
Hot Prospects, 253
House of Hunan, 25
House of Nagy, 159
Hunan by the Falls, 26
Hunan Coventry, 27
Hunan East, 27
Hunan Lion, 267
Hungarian Business and Tradesman Club, 160

I
I-ZU, 275
India Food & Spices, 88
Indian Jewel, 268
Indian Oven, 264
Indigo Indian Bistro, 72
Indo-American Foods, 88
International Foods, 167
Irish Cottage, 197
Iron Skillet, 278
Island Style Jamaican Cuisine, 207

J
Jack's Deli & Restaurant, 241
Jade Palace, 53
Jaipur Junction, 73
Japan West, 268
Jasmine Pita Bakery, 90
Jaworski's Meat Market & Deli, 172
Jimmy Daddona's, 116
John's Cafe, 152
Johnny Mango, 248
Johnny's Bar, 116
Johnny's Bistro, 184
Johnny's Downtown, 117
Juergen's Bakery and Restaurant, 263

K
K & K Meat Shoppe, 167
Kasba, 85
Kashmir Palace, 74

Kathy's Kolacke & Pastry Shop, 168
Katzinger's, 261
Kenmore Market Place, 168
Khiem's Vietnamese Cuisine, 54
Kihachi, 264
Kikyo, 265
Kim's Oriental Food, 63
Ko-Sho, 273
Kobawoo Oriental Food Market, 59
Korea House, 44
Korean Restaurant, 265
Krusinski Finest Meat Products, 172
Kuhar's, 188

L
L'Antibes, 262
L'Auberge, 276
La Borincana Foods, 225
La Fiesta, 214
La Gelateria, 117
La Michoacana, 226
La Petite France, 272
La Posadita, 215
La Tortilla Feliz, 204
Lake Road Market, 254
Lakshmi Plaza, 88
Lancer Steak House, 234
Las Piramides Mexican Restaurant, 272
Laurinda's, 169
Lax & Mandel Kosher Bakery, 244
Leach's Meats and Sweets, 254
Lelolai Bakery & Cafe, 227
Lelolai Bakery & Cafe, 222
Lemon Grass, 276
Lemon Grass Thai Cuisine, 47
Lenhardt's & Christy's, 274
Leo's Ristorante, 118
Let's Mango Tea Garden Restaurant, 206
Li Wah, 28
Little Budapest, 161
Little Orchid Cafe, 21
Little Saigon, 275
Lobby Lounge at the Ritz-Carlton Hotel, 183
Loma-Linda's Restaurant, 270
Long Phung, 29
Loretta Paganini School of Cooking, 254
Loretta Paganini School of Cooking, 249
Lozada's Restaurant, 222
Luchita's Mexican Restaurant, 215
Luchita's on the Square, 216
Lucy's Sweet Surrender, 170

M
Mad Greek, 102
Maharaja Restaurant, 75
Maisonette, 272
Malensek's Meat Market, 175
Mallorca Restaurant, 134
Mama Guzzardi's, 119

Mamma DiSalvo's Ristorante, 276
Mamma Santa's, 120
Manhattan West (soul food), 278
Manos Greek Restaurant, 268
Marbella Restaurant, 135
Marcelita's Mexican Restaurant, 216
Mardi Gras Lounge & Grill, 103
Maria's, 120
Marie's Restaurant, 155
Marinko's Firehouse, 161
Marta's, 153
Matsu Japanese Restaurant, 39
Max's Deli, 241
Meat Mart, 193
Mecklenberg Gardens, 272
Mediterranean Imported Foods, 255
Mehak-e-Punjab, 76
Mekong River, 47
Mertie's Hungarian Strudel Shop, 170
Mexican Village Restaurante y Cantinas, 217
Mi Pueblo, 226
Mi Pueblo, 218
Michael's Bakery, 194
Mickey Finn's Pub, 269
Middle East Restaurant, 84
Middle Eastern Deli, 277
Miles Farmers Market, 255
Min-Go Korean Restaurant, 265
Minh Anh Vietnamese Restaurant & Market, 54
Molinari's, 121
Molisana Italian Foods, 145
Mozart Restaurant, 180
Mozart's Pastries & Cafe, 261
Mughal Restaurant, 77

N
Nam Wah, 55
Nate's Deli & Restaurant, 84
Near East Market, 94
New Era Cafe, 155
New Wong's Chinese Restaurant, 30
Nicholson's Pub and Tavern, 274
Nicola's Ristorante, 273
Nighttown, 190
Niko's, 261
Ninni's Bakery, 145
Nino's, 121
Nipa Hut, 62
Nipa Hut, 35
Nuevo Acapulco, 220

O
Odessa European Market, 174
Old Country Sausage, 194
Old Country Smokehouse, 243
Old Prague Restaurant, 154
On The Rise—Artisan Breads and Pastries, 192
Oriental Food & Gifts, 59
Osteria, 122
Otani, 40

P

Pacific East, 41
Pacific Moon Cafe, 277
Pad Thai Restaurant, 48
Palazzo, 123
Pane E Vino, 273
Parker's New American Bistro, 185
Pat O'Brien's of Landerwood, 256
Patel Brothers, 89
Patria Imports, 175
Pearce Provisions, 194
Pearl of the Orient, 31
Peking Gourmet, 31
Peter's Market, 172
Petra Food, 94
Phil the Fire, 235
Phnom Penh Restaurant, 22
Pho Hoa, 55
Pho Little Saigon, 262
Piatto, 124
Pileggi's, 145
Pileggi's, 126
Pincus Bakery, 244
Players on Madison, 126
Polish American Cultural Center, 163
Porcelli's, 127
Portofino Ristorante, 127
Presti Bakery, 146
Presti Bakery, 128
Primavista, 273
Puritan Bakery, 199
Pyramid Restaurant, 85

R

R. Kaczur Meats, 170
Rachel's Caribbean Cuisine, 208
Raddell's Sausage Shop, Inc., 168
Raj Mahal Indian Cuisine, 77
Raj Mahal Indian Foods, 89
Rancheros Taqueria, 220
Refectory, 262
Rego's Lake Road Market, 257
Reinecker's Bakery, 195
Renee's French Bakery, 192
Reposteria Mana Homemade Bakery, 228
Resch's Bakery, 263
Restaurant Japan, 265
Ricky Ly's Chinese Gourmet, 32
Rincon Criollo, 223
Rincon Mexicano, 274
Ristorante Di Gianni, 129
Ristorante Giovanni's, 129
Rito's Italian Bakery, 146
Rudy's Quality Meats, 175
Rudy's Strudel & Bakery, 199
Ruthie & Moe's Diner, 249

S

Sachsenheim Hall, 195
Saffron Patch, 78
Saigon Palace, 266
Saigon Trading USA, 65
Samosky Home Bakery, 173

Sanabel Middle East Bakery, 95
Sans Souci, 133
Sapporo Wind, 265
Saree Mahal, 89
Sausage Shoppe, 195
Savannah, 238
Scali Ristorante, 267
Schmidt's Restaurant and Sausage Haus, 263
Seoul Garden, 45
Seoul Hot Pot, 45
Sergio's in University Circle, 250
Shinano Japanese Restaurant, 41
Shoku, 265
Shuhei Restaurant of Japan, 42
Siam Cafe, 56
Slyman's Deli, 242
Smokehouse Deli, 169
Sokolowski's University Inn, 163
Song Long, 279
Southeast Asian Food Market, 64
Spain Restaurant, 266
Spice Corner, 90
Starliner Diner, 267
'Stino da Napoli, 130
Stone Oven Bakery Cafe, 147
Sugarland Food Mart, 60
Sun Luck Garden, 33
Sun Tong Luck Tea House and Restaurant, 267
Sun-Land Oriental Foods, 60
Sunflower Chinese Restaurant, 262
Supermercado Rico, 228
Sushi 86, 42
Sushi on the Square Asian Grill, 43
Sushi Rock, 43
Swedish Pastry Shop, 197
Szechwan Garden, 34

T

T & T Sausage Market, 173
Tab West Indian American Restaurant, 209
Taj Mahal, 264
Taj Palace, 267
Tampico, 271
Tandoor India, 277
Tapatio, 265
TAT Ristorante di Famiglia, 264
Tea House Noodles, 21
Teak Thai Restaurant, 278
Thai Gourmet, 49
Thai Kitchen, 50
Thai Orchid, 266
Tibor's Quality Kosher Meat Market, 244
Tiger Lebanese Bakery and Restaurant, 269
Tink Hall Food Market, 60
Tlaquepaque Restaurant, 221
Tomatia's, 270
Tommy's Pastries, 171
Trattoria Roman Gardens, 130
Tuscany, 131

Tuscany Gourmet Foods, 147

U

Unger's Kosher Bakery & Food Shop, 245
United Asia Market, 64

V

V-Li's Thai Cuisine, 51
Vaccaro's Trattoria, 131
Valerio's Ristorante Cafe & Bar, 132
Vietnam Market, 65
Vine Valley Mediterranean Market, 95
Viva Barcelona, 135
Vivian's Restaurant, 236

W

West Point Market, 257
West Point Market, 251
West Side Bakery, 257
West Side Market, 258
Western Fruit Basket and Beverage, 137
Wixey Bakery, 268
Wojtilas Bakery, 176
Wu's Cuisine, 34

Y

Yeleseyevsky Deli, 174

Z

Za Za, 239
Zak's, 271
Zoss The Swiss Baker, 197

Index by Location *(Markets in italic)*

Downtown

CLEVELAND
Aladdin's Baking Company, 91
Alexandria's on Main, 233
Asia Tea House, 52
Fat Fish Blue, 237
Flannery's Pub, 188
Ginza Sushi House, 38
Greek Express, 102
Indigo Indian Bistro, 72
Johnny's Bistro, 184
Johnny's Downtown, 117
Lobby Lounge at the Ritz-Carlton Hotel, 183
Luchita's Mexican Restaurant, 216
Mallorca Restaurant, 134
Mardi Gras Lounge & Grill, 103
Middle East Restaurant, 84
Osteria, 122
Sans Souci, 133
Slyman's Deli, 242
Sushi 86, 42
Sushi Rock, 43
Tea House Noodles, 21

Near East Side

CLEVELAND
#1 Pho, 52
Anthony's, 139
Anthony's, 107
Asia Food Company, 57
Battuto Ristorante, 109
Bo Loong, 23
Bohemian Hall, 165
Bradford Restaurant, 234
Buettner's Bakery, 166
C & H Gertrude Bakery, 167
Cedarland at the Clinic, 79
Cleveland Food Co-op, 252
Corbo's Dolceria, 140
Dave's Supermarkets, 242
Empress Taytu Ethiopian Restaurant, 70
Europa Deli, 171
Ewa's Family Restaurant, 162
Felafel Cafe, 83
Frank Sterle's Slovenian Country House, 165
Gallucci Italian Food, 143
Golden Bakery, 61
Good Harvest Foods, 61
Guarino's Restaurant, 115
Halal Meats, 93
Jaworski's Meat Market & Deli, 172
John's Cafe, 152
Kim's Oriental Food, 63
Korea House, 44
Krusinski Finest Meat Products, 172
Lancer Steak House, 234
Li Wah, 28

Malensek's Meat Market, 175
Mamma Santa's, 120
Marie's Restaurant, 155
Mi Pueblo, 219
New Wong's Chinese Restaurant, 30
Old Country Smokehouse, 243
Pho Hoa, 55
Porcelli's, 127
Presti Bakery, 146
Presti Bakery, 128
Ruthie & Moe's Diner, 249
Seoul Hot Pot, 45
Sergio's in University Circle, 250
Siam Cafe, 56
T & T Sausage Market, 173
Tink Hall Food Market, 60
Trattoria Roman Gardens, 130
Valerio's Ristorante Cafe & Bar, 132
Vivian's Restaurant, 236

East Side

BEACHWOOD
D'Ici de Là, 224
D'Ici de Là, 203
Ristorante Giovanni's, 129
Shuhei Restaurant of Japan, 42

CLEVELAND
Clara's European Restaurant and Bakery, 158
Dailey's West Indian Food Mart, 224
Dailey's West Indian Food Mart, 206
Dave's Supermarkets, 243
Enterpride Restaurant, 207
Fanny's, 164
Gintaras Dining Room, 162
Luchita's on the Square , 216
Lucy's Sweet Surrender, 170
Patria Imports, 175
Phil the Fire, 235
Raddell's Sausage Shop, Inc., 168
Sushi on the Square Asian Grill, 43
Wojtilas Bakery, 176

CLEVELAND HEIGHTS
Aladdin's Eatery, 81
Cafe Tandoor, 71
Calabash African Market, 87
Hunan Coventry, 27
International Foods, 167
Kasba, 85
La Gelateria, 117
Lax & Mandel Kosher Bakery, 244
Lemon Grass Thai Cuisine, 47
Mad Greek, 102
Mekong River, 47
Nighttown, 190
On The Rise—Artisan Breads and Pastries, 192

Pacific East, 41
Stone Oven Bakery Cafe, 147
Sun Luck Garden, 33
Unger's Kosher Bakery & Food Shop, 245
Zoss The Swiss Baker, 197

EAST CLEVELAND
Island Style Jamaican Cuisine, 207

EUCLID
Barwulu/Hookes African Food Market, 86
Dave's Supermarkets, 243
Euclid Meat & Sausage Shop, 253
Kuhar's, 188
Marta's, 153
Wojtilas Bakery, 176

HIGHLAND HEIGHTS
DiStefano's Authentic Italian Foods, 141

LYNDHURST
Giovanni's Meats & Deli, 144
Thai Orchid, 50

MAYFIELD HEIGHTS
Arrabiata's, 108
Golden Swan, 25
Lakshmi Plaza, 88
Otani, 40
Sun-Land Oriental Foods, 60
Yeleseyevsky Deli, 174

MENTOR
Luchita's Mexican Restaurant, 216

PEPPER PIKE
Marbella Restaurant, 135
Pat O'Brien's of Landerwood, 256

RICHMOND HEIGHTS
Hunan East, 27
La Fiesta, 214
Maharaja Restaurant, 75
Shinano Japanese Restaurant, 41

SHAKER HEIGHTS
Balaton Restaurant, 156
Chandler and Rudd, 251
Matsu Japanese Restaurant, 39
Pearl of the Orient, 30
Saffron Patch, 78

SOUTH EUCLID
Alesci's of South Euclid, 139
Amir's Marketplace, 90
Amir's Marketplace Restaurant, 79
Felafel Cafe, 83
Gorby Grocery Store, 173
Oriental Food & Gifts, 59
Peking Gourmet, 31
Rachel's Caribbean Cuisine, 208
Za Za, 239

UNIVERSITY HEIGHTS
Boris's Kosher Meat, 243
Budapest Hungarian Cafe, 157
Jack's Deli & Restaurant, 241
Lax & Mandel Kosher Bakery, 244
Pincus Bakery, 244
Smokehouse Deli, 169
Tibor's Quality Kosher Meat Market, 244

WARRENSVILLE HEIGHTS
Tab West Indian American Restaurant, 209

WICKLIFFE
El Charrito, 212

WILLOUGHBY
Gavi's, 114

WILLOUGHBY HILLS
Marinko's Firehouse, 161

WILLOWICK
Rudy's Quality Meats, 175

WOODMERE VILLAGE
Corky and Lenny's, 240
Tuscany, 131
Tuscany Gourmet Foods, 147

Farther East

ASHTABULA
Swedish Pastry Shop, 197

AURORA
Cafe Tandoor, 72

BAINBRIDGE
Pearce Provisions, 194

BOARDMAN
Aladdin's Eatery, 82

BURTON
House of Nagy, 159

CHAGRIN FALLS
Hunan by the Falls, 26
Little Orchid Cafe, 21

CHESTER TOWNSHIP
Loretta Paganini School of Cooking, 254
Loretta Paganini School of Cooking, 249

EASTLAKE
Dubrovnik Garden Restaurant, 152

GENEVA
Ferrante Winery & Ristorante, 112

MADISON
His Majesty's Tea Room, 181

MANTUA
K & K Meat Shoppe, 167

MENTOR
Molinari's, 121

PAINESVILLE
Puritan Bakery, 199

SOLON
Akira Sushi & Hibachi, 36

Jimmy Daddona's, 116
Miles Farmers Market, 255

Near West Side

BROOKLYN
Agostino's Ristorante, 105
Aldo's, 107

CLEVELAND
Albelad Imported Food, 91
Ali Baba Restaurant, 82
Almadina Imports, 92
Asia Grocery & Gift, 58
Athens Pastries & Imported Foods, 136
Bruno's Ristorante, 110
Caribe Bake Shop, 227
Dave's Supermarkets, 225
Der Braumeister, 186
Der Braumeister Deli, 193
Dong Duong Indochina Grocery, 58
El Manantial, 205
El Taino Restaurant, 221
Farkas Pastry, 169
Gaelic Imports, 196
Hansa Import Haus, 193
Harp, 189
Hoan Nam Market, 58
Johnny Mango, 248
Johnny's Bar, 116
Kobawoo Oriental Food Market, 59
La Borincana Foods, 225
La Tortilla Feliz, 204
Lelolai Bakery & Cafe, 227
Lelolai Bakery & Cafe, 222
Long Phung, 29
Lozada's Restaurant, 222
Luchita's Mexican Restaurant, 215
Mediterranean Imported Foods, 255
Michael's Bakery, 194
Minh Anh Vietnamese Restaurant & Market, 54
Nate's Deli & Restaurant, 84
Palazzo, 123
Parker's New American Bistro, 185
Phnom Penh Restaurant, 22
Polish American Cultural Center, 163
Pyramid Restaurant, 85
Reposteria Mana Homemade Bakery, 228
Rincon Criollo, 223
Sachsenheim Hall, 195
Sausage Shoppe, 195
Sokolowski's University Inn, 163
Southeast Asian Food Market, 64
Supermercado Rico, 228
Vietnam Market, 65
West Side Market, 258

OLD BROOKLYN
Goodman's Sandwich Inn, 240

West Side

BAY VILLAGE
Fragapane Bakery & Deli, 142

BROADVIEW HEIGHTS
Cozumel, 211

CLEVELAND
Assad Bakery, 92
Holyland Imports, 93
Jasmine Pita Bakery, 90
Mi Pueblo, 226
Mi Pueblo, 218
Saigon Trading USA, 65

LAKEWOOD
Aladdin's Eatery, 81
Bavarian Pastry Shop, 198
Chinese Village, 53
El Tango Taqueria, 214
Irish Cottage, 197
Khiem's Vietnamese Cuisine, 54
Maria's, 120
Niko's, 103
Players on Madison, 126
Szechwan Garden, 34
Thai Kitchen, 50
Tommy's Pastries, 171
Wu's Cuisine, 34

NORTH OLMSTED
Aoeshi, 37
Asian Imports, 87
Columbia Asian Food & Gift, 63
Daishin Hibachi Steak House, 38
Fragapane Bakery & Deli, 142
Frankie's Italian Cuisine, 113
Hot Prospects, 253
Kashmir Palace, 74
Nuevo Acapulco, 220

NORTH RIDGEVILLE
Nino's, 121

OLMSTED TWP.
Donauschwaben German American Cultural Center, 186

ROCKY RIVER
Bucci's, 111
Casey's Irish Imports, 196
Lake Road Market, 254
Max's Deli, 241
Pearl of the Orient, 31
'Stino da Napoli, 130

WESTLAKE
Affamato Italian Deli and Market, 138
Affamato Italian Deli and Market, 104
Bovalino's Italian Ristorante, 110
Cafe Tandoor, 72
Daishin, 37
Frankie's Italian Cuisine, 114
Kathy's Kolacke & Pastry Shop, 168
Little Budapest, 161
Savannah, 238
Viva Barcelona, 135

Farther West

AVON
Fox & Crow Restaurant and Cafe, 101
Helen's Kitchen, 159

VERMILION
Chez Francois, 183
Old Prague Restaurant, 154

Southeast

BEDFORD
R. Kaczur Meats, 170

BROADVIEW HEIGHTS
Giganti's Imported Foods, 143

GARFIELD HEIGHTS
Charles Peters Bake Shop, 198
Peter's Market, 172

INDEPENDENCE
Aladdin's Eatery, 82

MACEDONIA
Reinecker's Bakery, 195

MAPLE HEIGHTS
Baraona's Baking Co., Inc., 140
Hungarian Business and Tradesman Club, 160
K & K Meat Shoppe, 167
Mehak-e-Punjab, 76
Old Country Sausage, 194
Saree Mahal, 89

NORTH RANDALL
Indo-American Foods, 88

Southwest

BEREA
Bucci's, 112
Nam Wah, 55

BROADVIEW HEIGHTS
Molisana Italian Foods, 145

CLEVELAND
Dave's Supermarkets, 225

MIDDLEBURG HEIGHTS
Fragapane Bakery & Deli, 143
Laurinda's, 169
Mertie's Hungarian Strudel Shop, 170
Patel Brothers, 89

NORTH ROYALTON
El Charro Restaurante, 213
Jaipur Junction, 73

PARMA
Cancun Restaurant & Lounge, 211
Colozza's Cakes & Pastries, 140
India Food & Spices, 88
Meat Mart, 193
Mexican Village Restaurante y Cantinas, 217
Rito's Italian Bakery, 146
Rudy's Strudel & Bakery, 199
Sugarland Food Mart, 60

PARMA HEIGHTS
Mughal Restaurant, 77
Nipa Hut, 62
Nipa Hut, 35
Samosky Home Bakery, 173

Farther South

AKRON
Bangkok Gourmet, 46
Bangkokville, 64
Big Mary's, 234
Crawdad's, 236
DeVitis & Sons, 141
Ellis Bakery, 92
Globe Cafe, 164
House of Hunan, 25
Jade Palace, 53
Kenmore Market Place, 168
La Michoacana, 226
La Posadita, 215
New Era Cafe, 155
Ninni's Bakery, 145
Odessa European Market, 174
Piatto, 124
Rancheros Taqueria, 220
Sanabel Middle East Bakery, 95
Spice Corner, 90
United Asia Market, 64
Vine Valley Mediterranean Market, 95
West Point Market, 257
West Point Market, 251
West Side Bakery, 257
Western Fruit Basket and Beverage, 137

BARBERTON
Al's Corner Restaurant, 154
Al's Quality Market, 166
Leach's Meats and Sweets, 254

BATH
Vaccaro's Trattoria, 131

BRUNSWICK
Heimatland Inn, 187

CANAL FULTON
Let's Mango Tea Garden Restaurant, 206
V-Li's Thai Cuisine, 51

CANFIELD
Renee's French Bakery, 192

CANTON
Athens Restaurant, 100
Bombay Sitar, 70
Canton Importing Company, 137
Desert Inn, 83
Dougardi's Italian Foods, 142
Mozart Restaurant, 180
Pileggi's, 145
Pileggi's, 126
Ricky Ly's Chinese Gourmet, 32
Tlaquepaque Restaurant, 221

CUYAHOGA FALLS
Asian Food Market, 58

Golden Dragon, 24
Near East Market, 94
Raj Mahal Indian Cuisine, 77
Raj Mahal Indian Foods, 89
Seoul Garden, 45

DELLROY
Casablanca, 100

FAIRLAWN
Continental Cuisine, 80

HUDSON
Marcelita's Mexican Restaurant, 216
Pad Thai Restaurant, 48

KENT
Henry Wahner's Restaurant & Lounge, 187
Ristorante Di Gianni, 129

MEDINA
Cancun Family Mexican Restaurant, 210

NILES
Alberini's, 106
Cork & More Shoppe, 141

NORTH CANTON
El Rincon Mexican Restaurant, 213
Mama Guzzardi's, 119

STOW
Thai Gourmet, 49

STRONGSVILLE
Portofino Ristorante, 127
Rego's Lake Road Market, 257

TALLMADGE
Petra Food, 94

WARREN
French Street Cafe, 191
Leo's Ristorante, 118

Index by Country or Ethnicity (Markets in italic)

Asterisk (*) indicates sub-specialty, not main focus of restaurant or market.

African
Barwulu/Hookes African Food Market, 86
Calabash African Market, 87

African-American/Southern
Alexandria's on Main, 233
Big Mary's, 234
Bradford Restaurant, 234
Dave's Supermarkets, 225*
Lancer Steak House, 234
Old Country Smokehouse, 243
Phil the Fire, 235
Vivian's Restaurant, 236

Argentinean
D'Ici de Là, 203

Austrian
Mozart Restaurant, 180

Brazilian
Sergio's in University Circle, 250*

British
Flannery's Pub, 188*
Gaelic Imports, 196*
His Majesty's Tea Room, 181
Lobby Lounge at the Ritz-Carlton Hotel, 183
Nighttown, 190*
Pincus Bakery, 244*
Puritan Bakery, 199*

Cajun/Creole
Alexandria's on Main, 233*
Crawdad's, 236
Fat Fish Blue, 237
Savannah, 238
Za Za, 239

Cambodian
Dong Duong Indochina Grocery, 58*
Phnom Penh Restaurant, 22
United Asia Market, 64*

Caribbean
Barwulu/Hookes African Food Market, 86*
La Borincana Foods, 225*
Let's Mango Tea Garden Restaurant, 206*
Rachel's Caribbean Cuisine, 208*
Supermercado Rico, 228*

Chinese
Asia Food Company, 57*
Asia Grocery & Gift, 58*
Asian Food Market, 58*
Bangkokville, 64*
Bo Loong, 23
Chinese Village, 53*
Columbia Asian Food & Gift, 63*

Dong Duong Indochina Grocery, 58*
Golden Bakery, 61
Golden Dragon, 24
Golden Swan, 25
Good Harvest Foods, 61
House of Hunan, 25
Hunan by the Falls, 26
Hunan Coventry, 27
Hunan East, 27
Jade Palace, 53*
Kobawoo Oriental Food Market, 59*
Li Wah, 28
Little Orchid Cafe, 21*
Long Phung, 29
Nam Wah, 55*
New Wong's Chinese Restaurant, 30
Nipa Hut, 62*
Pad Thai Restaurant, 48*
Pearl of the Orient, 30
Peking Gourmet, 31
Ricky Ly's Chinese Gourmet, 32
Saigon Trading USA, 65*
Southeast Asian Food Market, 64*
Sun Luck Garden, 33
Szechwan Garden, 34
Tea House Noodles, 21*
Thai Gourmet, 49*
Tink Hall Food Market, 60*
United Asia Market, 64*
Vietnam Market, 65*
Wu's Cuisine, 34

Croatian
Buettner's Bakery, 166*
Dubrovnik Garden Restaurant, 152
Marie's Restaurant, 155*
Patria Imports, 175*

Czech
Bohemian Hall, 165
John's Cafe, 152
Marta's, 153
Old Prague Restaurant, 154

Dominican
El Manantial, 205
Let's Mango Tea Garden Restaurant, 206

Ethiopian
Empress Taytu Ethiopian Restaurant, 70

Filipino
Asia Grocery & Gift, 58*
Bangkokville, 64*
Nipa Hut, 35
Tea House Noodles, 21*

Finnish
Puritan Bakery, 199*
Swedish Pastry Shop, 197*

French
Chez Francois, 183
French Street Cafe, 191
Johnny's Bistro, 184
On The Rise—Artisan Breads and Pastries, 192
Parker's New American Bistro, 185
Pincus Bakery, 244*
Renee's French Bakery, 192
Sans Souci, 133*
Zoss The Swiss Baker, 197*

German
Buettner's Bakery, 166*
Cancun Restaurant & Lounge, 211*
Der Braumeister, 186
Der Braumeister Deli, 193
Donauschwaben German American Cultural Center, 186
Europa Deli, 171*
Hansa Import Haus, 193
Heimatland Inn, 187
Helen's Kitchen, 159*
Henry Wahner's Restaurant & Lounge, 187
Kuhar's, 188
Marta's, 153*
Meat Mart, 193
Michael's Bakery, 194
Mozart Restaurant, 180*
Old Country Sausage, 194
Patria Imports, 175*
Pearce Provisions, 194
Pincus Bakery, 244*
Raddell's Sausage Shop, Inc., 168*
Reinecker's Bakery, 195
Sachsenheim Hall, 195
Sausage Shoppe, 195

Greek
Athens Pastries & Imported Foods, 136
Athens Restaurant, 100
Canton Importing Company, 137
Casablanca, 100
DeVitis & Sons, 141*
Fox & Crow Restaurant and Cafe, 101
Greek Express, 102
Holyland Imports, 93*
Mad Greek, 102
Mardi Gras Lounge & Grill, 103
Niko's, 103
Petra Food, 94*
Sans Souci, 133*

INDEXES

Smokehouse Deli, 169
Western Fruit Basket and
    Beverage, 137

Guatemalan
La Borincana Foods, 225*

Guyana
La Borincana Foods, 225*

Hungarian
Balaton Restaurant, 156
Budapest Hungarian Cafe, 157
Buettner's Bakery, 166*
Clara's European Restaurant and
    Bakery, 158
Farkas Pastry, 169
Helen's Kitchen, 159
House of Nagy, 159
Hungarian Business and Trades-
    man Club, 160
Kathy's Kolacke & Pastry Shop,
    168*
Laurinda's, 169
Little Budapest, 161
Lucy's Sweet Surrender, 170
Marinko's Firehouse, 161
Marta's, 153*
Mertie's Hungarian Strudel Shop,
    170
Pearce Provisions, 194*
Pincus Bakery, 244*
Puritan Bakery, 199*
R. Kaczur Meats, 170
Rudy's Quality Meats, 175*
Tommy's Pastries, 171

Indian
Albelad Imported Food, 91*
Amir's Marketplace, 90*
Asian Imports, 87
Bombay Sitar, 70
Cafe Tandoor, 71
Ellis Bakery, 92*
Holyland Imports, 93*
India Food & Spices, 88
Indigo Indian Bistro, 72
Indo-American Foods, 88
Jaipur Junction, 73
Kashmir Palace, 74
Lakshmi Plaza, 88
Mad Greek, 102*
Maharaja Restaurant, 75
Mehak-e-Punjab, 76
Mughal Restaurant, 77
Near East Market, 94*
Nipa Hut, 62*
Patel Brothers, 89
Petra Food, 94*
Raj Mahal Indian Cuisine, 77
Raj Mahal Indian Foods, 89
Saffron Patch, 78
Saree Mahal, 89
Spice Corner, 90

Indonesian
Tea House Noodles, 21*

Irish
Casey's Irish Imports, 196

Flannery's Pub, 188
Gaelic Imports, 196
Harp, 189
Irish Cottage, 197
Nighttown, 190

Israeli
Smokehouse Deli, 169*

Italian
Affamato Italian Deli and Market,
    138
Agostino's Ristorante, 105
Al's Quality Market, 166*
Alberini's, 106
Aldo's, 107
Alesci's of South Euclid, 139
Anthony's, 139
Arrabiata's, 108
Baraona's Baking Co., Inc., 140
Battuto Ristorante, 109
Bovalino's Italian Ristorante, 110
Bruno's Ristorante, 110
Bucci's, 111
Canton Importing Company, 137*
Colozza's Cakes & Pastries, 140
Corbo's Dolceria, 140
Cork & More Shoppe, 141
DeVitis & Sons, 141
DiStefano's Authentic Italian
    Foods, 141
Dougardi's Italian Foods, 142
Ferrante Winery & Ristorante, 112
Fragapane Bakery & Deli, 142
Frankie's Italian Cuisine, 113
Gallucci Italian Food, 143
Gavi's, 114
Giganti's Imported Foods, 143
Giovanni's Meats & Deli, 144
Guarino's Restaurant, 115
Jimmy Daddona's, 116
Johnny's Bar, 116
Johnny's Downtown, 117
La Gelateria, 117
Leo's Ristorante, 118
Mama Guzzardi's, 119
Mamma Santa's, 120
Maria's, 120
Molinari's, 121
Molisana Italian Foods, 145
Ninni's Bakery, 145
Nino's, 121
Osteria, 122
Palazzo, 123
Petra Food, 94*
Piatto, 124
Pileggi's, 126
Pincus Bakery, 244*
Players on Madison, 126
Porcelli's, 127
Portofino Ristorante, 127
Presti Bakery, 146
Ristorante Di Gianni, 129
Ristorante Giovanni's, 129
Rito's Italian Bakery, 146
Rudy's Quality Meats, 175*
Sans Souci, 133*

'Stino da Napoli, 130
Stone Oven Bakery Cafe, 147
Trattoria Roman Gardens, 130
Tuscany, 131
Tuscany Gourmet Foods, 147
Vaccaro's Trattoria, 131
Valerio's Ristorante Cafe & Bar,
    132
Zoss The Swiss Baker, 197*

Jamaican
Dailey's West Indian Food Mart,
    224
Enterpride Restaurant, 207
Island Style Jamaican Cuisine,
    207
Johnny Mango, 248*
Rachel's Caribbean Cuisine, 208
Tab West Indian American Res-
    taurant, 209

Japanese
Akira Sushi & Hibachi, 36
Aoeshi, 37
Asia Grocery & Gift, 58*
Asian Food Market, 58*
Columbia Asian Food & Gift, 63
Daishin, 37
Daishin Hibachi Steak House, 38
Ginza Sushi House, 38
Golden Dragon, 24*
Good Harvest Foods, 61*
Kobawoo Oriental Food Market,
    59*
Matsu Japanese Restaurant, 39
Nipa Hut, 62*
Otani, 40
Pacific East, 41
Ricky Ly's Chinese Gourmet, 32*
Shinano Japanese Restaurant, 41
Shuhei Restaurant of Japan, 42
Sushi 86, 42
Sushi on the Square Asian Grill,
    43
Sushi Rock, 43
Tea House Noodles, 21*

Jewish
Boris's Kosher Meat, 243
Corky and Lenny's, 240
Goodman's Sandwich Inn, 240
Jack's Deli & Restaurant, 241
Lax & Mandel Kosher Bakery, 244
Max's Deli, 241
Pincus Bakery, 244
Slyman's Deli, 242
Tibor's Quality Kosher Meat Mar-
    ket, 244
Unger's Kosher Bakery & Food
    Shop, 245

Korean
Asia Food Company, 57*
Asia Grocery & Gift, 58*
Asian Food Market, 58*
Columbia Asian Food & Gift, 63*
Good Harvest Foods, 61*
Kim's Oriental Food, 63

Kobawoo Oriental Food Market, 59*
Korea House, 44
Nipa Hut, 62*
Seoul Garden, 45
Seoul Hot Pot, 45

Laotian
Asia Food Company, 57*
Southeast Asian Food Market, 64*

Lebanese
Amir's Marketplace, 90
Amir's Marketplace Restaurant, 79
Cedarland at the Clinic, 79
Continental Cuisine, 80
Jasmine Pita Bakery, 90

Lithuanian
Gintaras Dining Room, 162
Raddell's Sausage Shop, Inc., 168*

Malaysian
Spice Corner, 90*

Mexican
Cancun Family Mexican Restaurant, 210
Cancun Restaurant & Lounge, 211
Cozumel, 211
El Charrito, 212
El Charro Restaurante, 213
El Rincon Mexican Restaurant, 213
El Tango Taqueria, 214
Johnny Mango, 248*
La Borincana Foods, 225*
La Fiesta, 214
La Michoacana, 226
La Posadita, 215
Luchita's Mexican Restaurant, 215
Luchita's on the Square, 216
Marcelita's Mexican Restaurant, 216
Mexican Village Restaurante y Cantinas, 217
Mi Pueblo, 226
Nuevo Acapulco, 220
Rancheros Taqueria, 220
Reposteria Mana Homemade Bakery, 228*
Supermercado Rico, 228*
Tlaquepaque Restaurant, 221

Middle Eastern
Aladdin's Baking Company, 91
Aladdin's Eatery, 81
Albelad Imported Food, 91
Ali Baba Restaurant, 82
Almadina Imports, 92
Assad Bakery, 92
D'Ici de Là, 203*
Desert Inn, 83
Ellis Bakery, 92
Felafel Cafe, 83
Halal Meats, 93
Holyland Imports, 93
Jasmine Pita Bakery, 90*

Middle East Restaurant, 84
Nate's Deli & Restaurant, 84
Near East Market, 94
Petra Food, 94
Pyramid Restaurant, 85
Sanabel Middle East Bakery, 95
Vine Valley Mediterranean Market, 95

Moroccan
Kasba, 85
Sans Souci, 133*

Pakistani
Spice Corner, 90*

Polish
Buettner's Bakery, 166*
Europa Deli, 171
Ewa's Family Restaurant, 162
International Foods, 167*
Jaworski's Meat Market & Deli, 172
K & K Meat Shoppe, 167*
Kathy's Kolacke & Pastry Shop, 168*
Krusinski Finest Meat Products, 172
Marta's, 153*
Patria Imports, 175*
Pearce Provisions, 194*
Peter's Market, 172
Polish American Cultural Center, 163
Rudy's Quality Meats, 175*
Samosky Home Bakery, 173
Sokolowski's University Inn, 163
T & T Sausage Market, 173

Portuguese
Mallorca Restaurant, 134*

Puerto Rican
Caribe Bake Shop, 227
El Taino Restaurant, 221
La Borincana Foods, 225*
Lelolai Bakery & Cafe, 222
Lozada's Restaurant, 222
Mi Pueblo, 226*
Reposteria Mana Homemade Bakery, 228
Rincon Criollo, 223
Supermercado Rico, 228

Russian
Globe Cafe, 164
Gorby Grocery Store, 173
International Foods, 167*
Odessa European Market, 174
Yeleseyevsky Deli, 174

Salvadoran
La Borincana Foods, 225*

Slovenian
Europa Deli, 171*
Fanny's, 164
Frank Sterle's Slovenian Country House, 165
K & K Meat Shoppe, 167*
Malensek's Meat Market, 175
Patria Imports, 175
Pearce Provisions, 194*
Raddell's Sausage Shop, Inc., 168*

Rudy's Quality Meats, 175
Wojtilas Bakery, 176

Spanish
Lelolai Bakery & Cafe, 222*
Mallorca Restaurant, 134
Marbella Restaurant, 135
Sans Souci, 133*
Viva Barcelona, 135

Swedish
Swedish Pastry Shop, 197

Swiss
Zoss The Swiss Baker, 197

Thai
Asia Food Company, 57*
Asia Grocery & Gift, 58*
Asian Food Market, 58*
Bangkok Gourmet, 46
Bangkokville, 64
Columbia Asian Food & Gift, 63*
Dong Duong Indochina Grocery, 58*
Good Harvest Foods, 61*
Johnny Mango, 248*
Lemon Grass Thai Cuisine, 47
Little Orchid Cafe, 21*
Mekong River, 47
Nipa Hut, 62*
Pad Thai Restaurant, 48
Pearl of the Orient, 30*
Ricky Ly's Chinese Gourmet, 32*
Siam Cafe, 56*
Southeast Asian Food Market, 64
Tea House Noodles, 21*
Thai Gourmet, 49
Thai Kitchen, 50
Thai Orchid, 50
United Asia Market, 64
V-Li's Thai Cuisine, 21
Vietnam Market, 65*

Ukranian
Globe Cafe, 164*

Vietnamese
#1 Pho, 52
Asia Food Company, 57*
Asia Tea House, 52
Bangkokville, 64*
Chinese Village, 53
Columbia Asian Food & Gift, 63*
Dong Duong Indochina Grocery, 58*
Good Harvest Foods, 61*
Jade Palace, 53
Khiem's Vietnamese Cuisine, 54
Little Orchid Cafe, 21*
Long Phung, 29
Minh Anh Vietnamese Restaurant & Market, 54
Nam Wah, 55
Pho Hoa, 55
Saigon Trading USA, 65
Siam Cafe, 56
Southeast Asian Food Market, 64*
United Asia Market, 64*
Vietnam Market, 65

Idea Indexes *(Markets in italic)*

Have a special need? Can't decide what you want? Here are some fun suggestions to try when you're not sure where to go. This is by no means a comprehensive list, but it should get you started.

100% Smoke-Free

Aladdin's Eatery, 81
Amir's Marketplace Restaurant, 79
Battuto Ristorante, 109
Cafe Tandoor, 72
Empress Taytu Ethiopian Restaurant, 70
Hunan by the Falls, 26
Jaipur Junction, 73
Kashmir Palace, 74
Lelolai Bakery & Cafe, 222
Nam Wah, 55
Phnom Penh Restaurant, 22
Rincon Criollo, 223
Sergio's in University Circle, 250
'Stino da Napoli, 130
Sun Luck Garden, 33
Sushi on the Square Asian Grill, 43
V-Li's Thai Cuisine, 51
Vaccaro's Trattoria, 131

A Room With a View

Location, location, location:

Bucci's, 112
Casablanca, 100
Chez Francois, 183
Ferrante Winery & Ristorante, 112
Harp, 189
Mallorca Restaurant, 134
Old Prague Restaurant, 154

A Sound Choice

Close to Severance Hall, these restaurants are used to diners who need to get to the concert hall on time. Reservations, of course, are a must:

Battuto Ristorante, 109
Guarino's Restaurant, 115
Mi Pueblo, 219
Porcelli's, 127
Sergio's in University Circle, 250
Valerio's Ristorante Cafe & Bar, 132

Added Attractions

These restaurants are not in big cities, but their locations put them close to interesting and entertaining destinations that can turn a meal into an all-day outing:

Casablanca, 100
Chez Francois, 183
Ferrante Winery & Ristorante, 112
His Majesty's Tea Room, 181
House of Nagy, 159
Hunan by the Falls, 26
Let's Mango Tea Garden Restaurant, 206
Little Orchid Cafe, 21
Old Prague Restaurant, 154
V-Li's Thai Cuisine, 51

Al Fresco

Restaurants offering seating in the great outdoors (when the weather obliges):

Chez Francois, 183
Donauschwaben German American Cultural Center, 186
Ferrante Winery & Ristorante, 112
Fox & Crow Restaurant and Cafe, 101
Harp, 189
His Majesty's Tea Room, 181
Lemon Grass Thai Cuisine, 47
Leo's Ristorante, 118
Luchita's on the Square, 216
Marinko's Firehouse, 161
Mozart Restaurant, 180
Nighttown, 190
Piatto, 124
Sergio's in University Circle, 250
Sushi on the Square Asian Grill, 43
Viva Barcelona, 135

Bakery/Cafes

Places to stock up on take-home goodies that also provide tables, chairs, and treats to eat on the premises:

Affamato Italian Deli and Market, 138
Clara's European Restaurant and Bakery, 158
D'Ici de Là, 203
French Street Cafe, 191
Golden Bakery, 61
Jasmine Pita Bakery, 90
Lelolai Bakery & Cafe, 222
Molisana Italian Foods, 145
Ninni's Bakery, 145
Presti Bakery, 128
Renee's French Bakery, 192
Stone Oven Bakery Cafe, 147
Tuscany Gourmet Foods, 147
West Side Bakery, 257

Buy in Bulk

Markets offering various food products in a self-serve setting; purchase as much or as little as you need:

Albelad Imported Food, 91
Almadina Imports, 92
Asia Food Company, 57
Cleveland Food Co-op, 252
Good Harvest Foods, 61
Holyland Imports, 93

By Dawn's Early Light

Early morning eats for those with the get up and go to get up and go there:

Athens Restaurant, 100
Cedarland at the Clinic, 79

Clara's European Restaurant and Bakery, 158
Corky and Lenny's, 240
Golden Bakery, 61
Jack's Deli & Restaurant, 241
Lelolai Bakery & Cafe, 222
New Wong's Chinese Restaurant, 30
Ruthie & Moe's Diner, 249
Savannah, 238

Call the Caterer

When you want someone else to do your cooking, many restaurants and chefs are happy to oblige:

Affamato Italian Deli and Market, 138
Anthony's, 107
Arrabiata's, 108
Caribe Bake Shop, 227
D'Ici de Là, 203
La Tortilla Feliz, 204
Phil the Fire, 235
Pileggi's, 126
Rachel's Caribbean Cuisine, 208
Savannah, 238
Thai Gourmet, 49

Cheap Eats, East & Downtown

Dinner entrees under $10:

Aladdin's Eatery, 81
Asia Tea House, 52
Clara's European Restaurant and Bakery, 158
Dailey's West Indian Food Mart, 206
Greek Express, 102
Island Style Jamaican Cuisine, 207
Marie's Restaurant, 155
New Era Cafe, 155
Pho Hoa, 55
Sushi 86, 42
Tea House Noodles, 21

Cheap Eats, West

Dinner entrees under $10:

Aladdin's Eatery, 81
El Manantial, 205
El Taino Restaurant, 221
El Tango Taqueria, 214
Minh Anh Vietnamese Restaurant & Market, 54
Pyramid Restaurant, 85
Thai Kitchen, 50
Wu's Cuisine, 34

Cheese Choices

The following stores are good choices if you're looking for some interesting examples of the cheesemaker's art:

Aladdin's Baking Company, 91
Canton Importing Company, 137
Chandler and Rudd, 251
Dave's Supermarkets, 225
French Street Cafe, 191
Gallucci Italian Food, 143
Giovanni's Meats & Deli, 144
Jasmine Pita Bakery, 90
Lake Road Market, 254
Mediterranean Imported Foods, 255
Miles Farmers Market, 255

Pat O'Brien's of Landerwood, 256
Rego's Lake Road Market, 257
West Side Market, 258

Come with Cash

Don't be caught short at these restaurants. Come prepared with greenbacks because they definitely don't take plastic:

Ali Baba Restaurant, 82
Bradford Restaurant, 234
Chinese Village, 53
Clara's European Restaurant and Bakery, 158
Dailey's West Indian Food Mart, 206
El Manantial, 205
Hungarian Business and Tradesman Club, 160
Khiem's Vietnamese Cuisine, 54
Marta's, 153
Minh Anh Vietnamese Restaurant & Market, 54
Nate's Deli & Restaurant, 84
New Era Cafe, 155
Phnom Penh Restaurant, 22
Rincon Criollo, 223
Slyman's Deli, 242
Tea House Noodles, 21

Desserts to die for

For some people the best part of a meal comes after the main course. These restaurants offer truly memorable endings:

Alexandria's on Main, 233
Balaton Restaurant, 156
Battuto Ristorante, 109
D'Ici de Là, 203
Gavi's, 114
Globe Cafe, 164
Johnny's Bistro, 184
Kashmir Palace, 74
La Gelateria, 117
Leo's Ristorante, 118
Maria's, 120
Max's Deli, 241
Osteria, 122
Palazzo, 123
Piatto, 124
Rachel's Caribbean Cuisine, 208
Sans Souci, 133
Sun Luck Garden, 33
Thai Gourmet, 49
Vaccaro's Trattoria, 131

Dip Into the Melting Pot

Multiple nationalities under one roof:

Cancun Restaurant & Lounge, 211
Chinese Village, 53
Golden Dragon, 24
Johnny Mango, 248
La Tortilla Feliz, 204
Little Orchid Cafe, 21
Mad Greek, 102
Nam Wah, 55
Sergio's in University Circle, 250
Siam Cafe, 56
Tea House Noodles, 21

Drams, Drinks, Potations & Libations

For the connoisseur and the enthusiast some restaurants offer really outstanding selections of fine wines, imported beers, and various other alcoholic pleasures:

Alberini's, 106
Flannery's Pub, 188
Gavi's, 114
Harp, 189
Johnny's Bistro, 184
La Tortilla Feliz, 204
Leo's Ristorante, 118
Mallorca Restaurant, 134
Matsu Japanese Restaurant, 39
Mozart Restaurant, 180
Parker's New American Bistro, 185
Savannah, 238
Thai Gourmet, 49
Viva Barcelona, 135
Za Za, 239

Eating as Entertainment

These locations host special events such as wine and food tastings, cigar parties, multi-course feasts, food ceremonies, and theme evenings (call for specific information):

Agostino's Ristorante, 105
Battuto Ristorante, 109
Chez Francois, 183
Empress Taytu Ethiopian Restaurant, 70
His Majesty's Tea Room, 181
Mozart Restaurant, 180
Nighttown, 190
Palazzo, 123
Sans Souci, 133
Sun Luck Garden, 33
Vaccaro's Trattoria, 131
West Point Market, 251

Everything's Jake

Convenient to Jacobs Field and Gund Arena:

Aladdin's Baking Company, 91
Fat Fish Blue, 237
Flannery's Pub, 188
Ginza Sushi House, 38
Middle East Restaurant, 84
Osteria, 122
Sushi Rock, 43

Exotic & Hard to Find Spices

Stores with an especially good selection:

Athens Pastries & Imported Foods, 136
Canton Importing Company, 137
Chandler and Rudd, 251
Cleveland Food Co-op, 252
Gallucci Italian Food, 143
Good Harvest Foods, 61
Hoan Nam Market, 58
Holyland Imports, 93
Hot Prospects, 253
India Food & Spices, 88
Mediterranean Imported Foods, 255
Molisana Italian Foods, 145
Nipa Hut, 62
Patel Brothers, 89
Petra Food, 94
Saree Mahal, 89
Spice Corner, 90

Foreign and Fascinating Fresh Produce

There's much more to fruits and vegetables than apples and broccoli. The following markets provide shoppers with an opportunity to sample the extraordinary variety of produce grown around the world:

Albelad Imported Food, 91
Cleveland Food Co-op, 252
Good Harvest Foods, 61
Hoan Nam Market, 58
La Borincana Foods, 225
Mi Pueblo, 226
Miles Farmers Market, 255
Nipa Hut, 62
Supermercado Rico, 228
Tink Hall Food Market, 60
West Side Market, 258

Good and Good For You

Most ethnic cuisines offer a variety of healthy alternatives to the Standard American Diet (also known as SAD), but some restaurants go out of their way to help diners with special dietary needs, offer lighter, leaner, low-fat dishes, or use local and organic products whenever possible. For more ideas about where to eat when you're counting calories or cholesterol, see the Great Choice for Vegetarians list.:

Cedarland at the Clinic, 79
Johnny Mango, 248
Matsu Japanese Restaurant, 39
Parker's New American Bistro, 185
Peking Gourmet, 31
Sun Luck Garden, 33
Thai Gourmet, 49

Great Choice for Vegetarians

Aladdin's Eatery, 81
Ali Baba Restaurant, 82
Amir's Marketplace Restaurant, 79
Bangkok Gourmet, 46
Bombay Sitar, 70
Cafe Tandoor, 71
Cedarland at the Clinic, 79
Cleveland Food Co-op, 252
Daishin, 37
Empress Taytu Ethiopian Restaurant, 70
Ginza Sushi House, 38
Jaipur Junction, 73
Kashmir Palace, 74
La Tortilla Feliz, 204
Lemon Grass Thai Cuisine, 47
Luchita's Mexican Restaurant, 215
Luchita's on the Square, 216
Marcelita's Mexican Restaurant, 216
Mehak-e-Punjab, 76
Mi Pueblo, 218
Minh Anh Vietnamese Restaurant & Market, 54
Nate's Deli & Restaurant, 84

Peking Gourmet, 31
Phnom Penh Restaurant, 22
Siam Cafe, 56
Tea House Noodles, 21
Wu's Cuisine, 34

Grocery Shop and Grab a Bite

Markets with on-site eateries:

Amir's Marketplace Restaurant, 79
Anthony's, 139
Der Braumeister Deli, 193
Mehak-e-Punjab, 76
Mi Pueblo, 226
Miles Farmers Market, 255
Minh Anh Vietnamese Restaurant & Market, 54
Odessa European Market, 174
Raj Mahal Indian Foods, 89
Saree Mahal, 89
Tuscany Gourmet Foods, 147
West Point Market, 257

Legal-Ease

Conveniently located near the Court House and the Justice Center. Atmosphere suitable for suits:

Flannery's Pub, 188
Johnny's Bistro, 184
Johnny's Downtown, 117
Mallorca Restaurant, 134
Osteria, 122
Sushi Rock, 43

Out-of-Cleveland Experience

Servers wear regional dress and/or decor recreates settings from faraway lands:

Daishin, 37
Empress Taytu Ethiopian Restaurant, 70
Frank Sterle's Slovenian Country House, 165
Ginza Sushi House, 38
Jaipur Junction, 73
Mexican Village Restaurante y Cantinas, 217
Mi Pueblo, 219
Shuhei Restaurant of Japan, 42

Perfect for Parties

Restaurants with private party rooms or facilities and services suitable for large groups:

Alberini's, 106
Bo Loong, 23
Der Braumeister, 186
Ferrante Winery & Ristorante, 112
Flannery's Pub, 188
Fox & Crow Restaurant and Cafe, 101
Frankie's Italian Cuisine, 114
Gintaras Dining Room, 162
His Majesty's Tea Room, 181
Leo's Ristorante, 118
Li Wah, 28
Nighttown, 190
Palazzo, 123
Peking Gourmet, 31
Ricky Ly's Chinese Gourmet, 32
Viva Barcelona, 135

Quick Lunch

For those who work in and around downtown, the following places get you seated, served, and back to work in less than an hour:

Ginza Sushi House, 38
Greek Express, 102
Lelolai Bakery & Cafe, 222
Mardi Gras Lounge & Grill, 103
Nate's Deli & Restaurant, 84
Pho Hoa, 55
Ruthie & Moe's Diner, 249
Slyman's Deli, 242
Sushi 86, 42
Tea House Noodles, 21

Romance

Where the atmosphere encourages hand-holding and the whispering of sweet nothings in each other's ears:

Bucci's, 112
Casablanca, 100
Chez Francois, 183
Guarino's Restaurant, 115
Mallorca Restaurant, 134
Mozart Restaurant, 180
Palazzo, 123
Portofino Ristorante, 127
Ristorante Di Gianni, 129
Sans Souci, 133
Valerio's Ristorante Cafe & Bar, 132

'Round Midnight

Places where it seems the kitchen almost never closes and you can get anything from a snack to a full meal long after the dinner hour:

Bo Loong, 23
Corky and Lenny's, 240
Crawdad's, 236
Fat Fish Blue, 237
Lancer Steak House, 234
Li Wah, 28
Mardi Gras Lounge & Grill, 103
New Wong's Chinese Restaurant, 30
Nighttown, 190
Niko's, 103
Savannah, 238
Za Za, 239

Serve Yourself

Buffets offer a chance to see what each dish looks like before you commit, and to sample freely. A great way to get acquainted with unfamiliar cuisines. Some buffets are open for lunch only, others on specific days of the week. Check listing or call for specific information.

Bangkok Gourmet, 46
El Charro Restaurante, 213
Heimatland Inn, 187
Indigo Indian Bistro, 72
Kashmir Palace, 74
Matsu Japanese Restaurant, 39
Mehak-e-Punjab, 76
Mughal Restaurant, 77
Nipa Hut, 35

Raj Mahal Indian Cuisine, 77
Shinano Japanese Restaurant, 41

Serving Sunday Brunch

Bucci's, 112
El Charro Restaurante, 213
Empress Taytu Ethiopian Restaurant, 70
Harp, 189
Johnny Mango, 248
Max's Deli, 241
Nighttown, 190
Phil the Fire, 235

Side Order of Live Music

Agostino's Ristorante, 105
Crawdad's, 236
Fat Fish Blue, 237
Flannery's Pub, 188
Frank Sterle's Slovenian Country House, 165
Harp, 189
La Tortilla Feliz, 204
Mardi Gras Lounge & Grill, 103
Mexican Village Restaurante y Cantinas, 217
Mi Pueblo, 219
Nighttown, 190
Niko's, 103
Savannah, 238

Smoker Friendly

These days it's becoming harder and harder to find restaurants that actually welcome smokers. The following places have no rules about lighting up. Those who still indulge will never be relegated to back corners, special rooms, or out on the sidewalk for a puff:

Jimmy Daddona's, 116
Johnny Mango, 248
La Posadita, 215
Marta's, 153
Mi Pueblo, 218
New Era Cafe, 155
New Wong's Chinese Restaurant, 30
Nino's, 121
Savannah, 238
Wu's Cuisine, 34
Za Za, 239

Sophisticated Side

Restaurants for impressing out-of-towners and entertaining business associates:

#1 Pho, 52
Akira Sushi & Hibachi, 36
Alexandria's on Main, 233
Gavi's, 114
Johnny's Bar, 116
Johnny's Bistro, 184
Osteria, 122
Parker's New American Bistro, 185
Piatto, 124
Ristorante Giovanni's, 129
Sans Souci, 133

Take the Kids

Restaurants where the atmosphere is tolerant, the staff accommodating, food includes things kids are sure to eat, and prices won't require a bank loan:

Cozumel, 211
El Charrito, 212
Ewa's Family Restaurant, 162
Fanny's, 164
Frankie's Italian Cuisine, 113
His Majesty's Tea Room, 181
Jimmy Daddona's, 116
Leo's Ristorante, 118
Li Wah, 28
Mamma Santa's, 120
Marcelita's Mexican Restaurant, 216
Max's Deli, 241
Mi Pueblo, 218
Sokolowski's University Inn, 163
Vaccaro's Trattoria, 131

Take More Than Your Share Home

These restaurants sell some of their most popular stuff by the pint, the quart, the pound, and the sheet:

Ali Baba Restaurant, 82
Anthony's, 107
Cedarland at the Clinic, 79
El Charrito, 212
Frankie's Italian Cuisine, 114
Harp, 189
Mi Pueblo, 218
New Era Cafe, 155
Nipa Hut, 35
Pileggi's, 126
'Stino da Napoli, 130

The Show Must Go On ... But Let's Eat First

Located near Playhouse Square, and just the right atmosphere for making it a very special occasion:

Johnny's Bistro, 184
Johnny's Downtown, 117
Mallorca Restaurant, 134
Osteria, 122
Sans Souci, 133

Wines To Go

Affamato Italian Deli and Market, 138
Alesci's of South Euclid, 139
Anthony's, 139
Canton Importing Company, 137
Chandler and Rudd, 251
Cork & More Shoppe, 141
Dougardi's Italian Foods, 142
French Street Cafe, 191
Gallucci Italian Food, 143
Giovanni's Meats & Deli, 144
Molinari's, 121
Pat O'Brien's of Landerwood, 256
West Point Market, 257
Western Fruit Basket and Beverage, 137

Eat Streets

(Markets in italic)

Sometimes where you eat and shop is determined by where you are. It's good to know that one street can offer many varied choices:

Eat Streets—Cedar

Aladdin's Eatery, 81
Boris's Kosher Meat, 243
Budapest Hungarian Cafe, 157
Nighttown, 190
Peking Gourmet, 31
Rachel's Caribbean Cuisine, 208
Smokehouse Deli, 169
Za Za, 239
Zoss The Swiss Baker, 197

Eat Streets—Detroit

Affamato Italian Deli and Market, 138
Aladdin's Eatery, 81
Fox & Crow Restaurant and Cafe, 101
Frankie's Italian Cuisine, 114
Halal Meats, 93
Harp, 189
Helen's Kitchen, 159
Hoan Nam Market, 58
Maria's, 120
Max's Deli, 241
Minh Anh Vietnamese Restaurant & Market, 54
Niko's, 103
Palazzo, 123
Pearl of the Orient, 31
Savannah, 238
'Stino da Napoli, 130
Szechwan Garden, 34
Vietnam Market, 65
Viva Barcelona, 135

Eat Streets—Lorain

Ali Baba Restaurant, 82
Almadina Imports, 92
Assad Bakery, 92
Athens Pastries & Imported Foods, 136
Der Braumeister, 186
Der Braumeister Deli, 193
Dong Duong Indochina Grocery, 58
Farkas Pastry, 169
Fragapane Bakery & Deli, 142
Hansa Import Haus, 193
Holyland Imports, 93
Jasmine Pita Bakery, 90
Mi Pueblo, 226
Nuevo Acapulco, 220
Phnom Penh Restaurant, 22
Pyramid Restaurant, 85
Saigon Trading USA, 65
Southeast Asian Food Market, 64
Supermercado Rico, 228

Eat Streets—Madison

Bavarian Pastry Shop, 198
Chinese Village, 53
El Tango Taqueria, 214
Khiem's Vietnamese Cuisine, 54

Players on Madison, 126
Thai Kitchen, 50
Tommy's Pastries, 171
Wu's Cuisine, 34

Eat Streets—Mayfield

Alesci's of South Euclid, 139
Amir's Marketplace, 90
Amir's Marketplace Restaurant, 79
Anthony's, 139
Arrabiata's, 108
Battuto Ristorante, 109
Corbo's Dolceria, 140
Giovanni's Meats & Deli, 144
Gorby Grocery Store, 173
Guarino's Restaurant, 115
Lakshmi Plaza, 88
Mamma Santa's, 120
Oriental Food & Gifts, 59
Otani, 40
Porcelli's, 127
Presti Bakery, 146
Sun-Land Oriental Foods, 60
Thai Orchid, 50
Trattoria Roman Gardens, 130
Valerio's Ristorante Cafe & Bar, 132
Yeleseyevsky Deli, 174

Eat Streets—Payne

Dave's Supermarkets, 242
Good Harvest Foods, 61
Li Wah, 28
New Wong's Chinese Restaurant, 30
Old Country Smokehouse, 243
Seoul Hot Pot, 45
Tink Hall Food Market, 60

Eat Streets—Pearl

Asia Grocery & Gift, 58
Fragapane Bakery & Deli, 143
Gaelic Imports, 196
Goodman's Sandwich Inn, 240
Kobawoo Oriental Food Market, 59
Patel Brothers, 89
Portofino Ristorante, 127
Samosky Home Bakery, 173

Eat Streets—Ridge

Agostino's Ristorante, 105
Bovalino's Italian Ristorante, 110
Cancun Restaurant & Lounge, 211
Casey's Irish Imports, 196
Colozza's Cakes & Pastries, 140
Daishin, 37
Dave's Supermarkets, 225
El Charro Restaurante, 213
India Food & Spices, 88
Kathy's Kolacke & Pastry Shop, 168

Little Budapest, 161
Rudy's Strudel & Bakery, 199
Sugarland Food Mart, 60

Eat Streets—S. Taylor
Cafe Tandoor, 71
Calabash African Market, 87
International Foods, 167
Kasba, 85
Lax & Mandel Kosher Bakery, 244
Sun Luck Garden, 33
Unger's Kosher Bakery & Food Shop, 245

Eat Streets—St. Clair
Asia Food Company, 57
Asia Tea House, 52
Bo Loong, 23
Empress Taytu Ethiopian Restaurant, 70
Marie's Restaurant, 155
Osteria, 122
Puritan Bakery, 199
Siam Cafe, 56
Slyman's Deli, 242
Wojtilas Bakery, 176

Eat streets—Superior
Golden Bakery, 61
Kim's Oriental Food, 63
Korea House, 44
Luchita's Mexican Restaurant, 216
Pho Hoa, 55

Eat Streets—W. 25th
El Manantial, 205
Lelolai Bakery & Cafe, 222
Lozada's Restaurant, 222
Mediterranean Imported Foods, 255
Nate's Deli & Restaurant, 84
West Side Market, 258

Tell me where to go!

Do you know of an *authentic* ethnic restaurant or market in Greater Cleveland that should have been included in this guide but wasn't? Well, that's what new editions are for! Tell me about your favorite place; if you were the first to suggest it and I add it to a future edition, you'll receive a free copy when it's published.

Send information (including your name) via email to:

cleveland.ethnic.eats@grayco.com

Or send a postcard to:

Cleveland Ethnic Eats
Gray & Company, Publishers
1588 E. 40th St., Suite 3A
Cleveland, OH 44103